2024

The Supreme Court Review

"Judges as persons, or courts as institutions, are entitled to no greater immunity from criticism than other persons or institutions . . . [J]udges must be kept mindful of their limitations and of their ultimate public responsibility by a vigorous stream of criticism expressed with candor however blunt."
—*Felix Frankfurter*

". . . while it is proper that people should find fault when their judges fail, it is only reasonable that they should recognize the difficulties. . . . Let them be severely brought to book, when they go wrong, but by those who will take the trouble to understand them."
—*Learned Hand*

THE LAW SCHOOL
THE UNIVERSITY OF CHICAGO

Volume 2024

The Supreme Court Review

EDITED BY
DAVID A. STRAUSS
GEOFFREY R. STONE
JUSTIN DRIVER
AND WILLIAM BAUDE

THE UNIVERSITY OF CHICAGO PRESS
CHICAGO AND LONDON

The Supreme Court Review, Volume 2024

Published annually by The University of Chicago Press.
www.journals.uchicago.edu/SCR/

University of Chicago Press's appointed EU Representative is Easy Access System Europe Oü, 16879218, Mustamäe tee 50, 10621 Tallinn, Estonia. Contact: gpsr.requests@easproject.com, +358 40 500 3575.

Subscriptions: For individual and institutional subscription rates, visit www.journals.uchicago .edu, email subscriptions@press.uchicago.edu, or call (877) 705-1878 (US) or (773) 753-3347 (international). Free or deeply discounted institutional access is available in most developing nations through the Chicago Emerging Nations Initiative (www.journals.uchicago.edu/inst/ceni).

Please direct subscription inquiries to Subscription Fulfillment, 1427 E. 60th Street, Chicago, IL 60637-2902. Telephone: (773) 753-3347 or toll free in the United States and Canada (877) 705-1878. Fax: (773) 753-0811 or toll-free (877) 705-1879. E-mail: subscriptions@press .uchicago.edu.

Standing orders: To place a standing order for this book series, please address your request to The University of Chicago Press, Chicago Distribution Center, Attn. Standing Orders/ Customer Service, 11030 S. Langley Avenue, Chicago, IL 60628. Telephone toll free in the U.S. and Canada: 1-800-621-2736; or 1-773-702-7000. Fax toll free in the U.S. and Canada: 1-800-621-8476; or 1-773-702-7212.

Single-copy orders: In the U.S., Canada, and the rest of the world, order from your local bookseller or direct from The University of Chicago Press, Chicago Distribution Center, 11030 S. Langley Avenue, Chicago, IL 60628. Telephone toll free in the U.S. and Canada: 1-800-621-2736; or 1-773-702-7000. Fax toll free in the U.S. and Canada: 1-800-621-8476; or 1-773-702-7212. In the U.K. and Europe, order from your local bookseller or direct from The University of Chicago Press, c/o John Wiley Ltd. Distribution Center, 1 Oldlands Way, Bognor Regis, West Sussex PO22 9SA, UK. Telephone 01243 779777 or Fax 01243 820250. E-mail: cs-books@wiley.co.uk.

The University of Chicago Press offers bulk discounts on individual titles to Corporate, Premium, and Gift accounts. For information, please write to Sales Department—Special Sales, The University of Chicago Press, 1427 E. 60th Street, Chicago, IL 60637 USA or telephone 1-773-702-7723.

This book was printed and bound in the United States of America.

ISSN: 0081-9557
E-ISSN: 2158-2459
ISBN: 978-0-226-84889-1 (cloth)
E-ISBN: 978-0-226-84891-4 (ebook)

IN MEMORIAM

FREDERICK SCHAUER

CONTENTS

JACK GOLDSMITH

THE PRESIDENCY AFTER TRUMP v. UNITED STATES

Two months after Special Counsel Jack Smith indicted then-former President Donald Trump for his efforts to alter the results of the 2020 presidential election, Trump's lawyers moved "to dismiss the indictment . . . with prejudice, based on Presidential immunity" for official acts.[1] The district court denied the motion and the court of appeals quickly affirmed in a decision that was widely described as obviously correct.[2] But the Supreme Court reversed, in an opinion written by

Jack Goldsmith is the Learned Hand Professor of Law at Harvard Law School.

Author's note: I thank Payvand Ahdout, William Baude, Robert Bauer, Matthew Gluck, John Harrison, Martin Lederman, Trevor Morrison, Saikrishna Prakash, Zachary Price, Robert Reinstein, Shalev Roisman, Thomas Schmidt, Adrian Vermeule, Edward Whelan, Alex Whiting, and University of Virginia workshop participants for comments, and Daniel Brickhill, Lev Cohen, Annabelle Hutchinson, Nicholas Nelson, Coy Ozias, Akhil Rajasekar, Mark Thomas, and Jeremiah Vroegop for research assistance. This Article draws in part on a Constitution Day Lecture delivered at the University of Michigan Law School on September 17, 2024.

[1] Motion to Dismiss Indictment Based on Presidential Immunity at 1, United States v. Trump, 704 F. Supp. 3d 196 (D.D.C. 2023) (No. 23-CR-00257), ECF No. 74.

[2] *Trump*, 704 F. Supp. 3d 196, *aff'd*, 91 F.4th 1173 (D.C. Cir. 2024). For laudatory commentary, see, for example, Scott R. Anderson, Quinta Jurecic, Anna Bower, Natalie K. Orpett & Benjamin Wittes, *Not So Immune: The D.C. Circuit's Forceful Rejection of Trump's Claim of Absolute Presidential Immunity*, Lawfare (Feb. 6, 2024, 6:24 PM), https://www.lawfaremedia.org/article/not-so-immune-the-d.c.-circuit-s-forceful-rejection-of-trump-s-claim-of-absolute-presidential-immunity; George T. Conway III, *An Airtight Ruling Against Trump*, Atlantic (Feb. 6, 2024), https://www.theatlantic.com/ideas/archive/2024/02/dc-circuit-court-ruling-on-trump-immunity/677367; Dahlia Lithwick & Mark Joseph Stern, *The Supreme Court Knows What It Must*

The Supreme Court Review, 2025.
 Published by The University of Chicago Press. https://doi.org/10.1086/735878

Chief Justice Roberts.[3] The Court held that a former President is absolutely immune from post-presidency prosecution for actions that fall in the President's exclusive constitutional authority, and at least presumptively immune for all other official presidential acts.

The decision in *Trump v. United States* was not well received.[4] A primary criticism has been that the Court's ruling portends a "lawless presidency."[5] This criticism, I will argue, rests on a misleading picture of how the criminal law operates inside the executive branch. Many factors other than the President's vulnerability to criminal law inform executive branch compliance with criminal law. One can certainly imagine a bad-man President after *Trump* engaging in widespread lawless criminal behavior. But, unfortunately, the bad-man President had many tools to skirt the criminal law before *Trump*, to which its uncertain immunity ruling added relatively little.

Which is not to say that the decision won't impact the presidency. It will, probably in a big way. But its impact will have less to do with the Court's immunity rulings than with its related rulings on the President's exclusive removal power and exclusive power over investigation and prosecution. These rulings, which were novel, expansive, and undertheorized, will play themselves out in litigation about the scope of presidential power for years. This Article, however, will mainly explore the slightly more tractable impact of the decision beyond judicial review and inside the executive branch, which will

Do with Trump's Immunity Ploy, SLATE (Feb. 6, 2024, 2:07 PM), https://slate.com/news-and-politics/2024/02/supreme-court-trump-immunity-john-roberts.html.

[3] Trump v. United States, 603 U.S. 593 (2024).

[4] *See, e.g.*, Akhil Reed Amar, *Something Has Gone Deeply Wrong at the Supreme Court*, ATLANTIC (July 2, 2024), https://www.theatlantic.com/politics/archive/2024/07/trump-v-united-states-opinion-chief-roberts/678877; Richard Lempert, Trump v. United States: *Explaining the Outrage*, BROOKINGS (July 12, 2024), https://www.brookings.edu/articles/trump-v-united-states-explaining-the-outrage; Laurence H. Tribe, *The Trump Decision Reveals Deep Rot in the System*, N.Y. TIMES (July 1, 2024), https://www.nytimes.com/2024/07/01/opinion/supreme-court-trump-immunity.html; Neil Siegel, *High Court's Immunity Case Protects the President, Not Democracy*, BLOOMBERG L. (July 5, 2024, 4:30 AM EDT), https://news.bloomberglaw.com/us-law-week/high-courts-immunity-case-protects-the-president-not-democracy.

[5] Kate Shaw, *The Supreme Court Creates a Lawless Presidency*, N.Y. TIMES (July 2, 2024), https://www.nytimes.com/2024/07/02/opinion/supreme-court-immunity-trump.html; *see also Trump*, 603 U.S. at 657–86 (Sotomayor, J., dissenting); *Trump*, 603 U.S. at 686–706 (Jackson, J., dissenting); Michael Stokes Paulsen, *A Lawless Court Gives Us a Lawless Presidency*, PUB. DISCOURSE (July 22, 2024), https://www.thepublicdiscourse.com/2024/07/95374; Patrick Marley, *Supreme Court's Trump Immunity Ruling Poses Risk for Democracy, Experts Say*, WASH. POST (July 1, 2024), https://www.washingtonpost.com/politics/2024/07/01/supreme-court-immunity-trump-democracy.

deploy the decision to help the President overcome legal constraints and win disputes with Congress.

Part I provides background to *Trump*. It shows that the Court's consequential rulings about exclusive presidential power were neither raised by Trump's lawyers in the courts below nor addressed by those courts and were addressed by the Supreme Court as a matter of first impression. Part I explores how and why this happened, and with what significance. Part II analyzes *Trump*, with special emphasis on the exclusive power rulings. It explains the novelty in these rulings and their potentially very broad implications. Part III assesses how *Trump* will impact presidential and executive branch compliance with criminal law and speculates how executive branch lawyers will use the exclusive power rulings in the decision to enhance executive branch power.

I. Background

The indictment against Trump alleged that he conspired with a Justice Department official and several private persons to overturn the results of the 2020 presidential election through public statements and through communication with and pressure on state officials, fraudulent state electors, Department of Justice officials, Vice President Mike Pence, and the joint session of Congress. It alleged that through this conduct Trump conspired to defraud the United States in violation of 18 U.S.C. § 371; conspired to obstruct an official proceeding in violation of 18 U.S.C. § 1512(k); obstructed and attempted to obstruct an official proceeding in violation of 18 U.S.C. §§ 1512(c)(2) and 2; and conspired to deny the rights of persons to vote and have their votes counted in violation of 18 U.S.C. § 241.[6]

Trump's lawyers claimed that Trump was immune from all charged conduct that involved official acts.[7] And yet, as I will explain below, they failed to raise in the lower courts what would turn out to be the most important separation of powers issue in the case: limits on Congress's power to criminalize presidential conduct. Ironically, the Special Counsel, arguing on behalf of the U.S. government,

---

[6] Indictment, *Trump*, 704 F. Supp. 3d 196 (No. 23-CR-00257), 2023 WL 4883396.

[7] Motion to Dismiss Indictment Based on Presidential Immunity, *supra* note 1, at 8–45. At oral argument, Trump's attorney appeared to concede that some of the charged conduct might have involved unofficial acts. *See* Transcript of Oral Argument at 29–30, *Trump*, 603 U.S. 593 (No. 23-939).

made this issue prominent in briefing and oral argument before the Court. These arguments were the basis for the Court's claim that the government "agree[d] with much of [the Court's] analysis" even if the Court reached conclusions sharply at odds with the government.[8] This Part explains this important background.

A. THE PRECEDENTS

Before *Trump*, the Supreme Court had never ruled on a former President's immunity from suit because no administration had ever prosecuted a former President before the Biden Administration prosecuted Trump through the quasi-independent Special Counsel.[9] The Court had addressed related issues, however. Three decisions were especially relevant in *Trump*.

First, *Youngstown Sheet & Tube Co. v. Sawyer* held that President Harry S. Truman lacked statutory or constitutional authority to direct the Secretary of Commerce to seize and operate certain steel mills during the Korean War.[10] Justice Jackson's concurrence articulated a three-tiered framework to assess presidential power claims "depending upon their disjunction or conjunction with those of Congress."[11] Jackson's third category concerned matters of "exclusive presidential

[8] *Trump*, 603 U.S. at 634.

[9] The criminal investigation of former President Trump in connection with both the January 6 matter and the Mar-a-Lago classified documents matter began under the supervision of Attorney General Merrick Garland. Garland appointed Special Counsel Jack Smith on November 18, 2022, "[b]ased on recent developments, including the former President's announcement that he is a candidate for President in the next election, and the sitting President's stated intention to be a candidate as well." Merrick B. Garland, Att'y Gen., U.S. Dep't of Just., Attorney General Merrick B. Garland Delivers Remarks on the Appointment of a Special Counsel (Nov. 18, 2022), https://www.justice.gov/archives/opa/speech/attorney-general-merrick-b-garland-delivers-remarks-appointment-special-counsel. Smith retained many lawyers and investigators who had worked on the January 6 case prior to his appointment and hired new staff. Perry Stein, *A Look at the Team Jack Smith Built to Try to Convict Donald Trump*, WASH. POST (Sept. 10, 2023), https://www.washingtonpost.com/national-security/2023/09/10/jack-smith-special-counsel-trump-investigations. Under Justice Department regulations, Smith had the powers of a U.S. Attorney and had to "comply" with Department rules and policies and "consult" with appropriate Department offices about them. 28 C.F.R. § 600.6–7(a) (2022). The Attorney General retained the authority to request from the Special Counsel "an explanation for any investigative or prosecutorial step," and the power to "conclude that the action is so inappropriate or unwarranted under established Departmental practices that it should not be pursued." *Id.* § 600.7(b). A Special Counsel is thus quasi-independent from the Attorney General, who is constitutionally subject to presidential direction but by virtue of norms—at least through the presidency of Joseph Biden—is independent of the White House. *See* Daphna Renan, *Presidential Norms and Article II*, 131 HARV. L. REV. 2187, 2207–13 (2018).

[10] 343 U.S. 579 (1952).

[11] *Youngstown*, 343 U.S. at 635 (Jackson, J., concurring).

control" that "disabl[e] the Congress from acting upon the subject."[12] Jackson provided little guidance on Category Three claims beyond suggesting that the President would rarely prevail on them.[13] The full Court adopted Jackson's tripartite framework three decades after *Youngstown*.[14] But it was not until 2015, in *Zivotofsky v. Kerry*, that the Court evaluated a presidential claim of exclusive authority under Jackson's third category.[15] It held that the President's recognition power was exclusive but did not mention or apply any presumption against presidential exclusivity.[16]

Second, *United States v. Nixon* recognized an Article II–based executive privilege protecting presidential and senior executive branch official communications from disclosure.[17] The Court explained: "Certain powers and privileges flow from the nature of enumerated powers; the protection of the confidentiality of Presidential communications has similar constitutional underpinnings."[18] The Court ruled that this executive privilege was not absolute, however, due to a countervailing Article III–based judicial duty "to do justice in criminal prosecutions."[19] The Court recognized a "presumptive privilege" for presidential communications that was "fundamental to the operation of Government and inextricably rooted in the separation of powers under the Constitution."[20] But it ruled that when the privilege is based on a "generalized interest in confidentiality" it "must yield to the demonstrated, specific need for evidence in a pending criminal trial."[21]

---

[12] *Id.* at 637–38.

[13] *Id.* at 638 ("Presidential claim to a power at once so conclusive and preclusive must be scrutinized with caution . . . ."); *id.* at 640 (explaining that claim is "most vulnerable to attack and in the least favorable of possible constitutional postures").

[14] *See* Dames & Moore v. Regan, 453 U.S. 654 (1981).

[15] Zivotofsky v. Kerry, 576 U.S. 1 (2015); *see also* Jack L. Goldsmith, Zivotofsky II *as Precedent in the Executive Branch*, 129 HARV. L. REV. 112, 121 (2015) (explaining that *Zivotofsky* was the first decision to evaluate exclusive authority in Jackson's third category).

[16] *Zivotofsky*, 576 U.S. at 10–32; *see also* Goldsmith, *supra* note 15, at 125–26.

[17] 418 U.S. 683 (1974).

[18] *Id.* at 705–06 (footnote omitted). The Court also recognized "the singularly unique role under Art. II of a President's communications and activities, related to the performance of duties under that Article." *Id.* at 715.

[19] *Id.* at 707.

[20] *Id.* at 708.

[21] *Id.* at 713. The Court did, however, indicate openness to the prospect that presidential privilege in the confidentiality of communications might prevail if based specifically on "a claim of need to protect military, diplomatic, or sensitive national security secrets." *Id.* at 706.

Third, *Nixon v. Fitzgerald* held that due to "the special nature of the President's constitutional office and functions," a President receives absolute immunity "from damages liability for acts within the 'outer perimeter' of his official responsibility."[22] It explained that a President's amenability to suit turned on a "balance [of] the constitutional weight of the interest to be served against the dangers of intrusion on the authority and functions of the Executive Branch."[23] Pointing to *Youngstown* and *United States v. Nixon*, the Court stated that "[w]hen judicial action is needed to serve broad public interests . . . the exercise of jurisdiction has been held warranted."[24] But, it concluded that in a "merely private suit for damages based on a President's official acts,"[25] the President receives the broad absolute immunity due to his important "discretionary responsibilities" and the extraordinary burden that inferior presidential immunity would entail.[26]

Three features of these foundational decisions warrant comment.

First, all three opinions interpret Article II to carve out areas of presidential power that are impervious to the intrusion of another branch, though in different ways and with different terminology. Jackson's *Youngstown* Category Three recognized the possibility of limits on *congressional power to regulate* areas of exclusive presidential power. By contrast, the *Nixon* cases recognized limitations *on judicial review*. *Nixon v. Fitzgerald* expressed this limitation in terms of a presidential *immunity* from suit for damages. *United States v. Nixon* expressed this limitation in terms of a presidential *presumptive privilege* against disclosure of presidential communications in court. The limits on congressional power contemplated by *Youngstown* go to the *legality* of presidential action, while the limit on judicial review contemplated by *Nixon v. Fitzgerald* accommodates the potential harms of judicial review on presidential action but does not affect the underlying legality of presidential conduct.[27]

---

[22] Nixon v. Fitzgerald, 457 U.S. 731, 756 (1982); *see also id.* at 749–51 (outlining the President's "unique position in the constitutional scheme" and his responsibility to "make the most sensitive and far-reaching decisions entrusted to any official under our constitutional system").

[23] *Id.* at 754. Importantly, this holding was premised on a suit based on implied causes of action; the Court left open the scope of immunity should Congress impose liability by statute on the President. *See infra* note 59 and accompanying text.

[24] *Fitzgerald*, 457 U.S. at 754 (first citing Youngstown Sheet & Tube Co. v. Sawyer, 343 U.S. 579, 579 (1952); and then citing *Nixon*, 418 U.S. at 703–13).

[25] *Id.*

[26] *Id.* at 756.

[27] This distinction is akin to the one Ann Woolhandler draws between the "legality" model of official action and the "discretion" model of official action. *See* Ann Woolhandler, *Patterns*

Second, neither the Jackson concurrence in *Youngstown*, nor the majority opinions in the *Nixon* cases, were examples of what we would today call originalism or even textualism. Jackson did not purport to discern constitutional meaning as fixed at the Founding but did poke fun at a few strands of what became modern originalism.[28] And, although he marched through the text of Article II, he did not rely on it in a serious way to deny the President's claims.[29] The *Nixon* opinions were not "textually based," as Michael Dreeben, the Counselor to the Special Counsel, said at the *Trump v. United States* oral argument.[30] Rather, they rested on "constitutional underpinnings," as the tapes case put it in the context of presidential communications.[31] And the *Nixon* opinions did not mention the views of the Founders, original public meaning, or any other originalist indicator of meaning.[32]

Third, all three opinions identified exclusive presidential power through functionalist, not formalist, methodology.[33] Jackson's tripartite

---

of Official Immunity and Accountability, 37 CASE W. RSRV. L. REV. 396 (1987). But it differs in several respects, especially as the Supreme Court used these lines of cases in *Trump*, and so I will not follow that terminology here. *But see* Thomas P. Schmidt, *Immunity After* Trump, 79 VAND. L. REV. (forthcoming 2026) (manuscript at 12–13) (on file with author) (using the Woolhandler distinction as a lens through which to understand *Trump*).

[28] *Youngstown*, 343 U.S. at 634 (Jackson, J., concurring) ("Just what our forefathers did envision, or would have envisioned had they foreseen modern conditions, must be divined from materials almost as enigmatic as the dreams Joseph was called upon to interpret for Pharaoh."); *see also id.* at 640 ("Some clauses could be made almost unworkable, as well as immutable, by refusal to indulge some latitude of interpretation for changing times.").

[29] *Id.* at 640–46.

[30] Transcript of Oral Argument, *supra* note 7, at 77.

[31] United States v. Nixon, 418 U.S. 683, 705–06 (1974).

[32] *Nixon v. Fitzgerald*, 457 U.S. 731 (1982), did say that its absolute presidential immunity was "a functionally mandated incident of the President's unique office, rooted in the constitutional tradition of the separation of powers and supported by our history." *Id.* at 749.

[33] By "formalist" I mean the idea that "[t]he Constitution sought to divide the delegated powers of the new federal government into three defined categories, legislative, executive, and judicial, to assure, as nearly as possible, that each Branch of government would confine itself to its assigned responsibility." INS v. Chadha, 462 U.S. 919, 951 (1983). A formalist approach to separation of powers identifies whether the exercise of governmental power is legislative, executive, or judicial, and that identification determines which branch may exercise the power. *See, e.g.*, Gary S. Lawson, *Territorial Governments and the Limits of Formalism*, 78 CALIF. L. REV. 853, 857–88 (1990). By contrast, a functionalist approach recognizes that the three branches do not "operate with absolute independence," Morrison v. Olson, 487 U.S. 654, 694 (1988) (quoting *Nixon*, 418 U.S. at 707), and that the Constitution requires only "safeguard[ing] against the encroachment or aggrandizement of one branch at the expense of the other," *id.* at 693 (quoting Buckley v. Valeo, 424 U.S. 1, 122 (1976)). *But see* Shalev Gad Roisman, *Balancing Interests in the Separation of Powers*, 91 U. CHI. L. REV. 1331, 1375 (2024) (reading classic functionalist cases to balance the interests of the branches, defined as the reasons behind their exercises of power, rather than the powers themselves).

approach to presidential power is famously anti-formalist.[34] While it recognized that Category Three housed exclusive presidential powers, it did not reason to such exclusivity by formalist methods. Rather, Jackson described the President's exclusive authority as the resolution of a clash of powers between the executive and other branches.[35] The *Nixon* opinions were overtly anti-formalist. They both balanced presidential claims of authority against the competing claims of the other branches, and they both reached their conclusions based on the Court's functional assessment of the impact of judicial actions on executive power.[36]

B. ARGUMENTS IN THE LOWER COURTS

Trump's lawyers argued from the outset that a former President is immune from criminal prosecution for conduct involving official acts unless he has been impeached and convicted for the same conduct.[37] They maintained that *Nixon v. Fitzgerald* should be extended to the criminal context and that *Marbury* and its progeny supported the President's immunity from criminal prosecution for public acts undertaken in office.[38] The focus was on *immunity from judicial review*, i.e., on "Article III courts lack[ing] the power to review the President's official acts under the separation of powers doctrine."[39] They

---

[34] *See, e.g.*, Harlan Grant Cohen, *Formalism and Distrust: Foreign Affairs Law in the Roberts Court*, 83 Geo. Wash. L. Rev. 380, 394 (2015). The majority opinion in *Youngstown*, by contrast, was famously formalist. *See, e.g.*, Stephen I. Vladeck, *Foreign Affairs Originalism in* Youngstown's *Shadow*, 53 St. Louis U. L.J. 29, 32 (2008).

[35] *See* Youngstown Sheet & Tube Co. v. Sawyer, 343 U.S. 579, 637 (1952) (Jackson, J., concurring) ("When the President takes measures incompatible with the expressed or implied will of Congress, his power is at its lowest ebb, for then he can rely only upon his own constitutional powers minus any constitutional powers of Congress over the matter."); *id.* at 640 (noting that the President can win in Category Three only if there is "any remainder of executive power" that survives after subtracting "such powers as Congress may have over the subject"). Jackson's rejection of the proposition that the seizure of wartime "strike-bound industries is within [the President's] domain and beyond control by Congress" was also mainly functionalist but is hard to categorize because the analysis was nuanced to the point of impressionistic. *Id.* at 640–54. *But see* Shalev Roisman, Trump v. United States *and the Separation of Powers*, 173 U. Pa. L. Rev. Online 33, 42 (2025) (arguing that "Justice Jackson's opinion operates in a formalist manner in Category Three").

[36] *See* Michael Stokes Paulsen, Nixon *Now: The Courts and the Presidency After Twenty-Five Years*, 83 Minn. L. Rev. 1337, 1375–81 (1999).

[37] Motion to Dismiss Indictment Based on Presidential Immunity, *supra* note 1, at 11–13.

[38] *Id.* at 13–15, 16.

[39] United States v. Trump, 91 F.4th 1173, 1189 (D.C. Cir. 2024).

did not argue that the Constitution's separation of powers prevented *Congress* from criminalizing presidential acts.[40]

The court of appeals, rushing to decision, rejected Trump's argument in broad terms—too broad.[41] Following Trump's lawyers' lead,

---

[40] Trump filed four motions to dismiss in the district court, none of which raised congressional separation of powers or *Youngstown* Category Three issues.

The motion to dismiss the indictment based on presidential immunity focused only on the line of cases involving immunity from federal judicial adjudication and did not raise separation of powers restraints on Congress. It mentioned Jackson's *Youngstown* concurrence only to emphasize that the President's organizing a slate of electors was an independent power in Jackson's Category Two, and it did not claim an exclusive and preclusive power in Category Three. Motion to Dismiss Indictment Based on Presidential Immunity, *supra* note 1, at 44 n.7; *see also* Reply Brief in Support of Motion to Dismiss the Indictment Based on Presidential Immunity, United States v. Trump, 704 F. Supp. 3d 196 (D.D.C. 2023) (No. 23-CR-00257), ECF No. 122.

The motion to dismiss on constitutional grounds mentioned separation of powers and the *Youngstown* majority opinion only in arguing that government could not second-guess Trump's acquittal on articles of impeachment. Motion to Dismiss the Indictment Based on Constitutional Grounds and Memorandum in Support at 23, *Trump*, 704 F. Supp. 3d 196 (No. 23-CR-00257), ECF No. 113.

The motion to dismiss on statutory grounds raised First Amendment constitutional avoidance arguments but none about the separation of powers. Motion to Dismiss the Indictment Based on Statutory Grounds and Memorandum in Support at 16–23, *Trump*, 704 F. Supp. 3d 196 (No. 23-CR-00257), ECF No. 114.

The motion to dismiss for selective and vindictive prosecution did not raise separation of powers issues at all. *See* Motion to Dismiss for Selective and Vindictive Prosecution, *Trump*, 704 F. Supp. 3d 196 (No. 23-CR-00257), ECF No. 116.

The Trump brief before the D.C. Circuit also did not raise separation of powers constraints on Congress or *Youngstown* Category Three issues. *See* Opening Brief of Defendant-Appellant President Donald J. Trump, *Trump*, 91 F.4th 1173 (No. 23-3228), 2023 WL 8874627; Reply Brief of Defendant-Appellant President Donald J. Trump, *Trump*, 91 F.4th 1173 (No. 23-3228), 2024 WL 36166. Trump's failure to discuss Category Three constraints on congressional power in the courts below is especially remarkable because the government had hinted at such constraints as a basis for immunity. *See, e.g.*, Response in Opposition to Defendant's Motion to Dismiss on Presidential Immunity Grounds at 35, *Trump*, 704 F. Supp. 3d 196 (No. 23-CR-00257), ECF No. 109.

One might speculate that Trump's lawyers declined to raise the issue of separation of powers vis-à-vis Congress because they viewed the argument as a defense on the merits to be raised at a different time and perhaps did not want to raise the issue at the motion to dismiss stage for fear that they would not be able to raise *Harlow*-type immunity on interlocutory appeal. But this speculation is implausible since, as explained above, the Trump team raised many other issues in the motions to dismiss that were clearly defenses and could clearly be appealed only after trial. In addition, as Justice Barrett wrote in her concurrence, there was a powerful argument that the separation of powers claim, even if a defense, was still subject to interlocutory review. *See* Trump v. United States, 603 U.S. 593, 651–55 (2024) (Barrett, J., concurring in part); *infra* note 67 and accompanying text.

[41] As the majority in *Trump* explained, "[d]espite the unprecedented nature of this case, and the very significant constitutional questions that it raises, the lower courts rendered their decisions on a highly expedited basis." 603 U.S. at 616. The court of appeals decided the case quickly in response to the government's proclamation of "the imperative public importance of a prompt resolution of this case." Answering Brief for the United States at 65, *Trump*, 91 F.4th 1173 (No. 23-3228), 2023 WL 9020632. The Supreme Court too, under similar appeal from the government to go fast, rushed to decision. It granted certiorari on February 28,

it focused on separation of powers constraints on the judiciary, not Congress. In concluding that the President lacked immunity for his public acts, the court of appeals stated that "[t]he separation of powers doctrine . . . *necessarily permits* the Judiciary to oversee the federal criminal prosecution of a former president for his official acts because the fact of the prosecution means that the former president has allegedly acted in defiance of the laws."[42] The Chief Justice at oral argument expressed "concern" that this statement, which he saw as a holding, meant that "a former president can be prosecuted because he's being prosecuted."[43] And that is indeed what the statement says.

C. THE ARGUMENT BEFORE THE SUPREME COURT

The government did not defend this reasoning by the court of appeals in the Supreme Court. When asked about it by Chief Justice Roberts at oral argument, the government's attorney, Dreeben, stated that it was not "the proper approach in this case" and "certainly not the government's approach."[44]

The government's more nuanced position on presidential immunity before the Supreme Court reflected what Dreeben described as "equities that are far beyond [the Trump] prosecution."[45] The Justice Department has duties to both protect the President's law enforcement prerogatives *and* to protect the presidency from encroachment by other branches. *Trump* was a highly unusual case because these interests were potentially in tension.[46] The Biden Administration had an interest in prosecuting the former President for his alleged crimes. But it also had an interest to prevent undue encroachments on future

2024, ordered expedited briefing, held oral argument on April 25, 2024, and issued the opinion on July 1, 2024.

[42] *Trump*, 91 F.4th at 1191 (emphasis added). The court additionally begged the question at the heart of the case by asserting that Trump had "no structural immunity" from criminal charges because his actions "allegedly violated generally applicable criminal laws, meaning those acts were not properly within the scope of his lawful discretion." *Id.* at 1192.

[43] Transcript of Oral Argument, *supra* note 7, at 73.

[44] *Id.* at 74.

[45] *Id.* at 143. Dreeben also made clear at oral argument that he had consulted with the Solicitor General and garnered her support behind the Special Counsel's position on presidential immunity before the Court. *See id.* at 142–43.

[46] *See also* United States v. Nixon, 418 U.S. 683 (1974) (special prosecutor squaring off against sitting President); Morrison v. Olson, 487 U.S. 654 (1988) (independent counsel investigating the head of the Office of Legal Counsel (OLC), with dueling briefs from the independent counsel and the Solicitor General).

presidencies by Congress and the courts (and, as the briefs made plain, from future Justice Department prosecutors).[47]

In reflection of this tension, and of the Court's role in protecting both interests, the government emphasized in the Supreme Court why its argument against immunity for Trump in the January 6 prosecution would not adversely impact future presidencies. One set of reasons concerned the practical barriers to prosecution, including internal Justice Department norms and the grand jury.[48] Another set of reasons concerned separation of powers limits *on Congress's power* to criminalize presidential actions, which the government had mentioned in passing in its briefs below but foregrounded before the Supreme Court. (It is not clear why Trump's lawyers failed to address these issues below; the best explanation appears to be, amazingly, that they just missed them.[49])

The centrality of separation of powers constraints on Congress to the government's argument was apparent in Dreeben's response to the first question he received at oral argument. Justice Thomas asked whether Dreeben was arguing that there was "no . . . presidential immunity, even for official acts." Dreeben gave a quick affirmative answer and then immediately shifted ground to a clearly pre-planned framing:

> Yes, Justice Thomas, but I think that it's important to put in perspective the position that we are offering the Court today. The president, as the head of the Article II branch, can assert as-applied *Article II objections to criminal laws* that interfere with an exclusive power possessed by the president or that prevent the president from accomplishing his constitutionally assigned functions. That is the constitutional doctrine that currently governs the separation of powers.[50]

In its brief and at oral argument, the government explained that "the position" it was "offering the Court" had several discrete components.[51]

First, Congress cannot interfere with the President's "conclusive and preclusive," i.e., exclusive, powers within the Jackson framework. This category, the government maintained, included the President's

---

[47] *See* Brief for the United States at 20–24, Trump v. United States, 603 U.S. 593 (2024) (No. 23-939).

[48] *Id.* at 20–21.

[49] *See* discussion and sources cited *supra* note 40.

[50] Transcript of Oral Argument, *supra* note 7, at 69–70 (emphasis added).

[51] *Id.* at 69–71; *see also* Brief for the United States, *supra* note 47, at 4–6.

authority to recognize foreign nations, to veto bills, to grant pardons, and to remove at will a principal officer of a single-headed agency.[52] Second, Congress also cannot enact a statute that as applied to the President would "impede the President's ability to carry out his constitutionally assigned duties."[53]

Third, and closely relatedly, federal courts must construe generally worded statutes to avoid serious questions of unconstitutionality under the first two rationales. This argument came in narrow and broad versions of constitutional avoidance. In some contexts, the government argued, the President can be carved out of a statute on a case-by-case basis. But other criminal statutes burden presidential power "in such a wide range of applications" that the President must be deemed excluded from the statute in every instance.[54] (The Trump lawyers raised this last component of the third argument for the first time in their brief in the Supreme Court but raised none of the other arguments for limits on Congress's power.[55])

These arguments for constitutional constraints on Congress's power to regulate the presidency were relevant because the government maintained that Congress had in fact criminalized Trump's allegedly illegal conduct and had the constitutional authority to do so.[56] The question of Congress's power to regulate the presidency was thus directly implicated in the case even if not raised by the defendant or

[52] Brief for the United States, *supra* note 47, at 11; Transcript of Oral Argument, *supra* note 7, at 87, 115–16.

[53] Brief for the United States, *supra* note 47, at 24. The government made a closely related if not identical argument early in its brief when explaining constitutional protections for the presidency. *See id.* at 11–12.

[54] Transcript of Oral Argument, *supra* note 7, at 121.

[55] Brief of Petitioner President Donald J. Trump at 37–40, Trump v. United States, 603 U.S. 593 (2024) (No. 23-939). Trump's lawyer, D. John Sauer, claimed at oral argument that Trump's district-court motion to dismiss based on statutory grounds, *see supra* note 40, set forth "a whole panoply of clear statement rules," Transcript of Oral Argument, *supra* note 7, at 65. But, as noted above, the motion did not in fact raise the clear statement or constitutional arguments based on separation of powers. When Justice Jackson noted that Trump "didn't raise" the clear statement or avoidance issue below, Sauer demurred and stated that the issue was "fairly included in the question presented." *Id.* As Dreeben correctly noted at oral argument, the argument "was not raised in the district court and it was not raised in the court of appeals." *Id.* at 122.

[56] This point is implicit in the prosecution, and Dreeben stated at oral argument that a "building block of [the government's] submission is that Congress actually did apply these criminal laws to official conduct." *Id.* at 124; *see also* Brief for the United States, *supra* note 47, at 24–26.

addressed below.[57] Dreeben, on behalf of the government, acknowledged at oral argument that the Court had "discretion to resolve that issue."[58]

It is important to understand why constitutional constraints on Congress's power were relevant to immunity in the criminal context in *Trump* but were not relevant to immunity from civil suit in *Fitzgerald*. In contrast to *Trump*, which was premised on congressional regulation of presidential conduct, the lawsuit in *Fitzgerald* was based on *judicially implied* statutory and constitutional causes of action. In recognizing a constitutionally based absolute immunity from judicial review of civil damages suits against the President, *Fitzgerald* assumed the validity of these implied causes of action but, under the canon of constitutional avoidance, declined to address Congress's power to create a cause of action for damages against the President.[59] The Court in *Fitzgerald* thus left open the possibility that Congress had the constitutional authority to enact a statute imposing civil damages liability on the President for official acts, but said not a word about how this authority might be limited by exclusive presidential power.

D. DEFENSE OR IMMUNITY?

The introduction at the Supreme Court of the issue of constitutional limits on Congress's power to criminalize official presidential acts raised a conceptual difficulty: Should such limits be treated as a defense to prosecution, or as an immunity from judicial review as in *Fitzgerald*?[60]

From one perspective, presidential immunity is a principle—like absolute immunity for judges, prosecutors, and legislators—that blocks "an otherwise valid legal rule [from being] enforced against a particular defendant in a particular context."[61] Since a criminal statute that

---

[57] Transcript of Oral Argument, *supra* note 7, at 121–22.

[58] *Id.* at 124; *see also* United States v. W. Pac. R.R. Co., 352 U.S. 59, 63 (1956) (exercising discretion to consider legal arguments raised by neither party or otherwise forfeited in the lower courts when they involve matters of "continuing public concern").

[59] 457 U.S. 731, 748 n.27 (1982); *see also* Schmidt, *supra* note 27 (manuscript at 15–16) (explaining this point).

[60] For a sophisticated analysis on the various types of immunity claims in *Trump v. United States*, see Carlos M. Vázquez, *What Is* Trump *Immunity?*, 100 NOTRE DAME L. REV. (forthcoming 2025) (on file with author).

[61] Trevor W. Morrison, *Moving Beyond Absolutes on Presidential Immunity*, LAWFARE (Mar. 18, 2024, 8:00 AM), https://www.lawfaremedia.org/article/moving-beyond-absolutes-on-presidential-immunity.

intrudes on an exclusive presidential power is *invalid*, it would be a defense rather than an immunity on this view.[62] By contrast, one might see any constitutional constraint on adjudication, including a Jackson Category Three constraint on Congress's power, as a presidential "immunity" in the sense of a constitutional bar on federal courts proceeding against the President. The Court has, in the federalism context at least, treated analogous constraints on state power to prosecute federal executive officials as an "immunity."[63]

Whether the constitutional constraint on Congress is treated as an "immunity" matters because "the essence of absolute immunity is its possessor's entitlement not to have to answer for his conduct."[64] If the constitutional constraint on Congress is a defense and not an immunity, then a President may have to suffer through trial under an unconstitutional law that would not be appealable until final judgment. The government had maintained this view in passing in the court of appeals and initially took that position at oral argument.[65]

But Justice Barrett at oral argument worried that an appeal on issues of this sort only after a jury trial and final judgment may come too late to protect the President.[66] Dreeben acknowledged that "the Court has the authority to craft procedural rules that implement its Article II concerns." This meant, he said, that the Court could treat a President's protection from an unconstitutional federal statute as an issue that the trial judge could address at the outset of a case and that could be subject to interlocutory review.[67]

E. A Fateful Choice

The government argued that its many concessions to presidential power vis-à-vis limits on Congress were not implicated by the Trump

[62] *Id.*

[63] *See id.*; Cunningham v. Neagle, 135 U.S. 1, 79 (1890).

[64] Mitchell v. Forsyth, 472 U.S. 511, 525 (1985).

[65] Answering Brief for the United States, *supra* note 41, at 45–46; Transcript of Oral Argument, *supra* note 7, at 78–80. At the same time, the government in places treated the issue of constitutional constraints on Congress's power to regulate the presidency as an "immunity." Brief for the United States, *supra* note 47, at 4; Response in Opposition to Defendant's Motion to Dismiss on Presidential Immunity Grounds, *supra* note 40, at 35.

[66] Transcript of Oral Argument, *supra* note 7, at 155.

[67] *Id.* at 155–59. Dreeben's concession has a basis in *Fitzgerald*, which had suggested that in the presidential context collateral orders could include "serious and unsettled issues" that "alleg[e] a threatened breach of essential Presidential prerogatives under the separation of powers." 457 U.S. 731, 743 (1982).

prosecution. All of Trump's conduct, it maintained, was covered by one of four validly enacted and applied federal criminal statutes. It offered its concessions as comfort to the Court about the implications for the presidency of denying Trump immunity in the case, and perhaps because it suspected the Court would be interested in these issues even though they were not addressed by the courts below.

But once the government put these issues on the Court's plate, several hard questions arose—questions that did not have firm answers in the Court's case law. Which and how many of the separation of powers theories offered by the government applied in the case, and how? What exactly is the scope of the President's exclusive Article II powers? How does the Court determine whether a federal criminal law unduly burdens a presidential power or prevents the President from accomplishing his constitutionally assigned duties?

The proper answers to these questions are notoriously underspecified in the Court's jurisprudence and contested among scholars. The government provided no concrete answers to these questions, and the Trump team did not address them. Also difficult and novel, as oral argument made clear, is the role the President's motives for conduct play in assessing these burdens, and in determining whether his action is official or unofficial.[68]

The Chief Justice asked Dreeben at oral argument whether, considering the D.C. Circuit's overbroad and erroneous reasoning, the Supreme Court should simply "send [the case] back to the court of appeals or issue an opinion making clear that [its reasoning is] not the law."[69] Dreeben did not answer that question. But in light of the hard and novel issues raised for the first time before the Court, and the rushed proceedings, the Court and the country might have been better off if the Court had taken the path suggested by the Chief Justice. Instead, it issued an opinion that, while resolving relatively little and deeply ambiguous in places, amounted to perhaps the most consequential disquisition ever on the law of the presidency.

II. The Majority Opinion

Everyone in the case agreed that a former President gets no immunity for private acts. The hard questions were about how to

[68] Transcript of Oral Argument, *supra* note 7, at 21–25, 31–33, 133–42, 154–55.

[69] *Id.* at 75.

distinguish a President's public from private acts, and what type of immunity, if any, a former President would receive for conduct related to public acts in office.

This Part analyzes the majority opinion's answers to these questions. It focuses primarily on the first element of the Court's immunity holding concerning the President's exclusive powers vis-à-vis Congress. It then assesses the Court's additional holding about the President's presumptive immunity for non-exclusive powers, and related issues. The concurring and dissenting opinions are discussed as pertinent.

A. EXCLUSIVE PRESIDENTIAL POWER VIS-À-VIS CONGRESS

The majority began with the issue that the government had teed up: the President's exclusive power vis-à-vis Congress. It described the President's protection from prosecution under an unconstitutional law as an "absolute immun[ity]" without bothering to engage the distinction between defense and immunity.[70] And then the Court staked out significant new ground—both from the government's argument and its precedents—when it applied these principles to Trump's attempt to pressure the Acting Attorney General, with threats of firing him, to convince states to replace their legitimate electors with Trump's fraudulent slates.

After asserting without explanation that these were public and not private acts, the Court ruled that the conduct implicated the President's exclusive authority and could not be criminalized by Congress.[71] It did so in part because the President's threatened firing of the Acting Attorney General, a central element of the charge of obstructing a congressional proceeding, implicated the President's exclusive removal power.[72] The Court also held that the effort to punish the President for obstruction due to his conversations with Justice Department officials implicated the President's exclusive power over the

[70] Justice Barrett's concurrence defended the treatment of the constitutional limit on congressional power as an immediately appealable issue but did not characterize the issue as an immunity. Trump v. United States, 603 U.S. 593, 651 (2024) (Barrett, J., concurring in part).

[71] *Id.* at 620 (majority opinion). The government appeared to acknowledge that the President's acts were official when it described them as "official conduct that was intertwined with his private means of attaining the conspiracy's aim." Brief for the United States, *supra* note 47, at 47.

[72] *See Trump*, 603 U.S. at 620–21.

investigation and prosecution of federal law, which the Court appeared to tie to the Take Care Clause. Specifically, the Court ruled that Congress could not make it a crime for the President to obstruct a congressional proceeding based on the President's efforts, however corrupt, to enforce federal election law.[73]

These were the most far-reaching rulings in the decision, and some of the most far-reaching pronouncements about presidential power in the Court's history. Four dimensions warrant comment.

1. *Formalism.* The Jackson Category Three element of *Trump* was, like Jackson's treatment in *Youngstown*, very light on textualism and originalism. But in contrast to Jackson's treatment, it was formalist in the extreme.[74] The Court determined that the President's communications with the Justice Department were exercises of the President's Article II removal power and take care duty. And that was that: Both Congress's Article I powers and the courts' Article III powers had to yield without any consideration of the scope of those powers, or how they might overlap with the President's own powers, and without any effort at balancing the interests or powers of the branches.[75]

This methodological approach tends to expand the category of exclusive presidential power because it does not consider any countervailing factor once an act is deemed to be an exercise of the exclusive presidential power. The approach is particularly significant because it goes to the underlying legality of presidential action and because the Court married it to novel extensions of the President's removal power and law enforcement discretion.

2. *Removal.* The Court amplified its removal jurisprudence to an uncertain but potentially large degree. The Court in three decisions before Trump had expanded the President's exclusive removal power in the face of statutory for-cause restrictions on presidential firings.[76] In *Seila Law LLC v. Consumer Financial Protection Bureau* in 2020, the

---

[73] *See id.* at 620–21, 626–27.

[74] *See* Roisman, *supra* note 35, at 42.

[75] *See Trump*, 603 U.S. at 608 ("[O]nce it is determined that the President acted within the scope of his exclusive authority, his discretion in exercising such authority cannot be subject to further judicial examination.").

[76] *See* Collins v. Yellen, 594 U.S. 220 (2021); Seila Law LLC v. Consumer Fin. Prot. Bureau, 591 U.S. 197 (2020); Free Enter. Fund v. Pub. Co. Acct. Oversight Bd., 561 U.S. 477 (2010). The Court had in various ways narrowed *Humphrey's Executor v. United States*, 295 U.S. 602 (1935), *Myers v. United States*, 272 U.S. 52 (1926), and *Morrison v. Olson*, 487 U.S. 654 (1988). For an explanation, see Daniel D. Birk, *Interrogating the Historical Basis for a Unitary Executive*, 73 Stan. L. Rev. 175, 189–92 (2021).

Court described its precedents as recognizing "only two exceptions to the President's unrestricted removal power": "one for multimember expert agencies that do not wield substantial executive power, and one for inferior officers with limited duties and no policymaking or administrative authority."[77]

Trump formally leaves these exceptions in place, though perhaps in a half-hearted way.[78] But the decision extends the President's exclusive removal power beyond its traditional domain of resisting for-cause limits on firings to a different context. The Court applied this exclusive power to deny Congress the authority to criminalize a President's use of the removal power to obstruct a congressional proceeding. That ruling is remarkable enough. But its logic appears to disable Congress from punishing the President for firing or threatening to fire a subordinate official in an effort to facilitate any crime.[79]

Congress now might be unable, for example, to criminalize a President's threatened or actual termination of a senior subordinate in order to obstruct justice or to use unlawful force or, possibly, to facilitate a bribe. I qualify this conclusion with respect to bribery because of an exchange between the Chief Justice and Justice Barrett about whether and how a President could be prosecuted for bribery, which opened up a possible yet ill-defined loophole to the majority's conclusion about exclusive presidential powers.[80] Even with this

[77] 591 U.S. at 204, 218.

[78] The Court in *Trump* stated that "Congress lacks authority to control the President's 'unrestricted power of removal' with respect to 'executive officers of the United States whom he has appointed,'" with a "cf." citation to the *Seila Law* exceptions. *Trump*, 603 U.S. at 608–09 (first quoting *Myers*, 272 U.S. at 106, 176; and then citing *Seila Law*, 591 U.S. at 215).

[79] The same logic appears to apply to other exclusive powers—for example, a presidential pardon in an effort to obstruct justice would not seem to be something Congress could criminalize.

[80] The Chief Justice maintained that the government could not introduce evidence of a President's official acts that were protected by immunity to prove crimes involving unprotected conduct. *Trump*, 603 U.S. at 630–32 ("Part III-C"). Justice Barrett disagreed, arguing that a President could be prosecuted (for example) for the crime of bribery because the Constitution "does not authorize a President to seek or accept bribes" and maintained that "excluding from trial any mention of the official act connected to the bribe would hamstring the prosecution." *Id.* at 655–66 (Barrett, J., concurring in part). The Chief Justice replied that "the prosecutor may point to the public record to show the fact that the President performed the official act" and "may admit evidence of what the President allegedly demanded, received, accepted, or agreed to receive or accept in return for being influenced in the performance of the act" but may not "admit testimony or private records of the President or his advisers probing the official act itself." *Id.* at 632 n.3 (majority opinion).

The upshot of this exchange on its own terms is hard to fathom. *See* Anna Bower & Benjamin Wittes, *What's Going on in Footnote 3?*, LAWFARE (July 23, 2024, 4:54 PM), https://

important caveat, the Court's removal holding is a significant and never-before-hinted-at expansion of the President's removal power that was nowhere briefed nor publicly discussed before the ruling. The scope of the principle going forward is unclear.[81]

3. *Take Care Clause.* Third, a broader and even more significant holding is that the President has "exclusive authority over the investigative and prosecutorial functions of the Justice Department and its officials."[82] The Court ostensibly tied this power to the Article II command that the President shall "take Care that the Laws be faithfully executed."[83]

The Court provided little support and no analysis for this conclusion. It cited cases about the President's broad civil and criminal law enforcement discretion that were inapposite because the Court had recognized that this discretion was subject to at least some forms of congressional regulation. The Court had previously ruled, for example, that Congress could "limit an agency's exercise of enforcement power if it wishes, either by setting substantive priorities or by circumscribing an agency's power to discriminate among issues or cases it will pursue."[84] It has also said that an "extreme case of nonenforcement arguably could exceed the bounds of enforcement discretion" even in the criminal context.[85]

---

www.lawfaremedia.org/article/what-s-going-on-in-footnote-3 (examining this dispute in detail). For purposes of the claim in the text, the upshot is even more uncertain since it involves a bribe *facilitated by the exercise of an exclusive presidential power*, a wrinkle that the Roberts-Barrett exchange did not consider. Also unclear is the basis for Justice Barrett's claim that the Constitution does not authorize the President to seek or accept bribes, since that does not appear to be the Court's test for official action, much less official action for conduct concerning an exclusive presidential power.

[81] It is unclear on its own terms and also due to Footnote Three of the majority opinion. *See* discussion and sources cited *supra* note 80.

[82] *Trump*, 603 U.S. at 621; *see also id.* at 620 ("[T]he Executive Branch has 'exclusive authority and absolute discretion' to decide which crimes to investigate and prosecute, including with respect to allegations of election crime." (quoting United States v. Nixon, 418 U.S. 683, 693 (1974))).

[83] *Id.*

[84] Heckler v. Chaney, 470 U.S. 821, 833 (1985); *see also id.* at 833 n.4 (mentioning the possibility of judicial review if "the agency has 'consciously and expressly adopted a general policy' that is so extreme as to amount to an abdication of its statutory responsibilities" (quoting Adams v. Richardson, 480 F.2d 1159, 1162 (D.C. Cir. 1973) (en banc))).

[85] United States v. Texas, 599 U.S. 670, 683 (2023) (making claim in standing context on assumption that the Executive Branch had "wholly abandoned its statutory responsibilities to make arrests or bring prosecutions"). The Court in *Texas* stated that a requirement that the government "shall" arrest certain noncitizens "does not entitle any particular plaintiff to enforce that mandate in federal court" in light of the "deep-rooted nature of law enforcement

Trump additionally stated, citing *United States v. Nixon*, that "the Executive Branch has 'exclusive authority and absolute discretion' to decide which crimes to investigate and prosecute."[86] But this was a dictum about prosecutorial discretion vis-à-vis *courts* uttered while rejecting justiciability objections to adjudication of the *Nixon* subpoena. The decision *Nixon* primarily relied on, *The Confiscation Cases*, made clear that Congress *could* constrain prosecutorial discretion.[87]

Nor did the Court say anything about how its ruling squared with its broader Take Care Clause jurisprudence. That Clause is the main source of presidential discretion whether and how to enforce civil and criminal law.[88] But it is also the source of "the President's duty to abide by and enforce the laws enacted by Congress" as part of a President's "duty to respect legislative supremacy and not to act *contra legem*."[89] The important case here is *Kendall v. United States*, where the Court denied that the Take Care Clause gave the President a "dispensing power" or "power to forbid [the laws'] execution," which, if accepted, "would be clothing the President with a power entirely to control the legislation of congress, and paralyze the administration of justice."[90]

The Court prior to *Trump* had never explained how the Take Care Clause's power-amplifying support for broad (but defeasible) presidential enforcement discretion squared with the Clause's power-constraining command that the President must abide by and enforce

---

discretion." *Id.* at 682 (quoting Town of Castle Rock v. Gonzales, 545 U.S. 748, 761, 764–65 (2005)). Without taking a firm position, the Court added that "an arrest mandate" might be enforceable in court, but only with "'stronger indication' from Congress that judicial review of enforcement discretion is appropriate. . . ." *Id.* (quoting *Castle Rock*, 545 U.S. at 761).

[86] *Trump*, 603 U.S. at 620 (citing *Nixon*, 418 U.S. at 693).

[87] The issue in *The Confiscation Cases*, 74 U.S. (7 Wall.) 454 (1868), was whether a federal attorney had discretion to dismiss a civil qui tam suit. The Court stated that he did, with a large caveat about congressional control: "Public prosecutions, until they come before the court to which they are returnable, are within the exclusive direction of the district attorney, and even after they are entered in court, they are so far under his control that he may enter a *nolle prosequi* at any time before the jury is empanelled [sic] for the trial of the case, *except in cases where it is otherwise provided in some act of Congress*." *Id.* at 457 (emphasis added). *Nixon* also cited the court of appeals decision in *United States v. Cox*, 342 F.2d 167 (5th Cir. 1965), which had affirmed only that *courts* (as opposed to Congress) could not interfere with federal prosecutorial discretion. *Nixon*, 418 U.S. at 693 (citing *Cox*, 342 F.2d at 171).

[88] *See, e.g.*, *Texas*, 599 U.S. at 678; United States v. Armstrong, 517 U.S. 456, 464 (1996); *Chaney*, 470 U.S. at 821.

[89] Jack Goldsmith & John F. Manning, *The Protean Take Care Clause*, 164 U. Pa. L. Rev. 1835, 1848 (2016).

[90] 37 U.S. (12 Pet.) 524, 612–13 (1838).

federal law. It had justified presidential enforcement discretion vis-à-vis *courts* as a pragmatic accommodation of (i) inevitable enforcement choices and tradeoffs in the face of over-legalization by Congress, (ii) changing public-welfare needs, (iii) executive branch resource constraints, and (iv) the judiciary's "lack [of] meaningful standards for assessing the propriety of enforcement choices."[91] At the same time, as noted above, the Court had suggested—but without specificity—that Congress might constrain at least some elements of executive enforcement discretion in the civil and criminal contexts.[92]

The Court mentioned none of this background, and none of it was discussed in the briefs or at oral argument. Yet its holding that the President has exclusive power to direct subordinates in investigations and prosecutions throws a bomb into this important corner of the law. It is hard to fathom what it might entail.

The first thing it might entail is the death knell for *Morrison*'s holding that Congress can "reduce[] the amount of control or supervision that the Attorney General and, through him, the President exercises over the investigation and prosecution of a certain class of alleged criminal activity."[93] This holding rested in part on the Court's approval of removal restrictions for an inferior officer in the Justice Department, a ruling that *Trump* technically does not address. But *Morrison* also held that congressional restrictions on presidential (and attorney-general) control over the prosecutorial discretion of a jurisdictionally constrained inferior officer did not violate the separation of powers because it did not unduly burden executive branch power.[94]

This latter holding is hard to square with *Trump*'s insistence that the President's control over investigation and prosecution is exclusive vis-à-vis Congress and thus (on *Trump*'s formalist analysis) not subject to any countervailing burden analysis.[95] In this regard, *Trump* quoted Justice Scalia's *Morrison* dissent that "'investigation and prosecution of crimes is a quintessentially executive function'" in order to explain why the allegations against Trump concerning his Justice

[91] *Texas*, 599 U.S. at 679; *see also* Zachary S. Price, *Enforcement Discretion and Executive Duty*, 67 Vand. L. Rev. 671, 681–83 (2014).

[92] *See Chaney*, 470 U.S. at 832–33; *Texas*, 599 U.S. at 683.

[93] Morrison v. Olson, 487 U.S. 654, 695 (1988).

[94] *See id.*

[95] Trump v. United States, 603 U.S. 593, 620–21 (2024).

Department efforts "plainly implicate Trump's 'conclusive and preclusive' authority."[96]

Trump might go further and call into question some applications of the proposition from *United States v. Perkins*, reaffirmed in *Myers*, that "when Congress by law vests the appointment of inferior officers in the heads of departments, it may limit and restrict the power of removal as it deems best for the public interest."[97] The basic idea that the removal power is linked to the appointments power is not affected by *Trump*. But *Trump* arguably undercuts *Perkins*' logic, not through the power of removal, but rather through the President's exclusive power to direct law enforcement activities, which is not tied to his power over appointments. If this power is truly exclusive, then it may not be limitable by Congress with respect to any executive branch action. To the extent that *Perkins* allows Congress through removal restrictions to prevent a President from directing the law enforcement actions of all subordinate executive branch officials, it might not survive *Trump*.[98]

More broadly, the law enforcement discretion ruling in *Trump* seems to mean that the President has the discretion to use law enforcement tools to achieve ends that Congress has otherwise made illegal. That is, after all, what happened in *Trump*: Congress had made it a crime to obstruct a congressional proceeding, but the Court held that Congress lacked the power to make this law applicable to the President's alleged sham investigation of state election fraud because the investigation implicated the President's exclusive investigative authority. The logic of the holding should extend beyond criminal law enforcement to civil law enforcement.[99] There seems to be no

[96] *Id.* at 620 (quoting Brief for the United States, *supra* note 47, at 19). The Court actually quoted Justice Scalia by quoting the government's brief that had quoted the statement Scalia had made in his *Morrison* dissent. *See* Brief for the United States, *supra* note 47, at 19 (quoting *Morrison*, 487 U.S. at 706 (Scalia, J., dissenting)).

[97] United States v. Perkins, 116 U.S. 483, 485 (1886).

[98] *Perkins* appears to survive the pre-*Trump* removal cases. *See, e.g.*, Seila Law LLC v. Consumer Fin. Prot. Bureau, 591 U.S. 197, 215, 217 (2020) (citing *Perkins*, 116 U.S. at 485).

[99] The Take Care Clause is the source of executive enforcement discretion in civil and criminal contexts. *See* U.S. Const. art. II, § 3. The Court cited a civil enforcement discretion case, *United States v. Texas*, 599 U.S. 670 (2023), in support of its rule. It also cited *Heckler v. Chaney*, 470 U.S. 821, 832 (1985). The Court's differential treatment of civil and criminal immunity for non-exclusive powers in a later section in *Trump* that discussed immunity for non-exclusive presidential acts, *see Trump*, 603 U.S. at 621–28, is not pertinent to its discussion of presidentially exclusive powers, which is based on a different constitutional logic.

reason why it would not extend beyond the Justice Department to the President's direction of all law enforcement activities around the executive branch.[100] Taken for all it is worth, the Take Care Clause discussion moves in the direction of a presidential dispensation power.

To get a flavor of the uncertainties about this aspect of the opinion, and what this holding might entail, imagine four situations:

1. Congress makes it a crime for the President to obstruct a congressional proceeding, and the President decides to enforce federal election law in a way that would otherwise be the crime of obstructing a congressional proceeding.
2. Congress in one law makes it a crime to transport one or more pounds of cocaine in interstate commerce and in a second law directs the Justice Department not to prosecute transportation of five pounds or less unless a gun was used in the violation.
3. Congress enacts a law that says it shall be a crime to transport (i) more than five pounds of cocaine in interstate commerce or (ii) less than five pounds of cocaine in interstate commerce if the crime was committed with a gun.
4. Congress bans TikTok from operating inside the United States and imposes large civil penalties for violations.[101]

Situation One is *Trump v. United States.* The Court held that the criminal prohibition against the President obstructing a congressional proceeding had to give way to his exclusive power to enforce federal election law. Although Situation Two is different from Situation One in expressly seeking to limit law enforcement discretion, it is like Situation One in seeking in one law to constrain the President's discretion to enforce another law. It is unclear how *Trump* operates in Situation Two, though one could argue that it means that the second law, the one that seeks to constrain presidential discretion, is unconstitutional.

Situation Two seems functionally similar to Situation Three. But in Situation Three, Congress has limited presidential enforcement

[100] To mention just a few examples, the Drug Enforcement Agency, the Bureau of Alcohol, Tobacco, and Firearms, U.S. Immigration and Customs Enforcement, the Transportation Security Administration, and the Internal Revenue Service all have law enforcement responsibilities, as do many traditional civil agencies, including independent ones like the Securities and Exchange Commission and the Federal Trade Commission.

[101] I thank Edward Whelan for discussion of these points.

power not by placing limits on enforcement discretion directly, but rather in the manner it has defined the crimes. Since a President has no crime-making power and cannot prosecute crimes that do not exist, congressional control of presidential enforcement discretion in Situation Three, though functionally like Situation Two, seems untouched by *Trump*.

Situation Four is the TikTok ban.[102] In an executive order (EO) on January 20, President Trump instructed the Attorney General to not enforce the act for seventy-five days so that Trump could assess the foreign policy implications of the ban and negotiate a work-around.[103] The President also ordered the Attorney General to inform the private firms that "there has been no violation of the statute and that there is no liability for any conduct" in violation of the statute during the seventy-five-day period (or after the effective date of the act and before the EO). This action, unlike *Trump*, is not the violation of a statute through enforcement of another but rather seems more like the assertion of a dispensation power not to enforce due to a policy objection. *Trump* may point in this direction but does not by its terms go this far. And Trump's TikTok order seems to blow through the Court's concerns about blanket non-enforcement in *Texas* and about a dispensation power in *Kendall*.

Justice Barrett noted in concurrence that she did "not understand the Court to hold that *all* exercises of the Take Care power fall within the core executive power," and the Court certainly did not insist or make clear otherwise.[104] So we do not know the scope of the Court's ruling on exclusive enforcement discretion or the extent to which it is tied to the Take Care Clause.[105] My only point is that the Court's ruling about the President's exclusive control over the investigative and prosecutorial function ostensibly tied to the Take Care Clause

[102] Protecting Americans from Foreign Adversary Controlled Applications Act of 2024, Pub. L. No. 118–50, 138 Stat. 955 (codified at 15 U.S.C. § 9901).

[103] Exec. Order No. 14,166, 90 Fed. Reg. 8611 (Jan. 20, 2025) ("I hereby order the Attorney General not to take any action on behalf of the United States to enforce the Act for 75 days from the date of this order.").

[104] *Trump*, 603 U.S. at 651 n.1 (Barrett, J., concurring in part). Justice Sotomayor appeared to read the majority's Take Care Clause analysis more broadly. *See id.* at 676 (Sotomayor, J., dissenting).

[105] The implications for this part of the opinion are further diminished by the uncertainties inherent in the back and forth between the majority and Justice Barrett about prosecuting a President for bribery, which presumably qualify the exclusive law enforcement discretion analysis as well. *See supra* note 80.

opens up a bevy of possible new implications about the scope of presidential power, both vertically within the executive branch and with respect to law enforcement in the world.

4. *Unitary Executive.* The theory of the unitary executive is that all of the executive power is vested in the President and the President, through removal or other tools, thus has the authority to manage and direct all executive branch officials.[106] The theory has a long history but came to prominence during the Reagan Administration.[107] Taken to its logical end, it entails that the President has control over every executive branch decision and that any congressional effort to deny him that power by preventing the President from ordering an action or firing an insubordinate official is unconstitutional.[108]

The Supreme Court has never fully embraced the unitary executive theory. *Trump* may be the closest it has ever come.[109] The Court reiterated that all of the executive power is vested in the President and that "unlike anyone else, the President is a branch of government, and the Constitution vests in him sweeping powers and duties."[110] It expands presidential removal power beyond prior baselines, as noted above.[111] The Court also underscored the President's "directive power" over subordinate official actions. It did so partly in reliance on the removal power, but also stated that the President's power to "supervise"

---

[106] *See generally* Steven G. Calabresi & Christopher S. Yoo, The Unitary Executive: Presidential Power from Washington to Bush (2008).

[107] *See id.*; *see also* Ashraf Ahmed, Lev Menand & Noah A. Rosenblum, *The Making of Presidential Administration*, 137 Harv. L. Rev. 2131, 2133 (2024).

[108] *See* Adrian Vermeule, *The Head and Body of Leviathan*, New Dig. (July 18, 2024), https://thenewdigest.substack.com/p/the-head-and-body-of-leviathan.

[109] *Myers v. United States*, 272 U.S. 52 (1926), endorsed a famously broad version of the unitary executive theory, but it contained qualifications. For example, *Myers* reserved the possibility that "if a statute 'specifically committed [a given set of decisions] to the discretion of a particular officer' or established a 'quasi-judicial . . . executive tribunal[] whose decisions after hearing affect [the] interests of individuals,' then Congress might properly foreclose the President from intervening in the decision of a particular case." Goldsmith & Manning, *supra* note 89, at 1840–41 (quoting *Myers*, 272 U.S. at 135). *Myers* also left in place the rule of *Perkins* that "when Congress, by law, vests the appointment of inferior officers in the heads of departments, it may limit and restrict the power of removal as it deems best for the public interest" because "[t]he constitutional authority in congress to thus vest the appointment implies authority to limit, restrict, and regulate the removal by such laws as congress may enact in relation to the officers so appointed." *Myers*, 272 U.S. at 160 (quoting United States v. Perkins, 116 U.S. 483, 485 (1886)); *see also id.* at 127, 161–62; *supra* notes 97–98 and accompanying text (examining the extent to which *Perkins* survives *Trump*).

[110] Trump v. United States, 603 U.S. 593, 639–40 (2024).

[111] *See supra* notes 76–81 and accompanying text.

the executive branch and "manage[]" at least "the most important of his subordinates" was exclusive.[112]

Perhaps most importantly, and cutting across all of the points above, the Court's ruling about the President's exclusive authority over enforcement discretion can now be seen as an important component of unitary executive power. The Court's holding about the President's exclusive control over how the executive branch enforces the law now adds to the President's removal power in enhancing the President's vertical control over executive branch action, especially since that vertical control gives the President expanded discretion from the pre-*Trump* baseline over when and how to enforce (and thus, perhaps, comply with) federal law.

B. FUNCTIONAL IMMUNITY FOR NON-EXCLUSIVE POWERS

The Court followed its formalist analysis of presidential "immunity" for exclusive presidential powers with a functional analysis of presidential immunity for non-exclusive presidential powers "shared with Congress."[113]

The Court resolved this issue by melding the two functionalist *Nixon* opinions about immunity from judicial review. Contrary to what *Nixon v. Fitzgerald* had suggested, the Court viewed the dangers of intrusion on the authority and functions of the presidency to be "greater" in the criminal context than in the civil context.[114] The Court acknowledged that the President faced many fewer criminal than civil trials but thought the more severe consequences of criminal sanction would have a greater deterrent impact on the presidency. Yet the Court did not recognize a definitive absolute immunity, as in *Nixon v. Fitzgerald*, due to the countervailing public interest—not present in *Fitzgerald*—in criminal law enforcement, including against the President. The Court cited *United States v. Nixon* as accommodating the public interest in criminal law enforcement vis-à-vis presidential claims of authority to resist the subpoena there by recognizing a defeasible "presumptive privilege."[115]

---

[112] *Trump*, 603 U.S. at 608, 621 (first quoting Seila Law LLC v. Consumer Fin. Prot. Bureau, 591 U.S. 197, 204 (2020); and then quoting Nixon v. Fitzgerald, 457 U.S. 731, 750 (1982)).

[113] *Id.* at 609–10.

[114] *Id.* at 613.

[115] *Id.* at 614; *see also* United States v. Burr, 25 F. Cas. 30, 33–34 (C.C.D. Va. 1807) (No. 14,692d); United States v. Burr, 25 F. Cas. 187, 192 (C.C.D. Va. 1807) (No. 14,694).

The Court resolved these "competing considerations" by recognizing at least a "presumptive immunity" from criminal prosecution for the outer perimeter of non-presidential public acts that rest on non-exclusive powers.[116] The Court said the immunity might ultimately be absolute but that it need not decide that question now. It instead ruled that the tentative "presumptive immunity" applied to the President's non-exclusive official acts "unless the Government can show that applying a criminal prohibition to that act would pose no 'dangers of intrusion on the authority and functions of the Executive Branch.'"[117] This "balancing" test seems more generous to the President than the *Fitzgerald* case that it quotes, since it leaves out *Fitzgerald*'s countervailing consideration of "the constitutional weight of the interest to be served."[118] Whatever its scope, the immunity here, as in *Fitzgerald* itself, did not concern the legality of the President's underlying acts, but rather shielded the President from adjudication due to the impact on the presidency.

This functional analysis has a made-up feel and is an analytical mess, though perhaps no more made up and no messier than the functional analyses in the two *Nixon* decisions on which it relied, or any functional separation of powers analysis.[119] The Court did not explain why the low chance of high-cost criminal prosecution and punishment "are plainly more likely to distort Presidential decisionmaking" than the many magnitudes greater possibility of civil damages liability. One can imagine this calculus cashing out in the opposite way, as the dissent suggested, though in truth there are no metrics here.[120] Nor did the Court explain why it could not decide at this stage if the Constitution demanded absolute or presumptive immunity in this

---

[116] *Trump*, 603 U.S. at 614–15.

[117] *Id.* at 615 (quoting *Fitzgerald*, 457 U.S. at 754).

[118] *Fitzgerald* had stated that "a court, before exercising jurisdiction, must balance the constitutional weight of the interest to be served against the dangers of intrusion on the authority and functions of the Executive Branch." 457 U.S. at 754. For criticisms of the Court's formulation, see Schmidt, *supra* note 27 (manuscript at 38); Trevor W. Morrison, *A Rule for the Ages, or a Rule for Trump?*, LAWFARE (July 11, 2024, 1:42 PM), https://www.lawfaremedia.org/article/a-rule-for-the-ages–or-a-rule-for-trump.

[119] *See, e.g.*, Roisman, *supra* note 33, at 1387; Martin H. Redish & Elizabeth J. Cisar, *The Need for Pragmatic Formalism in Separation of Powers Theory*, 41 DUKE L.J. 449, 450, 491 (1991); Suzanne Prieur Clair, *Separation of Powers: A New Look at the Functionalist Approach*, 40 CASE W. RSRV. L. REV. 331, 338 (1989).

[120] *See Trump*, 603 U.S. at 673–74 (Sotomayor, J., dissenting).

context.[121] *Nixon v. Fitzgerald* had relied on the "dangers of intrusion on the authority and functions of the Executive Branch" to establish a clear rule of absolute immunity against civil suits.[122] But the Court in *Trump* seemed to render this an as-applied standard, with the burden on the government, and without countervailing considerations, again without explaining the differences.[123]

In contrast to its exclusive presidential power analysis, the Court did not resolve any issues in the case on the basis of the functional immunity it recognized. But the Court did establish three additional propositions—none of which were briefed—that are vital to the scope of the presumptive immunity it recognized.

First, the Court provided guidance on how to distinguish official from unofficial acts.[124] This is a crucial distinction since many of Trump's alleged crimes were not obviously in one camp or the other, and since unofficial acts receive no immunity. *Trump* ruled that the President's official acts include everything he is authorized to do and more, since some official acts, like "speaking to and on behalf of the American people," are not authorized in any constitutionally conventional sense.[125] The Court thus concluded that the "outer perimeter" of official acts includes actions that are "not manifestly or palpably beyond [his] authority."[126] It further ruled that President Trump's communications with Vice President Pence to pressure him to "reject States' legitimate electoral votes or send them back to state legislatures for review" was an official act since the discussions involved their official conduct.[127] Trump was thus at least presumptively immune against this charge, though the Court remanded on the

[121] It is possible that a Justice in the majority did not agree on this question, and that the Chief Justice punted the issue to maintain a majority.

[122] *Fitzgerald*, 457 U.S. at 754.

[123] On countervailing considerations, see *supra* note 118 and accompanying text.

[124] The Court has distinguished between official and unofficial acts implicitly in its immunity cases but has never really explained the distinction. *Cf.* Trump v. Mazars, 591 U.S. 848, 868 (2020) (noting that "there is not always a clear line between [the President's] personal and official affairs" because "[t]he interest of the man" is often "connected with the constitutional rights of the place'" (quoting THE FEDERALIST No. 51, at 349 (James Madison) (Jacob E. Cooke ed., 1961))).

[125] *Trump*, 603 U.S. at 618.

[126] *Id.* (quoting Blassingame v. Trump, 87 F.4th 1, 13 (D.C. Cir. 2023)).

[127] *Id.* at 621–23.

question whether prosecution would unduly interfere with presidential power.

Second, the Court stated that "in dividing official from unofficial conduct, courts may not inquire into the President's motives," since that inquiry would "risk exposing even the most obvious instances of official conduct to judicial examination on the mere allegation of improper purpose, thereby intruding on the Article II interests that immunity seeks to protect."[128] The Court borrowed this idea from *Fitzgerald*, where it was used not as a basis to distinguish official from unofficial acts, but rather as a reason the President warranted absolute immunity for official conduct in a civil suit.[129]

Third, the Court ruled that in prosecuting a President for crimes committed in an unofficial capacity, the jury could not consider evidence concerning the President's official acts. Such consideration, the Court explained, "would permit a prosecutor to do indirectly what he cannot do directly—invite the jury to examine acts for which a President is immune from prosecution," thereby defeating the intended effect of immunity by "heighten[ing] the prospect that the President's official decisionmaking will be distorted."[130] Justice Barrett, who joined the rest of the majority opinion, did not join this analysis. She asserted (without further explanation) that the Constitution "does not require blinding juries to the circumstances surrounding conduct for which Presidents *can* be held liable," and claimed that the rules of evidence could accommodate any concerns about the impact on the presidency.[131] It was in this context that Justice Barrett and the Chief Justice had the hard-to-fathom dispute about whether the majority rule would or would not permit the President to be prosecuted for a bribe.[132]

C. THE DENOUEMENT, AND WHAT REALLY MATTERS

Trump technically decided very little—basically only that the President was immune in connection with the charge related to Justice Department communications, and that his communications with

[128] *Id.* at 618.

[129] *See* Nixon v. Fitzgerald, 457 U.S. 731, 756 (1982).

[130] *Trump*, 603 U.S. at 631.

[131] *Id.* at 655–56 (Barrett, J., concurring in part).

[132] *See supra* note 80.

Vice President Pence were official acts for which he might receive immunity. The scope of immunity it conferred was potentially broad but also possibly quite narrow, depending on how the opinion's ambiguities are resolved. Some critics claimed that the Court effectively immunized Trump from all criminal liability, but that is likely not true.[133] The government's superseding indictment on remand read *Trump* to permit every element of the original prosecution save the one involving communications with the Justice Department.[134] The government was not obviously wrong in its judgment. *Trump* was open-ended and inconclusive enough that it might well have permitted the government to surmount presidential immunity for all of the remaining charges.

We may never get clarity on the scope of the presidential immunity announced in *Trump*. Trump won the presidential election of 2024 and Smith dropped all of the charges. That means that many of the open questions in the opinion about presidential immunity will not be resolved by courts until, if ever, a former President is once against prosecuted.[135] Such unresolved issues could include the ultimate scope of presumptive immunity for official acts within the President's non-exclusive power, the related issue of the distinction between official and unofficial acts in this criminal law context, and the actual availability of official acts evidence to prove unofficial acts crimes.

This does not mean, however, that *Trump* will be irrelevant. Far from it. The immunity ruling, as uncertain as it is, could impact the calculus of executive branch actors even without further judicial clarification. And entirely independently of the Court's rulings about the scope of presidential immunity, the Court's discussion of the President's exclusive presidential power will have a large impact. It is to this issue that I now turn.

---

[133] *See, e.g.*, Sarah Fortinsky, *Schiff Says 'Of Course' He's Concerned About Trump's Personal Threats Against Him*, Hill (July 7, 2024, 10:53 AM ET), https://thehill.com/elections/4758532-adam-schiff-donald-trump-personal-attacks; Devon Ombres, *The Supreme Court Has Fully Embraced an Antidemocratic, Right-Wing Agenda*, Ctr. Am. Progress (July 3, 2024), https://www.americanprogress.org/article/the-supreme-court-has-fully-embraced-an-antidemocratic-right-wing-agenda.

[134] *See* Superseding Indictment, United States v. Trump, 704 F. Supp. 3d 196 (D.D.C. 2024) (No. 23-CR-00257), ECF No. 226.

[135] The immunity issue would be resolved in the first instance by the Justice Department contemplating a prosecution of a former President, and the Department could construe the immunities in *Trump* broadly to preclude prosecution even if the Court might not do so in a case presenting the issue.

III. How *Trump* Impacts the Presidency

Many critics claim that *Trump* opens the floodgates to a "lawless presidency." Justice Sotomayor in dissent, for example, said that the majority "effectively creates a law-free zone around the President, upsetting the status quo that has existed since the Founding."[136] Justice Ketanji Brown Jackson similarly argued that the majority opinion alters the "individual accountability model" that had previously guided Presidents and thus "undermines the constraints of the law as a deterrent for future Presidents who might otherwise abuse their power."[137] Critics of the opinion echoed these themes.[138] These claims must specifically concern presidential violation of criminal laws, since Presidents since *Fitzgerald* have had absolute immunity from civil suits over their official acts.

With so many loose ends in the undisciplined *Trump* opinion, it is impossible to assess these claims with certainty. They are surely overstated at least to the extent that they assume *Trump* clearly established a broad presidential criminal immunity. It did not. *Trump*'s diminishment of the deterrent effect of the criminal law, even on the critics' assumptions, is wildly uncertain.

This Part offers counterpoints to dominant claims about how *Trump* will impact the presidency. In Section III.A, I offer reasons to doubt that the decision will lead to rampant presidential criminality. The argument here might be unsatisfying to some, since it ultimately rests on the claim that a President had all the tools he needed to achieve rampant criminality long before *Trump*, to which the decision adds relatively little. In Section III.B, I focus on an area where I think *Trump* will have a larger impact: in expanding the scope of presidential power vis-à-vis Congress, not as a result of the immunity holding *per se*, but rather as a result of the Court's underlying rulings on the removal power, the take care duty, and exclusive presidential power more generally.

A. Criminal Law Inside the Executive Branch

1. *Subordinate Liability.* We do not have a great sense about how much, if at all, past Presidents pondered or might have been deterred

---

136 *Trump*, 603 U.S. at 684 (Sotomayor, J., dissenting).

137 *Id.* at 688, 697 (Jackson, J., dissenting).

138 *See supra* note 5.

by criminal liability in deciding whether to commit crimes. Richard Nixon knowingly committed crimes in his efforts to cover up the Watergate break-in, and he feared exposure and possibly jail even as he continued his criminal ways.[139] Presidents after Nixon have been accused of acting criminally, but we have little insight into how if at all fear of criminal liability influenced their decisions in office related to these allegations.[140] And the criminal law violations alleged in the indictment against Trump do not seem to have deterred him even though it was the official view of the executive branch, and widely believed at the time, that he could be prosecuted after office for crimes committed in office.[141]

Without a firm sense of whether or how much Presidents were deterred by criminal law prior to *Trump*, it is hard to assess the marginal impact of an uncertain immunity from prosecution on presidential behavior. But I have found no evidence that an "individual accountability model" influenced presidential behavior related to crime.[142]

[139] Evidence of knowing criminal action can be found in the "smoking gun" tape of June 23, 1972 and Nixon's "cancer on the presidency" tape of March 21, 1973. *See Transcript of a Recording of a Meeting Between the President and H.R. Haldeman in the Oval Office on June 23, 1972, from 10:04 to 11:39 AM*, Richard M. Nixon Presidential Libr., https://www.nixonlibrary.gov/sites/default/files/forresearchers/find/tapes/watergate/wspf/741-002.pdf; *Transcript of a Recording of a Meeting Among the President, John Dean, and H.R. Haldeman in the Oval Office, on March 21, 1973, from 10:12 to 11:55 AM*, Richard M. Nixon Presidential Libr., https://www.nixonlibrary.gov/sites/default/files/forresearchers/find/tapes/watergate/trial/exhibit_12.pdf. The March 21 transcript makes pretty clear, but not perfectly clear, that Nixon worried about criminal liability for himself during this period. And he clearly worried about prosecution and jail in 1974, especially in the run-up to his resignation. *See* Garrett Graff, Watergate: A New History 654, 659 (2022).

[140] For example, Bill Clinton faced potential criminal charges related to perjury and obstruction of justice in the Monica Lewinsky affair but was ultimately never charged. John F. Harris & Bill Miller, *In a Deal, Clinton Avoids Indictment*, Wash. Post (Jan. 19, 2001), https://www.washingtonpost.com/archive/politics/2001/01/20/in-a-deal-clinton-avoids-indictment/bb80cc4c-e72c-40c1-bb72-55b2b81c3065. George H.W. Bush was deeply implicated in elements of the Iran-Contra scandal as Vice President, and Independent Counsel Lawrence Walsh noted "a disturbing pattern of deception and obstruction that permeated the highest levels of the Reagan and Bush administrations." Walter Pincus, *Bush Pardons Weinberger in Iran-Contra Affair*, Wash. Post (Dec. 24, 1992), https://www.washingtonpost.com/archive/politics/1992/12/25/bush-pardons-weinberger-in-iran-contra-affair/912743a7-026b-4134-b63d-4c1c57948673. I have found no account of how the prospect of criminal liability influenced these men's official acts in office.

[141] *See, e.g.*, A Sitting President's Amenability to Indictment & Crim. Prosecution, 24 Op. O.L.C. 222, 255 (2000).

[142] It is conceivable that Presidents prior to *Trump* were not deterred by criminal liability when acting but that *Trump*, by making immunity explicit and salient, will encourage more criminality than previously would have occurred.

Even if one reads *Trump* to confer a broad presidential immunity, and even if a President is more motivated to commit a crime after *Trump* than before due to the reduced deterrent effect of criminal law, it does not follow that presidential crimes are easy to pull off. The reason is that normally, and for the vast majority of presidential criminal acts, a President must rely on executive branch subordinates who are not immune from criminal liability even if the President is immune.[143] The President cannot effectuate a coup or assassinate political rivals (to take two commonly mentioned examples) without the assistance of people who are subject to criminal law. Even issuing a corrupt pardon typically involves executive branch middlemen.

Subordinate liability is one reason why administrations do not engage in rampant violations of civil law. The President has absolute immunity for official acts, but subordinate officials have only qualified immunity for such acts.[144] Another reason is that various professional norms have (at least historically) constrained executive branch malfeasance to some degree.[145] For similar reasons, a principle of subordinate criminal liability, combined with associated executive branch norms of right behavior, have likely been the main historical determinants of executive branch compliance with criminal law.

To see how subordinate liability works, consider Justice Sotomayor's claim that a President would be immune from criminal liability if he or she ordered the Navy's Seal Team Six to assassinate a political rival. This does not follow from *Trump* because the assassination order would almost certainly not be an exclusive presidential power.[146] Thus, if the President ordered this action, and if it were an

---

[143] Zachary S. Price, *Even if the President Is Immune, His Subordinates Are Not*, YALE J. ON REGUL.: NOTICE & COMMENT (July 11, 2024), https://www.yalejreg.com/nc/even-if-the-president-is-immune-his-subordinates-are-not-by-zachary-s-price.

[144] *Compare* Nixon v. Fitzgerald, 457 U.S. 731, 749 (1982) ("[W]e hold that petitioner, as a former President of the United States, is entitled to absolute immunity from damages liability predicated on his official acts."), *with* Harlow v. Fitzgerald, 457 U.S. 800, 813 (1982) (denying absolute immunity to presidential aides but conferring qualified immunity).

[145] *See* Renan, *supra* note 9, at 2190.

[146] The Court would decide whether the assassination was an exclusive presidential power, but even under the pro-President OLC precedents it would not be. The hypothetical assassination would not be justified by war, but in any event OLC has recognized that the President's offensive war power is not exclusive, *see, e.g.*, April 2018 Airstrikes Against Syrian Chem.-Weapons Facilities, 42 Op. O.L.C. 39, 46–47 (2018), though it once without analysis asserted that Congress could not limit the President's self-defensive reactions to the 9/11 terrorist attacks, *see* The President's Const. Auth. to Conduct Mil. Operations Against Terrorists & Nations Supporting Them, 25 Op. O.L.C. 188, 214 (2001). In the domestic realm, OLC has recognized an

official act, it would fall at best in the category of presumptively immune and thus possibly be defeated by the balancing test. And even if the President is immune from prosecution for ordering the assassination, the soldiers could be prosecuted by the next President.

The potential criminal liability for subordinates is an important hurdle for a lawless President to carry out lawless acts. Consider Volume Two of the *Report on the Investigation into Russian Interference in the 2016 Presidential Election*, known as the "Mueller Report." The Report documented ten instances of then-former President Trump allegedly seeking to obstruct the ongoing FBI investigation into Russia's interference in the 2016 presidential election.[147] What is remarkable about these episodes is that Trump's "efforts to influence the investigation were mostly unsuccessful, . . . largely because the persons who surrounded the President declined to carry out orders or accede to his requests."[148]

These officials declined to carry out the President's instructions to impede the investigation in part, perhaps large part, out of fear of violating the criminal obstruction statute even though Trump himself was oblivious to it. The Mueller Report included a White House Counsel's Office note from March 2, 2017.[149] The note was written soon after Attorney General Jeff Sessions had recused himself from the Russia investigation in the face of pressure not to recuse from President Trump through White House Counsel Don McGahn.[150] The note stated: "No contact w/Sessions" and "No comms / Serious concerns about obstruction."[151] Journalistic treatments of this period

independent but not exclusive presidential power to use force during war. *See* Memorandum from John C. Yoo, Deputy Assistant Att'y Gen., Off. of Legal Counsel, & Robert J. Delahunty, Special Counsel, Off. of Legal Counsel, to Alberto R. Gonzales, Counsel to the President (Oct. 23, 2001), https://www.justice.gov/sites/default/files/olc/legacy/2009/08/24/memomilitaryforcecombatus10232001.pdf. It has also recognized an Article II "protective power" to "use troops for the protection of federal property and federal functions," Fed. Emps. by Mayday Demonstrations & Consequent Impairment of Gov't Functions, 1 Supp. Op. O.L.C. 343, 344 (1971), but has never suggested that it is exclusive.

[147] *See generally* Robert S. Mueller, III, *Report on the Investigation into Russian Interference in the 2016 Presidential Election, Vol. II of II*, U.S. Dep't of Just. (Mar. 2019), https://www.justice.gov/storage/report_volume2.pdf. *See also* John Cassidy, *Robert Mueller Says It's Up to Congress to Indict a President*, New Yorker (May 29, 2019), https://www.newyorker.com/news/our-columnists/robert-mueller-says-its-up-to-congress-to-indict-a-president.

[148] *See, e.g.*, Mueller, *supra* note 147, at 158.

[149] *Id.* at 50.

[150] *Id.*

[151] *Id.*

indicate that this obstruction concern permeated the White House Counsel's Office during this period.[152]

One can read *Trump* to weaken or possibly eliminate the principle of subordinate liability.[153] The Court in *Zivotofsky* ruled that a civil statute that impinged on an exclusive presidential power did not bind State Department subordinates.[154] The theory seems to be that a statute that prevents a subordinate from exercising an exclusive presidential power in effect prevents the President from exercising the power. On this view, if the Justice Department officials whom Trump tried to influence carried out his allegedly illegal scheme, they would benefit from his immunity because they are, in the words of *Trump*, "carry[ing] out his constitutional duties" to faithfully execute the law, an exclusive presidential power for which he received immunity.[155] This conclusion may be bolstered by *Trump*'s statement that "the interests that underlie Presidential immunity seek to protect not the President himself, but the institution of the Presidency," and by its occasional references to the "exclusive authority" of "the Executive Branch" in its discussion of Trump's immunity in connection with Department of Justice communications.[156]

This is a powerful argument but there are countervailing considerations. *Trump* nowhere hinted that it was extending immunity to subordinates. The Court emphasized that its decision turned on the unique position of the President in the constitutional scheme and the need to protect presidential decisionmaking, and its holding about immunity concerned only the President. Moreover, *Trump* emphasized presidential exclusivity in the context of "discuss[ing] potential investigations and prosecutions with the Attorney General and

---

[152] *See, e.g.*, Michael S. Schmidt, Donald Trump v. The United States: Inside the Struggle to Stop a President 5–6 (2020).

[153] An argument for this conclusion can be found in Vázquez, *supra* note 60.

[154] *See* Zivotofsky v. Kerry, 576 U.S. 1, 28–29 (2015). OLC has sometimes ruled that a federal statute does not apply to a subordinate executive branch official if it would violate an exclusive presidential power. *See, e.g.*, Statutory Restrictions on the PLO's Wash. Off., 42 Op. O.L.C. 108 (2018); Memorandum from David J. Barron, Acting Assistant Att'y Gen., Off. of Legal Counsel, to Joan E. Donoghue, Acting Legal Adviser, Dep't of State, Constitutionality of Section 7054 of the Fiscal Year 2009 Foreign Appropriations Act (June 1, 2009), https://www.justice.gov/sites/default/files/olc/opinions/2009/06/31/section7054.pdf.

[155] Trump v. United States, 603 U.S. 593, 614 (2024). Jeffrey Clark, a senior Justice Department official who helped Trump in his election fraud scheme, has made a version of this argument in his bar disciplinary proceeding. *See* Brief of Respondent at 20–23, *In re* Jeffrey B. Clark, No. 22-BD-039 (D.C. Bd. Pro. Resp. Oct. 28, 2024).

[156] *Trump*, 603 U.S. at 614–15, 632.

other Justice Department officials to carry out" his Take Care Clause duties.[157] It is possible after *Trump* that Congress cannot apply, say, the obstruction of justice statute to subordinates who advise the President on matters within his exclusive authority but could apply it to subordinates who go beyond advice and carry out a President's otherwise unlawful order to obstruct.

More fundamentally, any extension of *Trump* to eliminate subordinate liability for exclusive presidential actions would be contrary to the care the Court has taken, with respect to other remedies, to preserve subordinate liability even when granting absolute presidential immunity. For example, on the same day that *Nixon v. Fitzgerald* recognized absolute immunity from civil liability for the President, the Court in *Harlow v. Fitzgerald* rejected absolute immunity for senior executive branch officials for the same conduct and instead gave them only qualified immunity.[158] Similarly, the Court has held that it lacks jurisdiction to enjoin the President but it is commonplace to enjoin the lower-level officials, including cabinet officials, for the same conduct.[159] The availability of remedies against presidential subordinates even when the President receives absolute immunity accommodates the President's special position in the constitutional scheme with the need for government accountability to law.[160] The same

[157] *Id.* at 620.

[158] The Court emphasized that absolute immunity was inappropriate for high-level subordinate officials because "'[t]he greater power of high [non-presidential] officials affords a greater potential for a regime of lawless conduct.'" Harlow v. Fitzgerald, 457 U.S. 800, 809 (1982) (quoting Butz v. Economou, 438 U.S. 478, 506 (1978)). As previously discussed, the Court in *Nixon v. Fitzgerald*, 457 U.S. 731 (1982), did not address whether the President would be immune from civil damages had Congress expressly conferred civil liability on the President. *See supra* notes 23, 59 and accompanying text.

[159] On the absence of jurisdiction to award injunctive relief against the President, see Mississippi v. Johnson, 71 U.S. 475, 501 (1866); Franklin v. Massachusetts, 505 U.S. 788, 802–03 (1992) (plurality opinion) (quoting *Johnson*, 71 U.S. at 501); and *Franklin*, 505 U.S. at 827 (Scalia, J., concurring in part and in the judgment) (same). *Franklin* also discusses the availability of injunctive relief against subordinate executive officials in lieu of such relief against the President. *See Franklin*, 505 U.S. at 828 (noting that "[n]one of these conclusions" about the absence of injunctive relief against the President "in any way suggests that Presidential action is *unreviewable*" because "[r]eview of the legality of Presidential action can ordinarily be obtained in a suit seeking to enjoin the officers who attempt to enforce the President's directive"). *See generally* Schmidt, *supra* note 27 (analyzing all of these cases as they relate to *Trump*).

[160] *See* Schmidt, *supra* note 27 (manuscript at 6–9). *See generally* Richard H. Fallon & Daniel J. Meltzer, *New Law, Non-Retroactivity, and Constitutional Remedies*, 104 Harv. L. Rev. 1731 (1991) (arguing for a structure of constitutional remedies adequate to keep government within the bounds of law).

accommodation would serve the same aim in the criminal immunity context as well.

To the extent that subordinate liability survives *Trump*, it is, considered in isolation, a check on a lawless President. But it is only a check for a President who already possesses a sense of restraint due to law or norms or politics. If a President is determined to be lawless, then law cannot as a practical matter constrain him or her.

2. *The Powers of a Bad-Man President.* Those who think *Trump* leads to a lawless presidency are implicitly assuming a bad-man President who is oblivious to the norms and other non-legal expectations of the office, and who follows narrow self-interest right up to the point that the effective sanction of law allows it.[161] With the threatened sanction of criminal law gone, the critics think, the bad-man President is cut loose to do all sorts of awful illegal things that serve the President's narrow private interests.

The problem with this argument is that once we are in the world of a bad-man President, law (including the operation of subordinate criminal liability) cannot easily constrain him. Put differently, a bad-man President had the tools to effectuate widespread executive branch criminality with impunity long before *Trump*. I will focus on two such tools—the reliance on a legal interpretation and the pardon power—but there are others.

a. A Golden Shield. Since the beginning of the nation, clauses in Article II—"the executive Power" and the Take Care Clauses—have been interpreted to give the President the authority to interpret the law definitively for the executive branch. This power can be seen as an incident of the President's enforcement power: "Before the President can obey and enforce the laws, he must determine their meaning, what they authorize and prohibit, and how they fit together."[162] This power of interpretation includes the power "to interpret and apply the Constitution" and to disregard statutes that the President determines violates the Constitution.[163] The President typically delegates the interpretive power to the Attorney General,

---

[161] *See* Adrian Vermeule, "*Above the Law*," New Dig. (July 3, 2024), https://thenewdigest.substack.com/p/above-the-law.

[162] Goldsmith, *supra* note 15, at 134.

[163] The Const. Separation of Powers Between the President & Cong., 20 Op. O.L.C. 124, 128 (1996).

who in turn typically delegates it to the Office of Legal Counsel (OLC).[164]

The Attorney General and by delegation OLC have an underappreciated superpower. When they write the President or another executive branch official a legal opinion concluding that a course of action is lawful under a criminal statute, that President or executive branch official will not be prosecuted by a subsequent administration. Former Central Intelligence Agency (CIA) general counsel John Rizzo referred to this immunity-conferring power of the Justice Department legal interpretations as a "golden shield."[165] Rizzo was referring specifically to the effect of the notorious OLC opinions ruling that the criminal prohibition on torture did not forbid the CIA's brutal post-9/11 interrogation techniques. Those opinions were sought by the White House in a distorted process that aimed to greenlight the CIA program. They were badly legally flawed on multiple levels.[166]

And yet despite these deep flaws in process and substance, the golden shield worked. President Obama's Attorney General, Eric Holder, believed that the OLC opinions were appallingly bad and that elements of the CIA program were illegal. But when he ordered an investigation of the Bush-era CIA program, he made clear that he would, in his words, "not prosecute anyone who acted in good faith and within the scope of the legal guidance given by the Office of Legal Counsel regarding the interrogation of detainees."[167] There are many reasons why he might have reached this conclusion. But one reason was a legal doctrine called *entrapment by estoppel*.[168] Under this doctrine, it is a violation of due process to prosecute anyone who reasonably relies on an authorized government representative's claim that an action is lawful.

---

[164] 28 U.S.C. §§ 511–513; Judiciary Act of 1789, ch. 20, § 35, 1 Stat. 73, 93; General Functions, 28 C.F.R. § 0.25 (2014).

[165] *See* Jack L. Goldsmith, The Terror Presidency: Law and Judgment Inside the Bush Administration 144 (2007).

[166] *Id.* at 144–46.

[167] Press Release, U.S. Dep't of Just., Statement of the Attorney General Regarding Investigation into the Interrogation of Certain Detainees (June 30, 2011), https://www.justice.gov/archives/opa/pr/statement-attorney-general-regarding-investigation-interrogation-certain-detainees.

[168] Other reasons are canvassed in Note, *The Immunity-Conferring Power of the Office of Legal Counsel*, 121 Harv. L. Rev. 2086 (2008), which provides and analyzes the case law and commentary on entrapment by estoppel.

Entrapment by estoppel is the most powerful of a cluster of executive branch doctrines that undergird the immunity-conferring power of legal advice related to criminal statutes.[169] At oral argument in *Trump*, the government's attorney, Dreeben, held up entrapment by estoppel as an important protection for the President entirely independent of other immunity doctrines. He told the Justices that "it would be a due process problem to prosecute a President who received advice from the Attorney General that his actions were lawful absent the kind of collusion or conspiracy that itself represented a criminal violation, which I don't really see as being a realistic option."[170] Dreeben mentioned the limit on entrapment by estoppel—collusion or conspiracy—but they are uncertain and distant limits.[171] The permissive OLC torture opinions, to take one notorious example, did not come close to the level of a criminal conspiracy and had full legal effect as a golden shield.

Entrapment by estoppel in this context has critics. The Justice Department does not offer its legal advice at arm's length to the President so there is a danger of collusion (as mentioned above) or undue influence.[172] Entrapment by estoppel if too generous threatens to blur into a dispensing power.[173] And it is an odd inversion for the Attorney General, exercising interpretive power delegated from the President, to be able to protect the President from later criminal prosecution in ways that presidential auto-interpretation could not.[174]

---

[169] *See id.* at 2092–102. Entrapment by estoppel "has been recognized as an exception to the mistake of law rule." *U.S. Attorneys' Manual, Criminal Resource Manual Section 2055: Public Authority Defense*, U.S. Dep't of Just., https://www.justice.gov/archives/usam/criminal-resource-manual-2055-public-authority-defense.

[170] Transcript of Oral Argument, *supra* note 7, at 72; *see also id.* at 108 ("Mr. Dreeben: . . . [I]f a [sic] authorized government representative" (i.e., the attorney general) "tells you" (i.e., the President) "that what you are about to do is lawful, it would be a root violation of due process to prosecute you" (i.e., the President) "for that.").

[171] A related condition for the defense is that reliance on the legal opinion must be reasonable. *See* Note, *supra* note 168, at 2093.

[172] *Id.* at 2095; *cf.* Zachary S. Price, *Reliance on Executive Constitutional Interpretation*, 100 B.U. L. Rev. 197, 223 (2020) (noting that "executive-branch interpreters" are often "serving as a judge in one's own case").

[173] Price, *supra* note 172, at 223–24.

[174] James M. Burnham, *The Special Counsel Made a Dangerous Argument About Trump Immunity*, Wash. Post (May 1, 2024), https://www.washingtonpost.com/opinions/2024/05/01/jack-smith-argument-trump-immunity.

These are all fair points that might be relevant to the contours of an entrapment by estoppel defense to a federal prosecution.[175] But the real bite of reliance on an approving Justice Department opinion is that the Department likely will not bring such a prosecution absent collusion or conspiracy. This has to do with institutional reasons that transcend the best understanding of what due process requires at trial, including the government's need to promote reliance on authoritative legal opinions within the executive branch and inter-administration comity.[176]

It is easy to imagine a prescient bad-man President getting a golden-shield legal opinion from his Attorney General or OLC prior to January 6 to the effect that none of the statutes that former President Trump is charged with violating in the January 6 prosecution apply to the President's official acts. Such an opinion would rely on a different executive branch interpretive legal principle that was also discussed in the government's brief: the principle that generally worded criminal statutes that "arguably limit the President's constitutional role" or involve a "possible conflict with the President's constitutional prerogatives" do not apply to the President absent a plain statement.[177]

We do not have to speculate very much about whether this is a plausible scenario. Trump's first-term Attorney General William Barr in 2018, before he came back to office, wrote a famous memo that argued that the plain statement rule precluded Robert Mueller from applying the main obstruction of justice statute to the allegedly obstructing Trump acts he was investigating in the Russian collusion matter, at least as Barr understood those acts at the time.[178] This

---

[175] Price invokes some of these objections to conclude that entrapment by estoppel for reliance on OLC advice should apply "only insofar as the opinion's conclusions were objectively reasonable." Price, *supra* note 172, at 202, 244–47.

[176] *See* Note, *supra* note 168, at 2106–07. This is one important reason why, for the full impact of the golden shield to work, the legal advice with respect to criminal law should come from the Department of Justice. Legal advice to the President from the White House or outside lawyers might not have the same protective effect.

[177] Application of 28 U.S.C. § 458 to Presidential Appointments of Fed. Judges, 19 Op. O.L.C. 350, 351–52 (1995).

[178] *See* Quinta Jurecic, *Document: William Barr Memo on Obstruction Investigation*, LAWFARE (Dec. 20, 2018, 10:04 AM), https://www.lawfaremedia.org/article/document-william-barr-memo-obstruction-investigation.

is the very same statute that supports two of the four charges against Trump in the January 6 prosecution.

People can and do disagree about how the OLC plain statement rule *best applies* to the statutes Trump is charged with violating. The Special Counsel acknowledged the OLC principle in its brief and read it narrowly. The Court cited several of the relevant OLC opinions as evidence that the government "broadly agrees that the President's official acts are entitled to some degree of constitutional protection."[179] Justice Barrett said without explanation that she did not believe the OLC canon "applies in this circumstance."[180] As noted above, Barr took a robust view of the canon as applied to an obstruction statute.[181]

While the proper applicability of the canon is contested, what is not contestable is that a bad-man President's Attorney General could in good faith have advised the President that the plain statement rule rendered inapplicable all of the criminal statutes in Smith's indictment that "possibly" conflicted with Trump's constitutional prerogatives or "arguably" limited his constitutional role—a ruling that, on the entrapment by estoppel logic the government embraced at oral argument in *Trump*, would likely rule out all charges involving the President's official acts.

b. The Pardon Power. A second and even more robust presidential power that a bad-man President could use to defy criminal law is the pardon power. This one is easier to see, so I will be briefer.

As the Court noted in *Trump*, the pardon power is broad and exclusive.[182] "It extends to every offence known to the law, and may be exercised at any time after its commission, either before legal proceedings are taken or during their pendency or after conviction

---

[179] Trump v. United States, 603 U.S. 593, 635 (2024).

[180] *Id.* at 653 n.3 (Barrett, J., concurring in part).

[181] For my views of this canon in the context of the Mueller investigation, see Jack Goldsmith, *The Mueller Report's Weak Statutory Interpretation Analysis*, LAWFARE (May 11, 2019, 10:00 AM), https://www.lawfaremedia.org/article/mueller-reports-weak-statutory-interpretation-analysis; and Jack Goldsmith, *The Mueller Report's Weak Statutory Interpretation Analysis: Part II*, LAWFARE (May 23, 2019, 10:08 AM), https://www.lawfaremedia.org/article/mueller-reports-weak-statutory-interpretation-analysis-part-ii.

[182] *See Trump*, 603 U.S. at 608; *Ex parte* Garland, 71 U.S. (4 Wall.) 333, 380 (1866) (noting that the pardon power "is unlimited," except by the textual limitation for impeachments, and "cannot be fettered by any legislative restrictions").

and judgment."[183] A bad-man President could pardon subordinates who, for example, carried out an assassination or a coup, just as Trump on the evening of January 6 (or any time before leaving office) could have pardoned everyone involved who was later indicted, thereby precluding the indictments. Also, recall that Trump pardoned cronies who were investigated and convicted by Mueller.[184] Finally, no one knows if a President can pardon himself, but many commentators believe the President can.[185]

President Biden's recent "preemptive" pardons—i.e., pardons before charge or indictment—for officials whom he worried President Trump might prosecute is perhaps the best example of how pardons can operate to immunize criminal wrongdoing.[186] I am not suggesting that the government officials Biden pardoned committed crimes. But the same pardon power that Biden exercised can be deployed by a bad-man President to eliminate the criminal liability of subordinate officials who commit (or might have committed) actual crimes.[187] The pardon power could, for example, wipe out the criminal liability for one who on presidential command assassinates a political opponent. And the pardon power can be used on a very broad scale. Indeed, it does not appear to have limits of scale restricting the numbers of people who could be preemptively pardoned.[188]

---

[183] *Garland*, 71 U.S. (4 Wall.) at 380.

[184] *See* Josh Gerstein & Kyle Cheney, *'Any and All Possible Offenses': Trump Pardon Grants Flynn a Sweeping Reprieve*, Politico (Dec. 1, 2020, 2:10 PM EST), https://www.politico.com/news/2020/11/30/trump-flynn-pardon-reprieve-441527; Dan Mangan, *Trump Pardons 15, Including People Convicted in Mueller Probe*, CNBC (Dec. 23, 2020, 7:39 AM EST), https://www.cnbc.com/2020/12/22/-trump-pardons-15-including-people-convicted-in-mueller-probe-.html.

[185] For a range of views, see Jack Goldsmith, *A Smorgasbord of Views on Self-Pardoning*, Lawfare (June 5, 2018, 11:30 AM), https://www.lawfaremedia.org/article/smorgasbord-views-self-pardoning. A self-pardon, if valid, could be executed as a President's last act of office and wipe out all crimes committed in office.

[186] *See* Peter Baker & Michael D. Shear, *Biden in Final Hours Pardons Relatives and Others to Thwart Trump Reprisals*, N.Y. Times (Jan. 23, 2025), https://www.nytimes.com/2025/01/20/us/politics/biden-pardons-fauci-milley-cheney-jan-6.html.

[187] The President probably cannot issue a pardon preemptively, i.e., *before* the crime is committed. *See Garland*, 71 U.S. (4 Wall.) at 380 (noting that the pardon power "may be exercised at any time after [a crime's] commission"). This means that the bad-man President would need to convince subordinates *before* committing the crime that he will pardon them *after* its commission. The subordinates might lack certainty that the President will follow through, but the bad-man President would have every incentive to make his pledges credible.

[188] President Jimmy Carter pardoned many thousands of Vietnam draft dodgers. *See* Pres. Proc. No. 4483, 42 Fed. Reg. 4391 (Jan. 21, 1977); Exec. Order No. 11,967, 42 Fed. Reg. 4331 (Jan. 21, 1977). President Lincoln issued several amnesty proclamations during the

Congress before *Trump* might have been able to temper these abuses through statutes that criminalize overt presidential pardons used, for example, as bribes or to obstruct justice or as part of a conspiracy to commit a crime. A pardon (or other form of commutation) is "absolute" for the beneficiary of the pardon. As the Court stated in *Trump*, the "legislature cannot change *the effect* of . . . a pardon."[189] It might not follow, however, that a pardon affords the President, as grantor of the pardon, freedom from criminalization of bad acts in connection with the President's granting a pardon.[190]

The Court has never addressed this issue, though *Trump* did say, in dicta, that the President's "authority to pardon . . . is 'conclusive and preclusive,' 'disabling the Congress from acting upon the subject.'"[191] Given *Trump*'s broad and formalistic understanding of exclusive presidential powers, any criminal statute that purports to regulate the pardon power, and not just ones that regulate the "effect" of the pardon power, may be off limits. And even if Congress could in theory criminalize bad-act pardons in ways that did not limit the "effect" of a pardon, a President might well be able to issue blanket preemptive pardons to subordinates without running afoul of such statutes.

The pardon power, in short, is a massive criminal-law-evading mechanism in the hands of a bad-man President, right there on the face of Article II.

c. A More Realistic Picture. The point of this analysis of a bad-man President's robust law-skirting tools is to highlight the relative insignificance of the presidential immunity ruling in *Trump*. I have argued that Presidents were not obviously deterred by criminal law prior to *Trump* and thus that their decisional calculus in the face of criminal law might not change much after the decision; that executive

Civil War, the broadest of which was on December 8, 1863, and which pardoned rebels (with certain exceptions) and restored non-slave property upon the swearing of a prescribed oath. *See* Pres. Proc. No. 11, 13 Stat. 737 (1863). President Andrew Johnson issued an even broader pardon to rebels in his Christmas 1868 pardon. *See* Pres. Proc. No. 14, 15 Stat. 711 (1868).

[189] Trump v. United States, 603 U.S. 593, 608 (2024) (quoting United States v. Klein, 80 U.S. (13 Wall.) 128, 147–48 (1872)).

[190] *See* Bob Bauer & Jack Goldsmith, After Trump: Reconstructing the Presidency 171 (2020). Nor would it cover any separate crime committed by the grantee in seeking or accepting the pardon as part of a corrupt bargain. *Id.*

[191] *Trump*, 603 U.S. at 608 (quoting Youngstown Sheet & Tube Co. v. Sawyer, 343 U.S. 579, 637–38 (1952) (Jackson, J., concurring)).

branch compliance with criminal law to date has mainly been secured by norms and subordinate official liability; that a bad-man President had plenty of ways to weaken or eliminate the effect of norms and subordinate liability prior to *Trump*, including through golden shield legal opinions and through pardons; and thus, for all of these reasons, that the marginal impact of the uncertain immunity ruling on a bad-man President is unlikely to be significant. This is a different and I believe more realistic picture of presidential compliance with criminal law than one that sees post-presidency enforcement of criminal law against the President as the main check, and a significant one, on presidential criminality.

I am not claiming that the immunity ruling in *Trump* will have zero impact on presidential branch adherence to criminal law. Under various assumptions, the ruling could embolden a President to commit more criminal acts than before or to push subordinates harder to do so. One can imagine that a bad-man President who is inclined to pardon all criminality by subordinates, and to pardon himself, and to solicit maximal protective legal opinions, might nonetheless be marginally more inclined to commit a crime in light of the uncertain immunity conferred by *Trump* than before the decision due to the uncertainties in self-pardons and protective legal opinions and despite the uncertainties in *Trump*. But something like this analysis, and not a version of the individual accountability model, explains the incentives of the bad-man President.

I have discussed the bad-man President because I think it is an implicit assumption in the dissents in *Trump* and because I think it is a useful heuristic to explain the redoubtable power that the executive branch in theory has to engage in lawless criminal behavior if it really wants to, independent of and prior to the Court's immunity ruling. The larger lesson here is a sobering one: Criminal law cannot constrain a determined bad-man President. The potentially effective remedies for presidential criminality are impeachment and elections. As we have learned in recent years, those remedies are not terribly effective in checking a law-defying President.

B. *TRUMP*'S EXCLUSIVE POWER INSIDE THE EXECUTIVE BRANCH

While I do not think the immunity holding of *Trump* will have a large impact on the criminality of a bad-man presidency, I do believe that *Trump*'s analysis of exclusive presidential power vis-à-vis

Congress will have a large impact on the scope of presidential power in other respects. Some and perhaps many of these implications should be worked out in the months and years ahead in federal courts as a result of the second Trump Administration's aggressive assertions of presidential power on a number of fronts, many of which are potentially supported by *Trump*.[192] The Court might read the uncertainties in *Trump* broadly or narrowly, depending on the issues that come up and how they are framed. It is hard to predict.

But it is not hard to predict how *the executive branch* will use the *Trump* rulings, at least until they are later revised by courts. In litigation it will invoke them in support of broad presidential power. It will also invoke them inside the executive branch, in many contexts outside of judicial review, in deciding which executive branch actions are lawful, and in deciding, relatedly, which congressional statutes to disregard as unconstitutional.[193]

Executive branch lawyers do not interpret the law as courts do. They follow Supreme Court precedents when they are on point, but

---

[192] For example, the Trump Administration is setting up possible Supreme Court rulings on removal in its firing of the for-cause-protected member of the National Labor Relations Board and seventeen inspectors general, in its firings of civil servants in the Department of Justice, and in the Acting Solicitor General's announcement that the government has "determined that certain for-cause removal provisions that apply to members of multi-member regulatory commissions are unconstitutional" and will not be defended. Letter from Sarah M. Harris, Acting Solic. Gen., U.S. Dep't of Just., to Hon. Richard J. Durbin, Ranking Member, Comm. on the Judiciary (Feb. 12, 2025) (on file with author); Jonathan Stempel & Daniel Wiessner, *Former NLRB Member Sues Trump for Firing Her*, REUTERS (Feb. 5, 2025, 2:57 PM EST), https://www.reuters.com/legal/former-nlrb-member-sues-trump-administration-over-firing-2025-02-05; Jack Goldsmith, *Trump Fired 17 Inspectors General—Was It Legal?*, LAWFARE (Jan. 27, 2025, 9:25 AM), https://www.lawfaremedia.org/article/trump-fired-17-inspectors-general-was-it-legal; Perry Stein, Shayna Jacobs, Carol D. Leonnig & Ann E. Marimow, *Several Top Career Officials Ousted at Justice Department*, WASH. POST (Mar. 7, 2025), https://www.washingtonpost.com/national-security/2025/03/07/justice-department-trump-firings; *see also* Letter from Sarah M. Harris, Acting Solic. Gen., U.S. Dep't of Just., to Hon. Mike Johnson, Speaker, U.S. House of Reps. (Feb. 20, 2025) (on file with author) (announcing refusal to defend multiple layers of removal restrictions for administrative law judges (ALJs)). The Trump Administration will also implicate the law enforcement discretion ruling of *Trump* if it follows through on its pledge to assert a constitutional impoundment power. *See* Tony Romm & Jeff Stein, *White House Eyes Fight to Expand Trump's Power to Control Spending*, WASH. POST (Jan. 30, 2025), https://www.washingtonpost.com/business/2025/01/30/trump-impoundment-spending-control.

[193] This Section does not make strong assumptions about a bad-man presidency. Even a "normal" presidency—one that had internalized the importance of complying with law and norms, and with being perceived to have done so—would read *Trump* to counsel stronger executive branch positions vis-à-vis Congress. This point comes with the caveat, *see infra* p. 46, that Republican and Democratic executive branch lawyers on average have different views on the scope of the unitary executive and thus may read *Trump* differently on average.

they also give great weight to executive branch historical practice and executive branch legal opinions, both of which are often more salient.[194] Executive branch lawyers, and executive branch precedents, tend to view executive power in broader terms, often much broader, than do courts. Especially when there is no strictly controlling judicial precedent, executive branch lawyers "tend[] to rely on general principles embodied in Supreme Court dicta, especially ones that favor presidential power."[195] And they tend to construe dicta and legal ambiguities in the President's favor.[196]

One cannot say precisely how OLC lawyers or other executive branch lawyers will interpret *Trump* because lawyers across administrations take different interpretive approaches despite a common institutional outlook. As a general matter, Republican executive branch lawyers are more committed to a strong view of the unitary executive and will be more likely on average than their Democratic counterparts to run with *Trump*. And the lawyers in the Republican Trump Administration are pushing a maximalist version of the unitary executive theory.[197] There is no way to know the range of issues to which *Trump* may be relevant inside the executive branch. We can be certain, however, that they "will interpret the decision to favor the executive branch in its manifold interactions and disputes with Congress."[198] What follows are some of the contexts in which Justice Department lawyers can be expected to do so.

1. *Enforcement Discretion.* OLC has said that "The Executive . . . has the exclusive authority to enforce the laws adopted by Congress, and neither the Judicial nor Legislative Branches may directly interfere with the prosecutorial discretion of the Executive by directing the Executive to prosecute particular individuals."[199] No Supreme Court decision prior to *Trump* had gone that far, but *Trump* provides new support for this view. The executive branch will likely invoke

---

[194] Goldsmith, *supra* note 15, at 134–36.

[195] *Id.* at 135.

[196] *Id.* at 134–36.

[197] *See, e.g.*, Cass R. Sunstein, *This Theory Is Behind Trump's Power Grab*, N.Y. Times (Feb. 26, 2025), https://www.nytimes.com/2025/02/26/opinion/trump-roberts-unitary-executive-theory.html; Jack Goldsmith, *The President's Favorite Decision: The Influence of* Trump v. U.S. *in Trump 2.0*, Exec. Functions (Feb. 10, 2025), https://executivefunctions.substack.com/p/the-presidents-favorite-decision.

[198] Goldsmith, *supra* note 15, at 136.

[199] Cong. Subpoenas of Dep't of Just. Investigative Files, 8 Op. O.L.C. 252, 264 (1984).

Trump in disregarding or at least pushing back on congressional efforts to shape or delegate prosecutorial discretion or civil enforcement discretion.[200]

Relatedly, a major issue in recent presidencies is the extent to which the executive branch can use imaginative interpretations of bodies of federal law, combined with law enforcement discretion (including non-enforcement discretion), to achieve policy aims arguably in tension if not at odds with the statutes that are being enforced.[201] The Justice Department will likely use *Trump*'s discussion of the exclusive power over prosecution and investigation to push the bounds of this discretion. The decision will also give ammunition to constitutional arguments in favor of impoundment (i.e., exercising law enforcement discretion to decline to spend appropriated funds) on the theory that the President has enforcement discretion over appropriation laws.[202] It will also likely be invoked, more broadly, to support

---

[200] Several past examples will be amplified by *Trump*. *See* Comptroller Gen.'s Auth. to Relieve Disbursing & Certifying Offs. from Liab., 15 Op. O.L.C. 80, 84 (1991) (arguing that Congress's effort to "authorize the Comptroller General to relieve an executive branch official from liability for an improper payment" would deprive the executive branch "of the discretion to decide whether to bring suit to recover the funds from that official"); Constitutionality of the Qui Tam Provisions of the False Claims Act, 13 Op. O.L.C. 207, 229 (1989) (concluding that qui tam provisions that "permit a private citizen to sue on behalf of the government, even though the Attorney General may have decided for legitimate reasons not to prosecute the claim . . . removes from the executive branch the prosecutorial discretion that is at the heart of the President's power to execute the laws"); Prosecution for Contempt of Cong. of an Exec. Branch Off. Who Has Asserted a Claim of Exec. Privilege, 8 Op. O.L.C. 101, 114–28 (1984) (invoking Article II law enforcement discretion, in the context of an executive privilege response to a subpoena, to construe to the point of disregarding a statute that makes it a "duty" for a U.S. Attorney to bring before a grand jury any failure to comply with a subpoena).

[201] On the Deferred Action for Childhood Arrivals (DACA) policy, see Prioritizing & Deferring Removal of Certain Aliens Unlawfully Present in the U.S., 38 Op. O.L.C. 39, 39–41 (2014) (withdrawn). On the Obama Administration's policy of deprioritizing marijuana enforcement, see, for example, Memorandum on Guidance Regarding Marijuana Related Financial Crimes from James M. Cole, Deputy Att'y Gen., to U.S. Attorneys (Feb. 14, 2014) (on file with author); Memorandum on Guidance Regarding Marijuana Enforcement from James M. Cole, Deputy Att'y Gen., to U.S. Attorneys (Aug. 29, 2013) (on file with author). *See also* Exec. Order No. 13,765, 82 Fed. Reg. 8351 (2017) (directing the executive branch to "waive, defer, grant exemptions from, or delay the implementation of" the Affordable Care Act); Use of the HEROES Act of 2003 to Cancel the Principal Amounts of Student Loans, 46 Op. O.L.C., slip op. at 1–2 (2022) (arguing the President has the authority to not enforce loan repayment for a broad class of borrowers).

[202] In a 1969 opinion written by then-Assistant Attorney General William Rehnquist, OLC rejected the theory "that the President has a constitutional power to decline to spend appropriated funds." Presidential Auth. to Impound Funds Appropriated for Assistance to Federally Impacted Schs., 1 Op. O.L.C. 303, 309 (1969). *But see* Mark Paoletta & Daniel Shapiro, *The President's Constitutional Power of Impoundment*, CTR. FOR RENEWING AM. (Sept. 10, 2024), https://americarenewing.com/the-presidents-constitutional-power-of-impoundment

non-enforcement of particular statutes based largely on policy disagreements, despite contrary indications in Supreme Court case law.[203]

2. *Removal Authority and the Directive Power.* The Take Care Clause and the Vesting Clause are the primary bases on which the Court, and the Justice Department, have grounded the President's removal power.[204] As explained above, *Trump* expanded this power on a few dimensions. The early Trump Administration has engaged in a spree of firings that almost certainly rely on *Trump* for support beyond prior removal cases.[205] The courts will ultimately decide this issue, but until qualified or narrowed, *Trump* will assist the executive branch in disregarding all manner of congressional restrictions on removal.

The Trump Administration has already aggressively wielded the directive power, most notably in claiming broad dominion over independent agencies, including through full mandated Office of Management and Budget review and by mandating that every executive branch "employee" must "advance an interpretation of the law," including "the issuance of regulations, guidance, and positions advanced in litigation," that reflects the views ultimately of the President.[206] OLC had moved somewhat in this direction in the first Trump Administration.[207] The central Article II argument on which OLC's position rested was the President's power to "supervise the execution of federal

(current Trump Administration Office of Management and Budget General Counsel Mark Paoletta arguing prior to service in second Trump Administration that *Trump* justifies broad constitutional impoundment authority).

[203] For an early example that has not as of this writing been challenged in court, see Exec. Order No. 14,166, 90 Fed. Reg. 8611, 8611–12 (Jan. 20, 2025) (delaying enforcement of TikTok ban for seventy-five days). For contrary Supreme Court case law, see *supra* notes 85, 99. The Solicitor General during the Biden Administration argued in *United States v. Texas*, 599 U.S. 670 (2023), that no plaintiff has standing to challenge a President's decision to enforce a law she does not like. *See* Transcript of Oral Argument at 7, *Texas*, 599 U.S. 670 (No. 22–58). As explained above, *supra* note 85, the Court in *Texas* did not go that far.

[204] For Supreme Court case law, see *supra* pp. 17–23 and note 106. For Justice Department views, see Constitutionality of the Comm'r of Soc. Sec.'s Tenure Prot., 45 Op. O.L.C., slip op. at 5 (2021); Holdover & Removal of Members of Amtrak's Reform Bd., 27 Op. O.L.C. 163, 166 (2003); Common Legis. Encroachments on Exec. Branch Auth., 13 Op. O.L.C. 248, 252–53 (1989).

[205] *See supra* pp. 17–23.

[206] Exec. Order No. 14,215, 90 Fed. Reg. 10447, 10448–49 (Feb. 18, 2025).

[207] *See* Extending Regul. Rev. Under Exec. Order 12866 to Indep. Regul. Agencies, 43 Op. O.L.C. 232, 232–34 (2019) [hereinafter *Extending Regul. Rev.*] (concluding that a President can direct independent agencies to comply with cost-benefit analysis, as prescribed by Exec. Order No. 12866, 58 Fed. Reg. 51735 (Sept. 30, 1993)).

law."[208] This power, as noted above, received its fullest expression, and indeed was amplified, in *Trump*.[209]

One can imagine *Trump* being extended on this dimension in many ways. For example, the Trump Administration has not yet claimed full presidential control over every executive branch adjudication, but Trump's broad conception of the President's law enforcement power can be cited in support of this position.[210] More broadly, *Trump* opens the door for the President to challenge the once-standard view that "[w]hile the President must supervise the faithful execution of the laws, Congress has the authority to define the structure of the Executive Branch and the responsibilities of its officers."[211] *Trump* might lead executive branch lawyers to push back against the contours of this congressional authority, including in the organization and allocation of authority within agencies, especially when it interferes with what *Trump* described as the President's "exclusive authority over the investigative and prosecutorial functions of the Justice Department and its officials," and over executive branch law enforcement more generally.[212]

3. *Other Presidential Supervision Issues.* OLC has invoked the President's constitutional power of supervision over executive branch subordinates in other ways to block congressional encroachments on executive branch prerogatives. It has done this, for example, to resist certain reporting requirements to Congress, and disclosure requirements to the public, without executive branch clearance.[213] It has

---

208 *Id.* at 241.

209 Trump v. United States, 603 U.S. 593, 608–09 (2024).

210 The Administration has staked a claim against double for-cause removals of ALJs, *see supra* note 192, and has asserted dominion over "the issuance of regulations, guidance, and positions advanced in litigation," *see* Exec. Order No. 14,215, 90 Fed. Reg. 10447, 10449 (Feb. 18, 2025), but has not yet claimed direct presidential supervisory authority over all executive branch adjudications. For an argument that on "the maximalist logic" of the unitary executive view, "the President may either decide to exercise [adjudicative] power himself, or to command the adjudicator to rule one way or another by applying the relevant law as the President thinks warranted under that law," see Vermeule, *supra* note 108.

211 *Extending Regul. Review*, 43 Op. O.L.C. at 242; *see also* Constitutionality of the Comm'r of Soc. Sec.'s Tenure Prot., 45 Op. O.L.C., slip op. at 5 (2021); Centralizing Border Control Pol'y Under the Supervision of the Att'y Gen., 26 Op. O.L.C. 22, 23 (2002).

212 *Trump*, 603 U.S. at 621.

213 On reporting requirements, see, for example, Constitutionality of the Direct Reporting Requirement in Section 802(e)(1) of the Implementing Recommendations of the 9/11 Comm'n Act of 2007, 32 Op. O.L.C. 27, 27–28 (2008); Constitutionality of the OLC Reporting Act of 2008, 32 Op. O.L.C. 14, 14–17 (2008); and Auth. of Agency Offs. to Prohibit Emps. from Providing Info. to Cong., 28 Op. O.L.C. 79, 80–82 (2004). On disclosure requirements, see, for

invoked a similar power to rule that Congress cannot "compel an executive branch witness to appear without agency counsel and thereby compromise the President's constitutional authority" to control communications with Congress, and to disregard a congressional authorization to the Department of Housing and Urban Development to initiate enforcement proceedings against another executive branch agency.[214] *Trump* amplifies the underlying presidential power here.

4. *Executive Privilege.* OLC has long advised the President and his associates on whether they must respond to congressional subpoenas.[215] It frequently counsels in favor of an executive privilege or a testimonial immunity from congressional subpoenas but has acknowledged limitations on the privilege or immunity.[216] For example, in 1984, OLC acknowledged that the President cannot use executive privilege to conceal evidence of wrongdoing or criminal behavior.[217] That exception can now be questioned under *Trump* indirectly to the extent that the basis for the privilege is an exercise of an exclusive

example, Statute Limiting the President's Auth. to Supervise the Dir. of the Ctrs. for Disease Control in the Distrib. of an AIDS Pamphlet, 12 Op. O.L.C. 47, 56–58 (1988).

[214] Attempted Exclusion of Agency Couns. from Cong. Depositions of Agency Emps., 43 Op. O.L.C. 131, 132 (2019); Auth. of Dep't of Hous. & Urban Dev. to Initiate Enf't Actions Under the Fair Hous. Act Against Other Exec. Branch Agencies, 18 Op. O.L.C. 101, 105–08 (1994).

[215] *See, e.g.*, Testimonial Immunity Before Cong. of the Assistant to the President & Senior Couns. to the President, 43 Op. O.L.C. 186, 186 (2019); Immunity of the Assistant to the President & Dir. of the Off. of Pol. Strategy & Outreach from Cong. Subpoena, 38 Op. O.L.C. 1, 1–4 (2014); Assertion of Exec. Privilege Concerning the Dismissal & Replacement of U.S. Att'ys, 31 Op. O.L.C. 1, 1–2 (2007); Assertion of Exec. Privilege with Respect to Prosecutorial Documents, 25 Op. O.L.C. 1, 1 (2001); Assertion of Exec. Privilege with Respect to Clemency Decision, 23 Op. O.L.C. 1, 1–4 (1999); Assertion of Exec. Privilege for Memorandum to the President Concerning Efforts to Combat Drug Trafficking, 20 Op. O.L.C. 8, 8–9 (1996); Assertion of Exec. Privilege in Response to Cong. Demands for L. Enf't Files, 6 Op. O.L.C. 31, 31–32 (1982).

[216] For OLC's approach to balancing congressional and presidential interests in the context of executive privilege, see, for example, Assertion of Exec. Privilege in Response to a Cong. Subpoena, 5 Op. O.L.C. 27, 31 (1981) ("In cases in which the Congress has a legitimate need for information that will help it legislate and the Executive Branch has a legitimate, constitutionally recognized need to keep information confidential, the courts have referred to the obligation of each branch to accommodate the legitimate needs of the other."); and Response to Cong. Requests for Info. Regarding Decisions Made Under the Indep. Couns. Act, 10 Op. O.L.C. 68, 68 (1986) ("An assertion of executive privilege must be based upon an evaluation of the Executive Branch's interest in keeping the requested information confidential, the strength of Congress' need for the information, and whether those needs can be accommodated in some other way.").

[217] Cong. Subpoenas of Dep't of Just. Investigative Files, 8 Op. O.L.C. 252, 267 (1984) ("An additional limitation on the assertion of executive privilege is that the privilege should not be invoked to conceal evidence of wrongdoing or criminality on the part of executive officers.").

presidential power—such as discussing law enforcement issues with senior Justice Department officials—and thus Congress cannot probe that official act even if it is ostensibly contrary to federal criminal law.

More broadly, many OLC opinions on executive privilege and testimonial immunity reflect a balanced judgment about congressional need versus presidential prerogative.[218] To the extent that *Trump* recognizes a broader-than-ever exclusive presidential power related to discussions with the "investigative and prosecutorial functions of the Justice Department and its officials," executive branch lawyers can be expected to strike the balance even more frequently in favor of executive power.[219]

Conclusion

Trump made entirely new law on presidential immunity from criminal prosecution. Many elements of its immunity analysis were not briefed or addressed by the courts below, or by petitioner Trump in the Supreme Court. *Trump* also made entirely new law on the President's exclusive removal power and the President's exclusive power of investigation and prosecution. None of the issues addressed in the Court's exclusive power analysis were briefed or addressed by the courts below or briefed or discussed at oral argument by either party in the Supreme Court. The Court ruled on massively important issues of first impression about the nature and scope of presidential power in a short time frame and basically without any outside assistance.[220] The results of these unusual and possibly unprecedented circumstances, I have tried to show, were a confused mess.

Most of the concern about *Trump* has focused on the implications of its immunity rulings. I have argued that the generative element of the opinion is not the immunity ruling *per se*, but rather the exclusive power analysis that underlies the absolute immunity ruling. The Court has traditionally proceeded cautiously and carefully when marking out

---

[218] For examples of this balanced judgment in the context of executive branch law enforcement, see, for example, Assertion of Exec. Privilege over Audio Recordings of the Special Couns.'s Interviews of the President & His Ghostwriter, 48 Op. O.L.C., slip op. at 1, 5, 11 (2024); Cong. Requests for Info. from Inspectors Gen. Concerning Open Crim. Investigations, 13 Op. O.L.C. 77, 83 & n.9 (1989); and Confidentiality of the Att'y Gen.'s Commc'ns in Counseling the President, 6 Op. O.L.C. 481, 500 (1982).

[219] Trump v. United States, 603 U.S. 593, 621 (2024).

[220] On the Court's short time frame, see *supra* note 41.

exclusive presidential power because the President is known to run hard when the Court recognizes such power.[221] But it did the opposite in *Trump*. The Court issued an incautious and overly broad ruling on exclusive presidential powers that Presidents will use to their advantage against the other branches—especially Congress. This advantage will persist until the Court, in more considered reflection, acknowledges its imprudence and alters course.

[221] It was also generally believed, until relatively recently, that, as Jackson taught, a presidential claim of exclusive power in Category Three faced a "severe" test. Youngstown Sheet & Tube Co. v. Sawyer, 343 U.S. 579, 640 (1952) (Jackson, J., concurring). But in light of *Zivotofsky v. Kerry*, 576 U.S. 1 (2015), which recognized a broad and exclusive presidential recognition power without any presumption against exclusivity, *see* Goldsmith, *supra* note 15, at 125–26, and now *Trump*, which did the same for presidential removal and enforcement discretion, the idea of a "severe test" in Category Three can no longer be taken seriously.

MICHAEL W. McCONNELL

THE TRUMP DISQUALIFICATION CASE: THE HALLEY'S COMET OF CONSTITUTIONAL LAW

Section Three of the Fourteenth Amendment bars officials who "engaged in" an "insurrection" after taking an oath to support the Constitution of the United States from holding public office. Enacted immediately after the end of the Civil War, Section Three was designed to prevent the leadership class of the Confederate states from reassuming power after those states were readmitted to the Union, but its language was not limited to that historical context. It reads, in full:

> No person shall be a Senator or Representative in Congress, or elector of President and Vice-President, or hold any office, civil or military, under the United States, or under any State, who, having previously taken an oath, as a member of Congress, or as an officer of the United States, or as a member of any State legislature, or as an executive or judicial officer of any State, to support the Constitution of the United States, shall have engaged in insurrection or rebellion against the same, or given aid or comfort to the

Michael W. McConnell is the Richard and Frances Mallery Professor and Director of the Constitutional Law Center at Stanford Law School and a Senior Fellow at the Hoover Institution.

Author's note: I thank William Baude, Josh Blackman, Jud Campbell, Nathan Chapman, Derek Muller, Michael Stokes Paulsen, Richard Pildes, Seth Barrett Tillman, and Zachary Price for helpful comments on an earlier draft, and Charles Power, Collin Fredricks, and Thomas Archibald for able research assistance.

The Supreme Court Review, 2025.
 Published by The University of Chicago Press. https://doi.org/10.1086/735481

> enemies thereof. But Congress may by a vote of two-thirds of each House, remove such disability.[1]

The disqualification provision was sporadically enforced for about two years, after which Congress in 1872, by a two-thirds vote, passed an "Amnesty Act" lifting the disqualification for most violators.[2] No less a figure than Confederate Vice President Alexander Stephens was admitted to a seat in the House of Representatives in 1873, to the acclaim of his fellow Democrats.[3]

Prior to 2023, few Americans were aware of Section Three and almost no one—including constitutional law scholars—had given any serious thought to the possibility it could have modern application.[4] It was barely mentioned in the leading constitutional law casebooks.[5] The Biden Administration did not bring the case that would have made it relevant to the 2024 election. (That is, it did not charge former President Donald J. Trump with the crime of engaging in insurrection.) Then Section Three suddenly was discovered by two distinguished originalist scholars.[6] It blazed across the skies of courts and headlines, and it went to the Supreme Court, where two other important scholars declared it "perhaps one of the most important cases in American history."[7] Then it disappeared from public attention as rapidly as it had appeared. Section Three was the Halley's Comet of constitutional law.

---

[1] U.S. Const. amend. XIV, § 3.

[2] Act of May 22, 1872, ch. 193, 17 Stat. 142.

[3] 2 James G. Blaine, Twenty Years of Congress: From Lincoln to Garfield 546–47 (Norwich, Henry Bill Publ'g Co. 1886).

[4] The only full-length constitutional analyses of the issue before 2023 were Myles S. Lynch, *Disloyalty & Disqualification: Reconstructing Section 3 of the Fourteenth Amendment*, 30 Wm. & Mary Bill Rts. J. 153 (2021); and Gerard N. Magliocca, *Amnesty and Section Three of the Fourteenth Amendment*, 36 Const. Comment. 87 (2021). This Author covered the topic for half a day in his Stanford Law School course entitled *Reconstruction: Adding the Thirteenth, Fourteenth, and Fifteenth Amendments* (Winter 2021 & Spring 2023).

[5] Two casebooks contained brief discussions of Section Three, including the possibility of application to former President Trump, in their post-2020 editions. Michael Stokes Paulsen, Michael W. McConnell, Samuel L. Bray & William Baude, The Constitution of the United States 1380–81 (5th ed. 2023); Sanford Levinson, Jack M. Balkin, Akhil Reed Amar, Reva B. Siegel & Cristina Rodríguez, Processes of Constitutional Decisionmaking: Cases and Materials 366–67 (8th ed. 2022).

[6] William Baude of the University of Chicago Law School and Michael Stokes Paulsen of the University of St. Thomas School of Law. Both are close personal friends of the Author of this Article. *See* William Baude & Michael Stokes Paulsen, *The Sweep and Force of Section Three*, 172 U. Pa. L. Rev. 605 (2024).

[7] Brief of Akhil Reed Amar and Vikram David Amar as Amici Curiae in Support of Neither Party at 1, Trump v. Anderson, 144 S. Ct. 662 (2024) (No. 23-719).

Superstition held that Halley's Comet portended the defeat and destruction of a prominent leader, as happened to Harold Godwinson at the Battle of Hastings a few months after the comet appeared over England in 1066. Fingers were crossed for a repeat from 2023 to 2024, with former President Trump stepping in for the role of Harold. Supporters of Mr. Trump had forcibly entered the Capitol on January 6, 2021, threatened violence against Vice President Mike Pence and others, and delayed the counting of the electoral votes for more than five hours, spurred on by Mr. Trump's false claims that the election had been stolen.[8] Mr. Trump was not physically present at the Capitol incursion, but he had egged on the rioters at a rally nearby, with perfunctory admonitions to remain peaceful. Could it be said that the three-hour lawless disruption of congressional proceedings was an "insurrection" and that Mr. Trump "engaged in" it? If so, Mr. Trump's detractors thought, he could be stricken from the ballot and the danger of a second Trump presidency eliminated without need for consulting the voters.

Despite the novelty of the argument, many influential people were convinced that indeed Mr. Trump was ineligible to be on the ballot. A 4-3 majority of the all-Democrat-appointed Colorado Supreme Court held that Section Three disqualified Mr. Trump from the ballot.[9] The Secretary of State of Maine, also a Democrat, did the same.[10] The case hurtled toward the Supreme Court with remarkable speed. The Colorado Supreme Court issued its decision on December 19, 2023. Mr. Trump's lawyers petitioned for certiorari on January 3, and the Court granted the petition two days later. Oral argument was held

---

[8] Melissa Quinn et al., *Pence Announces Biden's Victory After Congress Completes Electoral Count*, CBS NEWS (Jan. 7, 2021, 7:05 AM EST), https://www.cbsnews.com/live-updates/electoral-college-vote-count-biden-victory.

[9] Anderson v. Griswold, 543 P.3d 283 (Colo. 2023). Interestingly, the split on the Colorado Supreme Court was not based on political party. All were appointed by Democratic governors. Nicholas Riccardi, *Colorado Supreme Court Declares Donald Trump Is Ineligible for the White House*, ASSOCIATED PRESS (Dec. 19, 2023, 9:56 PM ET), https://apnews.com/article/trump-insurrection-14th-amendment-2024-colorado-d16dd8f354eeaf450558378c65fd79a2. The Justices who had gone to elite out-of-state law schools voted to disqualify Mr. Trump. The dissenters were those who went to law school in-state. Kaelan Deese, *Justices Who Removed Trump from Colorado Ballot Attended Ivy League Law Schools*, WASH. EXAM'R (Dec. 20, 2023, 5:38 PM), https://www.washingtonexaminer.com/news/2644116/justices-who-removed-trump-from-colorado-ballot-attended-ivy-league-law-schools.

[10] Jordan Freiman, Katrina Kaufman & Grace Kazarian, *Maine Secretary of State Disqualifies Trump from Primary Ballot*, CBS NEWS (Dec. 29, 2023, 3:32 PM EST), https://www.cbsnews.com/news/trump-maine-primary-ballot-disqualified-secretary-of-state-shenna-bellows.

on February 8, and the decision came down less than a month later, on March 4—not coincidentally the day before the Colorado primary.

Once in the Supreme Court, the case for disqualifying the alleged insurrectionist had lost its dazzle. Not a single Justice—whether appointed by Republican or by Democratic Presidents—accepted the argument that Section Three kept the former President off the ballot. In an unsigned per curiam opinion joined by five Justices, accompanied by a concurrence by Justice Barrett and another concurrence by Justices Sotomayor, Kagan, and Jackson, the Court reversed the Colorado Supreme Court and held that states have no authority to enforce Section Three with respect to presidential candidates without empowerment by Congress, which has not been granted.[11] As a practical matter, because states control presidential electoral machinery, that rendered the effort to bar Mr. Trump from running for President defunct. Section Three then disappeared from the news as rapidly as it had appeared.[12] The idea that Mr. Trump is constitutionally disqualified dropped even from his opponents' campaign oratory. Like Halley's Comet, having streaked across the sky, the theory disappeared from sight and mind, leaving no trace on American politics.

That does not deprive the case of interest for students of constitutional law—not least as a case study in how the nine Justices of the Supreme Court respond when they are forced to decide a case of intense political consequence, with nothing but enigmatic text and no precedent to guide them. The case poses a host of unanswered or poorly answered questions in an intriguing corner of constitutional law. Again there is a similarity to the eponymous Comet in the centuries before Halley's scientific work: The immediate effect of the decision is clear for all to see, but its origins, its explanation, and its future are mostly a mystery.

I. Unanimity, Almost

Given the political stakes and the Court's well-known partisan divisions, it came as a surprise that the Justices decided the case unanimously. Six of the nine Justices were appointed by Republican Presidents, three of them by Mr. Trump himself, and three by Democrats.

---

[11] Trump v. Anderson, 144 S. Ct. 662, 671 (2024) (per curiam).

[12] The decision came down March 4, 2024. With the exception of end-of-Term retrospectives, no major newspaper mentioned Section Three again after March 7, 2024.

Yet all nine agreed that neither Colorado nor any other state could keep Mr. Trump off the ballot, even assuming he had "engaged in" an "insurrection" within the meaning of the Constitution—a contentious question that the Court, unsurprisingly, preferred to avoid. The reason for this unanimous outcome was almost certainly pragmatic rather than textual or historical. As Justices Sotomayor, Kagan, and Jackson stated in concurrence, "Allowing Colorado to [keep a presidential candidate off the ballot on the ground that he is an oathbreaking insurrectionist] would, we agree, create a chaotic state-by-state patchwork, at odds with our Nation's federalism principles."[13] The simple and unanimous holding of the case was that States have no role in enforcing Section Three with respect to the presidency.

Whether such a "patchwork" would in fact be at odds with "our Nation's federalism principles" will be discussed below; the answer is not obvious. It is more likely that pragmatics drove the decision. It must have weighed on the Justices' minds that throwing the leading presidential candidate of a major party off the ballot would cause a public uproar, especially when the rationale for doing so—that Mr. Trump "engaged in" an "insurrection"—is more a partisan Rorschach test than an objective determination. The Justices were not willing to deprive tens of millions of people of their right to vote for the candidate of their choice for anything less than clear and reasonably indisputable reasons; much less on the basis of a Delphic piece of text that had never been raised in connection with any presidential election or previously interpreted by the Court. Of course, that is not what the per curiam opinion actually said, but it was hard not to read that message between the lines.

For the Court to achieve unanimity in a case like *Trump v. Anderson*[14]—a case so riven by partisan animosity—was a considerable achievement. Public confidence in the integrity of the electoral process matters a great deal, and if all nine Justices, despite their different partisan appointments and presumed leanings, come to the same conclusion, this would demonstrate to the public that the result was not based on their political precommitments. Unanimity here would send the same signal as unanimity did in *Brown v. Board*[15] or *United*

---

[13] *Anderson*, 144 S. Ct. at 672 (Sotomayor, Kagan & Jackson, JJ., concurring in the judgment).

[14] *Id.* at 664 (per curiam).

[15] 347 U.S. 483 (1954).

States v. Nixon[16]—but was so grievously lacking in *Bush v. Gore*.[17] That these nine Justices (almost) did so in this wrenching case deserves more commendation than they received.

But the Justices squandered the benefits of unanimity by venturing into issues not before them. Despite being unanimous on the only thing that mattered to the case, the Court produced one of the most acrimonious minority opinions in history. Not only did three concurring Justices accuse the five-Justice per curiam of unnecessarily "decid[ing] novel constitutional questions"—an accusation that seems undeniably true—but they attributed to the majority base partisan motives. The five Justices in the majority took this unnecessary step, according to the three who joined this concurrence, for the purpose of "insulat[ing] this Court and petitioner [Mr. Trump] from future controversy."[18] More pointedly, they claimed that "[t]oday, the majority goes beyond the necessities of this case to limit how Section 3 can bar an oathbreaking insurrectionist from becoming President."[19] Needless to say, it was this split and this accusation that dominated news coverage of the decision.[20]

Justice Barrett, sounding every bit like a frustrated teacher trying to calm a class of squabbling children, chided the majority for "address[ing] the complicated question whether federal legislation is the exclusive vehicle through which Section 3 can be enforced," when it was "sufficient to resolve this case" to hold that "States lack the power to enforce Section 3 against Presidential candidates."[21] She likewise chided the other concurring Justices for raising such a fuss: "In my judgment, this is not the time to amplify disagreement with stridency. The Court

[16] 418 U.S. 683 (1974).

[17] 531 U.S. 98 (2000).

[18] *Anderson*, 144 S. Ct. at 672 (Sotomayor, Kagan & Jackson, JJ., concurring in the judgment).

[19] *Id.* at 674. In this sentence, the concurring Justices drop qualifying language like "alleged," and seem to presuppose that Mr. Trump actually *is* an "oathbreaking insurrectionist." *Id.*

[20] *See, e.g.*, Amy Howe, *Supreme Court Rules States Cannot Remove Trump from Ballot for Insurrection*, SCOTUSBLOG (Mar. 4, 2024, 12:09 PM), https://www.scotusblog.com/2024/03/supreme-court-rules-states-cannot-remove-trump-from-ballot-for-insurrection; Aaron Blake, *A Conspicuous Line on Trump from the Supreme Court's Left Flank*, WASH. POST (Mar. 5, 2024, 2:39 PM EST), https://www.washingtonpost.com/politics/2024/03/05/conspicuous-line-trump-supreme-courts-left-flank; Adam Liptak, *Trump Prevails in Supreme Court Challenge to His Eligibility*, N.Y. TIMES (Mar. 5, 2024), https://www.nytimes.com/live/2024/03/04/us/trump-supreme-court-colorado-ballot.

[21] *Anderson*, 144 S. Ct. at 671 (Barrett, J., concurring in part and concurring in the judgment).

has settled a politically charged issue in the volatile season of a Presidential election. Particularly in this circumstance, writings on the Court should turn the national temperature down, not up."[22] None of the other Justices joined her opinion.

II. What Exactly is the Holding of the Per Curiam Opinion?

For all the *sturm und drang*, it is not clear what exactly the per curiam Justices achieved in the non-unanimous parts of the opinion. Justice Barrett says that the per curiam opinion "address[ed] the complicated question whether federal legislation is the exclusive vehicle through which Section 3 can be enforced."[23] The other concurring Justices assert that the per curiam opinion "announces that a disqualification for insurrection can occur only when Congress enacts a particular kind of legislation pursuant to Section 5 of the Fourteenth Amendment."[24] "In doing so," they continue, "the majority shuts the door on other potential means of federal enforcement."[25] But those words do not appear in the per curiam opinion. At no point does the majority plainly state that Section Three can be enforced only by means of Section Five legislation. To be sure, the per curiam opinion contains language that strongly *hints* at that conclusion. It states that "[t]he Constitution empowers Congress to prescribe how those determinations should be made. *The* relevant provision is Section 5, which enables Congress, subject of course to judicial review, to pass 'appropriate legislation' to 'enforce' the Fourteenth Amendment."[26] The direct article "the" might be taken to suggest that Section Five is the *only* relevant provision. The per curiam opinion added that "Congress's Section 5 power is critical when it comes to Section 3."[27]

---

[22] *Id.*

[23] *Id.*

[24] *Id.* at 672 (Sotomayor, Kagan & Jackson, JJ., concurring in the judgment); *see also id.* at 674 (referring to the majority's "requirement that a Section 3 disqualification can occur only pursuant to legislation enacted for that purpose," which will "foreclose future efforts to disqualify a Presidential candidate under that provision").

[25] *Id.* at 672.

[26] *Id.* at 667 (per curiam) (emphasis added). It also states: "The terms of the Amendment speak only to enforcement by Congress, which enjoys power to enforce the Amendment through legislation pursuant to Section 5." *Id.* at 668. This sentence, which is literally true, does not explicitly deny that parts of the Constitution other than the Fourteenth Amendment itself might have relevance.

[27] *Id.* at 667.

What does "critical" mean? Does it mean "exclusive"?[28] To state that Section Five is "the" relevant provision and that it is "critical" to enforcement of Section Three does not—quite—say that Section Three cannot be enforced in any other way. Finally, the per curiam observes that the judicial gloss on Section Five announced in *City of Boerne v. Flores*[29]—that Section Five legislation limiting state power must "reflect 'congruence and proportionality' between preventing or remedying that conduct 'and the means adopted to that end'"[30]—"limits *congressional* legislation enforcing Section 3."[31] Surely the Court did not mean to suggest that the *Boerne* gloss applies to congressional powers outside Section Five, or to state power. What, then, was the point of referring to "congruence and proportionality"?[32]

It is usually a mistake for dissenters to make the majority out to be worse (from their point of view) than it actually is, because this can be a self-fulfilling prophecy. At one point, Justices Sotomayor, Kagan, and Jackson describe the Court's dicta as "musings" that are "as inadequately supported as they are gratuitous."[33] But elsewhere, they say that the majority Justices "decide" novel constitutional questions and that the per curiam "shuts the door on other potential means of enforcement."[34] Which is it? Musings? Decisions? Shutdowns? There are a number of reasons, canvassed below, to doubt that the majority meant to hold that Section Five is the exclusive vehicle for enforcement of Section Three. Why would the concurring Justices leap to that

---

[28] This is reminiscent of the Court's famous statement in *Marbury v. Madison*, 5 U.S. (1 Cranch) 137 (1803), that "it is emphatically the province and duty of the judicial department to say what the law is." *Id.* at 177. Does the adverb "emphatically" mean that no other department has such a power? Presumably not.

[29] 521 U.S. 507, 536 (1997).

[30] *Anderson*, 144 S. Ct. at 670 (quoting *Boerne*, 521 U.S. at 520).

[31] *Id.*

[32] The discussion of congruence and proportionality might seem to suggest that Section Five legislation enforcing Section Three must not extend farther than the strict terms of Section Three. But that is not the meaning of "congruence and proportionality" in *Boerne*. Congress is permitted to go beyond the strict terms of Section One (as interpreted by the Court) when this is appropriate as a means of enforcing the core. *See* Katzenbach v. Morgan, 384 U.S. 641 (1966). *See generally* Michael W. McConnell, Comment, *Institutions and Interpretation: A Critique of* City of Boerne v. Flores, 111 Harv. L. Rev. 153 (1997). Moreover, the per curiam cites Section 2383 approvingly as "*congressional* legislation enforcing Section 3" even though that criminal statute extends more broadly than the strict terms of Section Three. *Anderson*, 144 S. Ct. at 670. Among other things, Section 2383 extends to incitement and to giving "aid or comfort," as well as actual engagement in the insurrection. 18 U.S.C. § 2383.

[33] *Anderson*, 144 S. Ct. at 673 (Sotomayor, Kagan & Jackson, JJ., concurring in the judgment).

[34] *Id.* at 672.

construction, rather than saying that the Court had left open the difficult question of how to enforce Section Three at the federal level?

Here is a theory: Perhaps an earlier draft of the per curiam opinion *did* hold that Section Three could be enforced only by means of Section Five legislation. Perhaps the concurring Justices, who had voted to produce a unanimous decision, protested. Perhaps the authors of the per curiam opinion realized that such a holding would be an overstep, and amended the opinion draft to eliminate the objectionable parts, but failed to scrub the draft of language that might be susceptible to the prior interpretation. Here is the kicker: Perhaps the Justices ran out of time to work things out. For obvious reasons, the Court must have felt the need to issue the opinion before the Colorado primary, so that the voters of Colorado would know for sure whether votes for Mr. Trump would count. Under this speculative narrative of what might have happened, the majority removed any clear holding about the need for Section Five legislation, but did not have time to scrub the opinion for the remaining suggestive language; this was enough to goad the concurring Justices into their acrimonious separate opinion, and Justice Barrett into her frustrated rebuke of both sides. Or maybe it was the concurring Justices who did not have time to revise their work in light of the changes in the majority. In other words, the rush to issue an opinion before the Colorado primary prevented the Justices from coming together on a single unanimous text. That robbed the nation of what would have been a reassuringly unanimous and nonpartisan decision.

Why is it unlikely that the majority held that Section Five is the exclusive vehicle for enforcement of Section Three? Let us count the ways.

First, the Court unambiguously acknowledged that states have authority to enforce Section Three with respect to state candidates and officeholders. Of course that makes sense; "the States enjoy sovereign 'power to prescribe the qualifications of their own officers'" and "nothing in [the Fourteenth Amendment] plainly withdraws from the States this traditional authority."[35] This shows that, although Section Five empowers Congress to enforce the Amendment, there are other possible sources of enforcement authority, which are not erased by the existence of Section Five. Below, I will address whether Article II, Section One, Clause Two, which empowers state legislatures to set the

---

[35] *Id.* at 667 (per curiam) (quoting Taylor v. Beckham, 178 U.S. 548, 570–71 (1900)).

rules for selecting presidential electors, similarly empowers state enforcement of Section Three, notwithstanding Section Five.

Second, the Court recognized the persuasive force of historical practice during the period Section Three was enforced as evidence of its meaning.[36] The most conspicuous instances of enforcement of Section Three with respect to federal officeholders involved members of Congress. Article I designates each House of Congress as "the Judge of the . . . Qualifications of its own Members."[37] After the elections of 1870, both the House and the Senate decided challenges to the qualifications of men elected by Southern states to Congress on the ground that they had engaged in the Confederate insurrection after having taken an oath to support the Constitution of the United States. In some cases, the challenged individuals were seated and in other cases they were disqualified.[38] The jurisdiction of the two Houses to make these determinations was unchallenged—even though no Section Five legislation authorized the proceedings. This is proof positive that the Framers of the Fourteenth Amendment did not think that Section Five was the exclusive vehicle for enforcement of Section Three against federal officeholders.

Third, the per curiam opinion noted that the Confiscation Act of 1862 "effectively provided an additional procedure for enforcing disqualification" and went on to say that a "successor" to this legislation "remains on the books today. See 18 U.S.C. § 2383."[39] Section 2383, a criminal statute, provides that "[w]hoever incites, sets on foot, assists, or engages in any rebellion or insurrection against the authority of the United States or the laws thereof, or gives aid or comfort thereto, shall be fined under this title or imprisoned not more than ten years, or both; and shall be incapable of holding any office under the United States."[40] It would seem, by its terms, to be a straightforward way to enforce Section Three against an insurrectionist who may seek to hold a federal position, and the per curiam opinion seems to bless that reading. But as the per curiam opinion also notes, the Confiscation Act was not enacted pursuant to Section Five; indeed, it predated the

---

[36] *Id.* at 669–70.

[37] U.S. Const. art. I, § 5, cl. 1.

[38] *See infra* notes 82–89 and accompanying text.

[39] *Anderson*, 144 S. Ct. at 670.

[40] 18 U.S.C. § 2383.

Fourteenth Amendment by seven years.[41] If Section 2383 "effectively provided an additional procedure for enforcing disqualification" then it cannot be true that Section Five is the exclusive vehicle for enforcing disqualification.

Supreme Court opinions must be read to mean what they say. But they should not be read to mean more than they say, when that extra-textual meaning is in tension with other propositions in the opinion, and with the underlying evidence. Accordingly, *Trump v. Anderson* should be read to bar states from enforcing Section Three with respect to the presidency, and perhaps with respect to all federal offices, but it should not be read to make Section Five of the Fourteenth Amendment the exclusive vehicle for enforcement at the federal level—even though it was interpreted that way by the concurring Justices.

III. The Ratonale Not Offered: That Section Three Does Not Apply to Running for Office

Before turning to the basis for the Court's holding that states lack power to enforce Section Three for the presidency, we should note the existence of a straightforward, plain-language position that would have disposed of the Colorado case without need for any broader holding of constitutional law: that Section Three by its own terms does not address who can run for office. It addresses only who can "hold" office. The relevant language is: "No person shall *be* a Senator or Representative in Congress, or elector of President and Vice-President, or *hold* any office, civil or military, under the United States, or under any State, who . . . ."[42] The verbs are to "be" and to "hold."

That Section Three was not worded to apply to running for office should not be surprising. During this time, decades before adoption of the Australian ballot in the United States, states did not prepare a ballot for elections. Private entities—the political parties—printed and distributed ballots to the voters, and the voters were free to vote for whomever they wished.[43] It would not have occurred to the

---

[41] *Anderson*, 144 S. Ct. at 670.

[42] U.S. Const. amend. XIV, § 3 (emphases added).

[43] *See, e.g.*, Richard Franklin Bensel, The American Ballot Box in the Mid-Nineteenth Century 30 (2004); Erik J. Engstrom & Jason M. Roberts, The Politics of Ballot Design: How States Shape American Democracy 38–43 (2020).

Framers to word the Amendment to exclude insurrectionists from the ballot when there were no official ballots.

Historical experience supports this plain-language interpretation. The Enforcement Act of 1870 established a mechanism for removing oath-breaking insurrectionists from their offices, but it did not apply to mere candidates or to ballot access. Similarly, the Article I power of each House of Congress to judge the qualifications of its members kicks in only when those individuals seek to assume their positions in Congress, which is to say, after the election has taken place. So far as the historical evidence reveals (and our knowledge could be incomplete[44]), authorities enforcing Section Three at the state level did so when malefactors attempted to hold office, not when they ran for office.

Trump v. Anderson did not involve anyone attempting to "hold" an office, but rather exclusion of a candidate from the primary ballot. The Colorado proceeding was not, therefore, a direct enforcement of Section Three. Rather, it arose on the theory that either the Secretary of State or the state courts had legal authority to exclude from the ballot any candidate who would not be eligible to serve if elected.

The Colorado legislature has enacted an Election Code, which applies to presidential elections under the legislature's Article II authority to determine the "manner of choosing Electors." Under that law, candidates for office are required to attest that they "desire[] the office and [are] qualified to perform its duties if elected."[45] Mr. Trump filed the necessary attestation. The Election Code does not permit or require the Secretary of State to question the veracity of the candidate's attestation. As the Colorado Supreme Court put it:

> [I]f the contents of a signed and notarized statement of intent appear facially complete . . . the Secretary has no duty to further investigate the accuracy or validity of the information the prospective candidate has supplied. . . . To that extent, we agree with President Trump that the Secretary has no duty to determine, beyond what is apparent on the face of the required documents, whether a presidential candidate is qualified.[46]

---

[44] Evidence about actual enforcement in the Southern states is murky. *See* Magliocca, *supra* note 4, at 110.

[45] Colo. Rev. Stat. § 1-4-1101(1) (2017); *see* Anderson v. Griswold, 543 P.3d 283, 306–07 (Colo. 2023).

[46] *Anderson*, 543 P.3d at 306.

Hassan v. Colorado,[47] the oft-cited Tenth Circuit decision written by then-Circuit Judge Gorsuch, is not to the contrary. In that case, the presidential candidate, who was not a native-born citizen, did not attest that he was eligible for the office and was excluded from the ballot for that reason.[48]

The Colorado Supreme Court nevertheless held that, even though the Secretary of State had no state law duty to exclude Mr. Trump from the ballot, it was "wrongful" for her not to do so, on the *federal constitutional ground* that "President Trump is disqualified from holding the office of President under Section Three; because he is disqualified, it would be a wrongful act under the Election Code for the Secretary to list him as a candidate on the presidential primary ballot."[49] In other words, it is Section Three that compels the exclusion, not any state law enforcing Section Three. But as we have noted, Section Three does not address running for office, but only "holding" office. Whether or not Section Three *permits* states to exclude supposed insurrectionists from the ballot, it plainly does not take legal effect, by its own terms, until they attempt to hold the office. The claim that it was "wrongful" under Section Three for the Colorado Secretary of State not to exclude Mr. Trump from the ballot was therefore a clear error of federal constitutional law.

This would have been a narrow and textually grounded basis for the decision in *Anderson*. To be sure, this narrow holding would not have spoken to the state legislature's *power* to enforce Section Three at the ballot stage, but that question was not genuinely raised by the Colorado law as it exists.

Apart from this issue, there was a related technical complication also not mentioned in any of the opinions. Mr. Trump was not running in Colorado for President of the United States; he was running for the Republican nomination. The authority of states to limit the associational freedom of political parties to choose their candidates is disputed.[50] This is a problem not just of state law but of federal First

---

[47] 495 F. App'x 947 (10th Cir. 2012).

[48] *Id.* at 948.

[49] *Anderson*, 543 P.3d at 297.

[50] *See* Cousins v. Wigoda, 419 U.S. 477, 489–90 (1975); Democratic Party v. Wisconsin *ex rel.* La Follette, 450 U.S. 107, 108, 121–26 (1981); Derek T. Muller, *Administering Presidential Elections and Counting Electoral Votes After* Trump v. Anderson, 60 WAKE FOREST L. REV. (forthcoming 2025) (manuscript at 14–15 & n.43), https://ssrn.com/abstract=4916797.

Amendment law. No matter what the Colorado courts might have said, the Republican Party was entitled to nominate whomever it wished, and nothing would have required the Party to recognize delegate votes from Colorado if Colorado had kept a live candidate from the ballot. Thus, even if the primary-stage litigation had gone against Mr. Trump, it arguably would have had no practical effect.

And there is a further twist. Technically, candidates do not run for President in popular elections. Electors run, and they are the ones who actually elect the President. Section Three explicitly disqualifies oath-breaking insurrectionists from performing the office of elector. Should it be interpreted to disqualify candidates for elector on the ground that they plan to vote for an oath-breaking insurrectionist? That would seem to be the necessary implication of the view that Mr. Trump could be excluded at the election stage.

The Court did not mention any of these technical arguments. Perhaps that was a further product of the rushed character of the proceedings.

IV. What is the Reasoning Behind the Narrow, Unanimous Holding?

The Court unanimously held that states lack power to enforce Section Three against candidates for President. But why? The majority and the concurrences were in agreement about the reason as well as the result: States lack power to enforce Section Three against presidential candidates because this would create a "patchwork" at odds with basic federalism principles. Justices Sotomayor, Kagan, and Jackson put it this way: "Allowing Colorado to do so would, we agree, create a chaotic state-by-state patchwork, at odds with our Nation's federalism principles. That is enough to resolve this case."[51] The per curiam opinion elaborated the point at greater length, noting all the various ways different states might interpret differently the commands of Section Three. "The result could well be that a single candidate would be declared ineligible in some States, but not others, based on the same conduct (and perhaps even the same factual record). The 'patchwork' that would likely result from state enforcement would 'sever the direct link that the Framers found so critical between the National

[51] Trump v. Anderson, 144 S. Ct. 662, 672 (2024) (Sotomayor, Kagan & Jackson, JJ., concurring in the judgment).

Government and the people of the United States' as a whole . . . Nothing in the Constitution requires that we endure such chaos. . . ."[52]

No doubt that struck many people—maybe most people—as sensible. But is it an accurate account of the federalism principles of the Constitution? The Constitution explicitly and unambiguously provides for different rules for presidential elections in different states. Article II, Section One, Clause Two provides that each state will appoint electors "in such Manner as the Legislature thereof may direct."[53] There is no requirement that rules for presidential elections be uniform. Indeed, for many decades not all states had popular elections at all. Some had popular elections but some allowed the state legislatures to choose the electors, and thus to displace popular election. Today, some states award electoral votes on a winner-take-all basis, and some do it district-by-district.[54] Ballot access requirements vary from state to state (with some constraint arising from the First Amendment[55]), with the "result . . . that a single candidate [is] declared ineligible in some States, but not others"—the very outcome the Court found intolerable in the context of Section Three.[56] In 2024, the year of *Trump v Anderson*, Robert F. Kennedy, Jr. was on the ballot in some states and off the ballot in others (until he withdrew from the race); the same was true of Green Party candidate Jill Stein and Independent candidate Cornel West.[57] Whether a third-party candidate is on the ballot can profoundly affect the outcome of the election—not just for one state but for the country. This is truly a patchwork. But we cannot say the patchwork is at odds with "our Nation's federalism principles."[58] The "state-by-state resolution"[59] of how to select electors is one element of our federalism principles.

---

[52] *Id.* at 671 (per curiam) (quoting U.S. Term Limits, Inc. v. Thornton, 514 U.S. 779, 822 (1995)).

[53] U.S. Const. art. II, § 1, cl. 2.

[54] Maine and Nebraska award electoral votes by district, then allocate two votes each to the at-large winner of the state. *See Distribution of Electoral Votes*, Nat'l Archives (June 26, 2023), https://www.archives.gov/electoral-college/allocation.

[55] Anderson v. Celebrezze, 460 U.S. 780, 793–95 (1983).

[56] *Anderson*, 144 S. Ct. at 671.

[57] *See* Alyce McFadden, Taylor Robinson, Leanne Abraham & Rebecca Davis O'Brien, *Where R.F.K. Jr. and Independent Presidential Candidates Are on the Ballot*, N.Y. Times (Oct. 16, 2024), https://www.nytimes.com/interactive/2024/us/politics/presidential-candidates-third-party-independent.html.

[58] *Anderson*, 144 S. Ct. at 672 (Sotomayor, Kagan & Jackson, JJ., concurring in the judgment).

[59] *Id.* at 670 (per curiam).

The per curiam opinion states that "nothing in the Constitution delegates to the States any power to enforce Section 3 against federal officeholders and candidates."[60] It is true, of course, that "the text of the Fourteenth Amendment, on its face, does not affirmatively delegate such a power to the States. The terms of the Amendment speak only to enforcement by Congress, which enjoys power to enforce the Amendment through legislation pursuant to Section 5."[61] But what about Article II, Section One, Clause Two? As already noted, this Clause provides that each state will appoint electors "in such Manner as the Legislature thereof may direct."[62] On its face, that provision would seem to empower the state legislature to decide how to enforce the qualifications and disqualifications for being President, namely age, natural-born citizenship, two-term limit, and non-participation in an insurrection. Suppose that a state legislature enacts a law excluding violators of Section Three from running for President. Why does that not fall within the legislature's delegated power under Article II? (True, the Colorado Supreme Court held that the Colorado legislature has not enacted such a law, but for purposes of examining the authority of states with respect to Section Three it is a plausible hypothetical.)

Oddly, the *Anderson* opinion does not address whether and how states may enforce the other constitutional qualifications for presidential office—age, death, natural-born citizenship, and term limits. That would have been useful background information for the question whether and how they may enforce the disqualification from Section Three. Because of its highly contestable nature, Section Three might well present a different problem, leading to a different answer. But if so, the Court might have said so.

The per curiam opinion deals with the Article II, Section One, Clause Two question in a single laconic paragraph.[63] The concurring Justices, who agree as to the conclusion, say nothing at all. The paragraph begins by noting that "[t]he only . . . plausible constitutional sources of such a delegation [of power to the states to enforce Section Three against federal officeholders or candidates] are the Elections and Electors Clauses, which authorize States to conduct and regulate

[60] *Id.* at 668.

[61] U.S. Const. amend. XIV, § 5.

[62] *Id.* art. II, § 1, cl. 2.

[63] *Anderson*, 144 S. Ct. at 668.

congressional and Presidential elections, respectively."[64] Yes, but don't these Clauses explicitly delegate all authority to make rules for congressional and presidential elections? The per curiam answers this question in two sentences. The first is empty and unpersuasive: "But there is little reason to think that these Clauses implicitly authorize the States to enforce Section 3 against federal officeholders and candidates."[65] Why not? Textually they seem unlimited as to all questions regarding the manner of choosing members of Congress and electors. States have used these powers to exclude presidential candidates who violate the natural-born citizen restriction. Why not Section Three?

The paragraph's next sentence is more to the point: "Granting the States that authority would invert the Fourteenth Amendment's rebalancing of federal and state power."[66] If this is true, it would be a sound reason to reject the conclusion that state legislatures have the Article II power to make rules for enforcement of Section Three's disqualification provisions with respect to the presidency. This, then, is the most significant question raised by *Trump v. Anderson*: Would state enforcement of Section Three "invert the Fourteenth Amendment's rebalancing of federal and state power"?

V. Is State Power to Enforce Section Three in Presidential Elections Consistent with the Fourteenth Amendment?

If the reasoning in the preceding Part of this Article is correct, "our Nation's federalism principles" provide no support for the unanimous holding in *Trump v. Anderson*, even if all nine Justices said so. But that does not mean the holding is wrong. The per curiam's second rationale, resting squarely on the Fourteenth Amendment itself, has more substance. The Fourteenth Amendment is a nationalizing amendment to its toes: It nationalizes the definition of citizenship; it nationalizes the basic set of constitutional rights ("privileges or immunities") pertaining to citizens; it nationalizes the rule of law principles of due process; it creates for the first time a constitutional requirement of equality, which is national; it protects the national credit and discountenances the Confederate debt; and it gives the national legislature broad power to enforce all of that, with the ability

---

[64] *Id.*

[65] *Id.*

[66] *Id.*

to preempt inconsistent state law. Section Three is part and parcel of the Amendment's nationalizing project. Its clear purpose was to limit the ability of the states of the rebellion to re-empower officials who had betrayed their oaths of office. As legal historian Gerard Magliocca expresses it, the Framers of Section Three "embraced a theory that the political and military elites of the South were the only people who should bear constitutional responsibility for the Civil War. In making that judgment, . . . Congress limited a state's ability to choose its leaders and would force some of them to clean house."[67]

The per curiam opinion drew the logical conclusion that "[i]t would be incongruous to read this particular Amendment as granting the States the power—silently no less—to disqualify a candidate for federal office."[68] Imagine the shock if Alabama took upon itself to declare Ulysses Grant or some other Yankee general ineligible to run for President, on the ground that their violent assault on the seat of government in Montgomery amounted to an "insurrection." In no respect did the Fourteenth Amendment *increase* the states' power over the federal government. On this, the concurring Justices were in full agreement. Noting that "[t]he Reconstruction Amendments 'were specifically designed as an expansion of federal power and an intrusion on state sovereignty,'" Justices Sotomayor, Kagan, and Jackson wrote that "it would defy logic for Section 3 to give States new powers to determine who may hold the Presidency."[69]

There were no recorded statements during the time of the framing and enforcement of Section Three regarding the scope of authority of states to enforce, but as the per curiam opinion states, the "pattern of disqualification with respect to state, but not federal offices provides 'persuasive evidence of a general understanding' that the States lacked enforcement power with respect to the latter."[70] That pattern was clear and consistent: Federal and state authorities both were empowered to enforce the Section in the context of state officeholders, but only federal authorities enforced it against federal officials.

[67] Magliocca, *supra* note 4, at 99.

[68] *Anderson*, 144 S. Ct. at 668.

[69] *Id.* at 673 (Sotomayor, Kagan & Jackson, JJ., concurring in the judgment) (quoting City of Rome v. United States, 446 U.S. 156, 179 (1980)). It is not entirely clear whether the concurring Justices extended this principle to federal offices other than the presidency. In the quotation in text, they confine themselves to the presidency, but they then quote approvingly from the per curiam, which spoke of candidates for "federal office." *Id.* at 668 (per curiam).

[70] *Id.* at 669 (quoting U.S. Term Limits, Inc. v. Thornton, 514 U.S. 779, 826 (1995)).

Let us first examine the historical practice regarding enforcement at the state level. The First Military Reconstruction Act called for constitutional conventions in the ten rebel states, and provided that "no person excluded from the privilege of holding office by said proposed amendment to the Constitution of the United States, shall be eligible to election as a member of the convention to frame a constitution for any of said rebel States, nor shall any person vote for members of such convention."[71] The Second Military Reconstruction Act charged the Army with registering voters for those convention elections and required potential voters to swear that they were not subject to Section Three.[72] Congressional statutes readmitting certain of the rebel states required those states to bar officeholding by persons in violation of Section Three (even though it was not yet ratified).[73] Additionally, Congress instructed officers of the Union Army to remove some state officials who failed to take the so-called "Ironclad Oath" of loyalty to the Union, but subject to Congress's Section Three power to lift disabilities.[74] This was not, technically, an enforcement of Section Three, but it was closely related, and demonstrates Congress's intention to use federal power to clean house of former Confederates. Four new state constitutions excluded persons in violation of the terms of Section Three from voting and officeholding.[75] It bears mention that none of these enforcement measures were enacted pursuant to Section Five of the Fourteenth Amendment.

At the federal level, Congress passed the Enforcement Act of 1870, which applied to both state and federal offices.[76] This Act is the best evidence of how the Framers of the Fourteenth Amendment thought

---

[71] First Military Reconstruction Act, ch. 153, § 5, 14 Stat. 428, 429 (1867).

[72] Second Military Reconstruction Act, ch. 6, § 1, 15 Stat. 2, 2 (1867).

[73] *See, e.g.*, An Act to Admit States, ch. 70, § 3, 15 Stat. 73, 74 (1868) ("[N]o person prohibited from holding office under the United States, or under any State, by section three of the proposed amendment to the Constitution of the United States, known as article fourteen, shall be deemed eligible to any office in either of said States, unless relieved from disability as provided in said amendment. . . ."). This law appears to require enforcement by the state governments themselves.

[74] *See, e.g.*, S.J. Res. 8, 40th Cong., 15 Stat. 344 (1869).

[75] South Carolina, Texas, Alabama, and Arkansas each disenfranchised individuals in violation of Section Three and barred them from holding office. S.C. CONST. of 1868, art. VIII, § 2; TEX. CONST. of 1869, art. VI, § 1; ALA. CONST. of 1868, art. VII, § 3; ARK. CONST. of 1868, art. VIII, § 3; *see also* Magliocca, *supra* note 4, at 97–98.

[76] Enforcement Act of 1870 (First Ku Klux Klan Act), ch. 114, §§ 14–15, 16 Stat. 140, 143–44 (1870).

Section Three should be enforced. Section Fourteen authorized federal district attorneys to bring a *quo warranto*[77] proceeding in federal district court to remove anyone holding non-legislative office in violation of Section Three, and Section Fifteen added criminal penalties for those who refused to step down.[78] Note that these provisions vested authority to bring disqualification proceedings exclusively in the federal executive branch and final authority to decide the disqualification issue exclusively in the federal courts, subject to due process, rules of evidence, and appellate review. These provisions were repealed decades later, on the apparent assumption that Section Three had no more relevance after Congress passed the Amnesty Act in 1872.[79] These provisions applied to judges (and other judicial officers, such as clerks and marshals) and executive branch officers. By their terms, they did not apply to legislative positions. Whether they were understood to apply to the President and Vice President is a surprisingly difficult technical question, but it got almost no attention because it was obvious that neither President Grant nor Vice President Colfax were insurrectionists.[80]

The more important federal-level enforcement actions pertained to members of Congress. As already noted, Article I designates each House of Congress as "the Judge of the . . . Qualifications of its own Members."[81] Sections Fourteen and Fifteen of the Enforcement Act expressly excluded legislative offices from its scope, either on the ground that the Article I power to judge qualifications is exclusive as a constitutional matter or on the basis of a congressional judgment that it should be so. As the per curiam opinion noted, "[i]n the years following ratification, the House and Senate exercised their unique powers under Article I to adjudicate challenges contending that

---

[77] *Id.* § 14, 16 Stat. at 143. *Quo warranto* (Latin for "by what warrant?") was a common law writ challenging the right of a putative official to hold office. 2 William Blackstone, Commentaries *262–63.

[78] §§ 14–15, 16 Stat. at 143–44.

[79] Section Fifteen's criminal prohibition was repealed in the 1909 codification of the penal code. Act of Mar. 4, 1909, ch. 15, § 341, 35 Stat. 1088, 1153. The *quo warranto* provision in Section Fourteen was repealed during the 1948 codification of Title 28 of the U.S. Code. *See* Act of June 25, 1948, ch. 646, § 39, 62 Stat. 869, 992–93; *see also* Lynch, *supra* note 4, at 206 n.365; Baude & Paulsen, *supra* note 6, at 626 n.64. Another 1898 act removed Section Three disabilities "heretofore incurred." Act of June 6, 1898, ch. 389, 30 Stat. 432.

[80] For a discussion of the point, see *infra* notes 96–108 and accompanying text.

[81] U.S. Const. art. I, § 5, cl. 1. For historical context, see Magliocca, *supra* note 4, at 109 n.114.

certain prospective or sitting Members could not take or retain their seats due to Section 3."[82]

There were at least six such challenges, one in the Senate and five in the House. Zebulon B. Vance, a former U.S. Representative who had been a colonel in the Confederate Army and wartime governor of North Carolina, was barred from taking the senatorial seat to which he had been elected.[83] Two Representatives-elect were disqualified. John H. Christy of Georgia admitted to giving "aid, countenance, counsel, and encouragement to persons engaged in armed hostility" against the Union.[84] Interestingly, as the per curiam opinion pointed out in a footnote, the Governor had refused to commission Christy on Section Three grounds, which is the only known example of a state authority attempting to enforce Section Three against a federal officeholder. Christy nonetheless presented his credentials to the House in Washington, and the House made the final decision as to his eligibility. Christy's replacement, John A. Wimpy, was also disqualified. Wimpy had taken up arms as a soldier in the Confederate Army and thus was an easy case.[85] Two elected House members were seated despite claims that they had supported the insurrection. A Virginian, Lewis McKenzie, was permitted to take his seat in the House despite voting in favor of secession as a pre-war member of Virginia's House of Delegates and voting to appropriate funds to ready the State for armed hostilities with the Union.[86] The distinction appears to be that he did not take up arms, and thus did not "engage in" the rebellion. Similarly, John M. Rice of Kentucky was permitted to take his seat, despite having voted for secession as a member of his state legislature. Rice also had been a recruiter for the Confederate Army but not

---

[82] Trump v. Anderson, 144 S. Ct. 662, 669–70 (2024) (per curiam).

[83] 1 Asher Hinds, Precedents of the House of Representatives 478–86, §§ 459-463 (1907); *see also* Magliocca, *supra* note 4, at 108–11. According to the report in *The Globe*, the debate focused on whether the Senate could seat Zebulon B. Vance's runner-up or if the state legislature needed to re-vote. *See* Cong. Globe, 42d Cong., 2d Sess. 2387–90, 2431–34, 2676 (1872); *see id.* app. at 219–29, 234–67, 272, 79, 328–34; *see also* S. Rep. No. 42-58, at 34 (1872). The Senate Historian has written a helpful summary of the Vance controversy. *See The Election Case of Joseph C. Abbott v. Zebulon B. Vance and Matt W. Ransom of North Carolina (1872)*, U.S. Senate, https://www.senate.gov/about/origins-foundations/electing-appointing-senators/contested-senate-elections/059Abbott_Vance_Ransom.htm.

[84] 1 Hinds, *supra* note 83, at 470–72, § 459.

[85] *Id.*

[86] *Id.* at 440–41, § 446; *see also* Lynch, *supra* note 4, at 207–09 (explaining the House's report on Lewis McKenzie's pre-war conduct in more detail).

himself a participant.[87] While some House members thought these actions were disloyal and qualified as aid and comfort to the enemy, the full House voted to seat him.[88] Perhaps more strangely, the House voted to seat former Confederate Officer Alfred Waddell. Waddell had been the master of chancery in North Carolina before the war, an office which required him to take an oath to support the Constitution. Waddell's supporters argued that the state office was not "judicial in character," because it was a "clerical appointment," and thus that he had not taken an oath covered by Section Three. The House apparently accepted this argument.[89]

In conclusion: The Court's unanimous holding that states may enforce Section Three against their own officeholders but only federal authorities can enforce it against federal officeholders is not supported by "the Nation's federalism principles," but it is supported by the best reading of both the "nationalist spirit of the Fourteenth Amendment" and the historical practice.[90] The per curiam's further hint, short of an explicit holding, that federal enforcement must come in the form of congressional legislation pursuant to Section Five, lacks historical support. But as noted at the beginning of this Article, the *Trump v. Anderson* opinion appears not to be based on a textualist or originalist interpretive method, but on the pragmatic judgment that allowing states to exclude a major party candidate for President based on a debatable interpretation of Section Three would be disruptive to our democratic order. If that pragmatic conclusion contradicted the best evidence of historical meaning and practice, it would be problematic, but it does not. The holding may not truly rest on text and history, but it is consistent with text and history—more consistent with text and history than the opposite conclusion would have been.

Some commentators have criticized the Court's decision on the ground that it nullifies Section Three and insulates Mr. Trump from enforcement.[91] Even the three concurring Justices state that the

---

[87] 1 Hinds, *supra* note 83, at 472–73, § 460.

[88] Cong. Globe, 41st Cong., 2d Sess. 5442–47 (1870); H.R. Rep. No. 41-107 (1870).

[89] *See* 1 Hinds, *supra* note 83, at 441, § 447; Cong. Globe, 42d Cong., 1st Sess. 6–7 (1871).

[90] I borrow the term "nationalist spirit of the Fourteenth Amendment" from Gerard Magliocca. *See* Magliocca, *supra* note 4, at 95. The per curiam refers to the "the Fourteenth Amendment's rebalancing of federal and state power," *Trump v. Anderson*, 144 S. Ct. 662, 668 (2024) (per curiam), which is a less pointed way of saying the same thing.

[91] *See, e.g.*, J. Michael Luttig & Laurence H. Tribe, *Supreme Betrayal: A Requiem for Section 3 of the Fourteenth Amendment*, Atlantic (Mar. 14, 2024), https://www.theatlantic.com/ideas

decision"foreclose[s] future efforts to disqualify a Presidential candidate under that provision."[92] This is not entirely accurate. The Court explicitly noted that there is a provision of law that "remains on the books today," which authorizes prosecution for insurrection and bars convicted individuals from future office. This is Section 2383. As the per curiam opinion observes, Congress's enactment of Section 2383 "effectively provided an additional procedure for enforcing disqualification."[93] The House January 6 Commission officially recommended that the Department of Justice prosecute Mr. Trump under this provision,[94] but the Department did not do so, even though it brought a raft of other criminal charges against the former President. It is not known why the Department chose not to employ Section 2383 against Mr. Trump. In any event, the Court did not make Section Three unenforceable. The Biden Administration chose not to use the enforcement tool that was at hand.

VI. Post-Election Enforcement, and Whether Section Three Applies to the Presidency

The unanimous holding in *Trump v. Anderson* thus put an end to efforts to prevent former President Trump from running for President. States have no authority to enforce Section Three against presidential officeholders or candidates, and the Biden Administration chose not to bring a prosecution under the successor statute to the Confiscation Act: Section 2383. That exhausts the alternatives at the election phase. But there remain two possible ways, however unlikely as a practical political matter, that a President-elect's eligibility for office might be tested *after* the election—on the heuristic assumptions that he violated Section Three and that Section Three applies to former and future Presidents. First, it is possible that when Congress meets on January 6 to count electoral votes, it could exercise power under the Twelfth Amendment and the Electoral Count Act (as amended in 2023), to refuse to count electoral votes for a nominee in

/archive/2024/03/supreme-court-trump-v-anderson-fourteenth-amendment/677755; Mark Joseph Stern, *The Supreme Court's "Unanimous" Trump Ballot Ruling Is Actually a 5–4 Disaster*, Slate (Mar. 4, 2024, 11:56 AM), https://slate.com/news-and-politics/2024/03/supreme-court-trump-colorado-ballot-disaster.html.

92 *Anderson*, 144 S. Ct. at 674 (Sotomayor, Kagan & Jackson, JJ., concurring in the judgment).

93 *Id.* at 670 (per curiam).

94 H.R. Rep. No. 117-663, at 690 (2022).

violation of Section Three. Second, it is at least theoretically possible that a person with standing to sue could challenge the legality of an action of an executive officer appointed by a putative President with no right to hold office under Section Three. The concurring Justices Sotomayor, Kagan, and Jackson interpreted the per curiam opinion as foreclosing these avenues for enforcement of Section Three. This is what fueled the anger in their separate opinion.

There is no doubt that the Justices in the majority heartily disapprove of these two possibilities. Toward the end of the per curiam opinion, after bemoaning the prospect of "the 'patchwork' that would likely result from state enforcement" of Section Three, the Court commented that "the disruption would be all the more acute—and could nullify the votes of millions and change the election result—if Section 3 enforcement were attempted after the Nation has voted. Nothing in the Constitution requires that we endure such chaos. . . ."[95] That seems to say that once an election is over, Section Three should not be used to nullify the result.

This comment should not be taken to be part of the holding of the case. First, the statement is *obiter dictum.* The hypothetical possibility of post-election challenges was irrelevant to the case that was before the Justices, which involved disqualification from the ballot in Colorado. More importantly, it is evident from the text of Section Three that post-election enforcement *is* permissible. As discussed above, Section Three disqualifies those who violate the provision from *holding* office, not from running for office, and the Enforcement Act of 1870 provided for *quo warranto* proceedings to expel a violator from office.[96] The plain language of these provisions demonstrates beyond doubt that the Framers and enforcers of Section Three expected that it would be enforced *after* a would-be officeholder was elected or appointed. Moreover, several participants in the rebellion who were elected to Congress in 1870 were disqualified by the House and Senate after they presented their credentials in Washington.[97] If elected officeholders are unseated, it follows that the results of elections are nullified. However disruptive or chaotic the modern Court may think it is to nullify the results of an election, this was the original plan for enforcing Section Three.

---

[95] *Anderson*, 144 S. Ct. at 671.

[96] *See supra* notes 76–82 and accompanying text.

[97] *See supra* notes 82–89 and accompanying text.

But it remains to be seen what methods of post-election enforcement may be available under current law, since the Enforcement Act was repealed in relevant part. There are two possibilities: enforcement by Congress during the counting of electoral votes, and challenges to the legality of the actions taken by executive branch officials who are either insurrectionists themselves or were appointed by an insurrectionist President.

Note, however, that the availability of both of these alternatives depends on a prior interpretive point: that Section Three applies to former and future Presidents. That is not as obvious as it may seem. There are oddities in the language of Section Three that cast doubt on whether it applies to the presidency. Both the trial court and dissenting Justice Samour in the Colorado Supreme Court relied on these linguistic peculiarities in rejecting the case for disqualifying President Trump, and they were joined by amici in the Supreme Court including three former attorneys general,[98] and supported by research published by several scholars with expertise in these matters.[99] Their argument is as follows: Section Three bars violators from holding "any office, civil or military, *under* the United States. . . ."[100] They present evidence that the language "under the United States" is a term of art that, in the original Constitution, meant only appointed offices, which would suggest that the Framers of Section Three might not have understood that phrase to apply to future Presidents. Section Three uses different terminology in reference to the violator's past office, when he or she took the oath. There, it says "officer *of* the United States," which is used elsewhere in the Constitution in contexts that exclude the presidency.[101] For example, the Commission Clause provides that "[t]he

---

[98] Brief of Edwin Meese, et al. as Amici Curiae Supporting Petitioner at 6–18, *Anderson*, 144 S. Ct. 662 (No. 23-719).

[99] *See, e.g.*, Seth Barrett Tillman & Josh Blackman, *Offices and Officers of the Constitution, Part IV: The "Office . . . under the United States" Drafting Convention*, 62 S. Tex. L. Rev. 455, 459 (2023); Kurt Lash, *The Meaning and Ambiguity of Section Three of the Fourteenth Amendment*, 47 Harv. J.L. & Pub. Pol'y 309 (2024). Professors Tillman and Blackman leave open the possibility that, due to linguistic drift, the term "office under the United States" might not necessarily have the same meaning in Section Three as it did in the original Constitution. *See* Josh Blackman & Seth Barrett Tillman, *Sweeping and Forcing the President into Section 3*, 28 Tex. Rev. L. & Pol. 350, 563 (2024) [hereinafter Blackman & Tillman, *Sweeping and Forcing*].

[100] *See* U.S. Const. amend. XIV, § 3 (emphasis added).

[101] *See* Seth Barrett Tillman & Josh Blackman, *Is the President an "Officer of the United States" for Purposes of Section 3 of the Fourteenth Amendment*, 15 N.Y.U. J.L. & Liberty 1, 21–24, 31–34 (2021).

President . . . shall Commission all the Officers of the United States."[102] The President does not commission himself. Similarly, the Appointments Clause provides that the President shall appoint "all . . . Officers of the United States."[103] He does not appoint himself; the electors do that. This suggests that the term "Officers of the United States" might apply only to appointed positions, not to elected ones, and not to the presidency or vice presidency. Finally, the Section applies to persons who took an oath "to support the Constitution of the United States."[104] This language echoes the oath prescribed in Article VI, Section Three,[105] but Article II, Section One, Clause Eight prescribes a different oath for the President: He swears to "protect and defend the Constitution of the United States."[106]

These theories were widely disparaged in academic circles. Detractors rested primarily on the point that constitutional language, which is written by and for the People, should not be read in a hypertechnical fashion counter to its ordinary meaning, and that it makes little sense, in light of the purpose of Section Three, not to regard the presidency as an office "of" and "under" the United States.[107] There was little direct discussion during the time of framing and enforcement of whether Section Three covers past and future Presidents, since the issue had no practical payoff at the time. The only former President who supported the Confederacy, John Tyler, died in 1862, and it was politically inconceivable that a supporter of the rebellion could win a nationwide election. It was logically assumed that Section Three would have its practical effect in elections in Southern states, where the possibility that a participant in the rebellion could prevail in an election was anything but unlikely. Nonetheless, in the one reported discussion of the question in Congress, Senators Lot Morrill

---

[102] U.S. Const. art. II, § 3.

[103] *Id.* art. II, § 2, cl. 2.

[104] *Id.* amend. XIV, § 3.

[105] *Id.* art. VI, § 3.

[106] *Id.* art. II, § 1, cl. 8.

[107] *See, e.g.*, Baude & Paulsen, *supra* note 6, at 722–23, 725–27; James A. Heilpern & Michael T. Worley, *Evidence that the President is an "Officer of the United States" for Purposes of Section 3 of the Fourteenth Amendment*, 98 S. Cal. L. Rev. 65, 80–85 (2024); Mark A. Graber, *Of Course Presidents Are Officers of the United States*, Atlantic (Feb. 15, 2024), https://www.theatlantic.com/ideas/archive/2024/02/presidents-officers-supreme-court-case-trump-disqualification/677449; Brief of Akhil Reed Amar and Vikram David Amar as Amicus Curiae in Support of Neither Party, *supra* note 7, at 17.

and Reverdy Johnson agreed Section Three would bar a violator from becoming President.[108]

Although the issue was briefed to the Supreme Court, the Court made no reference to it. One hopes that it does not arise in the future. If it does, the Supreme Court is likely to adopt a non-technical definition, which includes the presidency. The remainder of this Article will assume that both past and future Presidents are covered.

VII. Congressional Enforcement in the Process of Counting Electoral Votes

The Twelfth Amendment, which in these respects exactly repeats the parallel provisions of Article II, Section One, requires electors to cast their votes and to send certificates attesting to those results to the seat of government. On the designated day (January 6 of the year following the election), the President of the Senate, who is the outgoing Vice President of the United States, is required to "open" these results in the presence of the newly elected Senate and House of Representatives, who will have taken office a few days earlier. The Amendment states "the votes shall then be counted."[109] This unhelpful use of the passive voice gave rise to a theory among Trump supporters in 2021 that the Vice President had authority to "count" the votes and hence to determine which putative results were valid. That is not what the Amendment says. The Vice President is instructed to "open" the certificates, but the shift to the passive voice suggests that he or she is not the one to "count" the votes. By default, counting (meaning resolution of which votes are legitimate) must be done by Congress. But the question remains what powers Congress has in connection with the count and which procedures to follow. The Constitution is frustratingly silent or ambiguous on these points.

The contested Hayes-Tilden election of 1876 brought these issues to the fore, leading Congress to enact the Electoral Count Act of 1887. That Act resolved some issues but not all. Ambiguities in the Electoral Count Act led to the confusion over the Trump-Biden election in 2020 and inspired the violence on January 6, 2021, when supporters of Mr. Trump invaded the Capitol, attempted to pressure members of Congress to recognize Trump as the winner (or perhaps to delay long enough to allow Republican legislatures to reverse the

---

108 Cong. Globe, 39th Cong., 1st Sess. 2899 (1866).

109 U.S. Const. amend. XII.

results in their states), threatened violence against Vice President Pence and members of Congress, assaulted law enforcement officers, and succeeded in delaying the electoral vote count for more than five hours.[110] In 2022, Congress amended the Electoral Count Act to reduce, but probably not eliminate, the opportunities for similar mischief in the counting of electoral votes in future years, including clarifying that the Vice President's role in the count is only "ministerial."[111] The amended Act governed the counting of votes in 2025.

The question of interest after *Trump v. Anderson* is whether Congress has authority to refuse to count the electoral votes cast in favor of a candidate it thinks is in violation of Section Three. As already discussed, there is language in the per curiam opinion that disapproves attempts to enforce Section Three against an elected officeholder after the election has taken place, and other language strongly suggesting (but not explicitly holding) that enforcement of Section Three can only take place via legislation passed pursuant to Section Five of the Fourteenth Amendment. We have already seen why those two propositions are (1) dictum and (2) almost certainly mistaken. We now ask what Congress's power is to enforce Section Three in the course of its electoral vote-counting function under the Twelfth Amendment and the Electoral Count Act.[112]

As required by Article II, each state conducts the selection of presidential electors in the manner directed by its legislature. For more than a century, all states have selected electors by popular vote, but the details vary from state to state. Under the Electoral Count Act, the governor must issue a "certificate of ascertainment" declaring which candidates for elector won the popular vote, unless the governor's determination is overridden by a state or federal court.[113] Congress

[110] *See* Quinn et al., *supra* note 8.

[111] Electoral Count and Presidential Transition Improvement Act of 2022, Pub. L. No. 117-328, § 108, 136 Stat. 5233, 5238.

[112] Readers are urged to read Professor Muller's exploration of this topic in Muller, *supra* note 50; and Derek T. Muller, *Electoral Votes Regularly Given*, 55 Ga. L. Rev. 1529 (2021) [hereinafter Muller, *Electoral Votes*]. *See also* Ned Foley, *Can Congress Disqualify Trump After the Supreme Court's Section 3 Ruling*, Lawfare (Mar. 14, 2024, 12:42 PM), https://www.lawfaremedia.org/article/can-congress-disqualify-trump-after-the-supreme-court-s-section-3-ruling. Interestingly, Professors Baude and Paulsen, whose 2023 article sparked the campaign to disqualify Mr. Trump under Section Three, are skeptical of the power of Congress not to count electoral votes cast for an oath-breaking insurrectionist. *See* Baude & Paulsen, *supra* note 6, at 640–42.

[113] Electoral Count Act, 3 U.S.C. § 5(a)(1) (as amended 2022).

must treat this certificate as conclusive as to which slate of electors was chosen. Because this selection process is governed by state law, and under the unanimous holding of *Trump v. Anderson* states have no role in enforcing Section Three against presidential candidates, allegations of insurrectionism should play no part in this stage of the process (unless electors themselves are insurrectionists).

The next stage of the proceedings is set by the Electoral Count Act, as amended in 2022. After the electors vote and transmit their certificates of election to the seat of government, the Vice President opens the certificate from the state in question in the presence of both the Senate and the House, then hands it to functionaries called "tellers" who announce the result to the assembled solons. The Act explicitly provides that "[t]he President of the Senate shall have no power to solely determine, accept, reject, or otherwise adjudicate or resolve disputes over the proper certificate of ascertainment of appointment of electors, the validity of electors, or the votes of electors."[114] Vice President Pence's admirable refusal to go along with the Trump lawyers' plan to use his authority to nullify Biden's electoral victory is thus now written into statutory law. After the tellers read the electoral votes from the state in question, the Vice President calls for objections. If, but only if, there is a written objection in proper form, signed by one fifth of the Senators and one fifth of the Representatives, the two Houses will separate and debate the objection for a period of no more than two hours. The objection is rejected unless *both* Houses affirmatively sustain the objection as valid, by majority vote. On the perhaps overly cynical assumption that partisan loyalty will typically dominate these determinations, that means that the electoral votes of a state will not be rejected unless the political party opposed to the candidate receiving those votes won majorities in both the House and the Senate.

Significantly, the Act provides that the "only grounds for objections shall be as follows":

> (I). The electors of the State were not lawfully certified under a certificate of ascertainment of appointment of electors according to section 5(a)(1).
>
> (II). The vote of one or more electors has not been regularly given.[115]

[114] *Id.* § 15(b)(2).

[115] *Id.* § 15(d)(2)(B)(ii).

The term "regularly given" derives from the original Electoral Count Act of 1887. What does it mean? In particular, does the claim that the vote was in favor of a person not eligible for the presidency, on the basis of age, natural-born citizen status, term limits, death, or engaging in an insurrection after swearing an oath to defend the Constitution, fall within the category of a vote "not regularly given"? There is no authoritative definition of the term "regularly given," and the amendments to the Electoral Count Act in 2022 did not clarify the meaning.

The first attempt in Congress to object to an electoral vote came in 1969, to a vote by a Republican-pledged elector for third-party candidate George Wallace. In this century, there have been objections from Democrats in Congress to electoral votes for every victorious Republican candidate for President, and of course, the objections by Republican members to Biden votes in 2021. With one dubious exception, all of these objections were based on events that allegedly occurred in the course of the election or the counting of the votes, such as long lines at voting places, supposed defects in voting machines, Russian interference, and the like.[116] These objections might be thought to be evidence of congressional interpretation or practice, which would be entitled to at least some interpretive weight, but all of them were roundly rejected—which is evidence of congressional interpretation or practice the other way. In truth there has been a lot of confusion and partisanship.

Most scholarly analyses of the issue, written both before and after the 2020 election, conclude that the term "regularly given" refers to "post-appointment controversies, not pre-appointment ones."[117] Significantly, these writings include one published in 1888, contemporaneous with the passage of the Act in 1887:

> [T]he law authorizes the two Houses by concurrent resolution to reject the votes of the electors for President and Vice-President if they agree that these have not been regularly given; i.e., the two Houses cannot reject the return on account of fraud or defect in the election of the electors or in the

[116] Professor Muller discusses these objections in Muller, *Electoral Votes*, *supra* note 112, at 1541–44.

[117] Professor Muller provides a helpful review of the literature. *See id.* at 1535–37. In addition to Muller, see Beverly J. Ross & William Josephson, *The Electoral College and the Popular Vote*, 12 J.L. & Pol'y 665, 729 (1996); and Stephen A. Siegel, *The Conscientious Congressman's Guide to the Electoral Count Act of 1887*, 56 Fla. L. Rev. 541 (2004).

> determination of a controversy thereover, but may do so on account of irregular action on the part of the electors themselves in giving their votes for President and Vice-President.[118]

This interpretation is confirmed by the 2022 amendments to the Act, which as already noted permit objections only on two grounds. The first is that "[t]he electors of the State were not lawfully certified under a certificate of ascertainment of appointment of electors according to section 5(a)(1)."[119] This kind of objection is confined to whether there was a lawful certificate of ascertainment, not to reconsidering whether that certificate should have been issued. It is like checking for a driver's license; this does not entail re-examining whether the driver really knows how to parallel park. All legal and factual issues bearing on the election results should have been brought and resolved in state or federal court before the certificate of ascertainment was signed, and the Electoral Count Act states unambiguously that the certificate of ascertainment "shall be treated as conclusive in Congress with respect to the determination of electors appointed by the State."[120] Whether the votes of the electors so certified were "regularly given" thus deals with the actions of the electors, not with the choice of electors.

This definition excludes objections based on allegations of fraud and other maladministration of the election, but includes challenges based on an elector's vote for an ineligible candidate.[121] The latter is an objection to the elector's vote, not to who is the elector. If this definition is correct, the objections made by Republicans in 2021 (as well as those made by Democrats in 2002, 2005, and 2017) were improper under the Electoral Count Act, but an objection based on Section Three would be proper (whether or not meritorious).

But how is this definition to be enforced? Individual members of Congress have been known to take a different view. The presiding officer, the Vice President, has no authority to declare an objection out of order. If the objection has the proper number of signatories and is otherwise procedurally proper, it will trigger separate meetings of the House and Senate, and those bodies will decide whether the

[118] John W. Burgess, *The Law of the Electoral Count*, 3 Pol. Sci. Q. 633, 649 (1888).

[119] 3 U.S.C. § 15(d)(2)(B)(ii) (as amended 2022).

[120] *Id.* § 5(c)(1)(A).

[121] Muller, *Electoral Votes*, *supra* note 112, at 1537–38. Professor Muller's article identifies four other types of objection to votes not "regularly given," in addition to objections based on qualification of the candidate. *Id.* at 1538–40.

objection is proper and meritorious. Whether they pay any attention to scholarly analyses or statutory textual clues is anyone's guess.

If this analysis of the Electoral Count Act is correct, there does exist a procedure by which members of Congress could properly raise the question of a candidate's eligibility to hold the presidency under Section Three, just as they may raise and resolve challenges to the eligibility of persons elected to the House and Senate. To be sure, such a proceeding would run counter to the per curiam's admonition about the "disruption" that would result if "enforcement were attempted after the Nation has voted."[122] Moreover, it would require a majority vote of both the newly elected Senate and the newly elected House to disqualify—and it seems, in general, unlikely as a political matter that a candidate would win the presidential election while his party fails to gain control of either House. This has not happened in more than fifty years.[123] But if both Houses find in favor of an objection to the President-elect's qualifications based on Section Three, that will almost certainly be the final word, whatever the Justices may think. Given the uncertainties in theory and precedent about the political question doctrine,[124] it would be rash to make a strong prediction, but the authority to count the electoral votes and decide disputed questions about qualifications seems to be as constitutionally committed to a coordinate branch of government as impeachment or the qualifications or election results of members of the House or Senate.[125] In *Roudebush v. Hartke*,[126] the Court held that the Senate's determination about who won a Senate election was a political question untouchable by the courts. It is hard to see why a decision by both Houses about who was elected President would be regarded as any more justiciable. Thus, if both Houses of Congress vote that electoral votes cast for a candidate were not "regularly given," the Supreme Court is not likely to say otherwise—no matter how "acute" the "disruption" they think this would entail.

---

[122] *See* Trump v. Anderson, 144 S. Ct. 662, 671 (2024) (per curiam).

[123] Richard Nixon, a Republican, was elected in a three-way race in 1968, while the Democrats took both Houses of Congress. Even when he won in a landslide in 1972, the Democrats retained control of both Houses.

[124] For one example among many, see Louis Henkin, *Is There a "Political Question" Doctrine?*, 85 Yale L.J. 597, 600–01 (1976).

[125] Baker v. Carr, 369 U.S. 186, 217 (1962); United States v. Nixon, 418 U.S. 683, 702 (1974); Roudebush v. Hartke, 405 U.S. 15, 19 (1972).

[126] *Roudebush*, 405 U.S. at 19.

Even this may not put an end to a candidate's prospects for election. Votes not counted on the ground that they were not "regularly given" are still electoral votes, and they must be included in the denominator in deciding whether a candidate got a majority of the electoral votes.[127] Discarding electoral votes favoring the candidate who initially got a majority will not increase the number of votes for other candidates; a candidate who did not get a majority before the vote count will still have less than a majority after objections to votes for the alleged insurrectionist have been validated. The result, under Article II, Section One, Clause Three and the Twelfth Amendment, will be to throw the election into the House of Representatives, with the delegations from each state having one vote. Congress's conclusion that some votes were not "regularly given" does not bind the House, operating on a different voting rule. And if the vote in the House is close, and some states split evenly and therefore cannot cast a vote, then the Twelfth Amendment tells us that the Vice President will be acting President. On the hypothesis that the disqualified candidate for President won a majority of the electoral votes and that his or her running mate is not an oath-breaking insurrectionist, that Vice President will be from the same party. The other party might well conclude that the effort is not worth the candle.

VIII. Section Three Challenges to the Legality of Acts by Executive Officials Appointed by an Alleged Oath-Breaking Insurrectionist

There is one final speculative possibility of how Section Three could be enforced, on the assumption that the alleged oath-breaking insurrectionist is elected by a majority of the people in states commanding a majority of the electoral votes and the Congress counts those votes and declares the alleged oath-breaking insurrectionist President. The possibility is this: In a proceeding where the legal rights of a person with standing are at stake, that person could appeal the result on the ground that the relevant official is disqualified under Section Three or that the official's appointment is constitutionally invalid because the appointing President was constitutionally disqualified from office by Section Three. Justices Sotomayor, Kagan,

---

[127] Muller, *Electoral Votes*, *supra* note 112, at 1551.

and Jackson give the example of "when a party is prosecuted by an insurrectionist and raises a defense on that score."[128] In other contexts—usually separation of powers—parties to administrative proceedings have been permitted to challenge administrative action on the ground that their agency adversary was improperly appointed.[129]

After *Trump v. Anderson*, this form of enforcement is unlikely to succeed. Unlike the electoral-vote-counting scenario, an attempt to enforce Section Three by disqualifying an officer will necessarily take place within the courts, where the case will quickly go to the Supreme Court, which has already expressed its opposition. To be sure, those comments in the per curiam opinion were *obiter dictum*, but if a case involving an actual disqualification issue goes to the Court, there is little doubt how it would be resolved.

Moreover, such a case faces three obstacles not faced by an electoral count challenge. First, the nature of the case presupposes that the alleged oath-breaking insurrectionist won the election, that the results of that election were recognized by Congress in its proceedings under the Twelfth Amendment, and that he or she has been sworn into office. There will be a strong argument that the Section Three issue has already been decided by appropriate political authorities. Even if the legitimacy of the officeholder's appointment is not technically a "political question" outside the jurisdiction of the courts, there will be a powerful judicial impulse to defer to those prior political decisions.

Second, this mode of enforcement would be systemically disruptive. Plaintiffs with standing could challenge every act that insurrectionist Presidents or their appointees take. This would effectively stop the government in its tracks for whatever time it took to sort things out. Even if a few of these proceedings succeed, there is no reason to think that the putative Presidents or their appointees would resign as a result. The courts would have no authority to depose either the Presidents or their appointees, but at most to set aside the particular agency action. (Even then, under the de facto officer doctrine, the courts might well refuse to take that step.) It is much harder to undo the acts of an illegitimate President than it would be to keep him or her out of office in the first place.

---

[128] Trump v. Anderson, 144 S. Ct. 662, 674 (2024) (Sotomayor, Kagan & Jackson, JJ., concurring in the judgment).

[129] *See, e.g.*, Seila Law LLC v. Consumer Fin. Prot. Bureau, 591 U.S. 197 (2020); Free Enter. Fund v. Pub. Co. Acct. Oversight Bd., 561 U.S. 477 (2010).

Third, there is precedent. *Griffin's Case*,[130] decided by Chief Justice Chase in 1869, contemporaneously with passage of the Fourteenth Amendment, involved almost precisely the scenario that the concurring Justices imagined. A criminal defendant was convicted in a court proceeding where the presiding state judge had been an open Confederate supporter. One federal judge granted the convicted man habeas corpus relief on the ground that the judge was not eligible to preside, based on Section Three. That decision was reversed on appeal, largely on the pragmatic ground that, at least in the context of a collateral challenge to a criminal conviction, "it must be ascertained what particular individuals are embraced by the definition [of engaging in an insurrection], before any sentence of exclusion can be made to operate."[131] The court went on: "To accomplish this ascertainment and ensure effective results, proceedings, evidence, decisions, and enforcements of decisions, more or less formal, are indispensable; and these can only be provided for by congress."[132]

It would overread *Griffin's Case* to think that its logic applies to all possible means of enforcing Section Three. Other avenues of enforcement, including Article I, Section Five and the Twelfth Amendment, have their own inherent procedure, and thus require no additional implementing legislation. We must be cautious about extending *Griffin's Case* beyond its context of challenging exercises of "official authority and power" by an official who is already seated and has never been adjudicated as an insurrectionist.[133] As Chief Justice Chase discussed at length, that particular context poses practical problems, which he termed "inconveniences."[134] It would be most reasonable to read *Griffin's Case* narrowly, as applying only to those circumstances. But the possibility under consideration here, namely a challenge by a litigant to the legitimate appointment status of government official imposing a penalty, is virtually on all fours with *Griffin's Case*.[135]

---

[130] 11 F. Cas. 7 (C.C.D. Va. 1869) (No. 5,815).

[131] *Id.* at 26.

[132] *Id.*

[133] *Id.* at 23.

[134] *Id.* at 25, 26.

[135] The only difference of significance is that *Griffin's Case* arose on habeas corpus, while the proposed alternative would likely come up on direct appeal from an order granting or denying a motion to dismiss the proceeding for want of a constitutionally proper tribunal.

As a circuit court decision, *Griffin's Case* is not binding precedent, and the per curiam opinion in *Anderson* did not treat it as such. The opinion quotes the Chief Justice's opinion merely as a description of the problem, not as a holding on a point of law. But the opinion in *Griffin's Case* should not lightly be dismissed. It was written by Chief Justice Chase, a prominent abolitionist who presumably was deeply immersed in the legal questions around Reconstruction and politically allied with the leading players. Chase was in as good a position to know how the new Amendment was expected to work as anyone—certainly better than we are today. Even though some current commentators are critical of the opinion,[136] there is no evidence that it was regarded as surprising or misguided at the time.[137] Moreover, much of the criticism directed at the opinion is predicated on its supposed inconsistency with Chase's opinion in the matter of Jefferson Davis's prosecution for treason[138]—but if there was inconsistency, it is more likely that his view on the law of treason was wrong than that *Griffin's Case* was wrong.

In any event, while this last possible avenue for enforcement may not be completely dismissed, its prospects are dim. Courts tend to be pragmatic, and if executive decisions by every appointee of the new President are illegitimate, government would come to a halt. If an individual has been elected by a majority of the people of states constituting a majority of the Electoral College, recognized by Congress as President, and sworn into the office, and if his or her nominees have been confirmed by the Senate, it seems unlikely that the courts will intervene, in defiance of dictum in *Trump v. Anderson* and contrary to a nearly identical case decided by a distinguished Chief Justice immediately after Section Three was added to the Constitution.

Conclusion

Like Halley's Comet, but with a different timeline, Section Three of the Fourteenth Amendment riveted the nation for a few years after its enactment and disappeared with the enactment of "amnesty" legislation in 1872, only to reappear in 2023 with the publication of

[136] *E.g.*, Magliocca, *supra* note 4, at 105–08; Baude & Paulsen, *supra* note 6, at 647–59.

[137] Blackman & Tillman, *Sweeping and Forcing*, *supra* note 99, at 426–27; Lash, *supra* note 99, at 72–73 & n.274.

[138] Magliocca, *supra* note 4, at 107; Baude & Paulsen, *supra* note 6, at 654.

an academic article and disappear in 2024 with the Supreme Court's decision in *Trump v. Anderson*. The attempt to disqualify Mr. Trump from running for President in 2024 deeply divided the nation. Was Section Three the hoped-for silver bullet that would rid the nation's political life of this oath-breaking insurrectionist for all time? Or was it yet another legal maneuver to rob the People of their right to choose the leader of their choice? It depended on whom you asked. But the Supreme Court did not divide. Despite its reputation for partisan division, the nine Justices unanimously held that these efforts to use the Constitution to disqualify Mr. Trump were contrary to our federal system and unanimously reversed the state supreme court decision expelling Mr. Trump from the ballot. Unfortunately, however, this unanimity was spoiled by strong hints in the majority's per curiam opinion that Congress is limited in its enforcement of Section Three to statutes passed pursuant to Section Five of the Fourteenth Amendment, and that post-election enforcement is illegitimate. If they were true, this would cut off other avenues for enforcement, including Congress's power to count electoral votes under the Twelfth Amendment. These suggestions, which were unnecessary to decide the case and very likely wrong as a textual and historical matter, angered the three Democrat-appointed Justices, leading them to accuse the majority of trying to insulate "the petitioner" (Mr. Trump) from the constitutional consequences of his actions.

This Article concludes that there was a reasonable basis for the unanimous holding that states lack power to enforce Section Three in connection with the presidency (and probably other federal offices). The reason, however, is not that such power would create a "patchwork" that is inconsistent with "this Nation's federalism," but that it is inconsistent with the nationalist thrust of the Fourteenth Amendment and what we know about the pattern of enforcement at the time—namely, that both federal and state governments would enforce Section Three against state officeholders, but only instrumentalities of the federal government would enforce it against federal officeholders.

In any event, the decision seemed to be driven more by pragmatic considerations than by textual or historical interpretation. Simply put, the Court was unwilling to take the choice of President out of the hands of the voters. While functionalist considerations should not prevail in the face of contrary text and history, the Justices were not wrong to show restraint when text and history are supportive, even if not dispositive.

As the concurring Justices say, the Court should have stopped with its unanimous holding that states lack the power, absent congressional authorization, to enforce Section Three with respect to the presidency. That holding was all that was needed to decide the case. The majority's forays into limitations on congressional enforcement power had nothing to do with the Colorado litigation, and most of what they had to say is questionable on the merits. In particular, the notion that Section Three cannot be enforced at the federal level without Section Five legislation is refuted by the practice of disqualifying would-be members of Congress under Article I, Section Five. And the notion that Section Three can be enforced only before the election flies in the face of the plain text of the provision, which forbids an oath-breaking insurrectionist to "hold" office—something that takes place only after the election. It follows that the *Trump v. Anderson* opinion should not be interpreted as foreclosing the possibility that Congress could, by a vote of both Houses, decide not to recognize electoral votes in favor of a candidate on the ground that he or she is not eligible for the office.

The rushed and uncertain quality of the per curiam opinion could have disruptive consequences in the future. Who knows when another person who supported a violent protest that temporarily shut down the operations of government will be elected President and challenged as an oath-breaking insurrectionist? If Halley's Comet is a portent, we should watch the skies after an election in about seventy-five years. Then, if that happens, we will not only have to argue over what constitutes an insurrection and what it means to engage in it, but we will also dispute what was dictum and what was holding in *Trump v. Anderson*. It could be ugly.

KATHERINE SHAW

HIDDEN HARMS: ABORTION AND THE SHADOW DOCKET

Introduction

Perusing last year's end-of-Term Supreme Court coverage, it was easy to get the impression that reproductive rights had largely prevailed in the Term's two major abortion cases. "Supreme Court Maintains Broad Access to Abortion Pill," blared one *New York Times* headline.[1] "Supreme Court Allows, for Now, Emergency Abortions in Idaho," proclaimed another.[2]

Katherine Shaw is a Professor of Law at the University of Pennsylvania Carey Law School.

Author's note: My thanks to Emily Bleiberg and Joshua Maymir for invaluable research assistance, and to Julia Kaye, Alexa Kolbi-Molinas, Serena Mayeri, Melissa Murray, and Steve Vladeck for generous comments and feedback.

[1] Abbie VanSickle, *Supreme Court Maintains Broad Access to Abortion Pill*, N.Y. Times (June 13, 2024), https://www.nytimes.com/2024/06/13/us/politics/supreme-court-abortion-pill-mifepristone-ruling.html; *see also* Laura Kusisto & Jess Bravin, *Supreme Court Rejects Abortion Pill Challenge, Preserving Wide Access to Drug*, Wall St. J. (June 13, 2024, 5:57 PM ET), https://www.wsj.com/us-news/law/supreme-court-abortion-pill-mifepristone-f78f3320.

[2] Abbie VanSickle, *Supreme Court Allows, for Now, Emergency Abortions in Idaho*, N.Y. Times (June 27, 2024), https://www.nytimes.com/2024/06/27/us/politics/supreme-court-idaho-abortion.html; *see also* Laura Kusisto, *Supreme Court Allows Emergency Abortions in Idaho but Leaves Big Questions Unresolved*, Wall St. J. (June 27, 2024, 2:43 PM ET), https://www.wsj.com/us-news/law/supreme-court-allows-emergency-abortions-in-idaho-but-leaves-big-questions-unresolved-7fae6427.

The Supreme Court Review, 2025.
 Published by The University of Chicago Press. https://doi.org/10.1086/735446

It is true that in both of the Term's merits cases involving access to abortion, *FDA v. Alliance for Hippocratic Medicine*[3] and *Moyle v. United States*,[4] the Court ultimately declined to upend a status quo that permitted *some* access to abortion in a post-*Dobbs* world. In the first case, *Alliance for Hippocratic Medicine*, the Court concluded that a group of anti-abortion physicians and organizations lacked Article III standing to challenge the FDA's regulation of mifepristone,[5] a medication that is widely used today for the termination of early pregnancies.[6] The Court dismissed the second case, *Moyle v. United States*, as "improvidently granted," with a per curiam order putting back into effect a district court injunction that directed Idaho to comply with the basic requirements of a federal statute, the Emergency Medical Treatment and Labor Act (EMTALA). EMTALA instructs doctors to provide "stabilizing care" to individuals experiencing medical emergencies—care that may in rare cases include the provision of emergency abortions.[7] For now, such care is again available in Idaho. But to view the results in these cases as unalloyed "wins" for access to abortion is profoundly misguided.

Indeed, one very plausible read of both cases is that, having seen *Dobbs*'s impact on the 2022 midterm elections, the Court's Republican appointees resolved the issues as they did in order to turn down the temperature on abortion in an election year. (The 2022 midterm elections represented one of the best midterm elections for the party in control of the White House in the last century, with twenty-seven percent of voters citing abortion as one of their top issues.[8]) And this abortion gambit may have worked: By November 2024, months after the disposition of these two cases, many voters were apparently unconcerned about the impact of federal elections on the future of abortion access, casting their ballots for Donald Trump and JD Vance

---

[3] FDA v. All. for Hippocratic Med., 602 U.S. 367 (2024).

[4] Moyle v. United States, 603 U.S. 324 (2024) (per curiam).

[5] *See All. for Hippocratic Med.*, 602 U.S. at 372.

[6] Mifepristone, together with another medication, misoprostol, is by far the most common way to terminate a pregnancy today. *See* Rachel K. Jones & Amy Friedrich-Karnik, *Medication Abortion Accounted for 63% of All US Abortions in 2023—An Increase from 53% in 2020*, Guttmacher Inst. (Mar. 19, 2024), https://www.guttmacher.org/2024/03/medication-abortion-accounted-63-all-us-abortions-2023-increase-53-2020.

[7] *Moyle*, 603 U.S. at 325.

[8] Harry Enten, *How Joe Biden and the Democratic Party Defied Midterm History*, CNN (Nov. 13, 2022, 1:43 PM EST), https://www.cnn.com/2022/11/13/politics/democrats-biden-midterm-elections-senate-house/index.html.

even as they identified their support for abortion as a top issue.[9] In addition, voters in seven states enshrined into law broad protections for abortion.[10] Strikingly, in some states, the electorate voted both to protect abortion under state law, and to return Trump to the White House.[11] Missouri was especially notable on this score. There, an initiative constitutionalizing a right to terminate a pregnancy to the point of fetal viability succeeded with nearly fifty-two percent of the vote, while Trump won the state's electoral votes with 58.5% statewide.[12] Given these results, the Justices' decision to take off-ramps in both of the Term's abortion cases may well have succeeded in achieving highly strategic electoral goals.

Whether or not this read of the Court's motivations is accurate,[13] the cases are significantly more important than their non-merits dispositions might suggest. First, looking beyond the Court's final action in both cases to consider earlier stages of the litigation—as well as other related disputes—reveals a Court willing to resort to shadow docket machinations and manipulation to thwart access to abortion, putting women's health and even lives at severe risk along the way. This is true even if the Court ultimately swerved to avoid direct encounters in *Alliance* and *Moyle*. Indeed, those earlier moves were as important as the cases' final resolutions. But the intense focus on the cases' final dispositions has largely elided the Court's earlier actions. The full saga of

[9] Sarah Varney, *They Split the Ticket. Meet the Abortion Rights Voters Who Also Went for Trump*, NPR (Nov. 9, 2024, 6:05 AM ET), https://www.npr.org/sections/shots-health-news/2024/11/08/nx-s1-5184539/trump-election-abortion-votes-harris.

[10] *See 2023 and 2024 Abortion-Related Ballot Measures*, BallotPedia, https://ballotpedia.org/2023_and_2024_abortion-related_ballot_measures (showing the success of 2024 abortion rights ballot measures in Arizona, Colorado, Maryland, Missouri, Montana, New York, and Nevada as well as failures in Florida, Nebraska, and South Dakota).

[11] *See id.*

[12] *See* Daniel Arkin, *Missouri Voters Approve Ballot Measure to Expand Abortion Rights*, NBC (Nov. 6, 2024, 2:07 AM EST), https://www.nbcnews.com/politics/2024-election/missouri-abortion-ban-amendment-3-pass-rcna177395; *Missouri Election Results*, NPR (Dec. 12, 2024, 10:58 AM ET), https://apps.npr.org/2024-election-results/missouri.html. *See generally* Melissa Murray & Katherine Shaw, Dobbs *and Direct Democracy*, 112 Va. L. Rev. (forthcoming 2026) (on file with author).

[13] Justice Jackson's partial concurrence and partial dissent in the *Moyle* case came close to explicitly endorsing this reading. She criticized the Court's decision to dismiss the case as improvidently granted, maintaining that this procedural device should not be "turned into a tool for the Court to use to avoid issues that it does not wish to decide," later suggesting that the Court was deferring answering the questions raised by the case until "a comparatively more convenient point in time. . . ." *See* Moyle v. United States, 603 U.S. 324, 339, 344 (2024) (Jackson, J., concurring in part and dissenting in part); *see also* Zachary D. Clopton & Katherine Shaw, *Public Law Litigation and Electoral Time*, 2023 Wisc. L. Rev. 1513, 1519.

each case, combined with related earlier moves involving pandemic-era access to mifepristone, Texas's S.B. 8, and *Dobbs* itself, may provide a more complete—and accurate—projection of how the Court will intervene in future abortion-related matters. Specifically, a wider lens suggests that future abortion disputes are very likely to be resolved through the Court's "shadow docket," rendering them less visible to the public scrutiny the Court's ordinary decisional processes ensure.[14] In addition, the writings in each case—Justice Kavanaugh's opinion for the Court in *Alliance* and two of the concurrences (covering six Justices) in *Moyle*—signal the Court's increasing interest in sweeping new "conscience" protections that would allow doctors to refuse to provide even urgently needed emergency care. These separate writings also suggest that in future cases more amenable to merits disposition, the Court may well be receptive to the underlying anti-abortion claims—whether in the shadows or in the open.

Widening the aperture to encompass other, seemingly unrelated cases the Court decided during the same Term as *Alliance* and *Moyle* may also provide additional insight into the future of access to abortion. While both *Alliance* and *Moyle* were about abortion, they were also about agency power. This was perhaps more obvious in *Alliance*, in which the challenge to the FDA's regulation of mifepristone represented a frontal assault on the agency's authority. But in many ways, *Moyle*, which concerned the interaction of the federal EMTALA statute with state laws, was also about agency power—namely, the Department of Health and Human Services' ability to enforce EMTALA to require emergency abortion care despite conflicting state law. Critically, both cases arose during a Term that inaugurated profound changes to the scope and nature of agency authority. These changes may have significant implications for the legal regulation of abortion access—in the executive branch as well as the courts.

This Article begins with a discussion of the ways the Court has used timing, inaction, and question selection to undermine access to abortion while evading accountability for its decisions—beginning with the litigation surrounding Texas's S.B. 8 and continuing through the pre-history of *Dobbs*. It then considers *Alliance* and *Moyle*—not just the final opinions, but each case's history (and in the case of *Alliance*, its

---

[14] *See generally* Stephen Vladeck, The Shadow Docket: How the Supreme Court Uses Stealth Rulings to Amass Power and Undermine the Republic (2023); William Baude, *Foreword: The Supreme Court's Shadow Docket*, 9 N.Y.U. J.L. & Liberty 1 (2015).

pre-history). The final Part looks ahead to assess what may be coming in light of the Court's resolution of these two cases. It also locates *Alliance* and *Moyle* in the broader context of the important administrative law cases that the Court decided in the 2023 Term. Together, these cases give the Court a powerful set of tools it may use to further restrict access to abortion—aggressively second-guessing agency determinations where those determinations operate to protect access to abortion, while remaining hands-off where it is sympathetic to agency choices that restrict abortion.

I. Abortion on the Shadow Docket Before the 2023 Term

Most media coverage of the post-*Roe* abortion landscape in the United States focuses on the Court's June 2022 decision in *Dobbs v. Jackson Women's Health Organization*. However, the most recent era in post-*Roe* law and politics arguably began months before *Dobbs*—on September 1, 2021.[15] That was the day the Supreme Court allowed Texas's S.B. 8, a private bounty-hunter bill that used a novel scheme to outlaw abortion after six weeks of pregnancy, to go into effect.[16] As Justice Sotomayor memorably wrote, the law was "flagrantly unconstitutional"[17] under *Roe v. Wade*[18] and *Planned Parenthood v. Casey*,[19] then the law of the land.[20] But S.B. 8's design was different from that of other legislative efforts that sought to undermine access to abortion: Rather than having the ban enforced by the traditional state officials (e.g., district attorneys) who would then be obvious defendants in a legal challenge, S.B. 8 empowered private individuals to bring civil suits against anyone who "performs or induces an abortion," or "aids or abets the performance or inducement of an abortion,"[21] with successful

[15] It is actually possible to argue that it started still earlier than that—in October 2020, just after Justice Ginsburg died and before she was replaced by Justice Barrett. *See infra* notes 73–97 and accompanying text.

[16] Whole Woman's Health v. Jackson, 141 S. Ct. 2494, 2499 (2021) (Sotomayor, J., dissenting) ("The applicants requested emergency relief from this Court, but the Court said nothing. The Act took effect at midnight last night.").

[17] *Id.* at 2498.

[18] 410 U.S. 113 (1973).

[19] 505 U.S. 833 (1992).

[20] *See* David A. Strauss, *Rights, Remedies, and Texas's S.B. 8*, 2022 Sup. Ct. Rev. 81, 84.

[21] Tex. Health & Safety Code Ann. § 171.208(a) (West 2021).

plaintiffs eligible for "statutory damages in an amount of not less than $10,000 for each abortion," in addition to attorneys' fees.[22]

Soon after S.B. 8's passage, abortion providers sought a federal court injunction against the law, naming as defendants a number of state officials, including judges, clerks, and the state licensing board.[23] The district court found that the case could proceed, at least as to some of the named defendants,[24] but on August 29, 2021, two days before the law was scheduled to take effect, the Fifth Circuit "administratively" stayed the district court order without any explanation.[25]

Texas abortion providers turned to the Supreme Court to block enforcement of the law. But as midnight on September 1 came and went, the Court stayed silent, allowing the law to go into effect.[26] It was not until well into the evening of September 1 that the Court finally issued a short order denying the providers' requests to enjoin the law and to vacate the Fifth Circuit's stay;[27] by that time, Texas abortion providers had already paused many of their services.[28] Despite the dramatic effects on the ground in Texas, the country's second most populous state, the Court's unsigned order merely noted the "complex

[22] *Id.* § 171.208(b).

[23] *See* Whole Woman's Health v. Jackson, 556 F. Supp. 3d 595, 607–08 (W.D. Tex. 2021), *aff'd*, No. 21-50792, 2021 WL 3919252 (5th Cir. Aug. 29, 2021), *rev'd*, 141 S. Ct. 2494 (2021) (listing as defendants a state judge, a state judicial clerk, the Texas Attorney General, and officers of the Texas Medical Board, Texas Board of Nursing, Texas Pharmacy Board, and Texas Health and Human Services Commission).

[24] *See id.* at 622 ("Plaintiffs have alleged that the Judicial Defendants' interests are sufficiently adverse to their own so as to satisfy the case or controversy requirement under Article III.").

[25] *See Whole Woman's Health*, 2021 WL 3919252, at *1. The Fifth Circuit provided no explanation until ten days later, on September 10. *See* Whole Woman's Health v. Jackson, 13 F.4th 434 (5th Cir. 2021); *see also* Vladeck, *supra* note 14, at 234.

[26] *See Whole Woman's Health*, 141 S. Ct. at 2499 (Sotomayor, J., dissenting) ("The applicants requested emergency relief from this Court, but the Court said nothing. The Act took effect at midnight last night."); *see also* Elizabeth Dias & Lisa Lerer, The Fall of *Roe* 317–26 (2024).

[27] *Whole Woman's Health*, 141 S. Ct. at 2495 ("The application for injunctive relief, or, in the alternative, to vacate stays of the district court proceedings . . . is denied.").

[28] *See* Adam Liptak, J. David Goodman & Sabrina Tavernise, *Supreme Court, Breaking Silence, Won't Block Texas Abortion Law*, N.Y. Times (Nov. 1, 2021), https://www.nytimes.com/2021/09/01/us/supreme-court-texas-abortion.html [https://perma.cc/22Y2-LQFL] ("[M]any [abortion clinics], in interviews, said they were [complying with S.B. 8]."); *see also* Eva Dinginger, Kate Coleman-Minahan, Jeanelle Sheeder & Nancy Z. Fang, *The Impact of the SB 8 Texas Abortion Ban on Pregnancy Duration at Time of Abortion in a Large Volume Colorado Clinic*, 143 Contraception 1, 1 (2024) ("In the month after SB 8 passed, the number of abortions performed in Texas decreased by 50%. . . .").

and novel antecedent procedural questions"[29] involved in the case, including whether "the named defendants in this lawsuit can or will seek to enforce the Texas law against the applicants. . . ."[30] In four separate writings, the dissenters virtually shouted their objections to the Court's order. In uncharacteristically sharp language, Chief Justice Roberts called S.B. 8 "unprecedented" and described it as designed "to insulate the State from responsibility for implementing and enforcing the regulatory regime."[31] Justice Sotomayor was even more blunt, describing S.B. 8 as "a breathtaking act of defiance—of the Constitution, of this Court's precedents, and of the rights of women seeking abortions throughout Texas."[32] She condemned the Court as "content to ignore its constitutional obligations to protect not only the rights of women, but also the sanctity of its precedents and of the rule of law."[33]

Although the Court may have hoped that its acquiescence in Texas's nullification of *Roe* would go unnoticed,[34] the criticism was swift and widespread.[35] Perhaps in response to the public outcry over its resolution of such a massive issue in so cursory a fashion and in the shadows, in late October the Court granted certiorari and set the case

---

[29] *Whole Woman's Health*, 141 S. Ct. at 2495.

[30] *Id.*

[31] *Id.* at 2496 (Roberts, C.J., dissenting).

[32] *Id.* at 2499 (Sotomayor, J., dissenting).

[33] *Id.* For a discussion of the on-the-ground impacts of S.B. 8 in Texas, see Shefali Luthra, Undue Burden: Life and Death Decisions in Post-*Roe* America (2024).

[34] *See* Jon D. Michaels & David L. Noll, *Vigilante Federalism*, 108 Cornell L. Rev. 1187, 1220 (2023) (describing the Court as "gutting *Roe* through a conclusory order entered on the so-called shadow docket").

[35] *See* Adam Serwer, *Five Justices Did This Because They Could*, Atlantic (Sept. 2, 2021), https://www.theatlantic.com/ideas/archive/2021/09/supreme-court-guts-roe-shadow-docket/619957 [https://perma.cc/5VYC-6AQX] ("The conservative majority on the Supreme Court was so eager to nullify *Roe v. Wade* . . . that it didn't even wait for oral arguments."); Charlie Savage, *Texas Abortion Case Highlights Concern over Supreme Court's Shadow Docket*, N.Y. Times (Sept. 4, 2021), https://www.nytimes.com/2021/09/02/us/politics/supreme-court-shadow-docket-texas-abortion.html ("[T]he [Supreme] [C]ourt is taking up weighty matters in a rushed way. . . ."). Politicians also criticized the hurried decision. *See* Press Release, Hank Johnson, Rep., House of Reps., Congressman Johnson Statement on SCOTUS Shadow Docket Ruling on Texas Law SB8 (Sept. 3, 2021), https://hankjohnson.house.gov/media-center/press-releases/congressman-johnson-statement-scotus-shadow-docket-ruling-texas-law-sb8 ("[T]his decision issued in the dead of night on the Supreme Court's 'shadow docket'. . . . The resulting one-paragraph, unsigned opinion is not appropriate for a wholesale change in . . . constitutional rights. . . ."); Press Release, Gregory W. Meeks, Rep., House of Reps., Meeks' Statement on Supreme Court Ruling on Texas Law S.B. 8 (Sept. 2, 2021), https://meeks.house.gov/media/press-releases/meeks-statement-supreme-court-ruling-texas-law-sb-8 ("By allowing the law to go into effect without a full briefing, oral arguments or providing a full, signed opinion is insulting to the rule of law.").

for highly expedited briefing and oral argument.[36] On November 1, 2021, it heard argument, and in early December, a 5-4 Court concluded that, for the most part, the provider plaintiffs could not proceed against the defendants they had named.[37] The Court purported to leave the door open to the possibility of the plaintiffs proceeding against the Texas medical licensing board.[38] But the Texas Supreme Court quickly slammed that door shut, clarifying that the licensing board had no role in enforcing S.B. 8.[39] On the same day that the U.S. Supreme Court ruled against the providers, the Court dismissed as improvidently granted a companion case brought by the federal government.[40] Despite the distinct jurisdictional issues raised by the federal government's case, the Supreme Court declined to address, let alone resolve, them.[41]

Shadow docket machinations also characterized the early history of *Dobbs*. The Court granted certiorari in that case in May 2021, which meant that *Dobbs* loomed over all of the Court's actions in the S.B. 8 cases.[42] In the end, of course, *Dobbs* formally overruled *Roe* and *Casey*,[43] allowing states to ban abortion outright rather than (or in addition to) facilitating vigilante action to prevent abortion through mechanisms like S.B. 8.[44] But before it issued its final merits decision in *Dobbs*, the Court's moves on the shadow docket significantly impacted both the trajectory of the case and national debates about access to abortion and about the Court itself.

At issue in *Dobbs* was the constitutionality of H.B. 1510, Mississippi's fifteen-week abortion ban. When the State enacted the ban in

---

[36] Whole Woman's Health v. Jackson, 142 S. Ct. 415 (2021) (mem.).

[37] Whole Woman's Health v. Jackson, 595 U.S. 30, 35 (2021) ("[S]uch an action is permissible against some of the named defendants but not others.").

[38] *See id.* at 51 ("[T]his case may proceed past the motion to dismiss stage against . . . defendants with specific disciplinary authority over medical licenses. . . .").

[39] Whole Woman's Health v. Jackson, 642 S.W.3d 569, 583 (Tex. 2022) ("Texas law does not grant the state-agency executives named as defendants . . . any authority to enforce the Act's [S.B. 8's] requirements. . . .").

[40] United States v. Texas, 595 U.S. 74, 75 (2021) (mem.).

[41] *Cf.* James E. Pfander, *Judicial Review of Unconventional Enforcement Regimes*, 102 Tex. L. Rev. 769, 803 (2024).

[42] Dobbs v. Jackson Women's Health Org., 141 S. Ct. 2619 (2021) (mem.).

[43] Dobbs v. Jackson Women's Health Org., 597 U.S. 215, 231 (2022) ("We hold that *Roe* and *Casey* must be overruled.").

[44] *See generally* Jon Michaels & David Noll, Vigilante Nation: How State-Sponsored Terror Threatens Our Democracy (2024).

2018, it was clear that the law was fatally inconsistent with *Roe* and *Casey*.[45] *Roe* concluded, and *Casey* reaffirmed, that the Constitution protected the right to terminate a pregnancy; whatever open questions surrounded the nature and scope of that right or state regulatory latitude, it was clear that those cases did not permit states to ban abortion prior to fetal viability. The Mississippi law, at the time the most restrictive in the nation, banned most abortions just fifteen weeks after a person's last menstrual period, far earlier than the point of viability, usually measured around twenty-three weeks.[46]

The lone abortion clinic operating in Mississippi quickly challenged the new law, and a district court permanently enjoined the law as a "facially unconstitutional ban on abortions prior to viability."[47] Even the Fifth Circuit was compelled to agree, noting that "the Supreme Court's abortion cases have established (and affirmed, and re-affirmed) a woman's right to choose an abortion before viability."[48] The court noted that while the State was entitled to regulate pre-viability abortions, it could not do so in ways that imposed an "undue burden" and it could not impose outright bans on pre-viability abortions.[49] In a separate concurrence, Judge James Ho agreed that "Supreme Court precedent require[s] affirmance," but registered his view that "[a] State has an unquestionably legitimate (if not compelling) interest in preventing gratuitous pain to the unborn."[50] He also detailed what he described as the "racial history of abortion advocacy as a tool of the eugenics movement."[51]

---

[45] Jessica Ravitz, *Mississippi Bans Abortions at 15 Weeks, Earliest in the Nation*, CNN (Mar. 19, 2018, 7:02 PM EDT), https://www.cnn.com/2018/03/19/health/mississippi-abortion-ban-15-weeks/index.html.

[46] *Id.*

[47] Jackson Women's Health Org. v. Currier, 349 F. Supp. 3d 536, 545 (S.D. Miss. 2018), *aff'd sub nom.* Jackson Women's Health Org. v. Dobbs, 945 F.3d 265 (5th Cir. 2019), *rev'd*, 597 U.S. 215 (2022). Judge Carlton Reeves in the district court was blunt in describing the State's likely motives in enacting the law: "The state chose to pass a law it knew was unconstitutional to endorse a decades-long campaign, fueled by national interest groups, to ask the Supreme Court to overturn *Roe v. Wade*." *Id.* at 542.

[48] *Dobbs*, 945 F.3d at 269.

[49] *Id.*

[50] *Id.* at 278 (Ho, J., concurring).

[51] *Id.* at 280; *see also* Melissa Murray, *Race-ing* Roe: *Reproductive Justice, Racial Justice, and the Battle for* Roe v. Wade, 134 HARV. L. REV. 2025 (2021) (documenting the speciousness of this argument).

When Mississippi first sought Supreme Court review of the Fifth Circuit's decision, it disclaimed any interest in directly confronting the Court's extant abortion precedents. The petition maintained that "the questions presented in this petition do not require the Court to overturn *Roe* or *Casey*."[52] Instead, the State argued that the Court could simply jettison *Casey*'s prohibition on all pre-viability abortions without overruling *Roe* and *Casey*.[53]

The State's petition was filed in June 2020.[54] It remained pending over the summer of 2020, when (as we now know) Justice Ruth Bader Ginsburg's health deteriorated until her death on September 18—less than two weeks before the Court was scheduled to discuss the *Dobbs* petition for the first time.[55] Justice Ginsburg was replaced by Justice Amy Coney Barrett less than a month later, during the waning days of the first Trump Administration. During Justice Barrett's initial months on the Court, in the fall of 2020, the newly constituted Court rescheduled the *Dobbs* petition for conference nine times.[56] When the case was finally discussed during the Court's January 8 conference, reporting by the *New York Times*' Jodi Kantor and Adam Liptak suggests that there were five votes to grant certiorari—Justices Thomas, Alito, Gorsuch, Kavanaugh, and the Court's newest member, Justice Barrett.[57] But although that number exceeded the four votes required to grant review, the Court did not immediately announce that it would hear the case.[58] Instead, according to Kantor and Liptak's reporting, Justice Kavanaugh succeeded in convincing his colleagues to "withhold the public announcement of its decision to take the case," and instead to wait to "announce the decision to move forward in the

[52] Petition for a Writ of Certiorari at 5, *Dobbs*, 597 U.S. 215 (No. 19-1392), 2020 WL 3317135.

[53] *See id.* ("[Mississippi] merely asks the Court to reconcile a conflict in its own precedents.").

[54] *See generally id.*

[55] *See No. 19-1392*, SupremeCourt.gov, https://www.supremecourt.gov/docket/docketfiles/html/public/19-1392.html (showing the first conference for the case was originally scheduled for September 29, 2020).

[56] *See id.* (showing the conference was rescheduled nine times).

[57] Jodi Kantor & Adam Liptak, *Behind the Scenes at the Dismantling of* Roe v. Wade, N.Y. Times (Dec. 15, 2023), https://www.nytimes.com/2023/12/15/us/supreme-court-dobbs-roe-abortion.html ("The five other conservatives voted in favor. . . .").

[58] *See No. 19-1392*, *supra* note 55 (showing the case was no longer rescheduled for conferences after the January 8, 2021 conference but continued to be relisted for subsequent conferences until May 17, 2021); Kantor & Liptak, *supra* note 57.

spring," deferring argument and decision in the case until the next Term.[59]

Perhaps based on Justice Kavanaugh's intervention, the petition was relisted for every conference from January 8 until May 17—nearly a year after the petition was filed—when the Court finally announced that it had granted the petition and would hear the case in the 2021 Term.[60] This had the effect of putting significantly more distance between Justice Ginsburg's death and replacement with Justice Barrett, and *Roe*'s overruling. And when, after this months-long delay, the Court finally announced that it would hear the case, it granted only one of the three questions presented in Mississippi's petition—the only one that required direct reconsideration of *Roe* and *Casey*.[61] Interestingly, however, the question did not *name* either of those precedents—perhaps contributing to limited public awareness that the cases were in the Court's crosshairs. Taken together, it certainly appears that the extraordinary delay in announcing the grant of certiorari, together with the decision to decline to take up the more limited questions presented, were designed to ease the Court's path to overruling *Roe* and *Casey* while simultaneously blunting public criticism.

When Mississippi filed its merits brief in July, its strategy had changed completely from the cert petition. Rather than argue that its ban could be maintained under *Roe* and *Casey*, the brief now called for their overruling, describing them as "egregiously wrong," "hopelessly unworkable" and "unprincipled decisions that have damaged the democratic process, poisoned our national discourse, plagued the law—and in doing so, harmed this Court."[62]

---

[59] Kantor & Liptak, *supra* note 57.

[60] *See No. 19-1392*, *supra* note 55 (showing the case was relisted twelve times between the January 8, 2021 and May 17, 2021 conferences). According to John Elwood, who tracks the Court's docketing practices closely, *Dobbs* was the second-most-relisted case the Court had ever agreed to hear. *See* John Elwood, *No New Relists, but You Should Read Anyway*, SCOTUSBLOG (May 19, 2021, 3:47 PM), https://www.scotusblog.com/2021/05/no-new-relists-but-you-should-read-anyway (describing *Dobbs* as "second only to *Masterpiece Cakeshop* . . . as the most-relisted case to be granted review").

[61] *See No. 19-1392*, *supra* note 55 ("Petition GRANTED limited to Question 1 presented by the petition."); *see also* Benjamin B. Johnson, *The Active Vices*, 74 ALA. L. REV. 917, 921 (2023) ("In *Dobbs*, the Court set aside questions that would allow the Justices to avoid reconsidering its entire abortion case law and limited review to a direct reconsideration of *Roe* and *Casey*.").

[62] Brief for Petitioners at 1–2, 4, Dobbs v. Jackson Women's Health Org., 597 U.S. 215 (2022) (No. 19-1392), 2021 WL 3145936; *see also* DIAS & LERER, *supra* note 26, at 311–13 (discussing brief).

The Court's decision in *Dobbs*, leaked in May 2022[63] and issued in virtually identical form the next month, reflected much of the brief's reasoning and rhetoric. The Court insisted that *Roe* represented an "abuse of judicial authority" and was "egregiously wrong from the start"; it also decried its "damaging consequences."[64] According to the Court, under a proper understanding of the Constitution, "guided by the history and tradition that map the essential components of our Nation's concept of ordered liberty," no right to abortion flowed from the Fourteenth Amendment.[65]

So it appears that in the S.B. 8 litigation and *Dobbs* the Court initially utilized inaction, delay, and a series of technical and unexplained orders, in part to modulate—and manipulate—the reactions of a public that, according to polls, largely agreed that *Roe* was rightly decided.[66]

When it finally considered and decided *Dobbs* on the merits, the Court insisted that principles of democracy and popular sovereignty demanded the overruling of *Roe* and *Casey*.[67] If these efforts to deflect responsibility were intended to preserve the Court's standing with the public, they do not appear to have succeeded: The Court's actions around S.B. 8 coincided with a precipitous decline in the Court's public approval rating.[68] These steps also emboldened abortion opponents to

---

[63] Josh Gerstein & Alexander Ward, *Supreme Court Has Voted to Overturn Abortion Rights, Draft Opinion Shows*, POLITICO (May 3, 2022, 2:14 PM EDT), https://www.politico.com/news/2022/05/02/supreme-court-abortion-draft-opinion-00029473.

[64] *Dobbs*, 597 U.S. at 231; *see also* Melissa Murray & Katherine Shaw, Dobbs *and Democracy*, 137 HARV. L. REV. 728, 731 (2024) ("On the majority's telling, its decision laying waste to nearly fifty years' worth of precedent was a necessary corrective to an egregious act of judicial overreach.").

[65] *Dobbs*, 597 U.S. at 241; *see also* Reva B. Siegel, *Memory Games:* Dobbs*'s Originalism as Anti-Democratic Living Constitutionalism—and Some Pathways for Resistance*, 101 TEX. L. REV. 1127, 1187 (2023); Reva B. Siegel, *The History of History and Tradition: The Roots of* Dobbs*'s Method (and Originalism) in the Defense of Segregation*, 133 YALE L.J.F. 99 (2023); Serena Mayeri, *The Critical Role of History After* Dobbs, 2 J. AM. CONST. HIST. 171, 267 (2024).

[66] *See Most Americans Support Legal Abortion with Some Restrictions*, AP-NORC (July 12, 2023), https://apnorc.org/projects/most-americans-support-legal-abortion-with-some-restrictions-ap-norc ("Most adults believe that abortion should be legal in all or most cases. . . . And 60% think Congress should pass a law guaranteeing access to legal abortion nationwide.").

[67] *See* Murray & Shaw, *supra* note 64, at 760 ("The *Dobbs* majority insisted that its opinion rested on and implemented principles of democracy.").

[68] *See Supreme Court*, GALLUP, https://news.gallup.com/poll/4732/supreme-court.aspx (showing a drop from forty-nine percent approval in July 2021 to forty percent in September 2021 with subsequent approval ratings all below forty-four percent); *see also Most Oppose Banning the Consideration of Race and Ethnicity in College and University Admissions*, AP-NORC (May 30, 2023),

pursue various strategies for limiting access to abortion, laying the groundwork for the two abortion-related cases the Court heard during the 2023 Term. As Karen Tani has observed, both *Alliance for Hippocratic Medicine* and *Moyle* were arguably "creatures of the docketing choice that produced *Dobbs*."[69]

II. Medication Abortion, Emergency Care, and the Shadow Docket

A. MEDICATION ABORTION

The first post-*Dobbs* abortion case the Court heard, *Alliance for Hippocratic Medicine*, involved the future availability of mifepristone, which has been approved by the FDA for ending early pregnancies since 2000.[70] The lower courts sided with a group of anti-abortion doctors and organizations who challenged various aspects of the FDA's regulation of mifepristone.[71] But the Supreme Court unanimously concluded that the plaintiffs could not satisfy the standing requirements of Article III.[72] This left mifepristone available on the terms set by the FDA—at least for now. But to fully appreciate the Court's willingness to intervene to set the terms on which mifepristone is available, it is necessary to examine mifepristone at the Court beginning significantly earlier—indeed, beginning with early COVID-era actions by district courts, the Supreme Court, and the executive branch.

---

https://apnorc.org/projects/most-oppose-banning-the-consideration-of-race-and-ethnicity-in-college-and-university-admissions ("Americans' confidence in the U.S. Supreme Court has been steadily declining since 2016 and has reached an all-time low."); Joseph Copeland, *Favorable Views of the Supreme Court Remain Near Historic Low*, Pew Rsch. Ctr. (Aug. 8, 2024), https://www.pewresearch.org/short-reads/2024/08/08/favorable-views-of-supreme-court-remain-near-historic-low ("[F]avorable views of the Supreme Court remain close to [the] three-decade low.").

[69] Karen M. Tani, *The Supreme Court, 2023 Term—Foreword: Curation, Narration, Erasure: Power and Possibility at the U.S. Supreme Court*, 138 Harv. L. Rev. 1, 20 (2024) ("The anti-abortion advocates behind the Alliance for Hippocratic Medicine took their cues not only from *Dobbs*, but also from recent religious freedom and administrative law cases. . . . *Moyle* . . . resulted from state legislators' belief that, following *Dobbs*, they were free to legislate abortion out of existence in their jurisdictions.").

[70] *See* FDA v. All. for Hippocratic Med., 602 U.S. 367, 375 (2024) ("In 2000, FDA approved a new drug application for mifepristone tablets. . . .").

[71] *See id.* at 377 (describing the case's procedural history).

[72] *See id.* at 374.

In May of 2020, during the early months of the COVID-19 pandemic, the American College of Obstetricians and Gynecologists (ACOG), leading a coalition of healthcare providers and reproductive justice advocates, sued the Trump Administration's FDA, challenging its continued enforcement of an in-person dispensing requirement for mifepristone.[73] As the plaintiffs noted, the federal government had already taken pandemic-driven steps to facilitate various forms of telemedicine to ensure that patients could "access healthcare they need from their home, without worrying about putting themselves or others at risk during the COVID-19 outbreak."[74] The CDC, for example, issued guidance encouraging providers to use telemedicine as "the best way to protect patients and staff from COVID-19."[75]

But the government had conspicuously failed to grant any exemption from the medication abortion protocols, which required patients to pick up the mifepristone tablet in person at a hospital, clinic, or medical office, rather than filling their prescription by mail or at a pharmacy, even if the patient's evaluation and counseling were entirely done through telehealth and there was no clinical reason for the visit.[76] In their suit, the plaintiffs presented evidence of "the challenges that COVID-19 presents to patients fulfilling the In-Person Requirements in order to obtain a medication abortion" and also attested to healthcare providers' ability to provide needed care through telemedicine.[77] In light of the obvious difficulty pregnant patients would face in complying with the in-person requirement, the district court concluded that continued enforcement of an in-person visit requirement likely constituted an undue burden under *Roe* and *Casey*, as well as under the more recent *Whole Woman's Health v. Hellerstedt*[78] and *June*

[73] Am. Coll. of Obstetricians & Gynecologists v. U.S. FDA (*ACOG*), 472 F. Supp. 3d 183 (D. Md.), *order clarified*, No. TDC-20-1320, 2020 WL 8167535 (D. Md. Aug. 19, 2020).

[74] Press Release, Alex Azar, Sec'y, Dep't of Health & Hum. Serv., Secretary Azar Announces Historic Expansion of Telehealth Access to Combat COVID-19 (Mar. 17, 2020), https://public3.pagefreezer.com/browse/HHS.gov/16-09-2020T14:35/https://www.hhs.gov/about/news/2020/03/17/secretary-azar-announces-historic-expansion-of-telehealth-access-to-combat-covid-19.html.

[75] *Prepare Your Practice for COVID-19*, Ctrs. For Disease Control & Prevention (June 12, 2020), https://www.supremecourt.gov/opinions/URLs_Cited/OT2020/20A34/20A34-3.pdf.

[76] *ACOG*, 472 F. Supp. 3d at 192.

[77] *Id.* at 195.

[78] 579 U.S. 582 (2016).

Medical Services v. Russo[79] cases. After considering the other factors set forth in *Winter v. Natural Resources Defense Council, Inc.*,[80] the district court preliminarily enjoined the in-person dispensing requirement.[81]

The federal government asked the Supreme Court to stay the district court's injunction,[82] and in October 2020—less than a month after Justice Ginsburg's death, and while Justice Barrett's nomination was pending before the Senate—the Court initially held the application in abeyance while it remanded the case for the district court "to promptly consider a motion by the Government to dissolve, modify, or stay the injunction, including on the ground that relevant circumstances have changed."[83]

On remand, the district court reaffirmed its opinion.[84] When the federal government renewed its request for a stay in the Supreme Court, the Court granted that request.[85] The Court did not explain how it justified the extraordinary step of staying a district court injunction. This was particularly troubling in light of the fact that the only change between the Court's initial remand order and its subsequent stay was that pandemic conditions had worsened dramatically in the interim. The Chief Justice concurred alone to provide some explanation for his vote. As he explained, he took no position on the question of whether the in-person dispensing requirement imposed an undue burden on women seeking medication abortions, but he contended that in the context of the pandemic, "courts owe significant deference to the politically accountable entities with the background, competence, and expertise to assess public health"[86]—

---

[79] 591 U.S. 299 (2020).

[80] 555 U.S. 7, 20 (2008).

[81] *ACOG*, 472 F. Supp. 3d. at 216 ("In light of the convergence of all of these factors stemming from the COVID-19 pandemic, the Court finds that the In-Person Requirements impose a substantial obstacle to abortion patients seeking medication abortion care.").

[82] Application for a Stay of the Injunction Issued by the United States District Court for the District of Maryland at 1, FDA v. Am. Coll. of Obstetricians & Gynecologists (*ACOG*), 141 S. Ct. 578 (2020) (No. 20A34).

[83] FDA v. Am. Coll. of Obstetricians & Gynecologists (*ACOG*), 141 S. Ct. 10, 11 (2020).

[84] *See* Am. Coll. of Obstetricians & Gynecologists v. FDA (*ACOG*), 506 F. Supp. 3d 328, 331 (D. Md. 2020) ("Defendants' Renewed Motion to Stay the Preliminary Injunction . . . will be DENIED.").

[85] *ACOG*, 141 S. Ct. at 578 (mem.) (granting the application for a stay).

[86] *Id.* at 579 (Roberts, C.J., concurring in the grant of application for stay).

here, the FDA.[87] Strikingly, the other Justices who voted to grant the stay did not attempt to explain their votes to subject women in pursuit of medication abortion to dramatic increases in health risks at the height of the pandemic. Their silence was especially conspicuous given their writings in other pandemic-related cases, where the same Justices were more than willing to override the judgments of elected officials when those judgments conflicted with the Court's position on other constitutional rights—in particular, the free exercise of religion.[88]

If the majority's silence in *FDA v. ACOG* was deafening, Justice Sotomayor's dissent featured both sound and fury. She charged that the Court had imposed "an unnecessary, irrational, and unjustifiable undue burden on women seeking to exercise their right to choose."[89] As she noted, at the time the Court issued its stay, over 350,000 Americans had died of COVID-19, a number that would continue to climb in the months that followed.[90] In light of the dangers in-person healthcare posed, the government had already taken a number of steps to facilitate telehealth, yet it and the Court "refused to extend that same grace to women seeking medication abortions,"[91] requiring women seeking to access medication abortion to expose themselves and their families to unnecessary and avoidable risk. Justice Sotomayor noted the significantly higher COVID mortality rates for Black and Hispanic women compared to white women. She noted the disparate effects of the in-person requirement on low-income women, who were both more likely to seek abortions and more likely to rely on public transportation to comply with the in-person requirement. Indeed, as the district court had observed, the pandemic already meant that as a result of closed medical offices, difficulties securing transportation and

[87] In fairness, this was the position Chief Justice Roberts maintained across pandemic cases. *See, e.g.*, South Bay United Pentecostal Church v. Newsom, 140 S. Ct. 1613, 1613 (2020) (Roberts, C.J., concurring in the denial of application for stay).

[88] *See, e.g.*, Tandon v. Newsom, 141 S. Ct. 1294, 1296 (2021) (per curiam) (invalidating California COVID regulations imposing limits on private gatherings and requiring masks and social distancing); *see also* Nelson Tebbe, *The Principle and Politics of Equal Value*, 121 Colum. L. Rev. 2397, 2462 (2021) (noting that in *ACOG*, the Court "refused the very same sort of emergency protection that it had repeatedly granted for free exercise during the same period in response to the same pandemic").

[89] *ACOG*, 141 S. Ct. at 585 (Sotomayor, J., dissenting).

[90] In May 2022, the United States exceeded one million COVID deaths. *See* Proclamation No. 10394, 87 Fed. Reg. 30095 (May 17, 2022).

[91] *ACOG*, 141 S. Ct. at 580 (Sotomayor, J., dissenting).

childcare, the economic downturn, or some combination of these factors, many women were unable to obtain their usual contraceptives—and were not in a position to carry a pregnancy to term if they found themselves unexpectedly pregnant.[92]

Finally, Justice Sotomayor observed that because "minority and low-income populations are more likely to live in intergenerational housing," traveling to secure mifepristone entailed the risk of "infecting not just themselves, but also elderly parents and grandparents."[93] In the end, she appeared to direct her message to the executive branch: "One can only hope that the Government will reconsider and exhibit greater care and empathy for women seeking some measure of control over their health and reproductive lives in these unsettling times."[94]

Justice Sotomayor was clearly aware of the timing of the Court's intervention—its stay issued on January 12, 2021, just over one week before the inauguration of a new President and less than one week after the January 6, 2021 attack on the U.S. Capitol. And indeed, soon after President Biden took office on January 20, 2021, the FDA suspended the in-person dispensing requirement.[95] In December 2021, the agency announced that it would be making the change permanent.[96] It also, for the first time, implemented a change that allowed pharmacists to prescribe mifepristone.[97]

December 2021 was also when the Court heard oral arguments in *Dobbs*. Within weeks of the Court's June 2022 release of the *Dobbs* decision, a group of anti-abortion doctors incorporated in Amarillo, Texas as a new organization calling itself the Alliance for Hippocratic

---

[92] Am. Coll. of Obstetricians & Gynecologists v. U.S. FDA (*ACOG*), 472 F. Supp. 3d 183, 197 (D. Md. 2020).

[93] *ACOG*, 141 S. Ct. at 582 (Sotomayor, J., dissenting).

[94] *Id.* at 585.

[95] *See* Letter from Patrizia A. Cavazzoni, Dir., Ctr. for Drug Evaluation & Rsch., to Donna J. Harrison, Exec. Dir., Am. Ass'n of Pro-Life Obstetricians & Gynecologists 4–5 (Dec. 16, 2021), https://www.regulations.gov/document/FDA-2019-P-1534-0016 [hereinafter Cavazzoni Letter]; *see also* Greer Donley, *Medication Abortion Exceptionalism*, 107 Cornell L. Rev. 627, 642 (2022).

[96] Cavazzoni Letter, *supra* note 95, at 6.

[97] *Mifeprex (Mifepristone) Information*, FDA (Mar. 23, 2023), https://www.fda.gov/drugs/postmarket-drug-safety-information-patients-and-providers/mifeprex-mifepristone-information [https://perma.cc/SH6R-SP66]; *see* Donley, *supra* note 95, at 640 (describing sequence of events); *see also* Rachel Rebouché, *Remote Reproductive Rights*, 48 Am. J.L. & Med. 244, 244 (2022).

Medicine.[98] Soon thereafter, the group filed a complaint in Amarillo—where the suit was guaranteed to be assigned to Trump appointee Judge Matthew Kacsmaryk, the lone federal judge in that division[99]—challenging both the FDA's original 2000 approval of mifepristone and recent rounds of FDA regulations loosening the restrictions on the drug. The suggestion that the FDA had been insufficiently attentive to safety concerns struck many as preposterous; if anything, from its initial 2000 approval of mifepristone, the FDA had been excessively cautious in its treatment of the drug compared to other drugs with similar risk profiles.[100]

Nevertheless, the plaintiffs challenged this original approval. They also challenged various FDA regulations, including the 2016 changes that extended the FDA-approved window for mifepristone use (from seven to ten weeks), permitted independent prescription of mifepristone by nurse practitioners, and reduced the in-person visits indicated in the labeling from three to one.[101] They also challenged the 2019 approval of a generic version of mifepristone. Finally, they challenged the 2021 elimination of the in-person dispensing requirement.[102] The plaintiffs prevailed in the district court, where Judge Kacsmaryk agreed that the plaintiffs had standing and purported to declare mifepristone

---

[98] *See* Melissa Gira Grant, *Who Exactly Is Behind the Supreme Court's Big Mifepristone Case?*, New Republic (Mar. 7, 2024), https://newrepublic.com/article/179626/mifepristone-abortion-supreme-court-alliance-hippocratic-medicine ("[T]he Alliance . . . is a newly incorporated anti-abortion group, hastily established in 2022 following the *Dobbs* decision in a jurisdiction that would be favorable to their case. . . .").

[99] Stephen I. Vladeck, *Don't Let Republican 'Judge Shoppers' Thwart the Will of Voters*, N.Y. Times (Feb. 5, 2023), https://www.nytimes.com/2023/02/05/opinion/republicans-judges-biden.html ("By filing [in Amarillo], . . . [there is] a 100 percent chance of having the case assigned to Judge Matthew Kacsmaryk. . . .").

[100] David S. Cohen, Greer Donley & Rachel Rebouché, *Abortion Pills*, 76 Stan. L. Rev. 317, 326 (2024) (arguing that when the FDA first approved mifepristone for terminating early pregnancies, "it required the manufacturer to adhere to distribution limitations that had been rarely applied to other drugs and that were, as many have argued, excessive in light of the drug's safety").

[101] *See* All. for Hippocratic Med. v. FDA, 668 F. Supp. 3d 507, 555 (N.D. Tex.), *aff'd in part, vacated in part*, 78 F.4th 210 (5th Cir. 2023), *rev'd*, 602 U.S. 367 (2024) (holding the regulatory changes allowing non-physicians to dispense the medication, extending the gestational age during which the medication could be used, and removing the in-person follow up exam requirement were arbitrary and capricious); Ctr. for Drug Evaluation & Rsch., FDA, Reference ID: 3909590, Medical Review(s) 5 (2016) (recommending the same regulatory changes to the original new drug application); *see also* FDA, Reference ID: 3909592, Mifeprex Risk Evaluation & Mitigation Strategy (REMS) (2016) (adopting the changes recommended in the medical review).

[102] *All. for Hippocratic Med.*, 668 F. Supp. 3d at 560.

an unauthorized drug, full stop.[103] As support for his conclusion that the FDA's original approval of mifepristone was contrary to law,[104] Judge Kacsmaryk reasoned that while the rule under which the FDA approved mifepristone applied to drugs used to treat "illness," pregnancy was not an illness but rather "a natural process essential to perpetuating human life."[105] He also claimed the approval was inconsistent with the governing regulation because "chemical abortion drugs do not provide a meaningful therapeutic benefit."[106] Judge Kacsmaryk proceeded to identify numerous other legal shortcomings in various FDA actions, including that the FDA's 2021 approval of mailing mifepristone violated the 1873 Comstock Act,[107] and that the FDA's pre-2021 regulations were arbitrary and capricious under the Administrative Procedure Act (APA).[108]

The federal government sought an immediate stay from the Fifth Circuit, which granted the request as to the FDA's original 2000 approval, but declined to stay the district court's injunction of the FDA's regulations dating from 2016 and 2021.[109] The federal government and the pharmaceutical company Danco—which manufactures mifepristone and had intervened early in the case—sought a stay in the Supreme Court.[110]

To the enormous relief of many, the Court put the district court decision on hold in its entirety—meaning mifepristone remained available on the terms set by the FDA while the Court considered

---

[103] *Id.* (finding that plaintiffs have standing and staying all FDA approvals of mifepristone).

[104] *Id.* at 543, 549.

[105] *Id.* at 543.

[106] *Id.* at 544 ("[T]o satisfy Subpart H, FDA deemed pregnancy a "serious or life-threatening illness[ ]" and concluded that mifepristone "provide[d] [a] meaningful therapeutic benefit to patients over existing treatments". . . . FDA was wrong on both counts.").

[107] *Id.* at 540–41 ("The Comstock Act declares . . . [mifepristone] . . . 'nonmailable.'").

[108] *Id.* at 549–56 (finding the FDA's actions were "not the product of reasoned decision-making"); *see* Leading Cases, *Article III—Standing—Comstock Act*—FDA v. Alliance for Hippocratic Medicine, 138 Harv. L. Rev. 295, 296–97 (2024).

[109] All. for Hippocratic Med. v. FDA, No. 23-10362, 2023 WL 2913725, at *1 (5th Cir. Apr. 12, 2023). When it later considered the case in the regular course, the Fifth Circuit agreed with Kacsmaryk that the challengers had standing and that the FDA's more recent regulation of mifepristone had been unlawful. All. for Hippocratic Med. v. FDA, 78 F.4th 210, 256 (5th Cir. 2023), *rev'd*, 602 U.S. 367 (2024) ("Mifeprex will remain available under the safety restrictions that were in effect prior to 2016.").

[110] *See* Emergency Application for Stay of Preliminary Injunction Pending Appeal, Danco Lab'ys, L.L.C. v. All. for Hippocratic Med., 143 S. Ct. 1075 (2023) (No. 22A901), 2023 WL 3122097 (requesting stay).

and decided the case.[111] This was shadow docket activity that pointed in the opposite direction from the Court's actions on S.B. 8 and its earlier actions vis-à-vis mifepristone—that is, here the Court acted to preserve rather than restrict abortion access. And it was clearly correct for the Court to have taken this step in light of the fundamental errors the Court later unanimously identified in the standing analyses of both the district court and the court of appeals. But the Court should have explained itself in granting the request for a stay—perhaps pointing to the likelihood that no plaintiff had Article III standing to challenge the FDA's decision. It also could have emphasized the danger—which the Court later elaborated in its full opinion—of permitting parties without cognizable interests to use litigation to successfully suspend access to pharmaceutical drugs. In all events, it should have acknowledged the significance of the step it was taking to override determinations made by the lower courts, and it should have offered some explanation. The Court's silence was especially conspicuous in light of Justice Alito's intemperate dissent from the Court's decision to grant the stay.[112]

After the Supreme Court's early intervention, the Fifth Circuit considered and decided the case on the merits—siding, as it had on the stay application, with the district court on both standing and the unlawfulness of the FDA's post-2016 regulations. However, it disagreed with the district court that the challenge to the FDA's original 2000 approval was timely.[113] The Supreme Court granted the cert petitions filed by the federal government and Danco regarding the lawfulness of the 2016 and 2021 regulations[114] and heard oral arguments in March

---

[111] *See Danco Lab'ys*, 143 S. Ct. at 1075 (granting stay).

[112] Justice Alito's solo dissent (Justice Thomas also noted his dissent but did not join Justice Alito) included charges that the majority had acted hypocritically in granting the stay; it also levied baseless claims that the FDA had acted inequitably and might in any event not comply with the district court's order. *See Danco Lab'ys*, 143 S. Ct. at 1075–76 (Alito, J., dissenting from grant of applications for stays); *see also* Steve Vladeck, *Justice Alito and the Shadow Docket*, ONE FIRST (Apr. 24, 2023), https://www.stevevladeck.com/p/24-justice-alito-and-the-shadow-docket.

[113] *All. for Hippocratic Med.*, 78 F.4th at 256 ("We vacate the component of the order that stayed the . . . 2000 Approval and the 2019 Generic Approval. . . . We affirm . . . the stay . . . regarding the 2016 Amendments and the 2021 Non-Enforcement Decision.").

[114] *See* FDA v. All. for Hippocratic Med., 144 S. Ct. 537 (2023) (mem.) (granting the federal government's petition for certiorari); Danco Lab'ys, L.L.C. v. All. for Hippocratic Med., 144 S. Ct. 537 (2023) (mem.) (granting Danco Laboratories' petition for certiorari). At the same time, the Court denied the cross-petition brought by the Alliance challenging the Fifth Circuit's decision as to the original 2000 approval decision. *See* All. for Hippocratic

2024. Ultimately, the Court unanimously concluded that the plaintiffs lacked standing.[115] On the Court's description,

> the plaintiffs do not prescribe or use mifepristone. And FDA is not requiring them to do or refrain from doing anything. The plaintiffs want FDA to make mifepristone more difficult for other doctors to prescribe and for pregnant women to obtain. Under Article III of the Constitution, a plaintiff's desire to make a drug less available *for others* does not establish standing to sue.[116]

The Court went on to reject the plaintiffs' argument that the FDA's actions had caused them to divert resources to care for complications caused by mifepristone,[117] and similarly to reject their arguments for organizational standing.[118]

Significantly, the Court also rejected the plaintiffs' arguments that the FDA's regulations would cause them "conscience injuries." The plaintiffs argued that the FDA's relaxed mifepristone regulations would result in complications for some women, and that some of the plaintiffs would need to participate in addressing those complications in an emergency room setting. The Court reasoned that this was not a realistic possibility in light of the federal government's position that federal law would protect objecting doctors in such circumstances.[119]

This final aspect of the Court's analysis, though brief, could have profoundly dangerous implications for patients in need of emergency care in conjunction with mifepristone. The Court's discussion of conscience objections appeared both blind to the realities of emergency medicine and wildly callous about the health effects on women of refusals to provide care in the case of medical emergencies. As the Court noted, the plaintiffs argued that "emergency room doctors summoned to provide emergency treatment may not have time to

Med. v. FDA, 144 S. Ct. 537 (2023) (mem.) (denying the Alliance's petition for certiorari); Conditional Cross-Petition for a Writ of Certiorari, FDA v. All. for Hippocratic Med., 602 U.S. 367 (2024) (Nos. 23-235 & 23-236), 2023 WL 6847567.

[115] *See All. for Hippocratic Med.*, 602 U.S. at 372.

[116] *Id.* at 374.

[117] *See id.* at 391–92 ("[D]octors have never had standing to challenge FDA's drug approvals simply on the theory that use of the drugs by others may cause more visits to doctors.").

[118] *See id.* at 394 ("An organization cannot manufacture its own standing. . . .").

[119] *See id.* at 386–90; *id.* at 387 ("[F]ederal conscience laws definitively protect doctors from being required to perform abortions. . . .").

invoke federal conscience protections."[120] But not to worry, the Court responded: "[D]octors need not follow a time-intensive procedure to invoke federal conscience protections. A doctor may simply refuse; federal law protects doctors from repercussions when they have 'refused' to participate in an abortion."[121]

The Court's discussion of "repercussions" was quite notably limited to doctors; repercussions for patients denied care, perhaps care that is necessary to preserve fertility or even life, were wholly absent from the Court's consideration.

It is worth pausing to consider the full import of this aspect of the Court's reasoning. A patient has taken mifepristone. This may have been to terminate an early pregnancy; it may also have been because mifepristone is regularly used as part of the treatment regimen for medical management of early miscarriage.[122] If she experiences a medical emergency as a result of complications, the Court's insistence that there are no limits on the ability to refuse care suggests that the law would affirmatively protect a doctor who stood by as the patient deteriorated and potentially died.[123]

To note the Court's failure to consider repercussions for patients denied care is not to suggest that the Court should have disregarded physicians' conscience objections.[124] But not long ago, the Court's consideration of conscience objections grappled with the third-party harms caused by such objections.[125] There is no indication of interest in such effects in *Alliance*.

Later in the *Alliance* opinion, the Court again discussed the issue of complications that require emergency care, this time in its discussion of EMTALA, which the plaintiffs suggested "might be interpreted to

---

[120] *Id.* at 389.

[121] *Id.*

[122] *See, e.g.*, Justin Chu et al., *Mifepristone and Misoprostol Versus Misoprostol Alone for the Management of Missed Miscarriage (MifeMiso): A Randomised, Double-Blind, Placebo-Controlled Trial*, 396 LANCET 770 (2020) (discussing use of mifepristone for miscarriage management).

[123] *See* Reva Siegel & Mary Ziegler, *The Supreme Court Just Created a Road Map for Trump to Ban Abortion Nationwide*, SLATE (June 14, 2024, 1:54 PM), https://slate.com/news-and-politics/2024/06/supreme-court-road-map-trump-national-abortion-ban-2024.html ("Justice Brett Kavanaugh's opinion for the court discusses federal conscience protections more expansively than SCOTUS has before. . . . *Alliance* speaks of complicity claims of this kind as if they have no limits.").

[124] *See* Elizabeth Sepper, *Taking Conscience Seriously*, 98 VA. L. REV. 1501, 1505 (2012).

[125] Douglas NeJaime & Reva B. Siegel, *Conscience Wars: Complicity-Based Conscience Claims in Religion and Politics*, 124 YALE L.J. 2516, 2519 (2015).

override . . . federal conscience laws and to require individual emergency room doctors to participate in emergency abortions in some circumstances."[126] Once again, the Court was at pains to convey the breadth of its conception of conscience objections. Referencing concessions in the federal government's brief and at the *Alliance* oral argument, the Court emphasized that "EMTALA does not require doctors to perform abortions or provide abortion-related medical treatment over their conscience objections because EMTALA does not impose obligations on individual doctors."[127] The Court elaborated, seizing on a concession by the federal government, that "[s]trong protection for conscience remains true even in a so-called healthcare desert, where other doctors are not readily available."[128]

B. ABORTION AND MEDICAL EMERGENCIES

Issues of conscience objections were, if anything, even more front and center in the Term's second abortion case, *Moyle v. United States*.[129] *Moyle* concerned the interaction of the federal EMTALA statute with state laws that ban or severely restrict access to abortion.[130] Enacted in 1986, EMTALA requires Medicare-funded hospitals to provide "stabilizing care" to any individual experiencing a medical emergency.[131] After taking the highly unusual step of granting "cert before judgment"—taking the case directly from the district court—the Court ultimately dismissed the writ as "improvidently granted."[132] But like *Alliance for Hippocratic Medicine*, the Court's actions leading up to its dismissal of *Moyle*, as well as clues contained in various writings, are every bit as important as the case's bottom-line disposition.

---

[126] *All. for Hippocratic Med.*, 602 U.S. at 389.

[127] *Id.*

[128] *Id.* at 388; *see* Transcript of Oral Argument at 18, *All. for Hippocratic Med.*, 602 U.S. 367 (Nos. 23-235 & 23-236) ("General Prelogar: The federal government has never taken the position that EMTALA would override an individual doctor's conscience objections. . . . [W]e understand the conscience protections to continue to apply and shield a doctor who doesn't want to provide care in violation of those protections."); *id.* (Barrett, J.) ("Would that be true in a healthcare desert as well? General Prelogar: Yes.").

[129] 603 U.S. 324 (2024) (per curiam).

[130] *See id.* at 325–36 (Kagan, J., concurring) (discussing the interaction of Idaho's abortion law and EMTALA).

[131] *Id.* at 326–27 ("[EMTALA] requires a Medicare-funded hospital to provide essential care to patients experiencing medical emergencies.").

[132] *See id.* at 325 (per curiam) (dismissing the writs as improvidently granted).

Moyle arose in Idaho, one of the states that passed a near-total ban on abortion in the wake of *Dobbs*.[133] Shortly after *Dobbs*, as Idaho and other states moved to severely restrict or ban abortion, the federal government issued guidance reiterating the federal government's longstanding position that EMTALA's requirement of stabilizing care in medical emergencies could, in rare cases, include an abortion, regardless of the state in which the emergency arose.[134] Most states that imposed restrictions or bans in the wake of *Dobbs* included exceptions for abortions that are necessary to preserve the health of the pregnant woman; Idaho did not. So in August 2022, the federal government filed suit in an Idaho district court, invoking both EMTALA's express preemption clause and also basic principles of federal supremacy to argue that EMTALA preempted Idaho's abortion law in a narrow class of cases: those where state law purported to bar hospitals from performing an abortion needed to prevent serious health harms like the loss of an organ, or the prospect of future fertility.[135] The district court sided with the federal government and enjoined the enforcement of Idaho's ban "as applied to medical care required by [EMTALA]."[136]

The district court was bracingly direct about the physical reality of pregnancy complications, opening the opinion with a detailed description of the sorts of emergencies that might land a pregnant patient in an emergency room:

> The patient might be spiking a fever, experiencing uterine cramping and chills, contractions, shortness of breath, or significant vaginal bleeding. The ER physician may diagnose her with, among other possibilities, traumatic placental abruption, preeclampsia, or a preterm premature rupture of the membranes. In those situations, the physician may be called upon to make complex, difficult decisions in a fast-moving, chaotic environment. She may conclude that the only way to prevent serious harm to the patient or save

[133] Idaho Code Ann. § 18–622 (West 2023).

[134] *See* Memorandum from the Dirs., Quality, Safety, & Oversight Grp., to State Surv. Agency Dirs. 1 (Aug. 25, 2022), https://www.cms.gov/files/document/qso-22-22-hospitals.pdf ("If a physician believes that . . . abortion is the stabilizing treatment necessary . . . the physician must provide that treatment. . . . [S]tate law is preempted.").

[135] *See* United States v. Idaho, 623 F. Supp. 3d 1096, 1101 (D. Idaho 2022), *cert. granted sub nom.* Moyle v. United States, 144 S. Ct. 540 (2024) ("[T]he Supremacy Clause says state law must yield. . . .").

[136] *Id.* (granting the United States' motion for a preliminary injunction).

> her life is to terminate the pregnancy—a devastating result for the doctor and the patient.[137]

The court continued by noting that when the appropriate stabilizing care for such a patient is an abortion, Idaho law placed the doctor in an impossible position: compliance with the obligations of EMTALA and exposure to felony prosecution under state law for providing needed care, or denial of appropriate stabilizing care in violation of EMTALA, exposing the patient to consequences that could include "severe sepsis requiring limb amputation, uncontrollable uterine hemorrhage requiring hysterectomy, kidney failure requiring lifelong dialysis, hypoxic brain injury, or even death."[138] It could also expose the hospital to liability for civil penalties, loss of federal funds, and individual damages suits.

The court concluded that the Federal Constitution supplied a straightforward answer for resolving the conflict between the obligations of state and federal law: "[T]he Supremacy Clause says state law must yield to federal law when it's impossible to comply with both."[139] The court accordingly preliminarily enjoined the enforcement of the Idaho law to the extent it conflicted with EMTALA.[140]

When Idaho asked the Supreme Court to stay the district court's injunction, the Court agreed,[141] construing the State's request as a petition for certiorari before judgment, granting that petition, and putting the district court injunction on hold, leaving Idaho free to enforce a ban the district court had found preempted by federal law.[142] Just as the Court had declined to explain its decision to reverse the careful district court opinion enjoining the in-person dispensing requirement for mifepristone, the Court said not a word about the justifications for overriding the district court's conclusion.

---

137 *Id.* at 1096.

138 *Id.* at 1101.

139 *Id.*

140 *Id.* at 1102 ("[T]he state of Idaho will be enjoined . . . to the extent that statute conflicts with EMTALA. . . .").

141 *See* Moyle v. United States, 144 S. Ct. 540 (2024) (mem.) (granting Idaho certiorari before judgment). Some proceedings had actually occurred in the Ninth Circuit—a panel opinion staying the district court's injunction, and an en banc opinion vacating the stay—but no proceedings on the merits. *See* United States v. Idaho, 83 F.4th 1130 (9th Cir.), *reh'g en banc granted, opinion vacated*, 82 F.4th 1296 (9th Cir. 2023).

142 *Moyle*, 144 S. Ct. at 540 ("The preliminary injunction issued on August 24, 2022, by the United States District Court for the District of Idaho . . . is stayed.").

But while the human costs of the Court's unreasoned intervention in the earlier mifepristone litigation were difficult to quantify, the toll of the Court's intervention in Idaho was clear. While the Court's stay was in effect, women in Idaho were airlifted out of state *every other week* for emergency abortion care.[143] That was in contrast to only one pregnant patient being airlifted in the preceding year, while the preliminary injunction was in effect.[144] One Idaho woman described to the *New York Times* a harrowing ordeal of being airlifted to Utah for an emergency abortion after she began hemorrhaging following a placental abruption and premature breaking of waters; nurses reported that when she arrived in Salt Lake City, fourteen hours after she first sought emergency care in Idaho, she told them: "I just need to stay alive so I can be around for my two other kids."[145]

"Cert before judgment" allows the Court to take cases straight from trial courts where those cases, in the Court's view, are of "such imperative public importance as to justify deviation from normal appellate practice and to require immediate determination in this Court."[146] This was once a rarely used device, but there has been an enormous uptick in the past five years.[147] But that increase has been highly selective. For example, in December 2023—the same month Idaho asked the Court to consider its request that it be able to enforce its harsh abortion law without regard to EMTALA—Special Counsel Jack Smith asked the Court to take up immediately, rather than wait

---

[143] *See* Julie Luchetta, *As Emergency Airlifts for Pregnant Patients Increase in Idaho, U.S. Supreme Court Abortion Case Starts*, Boise St. Pub. Rad. News (Apr. 24, 2024, 10:31 AM MDT), https://www.boisestatepublicradio.org/health/2024-04-24/moyle-idaho-supreme-court-airlift-abortion-emergency ("In the three months since the injunction was lifted . . . that number [of pregnant patients airlifted out of state] rose to six.").

[144] Sabrina Talukder, *Supreme Court Dismisses* Idaho v. United States *Without Making a Decision on Emergency Abortion Care*, Ctr. for Am. Progress (June 27, 2024), https://www.americanprogress.org/article/supreme-court-dismisses-idaho-v-united-states-without-making-a-decision-on-emergency-abortion-care ("[F]or the entirety of 2023 . . . only one pregnant patient was airlifted.").

[145] Kate Zernike, *She Needed an Emergency Abortion. Doctors in Idaho Put Her on a Plane*, N.Y. Times (June 28, 2024), https://www.nytimes.com/2024/06/28/us/emergency-abortion-idaho-mother.html; *cf.* Sarah Zhang, *That's Something That You Won't Recover from as a Doctor*, Atlantic (Sept. 12, 2023), https://www.theatlantic.com/magazine/archive/2024/10/abortion-ban-idaho-ob-gyn-maternity-care/679567 (recounting stories of additional Idaho women forced to leave the state for emergency abortions).

[146] Sup. Ct. R. 11.

[147] *See* Stephen I. Vladeck, *A Court of First View*, 138 Harv. L. Rev. 533, 545 (2024) (identifying twenty-one grants of certiorari before judgment between 2019 and 2024, compared to three total such grants in the preceding thirty years).

for the court of appeals to first answer, the question of whether former Presidents are immune from prosecution even after they leave office.[148] Although the Special Counsel clearly laid out the pressing national interest in an expedited resolution to that question, the Court declined his request.[149]

Two months after the oral argument in *Moyle*, the Court dismissed the writ as improvidently granted (colloquially, a DIG).[150] Often, a DIG provides limited or no clues about the Court's reasoning. Here, though, each Justice signed on to a separate writing—a concurrence, partial concurrence and dissent, or dissent—making it easier than usual to piece together the Court's motivations and the likely future trajectory of disputes involving conflicts between EMTALA and state abortion bans.[151]

Justice Kagan concurred in the dismissal, joined by Justice Sotomayor and in part by Justice Jackson, explaining that the Court should not have taken up the case prematurely, because "Idaho's arguments about EMTALA do not justify, and have never justified, either emergency relief or our early consideration of this dispute."[152] Although her concurrence was technically only in the Court's decision to dismiss the case and dissolve the stay, she also made clear that her view aligned with the district court that "EMTALA requires hospitals to provide abortions that Idaho's law prohibits. When that is so, Idaho's law is preempted."[153]

Justice Jackson agreed with the Court's decision to dissolve the stay, charging the Court with having created a "months-long catastrophe

---

[148] *See* Petition for a Writ of Certiorari Before Judgment, United States v. Trump, 144 S. Ct. 539 (2023) (No. 23-624), 2023 WL 8601421 (petition by Special Counsel Jack Smith for certiorari before judgment).

[149] *Trump*, 144 S. Ct. at 539 (denying writ of certiorari before judgment).

[150] *See* Moyle v. United States, 603 U.S. 324, 325 (2024) (dismissing the grant of certiorari as improvidently granted).

[151] Interestingly, like *Dobbs*, the opinion in *Moyle* saw the light of day before the final opinion in the case was issued—not as a result of a leak, but an apparent "glitch" that resulted in the opinion being briefly posted to, and then removed from, the Court's website before its formal release. *See* Steve Vladeck, *Bonus 86: The EMTALA Glitch*, One First (June 27, 2024), https://www.stevevladeck.com/p/bonus-86-the-emtala-glitch.

[152] *Moyle*, 603 U.S. at 327 (Kagan, J., concurring).

[153] *Id.* at 328; *see* Reva Siegel & Mary Ziegler, *Amy Coney Barrett Signaled Something Very Scary About Where Abortion Bans Will Go Next*, Slate (July 2, 2024, 5:45 AM), https://slate.com/news-and-politics/2024/07/amy-coney-barrett-next-abortion-bans.html (noting that Justice Kagan's concurrence channeled "the perspective of medical science: that abortion is an ordinary and valuable form of health care, especially in cases of medical emergency").

[that] was completely unnecessary."[154] And she co-signed Justice Kagan's statutory and preemption analyses. But rather than dismiss the writ, she would have affirmed the district court's decision.[155]

Justice Barrett, joined by the Chief Justice and Justice Kavanaugh, also concurred, contending that the dismissal was appropriate because "the shape of these cases has substantially shifted since we granted certiorari."[156] Justice Barrett pointed to developments in Idaho law since the Court's intercession in the case, including legislative amendment and construction by the state supreme court.[157] She also noted that for the first time in the Supreme Court a question had arisen as to whether a law passed under Congress's Spending Clause authority *could* preempt state law.[158] But she seemed to place the most weight on what she described as two important concessions by the federal government that fundamentally changed the case—and that prompted a reassessment of the Court's decision to stay the district court injunction. The first was that, according to Justice Barrett, the federal government "emphatically disavowed the notion that an abortion is ever required as stabilizing treatment for mental health conditions."[159]

The second, Justice Barrett explained, was the federal government's representation that "federal conscience protections, for both hospitals and individual physicians, apply in the EMTALA context."[160] Justice Barrett intimated that when Idaho first came to the Court seeking emergency relief, the Court had credited Idaho's representation that an interpretation of EMTALA that would allow abortions in cases of serious jeopardy to mental health would convert Idaho emergency rooms to "federal abortion enclaves governed not by state law, but by

---

[154] *Moyle*, 603 U.S. at 339 (Jackson, J., concurring in part and dissenting in part).

[155] *Id.* at 343 ("We permitted Idaho's law to go into effect by staying the District Court's injunction in the first place, then allowed this matter to sit on our merits docket for five months while we considered the question presented. It is too little, too late for the Court to take a mulligan and just tell the lower courts to carry on as if none of this has happened. As the old adage goes: The Court has made this bed so now it must lie in it—by proceeding to decide the merits of the critical pre-emption issue this case presents.").

[156] *Id.* at 332 (Barrett, J., concurring).

[157] *Id.* at 333.

[158] *See id.* at 336–37 ("[P]etitioners have raised a difficult and consequential argument . . . whether Congress, in reliance on the Spending Clause, can obligate recipients of federal funds to violate state criminal law.").

[159] *Id.* at 335.

[160] *Id.*

physician judgment, as enforced by the United States's mandate to perform abortions on demand,"[161] and would also "threate[n] religious healthcare providers."[162] Although the Court had of course provided no reasoning at the time, Justice Barrett now clarified that "[b]oth of these points were relevant to the Court's assessment of the irreparable harm that Idaho would suffer from the preliminary injunction, . . . as well as the need for 'immediate determination in this Court.'"[163] This revealing passage clarified what drove the Court in its decision to grant certiorari before judgment and to stay the injunction—and suggested that the votes of Justices Barrett, Roberts, and Kavanaugh to dismiss the case were largely predicated on the same broad conception of conscience protections the Court had announced in *Alliance*. In no way did their vote signal their alignment with Justices Kagan, Sotomayor, and Jackson as to the interaction of EMTALA and state law.

Justice Alito, joined in full by Justice Thomas and in part by Justice Gorsuch, accused the Court of having "lost the will to decide the easy but emotional and highly politicized question that the case presents."[164] The case was "easy," according to Justice Alito, because the statute's reference to "unborn child" meant that EMTALA *never* authorized Medicare-funded hospitals to perform abortions[165]—perhaps not even, at least as Justice Kagan understood Justice Alito to maintain, if an abortion was required to prevent a pregnant patient's death.[166] In addition to the statute's reference to "unborn child," Justice Alito drew for support on a speech by President Reagan to the Annual "March for Life"[167] and separate provisions of the federal Hyde Amendment—but

---

161 *Id.* at 334–35 (citing Idaho's reply brief).

162 *Id.* at 335.

163 *Id.*

164 *Id.* at 348 (Alito, J., dissenting).

165 *Id.* at 349 ("At no point in its elaboration of the screening, stabilization, and transfer requirements does EMTALA mention abortion. Just the opposite is true: EMTALA requires the hospital at every stage to protect an 'unborn child' from harm.").

166 *Id.* at 329 (Kagan, J., concurring); *see also* Reva B. Siegel & Mary Ziegler, *Abortion's New Criminalization—A History-And-Tradition Right to Healthcare Access After* Dobbs, 111 Va. L. Rev. (forthcoming 2025) (manuscript at 18–19), https://ssrn.com/abstract=4881886 (explaining that Justice Alito, dissenting in *Moyle*, "read[] into the law a particular movement perspective on personhood, one that erases the pregnant patient at the mere mention of the term 'unborn child'").

167 *Moyle*, 603 U.S. at 353 (Alito, J., dissenting) ("Less than three months before signing EMTALA, President Reagan told participants in the annual March for Life that 'the resources of government are not [to be] used to promote or perform abortions.'").

not the overall statutory scheme created by EMTALA, nor the context in which the law was enacted.

In the final portion of his dissenting opinion, Justice Alito made the curious choice to opine at length on various aspects of obstetric care. This included a lengthy disquisition on how doctors were to proceed in the context of pre-term, premature rupture of membranes (PPROM). Although Justice Alito allowed that when PPROM occurs prior to the thirty-fourth week of pregnancy, a pregnant woman "may experience conditions such as an infection of the amniotic fluid, inflammation of the uterine lining, hemorrhage, or sepsis," he also mused that because "life-threatening complications are not inevitable," and "death is 'extremely rare,'" instances of PPROM did not necessarily justify emergency abortions, and evidently did not remove doctors' obligations to take whatever steps are necessary to preserve the life of the "unborn child."[168]

These observations were, to be clear, chilling. Under the best of circumstances, pregnancy takes a serious toll on the body.[169] When a pregnancy goes wrong, the stakes can be catastrophic. Doctors may be able to act to protect a woman's health and, especially later in a pregnancy, to also increase the chances of a successful delivery. But Justice Alito's casual engagement with the question of this type of care appeared clueless or indifferent to the practice of medicine in the high-stakes environment of emergency rooms in which split-second decisions are standard and physicians are accustomed to treating (and view themselves as obligated to treat) the patient before them.

So *Moyle* is chock full of ominous signals about the future of abortion before the Court. And while it is likely that the Court has not said its final word on EMTALA's interaction with state law, it is not entirely clear how and when another such case will make its way to the Court. Several months after the Court dismissed the petition in *Moyle*, it denied certiorari in another, similar, case—this one arising

---

[168] *Id.* at 364; *see also* Duncan Hosie, *Samuel Alito's Recent Cosplay as a Scientific Expert Is a Glimpse onto the Future of America Law*, S.F. Chron. (June 30, 2024), https://www.sfchronicle.com/opinion/openforum/article/supreme-court-conservative-law-alito-chevron-19546140.php.

[169] Cat Bohannon, Eve: How the Female Body Drove 200 Million Years of Human Evolution 114 (2023) ("Pregnancy is inherently dangerous and can have crippling long-term side effects on women."); *see also* Annie Lowery, *American Motherhood*, Atlantic (Aug. 1, 2022), https://www.theatlantic.com/ideas/archive/2022/08/pregnancy-birth-complication-abortion-life-of-mother/671006 (noting that "bearing a child remains startlingly dangerous").

out of a Texas suit against the Department of Health and Human Services challenging the federal government's EMTALA guidance.[170] The Fifth Circuit had ruled against the federal government, finding that EMTALA did not preempt Texas's "Human Life Protection Act."[171] The federal government challenged that decision in a cert petition the Supreme Court held as it considered *Moyle*.[172] After the *Moyle* dismissal, the federal government asked the Court to "grant certiorari, vacate the Fifth Circuit's decision, and remand (GVR)" so that the lower courts could reconsider their prior determinations in light of *Moyle*.[173] The Court, without providing any reasons, declined to take even this modest step, suggesting that it may be content to let lower courts nullify EMTALA—and that only if and when another lower court takes a more expansive view of EMTALA will the Court again step in.

III. Looking Ahead

Both decisions, then, signal openness to limiting—or themselves operate to meaningfully limit—access to abortion care even where the law on its face continues to permit it. And both make clear that the questions the Court did not squarely answer could return. In *Alliance*, the Court broadcast its receptivity to a future case brought by plaintiffs with a more plausible claim of injury caused by the FDA, writing, "[I]t is not clear that no one else would have standing to challenge FDA's relaxed regulation of mifepristone."[174] And several states have already launched a new effort in Amarillo, seeking to assert injuries that might fare better than those of the physicians and organizations in *Alliance*.[175] Among other things, this new litigation might

---

[170] Becerra v. Texas, 145 S. Ct. 139 (2024) (mem.) ("Petition for writ of certiorari . . . [is] denied.").

[171] *See* Texas v. Becerra, 89 F.4th 529, 533 (5th Cir. 2024) (affirming district court's holding that EMTALA did not preempt state abortion ban).

[172] *See* Petition for a Writ of Certiorari at 6, *Becerra*, 145 S. Ct. 139 (No. 23-1076), 2024 WL 1469612.

[173] *See* Reply Brief for the Petitioners at 2, *Becerra*, 145 S. Ct. 139 (No. 23-1076), 2024 WL 4101404.

[174] FDA v. All. for Hippocratic Med., 602 U.S. 367, 396 (2024).

[175] *See* Amended Complaint at 197, Missouri v. FDA, No. 22-CV-00223 (N.D. Tex. Oct. 11, 2024), https://storage.courtlistener.com/recap/gov.uscourts.txnd.370067/gov.uscourts.txnd.370067.195.1.pdf ("Plaintiff States respectfully request that the Court . . . order[] Defendants to withdraw Defendants' actions to deregulate these abortion drugs."); Chris Geidner, *Judge Who Wanted to Ban Mifepristone Refuses to Dismiss Case*, Ms. Mag. (Jan. 17, 2025), https://msmagazine.com/2025/01/17/judge-ban-mifepristone-matthew-kacsmaryk-texas.

permit the Court to consider the argument that mailing mifepristone violates the Comstock Act, the 1873 anti-vice statute that made several appearances at the *Alliance* oral argument, though it was absent from the final opinion in the case.[176] And the various writings in *Moyle* make clear that the Court may yet do more than identify expansive conscience protections that seemingly negate any interests in patient life or care; it may more directly nullify EMTALA insofar as EMTALA recognizes that abortions can sometimes be stabilizing care for individuals experiencing medical emergencies.

If the Court does again consider the issues in either case, the 2023 Term's administrative law cases—of which there were many—might play important roles. First, one of the Term's lower-profile administrative law cases, *Corner Post v. Board of Governors*,[177] could revive the prospects of the broadest possible challenges to mifepristone. Recall that the most sweeping challenge brought by the *Alliance* plaintiffs to the FDA's original 2000 approval of mifepristone was dismissed by the Fifth Circuit as untimely[178] based on the six-year statute of limitations set forth in the APA.[179] But in *Corner Post*, Justice Barrett, writing for a six-Justice majority, held that the APA's six-year statute of limitations does not begin to run until a particular entity is injured by agency action, rather than when the agency actually *takes* the action.[180] This ruling, upending decades of settled practice, could mean that new entities like the Alliance for Hippocratic Medicine—or existing entities asserting new injuries in a post-*Dobbs* world—might be able to proceed with their challenges to the FDA's 2000 approval of mifepristone.

---

[176] *See* Siegel & Ziegler, *supra* note 166 (manuscript at 20) ("During argument of the case, two Justices appeared to credit these Comstock claims; but the Court's final decision was conspicuously silent—neither encouraging nor foreclosing future claims of this kind."); *see also* Reva B. Siegel & Mary Ziegler, *Comstockery: How Government Censorship Gave Birth to the Law of Sexual and Reproductive Freedom, and May Again Threaten It*, 134 YALE L.J. 1068 (2025); Project 2025, *Mandate for Leadership: The Conservative Promise*, HERITAGE FOUND. 459 & n.16 (2023), https://static.project2025.org/2025_MandateForLeadership_FULL.pdf (calling on FDA to "[s]top promoting or approving mail-order abortions in violation of long-standing federal laws that prohibit the mailing and interstate carriage of abortion drugs").

[177] Corner Post, Inc. v. Bd. of Governors of the Fed. Rsrv. Sys., 603 U.S. 799 (2024).

[178] All. for Hippocratic Med. v. FDA, 78 F.4th 210, 242 (5th Cir. 2023) ("[T]hey did not raise a claim [regarding the 2000 Approval] . . . within six years, as required. . . .").

[179] *See* 28 U.S.C. § 2401 (requiring civil actions to be filed within six years after the claim accrues).

[180] *See Corner Post*, 603 U.S. at 825 ("[A] claim does not 'accrue' as soon as the defendant acts, but only after the plaintiff suffers the injury required to press her claim in court.").

In addition, the long-standing principle of judicial deference to administrative agencies set forth in the 1984 *Chevron* decision was repudiated in the 2024 case *Loper Bright Enterprises v. Raimondo*;[181] insofar as past challenges to agency action might have had to overcome modes of deference set forth in *Chevron* or its progeny, those doctrines may no longer pose any meaningful obstacle to judicial invalidation of agency action.[182] In theory, this change could cut in either direction when it comes to the future of judicial review of agency action as to either mifepristone or EMTALA. *Loper Bright*'s assertion of the Court's primacy in the interpretation of law should mean that agency actions inconsistent with statutes enacted by Congress are vulnerable to judicial invalidation. This should mean that if future agency action is taken to restrict access to abortion for reasons other than those set forth in statutes passed by Congress, such actions should fail. At least Justice Alito, however—and perhaps a majority of the other Justices—appears determined to read statutes in ways that are fundamentally hostile to access to abortion.

In the context of future agency action—in particular, a possible move by the FDA to reconsider the terms on which mifepristone is available, or even to revisit its original approval—another case from the same Term could come into play. In that case, *Ohio v. EPA*,[183] the Court used an aggressive form of "arbitrary and capricious review" to stay an EPA rule governing interstate air pollution in the context of federal air quality standards. *Ohio v. EPA* involved rulemaking, so it is not entirely clear how its logic will apply to other forms of agency action. But the case, in addition to a number of other recent cases deploying arbitrary and capricious review to invalidate various agency actions,[184] should mean that the FDA gets a genuinely "hard look" if it seeks to fundamentally overhaul access to mifepristone, in light of the Federal Food, Drug, and Cosmetic Act's directive to agencies to use safety and efficacy as the criteria for drug approval and regulation.[185]

---

[181] 603 U.S. 369 (2024).

[182] Rachel E. Sachs & Erin C. Fuse Brown, *Supreme Power—The Loss of Judicial Deference to Health Agencies*, 391 New Eng. J. Med. 777, 778 (2024) ("The decision could open the door to more, and broader, challenges to actions taken by health agencies, such as the Centers for Medicare and Medicaid Services . . . and the Food and Drug Administration.").

[183] 603 U.S. 279 (2024).

[184] Dep't of Homeland Sec. v. Regents of the Univ. of Cal., 591 U.S. 1 (2020); Dep't of Com. v. New York, 588 U.S. 752 (2019).

[185] *See* 21 U.S.C. § 355(d) (requiring the FDA to evaluate safety and efficacy when approving a new drug).

Conclusion

Viewed in their entirety, these episodes reveal a Court that is testing possibilities for what Reva Siegel and Mary Ziegler describe as the invention of a harsher new regime when it comes to punitive and even lethal abortion policies.[186]

As the sequence of events in *Alliance* made clear, it is the Court that will decide who has access to mifepristone and who does not—whether in the shadows or in the open. And the Court's willingness to use the shadow docket to allow Idaho to suspend EMTALA recalled its use of the shadow docket to restrict mifepristone during the pandemic, and also to allow Texas's S.B. 8 to override federal constitutional protections announced in *Roe*. Just as the Court's shadow docket decision in S.B. 8 presaged its ultimate decision in *Dobbs*, it is quite possible that the Court will make permanent in a future case what it permitted in the run-up to *Moyle*.[187]

One of the rare bright spots for access to abortion in the post-*Dobbs* era has been the widespread use of direct democracy, in which voters have bypassed legislatures and directly enshrined abortion protections into law.[188] But those state-law guarantees will do little to protect access to mifepristone if the federal government or the courts accept the argument that the Comstock Act bans mailing abortion pills,[189] or to guard against an interpretation of EMTALA that requires doctors to protect fetal life above all else.

---

[186] Siegel & Ziegler, *supra* note 166 (manuscript at 8–14); *see also Two Years Post-*Dobbs*: The Nationwide Impact of Abortion Bans*, U.S. Senate 4 (2024), https://www.cantwell.senate.gov/imo/media/doc/2024_dobbs_anniversary_national_report_final.pdf (explaining how, according to Alabama State Director at Planned Parenthood Southeast Stephen Stetson, bans with very limited health exceptions require doctors "'to watch patients go into sepsis . . . and deteriorate, because they are afraid that the person isn't sick enough to qualify for the medical exemption'"). The report indicates that even in jurisdictions where statutes permit abortions for medical emergencies, the number of legal abortions performed is far below the level expected. *See Two Years Post-*Dobbs, *supra*, at 4. Consequently, patients must bear—and sometimes suffer—serious health risks before doctors are able to perform necessary procedures.

[187] Alito's dissent in particular seemed to echo the Court's disposition of Texas's S.B. 8: At least where federal law protects and state law restricts access to abortion, states apparently have free rein to nullify federal law.

[188] *See generally* Murray & Shaw, *supra* note 12.

[189] *See* Mayeri, *supra* note 65, at 267 (noting that state constitutional guarantees of reproductive freedom, including those adopted via direct democracy, may be "on a collision course with . . . a revitalized Comstock Act, a future nationwide abortion ban, [or] a constitutional fetal personhood decision").

For now, the Court has a potent set of tools at its disposal. If it does directly return to the issues raised in these cases, it can deploy a new set of rules that give it broad powers over federal agencies and the choices they make. And it can continue to use the shadow docket strategically—to evade public scrutiny, and to desensitize the public to a status quo it has allowed but not proclaimed.

JACK M. BALKIN

MOODY v. NETCHOICE: THE SUPREME COURT MEETS THE FREE SPEECH TRIANGLE

Concerned that large social media companies discriminated against conservative voices, Texas and Florida passed laws regulating how social media companies could moderate posts, sanction speakers, and promote or demote content. Conservative politicians in the two states were deeply suspicious of the large social media companies headquartered in the Bay Area of liberal California. They believed that these social media companies, Meta, YouTube, and Twitter, were unfairly removing conservative speech, demoting it in social media feeds, or de-platforming conservative speakers. Texas and Florida sought to restore online ideological balance and prevent what they considered censorship by the companies' progressive employees.[1]

Jack M. Balkin is the Knight Professor of Constitutional Law and the First Amendment at Yale Law School.

AUTHOR'S NOTE: Thanks to Justin Driver, Daphne Keller, and Robert Post for their comments on previous drafts. The Author participated in an amicus brief in *Moody v. NetChoice*. *See* Brief of Amicus Curiae Francis Fukuyama in Support of Respondents in No. 22-277 and Petitioners in No. 22-555, Moody v. NetChoice, LLC, 603 U.S. 707 (2024) (Nos. 22-277 & 22-555).

[1] *See* Press Release, Off. of the Tex. Governor, Governor Abbott Signs Law Protecting Texans From Wrongful Social Media Censorship (Sept. 9, 2021), https://gov.texas.gov/news/post/governor-abbott-signs-law-protecting-texans-from-wrongful-social-media-censorship [https://perma.cc/3U57-3BDD] (quoting Governor Greg Abbott stating that "there is a dangerous movement

The Supreme Court Review, 2025.
 https://doi.org/10.1086/735007

The states argued that in curating and organizing content social media companies were not actually engaged in First Amendment speech; they were only engaged in private censorship.[2] In the alternative, the states argued that they could treat social media platforms as common carriers or otherwise subject the platforms to nondiscrimination rules to promote a diversity of ideas and opinions.[3]

Because the state statutes were so broadly (and badly) drafted, the Supreme Court did not rule on the merits but instead sent the cases back to the lower courts with instructions about the First Amendment rights of social media companies. Justice Elena Kagan's majority opinion in *Moody v. NetChoice, LLC*[4] held that when social media companies curate posts, they make "editorial judgments" and create an "expressive product" protected by the First Amendment.[5]

The Supreme Court began considering internet speech cases almost three decades ago, in *Reno v. American Civil Liberties Union*.[6] But social media companies as we know them today did not exist in 1997. *Moody* was the Court's first attempt at explaining how the First Amendment applied to the business models of the social media companies that now dominate the digital public sphere. *Moody* was also the Court's first attempt at thinking through the problems of a digital public sphere in which states are no longer the only governors and regulators of free expression and must contend with powerful global corporations that shape public opinion and dominate democratic life. Finally, *Moody* also

---

by social media companies to silence conservative viewpoints and ideas"); News Release, Governor of Fla., Governor Ron DeSantis Signs Bill to Stop the Censorship of Floridians by Big Tech (May 24, 2021), https://www.flgov.com/2021/05/24/governor-ron-desantis-signs-bill-to-stop-the-censorship-of-floridians-by-big-tech [https://perma.cc/HN24-YW3K] (quoting Governor Ron DeSantis's statement that "we took action to ensure that . . . real Floridians across the Sunshine State . . . are guaranteed protection against the Silicon Valley elites. . . . If Big Tech censors enforce rules inconsistently, to discriminate in favor of the dominant Silicon Valley ideology, they will now be held accountable").

[2] NetChoice, LLC v. Att'y Gen., 34 F.4th 1196, 1208 (11th Cir. 2022); NetChoice, L.L.C. v. Paxton, 49 F.4th 439, 482 (5th Cir. 2022).

[3] *See NetChoice*, 34 F.4th at 1219–20 (describing Florida's argument that platforms are either common carriers or can be treated as common carriers); *Paxton*, 49 F.4th at 445 (reciting the Texas' Legislature's findings that social media companies are common carriers); *Paxton*, 49 F.4th at 482 (describing Texas's argument that the law is a content-neutral time, place, and manner regulation).

[4] 603 U.S. 707 (2024). *Moody v. NetChoice* arose out of a challenge to Florida's statute. The companion case from Texas was *NetChoice v. Paxton.*

[5] *Id.* at 718, 731.

[6] Reno v. ACLU, 521 U.S. 844 (1997).

offered brief hints about how the First Amendment might apply to content produced by algorithms and artificial intelligence (AI).

In this Article, I explain how the digital public sphere differs from the world that produced most of the Court's First Amendment doctrine. I then explain how the Court both recognized and failed to recognize those changes. *Moody*'s reasoning displays many of the limitations of American First Amendment doctrine. It asks whether states are abridging the speech of platforms, but it does not consider the free speech interests of end users. Focusing on platforms as speakers, it plays less attention to platforms as governors. Although *Moody* does not close the door on regulations designed to check the governing power of digital platforms, it bestows significant First Amendment protections on the ways that social media platforms govern end users.

I. The Pluralist System of Speech Regulation

In the older, pre-digital world, the system of speech regulation was *dyadic*. It had two basic kinds of players: the state and private speakers, including media companies like newspapers, broadcasters, and cable providers. The digital age, by contrast, has a *pluralist* system of speech regulation.[7] By this I mean that there are many different speech regulators in addition to governments. These new regulators are the owners of private infrastructure that are situated up and down the "tech stack."[8] The tech stack includes broadband and cellular providers, domain name companies, caching services, cybersecurity and defense services, webhosting services, app stores, and applications. You can think of these companies as occupying successive layers in a stack of digital services that make digital communication possible.

---

[7] Jack M. Balkin, *Free Speech in the Algorithmic Society: Big Data, Private Governance, and New School Speech Regulation*, 51 U.C. Davis L. Rev. 1149, 1186–87 (2018) [hereinafter Balkin, *Free Speech in the Algorithmic Society*]; Jack M. Balkin, *Free Speech Is a Triangle*, 118 Colum. L. Rev. 2011, 2013 (2018) [hereinafter Balkin, *Free Speech Is a Triangle*].

[8] Geoffrey A. Fowler & Chris Alcantara, *Gatekeepers: These Tech Firms Control What's Allowed Online*, Wash. Post (Mar. 24, 2021), https://www.washingtonpost.com/technology/2021/03/24/online-moderation-tech-stack [https://perma.cc/PKW4-GUG3] (describing how content moderation occurs up and down the various parts of the technology stack); Joan Donovan, *Navigating the Tech Stack: When, Where and How Should We Moderate Content?*, Ctr. for Int'l Governance Innovation (Oct. 28, 2019), https://www.cigionline.org/articles/navigating-tech-stack-when-where-and-how-should-we-moderate-content [https://perma.cc/U3QX-J7VC] ("At every level of the tech stack, corporations are placed in positions to make value judgments regarding the legitimacy of content, including who should have access, and when and how.").

Social media platforms are applications that sit at the top of the tech stack in the "application layer."[9]

Each of the players in the tech stack has the ability to block, slow down, or moderate speech by end users, although their techniques and abilities differ.[10] The social media companies at the top of the tech stack have the most elaborate bureaucracies and systems for speech regulation, which is one reason why they have drawn the most attention.

In general, platform companies like social media have the ability to govern their end users by creating and enforcing rules and norms for appropriate behavior on the platform.[11] In many cases, these companies and other private infrastructure owners can surveil and regulate speech more quickly and effectively than territorial governments can.[12] There is simply too much speech and much of it is anonymous or beyond territorial governments' borders. As a result, territorial governments often try to coerce or co-opt private infrastructure owners to surveil and regulate speech for them.[13] Moreover, because some of these infrastructure owners are global corporations, territorial governments and the European Union, through their internet policies, can affect how these global companies regulate speech in other parts of the world.[14]

This pluralist system of speech regulation is far more complicated than the dyadic system that produced First Amendment law in the twentieth century. But for convenience, we can think of the new system as a kind of triangle of three different kinds of relationships. Together, these relationships form the free speech triangle.[15]

---

[9] Evelyn Douek, Moderated Content, *Content Moderation in the Stack*, Stanford L. Sch. (Oct. 27, 2022), https://law.stanford.edu/podcasts/content-moderation-in-the-stack [https://perma.cc/GS3S-YRL6] ("When we talk about content moderation, we often focus on companies at the application layer of the internet, like the Facebooks and Twitters of the world.").

[10] Fowler & Alcantara, *supra* note 8.

[11] Kate Klonick, *The New Governors: The People, Rules, and Processes Governing Online Speech*, 131 Harv. L. Rev. 1598, 1635–48 (2018) (describing the development of content moderation bureaucracies at Facebook, YouTube, and Twitter).

[12] Balkin, *Free Speech Is a Triangle*, *supra* note 7, at 2019–20.

[13] *Id.*

[14] Jack M. Balkin, *Free Speech Versus the First Amendment*, 70 UCLA L. Rev. 1206, 1220–21 (2023) [hereinafter Balkin, *Free Speech Versus the First Amendment*]; Daphne Keller, *Who Do You Sue? State and Platform Hybrid Power over Online Speech*, Hoover Inst. 7 (Jan. 29, 2019), https://www.hoover.org/sites/default/files/research/docs/who-do-you-sue-state-and-platform-hybrid-power-over-online-speech_0.pdf [https://perma.cc/2KE7-6JUW] (describing cross-border effects of speech regulation).

[15] Balkin, *Free Speech Is a Triangle*, *supra* note 7, at 2012.

First, governments continue to regulate the speech of private individuals (or privately owned media). This is "old-school" speech regulation and it is the traditional subject of most of First Amendment speech and press law.[16]

Second, governments attempt to regulate the owners of private infrastructure up and down the tech stack in order to harness the latter's superior capacities for surveillance and speech regulation. This is "new-school" speech regulation, and it is one of the central concerns of free speech theory in the digital age.[17]

Countries often engage in new-school speech regulation because they want global platform owners to find and take down or demote content that is illegal in their jurisdiction or that they otherwise do not like. The European Union has elaborate rules of this kind, and it has effectively harnessed the largest digital media companies to act as a sort of private bureaucracy of first resort for speech regulation.[18] On the other hand, populist politicians, especially on the right, may regulate platforms in the opposite direction: They may try to prevent platforms from removing or demoting certain content.[19] That is because they fear that social media companies are biased and will discriminate against their ideological supporters and political allies. The Texas and Florida statutes at issue in *Moody* involve this kind of new-school speech regulation.

The third set of relationships in the free speech triangle is the relationship between the owners and operators of digital infrastructure and end users. This is a relationship of private governance,[20] and it is also at issue in *Moody*. By governance, I simply mean the ability to establish rules and norms and enforce them against other people in a community or an organization.[21]

Infrastructure owners govern what end users do by establishing rules and policies through a combination of contract and software

[16] *Id.* at 2015.

[17] *Id.* at 2015–16.

[18] *Id.* at 2030; *see also* Hannah Bloch-Wehba, *Global Platform Governance: Private Power in the Shadow of the State*, 72 SMU L. Rev. 27, 29 (2019) ("[P]latforms are acting as regulators or bureaucracies—implementing the favored policy solutions of executive and legislative branch actors—on a global scale.").

[19] Balkin, *Free Speech Versus the First Amendment*, *supra* note 14, at 1217.

[20] Balkin, *Free Speech in the Algorithmic Society*, *supra* note 7, at 1182–84; Balkin, *Free Speech Is a Triangle*, *supra* note 7, at 2021–25.

[21] Balkin, *Free Speech Is a Triangle*, *supra* note 7, at 2021.

code. Through a bureaucracy of content moderators, an army of programmers, and a collection of algorithms, large social media platforms can promote, demote, slow down, block, remove, or label end-user content. They can suspend end users temporarily or kick them off the platform entirely.[22] In fact, most of the companies up and down the tech stack can govern and affect access to end-user content, but social media platforms have the most methods at their disposal.

Although platforms are governors, it is important to recognize how different they are from states. The private governors of the digital public sphere have fewer and less potent sanctions than territorial governments. They can kick people off their sites but they cannot put them in jail, for example. They also lack democratic legitimacy to enforce their norms and rules. Their right to govern ultimately depends on the laws of the states in which they operate. *Moody* involves an attempt by two states to change the rules of private governance.

First Amendment law was designed for a dyadic system of speech regulation, in which the state is the central threat to freedom of expression. It was not designed for a pluralist system in which some private actors are both speakers and governors of the speech of large populations. In some cases that difference does not matter too much. Sometimes the free speech interests of end users and platforms are aligned, for example, when governments order internet service providers to filter content or hold social media companies liable for hosting speech.[23] In these cases of new-school speech regulation, courts are likely to recognize free speech rights both in end users and in private digital companies. These situations are akin to laws that pressure distributors like book stores and movie theaters not to sell or display the speech of others.[24] The existing free speech doctrines built for a dyadic model of speech regulation work tolerably well in these situations.

---

[22] *See* Eric Goldman, *Content Moderation Remedies*, 28 MICH. TECH. L. REV. 1, 23–40 (2021) (cataloging the alternatives available to digital companies).

[23] *See, e.g.*, Woodhull Freedom Found. v. United States, 948 F.3d 363, 371–74 (D.C. Cir. 2020) (individual speakers had standing to raise challenge to modifications to Section 230 intermediary immunity rules); Ctr. for Democracy & Tech. v. Pappert, 337 F. Supp. 2d 606, 611 (E.D. Pa. 2004) (upholding individual speakers' First Amendment challenge to a Pennsylvania state statute requiring internet service providers (ISPs) to block access to websites displaying child pornography).

[24] Bantam Books, Inc. v. Sullivan, 372 U.S. 58 (1963) (striking down informal censorship system); Smith v. California, 361 U.S. 147 (1959) (striking down law holding bookstore owner criminally liable for obscene publications).

But there are many cases in which the free speech interests of end users and digital companies are not aligned—for example, when end users complain that social media companies are censoring or demoting their content. Then the differences between the older dyadic and the newer pluralist system may matter a great deal. In fact, the free speech triangle perpetually generates conflicts between private infrastructure owners and end users.[25] In particular, social media companies and end users often assert conflicting free speech interests. The companies claim that they have a free speech right to organize and govern the content that appears on their sites. End users argue that they have a right to speak free from interference by the platforms.

Generally speaking, U.S. First Amendment law has a difficult time addressing situations in which two private parties claim conflicting free speech interests.[26] That is because it normally views free speech rights as something that private parties have against governments, and not against other private parties. By contrast, European law recognizes that constitutional provisions may have a horizontal effect that imposes certain constitutional norms on private actors.[27] Between the 1940s and 1960s, the U.S. Supreme Court flirted with a similar idea through

---

[25] Balkin, *Free Speech Versus the First Amendment*, *supra* note 14, at 1221–22.

[26] An important example is *Denver Area Educational Telecommunications Consortium, Inc. v. FCC*, 518 U.S. 727 (1996), which produced multiple opinions. Justice Breyer's plurality opinion explained the problem that standard First Amendment doctrine faces:

> We recognize that the First Amendment, the terms of which apply to governmental action, ordinarily does not itself throw into constitutional doubt the decisions of private citizens to permit, or to restrict, speech—and this is so ordinarily even where those decisions take place within the framework of a regulatory regime such as broadcasting. Were that not so, courts might have to face the difficult, and potentially restrictive, practical task of deciding which, among any number of private parties involved in providing a program (for example, networks, station owners, program editors, and program producers), is the "speaker" whose rights may not be abridged, and who is the speech-restricting "censor."

Denver Area Ed. Telecomms. Consortium, 518 U.S. at 737 n.1.

[27] *See* András Koltay, *The Protection of Freedom of Expression From Social Media Platforms*, 73 MERCER L. REV. 523, 564–67 (2022) (describing how German law applies free speech norms horizontally to social media companies); Stephen Gardbaum, *The "Horizontal Effect" of Constitutional Rights*, 102 MICH. L. REV. 387, 388 (2003) ("In recent years, the horizontal position has been adopted to varying degrees, and after systematic scholarly and judicial debate, in Ireland, Canada, Germany, South Africa, and the European Union, among others."); Giovanni De Gregorio, *From Constitutional Freedoms to the Power of the Platforms: Protecting Fundamental Rights Online in the Algorithmic Society*, 11 EUR. J. LEGAL STUD. 65, 101 (2019) (arguing for horizontal effect of constitutional norms against privately owned platforms because they exercise public functions).

relaxing the doctrine of state action and applying First Amendment norms to private actors like company towns and shopping malls.[28] But the Court eventually abandoned the attempt and moved to a fairly rigid distinction between public and private action.[29]

As a result of the inflexibility of American First Amendment law, if two private parties claim conflicting speech rights, courts are likely to award First Amendment rights, if at all, only to one of them.[30] End users can communicate with each other on social media only because social media companies allow them to use the companies' property. Current First Amendment doctrine tends to identify free speech rights with the ownership of private property.[31] That means that when the free speech claims of end users and digital companies conflict, U.S. courts are likely to assign First Amendment rights to digital companies and not to end users.[32]

That is not the only possible solution, of course. Courts could hold that the property rights of digital companies do not encompass full rights to govern or exclude and award First Amendment rights against them to end users. But that has not been the tendency of U.S. courts at least since the 1960s. The one major exception has been broadcast regulation, where the Supreme Court has held that

---

[28] Amalgamated Food Emps. Union Loc. 590 v. Logan Valley Plaza, Inc., 391 U.S. 308, 317 (1968) (holding that a private shopping mall could not prevent individuals from peacefully picketing on the premises); Marsh v. Alabama, 326 U.S. 501, 509 (1946) (holding that leafleters had First Amendment rights to distribute literature in a privately owned company town).

[29] *See* Jackson v. Metro. Edison Co., 419 U.S. 345, 352 (1974) (holding that *Marsh* applies only "in the exercise by a private entity of powers traditionally exclusively reserved to the State"); Manhattan Cmty. Access Corp. v. Halleck, 587 U.S. 802, 812 (2019) (upholding cable company's right to refuse access to speakers because a "private entity is not ordinarily constrained by the First Amendment"); Pac. Gas & Elec. Co. v. Pub. Utils. Comm'n, 475 U.S. 1, 20–21 (1986) (plurality opinion) (rejecting right of access to mailings by privately owned public utility company); Columbia Broad. Sys., Inc. v. Democratic Nat'l Comm., 412 U.S. 94, 126–28 (1973) (rejecting right of access to broadcasting networks); Hudgens v. NLRB, 424 U.S. 507, 520 (1976) (rejecting right of access to shopping malls for protest).

[30] Balkin, *Free Speech Versus the First Amendment*, *supra* note 14, at 1222.

[31] For the classic argument against this confusion of speech and private property, see Owen M. Fiss, *Free Speech and Social Structure*, 71 Iowa L. Rev. 1405, 1414 (1986) ("The state of affairs protected by the first amendment can just as easily be threatened by a private citizen as by an agency of the state. A corporation operating on private capital can be as much a threat to the richness of public debate as a government agency.").

[32] Balkin, *Free Speech Versus the First Amendment*, *supra* note 14, at 1225–26; *see also* Niva Elkin-Koren, Giovanni De Gregorio & Maayan Perel, *Social Media as Contractual Networks: A Bottom up Check on Content Moderation*, 107 Iowa L. Rev. 987, 1013–14 (2022) (noting that American courts have so far refused to give horizontal effect to First Amendment rights against privately owned social media companies).

the rights of listeners sometimes may take precedence over the free speech and property rights of broadcasters. That is the point of the doctrine of *Red Lion v. FCC*,[33] which held that "[i]t is the right of the viewers and listeners, not the right of the broadcasters, which is paramount."[34] But that doctrine is best justified on the grounds that broadcasters gain access to spectrum through a license with the government, and the government may, as a condition of the license, require the broadcaster to act in the interests of listeners.[35] Five years after *Red Lion*, the Court famously declined to extend that reasoning to privately owned newspapers in *Miami Herald Publishing Co. v. Tornillo*.[36] Because newspapers did not need government licenses to operate, the Court retreated to its usual conflation of speech and property rights.

Digital companies try to use the First Amendment as an anti-regulatory device.[37] This strategy is not limited to social media companies, of course. Over the past half century, more and more businesses have figured out ways to use the First Amendment to attack government regulations of their businesses.[38] But digital media companies find this strategy especially attractive. Because they are in the business of hosting and curating speech, they will try to claim that regulations of their business models violate their free speech and press rights under the First Amendment.

In response, people who want to reform social media will try to neutralize these First Amendment claims. For the reasons stated above, they are unlikely to succeed in getting courts to create European-style

---

[33] 395 U.S. 367 (1969).

[34] *Id.* at 390.

[35] *See id.* at 379–80, 391, 394.

[36] 418 U.S. 241 (1974).

[37] *See* Jack M. Balkin, *Digital Speech and Democratic Culture: A Theory of Freedom of Expression for the Information Society*, 79 N.Y.U. L. Rev. 1, 26–27 (2004) (arguing that in the Second Gilded Age, "[t]he right to speak has been recast as a right to be free from business regulation," and that "[f]reedom of speech is becoming a generalized right against economic regulation of the information industries," while "[p]roperty is becoming the right of the information industries to control how ordinary people use digital content").

[38] Robert Post & Amanda Shanor, *Adam Smith's First Amendment*, 128 Harv. L. Rev. F. 165, 166–67 (2015) ("Across the country, plaintiffs are using the First Amendment to challenge commercial regulations, in matters ranging from public health to data privacy. It is no exaggeration to observe that the First Amendment has become a powerful engine of constitutional deregulation." (footnote omitted)); Jack M. Balkin, *Some Realism About Pluralism: Legal Realist Approaches to the First Amendment*, 1990 Duke L. Rev. 375, 384, 386 (predicting the "ideological drift" of the free speech principle to serve conservative and business interests).

doctrines of horizontal effect that recognize constitutional speech rights on both sides. Therefore reformers on both the left and the right will pursue a strategy of *de-constitutionalization*. That is, they will try to get the courts to adopt legal theories that turn conflicts over speech claims into non-constitutional questions of statutory or administrative law or technological design.[39] That is what Texas and Florida tried to do in *Moody*. The two states passed laws that, in effect, gave end users statutory free speech and due process rights against digital media companies. The point of de-constitutionalization is judicial restraint. It relies on the political branches to enforce free speech rights; in this case, against the private platforms that govern speech in the digital age.[40]

In its current form, American First Amendment doctrine is ill-suited to deal with many of the complexities of the new pluralist system and the free speech triangle. There is a strong tendency to try to wish away the problem by forcing speech questions into the mold of the older, dyadic system of speech regulation.

For example, *Murthy v. Missouri*,[41] decided the same Term as *Moody*, presented a fairly standard question of new-school speech regulation. The government put pressure on social media companies to take down or demote content about public health that the government found misleading, false, or otherwise problematic. The plaintiffs tried to avoid the complications of the free speech triangle by arguing that the social media companies had not acted independently but only out of government pressure.[42] This reduced the number of relevant parties to two—the state and the end users—with social media companies treated as mere instruments of the state. Plaintiffs requested an injunction against future communications between the state and social media companies to prevent the government from directing social media companies in the future.[43]

The Supreme Court held that the plaintiffs lacked standing because, among other things, social media companies were not mere puppets of the state but independent actors. They did not always accede to the government's wishes. Their own rules and norms gave

[39] Balkin, *Free Speech Versus the First Amendment*, *supra* note 14, at 1211.

[40] *Id.*

[41] 603 U.S. 43 (2024).

[42] *Id.* at 49–50.

[43] *Id.* at 54.

social media companies independent reasons for blocking and demoting content, and there was no guarantee that they would do the state's bidding in the future.[44] Thus, the plaintiffs lacked standing because the relief they requested would not clearly redress the harms they complained of.[45] Getting an injunction against the government would not necessarily give them what they actually wanted: namely, stopping powerful privately owned social media companies from regulating their speech. The attempt to fit the case into the old dyadic model failed because the Court recognized that there were two different sets of speech regulators who sometimes cooperated and sometimes did not. That is, it recognized one of the new realities of the free speech triangle. In the process, however, the Court made it harder to sue the government for unconstitutionally pressuring social media platforms.

The problem of the free speech triangle was also front-and-center in *Moody*. It involved a conflict between the speech claims of platforms and of end users, with the states attempting to protect their citizens' speech through new-school speech regulation. But once again, the litigants tried to force the issues into the older, dyadic model. Texas and Florida sought to protect end users' free speech rights through a strategy of deconstitutionalization. They argued that the platforms were not exercising First Amendment rights at all and therefore the states could adjust private rights between the two sides.[46] In the alternative, Texas and Florida argued that their laws were content-neutral regulations of time, place, and manner or regulations of commercial speech that survived First Amendment scrutiny.[47] The platforms, by contrast, argued that their activities were fully First Amendment-protected, while the speech rights of end users had no constitutional relevance. In fact, it was unconstitutional for states to try to protect end users' speech rights.

Faced with these conflicting approaches, the Court temporized. It sent the case back to the lower courts with a series of instructions.[48] The Court's opinion gave social media companies much of what they wanted. But it left open many important questions about permissible regulation of digital platforms.

---

[44] *Id.* at 73–74.

[45] *Id.*

[46] NetChoice, LLC v. Att'y Gen., 34 F.4th 1196, 1208 (11th Cir. 2022); NetChoice, L.L.C. v. Paxton, 49 F.4th 439, 482 (5th Cir. 2022).

[47] *See NetChoice*, 34 F.4th at 1208; *Paxton*, 49 F.4th at 445, 482.

[48] Moody v. NetChoice, LLC, 603 U.S. 707, 717–19 (2024).

II. The Texas and Florida Statutes

To explain what the Court did and why, we have to understand the complexities of the Florida and Texas statutes.

Florida's law regulates "social media platforms," defined as those that have annual gross revenue of over $100 million or more than 100 million monthly active users.[49] Florida requires that social media platforms must apply their standards for disciplining end users and their standards for content moderation, recommendation, and prioritization "in a consistent manner among its users on the platform."[50] It also requires written notice within seven days with a "thorough rationale" for its decision whenever a social media platform censors or limits exposure to content or de-platforms a user.[51] The company must also include "a thorough explanation" of any algorithms used "to identify or flag the user's content or material as objectionable."[52] It creates a private right of action with statutory and punitive damages to enforce these provisions.[53]

Notwithstanding the requirement of consistency, Florida's law has special rules for "journalistic enterprises,"[54] which include most newspapers, cable channels, broadcast media, and popular video channels that "[p]ublish[] 100 hours of audio or video available online with at least 100 million viewers annually."[55] Social media platforms "may not take any action to censor, deplatform, or shadow ban [i.e., limit exposure to] a journalistic enterprise based on the content of its publication or broadcast."[56] However, journalistic enterprises can pay social media companies to prioritize their content, which, in effect, can give them favored exposure over other journalistic enterprises and end users.[57] Florida also has special rules for political candidates. Social media platforms may not prioritize or demote content *by* candidates or *about* candidates.[58]

---

[49] Fla. Stat. § 501.2041(1)(g) (2023).

[50] *Id.* § 501.2041(2)(b).

[51] *Id.* § 501.2041(2)(d)–(3)(d). "[S]hadow-banning" is defined as any action that limits exposure to content. *Id.* § 501.2041(1)(f).

[52] *Id.* § 501.2041(3)(d).

[53] *Id.* § 501.2041(6).

[54] *Id.* § 501.2041(2)(h).

[55] *Id.* § 501.2041(1)(d).

[56] *Id.* § 501.2041(2)(j). There is an exception for moderating obscene content. *Id.*

[57] *Id.*

[58] *Id.* § 501.2041(2)(h).

Florida's law was clearly aimed at social media companies like Facebook or YouTube that provide feeds of content to end users. But the statute is very badly drafted, and so it turns out that Florida's definition of social media platforms is much broader. It includes "any information service, system, Internet search engine, or access software provider [that] [p]rovides or enables computer access by multiple users to a computer server" that has enough revenue and customers.[59] This would include email services, online stores, ride-share services like Uber, and a host of other applications.

Texas regulates "social media platform[s]" with over fifty million monthly active users.[60] It defines a "social media platform" as any "Internet website or application that is open to the public, allows a user to create an account, and enables users to communicate with other users for the primary purpose of posting information, comments, messages, or images."[61]

Texas's law provides that "[a] social media platform may not censor a user, a user's expression, or a user's ability to receive the expression of another person" based on viewpoint.[62] To "censor" means "to block, ban, remove, deplatform, demonetize, de-boost, restrict, deny equal access or visibility to, or otherwise discriminate against expression."[63] When a platform removes content (as opposed to other forms of "censor[ship]"), Texas requires that "concurrently with the removal" the platform must "notify the user" and "explain the reason the content was removed."[64] Users have a right to appeal the decision, and the platform must respond to the user's appeal within fourteen days.[65]

Like Florida, Texas makes exceptions to its ban on viewpoint discrimination.[66] In addition to censoring illegal content, social media platforms are free to censor content that "directly incites criminal activity" or that "consists of specific threats of violence targeted against

---

[59] *Id.* § 501.2041(1)(g).

[60] Tex. Bus. & Com. Code Ann. §§ 120.001(1), 120.002(b) (West 2023).

[61] *Id.* § 120.001(1).

[62] Tex. Civ. Prac. & Rem. Code Ann. § 143A.002(a) (West 2023).

[63] *Id.* § 143A.001(1).

[64] Tex. Bus. & Com. Code Ann. § 120.103(a)(1) (West 2023).

[65] *See id.* §§ 120.103(a)(2), 120.104. The right of appeal does not apply when a platform cannot locate a user or when the content is the basis of a law enforcement investigation. *Id.* § 120.103(b).

[66] Tex. Civ. Prac. & Rem. Code Ann. § 143A.006 (West 2023).

a person or group because of their race, color, disability, religion, national origin or ancestry, age, sex, or status as a peace officer or judge."[67] Platforms may also censor based on referrals from organizations that seek to "prevent[] the sexual exploitation of children and protect[] survivors of sexual abuse from ongoing harassment."[68]

III. What Kind of Challenge?

Although Texas's and Florida's laws were clearly aimed at the largest social media sites like Facebook and YouTube, they defined "social media platforms" in ways that reach well beyond those companies and include a host of online applications and services.[69] This definition created a problem for the Justices in *Moody*. If, as the Justices believed, NetChoice was raising a First Amendment facial challenge, it would have to show that Texas's and Florida's laws were substantially overbroad.[70] This meant showing that "a substantial number of [the challenged law's] applications are unconstitutional, judged in relation to the statute's plainly legitimate sweep."[71] This test is more forgiving than the general rule for facial challenges that do not involve the First Amendment. The latter doctrine, as explained in *United States v. Salerno*, requires showing that there is "no set of circumstances . . . under which the [law] would be valid."[72] Even under the First Amendment test of substantial overbreadth, however, the Justices believed that there might be a large number of covered applications where a nondiscrimination rule might be constitutional.[73]

Apparently, the issue was raised for the first time in oral argument before the Court.[74] The resulting uncertainty led the Justices to vacate

---

[67] *Id.*

[68] *Id.*

[69] Texas sought to limit the reach of its law by specifying that it did not cover ISPs, email providers, nor any online service, website, or app consisting "primarily of news, sports, entertainment, or other information or content that is not user generated but is preselected by the provider." Tex. Bus. & Com. Code Ann. § 120.001(1) (West 2023). Even so, the statute covers a wide range of online applications for sending and posting messages.

[70] Moody v. NetChoice, LLC, 603 U.S. 707, 723–24 (2024); United States v. Hansen, 599 U.S. 762, 769–70 (2023).

[71] Ams. for Prosperity Found. v. Bonta, 594 U.S. 595, 615 (2021).

[72] United States v. Salerno, 481 U.S. 739, 745 (1987).

[73] *Moody*, 603 U.S. at 724–26; *id.* at 787–88 (Alito, J., concurring in the judgment).

[74] *Id.* at 724 (majority opinion); Transcript of Oral Argument at 6, 29, 67, 125–26, 151–53, *Moody*, 603 U.S. 707 (Nos. 22-277 & 22-555).

the decisions below and send the cases back to the lower courts for clarification about which applications were covered and therefore whether a facial challenge could succeed.[75]

In fact, there was a way to dispose of the cases on the merits that avoided these problems. One can challenge a statute facially either because a large proportion of its applications are unconstitutional or because the law imposes an unconstitutional requirement on its face.[76] That is how the Court deals with laws that, on their face, make content-based, viewpoint-based, and speaker-based distinctions. The Court normally does not ask whether these laws have a significant number of constitutional applications; rather, it simply applies strict (or heightened) scrutiny and (usually) strikes the statute down.[77] A good analogy is to equal protection doctrine. If a statute on its face classifies on the basis of race or sex, the Court does not first ask whether there are a substantial number of constitutional applications. It applies strict or heightened scrutiny.[78]

The Florida statute makes content-based and speaker-based distinctions. Florida tells platforms that they must apply their content moderation and recommendation rules consistently except for posts by a political candidate (a speaker-based rule) or about a political candidate (a content-based rule). Platforms may not demote or deprioritize these posts.[79] Florida also exempts content by "journalistic enterprises" from removal, demotion, and prioritization rules entirely (a speaker-based exemption).[80]

---

[75] *Moody*, 603 U.S. at 724–26. As Evelyn Douek and Genevieve Laker have pointed out, this application of the substantial overbreadth doctrine rewarded bad legislative drafting. The states avoided a facial challenge because they used such broad and unclear terms, which is normally what overbreadth doctrine is designed to prevent. Evelyn Douek & Genevieve Lakier, *Lochner.com?*, 138 Harv. L. Rev. 100, 167–68 (2024).

[76] *See, e.g.*, City of Austin v. Reagan Nat'l Advert. of Austin, LLC, 596 U.S. 61, 69 (2022) (finding that a regulation of speech is facially content-based under the First Amendment if it "target[s] speech based on its communicative content"—that is, if it "applies to particular speech because of the topic discussed or the idea or message expressed" (quoting Reed v. Town of Gilbert, 576 U.S. 155, 163 (2015))); R.A.V. v. City of St. Paul, 505 U.S. 377, 381–82 & n.3 (1992) (explaining that a showing of substantial overbreadth is not necessary for facial invalidity when a statute is invalid on its face because it makes content-based distinctions).

[77] *E.g.*, *Reed*, 576 U.S. at 163.

[78] *See* Katie Eyer, *As-Applied Equal Protection*, 59 Harv. C.R.-C.L. L. Rev. 49, 50 (2024) (noting that "the vast majority of Equal Protection claims have been brought—and decided—as facial challenges").

[79] Fla. Stat. § 501.2041(2)(h) (2023).

[80] *Id.* § 501.2041(2)(j); *see* Barr v. Am. Ass'n of Pol. Consultants, Inc., 591 U.S. 610, 621 (2020) (holding that a restriction on all robocalls except for those that attempted to collect

Texas's statute makes viewpoint-based distinctions. It prohibits social media from viewpoint-based moderation and recommendations. But it makes exceptions for threats based on certain viewpoints—"because of . . . race, color, disability, religion, national origin or ancestry, age, sex, or status as a peace officer or judge."[81] To be sure, threats are generally unprotected expression.[82] But Texas does not relax its rule for all threats, only for threats based on specified disfavored criteria. In *R.A.V. v. City of St. Paul*,[83] the Court held that similar distinctions in a ban on fighting words were viewpoint-based: "Displays containing abusive invective, no matter how vicious or severe, are permissible unless they are addressed to one of the specified disfavored topics."[84]

Texas's statute also makes speaker-based distinctions. It makes an exception to the general ban on viewpoint-based moderation when a social media platform acts according to a referral from an organization that seeks to "prevent[] the sexual exploitation of children and protect[] survivors of sexual abuse from ongoing harassment."[85] This rule does not actually require that the referral be about a post that contains child sexual abuse material or harassment, only that the source of the referral comes from a favored speaker. Referrals from any other source—even about the very same content—receive no exemption.

Thus, without remanding, the Court could have applied heightened or strict scrutiny, and, if the statutes failed the test, struck them down.[86] Why didn't the Court take this path? This resolution would not have decided what for most of the Justices was the crucial question—whether social media content moderation and recommendation systems are akin to editorial judgments protected by the First Amendment. The Fifth Circuit had denied that social media companies were engaged in protected First Amendment expression at all. Rather, the Fifth Circuit argued, they were only engaged in

---

government debts was content-based and subject to strict scrutiny); *Barr*, 591 U.S. at 619–20 ("'[L]aws favoring some speakers over others demand strict scrutiny when the legislature's speaker preference reflects a content preference.'" (quoting *Reed*, 576 U.S. at 170)).

[81] Tex. Civ. Prac. & Rem. Code Ann. § 143A.006 (West 2023).

[82] Virginia v. Black, 538 U.S. 343, 359 (2003); Watts v. United States, 394 U.S. 705, 708 (1969) (per curiam).

[83] 505 U.S. 377 (1992).

[84] *Id.* at 391.

[85] Tex. Civ. Prac. & Rem. Code Ann. § 143A.006 (West 2023).

[86] *See* Barr v. Am. Ass'n of Pol. Consultants, Inc., 591 U.S. 610, 619–21 (2020). Note that the offending parts of the statutes might be severable, leaving the rest in place.

censorship.[87] As is obvious from Justice Kagan's majority opinion, many of the Justices wanted to send a strong signal that this was not a correct understanding of the First Amendment.[88] Otherwise the Fifth Circuit might continue to apply the same (incorrect) views in deciding whether the statutes were substantially overbroad.[89] Conversely, Justices Samuel Alito, Clarence Thomas, and Neil Gorsuch wanted to preserve the possibility that states could impose nondiscrimination rules on social media companies or treat them like common carriers.[90] This would greatly restrict the companies' ability to make moderation and recommendation decisions. However, the content-based, viewpoint-based, and speaker-based exemptions in the two statutes undermined the claim that they were genuine common carrier regulations.

IV. Editorial Choices and Expressive Products

Because the Fifth Circuit had held that platforms were not engaged in speech when they engaged in content moderation and recommendations,[91] Justice Kagan's majority opinion sought to clarify the relevant First Amendment principles. When governments "order[] a party to provide a forum for someone else's views,"[92] she explained, this "implicates the First Amendment . . . if, though only if, the regulated party is engaged in its own expressive activity, which the mandated access would alter or disrupt."[93] And "expressive activity includes presenting a curated compilation of speech originally created by others."[94]

Justice Kagan argued that "[t]o the extent that social-media platforms create expressive products, they receive the First Amendment's protection."[95] When social media moderate content and recommend

---

[87] NetChoice, L.L.C. v. Paxton, 49 F.4th 439, 445 (5th Cir. 2022).

[88] Moody v. NetChoice, LLC, 603 U.S. 707, 726–27 (2024).

[89] *Id.* at 727. Justice Ketanji Brown Jackson concurred on the basic statement of first principles but did not join in the majority's application of them to social media companies. *Id.* at 748 (Jackson, J., concurring in part and concurring in the judgment).

[90] *Id.* at 782 n.17, 785 n.19 (Alito, J., concurring in the judgment); *id.* at 794 (Thomas, J., concurring in the judgment).

[91] *Id.* at 726–27 (majority opinion) (citing *Paxton*, 49 F.4th at 482, 494).

[92] *Id.* at 728.

[93] *Id.*

[94] *Id.*

[95] *Id.* at 716.

content to end users, are they producing an "expressive product?" Yes, Kagan held. "Deciding on the third-party speech that will be included in or excluded from a compilation—and then organizing and presenting the included items—is expressive activity of its own. And that activity results in a distinctive expressive product."[96]

Kagan repeatedly described content moderation and recommendations as "editorial choice[s]," analogizing what social media companies do to what newspaper editors do.[97] Therefore the central precedent was *Tornillo*,[98] in which the Court struck down a Florida right-of-reply requirement for newspapers because it interfered with newspapers' editorial judgments. The First Amendment, Kagan explained, "offers protection when an entity engaging in expressive activity, including compiling and curating others' speech, is directed to accommodate messages it would prefer to exclude. '[T]he editorial function itself is an aspect of speech.'"[99]

It does not matter that "a compiler includes most items and excludes just a few."[100] Kagan pointed to *Hurley v. Irish-American Gay, Lesbian and Bisexual Group of Boston, Inc.*,[101] which upheld the right of the organizers of a St. Patrick's Day parade to accept almost everyone as a participant except a gay and lesbian group seeking to convey a gay pride message.[102] Social media companies may want to allow the vast majority of speakers and messages on their sites—after all, their profits depend on amassing as large an audience as possible. But they still retain the right to remove content they do not like and speakers who violate their community standards. It also does not matter whether or not people "wrongly attribute to [the platforms] the views in an individual post."[103] First Amendment protection (or the lack thereof) does not turn on the risk of misattribution.[104]

Justice Alito, concurring only in the judgment that the cases should return to the lower courts, offered a narrower, three-part test

---

[96] *Id.* at 731. Justice Jackson did not join in this part of the opinion.

[97] *Id.* at 717, 726, 729, 732, 739.

[98] 418 U.S. 241 (1974).

[99] *Moody*, 603 U.S. at 731 (quoting Denver Area Ed. Telecomms. Consortium, Inc. v. FCC, 518 U.S. 727, 737 (1996) (plurality opinion)).

[100] *Id.* at 732.

[101] 515 U.S. 557 (1995).

[102] *Id.* at 561.

[103] *Moody*, 603 U.S. at 739.

[104] *Id.* at 739–40.

for First Amendment protection. "First, a claimant must establish that its practice is to exercise 'editorial discretion in the selection and presentation' of the content it hosts."[105] "Second, the host must use the compilation of speech to express 'some sort of collective point'—even if only at a fairly abstract level."[106] "Finally, a compiler must show that its "own message [is] affected by the speech it [is] forced to accommodate."[107] In short, "the First Amendment protects only those compilations that are 'inherently expressive' in their own right, meaning that they select and present speech created by other persons in order 'to spread [the compiler's] own message.'"[108]

Under Justice Alito's test, it is unclear whether social media companies would enjoy First Amendment protection for their content moderation and recommendation systems. First, because of the sheer volume of traffic that platforms must handle, much—if not most—content escapes notice and is never moderated. Second, social media platforms are not trying to send a single message; rather their goal is to allow end users to speak to each other consistent with the company's terms of service and community standards. Finally, because social media platforms are not trying to convey a single message, that message is not compromised by the inclusion of unmoderated content. Justice Alito, like Justice Thomas, wanted to keep open the possibility that states could subject large social media platforms to antidiscrimination rules or treat them like common carriers.[109] But Justice Kagan's majority opinion, which bestows First Amendment protection on content moderation and recommendation systems, rejects that possibility.

Because Facebook, YouTube, and Twitter had such an enormous impact on public opinion, Texas and Florida feared that the companies could use their power to silence people they disagreed with and elevate voices they supported. This would make them powerful and effective propagandists. Although Texas and Florida wanted to

---

[105] *Id.* at 782 (Alito, J., concurring in the judgment) (first citing Ark. Ed. Television Comm'n v. Forbes, 523 U.S. 666, 674 (1998); and then citing *Hurley*, 515 U.S. at 574).

[106] *Id.* at 783 (citing *Hurley*, 515 U.S. at 568).

[107] *Id.* at 784 (citing Rumsfeld v. F. for Acad. & Institutional Rights, Inc. (*FAIR*), 547 U.S. 47, 63 (2006)).

[108] *Id.* at 781 (first citing *FAIR*, 547 U.S. at 66; and then citing Pac. Gas & Elec. Co. v. Pub. Utils. Comm'n of Cal., 475 U.S. 1, 10 (1986) (plurality opinion)).

[109] *Id.* at 782 n.17, 785 n.19; *id.* at 794 (Thomas, J., concurring in the judgment).

protect conservative voices from liberal domination, these fears were soon realized in the opposite ideological direction. In 2022, while the NetChoice litigation was ongoing, one of the world's richest people, Elon Musk, purchased Twitter and eventually renamed it X. Although he claimed that he would defend freedom of speech against the "woke mind virus," he soon abandoned any pretense of neutrality and used his control over the platform to favor conservative voices and promote Donald Trump in the 2024 election.[110] He also throttled traffic to news media he disliked.[111]

Justice Kagan emphasized that concerns about the power of social media companies to skew public opinion and throttle access to speech by disfavored voices could not justify regulating how social media moderated and prioritized content. She explained that social media companies are private actors who enjoy the same First Amendment rights as all other private parties. "[A] State may not interfere with private actors' speech to advance its own vision of ideological balance."[112] That issue was settled long ago, Kagan explained. In *Tornillo*, the "Court devoted six pages of its opinion to recounting a critique of the then-current media environment—in particular, the disproportionate 'influen[ce]' of a few speakers—similar to one heard today. It made no difference."[113] Today's social media companies may be far more wealthy and powerful than earlier media barons could have dreamed of. But greater power does not allow government to impose a greater responsibility.

"On the spectrum of dangers to free expression," Kagan insisted, "there are few greater than allowing the government to change the speech of private actors in order to achieve its own conception of speech nirvana. That is why we have said in so many contexts that the government may not 'restrict the speech of some elements of our society in order to enhance the relative voice of others.'"[114] Here

---

[110] Philip Bump, *The Demise of the 'Public Square' Argument for X*, Wash. Post (Nov. 27, 2024), https://www.washingtonpost.com/politics/2024/11/27/musk-twitter-bluesky-trump [https://archive.ph/HBHxU]; Tim Higgins, *Why Elon Musk Won't Stop Talking About a 'Woke Mind Virus,'* Wall St. J. (Dec. 23, 2023, 5:30 AM ET), https://www.wsj.com/tech/elon-musk-woke-mind-virus-41576aa6 [https://archive.ph/WfLaa].

[111] Jeremy B. Merrill & Drew Harwell, *Elon Musk's X Is Throttling Traffic to Websites He Dislikes*, Wash. Post (Aug. 16, 2023), https://www.washingtonpost.com/technology/2023/08/15/twitter-x-links-delayed [https://archive.ph/qlQBZ].

[112] *Moody*, 603 U.S. at 741.

[113] *Id.* at 733.

[114] *Id.* at 742 (quoting Buckley v. Valeo, 424 U.S. 1, 48–49 (1976) (per curiam)).

Kagan quoted *Buckley v. Valeo*, a 1976 campaign finance decision that symbolizes the Court's conflation of freedom of speech with property rights.

V. Structural Regulation of Digital Media

Although *Moody* holds that social media recommendations and content moderation are First Amendment protected activities, it did not hold that all regulations that affect these activities are unconstitutional, much less that strict scrutiny always applies.

In particular, Justice Kagan distinguished the two *Turner Broadcasting System, Inc., v. FCC* decisions,[115] in which the Court held that Congress could require cable operators to carry local broadcast channels. These "must-carry" rules "interfere[d]" with the cable operators' "editorial discretion over which stations or programs to include in [their] repertoire."[116] But the Court applied intermediate scrutiny and upheld the rules even though they required cable operators to include channels they did not wish to carry. Congress's purpose, the Court explained, was not to interfere with editorial discretion—that would have been a content-based regulation that triggered strict scrutiny. Rather, Congress's goals were to "(1) preserv[e] the benefits of free, over the air local broadcast television, (2) promot[e] the widespread dissemination of information from a multiplicity of sources, and (3) promot[e] fair competition in the television programming market."[117] As Justice Kagan explained in *Moody*, Congress sought "to save the local-broadcast industry, so that it could continue to serve households without cable."[118] The loss of this industry would rob the public of important sources of information. But because cable companies held a "'monopolistic,' gatekeeping position," they could refuse to provide local broadcasting content to cable subscribers, threatening broadcasters' financial survival.[119] Congress's interest in preserving the benefits of free local broadcasting "was 'unrelated to

---

[115] Turner Broad. Sys., Inc. v. FCC (*Turner I*), 512 U.S. 622 (1994); Turner Broad. Sys., Inc. v. FCC (*Turner II*), 520 U.S. 180 (1997).

[116] *Turner I*, 512 U.S. at 636, 643–44.

[117] *Id.* at 662; *Turner II*, 520 U.S. at 189.

[118] *Moody*, 603 U.S. at 742 n.10.

[119] *Id.* (quoting Hurley v. Irish-Am. Gay, Lesbian & Bisexual Grp. of Bos., Inc., 515 U.S. 557, 577 (1995)).

the content of expression' disseminated by either cable or broadcast speakers."[120] Because "the Government's interest was 'not the alteration of speech' . . . the prospects of permissible regulation are entirely different."[121]

Moody thus leaves available structural regulation of digital media for reasons unrelated to the direct regulation of content and editorial judgment.[122] First, it preserves regulations designed to protect end-user privacy. Second, it preserves regulations designed to open up the market for social media services and promote competition and innovation.

The power that social media companies have over the digital public sphere is connected to their collection and control of data. They have collected and continue to collect enormous amounts of end-user data, which they can use to attract advertisers and employ in other applications and services. Most if not all of Google's and Meta's free services and applications are designed to collect data from end users. It is not too much of a stretch to say that Alphabet (Google's parent company) and Meta (which owns Facebook and Instagram) are actually global data collection and surveillance companies that offer social media products on the side. Congress can protect consumer privacy in digital media and regulate the collection and use of end-user data without second-guessing the editorial judgments of these companies. In general, courts treat regulations of the collection, collation, and use of consumer data—as opposed to regulations of the sale or distribution of data—either as regulations of conduct or as content-neutral, time, place, and manner regulations subject to intermediate scrutiny.[123]

---

[120] *Id.* (quoting *Turner I*, 512 U.S. at 647).

[121] *Id.* (quoting *Hurley*, 515 U.S. at 577).

[122] *See* C. Edwin Baker, Turner Broadcasting: *Content-Based Regulation of Persons and Presses*, 1994 Sup. Ct. Rev. 57, 81 (noting that structural regulation of communications industries "to advance its conception of a desirable communications order" has been ubiquitous).

[123] *See, e.g.*, Jack M. Balkin, *The Fiduciary Model of Privacy*, 133 Harv. L. Rev. F. 11, 30 (2020) ("Courts are more likely to treat restrictions on collection or use as not raising First Amendment questions at all, because they aim at conduct. In the alternative, courts may treat them as content-neutral time, place, and manner regulations." (footnotes omitted)); Neil M. Richards, *Reconciling Data Privacy and the First Amendment*, 52 UCLA L. Rev. 1149, 1182–86, 1190–92 (2005) (noting the ubiquity of collection and use restrictions that do not violate the First Amendment); *cf.* Bartnicki v. Vopper, 532 U.S. 514, 526 (2001) (treating privacy regulations as content-neutral); *Bartnicki*, 532 U.S. at 544 (Rehnquist, C.J., dissenting) (agreeing that restrictions on interception and disclosure were content-neutral); *see also* TikTok Inc. v. Garland, 145 S. Ct. 57 (2025) (holding that requiring divestiture to prevent data collection from a foreign adversary was a content-neutral regulation).

Regulating the collection and use of end-user data may have downstream effects on social media business models, and thus on the kinds of content they curate and recommend, but those effects in and of themselves do not trigger strict scrutiny under *Tornillo*, *Hurley*, or *Moody*.

Perhaps equally important, even after *Moody*, governments can regulate the various players in digital industries to promote fair competition, prevent information bottlenecks, and prevent monopolization of digital media.[124] Although these regulations may affect the relative communicative power of participants, this does not by itself violate the First Amendment.

Texas and Florida were worried that a small number of social media companies with ideological views hostile to their own enjoyed outsized influence in the digital public sphere. Instead of directly regulating the platforms' judgments about content, they should have tried to open up the platforms to allow for greater user choice about content moderation and recommendation systems. In fact, Florida's legislation does this in a very limited way. It gives end users the right to opt out of a platform's recommendation systems and receive "sequential or chronological posts and content."[125]

This provision is one example of a much larger strategy of structural regulations that give end users the option to implement user controls. User controls place decisions about which content end users receive with end users themselves. The Supreme Court has repeatedly pointed to user controls as a less restrictive alternative to content-based regulation of electronic media.[126]

There are two basic strategies that governments might pursue. First, governments could impose structural regulations that require large social media platforms to offer end users the choice to use "middleware."[127]

[124] *Moody*, 603 U.S. at 742 n.10; *Turner I*, 512 U.S. at 657, 661–62; Turner Broad. Sys., Inc. v. FCC (*Turner II*), 520 U.S. 180, 189–90, 192–93 (1997).

[125] Fla. Stat. § 501.2041(2)(f)(2) (2023). Platforms must also "provide users with an annual notice on the use of algorithms for post-prioritization and shadow banning and reoffer annually the opt-out opportunity." *Id.* § 501.2041(2)(g).

[126] United States v. Playboy Ent. Grp., Inc., 529 U.S. 803, 815–18 (2000) (holding that content regulation of adult content was unconstitutional if cable companies could block adult content at customer request); Reno v. ACLU, 521 U.S. 844, 877–78 (1997) (existence of user-based software to block material inappropriate for minors is a less restrictive alternative).

[127] *Shaping the Future of Social Media with Middleware*, Found. for Am. Innovation (Dec. 2024), https://repository.library.georgetown.edu/bitstream/handle/10822/1089126/Shaping_Future_Social_Media_Middleware.pdf [https://perma.cc/3XEH-3TYF]; Daphne Keller, *Amplification and Its Discontents: Why Regulating the Reach of Online Content Is Hard*, 1 J. Free

Middleware companies provide alternative content moderation and recommendation services. Platforms would still moderate and recommend content as before, but end users could also choose different companies to perform these tasks.

This kind of structural regulation would create a market for third-party middleware companies to connect with the largest platforms. It would allow end users whose speech would otherwise be blocked or demoted by a platform to reach willing listeners that subscribe to a middleware service with different rules and norms. Finally, it would allow end users to enjoy the benefits of the global communities that large platforms create without being locked into a single service for content moderation and recommendations.

A second structural solution is to require large social media platforms to be interoperable with other social media platforms.[128] This means that they would employ common technical standards for sharing, interpreting, and presenting data. Common technical standards would not require platforms to select, present or curate data in any particular way. Any platform that used these common standards could receive content posted on other platforms and share content with other platforms while presenting and curating content however it liked. This is how email works today. People using different email providers can send and receive messages to each other because the providers use common standards.

Like middleware solutions, an interoperability requirement would give end users all the benefits of belonging to large digital communities; and they could also communicate with people who belonged to other social media platforms. Interoperability would lower barriers to entry for new social media platforms that might have trouble gaining new users because network effects keep people on existing platforms. Finally, interoperability could also create a market for third-party content moderation and recommendation systems that would allow

---

Speech L. 227, 268 (2021); Daphne Keller, *Lawful but Awful? Control over Legal Speech by Platforms, Governments, and Internet Users*, U. Chi. L. Rev. Online (June 28, 2022), https://lawreviewblog.uchicago.edu/2022/06/28/keller-control-over-speech [https://perma.cc/5ZYJ-YLHC]; Francis Fukuyama, *Making the Internet Safe for Democracy*, 32 J. Democracy 37, 41–43 (2021); Francis Fukuyama, Barak Richman, Ashish Goel, Marietje Schaake, Roberta R. Katz & Douglas Melamed, *Report of the Working Group on Platform Scale*, Stanford Cyber Pol'y Ctr. (Nov. 17, 2020), https://cyber.fsi.stanford.edu/publication/report-working-group-platform-scale [https://perma.cc/ASX3-DUEV].

[128] Mike Masnick, *Protocols, Not Platforms: A Technological Approach to Free Speech*, Knight First Amend. Inst. (Aug. 21, 2019), https://knightcolumbia.org/content/protocols-not-platforms-a-technological-approach-to-free-speech [https://perma.cc/UPY2-CRL6].

end users to escape the largest platforms' control over what they say, see, and hear.

These possibilities are not speculative. A third party middleware company, Block Party, once gave Twitter users the power to block harassing or threatening posts until the new ownership prevented its operation.[129] The social media platform Bluesky has been designed to accommodate customized content moderation.[130] Another platform, Mastodon, is premised on interoperability between different nodes that can have different content moderation and recommendation rules.[131]

The power of social media platforms over the digital public sphere comes in large part from network effects: The more people belong to a platform, the more valuable the platform is and the harder it is to exit from it. That gives enormous advantages to the largest companies and helps maintain their dominance over public discussion. Middleware and interoperability mandates allow users to enjoy the benefits of network effects while also allowing them to choose other platforms or middleware companies with different values and moderation standards. These mandates also promote industry competition because they lower barriers to entry for new social media companies that might offer new kinds of services.

Regulations facilitating middleware and interoperability do not attempt to regulate social media companies' editorial judgments. They do not require social media companies to remove, restore, promote or demote any content. Instead, they alter the competitive structure of the industry. For this reason, *Turner I* and *II*, and not *Tornillo* and *Hurley*, are the relevant First Amendment precedents.

The Supreme Court held in *Turner I* and *II* that "promoting the widespread dissemination of information from a multiplicity of sources" is an important purpose that is unrelated to the suppression of free expression and therefore does not trigger strict scrutiny.[132]

---

[129] Tracy C. Chou, *The Path to a Better Internet for Everyone*, Block Party Newsl. (Mar. 3, 2022), https://blog.blockpartyapp.com/p/a-better-internet-for-everyone [https://perma.cc/LF77-YQ2W].

[130] *See generally* Martin Kleppmann et al., *Bluesky and the AT Protocol: Usable Decentralized Social Media*, arXiv (Oct. 16, 2024), https://arxiv.org/abs/2402.03239 [https://perma.cc/2XFQ-R8QF] (describing how Bluesky permits custom feeds for content moderation).

[131] *See* Alan Z. Rozenstein, *Moderating the Fediverse: Content Moderation on Distributed Social Media*, 3 J. Free Speech L. 217, 218 (2023).

[132] Turner Broad. Sys., Inc. v. FCC (*Turner I*), 512 U.S. 622, 662 (1994); Turner Broad. Sys., Inc. v. FCC (*Turner II*), 520 U.S. 180, 189 (1997).

This phrase originally comes from Justice Black's opinion in *Associated Press v. United States*,[133] which argued that the government could apply the antitrust laws to a publisher's association that restricted the sale of news stories to non-members.[134] This language might seem to be in tension with the position stated in *Buckley* and reaffirmed in *Moody* that the "government may not 'restrict the speech of some elements of our society in order to enhance the relative voice of others.'"[135] But as the Court explained in *Turner I*, the two ideas are consistent. The government may regulate industry structure and shape the rules of market competition to increase the number and diversity of voices in the public sphere as long as it does not aim at restricting anyone's expression because the government objects to its content.[136]

VI. *Moody* and the Technology Stack

Moody gives social media companies First Amendment protection to edit and curate end-user content to the extent that by doing so they produce "expressive products." What *Moody* leaves open is First Amendment protection for other kinds of internet services. These include other services at the application layer like email, Uber, or eBay, and services further down the tech stack, like broadband, app stores and web hosting services.

Note once again that when governments regulate infrastructure owners in order to get them to block or censor end-user content, courts may recognize that infrastructure owners have First Amendment rights even if they are not independent speakers or editors because they make possible the distribution of end-user content. But here, as in *Moody*, the question is whether infrastructure owners have independent First Amendment rights to edit, block, or censor end-user content.

---

[133] 326 U.S. 1, 20 (1945) ("The First Amendment . . . rests on the assumption that the widest possible dissemination of information from diverse and antagonistic sources is essential to the welfare of the public, that a free press is a condition of a free society.").

[134] *Id.* at 20 ("Freedom of the press from governmental interference under the First Amendment does not sanction repression of that freedom by private interests.").

[135] Moody v. NetChoice, LLC, 603 U.S. 707, 742 (2024) (quoting Buckley v. Valeo, 424 U.S. 1, 48–49 (1976) (per curiam)).

[136] *Turner I*, 512 U.S. at 658 ("*Buckley* thus stands for the proposition that laws favoring some speakers over others demand strict scrutiny when the legislature's speaker preference reflects a content preference.").

Start first with the application layer. Not all digital services produce the equivalent of social media feeds. But digital applications are protean. Their designs can change rapidly and they can offer many different features and affordances. Many applications allow end users to communicate with each other on the platform, either by sending messages or by posting ratings and comments. As soon as platforms allow end-user communication, they will find it necessary to engage in content moderation.[137] As a result, content moderation is ubiquitous on platforms, whether or not they resemble Facebook or YouTube. Even applications that seem resistant to content moderation, like encrypted messaging apps, can be moderated.[138] Moreover, some modern messaging apps allow broadcasting messages to hundreds of other users, which blurs distinctions between their services and social media feeds.[139]

Moody's focus on the existence of an "expressive product" is not well-designed to address the variety and complexity of digital applications. That is perhaps the best reason to read *Moody* fairly narrowly—as giving lower courts an example of what is protected by the First Amendment without establishing necessary and sufficient conditions for all digital platforms and applications.

At oral argument the Justices gave the example of email as an application for which common carriage or nondiscrimination rules might be constitutional.[140] Their assumption was that given the nature of the service, email providers had no good reason to engage in content discrimination—for example, banning all emails by conservatives.[141] But that is not what email services actually do. In fact, email services are among the earliest content moderators on the internet. They try to identify and block spam, because if they did not do so, they would quickly be overrun with it. Most spam is commercial solicitation (much of it fraudulent) but not all of it is commercial, and the category is

---

[137] *See* James Grimmelmann, *The Virtues of Moderation*, 17 Yale J.L. & Tech. 42, 51–53 (2015) (explaining that, because online communities are a shared resource, they are liable to abuse).

[138] Charles Duan & James Grimmelmann, *Content Moderation on End-to-End Encrypted Systems: A Legal Analysis*, 8 Geo. L. Tech. Rev. 1 (2024).

[139] *See generally* Akriti Gaur, Social Media Shapeshifters: The Emergence of a "Public-Private Hybrid" (2023) (unpublished manuscript) (on file with author).

[140] Transcript of Oral Argument at 70–80, *Moody*, 603 U.S. 707 (Nos. 22-277 & 22-555).

[141] *See id.* at 79–80 (Barrett, J.) ("I'm not sure I agree with you about DMs and—and Gmail . . . it's not obvious to me anyway that . . . they can't qualify as common carriers.").

notoriously difficult to define. Email services moderate and organize content in other ways, too: Gmail, for example, now sorts incoming emails into content-based categories like "primary," "social," and "promotions."[142] End users can change this system, but content moderation occurs as a default.

If one reads *Moody* narrowly to protect only "expressive products" that resemble social media feeds, then states could impose nondiscrimination rules for other kinds of platforms and applications. States could also create carve-outs to allow for specific kinds of content moderation—for example, eliminating spam—without running afoul of the First Amendment because they are not interfering with editorial judgment nor is it their goal to do so. It is true that states could wreak havoc with platforms if their regulations are ham-handed and intrusive. But the First Amendment is not always the most flexible tool for separating out good platform policies from bad ones.

Now consider applications lower in the internet stack—broadband companies, domain name companies, and web hosting services. Here is where nondiscrimination or common carriage rules make the most sense. After all, the central purpose of the services lower in the stack is to get bits of information from one part of the internet to the other as quickly and efficiently as possible. Moreover, services lower in the stack are generally less adept at granular moderation of content.[143] For example, domain name companies can block all content hosted under a single domain name (e.g., facebook.com), but they cannot make finer distinctions.

Even so, some services lower in the tech stack do regulate content directly or indirectly. App stores may refuse to carry applications unless the latter have appropriate content moderation and safety policies.[144]

---

[142] Matthew Izatt, *Making Gmail's Tabbed Inbox Work Better for You*, Google Workspace Blog (Jan. 16, 2020), https://workspace.google.com/blog/productivity-collaboration/how-gmail-sorts-your-email-based-on-your-preferences [https://perma.cc/V7H2-JYZY].

[143] *See* Jack M. Balkin, *How to Regulate (and Not Regulate) Social Media*, 1 J. Free Speech L. 71, 73 (2021) (arguing that, in general, services lower in the stack should not engage in content discrimination); Goldman, *supra* note 22, at 49–50 ("Services with limited remedy options are not in good positions to redress user violations. . . . [T]he coarseness of the remedy options increases the odds that any remedial actions will be miscalibrated or will have adverse collateral consequences."); Annemarie Bridy, *Remediating Social Media: A Layer-Conscious Approach*, 24 B.U. J. Sci. & Tech. L. 193, 205 (2018) (arguing that control over content should occur at the edge of the network or at the application layer).

[144] *See App Review Guidelines*, Apple Dev. (June 5, 2023), https://developer.apple.com/app-store/review/guidelines [https://perma.cc/56EW-T2U2] (specifying content moderation requirements for apps available on the Apple App Store); *Restricted Content Policy*, Amazon

Web hosting services may refuse to host applications that encourage violence or terrorist activity, and so on.[145] *Moody* does not tell us whether the First Amendment protects these decisions. Web hosting services do not appear to offer a single expressive product, because people do not experience the collection of websites the companies host as a product. The same would also seem to apply to domain name servers and caching services. App stores may be a closer call: They are applications in their own right that appear on people's phones and they offer end users a list of applications that the store is willing to host, including games and entertainment. Even so, when states are trying to promote efficiency and nondiscrimination in the delivery of digital services lower in the tech stack, there is good reason to read *Moody* narrowly. If *Moody* does not apply, states can easily create carve-outs from nondiscrimination rules to allow companies to prevent the misuse of their platforms and services.

What about network neutrality rules for broadband providers? These rules classify broadband providers as "telecommunications services" and require, in essence, that broadband providers may not discriminate against content or applications traveling through their facilities.[146] The FCC adopted network neutrality rules during the Obama Administration but subsequently eliminated them during the Trump Administration.[147]

When he served on the D.C. Circuit, Justice Brett Kavanaugh argued that network neutrality rules violated the First Amendment, because broadband providers might want to engage in content moderation just like Facebook. To be sure, the government might impose must-carry obligations to promote fair competition as in *Turner I* and *II*. But "[a]bsent a showing of market power," Kavanaugh argued, "the Government may not tell Internet service providers how to exercise

---

Appstore (Nov. 17, 2021), https://developer.amazon.com/docs/policy-center/restricted-content.html [https://perma.cc/2MPU-DYS9] ("[A]pps that include or link to user-generated content must include a method for filtering objectionable content, an age verification system, and a mechanism to report and remove offensive content.").

[145] *See AWS Acceptable Use Policy*, Amazon Web Servs. (July 1, 2021), https://aws.amazon.com/aup [https://perma.cc/5NF2-DA9N] (listing content restrictions for use of AWS services).

[146] *See* Protecting and Promoting the Open Internet, 30 FCC Rcd. 5601, ¶ 4 (2015) (imposing rules at the network layer prohibiting providers from blocking lawful content, throttling lawful content, or discriminating against lawful content on the basis of its source or destination).

[147] The FCC promulgated its network neutrality rules once again during the Biden Administration, but the Sixth Circuit rejected them as inconsistent with the Telecommunications Act of 1996. *See In re* MCP No. 185, 124 F.4th 993, 1009 (6th Cir. 2025).

their editorial discretion about what content to carry or favor any more than the Government can tell Amazon or Politics & Prose what books to promote; . . . or tell Twitter or YouTube what videos to post; or tell Facebook or Google what content to favor."[148]

Nondiscrimination rules such as network neutrality make sense for services beneath the application layer because the central goal of these services is speedy and efficient distribution of digital information. Once again, governments can make exceptions to general nondiscrimination rules to ensure efficient network management. If content moderation occurs at all, it should primarily occur at the application layer, or better still, through choices made by end users at the edge of the network. (This is another justification for middleware). This is why Kavanaugh's First Amendment arguments against network neutrality miss the mark. They do not seem to recognize the different functions played by the different parts of the tech stack.

Moody cites Kavanaugh's D.C. Circuit dissent for the general proposition that the government ordinarily may not interfere in the editorial choices of private actors, although it may regulate them to promote fair competition.[149] If *Moody* meant to incorporate all of Kavanaugh's reasoning, however, it would be especially unfortunate, because that would prevent governments from ensuring nondiscrimination lower in the tech stack. The D.C. Circuit has upheld network neutrality against a First Amendment challenge,[150] but the Supreme Court has never decided the issue. *Moody* complicates that question but does not answer it. It remains unclear whether the Court will view the stream of bits that flows through a broadband provider's facilities as an "expressive product" like a social media feed or a St. Patrick's Day Parade.

VII. The Speech Rights of End Users—Informed Consumers or Due Process?

Texas and Florida also created procedural requirements to prevent arbitrary decision making by social media platforms. Texas

[148] U.S. Telecom Ass'n v. FCC, 855 F.3d 381, 435 (D.C. Cir. 2017) (Kavanaugh, J., dissenting from the denial of rehearing en banc).

[149] Moody v. NetChoice, LLC, 603 U.S. 707, 742 (2024) (citing *U.S. Telecom Ass'n*, 855 F.3d. at 432 (Kavanaugh, J., dissenting from the denial of rehearing en banc)).

[150] U.S. Telecom. Ass'n v. FCC, 825 F.3d 674, 739, 741–42 (D.C. Cir. 2016), *reh'g denied*, 855 F.3d 381 (D.C. Cir. 2017), *cert. denied sub nom.* Berninger v. FCC, 586 U.S. 994 (2018).

requires social media companies to provide an explanation when content is removed.[151] It also requires a right of appeal and a written determination of the decision on appeal.[152]

Florida requires that social media companies explain each moderation and recommendation decision that affects an end user by "a thorough rationale explaining the reason that the social media platform censored the user," and "a precise and thorough explanation of how the social media platform became aware of the censored content or material, including a thorough explanation of the algorithms used, if any, to identify or flag the user's content or material as objectionable."[153]

Florida allows end users a private right of action to sue for actual, statutory, and punitive damages if the platform's explanation for its content moderation or recommendation decision is inadequate.[154] Finally, Florida requires that "[a] social media platform must inform each user about any changes to its user rules, terms, and agreements before implementing the changes and may not make changes more than once every 30 days."[155]

The Court did not resolve the First Amendment issues presented by these elements of the statutes and sent them back to the lower courts.[156] The Court assumed, although it did not squarely hold, that lower courts should analyze these questions according to the Court's decision in *Zauderer v. Office of Disciplinary Counsel of Supreme Court of Ohio*,[157] which announced the basic doctrines for compelled commercial speech. As Justice Kagan explained, "for the individualized-explanation provisions" lower courts must ask "whether the required disclosures unduly burden expression," citing *Zauderer*.[158] (Kagan did

[151] TEX. BUS. & COM. CODE ANN. § 120.103(a)(1) (West 2023).

[152] *Id.* § 120.103(a)(2).

[153] FLA. STAT. § 501.2041(3)(c)–(d) (2023); *id.* § 501.2041(2)(a)–(e).

[154] *Id.* § 501.2041(6).

[155] *Id.* § 501.2041(2)(c).

[156] Moody v. NetChoice, LLC, 603 U.S. 707, 725–26 (2024).

[157] 471 U.S. 626 (1985).

[158] *Moody*, 603 U.S. at 725 (citing *Zauderer*, 471 U.S. at 651); *see also id.* at 727 n.3 ("[R]equirements [like the individualized-explanation provisions] violate the First Amendment if they unduly burden expressive activity."); *id.* at 750–51 (Thomas, J., concurring in the judgment) (noting that the Court has assumed that *Zauderer* applies but arguing that the Court should revisit *Zauderer*); *id.* at 791 n.46 (Alito, J., concurring in the judgment) ("If, on remand, the States show that the platforms have been able to comply with [European law] without having to forgo 'exercising editorial discretion at all,' . . . then that might help them prove that their disclosure laws are not 'unduly burdensome' under *Zauderer*." (citation omitted)); *id.* at

not address Texas's appeal provision or Florida's thirty-day requirement separately).

There are two problems here. First, the use of commercial speech doctrine fits awkwardly with the Court's argument that the platforms are engaged in editorial judgment like newspapers. Second, commercial speech doctrine is a poor proxy for addressing what is really at stake. The point of Texas's and Florida's statutes is not simply informing consumers. They are offering procedural protections against arbitrary governance by platforms.

Here is why the difference in characterization matters. In the pluralist model, end users have free speech interests against governments *and* against the platforms that host their speech, because both states and platforms regulate end-user speech. The substantive doctrines of the First Amendment constrain governments; however, because of the Court's state action doctrines, they do not constrain platforms. Private parties may impose whatever content-based and viewpoint-based limits on speech they like. *Moody* reaffirms this principle, at least for social media companies.

Because of this difference between public and private governance, enforceable end-user speech interests turn out to be mostly procedural guarantees. Platforms must state their content moderation standards publicly, and apply them consistently, even-handedly, and non-arbitrarily. Where private governance is concerned, freedom of speech is largely a matter of due process.[159]

Commercial speech doctrine emerged out of the dyadic model of speech regulation characteristic of the twentieth century. Platforms claim a First Amendment right to be free from state regulation, and the state justifies disclosure because it informs consumers. The speech interests of end users are left completely out of the picture. Now consider the problem from the standpoint of the free speech triangle. The issue is not that platforms are giving consumers incomplete information. It is that platforms are governing end users by creating and

796 n.57 ("[I]n the Florida case in particular, NetChoice did not contest—and accordingly forfeited—whether *Zauderer* applies here.").

[159] Balkin, *Free Speech in the Algorithmic Society*, *supra* note 7, at 1196–98 (arguing that the shift from the dyadic to the pluralist model makes due process especially important to end users); Matthew Prince, *Why We Terminated Daily Stormer*, Cloudfare (Aug. 16, 2017), https://blog.cloudflare.com/why-we-terminated-daily-stormer [https://perma.cc/3447-JVV6] (arguing that "Freedom of Speech < Due Process" in "[t]he issue of who can and cannot be online").

enforcing rules and standards. The danger is not that end users will be misinformed. It is that they will be unfairly governed without procedural protections. End users want the right to speak on the platform, and they do not want to be governed arbitrarily when they do so.

Under the dyadic model, what is at stake is consumer information. Under the pluralist model, it is due process. One can describe both of these concerns as issues of "consumer protection." But what is protected is different. In the first case, the law protects consumers from deception and lack of knowledge. In the second case, the law protects end users from abuses of private governance.

The *NetChoice* litigation in Texas and Florida suggests that in the short run at least, the federal courts will cling to the dyadic model. They will think and talk about the issues in terms of access to consumer information.[160] That is how the parties argued the cases and how the lower courts and the Supreme Court initially conceptualized the question. That is hardly surprising because the interests of end users went unrepresented in the *NetChoice* litigation.[161] But commercial speech doctrine is only an imperfect proxy for the deeper questions raised by private governance. At some point, the courts will have to focus on the real problems created by the free speech triangle and not on how commercial speech doctrine imagines them.

For the moment, however, the commercial speech model will prevail. Yet even that model reveals problems with the Court's holding that platforms are editors. For it suggests that what social media companies are doing is importantly different from newspapers or organizers of parades.[162] If social media companies really were engaged

---

[160] *But see* X Corp. v. Bonta, 116 F.4th 888, 897–98, 901 (9th Cir. 2024) (striking down as compelled non-commercial speech California law requiring social media companies to issue reports on their content moderation policies). The Ninth Circuit argued that *Zauderer* did not apply because "the Content Category Reports are not commercial speech. They require a company to recast its content-moderation practices in language prescribed by the State, implicitly opining on whether and how certain controversial categories of content should be moderated." *Id.* at 901.

[161] This is a recurrent problem in platform regulation cases, in which either platforms or end users appear before the courts but not both. *See* Daphne Keller, *The Three-Body Problem: Platform Litigation and Absent Parties*, LAWFARE (May 4, 2023, 9:00 AM), https://www.lawfaremedia.org/article/the-three-body-problem-platform-litigation-and-absent-parties [https://perma.cc/HT5C-TR3Z].

[162] *See* Daphne Keller, *Platform Transparency and the First Amendment*, 4 J. FREE SPEECH L. 1, 4 (2023) (arguing that the newspaper analogy is flawed because platforms process enormous amounts of information and "have far less commercial or editorial interest in defending any particular user's posts than a newspaper has in defending its articles").

in editorial judgments like newspapers, and in producing "expressive products" like the authors of anthologies, it would seem contrary to the First Amendment to ask them to defend their choices of which content to exclude, promote, or demote, or require them to create appeal procedures. Under current precedents, it would be unconstitutional for a state to require the *New York Times* to offer explanations for each rejection of a letter to the editor, or to require the *New Yorker* to create an appeal process for authors whose articles, short stories, and cartoons are rejected. It would also be unconstitutional to require that a newspaper wait thirty days before changing any aspect of its editorial standards. And under *Hurley*, it is doubtful that Massachusetts could require the organizers of the St. Patrick's Day parade to publish their rules for inclusion in the parade publicly in advance and offer explanations and an appeal process for rejected participants.

Editors normally enjoy First Amendment rights to speak or not to speak without having to justify their editorial choices to the state. But the assumption underlying a requirement of explanation or appeal is that editors must act reasonably in deciding what to include in their expressive products according to publicly available criteria stated in advance. This raises problems of compelled speech and even prior restraint. But beyond this, the idea that editors must justify their creative process to the state seems foreign to the rights of expression that the First Amendment guarantees. Moreover, because the goal of Texas's and Florida's statutes is to coax social media companies to publish or restore some content that they would otherwise remove, these procedural guarantees would also seem to violate the *Buckley* principle on which Kagan relies: restricting the voice of some (social media companies) to enhance the voices of others (end users).

Redescribing the statutes' procedural guarantees as purely informational measures—and thus as governed by commercial speech doctrine—seeks to avoid these problems, although, as we shall see, it does not really eliminate them. The basic idea is that states are simply requiring the platforms to "provide somewhat more information [about their services] than they might otherwise be inclined to present"[163] and "include . . . purely factual and uncontroversial information about the terms under which [their] services will be available."[164] The platforms

[163] *Zauderer*, 471 U.S. at 650.

[164] *Id.* at 651.

enter into consumer contracts with end users that incorporate their community standards by reference. States should be able to require platforms to explain why end users have violated these contracts and are subject to content moderation or even exclusion. By contrast, parade organizers do not have contracts with potential participants and newspapers do not have contracts with people submitting letters to the editor.[165] In other words, states can require disclosure because of an ongoing commercial relationship.

This theory faces a number of hurdles. First, *Zauderer* was a case about compelling information from advertisers to avoid misleading or deceiving consumers.[166] The disclosures required here go well beyond this. However, lower courts have generally held that compelled commercial disclosures are not limited to preventing deception in advertising, although the Supreme Court has yet to address the matter squarely.[167]

Second, one would have to show that disclosure of the grounds for moderating content was "factual and uncontroversial."[168] *Why* a social media platform moderated content would seem to be a question of fact that is easily available to the platform. The only wrinkle is the "uncontroversial" requirement. In *National Institute of Family and Life Advocates (NIFLA) v. Becerra*, the Court glossed this part of the test.[169] It held that requiring a crisis pregnancy center—dedicated to preventing abortions—to disclose the availability of abortion services is not consistent with *Zauderer* because "information about state-sponsored services . . . including abortion [is] anything but an 'uncontroversial' topic."[170]

At first glance this might mean that *Zauderer* does not apply to mandatory disclosures about content moderation, because platforms

---

[165] *See* Brief of the Knight First Amendment Institute at Columbia University as Amicus Curiae in Support of Neither Party at 26–27 & n.18, Moody v. NetChoice, LLC, 603 U.S. 707 (2024) (Nos. 22-277 & 22-555) (explaining why disclosure rules are compelled commercial speech).

[166] *Zauderer*, 471 U.S. at 651 ("[A]n advertiser's rights are adequately protected as long as disclosure requirements are reasonably related to the State's interest in preventing deception of consumers.").

[167] *See, e.g.*, CTIA – The Wireless Ass'n v. City of Berkeley, 928 F.3d 832, 844 (9th Cir. 2019) (collecting cases from the various circuits); *cf.* Nat'l Inst. of Family & Life Advocs. v. Becerra (*NIFLA*), 585 U.S. 755, 775 (2018) ("[W]e do not question the legality of health and safety warnings long considered permissible, or purely factual and uncontroversial disclosures about commercial products.").

[168] *Zauderer*, 471 U.S. at 651.

[169] *NIFLA*, 585 U.S. 755.

[170] *Id.* at 769 (emphasis omitted).

make moderation decisions about controversial topics all the time, including hate speech, sexuality, and misinformation. But one might distinguish *NIFLA* as follows: There the state was forcing the crisis pregnancy center to talk about services provided by the state, and not its own services. Moreover, it required the center to convey a controversial message about abortion that was inconsistent with the center's mission.[171] These concerns do not apply to disclosures about a platform's own content moderation decisions. They are central to what the platform does. Even if the subject of a post is controversial, and even if the platform's judgment about the post is controversial, it is not controversial that the platform moderated the content for a particular reason based on its terms of service or community standards.

Zauderer places some limits on the government's ability to compel commercial speech. Mandated disclosures cannot be "unjustified or unduly burdensome."[172] In his concurrence in the judgment in *Moody*, Justice Alito pointed out that the largest platforms already comply with the disclosure provisions of the European Union's Digital Services Act (DSA), and he suggested that "complying with that law does not appear to have unduly burdened each platform's speech in those countries."[173] But the fact that global platforms must adhere to DSA rules as a cost of doing business in the European Union does not mean that the regulations are not unduly burdensome under *Zauderer*.[174] The test cannot be whether a regulation causes or does not cause a company to close up shop.

Because of the enormous scale of the content that flows through the platforms every day and the millions of violations that platforms identify each quarter,[175] it would be very difficult for platforms to do

---

[171] *See* Robert Post, NIFLA *and the Construction of Compelled Speech Doctrine*, 97 Ind. L.J. 1071, 1092–93 (2022) ("[T]he mandated notices . . . potentially undermine[d] . . . the [crisis pregnancy centers'] efforts to persuade women to repudiate abortions.").

[172] *Zauderer*, 471 U.S. at 651.

[173] Moody v. NetChoice LLC, 603 U.S. 707, 797–98 (2024) (Alito, J., concurring in the judgment).

[174] Article 17 of the Digital Services Act requires platforms to offer a "statement of reasons" explaining their content moderation decisions. Platforms can provide automated responses as long as they are "clear and specific." Regulation 2022/2065 of the European Parliament and of the Council of 19 October 2022 on a Single Market for Digital Services and amending Directive 2000/31/EC (Digital Services Act), art. 17, 2022 O.J. (L 277) 1, 51–52.

[175] YouTube's latest transparency report states that the company removed nine million individual videos and 4.8 million channels (constituting seventy-two million videos) from July 2024 to September 2024. *YouTube Community Guidelines Enforcement*, Google Transparency

much more than provide automated responses that identity the specific part of the platform's community standards violated and describe the basic category of content at issue (for example, hate speech). As a result, disclosure requirements will have to be relatively modest to remain constitutional.[176]

In addition, constitutional disclosure rules under *Zauderer* must not deter content moderation and curation, leading digital companies to refrain from promulgating and enforcing content standards (or water them down) in order to avoid costly lawsuits and intrusive discovery. *Moody* states that content moderation and curation are expressive activity protected by the First Amendment. But litigants, including fiercely partisan state attorneys general, may try to use litigation about whether disclosures are adequate to fight over platforms' definitions of hate speech, sexual orientation discrimination, and other aspects of community standards linked to the culture wars.[177] In response, platforms may decide that enforcing their community standards is not worth the trouble and discard them or water them down. For commercial speech doctrine to work consistently with *Moody*, disclosure rules cannot become a tool for chilling editorial judgment.

Florida's disclosure rules exemplify these problems of burdensome costs and chilling effects. Whereas Texas's disclosure rules apply only to removals of content, Florida's rules are much broader. They apply to every act of moderating content and every decision about what content to promote or demote. Moreover, they require "a thorough rationale explaining the reason that the social media platform censored the user," and "a precise and thorough explanation of how the social media platform became aware of the censored content or material, including a thorough explanation of the algorithms used, if any, to identify or flag the user's content or material as objectionable."[178] It would be very difficult if not impossible to perform this kind of

---

Rep., https://transparencyreport.google.com/youtube-policy/removals [https://perma.cc/MVF9-88LF].

[176] *See* Evelyn Douek, *Content Moderation as Systems Thinking*, 136 Harv. L. Rev. 526, 577–83 (2022) (explaining why traditional conceptions of due process do not work well for content moderation systems).

[177] *See* Daphne Keller, *State Abuse of Transparency Laws and How to Stop It*, Ctr. for Internet & Soc'y (Sept. 19, 2022), https://cyberlaw.stanford.edu/blog/2022/09/state-abuse-transparency-laws-and-how-stop-it [https://perma.cc/C35F-R296] ("State actors who are licensed to examine the adequacy of platform transparency will have unique leverage to influence the substantive speech policies applied to users.").

[178] Fla. Stat. § 501.2041(3)(c)–(d) (2023); *id.* § 501.2041(2)(a)–(e).

reporting at scale. Moreover, these rules, combined with a right of private action that allows awards of statutory and punitive damages for each instance of inadequate disclosure, seem designed more to bully the platforms into changing their editorial policies than to informing consumers.[179]

So far, I've considered whether one might justify laws like Texas's and Florida's through compelled commercial speech doctrine. Texas's law, however, does more than mandate disclosure. Whenever platforms remove content, Texas also provides for a right to appeal and the right to a written explanation of the decision reached.[180] This provision shows what Texas's statute is really about. It does not simply inform consumers about the nature of commercial services. Rather, it involves the rudiments of due process. This casts the disclosure provisions in a different light. Texas is trying to protect end users' speech interests by giving them a right to non-arbitrary decisionmaking by the platforms. It is responding, albeit in a haphazard way, to the problems of the free speech triangle. And the statute shows, once again, why commercial speech doctrine is an imperfect proxy for safeguarding the interests of end users.

VIII. Conclusion: *Moody*, Artificial Intelligence and Algorithmic Speech

Moody raises a final set of issues that will only grow in importance in the years to come. In a very preliminary way, *Moody* begins to discuss the First Amendment status of expression produced by algorithms and artificial intelligence. That question is of enormous importance generally, but here are the stakes for social media companies. Suppose that using automated systems—including artificial intelligence—to engage in content moderation and recommendation is unprotected by the First Amendment. Then the social media companies that employ automated systems might be sued—or otherwise regulated—because of the harmful effects that their moderation and recommendation systems produce on populations. This assumes, of course, that they are not otherwise immune from suit under Section 230

---

[179] *See* Keller, *supra* note 162, at 4 (arguing that burdensome transparency requirements give platforms incentives to change their editorial practices).

[180] Tex. Bus. & Com. Code Ann. § 120.103(a)(2) (West 2023).

of the Telecommunications Act of 1996, which the Court did not consider in *Moody*.[181]

Digital companies have sought to protect as much of their operations as possible under the shield of the First Amendment (and Section 230). To the extent that companies' use of artificial intelligence (or algorithms more generally) is unprotected, it will have major consequences for this strategy.

In *Moody*, Justice Kagan noted that much social media curation occurs through algorithms; these remove or demote content based on predictions of whether the content matches end users' interests and activities and whether the content violates a platform's community guidelines or standards.[182] Kagan assumed that this use of algorithms is part of a platform's editorial judgment and is therefore protected by the First Amendment.[183] That assumption is one of *Moody*'s most important holdings, a holding that litigators will try to build on (or distinguish) in future cases involving algorithmic speech and artificial intelligence. Read broadly, *Moody* might suggest that where programs further a human being's expressive goals, their use is protected by the First Amendment.

At the same time, Kagan expressed no opinion about situations in which "algorithms respond solely to how users act online—giving them the content they appear to want, without any regard to independent content standards."[184] Justice Amy Coney Barrett offered a similar caveat in her concurrence: "[I]f a platform's algorithm just

---

[181] 47 U.S.C. § 230(c); *see* Moody v. NetChoice LLC, 603 U.S. 707, 771 n.8 (2024) (Alito, J., concurring in the judgment) (noting that the Eleventh Circuit declined to pass on the Section 230 issues in the case).

[182] *Moody*, 603 U.S. at 734–36 & n.5.

[183] *Id.* at 734–35 ("The key to the scheme is prioritization of content, achieved through the use of algorithms. . . . The platforms write algorithms to implement [their community] standards. . . ."). Justice Barrett makes a similar argument in her concurrence:

> Assume that human beings decide to remove posts promoting a particular political candidate or advocating some position on a public-health issue. If they create an algorithm to help them identify and delete that content, the First Amendment protects their exercise of editorial judgment—even if the algorithm does most of the deleting without a person in the loop. In that event, the algorithm would simply implement human beings' inherently expressive choice "to exclude a message [they] did not like from" their speech compilation.

Id. at 746 (Barrett, J., concurring) (quoting Hurley v. Irish-Am. Gay, Lesbian & Bisexual Grp. of Bos., Inc., 515 U.S. 557, 574 (1995)).

[184] *Id.* at 736 n.5 (majority opinion).

presents automatically to each user whatever the algorithm thinks the user will like—e.g., content similar to posts with which the user previously engaged . . . [t]he First Amendment implications . . . might be different. . . ."[185]

This distinction, however, does not work. After all, the algorithms maximize engagement because human beings programmed them to do so; they are furthering human goals in producing an "expressive product." People often tailor their expression—including their choices of what to say and when to say it—based on what they think their audiences will like, and there is no doubt that they have a First Amendment right to do so. Musicians order their concert playlists to keep their audiences entertained. Newspapers decide which stories to cover and where to place them based on expectations about reader engagement. Local television news shows frontload attention-grabbing violent stories according to the dictum "if it bleeds, it leads."[186] Motion picture producers test audience reactions to the endings of movies and the inclusion or exclusion of certain scenes or characters, and so on.

In the attention economy of the digital age, it should be obvious that a central object of much popular expression and entertainment is audience engagement, and that producers, composers, editors, and publishers employ algorithms and other computer programs as tools to maximize the same.[187] If a musician, for example, uses artificial intelligence to program a concert *solely* to please her audience and maximize engagement (and revenues), this is still protected by the First Amendment.

One might respond that these situations involve ordering a speaker's *own* content. People have a right to choose from their own compositions solely for the purpose of maximizing audience engagement. The concert musician picks the order of her own songs; the newspaper chooses from among possible stories to put on the front

---

[185] *Id.* at 746 (Barrett, J., concurring).

[186] *If It Bleeds, It Leads*, TvTropes, https://tvtropes.org/pmwiki/pmwiki.php/Main/IfItBleeds ItLeads [https://perma.cc/A8QC-AC5W].

[187] *See, e.g.*, The NYT Open Team, *How The New York Times Incorporates Editorial Judgement in Algorithms to Curate Home Screen Content*, Medium (Oct. 2, 2024), https://open.nytimes.com /how-the-new-york-times-incorporates-editorial-judgement-in-algorithms-to-curate-home -screen-content-85f48209fdad [https://perma.cc/YD57-ZB55]; Emmet McDermott, *AI Decision-Making in Hollywood Is Already Here, Now What?*, Hollywood Rep. (May 4, 2023, 10:21 AM), https://www.hollywoodreporter.com/business/digital/ai-filmmaking-algorithm-documentaries -non-fiction-1235478174 [https://perma.cc/2RSB-VV28] (describing how filmmakers use algorithms to choose subjects for films).

page; movie studios decide how to end their own movies; stand-up comedians include or discard jokes from their own stable of material, and so on. And a musician, a newspaper, a movie studio, or a comedian does not lose First Amendment protection if they employ an algorithm or other predictive tool to figure how to maximize engagement.

By contrast, Kagan and Barrett are pointing to algorithms that compile *other* people's content solely on the grounds that people will like it or be engaged with it. But *Moody* already holds that producing a compilation consisting solely of other people's speech creates an "expressive product" and that the right to create such a product is protected by the First Amendment. If so, then choosing which posts to present and in which order should also be protected as part of the compilation if it furthers the expressive and editorial goals of human beings. And if using algorithms to remove posts from a feed is a permissible tool for creating an "expressive product," so too would be choosing which posts to promote and in what order to encourage audience engagement.

Justice Barrett, however, expressed a deeper concern. Platforms might use artificial intelligence programs to substitute for human judgment more generally. "[A] platform's owners [might] hand the reins to an AI tool and ask it simply to remove 'hateful' content" based "on large language models to determine what is 'hateful' and should be removed. . . ."[188] If so, "has a human being with First Amendment rights made an inherently expressive 'choice . . . not to propound a particular point of view?'"[189] "[T]he way platforms use this sort of technology might have constitutional significance," Barrett argued, because "technology may attenuate the connection between content-moderation *actions* . . . and human beings' constitutionally protected right to '*decide for [themselves]* the ideas and beliefs deserving of expression, consideration, and adherence.'"[190] Barrett argues that at some point human input into the work of an AI agent is so small that we should not say that what results is a human being's "expressive product"[191] that is protected by the First Amendment.

188 *Moody*, 603 U.S. at 746 (Barrett, J., concurring).

189 *Id.* (quoting Hurley v. Irish-Am. Gay, Lesbian & Bisexual Grp. of Bos., Inc., 515 U.S. 557, 575 (1995)).

190 *Id.* (quoting Turner Broad. Sys., Inc. v. FCC (*Turner I*), 512 U.S. 622, 641 (1994)).

191 *Id.* Justice Alito was equally concerned. *Id.* at 795 (Alito, J., concurring in the judgment) ("[W]hen AI algorithms make a decision, 'even the researchers and programmers creating them don't really understand why the models they have built make the decisions they make.' Are such decisions equally expressive as the decisions made by humans? Should we at least

What kind and degree of human input is necessary to enjoy First Amendment protection? Justice Barrett seems to suggest that simply articulating substantive goals in training such as "get rid of hate speech" and asking the AI agent to perform these goals is not sufficient to bestow First Amendment protection. But that argument is in some tension with Justice Kagan's assumption that most content moderation is and will be performed by automated systems. These systems are programmed and trained by human beings and they reflect human judgments about content.

Perhaps the line might be drawn between different kinds of automated systems, for example, between algorithms that do not employ machine learning and artificial intelligence systems that do. But if there is a line to be drawn here, the Justices do not take us very far in articulating it. For example, platforms already use artificial intelligence to manage spam and identify bots.[192] If this furthers the company's editorial goals it is not clear why the company should lose First Amendment protection under *Moody*. Finally, the fact that automated processes are opaque to humans cannot be the sole deciding criterion. The algorithms that social media companies employ may already be opaque to their content moderation teams.

The larger problem that the Justices are pointing at—even if they cannot yet draw workable lines—is how best to make companies' use of new technology accountable. A company's automated systems might produce significant harms to populations without the company understanding how or why it is happening, but the company might then turn around and use the First Amendment as a shield against liability or regulation. The First Amendment should not become a general defense against health and safety regulation. How to ensure the necessary accountability for artificial intelligence while still protecting First Amendment freedoms is a crucial question for the future.[193] *Moody* points vaguely at the problem but does not yet provide the tools to answer it.

---

think about this?" (footnote omitted) (quoting Tammy Xu, *AI Makes Decisions We Don't Understand. That's a Problem.*, BuiltIn (July 19, 2021), https://builtin.com/artificial-intelligence/ai-right-explanation [https://perma.cc/T6A4-45U3])).

[192] *See, e.g.*, *Navigating the Impact of Artificial Intelligence in Social Media Management*, SG Analytics (Nov. 8, 2024), https://us.sganalytics.com/blog/artificial-intelligence-in-social-media-management [https://perma.cc/U6FW-KWML].

[193] *See* Ian Ayres & Jack M. Balkin, *The Law of AI Is the Law of Risky Agents Without Intentions*, U. Chi. L. Rev. Online (Nov. 27, 2024), https://lawreview.uchicago.edu/online-archive/law-ai-law-risky-agents-without-intentions [https://perma.cc/HMB9-WPUQ].

WILLIAM BAUDE

FEAR OF BALANCING

Introduction

As a new Supreme Court majority settles into a new era of constitutional adjudication, the Justices will confront important methodological questions. How are they to go about interpreting the Constitution? In the Second Amendment case of *United States v. Rahimi*,[1] many of the Justices wrote separately to debate broader methodological questions about constitutional interpretation. They expressed a shared desire to turn away from judicial "balancing" of interests in adjudicating constitutional rights in favor of Founding Era understandings. That is a healthy instinct, but Founding Era understandings may in truth lead to balancing, so maintaining an originalist approach and an opposition to balancing is trickier than it seems. In future cases the Justices may need to resolve this tension by emphasizing the presumption of constitutionality, by making greater

William Baude is the Harry Kalven, Jr. Professor of Law at the University of Chicago Law School.

Author's note: Thanks to Sam Bray, Jud Campbell, Justin Driver, Sherif Girgis, Genevieve Lakier, Robert Leider, Haley Proctor, Richard Re, Steve Sachs, Francisco Urbina, and participants in the Notre Dame Law School Faculty Colloquium for helpful comments; to Will Horvath for helpful research assistance; and to the Stuart C. and JoAnn Nathan Faculty Fund for research support.

[1] 602 U.S. 680 (2024).

The Supreme Court Review, 2025.
 Published by The University of Chicago Press. https://doi.org/10.1086/735642

use of the principles of general law, or by crafting more rule-like doctrines for adjudication.

I. *Rahimi* as Methodology

The question presented in *Rahimi* had a straightforward answer that the Court got right. What is more significant, however, is what the Justices had to say about problems of constitutional interpretation that go well beyond the question presented in *Rahimi*, and well beyond the Second Amendment.

A. THE SECOND AMENDMENT QUESTION

18 U.S.C. § 922(g)(8)(C)(i) makes it a federal crime for a person to possess a gun if he is the subject of a domestic violence restraining order that "includes a finding that such a person represents a credible threat to the physical safety of [a covered] intimate partner or child."[2]

The Second Amendment to the Constitution says that "[a] well regulated Militia, being necessary to the security of a free State, the right of the people to keep and bear Arms, shall not be infringed."[3] In *District of Columbia v. Heller*,[4] the Supreme Court interpreted the Second Amendment to protect an individual right not limited to service in an organized militia. And in *New York State Rifle and Pistol Association, Inc. v. Bruen*,[5] the Court concluded that the scope of that individual right should be derived from historical practice.

In *Rahimi*, the Court concluded that Section 922(g)(8)(C)(i) was consistent with the Second Amendment as interpreted in *Heller* and *Bruen*.[6] In my view, this was straightforwardly correct, for three reasons that Professor Robert Leider and I sketched out shortly before *Rahimi* was decided.[7]

First, the Second Amendment (and the Fourteenth Amendment) protect a pre-existing right to keep and bear arms, whose scope was

---

[2] 18 U.S.C. § 922(g)(8)(C)(i).

[3] U.S. Const. amend. II.

[4] 554 U.S. 570 (2008).

[5] 597 U.S. 1 (2022).

[6] *Rahimi*, 602 U.S. at 699–700.

[7] *See* William Baude & Robert Leider, *The General-Law Right to Bear Arms*, 99 Notre Dame L. Rev. 1467, 1509–14 (2024).

generally expounded by general law at the time of the Founding and Reconstruction.[8]

Second, *Bruen*'s references to historical and analogical reasoning were a call for courts to perform a version of that general law inquiry—an inquiry into "the law of the past"[9]—to understand the principles under which a legislature could regulate the right to keep and bear arms.[10]

Third, there was strong historical evidence that one such principle was that legislatures could limit the use of weapons by those who had been proven to be dangerous, as then-Judge Barrett had argued in a prominent dissenting opinion in the Seventh Circuit.[11]

Under those basic premises, *Rahimi* was a straightforward case.[12] This is more or less what Chief Justice Roberts said in his opinion for an eight-Justice majority. The Court reiterated that, under *Bruen*, "the appropriate analysis involves considering whether the challenged regulation is consistent with the principles that underpin our regulatory tradition,"[13] and that judges must "'apply[] faithfully the balance struck by the founding generation to modern circumstances.'"[14] It reiterated that "when a challenged regulation does not precisely match its historical precursors, 'it still may be analogous enough to pass constitutional muster.' The law must comport with the principles underlying the Second Amendment, but it need not be a 'dead ringer' or a 'historical twin.'"[15] The Court then employed this methodology to quickly survey historical examples that "confirm what common sense suggests: When an individual poses a clear threat of physical violence to another, the threatening individual may be disarmed."[16]

Justice Thomas, the author of *Bruen*, did not believe that the historical examples supported a general dangerousness principle. In his

---

[8] *Id.* at 1470–82.

[9] *See Bruen*, 597 U.S. at 25 n.6 (quoting William Baude & Stephen E. Sachs, *Originalism and the Law of the Past*, 37 LAW & HIST. REV. 809, 810–11 (2019)).

[10] *See* Baude & Leider, *supra* note 7, at 1485–95.

[11] Kanter v. Barr, 919 F.3d 437, 451 (7th Cir. 2019) (Barrett, J., dissenting).

[12] *See* Baude & Leider, *supra* note 7, at 1509–14.

[13] United States v. Rahimi, 602 U.S. 680, 692 (2024) (citing *Bruen*, 597 U.S. at 26–31).

[14] *Id.* (quoting *Bruen*, 597 U.S. at 29).

[15] *Id.* (citation omitted) (quoting *Bruen*, 597 U.S. at 30); *see also id.* at 691 (observing that *Heller* and *Bruen* "were not meant to suggest a law trapped in amber").

[16] *Id.* at 698.

view, historical laws disarming dangerous persons "were driven by . . . quashing treason and rebellion," rather than "preventing interpersonal violence."[17] Other laws, such as sureties, did aim to prevent interpersonal violence, but did not disarm individuals.[18] These are fair quibbles, which Professor Leider and I bracketed in our earlier work,[19] but ultimately my view is that unless one is trying to distill the general law to an artificially low level of abstraction,[20] the more natural inference is that legislatures could use their regulatory authorities to provide for the disarmament of dangerous people. That is what Section 922(g)(8)(C)(i) does, and so it is constitutionally permissible.

B. METHODOLOGICAL FIRST PRINCIPLES

If the fate of Section 922(g)(8)(C)(i) were all that were at stake in *Rahimi*, there would be little more to say. But Chief Justice Roberts's eighteen-page opinion was followed by forty-nine pages of concurrences which focused less on the fate of the statute and more on a broader question: How should the Court interpret the Second Amendment in general, and, for that matter, the Constitution in general?

There is a reason that *Rahimi* generated such a robust methodological debate. The Second Amendment presents today's Justices with a doctrinal blank slate. Without the path dependence of numerous precedents, the Justices see an opportunity to describe from first principles how the adjudication of constitutional rights ought to work—to borrow from what they see as working well in other areas of law and to reject what they believe is not.

The Court's opinion in *Bruen*, for instance, contained several central analogies to recent decisions championing a categorical historical approach to the First Amendment;[21] it also endorsed the originalist

[17] *Id.* at 755–57 (Thomas, J., dissenting).

[18] *Id.* at 764; *cf.* George A. Mocsary, *In Denial About the Obvious: Upending the Rhetoric of the Modern Second Amendment*, 2024 Cato Sup. Ct. Rev. 201, 215 ("Justice Thomas's disagreement with the majority was about *Bruen*'s application, not *Bruen*'s method.").

[19] Baude & Leider, *supra* note 7, at 1510 n.258.

[20] *Cf. infra* note 58.

[21] N.Y. State Rifle & Pistol Ass'n, Inc. v. Bruen, 597 U.S. 1, 24–25 (2022) (citing United States v. Stevens, 559 U.S. 460, 468–71 (2010)); *id.* at 17, 24 (quoting Konigsberg v. State Bar, 366 U.S. 36, 50 n.10 (1961)); *id.* at 36 (citing Espinoza v. Mont. Dep't of Revenue, 591 U.S. 464, 480–82 (2020)); *id.* at 37 (citing Nev. Comm'n on Ethics v. Carrigan, 564 U.S. 117, 122–25 (2011)); *id.* at 70–71; *see also id.* at 82 (Barrett, J., concurring) (citing *Espinoza*, 591 U.S. at 482); *Rahimi*, 602 U.S. at 716–17 (Kavanaugh, J., concurring); *id.* at 724 (citing Republican

approach to the Confrontation Clause of the Sixth Amendment led by Justice Scalia in various opinions for the Court.[22] And by counterpoint, the Justices have also used Second Amendment cases to express their skepticism of doctrinal tools such as the tiers of scrutiny well known to First Amendment and Fourteenth Amendment case law.[23]

The opinions in *Rahimi* therefore present an especially rich opportunity to debate and analyze how to interpret the Constitution. Those debates will affect not just the future of the right to keep and bear arms, but the future of many other constitutional rights as well.

What they reveal is a pivotal phalanx of Justices who are openly committed to two things: an originalist method of constitutional interpretation, and an opposition to judicial "balancing" in constitutional adjudication. But it will be trickier for the Justices to maintain both of those commitments than their opinions in *Rahimi* let on.[24]

II. Methodological Commitments

A central debate that emerged from the *Rahimi* opinions involved the role of judicial "balancing" in constitutional adjudication.

Three of the Justices who joined the *Rahimi* majority opposed *Bruen*'s project in the first place. Justice Sotomayor, who dissented in *Bruen*,[25] penned a concurrence saying that while "[e]ven under *Bruen*, this is an easy case," she "remain[ed] troubled by *Bruen*'s myopic focus on history and tradition," and preferred "the means-end scrutiny that this Court rejected in *Bruen*. . . ."[26] Justice Kagan, also a *Bruen*

Party of Minn. v. White, 536 U.S. 765, 785 (2002)); *id.* at 728 (citing Kennedy v. Bremerton Sch. Dist., 597 U.S. 507, 535–36 (2022)); *id.* at 738 (Barrett, J., concurring) (citing Vidal v. Elster, 602 U.S. 286, 322–24 (2024) (Barrett, J., concurring in part)).

[22] *Bruen*, 597 U.S. at 25 (quoting Giles v. California, 554 U.S. 353, 358 (2008)); *id.* at 37 (citing Crawford v. Washington, 541 U.S. 36, 42–50 (2004)); *id.* at 71; *see also Rahimi*, 602 U.S. at 710 (Gorsuch, J., concurring) (citing *Crawford*, 541 U.S. at 54); *id.* (citing *Giles*, 554 U.S. at 358–61); *id.* at 728 (Kavanaugh, J., concurring) (citing *Crawford*, 541 U.S. at 47–50).

[23] *Bruen*, 597 U.S. at 17–25; *id.* at 29 n.7; *see also Rahimi*, 602 U.S. at 710–11 (Gorsuch, J., concurring); *id.* at 712–13; *id.* at 731–32 (Kavanaugh, J., concurring); District of Columbia v. Heller, 554 U.S. 570, 634–35 (2008).

[24] For other recent analyses of the tensions and omissions in these opinions, see Stephen Breyer, *Pragmatism or Textualism*, 138 Harv. L. Rev. 717, 765–69 (2025); and Reva B. Siegel, *The Levels-of-Generality Game: "History and Tradition" in the Roberts Court*, 47 Harv. J.L. & Pub. Pol'y 563, 599–604 (2024).

[25] *See Bruen*, 597 U.S. at 83 (Breyer, J., dissenting).

[26] *Rahimi*, 602 U.S. at 703, 706 (Sotomayor, J., concurring).

dissenter,[27] joined the concurrence.[28] Justice Jackson was not on the Court when *Bruen* was decided, but her *Rahimi* concurrence declared that she "disagree[d] with the methodology of that decision" and "would have joined the dissent had I been a Member of the Court at that time."[29] These Justices appear to be comfortable with the Second Amendment balancing tests that had prevailed in the lower courts before *Bruen*.

But in *Rahimi*, the Justices who *joined Bruen* expressed a different methodological theme—one that centered an originalist approach to constitutional interpretation and also rejected judicial balancing of constitutional rights.

A. ORIGINALISM

Justices Gorsuch, Barrett, and Kavanaugh each professed fidelity to originalist interpretations of the Constitution, though each with their own spin.

Justice Gorsuch emphasized that the Constitution's core commands are "the people's directions in the Constitution—directions that are 'trapped in amber.'"[30] He amusingly co-opted this quotation from the Chief Justice's majority opinion, where the Chief had emphasized that constitutional doctrine was *not* trapped in amber.[31]

Justice Barrett invoked a more explicitly positivist strain of originalism—one that was "built on two core principles."[32] First, "that the meaning of constitutional text is fixed at the time of its ratification,"[33] and second, that that meaning "'remains law until lawfully altered.'"[34] She also correctly recognized that historical evidence was relevant both to "elucidat[ing] how contemporaries understood the text" but also to "the more complicated role of determining the pre-existing right that the people enshrined in our fundamental law," which one

---

[27] *Bruen*, 597 U.S. at 83 (Breyer, J., dissenting).

[28] *Rahimi*, 602 U.S. at 702 (Sotomayor, J., concurring).

[29] *Id.* at 741 (Jackson, J., concurring).

[30] *Rahimi*, 602 U.S. at 709 (Gorsuch, J., concurring) (quoting *id.* at 691 (majority opinion)).

[31] *Id.* at 691 (majority opinion).

[32] *Id.* at 737 (Barrett, J., concurring).

[33] *Id.*

[34] *Id.* (quoting Stephen E. Sachs, *Originalism: Standard and Procedure*, 135 HARV. L. REV. 777, 782 (2022)).

might call "'original contours' history."[35] The Second Amendment protects a pre-existing right, and so we must understand history—the law of the past—to know what it is that it protects.[36]

Justice Kavanaugh delivered the most extensive essay on the role of text, history and tradition in constitutional interpretation. This essay emphasized originalism as a constraint on judges, citing classic works by Judge Bork and Justice Scalia.[37] Justice Kavanaugh first stressed the importance of following the Constitution's text in cases where it is clear and specific, supplying an almost comically long list of examples from the document.[38] He then discussed the importance of using history, rather than judicial policymaking, in resolving disputes about the meaning of the text in cases where it is less clear or less specific. His essay ranged from the use of pre-Founding background history, to Founding Era history probative of original meaning, to post-Founding practice more relevant to liquidation, gloss, and the like.[39]

B. FEAR OF BALANCING

A second common denominator that emerged from these opinions was opposition to balancing. Justices Gorsuch, Kavanaugh, and Barrett all insisted that they were not deciding the merits of gun control provisions or determining the importance of the right to bear arms.

Justice Gorsuch emphasized that it was "the people [who] ratified the Second Amendment" who had decided that gun rights were "vital to the preservation of life and liberty" even though "an arms-bearing citizenry posed some risks."[40] By contrast, he wrote, today's judges "have no authority to question that judgment" and their "only lawful role is to apply" it.[41] And while Justice Gorsuch did not deny that

---

[35] *Id.* at 738–39.

[36] *Accord* Baude & Leider, *supra* note 7, at 1486–95.

[37] *Rahimi*, 602 U.S. at 718 (Kavanaugh, J., concurring) (first quoting Robert Bork, *Neutral Principles and Some First Amendment Problems*, 47 Ind. L.J. 1, 8 (1971); then quoting Antonin Scalia, *Originalism: The Lesser Evil*, 57 U. Cin. L. Rev. 849, 864 (1989); and then quoting Antonin Scalia, *The Rule of Law as a Law of Rules*, 56 U. Chi. L. Rev. 1175, 1183 (1989)).

[38] *Id.* at 715.

[39] *Id.* at 719–30. Professor Sherif Girgis highlights that the theoretical differences between Justice Kavanaugh and Justice Barrett, which "track[ ] an old cleavage in legal conservatism," also explain their different attitudes toward post-ratification tradition. Sherif Girgis, *Originalism's Age of Ironies*, 138 Harv. L. Rev. F. 1, 13 (2024).

[40] *Rahimi*, 602 U.S. at 709 (Gorsuch, J., concurring).

[41] *Id.*

originalist reasoning "may sometimes be difficult," he concluded that "that path offers surer footing than any other this Court has attempted. . . ."[42] "Come to this Court with arguments from text and history," he proposed, "and we are bound to reason through them as best we can. . . . Allow judges to reign unbounded by those materials, or permit them to extrapolate their own broad new principles from those sources, and no one can have any idea how they might rule."[43]

Justice Kavanaugh argued that when dealing with "vague constitutional text" without established judicial precedent, "there are really only two potential answers to the question of how to determine exceptions to broadly worded constitutional rights: history or policy."[44] History was better, Justice Kavanaugh argued, because it "establishes a 'criterion that is conceptually quite separate from the preferences of the judge himself.'"[45]

Justice Kavanaugh emphasized this dichotomy and his allergy to judicial balancing many times throughout his concurrence. To quote only a few choice passages:

> When the text is vague and the pre-ratification history is elusive or inconclusive, post-ratification history becomes especially important. Indeed, absent precedent, there can be little else to guide a judge deciding a constitutional case in that situation, unless the judge simply defaults to his or her own policy preferences.[46]

> [T]hat kind of balancing approach to constitutional interpretation departs from what Framers such as Madison stated, what jurists such as Marshall and Scalia did, what judges as umpires should strive to do, and what this Court has actually done across the constitutional landscape for the last two centuries.[47]

> The subjective balancing approach forces judges to act more like legislators who decide what the law should be, rather than judges who "say what the law is."[48]

---

[42] *Id.* at 711, 712.

[43] *Id.* at 712.

[44] *Id.* at 717 (Kavanaugh, J., concurring).

[45] *Id.* at 718 (quoting Antonin Scalia, *Originalism: The Lesser Evil*, 57 U. Cin. L. Rev. 849, 864 (1989)).

[46] *Id.* at 723.

[47] *Id.* at 731.

[48] *Id.* at 732 (quoting Marbury v. Madison, 5 U.S. (1 Cranch) 137, 177 (1803)).

> Deciding constitutional cases in a still-developing area of this Court's jurisprudence can sometimes be difficult. But that is not a permission slip for a judge to let constitutional analysis morph into policy preferences under the guise of a balancing test that churns out the judge's own policy beliefs.[49]

This shared opposition to balancing is also what drove the biggest methodological cleavage between these Justices—the cleavage about how much to rely on history and tradition when the original meaning of the Constitution has run out.

As noted above, Justice Kavanaugh's answer was: *very much*. To him, the only real choices are "history or policy,"[50] so judges who wish to avoid making policy decisions must use history—history to figure out the original meaning of the Constitution, and still more history (however late in the day) to close the gap.

Justice Barrett, by contrast, reiterated her longstanding skepticism of "'freewheeling reliance on historical practice'"[51] and rejected the view that "'tradition,' standing alone, is dispositive."[52] Justice Barrett had voiced that skepticism in earlier separate opinions in *Bruen*,[53] *Samia v. United States* (a self-incrimination case),[54] and *Vidal v. Elster* (a free speech case).[55] On Justice Barrett's more specifically positivist view, judges should turn to history only when a legal rule tells them to do so—such as originalism, liquidation, stare decisis, and so on.[56] History without law to drive it does not make the judge's task any easier or better.

But again, despite this important dispute between Justice Kavanaugh and Justice Barrett about the relevance of post-Founding history in constitutional interpretation (a dispute in which I favor Justice Barrett's view, for what it is worth),[57] what is especially striking is

---

[49] *Id.* at 736.

[50] *Id.* at 717.

[51] *Id.* at 738 (Barrett, J., concurring) (quoting N.Y. State Rifle & Pistol Ass'n, Inc. v. Bruen, 597 U.S. 1, 83 (2022) (Barrett, J., concurring)).

[52] *Id.*

[53] *Bruen*, 597 U.S. at 81–83 (Barrett, J., concurring).

[54] Samia v. United States, 599 U.S. 635, 656–57 (2023) (Barrett, J., concurring in part and concurring in the judgment).

[55] Vidal v. Elster, 602 U.S. 286, 322–25 (2024) (Barrett, J., concurring in part).

[56] *Rahimi*, 602 U.S. at 738 (Barrett, J., concurring).

[57] Because I share Justice Barrett's view that the central reason to follow the original meaning of the Constitution is that it is the law, rather than because it is especially good at constraining judges, *compare* William Baude, *Is Originalism Our Law?*, 116 Colum. L. Rev. 2349, 2391–97 (2015), *with* William Baude, *Originalism as a Constraint on Judges*, 84 U. Chi. L. Rev. 2213, 2228–29 (2017), I share her view that we ought to focus on whether and when the law gives special status to post-ratification practices. *Accord* Girgis, *supra* note 39, at 13.

what both sides of the dispute have in common. Both of them saw it as common ground that judges should avoid freewheeling analysis in which judges pick and choose their sources or preferred outcomes, even while they disagreed on exactly how methodologically to accomplish that goal.[58]

C. TENSIONS

In my view, the Justices' willingness to embrace originalism as the central task of constitutional interpretation, and their unwillingness to embrace judicial balancing, are both very good things. The problem is that these commitments are in tension with one another.

One aspect of this tension, highlighted by the Kavanaugh/Barrett dispute, is that sometimes the original meaning of a specific constitutional provision can be too hard to discern, or too indeterminate. Justice Kavanaugh is right that when the original meaning of the constitutional text is vague or ambiguous, judges need some way to decide the cases nonetheless, and their own policy views about the justice of the cause are not good material for filling the gap. Especially in a world of political and judicial polarization, it is better for judges deciding constitutional cases to try to decide them on the basis of something other than their policy preferences. But Justice Barrett is right that "history," without a more defined legal methodology, is not a sufficient way to fill that gap either. And she is right that a judge, whose job is to follow the law, needs not just *some* gap-filler, but a *legal* gap-filler.

A second aspect of this problem, which is more fundamental, is that the original understanding of constitutional rights *was not hostile to balancing*. Among the many works of legal scholarship cited in the *Rahimi* opinions and for that matter in the *Bruen* opinions, perhaps the most glaring omissions were works by Professors Jamal Greene, Jud Campbell, and others illustrating that many Founding Era

[58] Finally, it is worth noting that Justice Thomas's dissent, while less focused on methodology, also reflected an opposition to the use of "generalized principles," *Rahimi*, 602 U.S. at 775 (Thomas, J., dissenting), arguing that the government's approach—"and indeed any similar, principle-based approach—would hollow out the Second Amendment of any substance," *id.* at 775. It expressed concern that the majority's approach to synthesizing the historical materials would result in "the exact sort of 'regulatory blank check' that *Bruen* warns against and the American people ratified the Second Amendment to preclude." *Id.* at 772 (quoting *Bruen*, 597 U.S. at 30).

constitutional rights were not absolutes and relied on a notion of balancing.[59]

At and after the Founding, legislatures were expected to make reasonable determinations about how to regulate individual liberty in order to better protect and preserve the liberty of all. This was a basic tenet of social contract theory that formed a backdrop to reading the constitutional bills of rights.[60]

To be sure, constitutional rights still constrained the power to legislate. If the legislature trenched on the core of a protected constitutional right, the legislation was unconstitutional. If the legislature trenched on a constitutional right that had been expounded with specificity through precedent and practice, the legislation was unconstitutional. And if the legislature regulated a constitutional right in unreasonable ways, the legislation was unconstitutional. But these inquiries, especially the latter, entailed a great degree of balancing—balancing the rights of each individual against the common good. The now-familiar intuiting that rights are necessarily "trumps" is a modern one.[61]

So too the obsession of today's originalist judges with avoiding any policy determinations is somewhat anachronistic. Though that does not mean it is wrong. Judges at the time of the enactment of the Bill of Rights or the Fourteenth Amendment lived in a different legal environment—one that could still take for granted various unwritten principles of law, even of fundamental rights, as being widely shared

---

[59] *See, e.g.*, Jud Campbell, *Natural Rights and the First Amendment*, 127 Yale L.J. 246, 268–80 (2017) [hereinafter Campbell, *Natural Rights and the First Amendment*]; Jud Campbell, *Republicanism and Natural Rights at the Founding*, 32 Const. Comment. 85, 90–98 (2017) [hereinafter Campbell, *Republicanism and Natural Rights at the Founding*]; Jamal Greene, How Rights Went Wrong: Why Our Obsession with Rights Is Tearing America Apart 7–31 (2021).

[60] *See* Campbell, *Republicanism and Natural Rights at the Founding*, *supra* note 59, at 87–92; Jud Campbell, *Determining Rights*, 138 Harv. L. Rev. 921, 929–37 (2025) [hereinafter Campbell, *Determining Rights*].

[61] *See* Jamal Greene, *The Supreme Court, 2017 Term—Foreword: Rights as Trumps?*, 132 Harv. L. Rev. 28, 109–10 (2018); Campbell, *Determining Rights*, *supra* note 60, at 979–81. For a canonical modern formulation, see Ronald Dworkin, Taking Rights Seriously 191–92 (1977). To be sure, there were *some* Founding Era rights that were closer to absolutes, for instance because they were grounded in a specific positive law custom or because they were seen as inalienable. *See* Campbell, *Natural Rights and the First Amendment*, *supra* note 59, at 280–90; *see also* William Baude & Stephen E. Sachs, *The "Common-Good Manifesto,"* 136 Harv. L. Rev. 861, 892 (2023) (reviewing Adrian Vermeule, Common Good Constitutionalism (2022)).

across Anglo-American jurisdictions.[62] It was perhaps easier for them to apply well-settled policies of unwritten law, without worrying that in doing so they were *applying the judge's own views*, because of this generally shared legal culture.

Approaching this problem today poses greater difficulties for judges. Some may be skeptical that there is such a thing (if there ever was) as well-settled principles of unwritten law shared across jurisdictions. Others may believe such principles exist but doubt that judges will really try to follow them. Still others may believe that judges will *try*, but doubt that they will succeed in doing anything other than following their own hearts. If any of this is true, then today's originalist judges need to think harder—or at least to think differently—about how to ensure that they are neutrally and fairly adjudicating cases under our inherited Constitution.

III. Alternatives to Balancing

Now some say that balancing is simply inevitable. That is Professor Sherif Girgis's analysis, at least when it comes to "general liberties … defined by reference to conduct to be shielded from regulations of various sorts," such as free speech and arms bearing.[63] But there are strategies the Justices can use to reduce the need for judicial balancing, if they are as serious about it as they claim.

I will briefly describe three: deference, the general law approach, and the construction of rules.

A. The Presumption of Constitutionality

For all that the *Rahimi* opinions denied judicial balancing, they gave almost no attention to one of the oldest and most straightforward ways of avoiding it: judicial deference. On this view, when other legal materials run out, judges should decide constitutional cases with the presumption of constitutionality—by deferring to the legislature's decision. There is much to be said for this approach.

First, at a conceptual level, this is a straightforward alternative to the other options canvassed in *Rahimi*—namely, the broad use of

---

[62] *See* William Baude, Jud Campbell & Stephen E. Sachs, *General Law and the Fourteenth Amendment*, 76 Stan. L. Rev. 1185, 1193–1206 (2024).

[63] Sherif Girgis, *Unfinished Liberties, Inevitable Balancing*, 125 Colum. L. Rev. (forthcoming 2025) (manuscript at 3) (on file with author).

postenactment history and judicial policymaking. Justice Kavanaugh's repeated insistence that those were really the only two alternatives is a false dichotomy. A rule that judges should defer to legislative regulations of rights in cases of doubt does not call for judicial policymaking; it calls for judges to permit the products of *legislative* policymaking. And rather than defer to the traditions of a rolling period of the past, it defers to the decisions of legislators whose enactments remain law in the present.[64]

Second, and importantly, some form of deference to legislators in constitutional cases is *itself* sanctioned by text, history and tradition. The presumption of constitutionality can potentially be stated as a correlate of the constitutional text itself: "[I]t is simply that, as a matter of correct interpretation of the text, the proper hermeneutic principle is that indeterminacy does not warrant judicial invalidation of legislation or executive actions that fall within the range of meaning of the specific text at issue."[65]

Additionally, as discussed above, Professors Greene and Campbell argue that the Founding Era conception of rights was one that centered on the role of legislatures, representative of the people, to regulate individual rights where necessary for the common good.[66] The very idea of retaining natural rights entailed self-determination, so while judicial review was present in this system, it was limited.[67]

Still further, as Professor Christopher Green has demonstrated, in the early republic judges insisted that statutes could be set aside only when they were clearly unconstitutional, which they grew to equate with a standard of unconstitutionality beyond a "reasonable doubt."[68] And as Professor Derek Webb has more recently expanded, a "'triple helix' of judicial restraint"—"(1) the presumption of constitutionality,

---

[64] *See id.* (manuscript at 62–66).

[65] Michael Stokes Paulsen, *The Text, the Whole Text, and Nothing but the Text, So Help Me God: Un-Writing Amar's* Unwritten Constitution, 81 U. Chi. L. Rev. 1385, 1436 (2014) (reviewing Akhil Reed Amar, America's Unwritten Constitution (2012)).

[66] *See* Greene, *supra* note 59, at 12–13, 30–31; Campbell, *Natural Rights and the First Amendment*, *supra* note 59, at 253, 263, 270–76.

[67] *See* Greene, *supra* note 59, at 30; Campbell, *Natural Rights and the First Amendment*, *supra* note 59, at 287, 302, 305, 316; Campbell, *Republicanism and Natural Rights at the Founding*, *supra* note 59, at 86–87, 98–103, 106–08, 112.

[68] Christopher R. Green, *Clarity and Reasonable Doubt in Early State-Constitutional Judicial Review*, 57 S. Tex. L. Rev. 169, 172–88 (2015).

(2) the clear error rule, and (3) the reasonable doubt standard"—was firmly "liquidated" over the course of the nineteenth century.[69]

To the extent that the opinions in *Rahimi* acknowledged this approach at all they did so with an equivocal shrug. "Some judges will apply heightened scrutiny with a presumption in favor of deference to the legislature. Other judges will apply heightened scrutiny with a presumption in favor of the individual right in question," Justice Kavanaugh lamented.[70] Or they did so with a hand-waving invocation of the burden of proof: "A regulation is constitutional only if the government affirmatively proves that it is 'consistent with the Second Amendment's text and historical understanding,'" Justice Barrett said, quoting *Bruen*.[71] But if the Justices are serious about both being originalists and avoiding judicial policymaking, they would do well to more seriously contemplate the longstanding approach that their predecessors developed for doing both.

To be sure, doctrines of judicial deference have themselves evolved over time. The classical doctrines of judicial restraint rested on two institutional premises: one judicial and one legislative.[72] The judicial premise was that judicial review should be exercised with delicacy because taking a judgment out of the hands of the legislature was a matter of high stakes—with no easy way to correct a mistaken decision. That view remains true. The legislative premise was that legislatures took very seriously their obligations to the Constitution, and so legislation was only enacted after it had survived serious constitutional scrutiny. That premise is much more contestable and indeed often false today.[73]

---

[69] Derek A. Webb, *The Lost History of Judicial Restraint*, 100 Notre Dame L. Rev. 289, 294, 302–03 (2024).

[70] United States v. Rahimi, 602 U.S. 680, 733 (2024) (Kavanaugh, J., concurring).

[71] *Rahimi*, 602 U.S. at 737 (Barrett, J., concurring) (quoting N.Y. State Rifle & Pistol Ass'n, Inc. v. Bruen, 597 U.S. 1, 26 (2022)). To be fair, one might conclude that this burden-shifting is entailed by *Bruen*'s two-part test, especially if one reads *Bruen* to say (at "Step One") that any regulation that falls within the unqualified text of the Second Amendment is presumptively unconstitutional, and then to say that the regulation can only be saved if (at "Step Two") the government rebuts the presumption of unconstitutionality with historical evidence. J. Joel Alicea, Bruen *Was Right*, 174 U. Pa. L. Rev. (forthcoming 2025) (manuscript at 9–10, 30–32), https://ssrn.com/abstract=5122492.

[72] *See* Green, *supra* note 68, at 192–97.

[73] *See* Note, *Should the Supreme Court Presume that Congress Acts Constitutionally? The Role of the Canon of Avoidance and Reliance on Early Legislative Practice in Constitutional Interpretation*, 116 Harv. L. Rev. 1798, 1804–08 (2003); *see also* Keith E. Whittington, *James Madison Has Left the Building*, 72 U. Chi. L. Rev. 1137, 1148–58 (2005) (reviewing J. Mitchell Pickerill,

Perhaps relatedly, many courts no longer adhere to the "reasonable doubt" standard of judicial review.[74] Indeed, the standard is sufficiently eyebrow raising that when the Wisconsin Supreme Court recently employed the reasonable doubt rule to deny a religious challenge to the state's unemployment tax,[75] the Catholic Charities Bureau sought certiorari on the reasonable doubt standard, arguing that it was something between "a hortatory expression" and simply "'dead' in federal courts."[76] The Supreme Court even briefly agreed to review the standard when it granted the Catholic Charities Bureau's petition, but then quickly beat a retreat, amending the cert grant to include only the merits and not the presumption of constitutionality.[77] Perhaps that is just as well for now, as the Court does not appear ready to fully appreciate the tradition of judicial deference to legislation, but this is something the anti-balancing Justices will need to confront someday.

In any event, even if neither law nor logic calls for a presumption of constitutionality that is so strong as to require proof beyond a reasonable doubt, they could still call for *some* presumption—at least one strand of Webb's "triple helix"[78] remains unbroken. The Justices should give that presumption some attention in constitutional cases and recognize that, beyond "history or policy,"[79] another approach to resolving close constitutional cases is to let legislatures resolve them.[80]

Constitutional Deliberation in Congress: The Impact of Judicial Review in a Separated System (2004)).

[74] *See* Hugh Spitzer, *Reasoning v. Rhetoric: The Strange Case of "Unconstitutional Beyond a Reasonable Doubt,"* 74 Rutgers U. L. Rev. 1429, 1440–45 (2022).

[75] Cath. Charities Bureau, Inc. v. Wis. Lab. & Indus. Rev. Comm'n, 3 N.W.3d 666, 686 (Wis. 2024).

[76] Petition for Writ of Certiorari at 32–33, Cath. Charities Bureau, Inc. v. Wis. Lab. & Indus. Rev. Comm'n, No. 24-154 (U.S. Aug. 9, 2024), 2024 WL 3815281 (first quoting Spitzer, *supra* note 74, at 1460; and then quoting Richard A. Posner, *The Rise and Fall of Judicial Self-Restraint*, 100 Calif. L. Rev. 519, 553 (2012)).

[77] Cath. Charities Bureau, Inc. v. Wis. Lab. & Indus. Rev. Comm'n, No. 24-154, 2024 WL 5100663, at *1 (U.S. Dec. 13, 2024), *amended by* No. 24-154, 2024 WL 5112872 (U.S. Dec. 16, 2024).

[78] *See* Webb, *supra* note 69, at 294.

[79] United States v. Rahimi, 602 U.S. 680, 717 (2024) (Kavanaugh, J., concurring).

[80] I cannot resist observing that making use of the presumption of the constitutionality more frequently would also help the Court address another recurring problem it discussed in a slate of concurrences last year: "the best processes for analyzing likelihood of success on the merits" when considering "emergency applications in cases . . . where a party has sought to enjoin enforcement of a new state or federal law." Labrador v. Poe, 144 S. Ct. 921, 928 (2024)

B. THE GENERAL LAW APPROACH

The presumption of constitutionality is simply a presumption, and it will never be able to eliminate all hard cases—at best it can only reduce them by relocating them to a new boundary. And even in the days of deep deference, judicial review of individual rights was still alive and important. When a legislature abridged the core of an individual right, or regulated it in sufficiently unreasonable ways, courts would uphold individual rights by saying so.[81] So beyond the presumption of constitutionality, originalist Justices might engage in more searching judicial review by reviving the techniques of their forebears.

In the nineteenth century, constitutional rights were seen and adjudicated partly through the lens of "what we now call general law. Though referred to by different names, this shared body of unwritten law was not derived from any enactment by a single sovereign but instead 'existed by common practice and consent among a number of sovereigns.'"[82] These general law rights were secured by the Privileges or Immunities Clause of the Fourteenth Amendment and the provisions of the Bill of Rights that were understood to codify pre-existing customary and natural rights, such as freedom of speech, freedom of the press, and the right to keep and bear arms.[83]

Judges who wish to pursue an originalist approach to rights adjudication could look to the practices and constitutional decisions of the states over time to help understand the contours of those rights. As discussed above, in the case of the right to keep and bear arms, this method could point to something very much like the approach taken in *Rahimi*: the recognition that disarming those proven to be

(Kavanaugh, J., concurring in the grant of stay). Justice Kavanaugh has expressed doubt about the usefulness of the maxim that courts "should simply try to 'preserve the status quo,'" arguing that "[t]here is no good blanket answer to the question of what the status quo is. Each conception of the status quo is defensible, but there is no sound or principled reason to pick one over another. . . ." *Id.* at 930. The presumption of constitutionality provides a sound and principled reason to treat newly enacted legislation as the status quo. This presumption would of course be subject to rebuttal for "plainly unconstitutional . . . laws." *Id.* at 931. Whether that same presumption would apply to administrative actions is another matter.

[81] Baude & Leider, *supra* note 7, at 1489.

[82] Baude, Campbell & Sachs, *supra* note 62, at 1190 (footnote omitted) (quoting William A. Fletcher, *The General Common Law and Section 34 of the Judiciary Act of 1789: The Example of Marine Insurance*, 97 Harv. L. Rev. 1513, 1517 (1984)).

[83] *Id.* at 1235–36.

dangerous was a reasonable regulation of the right to bear arms.[84] But in other cases—such as permanent disarmaments,[85] the exclusion of guns from "sensitive places,"[86] the regulation of gun length or magazine size,[87] and so on—courts would have to make judgments about the reasonableness of the regulations, their purposes, and the burdens they impose. That would be the originalist and traditionalist approach.

This approach will look uncomfortably like balancing, but it is not of the same kind as the tiers of scrutiny that Justice Kavanaugh seems to especially disfavor.[88] As Professor Leider and I have described it:

> [W]hat the traditional approach permitted was a sort of *rights-based* interest balancing, where the state could regulate a right for limited purposes, such as to protect the rights of others. It did not necessarily allow legislatures to restrict a right simply out of disagreement with the value of the right. And even when the legislature had the power to restrict rights out of public necessity, restrictions could not be so severe as to amount to a nullification of the right.[89]

And it is not the "freewheeling" use of history that Justice Barrett has especially rejected.[90] Rather, judges consider the history and tradition of regulation of particular individual rights under a specific legal theory: the theory that those individual rights were understood to have a scope defined by the principles of "general law," and that these cases and statutes can be used as evidence of what those general law principles were. But as noted above, this way of thinking about the law has become so unfashionable today that it may be quite some time before judges are ready to ask it to bear all of the weight in constitutional cases.

---

[84] Baude & Leider, *supra* note 7, at 1509–14.

[85] *Id.* at 1510 n.258, 1511–12.

[86] *Id.* at 1506–08.

[87] *Id.* at 1504–05.

[88] *See* United States v. Rahimi, 602 U.S. 680, 731–34 (2024) (Kavanaugh, J., concurring).

[89] Baude & Leider, *supra* note 7, at 1491 (footnotes omitted); *see also* T. Alexander Aleinikoff, *Constitutional Law in the Age of Balancing*, 96 Yale L.J. 943, 948–52 (1987) (emphasizing the sharp break between the now-familiar "balancing" approach that emerged in the mid-twentieth century and the traditional approach that prevailed before that).

[90] *Rahimi*, 602 U.S. at 738 (Barrett, J., concurring) (quoting N.Y. State Rifle & Pistol Ass'n, Inc. v. Bruen, 597 U.S. 1, 83 (2022) (Barrett, J., concurring)).

C. CONSTRUCTING RULES

A third strategy the Justices might use to avoid the balancing of individual rights is to construct a series of doctrinal rules as they decide a series of cases over time. These rules would hopefully be grounded in historical sources and constitutional principles but presented in more easily administrable ways. The doctrine could take on a life of its own.

Something like this may describe the Court's approach to many aspects of free speech doctrine today. Today the Court has demarked "historic and traditional categories" of unprotected speech that trace "[f]rom 1791 to the present ... in a few limited areas. . . ."[91] The original and historical understanding of free speech did not necessarily have such sharp contours between completely protected and unprotected speech, making the modern doctrine something of a translation or extrapolation.[92]

Today the Court frequently employs rules of viewpoint and content neutrality to determine which speech restrictions are constitutionally suspected. But as discussed, the original and historical understanding of free speech did not have a strong neutrality principle, instead turning on the reasonableness of legislative regulations in pursuance of the common good.[93] The modern doctrine of neutrality arose in part as a reaction to the anxieties of legal realism and the need for judges to articulate more neutral principles in deciding which restrictions on speech they would uphold and which they would not.[94]

One could imagine the Court pursuing a similar strategy over time with other individual rights. There are at least three major challenges with such a strategy, however.

The first is that it is a difficult approach for an originalist to justify. As the free speech examples show, there is often a noticeable difference between the modern doctrinal rule and the law of the past,

---

[91] United States v. Stevens, 559 U.S. 460, 468 (2010) (first quoting Simon & Schuster, Inc. v. Members of N.Y. State Crime Victims Bd., 502 U.S. 105, 127 (1991) (Kennedy, J., concurring in the judgment); and then quoting R.A.V. v. City of St. Paul, 505 U.S. 377, 382–83 (1992)).

[92] *See* Genevieve Lakier, *The Invention of Low-Value Speech*, 128 Harv. L. Rev. 2166, 2177–79, 2201–03, 2214–18 (2015).

[93] *See supra* note 62 and accompanying text.

[94] *See* Jud Campbell, *The Emergence of Neutrality*, 131 Yale L.J. 861, 892–93, 928–43 (2022).

and the originalist grounding for modern doctrine is thought to be very weak.[95] I suspect that most modern free speech doctrine can still be grounded in originalism—this depends on the details of the differences, the legal changes that might justify them, and on the relationship between constitutional standards and constitutional decision procedures[96]—but it is true that it is a *difficult* approach to justify.[97]

The second challenge is that the Court has not been especially consistent in pursuing that strategy even where it claims to do so. While the *Bruen* majority invoked the Court's categorical historical approach to the First Amendment as a favorable analogy, it downplayed the fact that other aspects of First Amendment doctrine also frequently employ means-ends scrutiny through forms of heightened scrutiny that the majority and especially Justice Kavanaugh disfavored.[98] This may be a bad omen. Just as the Court's First Amendment doctrine has not proven as categorical or rule-based as sometimes advertised, it is easy to imagine that the same thing might happen in the Second Amendment and other areas.

The third challenge is that articulating such rules requires the Court to decide a reasonably plentiful number of cases on the topic. The First Amendment rules emerged over many decades of adjudication of many free speech claims. In the past twenty years, the Court has decided only five Second Amendment cases, and has only begun to address the most basic questions about the scope of the right.[99] And it does not seem to be interested in picking up the pace. After *Rahimi*, the Solicitor General asked the Court to immediately resolve three pending petitions about the scope of Section 922(g)'s ban on felons possessing firearms, observing that the range of

[95] *See, e.g.*, Richard H. Fallon, Jr., *Selective Originalism and Judicial Role Morality*, 102 Tex. L. Rev. 221, 251–52 (2023); David A. Strauss, *Freedom of Speech and the Common-Law Constitution*, *in* Eternally Vigilant: Free Speech in the Modern Era 33 (Lee C. Bollinger & Geoffrey R. Stone eds., 2002).

[96] On originalist standards and decision procedures, see generally Stephen E. Sachs, *Originalism: Standard and Procedure*, 135 Harv. L. Rev. 777 (2022).

[97] *Cf.* William Baude & Michael Stokes Paulsen, *The Sweep and Force of Section Three*, 172 U. Pa. L. Rev. 605, 670 n.259 (2024) (suggesting that "modern First Amendment doctrine . . . often captures the original meaning of freedom of speech and freedom of the press, as applied to modern circumstances" and that "one might construct a truly marvelous proof of this, which this margin is too narrow to contain").

[98] *See* N.Y. State Rifle & Pistol Ass'n, Inc. v. Bruen, 597 U.S. 1, 22–25 (2022); United States v. Rahimi, 602 U.S. 680, 731 (2024) (Kavanaugh, J., concurring).

[99] Those five cases are, in order, *Heller*, *McDonald v. City of Chicago*, 561 U.S. 742 (2010), *Caetano v. Massachusetts*, 577 U.S. 411 (2016), *Bruen*, and *Rahimi*.

pending petitions would help the Court articulate a rule that would guide the lower courts.[100] The Court summarily granted, vacated, and remanded them all without opinion.[101] Sometimes it seems that fear of balancing might lead to a fear of opining in the first place.

D. MIXED METHODS

None of these approaches are a complete and sufficient alternative to all kinds of judicial balancing in all cases. Deference to legislatures allows legislatures to balance rights in many cases and still requires judges to decide when the legislature has gone too far. The general law approach still requires courts to compare the legislature's purpose in regulating the right to the scope of the burden it has imposed. Constructing a doctrine still requires the Court to decide what kind of doctrine to construct.

But each of these approaches responds to a different potentially troubling element of judicial balancing. Deference to legislatures replaces some judicial balancing with legislative balancing; it makes balancing more democratic and authoritative. The general law approach constrains balancing with a historically guided and rights-oriented approach; it makes balancing more lawful and legitimate. Constructing doctrine replaces case-by-case or ad hoc balancing with the ex ante elaboration of neutral principles; it makes balancing more predictable and impersonal.

Indeed, analysis of these approaches in combination helps to remind us that the disfavored concept of balancing entails several different but related judicial approaches. Different judges might disfavor different parts of balancing and for different reasons. Over time, the Justices may find that these frameworks will let them define and avoid whatever is especially bad about balancing while accepting the parts that are inevitable or even desirable.

Interestingly, in *Rahimi* the Court's decision can be justified by all three of these approaches, perhaps in combination. The Court articulated, as if through construction, the principle that legislatures may regulate firearms so as to disarm the dangerous. That principle

---

[100] Supplemental Brief for the Federal Parties at 6–7, Garland v. Range, 144 S. Ct. 2706 (2024) (No. 23-374).

[101] *Range*, 144 S. Ct. 2706; Doss v. United States, 144 S. Ct. 2712 (2024) (mem.); Jackson v. United States, 144 S. Ct. 2710 (2024) (mem.).

can be derived from the general law approach. And it led the Court to uphold the constitutionality of a federal statute.[102] But of course many harder cases will await the Justices where the relative power of these approaches will be put to a greater test.

Conclusion

It might seem overly credulous to put so much stock in the Justices' methodological statements. When we see the Justices insisting on their adherence to originalism, or denying that the most powerful judges in the country engage in policymaking, we might hear Ralph Waldo Emerson in the background: "[T]he louder he talked of his honor, the faster we counted our spoons."[103]

But methodologies lay down a marker. They invite readers to judge the judges, to see if they have lived up to their promises or fallen short.[104] The opinions in *Rahimi* lay down markers for originalism and opposition to judicial balancing, thus inviting us all to judge over the next few decades whether their authors can manage to live up to both.

---

[102] Indeed, the chief methodological critique of the dissent was that the majority's approach would lead the government to win too many cases. *Rahimi*, 602 U.S. at 772 (Thomas, J., dissenting); *cf. supra* note 58.

[103] Ralph Waldo Emerson, The Conduct of Life 184 (1867).

[104] *See* Stephen E. Sachs, Life After *Erie* 1 (Nov. 1, 2023), https://ssrn.com/abstract=4633575.

RISA GOLUBOFF AND
RICHARD SCHRAGGER

GRANTS PASS AND THE VAGRANCY REVOLUTION REVISITED

Introduction

City of Grants Pass v. Johnson[1] was an easy case for the Roberts Court. For one of the most conservative courts in U.S. history, the case must have loomed like a giant softball. The recognition of a right for the homeless to camp and sleep in public places likely resembled old-fashioned Warren Court-style judicial activism, an outlier from the Ninth Circuit where even liberal state and local elected officials filed briefs urging the Supreme Court to reverse.[2] Homelessness is worse than ever, and the causes of homelessness are complex and varied. Local governments require flexibility in responding to difficult policy challenges. Judges are not well suited to devise responses to pressing

Risa Goluboff is the David and Mary Harrison Distinguished Professor of Law at the University of Virginia School of Law. Richard Schragger is the Walter L. Brown Professor of Law at the University of Virginia School of Law.

Authors' note: Many thanks to Brian Ziegler and Joshua Adamson for excellent research assistance and to Justin Driver for his editorial wisdom.

[1] City of Grants Pass v. Johnson, 144 S. Ct. 2202 (2024).

[2] *See, e.g.*, Brief for California Governor Gavin Newsom as Amicus Curiae Supporting Petitioner, *Grants Pass*, 144 S. Ct. 2202 (No. 23-175); City and County of San Francisco as Amicus Curiae Supporting Petitioner, *Grants Pass*, 144 S. Ct. 2202 (No. 23-175).

The Supreme Court Review, 2025.
 https://doi.org/10.1086/734709

social questions. All of which is what the Supreme Court, in an opinion by Justice Gorsuch, ultimately concluded. The Court reversed the Ninth Circuit's holding that the Constitution prevents governments from criminalizing sleeping in public places or in cars when there is otherwise no other place to go.[3]

The liberal Justices dissented, more vigorously perhaps than one may have predicted, given that so many progressive city and state leaders had lined up to defend the ordinances. Justice Sotomayor, joined by Justices Kagan and Jackson, treated homelessness as a "complex and heartbreaking crisis."[4] The abiding tragedy of homelessness linked the majority and dissenting opinions. What divided them was a doctrinal disagreement about the Eighth Amendment's Cruel and Unusual Punishments Clause,[5] which the Court had previously read to prevent people from being criminalized for things they "are" rather than things they "do." The dissent urged basic fidelity to that constitutional precedent—with special concern for the homeless as an insular and highly vulnerable population. They argued that penalizing homeless people for sleeping in public violated previous understandings of the Eighth Amendment.[6]

That disagreement could appear to be limited to the policies at issue in the case, but there are deep structural principles—of both constitutional doctrine and political economy—at work here, too. A key question in the jurisprudence of the Warren and Burger Courts—and one that continues to reverberate today—concerns the discretionary power that low-level criminal laws like vagrancy and loitering give the police to stop, arrest, or move people along simply for being out of place in some way.[7] That large groups of people lack shelter in a propertied society is structural too. By that we mean that "homelessness" is not some new policy problem, suddenly sprung on twenty-first-century cities surprised by the absence of mental health services, the scourge of fentanyl, or the high cost of housing. Rather, "homeless" or "unhoused" are just the most recent names given to the "vagrant," the "loiterer," the "vagabond," the "habitual loafer," the "lewd," the

[3] *See* Johnson v. City of Grants Pass, 72 F.4th 868 (9th Cir. 2023).

[4] *Grants Pass*, 144 S. Ct. at 2243 (Sotomayor, J., dissenting).

[5] U.S. Const. amend. VIII.

[6] *Grants Pass*,144 S. Ct. at 2233–34 (Sotomayor, J., dissenting).

[7] *See infra* pp. 194–205.

"willfully unemployed," to "disorderly persons," "common drunkards," or "rogues"—categories of people it was illegal to be first in England and then in all U.S. states until the late twentieth century.[8] And the seemingly perpetual existence of the shelter-less, the wanderers, the tent-livers, is key to understanding the long narrative, written by the Court and society alike, of the policing of the marginal, the unattached, or the deviant. The vulnerable and heavily policed existence of those deemed "other" has been integral to the non-policed existence of those deemed respectable or mainstream. During the Warren and Burger Courts, constitutional law came to recognize that to some degree—even to the point of deploying constitutional doctrines connecting the right to be allowed to wander unmolested to the right to bodily autonomy and to terminate a pregnancy.[9]

None of that is apparent from the *Grants Pass* case, which does not scream "constitutional revolution!" But it augurs one. And to understand *that* we have to recover the historic role that vagrancy law played and still plays both in the structure of constitutional law and in the larger social order that has for centuries demanded the policing of those deemed out of place.[10] This history does not make it into the *Grants Pass* opinion. The question of the constitutional status of the vagrant, which shaped post-war American constitutional rights, is reduced to a local policy problem, detached from the wider constitutional canon and from the social facts that have shaped the American landscape in the twentieth and now the twenty-first centuries. This erasure is not surprising; even at the height of the Warren and Burger Courts, it was not easy to see how vagrancy regulation was the thread running through disparate social movements' demands for fair treatment. The lawyers got there, eventually, as did the Court. In a

---

[8] Risa Goluboff, Vagrant Nation: Police Power, Constitutional Change, and the Making of the 1960s 1–2 (2016) [hereinafter Goluboff, Vagrant Nation]. We will generally use "homeless" and "homelessness" throughout this Article, following the Supreme Court's choice of terms, though we do not mean to take a position on their appropriateness. We recognize that the various terms—vagrant, vagabond, mobile poor, shelter-less, unhoused—that have been and are currently used to describe the "homeless" (and which we will also sometimes use below) are historically contingent and unevenly applicable to the many types of people with limited access to a permanent home. Those terms are also inevitably ideologically loaded, something we mean to highlight here.

[9] *Id.* at 318–22; Papachristou v. City of Jacksonville, 405 U.S. 156 (1972); Eisenstadt v. Baird, 405 U.S. 438 (1972); Roe v. Wade, 410 U.S. 113, 153 (1973).

[10] *See generally* Goluboff, Vagrant Nation, *supra* note 8.

series of cases culminating in *Papachristou v. City of Jacksonville*[11] in 1972, the Court created a set of overlapping constitutional doctrines that both spawned laws like the ones at issue in *Grants Pass* and formed the doctrinal background for the Ninth Circuit's decision in the case. It is that set of doctrines that the Supreme Court's conservative majority, in both what it has said and what it has ignored, has now tightly circumscribed.

This Article thus first looks backward, placing *Grants Pass* in the historical context of the policing of the vagrant, from Elizabethan poor laws on—though with special emphasis on Warren and Burger Court developments, which sought to establish a clearer line between status and conduct, between the socially undesirable and the actual criminal. By erasing the history of vagrancy law and the vagrancy revolution of the late twentieth century, the Court makes it nearly impossible to see what is at stake in *Grants Pass*. That is what concerns us in the rest of this Article. The vagrant's status—how we treat the unhoused poor in a propertied society—is central to how we conceptualize fundamental rights, not only for the homeless but for everyone. Moreover, by reducing the issue of "homelessness" to a temporary and acute policy problem, not a longstanding and endemic structural one, the Court obscures the economic and social underpinnings of the urban policies that simultaneously create the conditions for homelessness and require its criminal regulation. *Grants Pass* erases the fact that there have always been large numbers of mobile poor people prior to the current moment and ignores the constitutional law that long allowed and then prevented their criminalization. All of this made the *Grants Pass* decision *too easy* for the Roberts Court. For hundreds of years, Anglo-American jurisprudence authorized the criminal regulation of the poor and socially marginal, despite recognizing its exceptional nature.[12] It seems to be where we and the Court are again at this historical moment.

I. Vagrancy Law and the Making of the Post-War Constitutional Order

Let us begin with Isidore Edelman, who spent his days in the late 1940s preaching his own brand of Communism from a park

[11] *Papachristou*, 405 U.S. 156; *see infra* pp. 202–04.

[12] Goluboff, Vagrant Nation, *supra* note 8, at 1–4.

bench in Pershing Square, Los Angeles. He was arrested some sixty-three times in quick succession for a variety of low-level infractions and then, because he had been arrested before, the police deemed him "dissolute" and therefore a vagrant.[13] Or "Shuffling" Sam Thompson, arrested more than fifty times in the late 1950s by the Louisville, Kentucky, police, variously for loitering, vagrancy, disorderly conduct, public drunkenness and "perversion"—mostly for being visibly unemployed and hanging around the Union Bus Station.[14] Or consider Margaret "Lorraine" Papachristou, arrested pursuant to a Jacksonville, Florida, ordinance that defined vagrants as

> [r]ogues and vagabonds, or dissolute persons who go about begging; common gamblers, persons who use juggling or unlawful games or plays, common drunkards, common night walkers, thieves, pilferers or pickpockets, traders in stolen property, lewd, wanton and lascivious persons, keepers of gambling places, common railers and brawlers, persons wandering or strolling around from place to place without any lawful purpose or object, habitual loafers, disorderly persons, persons neglecting all lawful business and habitually spending their time by frequenting houses of ill fame, gaming houses, or places where alcoholic beverages are sold or served, persons able to work but habitually living upon the earnings of their wives or minor children. . . .[15]

Papachristou was none of those things. But she was white, tall, and blond, and in April 1969, she was in a car in Jacksonville with another white woman and two "Negro males" (using the language of the stipulated facts). All were charged with a type of vagrancy not on that very long list: "prowling by auto."[16]

The vagrant could be anyone, but they were usually people deemed to be outside the mainstream in some way—economically, culturally, socially, racially, sexually, or politically. The breadth and vagueness of vagrancy laws enabled officials to use them against any new threat to the social order that might arise. In sixteenth- and seventeenth-century England, vagrancy was used largely to control untethered labor—to suppress wage demands in tight labor markets and prevent the poor from extracting relief from local governments not obligated

---

[13] *Id.* at 12–14.

[14] *Id.* at 74–77.

[15] *Id.* at 1, 300 (quoting *Papachristou*, 405 U.S. at 156 n.1).

[16] *Id.* at 304 (quoting *Papachristou*, 405 U.S. at 159).

to support them. A man was supposed to work where "he happened to be and must take the wages offered to him on the spot."[17]

Who that "anyone" *was* changed over time and place. In the American colonies and the early years of the American republic, localities actively excluded poor strangers, and fought over who was responsible for their upkeep, while keeping close tabs on and requiring work from the local poor. In the antebellum South, states aggressively policed the mobility of free Blacks, and in the aftermath of the Civil War a new generation of vagrancy laws in the Black Codes intensified such regulation. The transient propertyless exploded after the war into a virtual army of underemployed and mobile men. By the end of the nineteenth century, the problem of wandering American men—white and Black in the South and mostly white in the North, Midwest and West—produced a vagrancy regulation avalanche, designed to discipline those who might, "by begging or shunning regular work, flout the wage labor system."[18] These were the hobos and tramps of the "main stem" who, in romantic lore, rode the rails seeking work. In less romantic lore, they were subversive, deviant, a threat to social and moral stability and the economic order. Many laws, including the law later at issue in *Papachristou*, specifically targeted "persons able to work but habitually living upon the earnings of their wives or minor children and all able bodied male persons over the age of eighteen years who are without means of support and remain in idleness."[19]

The numbers of propertyless wanderers in the U.S. starting in the late 1800s are striking: In 1893, an estimated 90,000 men were homeless; between 1890 and 1925, between 100,000 to 500,000 individuals "rode the rails"; and by 1933, anywhere from one to five million people were on skid rows or otherwise homeless.[20] Large-scale economic dislocations like the Great Depression dispossessed many Americans: those derogatorily called "Okies" who moved west to escape the Dust Bowl; the countless individuals who filled the Hoovervilles that dotted the urban landscape; the tens of thousands

[17] *Id.* at 15 (quoting 3 Sir James Fitzjames Stephen, A History of the Criminal Law of England 267 (1883)).

[18] *Id.* at 15.

[19] *Id.* at 300 (quoting Fla. Stat. § 856.02 (1965)).

[20] Ellen Bassuk & Deborah Franklin, *Homelessness Past and Present: The Case of the United States, 1890–1925*, 8 New Eng. J. Pub. Pol'y 67, 71 (1992); Samuel E. Wallace, Skid Row as a Way of Life 21–22 (1965).

of unemployed World War I veterans who made up the Bonus Army that marched on Washington in 1932.

Much vagrancy regulation into the mid-twentieth century was directed not only at those made homeless by the Depression but also anyone without stable housing and often with mental health or substance abuse problems. Notably, policing the idle poor was a lot of what police *did*. In 1946, San Francisco spent approximately thirty percent of its budget on the arrest and jailing of drunks; in 1957, half of all the arrests in Minneapolis were for public order offenses on skid row; in early 1960s Chicago, nearly one-quarter of all arrests took place on skid row.[21] The Louisville police court where Sam Thompson was convicted in 1959 processed some 25,000 cases like Thompson's *every year*, largely without trials, appeals, counsel for the defendants, or transcripts of the proceedings.[22] Convictions in local police courts often came in batches of fifty or sixty men at a time. Even after the Supreme Court began to impose constitutional oversight of criminal procedures in the mid-twentieth century, vagrancy prosecutions continued to fly under the constitutional radar. The lack of procedural regularity or protections kept visibility low, defendants detained, and oversight elusive.

The broad and vague nature of vagrancy laws enabled officials to deploy them not only against vagrants proper, but against any threat to the social order—the cultural nonconformist, the unemployed, the substance abuser, the racial minority, the civil rights or anti-war activist, the sexual or gender minority. Vagrancy was understood to be "one of the most effective weapons in the arsenal of law enforcement"—enabling the police to "vag" anyone suspicious, troublesome, deviant, out of place, or just plain poor. Officials put vagrancy laws to political use to attack and imprison labor organizers, Wobblies, anarchists, strikers, and Communists; and to social, cultural, and political use to harass the Beats in the 1950s and later the hippies and antiwar protestors in the 1960s.[23] Vagrancy was also a primary tool for enforcing sexual mores. Female vagrants might be prostitutes, but just

---

[21] Goluboff, Vagrant Nation, *supra* note 8, at 83; *see also* Robert C. Ellickson, *Controlling Chronic Misconduct in City Spaces: Of Panhandlers, Skid Rows, and Public-Space Zoning*, 105 Yale L.J. 1165, 1209 (1996) (noting that fifty percent of arrests in large cities, many for drunkenness, occurred on skid row).

[22] Goluboff, Vagrant Nation, *supra* note 8, at 89.

[23] *Id.* at 59 (quoting Letter from Ernest Besig, Exec. Dir. N. Cal. ACLU, to Edmund G. Brown, Governor of Cal. (July 10, 1959) (on file with the California Historical Society ACLU Papers)); *id. passim*.

as easily women who flouted conventional norms of female sexuality, who were seen in the company of men, or who were merely perceived as promiscuous or "lewd." "Vag-lewd," or the charge of being "lewd and dissolute," was also used to arrest gay men, lesbians, and gender nonconformists; challenges to that use of vagrancy would shape the gay and trans rights movements and the ensuing due process and privacy revolutions.[24] So, too, vagrancy was a crucial tool for racial subordination long after slavery, used to coerce the formerly enslaved to work in the South as sharecroppers and peons, or simply to enforce Jim Crow's punitive apartheid.[25] "Cotton is ripening. See that the 'vags' get busy," admonished the *Atlanta Constitution* in 1904.[26] Vagrancy arrests served as a prime weapon against the civil rights movement; in one case the police arrested civil rights leaders inside their colleague's *own home*.[27] "For integration? You're a Vagrant" is how *The Baltimore Afro-American* put it, as legions of civil rights activists were booked on vagrancy and related charges.[28]

For centuries, none of this seemed particularly troublesome to either law enforcement or judges. As for the poor, initially the Supreme Court, in *New York v. Miln*, deemed it unremarkable for the state to take measures against the "moral pestilence of paupers, vagabonds, and possibly convicts."[29] Treating the poor as morally deficient began to look suspect, however, in light of the Great Depression. In *Edwards v. California*, which struck down a law that made it a crime to bring an indigent person into California,[30] the Court repudiated that aspect of *Miln*.[31] Around the same time, the Court first began to question other laws related to the vagrancy law regime. In *Lanzetta v. New Jersey*, the Court invalidated a law that allowed the police to designate a person a "gangster." The Court both noted the similarity between the law at issue and traditional vagrancy laws and

---

[24] *Id.* at 46–52, 164–76. *See generally* Kate Redburn, *Before Equal Protection: The Fall of Cross-Dressing Bans and the Transgender Legal Movement, 1963–86*, 40 LAW & HIST. REV. 679 (2022).

[25] GOLUBOFF, VAGRANT NATION, *supra* note 8, at 115–17.

[26] *Id.* at 116–17 (quoting *Editorial Article 1*, ATLANTA CONST., Sept. 2, 1904, at 6).

[27] *Id.* at 112.

[28] *Id.* at 123 (quoting *For Integration? You're a Vagrant*, BALT. AFRO-AM., Jan. 19, 1963, at 12); *id.* at 127.

[29] *Id.* at 81 (quoting Mayor of New York v. Miln, 36 U.S. (11 Pet.) 102, 142–43 (1849)).

[30] Edwards v. California, 314 U.S. 160 (1941).

[31] *Id.* at 177; *id.* at 178 (Douglas, J., concurring).

criticized the law for "condemn[ing] no act or omission."[32] These and other cases set the stage for a more comprehensive challenge to vagrancy laws.[33]

Over the next two decades, many of those subject to vagrancy law's unfettered discretion gained social movement power and access to new forms of legal support from legal aid societies, public defenders' offices, and organizations like the ACLU and the NAACP. They began to identify vagrancy laws as an obstacle to their other social movement goals, and they began to see the possibility of constitutional challenges to such laws. The social revolutions of the 1950s, 1960s, and 1970s—civil rights, women's liberation, LGBTQ rights, the rights of the poor—became by necessity revolutions against unfettered police power. The foundational question vagrancy laws posed for post-war constitutional law was whether and to what extent the state could use the criminal law to enforce moral and racial norms, corral undesirables, and manage the mobile unemployed and poor.

Vagrancy was the all-purpose criminalization of everything, and both substantive criminal law and criminal procedure were implicated by its use. The disparate and mostly unconnected lawyers representing disparate and mostly unconnected clients—union organizers, civil rights protestors, gay men, hippies, poor people—came to understand this problem. Edelman was a client of the first ACLU affiliate in Southern California, which had emerged in the aftermath of a Los Angeles dock workers' strike that saw the arrest of 400 Wobblies on vagrancy and other charges in 1923.[34] Shuffling Sam Thompson's lawyer turned out to be Louis Lusky, first in his class at Columbia Law School and law clerk to Justice Stone (of the famous *Carolene Products* footnote four, which Lusky drafted).[35] Lusky was connected to Thompson through a mutual acquaintance and member of the Kentucky Civil Liberties Union. These lawyers and many others, some attached to local or national ACLUs, some working for the NAACP's Legal Defense Fund, and others simply representing clients in private practice, began to coalesce around the problem of vagrancy law.

---

[32] Lanzetta v. New Jersey, 306 U.S. 451, 458 (1939).

[33] *See* Thornhill v. Alabama, 310 U.S. 88 (1940) (striking down loitering laws aimed expressly at labor picketers); Carlson v. California, 310 U.S. 106 (1940) (same).

[34] Goluboff, Vagrant Nation, *supra* note 8, at 20.

[35] *Id.* at 77–78; *see* Louis Lusky, *Footnote Redux: A* Carolene Products *Reminiscence*, 82 Colum. L. Rev. 1087, 1093 (1982).

The law's unlimited reach was the problem, as a young Anthony Amsterdam, who became the intellectual voice of the anti-vagrancy law movement, would realize. Amsterdam, who clerked for Justice Frankfurter, would go on to become a distinguished civil rights lawyer and influential law professor.[36] In 1960, he was still a law student when he published a "note" that became one of the most cited law review articles of all time—*The Void-for-Vagueness Doctrine in the Supreme Court*—which raised questions about the enforcement of catch-all criminal statutes like vagrancy.[37] Such laws failed to give fair warning to potential violators or sufficient guidance to law enforcement, who consequently enforced the laws in an arbitrary or discriminatory fashion. In 1967, he even more directly addressed the problem of vagrancy laws and vagrancy-like statutes in an article titled *Federal Constitutional Restrictions on the Punishment of Crimes of Status, Crimes of General Obnoxiousness, Crimes of Displeasing Police Officers, and the Like*.[38] He argued that loitering and vagrancy laws were constitutionally suspect for a panoply of reasons. When used to suppress speech protected by the First Amendment, the laws could be challenged as overbroad or void for vagueness; when suppressing mobility, they could be challenged as violating the right to travel or to move more generally. He further argued that vagrancy laws violated the prohibition on involuntary servitude under the Thirteenth Amendment; the Equal Protection and Due Process Clauses of the Fourteenth Amendment; rights of criminal defendants under the Fourth and Fifth Amendments; and the Eighth and Fourteenth Amendments by criminalizing status and essentially condoning banishment.[39]

Versions of these various constitutional claims eventually made their way into lawyers' briefs and arguments, and then into judicial decisions across the country. These cases, arising from different circumstances and relying on different constitutional provisions, are often thought to be largely unrelated. But they were, in fact, closely

[36] Goluboff, Vagrant Nation, *supra* note 8, at 135, 137.

[37] *Id.* at 133; *see* Note, *The Void-for-Vagueness Doctrine in the Supreme Court*, 109 U. Pa. L. Rev. 67 (1960).

[38] Goluboff, Vagrant Nation, *supra* note 8, at 135; *see* Anthony G. Amsterdam, *Federal Constitutional Restrictions on the Punishment of Crimes of Status, Crimes of General Obnoxiousness, Crimes of Displeasing Police Officers, and the Like*, 3 Crim. L. Bull. 207, 233 (1967).

[39] Amsterdam, *supra* note 38, at 233.

connected. Taken together, they produced a significant body of legal doctrine, in both the Supreme Court and the state and lower federal courts, that seemingly rejected the vagueness of vagrancy laws, crimes of status, the criminalization of poverty, and unfettered police discretion. The process was incremental and initially piecemeal. In 1960, the Court decided *Thompson v. City of Louisville* (Shuffling Sam Thompson's case) dismissing charges of loitering and disorderly conduct for lack of evidence.[40] Three years earlier, in *Lambert v. California*, the Court rekindled the interest it had begun to show in status crimes in 1939's *Lanzetta* case. The Court held that the law at issue in *Lambert*, which criminalized the failure of a person convicted of a crime to register with the police, violated due process because it was based on "conduct that was wholly passive."[41] Two years later, it further developed that idea in *Robinson v. California*, the Eighth Amendment case at issue in *Grants Pass*. *Robinson* held that addiction to narcotics—being a drug addict—could not in itself be criminalized.[42] Later, in *Powell v. Texas*, in 1968, the Court upheld a public drunkenness law against a similar Eighth Amendment challenge. While a majority of the Justices concluded that being drunk in a public place was conduct that could be criminalized, they continued to maintain that an involuntary status, like being an alcoholic, could not itself be criminalized.[43]

The Court's interest in such cases arose in tandem with social movement organizing among poor people, and it was simultaneously engaged in a project of identifying whether, when, and how the Constitution might provide other protections against the harms that people living in poverty faced. Beginning with *Griffin v. Illinois* in 1956, a case challenging an Illinois law that required payment for trial transcripts to access a criminal appeal, the Court began to articulate the view that "a State can no more discriminate on account of poverty than on account of religion, race, or color."[44] Over the next fifteen years, the Warren and then the early Burger Courts experimented with numerous doctrinal formulations that might provide criminal procedure

[40] Thompson v. City of Louisville, 362 U.S. 199 (1960).

[41] Lambert v. California, 355 U.S. 225, 228 (1957).

[42] Robinson v. California, 370 U.S. 660, 667 (1962).

[43] Powell v. Texas, 392 U.S. 514, 537, 532 (1968).

[44] Griffin v. Illinois, 351 U.S. 12, 17 (1956).

protections, access to civil justice, family law, and voting, and rights concerning welfare, food stamps, education, medical care, and travel.[45] The Court never ended up coalescing around a single theory, and by the early 1970s, the project had stalled.[46] But that the Court was engaged in this project at the same time that it was questioning the vagrancy laws was no coincidence.

The Court developed its anti-vagrancy law stance in cases far beyond poverty and addiction as well. In *Shuttlesworth v. City of Birmingham*, the Court invalidated a loitering conviction of the Reverend Fred Shuttlesworth, one of the founders and leaders of the Southern Christian Leadership Conference.[47] Shuttlesworth had been arrested as he paused on a Birmingham street corner while leading a boycott against downtown department stores at the height of the civil rights movement.[48] Much less visible were an unusual number of vagrancy cases the Supreme Court "dismissed as improvidently granted."[49] Though these cases did not themselves develop constitutional doctrine, the opinions dissenting from the dismissals that various Justices authored both highlighted the breadth of the vagrancy law problem and identified the myriad constitutional infirmities with those laws.[50] One of these was Edelman's case in 1953.[51] Another was that of Eddie Hicks, a hippie arrested for playing his guitar in Washington D.C.'s Dupont Circle.[52] The Court also took and then dismissed *Arceneaux v.*

---

[45] *See* Gideon v. Wainwright, 372 U.S. 335 (1963) (right to assistance of counsel for indigent criminal defendants); Harper v. Va. State Bd. of Elections, 383 U.S. 663 (1966) (poll tax unconstitutional); Shapiro v. Thompson, 394 U.S. 618 (1969) (right to travel); Goldberg v. Kelly, 397 U.S. 254 (1970) (evidentiary hearing required before termination of welfare benefits); Boddie v. Connecticut, 401 U.S. 371 (1971) (fee for divorce filing violated due process).

[46] *See generally* Michael J. Graetz & Linda Greenhouse, The Burger Court and the Rise of the Judicial Right (2016).

[47] Shuttlesworth v. City of Birmingham, 382 U.S. 87 (1965).

[48] *Id.* at 148–49. Though the 1970 case of *Adickes v. Kress* eventually turned on other issues, central to the case was the fact that white schoolteacher and civil rights protestor Sandra Adickes and others had been arrested for vagrancy as they tried to integrate the Kress lunch counter in Hattiesburg, Mississippi. Adickes v. S.H. Kress & Co., 398 U.S. 144 (1970).

[49] Goluboff, Vagrant Nation, *supra* note 8, at 31–39, 178, 196, 228–30, 208–09, 212; *see* Edelman v. California, 344 U.S. 357 (1953); Arceneaux v. Louisiana, 376 U.S. 336 (1964); Hicks v. District of Columbia, 383 U.S. 252 (1966); Wainwright v. City of New Orleans, 392 U.S. 598 (1968).

[50] *See Edelman*, 344 U.S. at 362–66 (Black, J., dissenting); *Hicks*, 383 U.S. at 252–58 (Douglas, J., dissenting); *Wainwright*, 392 U.S. at 600–10 (Warren, C.J., dissenting).

[51] *Edelman*, 344 U.S. at 362 (Black, J., dissenting).

[52] *Hicks*, 383 U.S. at 258 (Douglas, J., dissenting).

Louisiana, in which a rural farmworker in Cajun Country was arrested for vagrancy after a dispute with his landlord over his wages,[53] and *Wainwright v. City of New Orleans*, in which a law student was arrested for vagrancy because, though he resembled a murder suspect, the police lacked probable cause to arrest him for murder.[54] By the late 1960s, the lawyers who brought these cases, along with lower court judges increasingly sympathetic to their arguments,[55] had educated the Court about the vast reach of vagrancy laws. A number of the Justices were clearly interested in taking cases that would enable the Court to invalidate them.[56]

A quartet of cases in the early 1970s crystallized the Court's condemnation of vagrancy and related laws.[57] In 1971, the Court decided *Palmer v. Euclid*, holding that a statute that criminalized being "a suspicious person" was unconstitutionally vague.[58] In *Coates v. Cincinnati*, it struck down an ordinance making it illegal for three or more persons to "conduct themselves in a matter annoying to persons passing by"—again, on void-for-vagueness grounds.[59] Finally, in December of 1971, the Court heard two cases from Florida, *Smith v. Florida*[60] and *Papachristou*,[61] the case challenging the Jacksonville vagrancy ordinance that was the basis for Papachristou's conviction for "prowling by auto." Justice Douglas wrote unanimous opinions striking down both laws.[62]

Douglas identified with the vagabonds and wanderers—he claimed to have ridden the rails himself and was an honorary member of the Hoboes of America, who made him a "Knight of the Open Road" in 1939—and his sympathies were apparent in the main case of *Papachristou*.[63] Douglas included in the fundamental rights he would deem constitutionally protected "walking, strolling, wandering, [and] loafing" as well as "unwritten amenities" like "the right of dissent," "the right to

[53] *Arceneaux*, 376 U.S. at 336–38.

[54] *Wainwright*, 392 U.S. at 600–05 (Warren, C.J., dissenting).

[55] Goluboff, Vagrant Nation, *supra* note 8, at 239–57, 298–99.

[56] *See also* Shevin v. Lazarus, 401 U.S. 987 (1971) (mem.).

[57] Goluboff, Vagrant Nation, *supra* note 8, at 258–332.

[58] Palmer v. City of Euclid, 402 U.S. 544, 545 (1971).

[59] Coates v. City of Cincinnati, 402 U.S. 611, 614 (1971).

[60] Smith v. Florida, 405 U.S. 172 (1972).

[61] Papachristou v. City of Jacksonville, 405 U.S. 156 (1972).

[62] Justices Powell and Rehnquist joined the Court after oral argument in the case and so did not participate. Goluboff, Vagrant Nation, *supra* note 8, at 314.

[63] *Id.* at 32.

be nonconformists and the right to defy submissiveness."[64] Such rights, to Douglas, "have encouraged lives of high spirits rather than hushed, suffocating silence."[65] Though Douglas initially based his *Papachristou* opinion on fundamental rights located alternately in the Ninth and Fourteenth Amendments, the case ultimately turned on the void-for-vagueness doctrine of the Fourteenth Amendment.[66] As Amsterdam had described, that doctrine finds constitutional infirmity in laws that provide insufficient notice to potential defendants about what the criminal law prohibits, as well as insufficient guidance to those charged with enforcing the law so as to prevent discriminatory or arbitrary enforcement.

Douglas wrote at a time when the post-war constitutional order was being formed, and the idea of a right to nonconformity was of serious constitutional consideration. It was a moment when the Court concerned itself with policing majorities' "bare . . . desire to harm . . . politically unpopular group[s]," as the food stamp case of *United States Department of Agriculture v. Moreno*[67] put it, and it was open to a broad definition of who those unpopular minorities were. Indeed, conservative and moderate legal scholars J. Harvie Wilkinson III (appointed to the federal bench by President Reagan in 1984)[68] and G. Edward White saw an ongoing trend of greater *Constitutional Protection for Personal Lifestyles*, as the title of their 1977 article proclaimed.[69] The social movements of the period attacked vagrancy laws because they stood in the way of equality and individual freedom, and these developments show those movements to have succeeded at least in part.

Even so, neither *Papachristou* nor the other cases ended the discretionary policing that vagrancy laws had facilitated. The 1968 case of *Terry v. Ohio*, which authorized police to "stop and frisk" suspects on the basis of the lower standard of "reasonable suspicion" rather than the "probable cause" required to make an arrest,[70] had already

---

[64] *Id.* at 315 (quoting William Douglas, Draft Opinion in Papachristou v. City of Jacksonville (1971) (on file with William O. Douglas Papers, Box 1558, Folder 70-5030)).

[65] *Id.*

[66] *Id.* at 314–22; *Papachristou*, 405 U.S. at 162.

[67] U.S. Dep't of Agric. v. Moreno, 413 U.S. 528, 534 (1973).

[68] Goluboff, Vagrant Nation, *supra* note 8, at 329.

[69] *See* J. Harvie Wilkinson III & G. Edward White, *Constitutional Protection for Personal Lifestyles*, 62 Cornell L. Rev. 563 (1977).

[70] Goluboff, Vagrant Nation, *supra* note 8, at 186–220; Terry v. Ohio, 392 U.S. 1, 27 (1968).

made sure of that. Before the Court removed broad, vague, and largely invisible vagrancy laws as police authority for maintaining social control, *Terry* had ensured that police would continue to have authority necessary for crime control.

Nor did, or could, the Court's decision in *Papachristou* end the question of vagrancy regulation once and for all.[71] To be sure, because the essence of vagrancy laws was their breadth and vagueness, they could not be fully replicated (except by another vagrancy law). But the Supreme Court's void-for-vagueness holding invited cities and states to target specific acts and behaviors instead. Indeed, states and localities responded to the demise of vagrancy laws by passing a panoply of other criminal prohibitions that were more specific and that police could newly deploy to control the poor and homeless, the mobile and the unattached. These new laws included no-camping and public-sleeping bans like those at issue in *Grants Pass*.[72]

II. The *Grants Pass* Erasure

None of the preceding history makes it into the *Grants Pass* opinion. Indeed, Justice Gorsuch's opinion for the majority makes much of the fact (stated with some alarm) that "homelessness in this country has reached its highest levels since the government began reporting data on the subject in 2007."[73] The lack of historical awareness is striking—not only about the continual existence of masses of shelter-less and displaced people in the U.S. (since well before 2007), and not only about the constant surveillance and regulation of those propertyless masses throughout American history, but also about the increased constitutional protection for the poor that had marked the late twentieth century.

Grants Pass is an act of erasure. The Court's opinion reads as if the Ninth Circuit's "experiment" in a limited right to shelter came out of nowhere historically, economically, and constitutionally. So here in the third decade of the twenty-first century, long after the constitutional interventions of the 1970s, we have, judicially and socially, again come back around to vagrancy and the status/conduct distinction.

---

[71] Goluboff, Vagrant Nation, *supra* note 8, at 338.

[72] *Id.* at 342.

[73] City of Grants Pass v. Johnson, 144 S. Ct. 2202, 2208 (2024).

Gorsuch begins with the problem of large numbers of homeless persons, some mentally ill, some dependent on narcotics, many forced by economic circumstances onto the streets and sidewalks and into parks. He recognizes that the initial act of becoming shelter-less is usually involuntary, and he expresses sympathy for the "down-and-out."[74] But he also observes at length that choosing to *remain* without shelter—to decline social and rehabilitative services—is a choice. He further emphasizes how homeless people have often chosen to live in groups, in encampments.[75] Those encampments raise problems of criminality, public order, and disease. Echoing the view of previous critics of the main stem and skid rows, Gorsuch argues that large collections of homeless people contribute to crime, drug use, and disease ("typhus, shigella, trench fever"[76]), while overwhelming the neighborhoods where they are located.

Much of the majority opinion addresses the various "tools" (including the criminal law) available to cities and towns in managing their homeless populations, tools meant "to encourage" the inhabitants to accept shelters, drug treatment, or admission to mental-health facilities.[77] In Gorsuch's telling, local governments generally have made these services widely available (through charitable organizations), are eager to assist the homeless, and use the criminal law only as a last resort, "tak[ing] a light touch" to "persuade" uptake.[78] This is a decidedly benign view of what local governments are doing, perhaps true in places, but also quite partial.

Undoubtedly, there were serious problems with the old skid rows—and there are serious problems with the new ones. Gorsuch argues that the Ninth Circuit's 2019 opinion in *Martin v. City of Boise*,[79] which established the Eighth Amendment limitation that was applied in *Grants Pass*, led to an explosion of homelessness and ancillary social disorder and the inability of cities like San Francisco to address them.[80] As Gorsuch is at pains to point out, local government amici from all

---

[74] *Id.*

[75] *Id.* at 2208–10. On encampments, see Mila Versteeg, Kevin L. Cope & Gaurav Mukherjee, *The New Homelessness*, 113 Calif. L. Rev. (forthcoming 2025), https://ssrn.com/abstract=4718929.

[76] *Grants Pass*, 144 S. Ct. at 2209.

[77] *Id.* at 2210.

[78] *Id.* at 2212–13.

[79] Martin v. City of Boise, 920 F.3d 584 (9th Cir. 2019).

[80] *Grants Pass*, 144 S. Ct. at 2211–12.

over California, the rest of the Ninth Circuit, and the country agreed that removing the "tool" of criminalization in *Martin* "wreak[ed] havoc on local governments, residents, and businesses."[81]

But the causation is a little tricky, especially if one is attentive to history before the turn of the twenty-first century. As Part I discussed, the existence of skid rows is not new—cities and towns have encountered and tried to regulate shelter-less people for hundreds of years. Making those people criminals did not prevent them from having to exist somewhere—it just led to their repeated arrest, sometimes banishment, and the creation of informal urban spaces where they were tolerated. Before *Martin*, there were plenty of people living on the streets in cities and towns in the Ninth Circuit, but also outside of the Circuit, in the vast majority of places not subject to *Martin*'s constitutional rule.[82]

It is possible, as many of the amici argued, that *Martin* made "solving" the homelessness crisis "harder" in the Ninth Circuit. But that assertion is based on two assumptions that history shows are at least questionable: (1) that the crisis of shelter-less people is otherwise "solvable" and (2) that cities and towns are generally acting in good faith to "solve" it. As to the first, it is apparent that the country's social welfare system has always been and continues to be inadequate to address the needs of the very poor, the very troubled, and the very addicted. This might be because of cycles of boom and bust, the ineradicability of unemployment, the lack of sustained investment in health care, or a housing system that relies principally on "free" markets that do not serve those without money.

As to the second, "solving" the crisis could mean providing homes for the homeless, but it might also involve many tactics short of providing housing, especially if the goal is to eliminate the ancillary social harms that come with having large numbers of people encamped in the outdoors. In particular, solving the crisis could also mean dispersing the homeless or moving them down the road. Vagrancy and loitering

---

[81] *Id.* at 2211 (quoting *Martin*, 920 F.3d at 590 (Smith, J., dissenting from denial of rehearing en banc)).

[82] *See, e.g.*, Emma Goldberg, *When Kentucky Bans Homeless Camps, Where Do People Go?*, N.Y. Times (Nov. 5, 2024), https://www.nytimes.com/2024/11/05/business/kentucky-homeless-camps.html. It is notable that Canadian courts have recognized a *Martin*-like right to camp in public places absent adequate shelter beds since 2008, reaffirmed most recently in The Regional Municipality of Waterloo v. Persons Unknown and to Be Ascertained, 2023 ONSC 670 (Can. Super. Ct.).

laws were similarly characterized as indispensable tools for managing prior crises of shelter-less people—that is, before those laws were deemed unconstitutional and new tools were sought. These new "tools" of the criminal law may be used just as easily, as they have been historically, to "solve" the homelessness crisis not so much by helping the homeless as by forcing shelter-less people elsewhere, keeping them under constant threat of arrest, and otherwise harassing and containing them.

In any case, whether the tool of the criminal law is useful to assist the homeless—or for any policy purpose—cannot answer the question of a given tool's constitutionality. In *Grants Pass*, the answer to that question appears to turn mostly on a reading of one case: *Robinson*.[83] Justice Gorsuch dedicates considerable energy to analyzing *Robinson* and for good reason: It stands for the proposition that the Eighth Amendment's prohibition against the imposition of "cruel and unusual" punishments prevents the criminalization of status.[84] In *Robinson*, the Court struck down a California law that declared that "no person shall be addicted to the use of narcotics."[85]

Gorsuch is skeptical that the Eighth Amendment applies by its terms to limit substantive criminal law. He is sympathetic to the argument Justice Thomas offers in a brief lone concurrence—that the Eighth Amendment only restricts the kinds of *punishments* that can be imposed for a given crime.[86] Thomas would have held that *Robinson* was wrongly decided.[87]

Gorsuch, by contrast, only casts doubt on *Robinson*, highlighting how the decision was unprecedented to that point and the Court has not used it since. He emphasizes its Eighth Amendment basis, which seemed to come as some surprise even to the advocates at the time.[88] He recognizes, however, that no one has asked the Court to reconsider *Robinson* and that due process principles might be read to prevent the criminalization of status in any case (as the 1957 case of *Lambert* suggested, but which Gorsuch fails to cite).[89] As he notes, common-law

[83] Robinson v. California, 370 U.S. 660 (1962).

[84] *Id.* at 665–67.

[85] *Id.*

[86] *Grants Pass*, 144 S. Ct. at 2215–16.

[87] *Id.* at 2226–27 (Thomas, J., concurring).

[88] *Id.* at 2217 (majority opinion).

[89] *Id.* at 2218.

principles of criminal law generally require both a bad act and bad intent—something that is lacking when the state criminalizes *being* something unconnected to *doing* something.[90]

Gorsuch does not need to belabor the point, however, because, he argues, *Robinson* is easily distinguishable. The Grants Pass ordinances do not criminalize the status of being homeless, he asserts, but rather the conduct of camping on public lands, sleeping on the streets or in parks or one's car. These are clearly "conduct" and thus do not fall under *Robinson*'s prohibition. Gorsuch (probably inadvertently) echoes Anatole France's famous observation that "the majestic equality of the la[w] . . . forbid[s] rich and poor alike to sleep under bridges, to beg in the streets, and to steal their bread"[91] when he notes that not only are the "homeless" forbidden from sleeping outdoors, but so is everyone else.[92] Furthermore, he observes, the Court in *Powell* already determined that the government can criminalize acts (in that case, "get[ting] drunk or be[ing] found in a state of intoxication in any public place") that are caused by or are a direct result of an involuntary condition (being an alcoholic).[93]

Robinson and *Powell* are the beginning and the end for Gorsuch—all that is necessary to decide the case. His opinion cites almost no other cases. There is no mention of *Papachristou* or any of the vagrancy-related cases. There is no mention of the watershed moment in the 1960s and 1970s of treating the indigent with greater humanity and providing them with greater constitutional protection.

Instead, after addressing *Robinson*, Gorsuch returns to policy. He describes the myriad difficulties that arise under the Ninth Circuit's *Martin/Grants Pass* rulings.[94] These difficulties include determining who is "involuntarily homeless," the number of homeless in any given city on any given day, the number of shelter beds that are available, and the conditions that make a shelter bed an acceptable alternative such that the homeless can be required to accept it on pain of the criminal law. These problems, argues Gorsuch, are insurmountable, for they require courts to delve too deeply into complicated social policy. The

[90] *Id.* at 2217.

[91] ANATOLE FRANCE, THE RED LILY 95 (Winifred Stephens trans., 6th ed. 1922).

[92] *Grants Pass*, 144 S. Ct. at 2218.

[93] *Id.* at 2219.

[94] *Id.* at 2221–24.

Martin/Grants Pass experiment, Gorsuch concludes, has been a disaster, for cities and for the homeless themselves. And he urges respect for federalism and the benefits of local experimentation: "[I]nstead of encouraging productive dialogue and experimentation, through our democratic institutions, courts have frozen in place their own formulas by fiat."[95]

Authored by Justice Sotomayor, and joined by Justices Kagan and Jackson, the dissenting opinion contests every one of the majority's arguments, with special attention to *Robinson*.[96] Here too, the multi-century history of vagrancy enforcement and more recent constitutional protection goes mostly unremarked. And yet the dissent's arguments against criminalizing those once called the "vagrant," the "vagabond," and now called the "homeless," track fairly well those decisions made fifty years ago. Criminalization, Sotomayor argues, does not help the homeless or solve the homelessness problem, which she attributes to myriad structural factors, including stagnant wages, domestic abuse, mental illness, and rising housing costs. She highlights the particular vulnerability of veterans, victims of domestic abuse, teenagers, and the disabled to becoming homeless.[97] These groups are a portrait of the "involuntary homeless,"[98] which Sotomayor fills out with specific accounts of people being repeatedly arrested and harassed by the police. On this account, criminalization does not "encourage" or "persuade" the homeless to enter shelters and get off the streets. It does not deter undesirable behaviors or even prevent crime—which is often perpetrated against the homeless, who will not report it for fear of becoming police targets themselves.

The "tool" of the criminal law, argues Sotomayor, fails to do anything for the homeless—even though that is what the majority and the many local government amici assert. Fines, threats of jail time, jail itself, police harassment, destruction of tents, and seizures of possessions only exacerbate the difficulties the homeless face.[99] As Sotomayor points out, when faced with a "move-along" order, the homeless usually just move a few blocks down the road. What else are they

---

[95] *Id.* at 2224.

[96] Robinson v. California, 370 U.S. 660 (1962); *Grants Pass*, 144 S. Ct. at 2233–34 (Sotomayor, J., dissenting).

[97] *Grants Pass*, 144 S. Ct. at 2229–30 (Sotomayor, J., dissenting).

[98] *Id.* at 2237.

[99] *Id.* at 2230–31.

supposed to do?[100] "Vag 'em," the police would have said in the 1940s or 1960s—and they would have known that what they were doing was sending the homeless to jail in the short term and pushing them to go someplace else in the longer term. Indeed, the "revolving door" of criminal justice involvement that Sotomayor references in her dissent has been a feature of homelessness in the United States since long before 1962, when Judge Murtagh coined the term.[101]

Sotomayor recounts a story of one homeless man who was arrested 198 times for petty offenses while he was awaiting assistance to obtain shelter.[102] His outreach worker made him a t-shirt that read: "Please do not arrest me, my outreach worker is working on my housing."[103] Shuffling Sam Thompson had a comparable experience even after he won his Supreme Court case against the City of Louisville in 1960. According to his lawyer, Lusky, Thompson kept a copy of the Court's decision, *Thompson v. Louisville*, with him at all times. Though it did not always work to insulate him, he would show it to the police when they threatened further arrests.[104]

For Sotomayor, like Gorsuch, *Robinson* and *Powell* are the beginning and end of the case. Their disagreement is straightforward: Gorsuch argues that public-sleeping bans regulate conduct; Sotomayor argues that they regulate status, since the conduct (sleeping outdoors) is co-extensive with the status of being homeless. For people without access to shelter, laws making it illegal to sleep outside in public places or in their cars "punish[] them for being homeless."[105] They have no choice but to sleep (as well as engage in other bodily functions) *somewhere*. Moreover, writes Sotomayor, the city's public-sleeping restrictions essentially set up a binary: Either you sleep in a shelter or you break the law by sleeping outdoors. If there are no shelter beds available, the first option is not available to the homeless person—they would have to leave the jurisdiction to comply or simply remain awake at all times. "Under the majority's

---

[100] *Id.* at 2231.

[101] *Id.* at 2230; John M. Murtagh, *The Derelicts of Skid Row*, ATLANTIC, Mar. 1962, at 77, 80.

[102] *Grants Pass*, 144 S. Ct. at 2231 (Sotomayor, J., dissenting).

[103] *Id.*

[104] GOLUBOFF, VAGRANT NATION, *supra* note 8, at 108; Thompson v. City of Louisville, 362 U.S. 199 (1960).

[105] *Grants Pass*, 144 S. Ct. at 2228 (Sotomayor, J., dissenting).

logic," Sotomayor writes, "cities cannot criminalize the status of being homeless, but they can criminalize the conduct that defines that status. The Constitution cannot be evaded by such formalistic distinctions."[106]

As for *Powell*, Sotomayor dismisses it as a "strawman."[107] With four Justices upholding Powell's conviction and four dissenting on the basis that *Robinson* applied to any "condition [a defendant] is powerless to change," Sotomayor deems Justice White's fifth vote for upholding as the key. White's view was that, because Powell had not shown his presence in public to be involuntary, it was unnecessary to address the involuntariness of his intoxication. Had Powell established that he was homeless, the case would have come out differently. Moreover, as Sotomayor points out, even Justice Marshall's plurality opinion agreed that "*Robinson* prohibited enforcing laws criminalizing 'a mere status.'"[108] In other words, though *Powell* declined to extend *Robinson*, neither did it undermine *Robinson*'s holding or reasoning.

Sotomayor also takes up the majority's policy arguments about the problems encampments create and the workability of the *Martin/Grants Pass* rule.[109] As to the former, Sotomayor decries the majority's focus on the problems caused by encampments and the emphasis on "violent crime, drug overdoses, disease, fires, and hazardous waste."[110] Even under the *Grants Pass* injunction, the city may prohibit all of those things, she observes. As to the latter, Sotomayor argues that courts can easily fashion workable rules that give cities due notice of what they are required to do.[111] Sotomayor's view of the *Grants Pass* injunction is narrow: It only kicks in if there are not enough shelter beds, and everyone seems to admit that there are not. Even counting the beds provided by religious charities, the number

---

[106] *Id.* at 2236.

[107] *Id.* at 2239.

[108] *Id.* at 2240. *But see* Justin Driver, *The Constitutional Conservatism of the Warren Court*, 100 Calif. L. Rev. 1101, 1139–48 (2012) (arguing that *Powell* narrows *Robinson* and noting that the decision surprised some observers who had believed that the Court would decriminalize public drunkenness).

[109] *Grants Pass*, 144 S. Ct. at 2237–41 (Sotomayor, J., dissenting).

[110] *Id.* at 2239.

[111] *Id.*

does not come close to the estimated numbers of homeless in Grants Pass, by a long shot.[112]

The dissent thus mostly addresses, and refutes, the majority's policy arguments. In two key ways, however, one can glimpse the larger political and historical context, and additional doctrinal possibilities, in the opinion. First, Sotomayor contests the good intentions that the majority ascribes to local officials. She argues that the city council meant to target the homeless, and she quotes, among others, the city council president as saying that "the point is to make it uncomfortable enough for [homeless people] in our city so they will want to move on down the road."[113] Sotomayor points out that the council was not interested in regulating the behavior of "infants napping in strollers, Sunday afternoon picnickers, or nighttime stargazers"—all of whom might use a blanket or end up sleeping in public places, but none of whom would be arrested for doing so.[114] What matters to the Grants Pass ordinance is the "intent" to live in public, and only the homeless would have such an intent. Though Sotomayor cites neither the specific Warren and Burger Court precedents condemning intentional discrimination against the indigent nor the more general prohibition from *Moreno* against targeting unpopular groups,[115] one can hear echoes of those arguments in her dissent.

Second, *Papachristou* and the panoply of constitutional arguments made during the heyday of the anti-vagrancy law movement become visible, briefly, at the tail end of her opinion. Sotomayor considers other ways of challenging no-sleeping ordinances, using the Excessive Fines Clause, the Due Process Clause, the right to travel, the Fourteenth Amendment, and the constitutional rule against banishment.[116] And here, Sotomayor *does* mention vagrancy and the void-for-vagueness doctrine, citing *Kolender v. Lawson*[117] and, tellingly,

---

[112] *Id.*

[113] The dissent observes that the city councilors of Grants Pass also considered other "tools" to manage the local homeless population, including buying them bus tickets out of town, transporting them elsewhere and leaving them there, or denying them basic social services by publishing "do not serve" lists. *Id.* at 2234–35.

[114] *Id.* at 2235.

[115] U.S. Dep't of Agric. v. Moreno, 413 U.S. 528, 534 (1973).

[116] *Grants Pass*, 144 S. Ct. at 2241–43 (Sotomayor, J., dissenting).

[117] Kolender v. Lawson, 461 U.S. 352, 361–62 (1983).

Papachristou.[118] This list echoes Amsterdam's articulation of vagrancy law infirmities in his celebrated law review article.[119]

Sotomayor thus alludes to the more capacious individual rights that Justice Douglas championed, though she largely accepts the majority's narrow framing of the case. Compare her dissent to what Douglas might have written in *Grants Pass*. (We have a good idea because he already wrote it in *Papachristou*.[120]) Douglas articulated an affirmative right to be "out of place," not simply a limited right to avoid criminal prosecution for something one has no choice but to do. Though *Papachristou*'s holding was based in void-for-vagueness doctrine, the case espoused a broad-based concept of liberty, which tried to create space not only for survival, but also for thriving—those "lives of high spirits."[121]

As the ongoing dynamic of constitutional oversight and criminal law response has proceeded over the last fifty years, however, states and localities have passed new laws, targeting specific populations, in particular the homeless and indigent. The homeless have become more isolated politically and legally. *Grants Pass* has now clarified that conduct regulation can do much of the work that status regulation once performed, at least for those who must live without permanent shelter. The majority opinion offers this as a form of compassion—to assist the homeless—while the dissent bemoans the Court's cruelty. In the conclusion to her dissent, Justice Sotomayor criticizes the Court for "abdicat[ing]" its constitutional obligations and entreats us to take responsibility for society's most vulnerable.[122]

III. The City and the Poor

What are we to make of the return of vagrancy? One possibility (and this is the lesson that history seems to teach) is that it never really went away. Large numbers of shelter-less people have been

---

[118] Papachristou v. City of Jacksonville, 405 U.S. 156, 161–62 (1972); *Grants Pass*, 144 S. Ct. at 2244 (Sotomayor, J., dissenting).

[119] *See generally* Amsterdam, *supra* note 38.

[120] *Papachristou*, 405 U.S. at 164.

[121] *Id.*

[122] *Grants Pass*, 144 S. Ct. at 2244 (Sotomayor, J., dissenting). On the Court's erasure of the most vulnerable from its docket generally and in *Grants Pass* specifically, see Karen M. Tani, *The Supreme Court, 2023 Term—Foreword: Curation, Narration, Erasure: Power and Possibility at the U.S. Supreme Court*, 138 Harv. L. Rev. 1, 13, 80 (2024).

ever-present in American history. The demand to control mobile populations and to move along the poor, the destitute, and the 'down-and-out' regularly reemerges in periods when the city's streets appear to be ungovernable, out of control. But resort to vagrancy also arises when perceived disorder begins to spill over into "nicer" neighborhoods, the business district, or into those urban locations that have become more recently desirable or where those who benefit from higher land values see an opportunity.

Vagrancy law and its analogs have been historically used to police certain populations, but the location of enforcement is importantly territorial. Vagrancy regulation is about urban *space*: The shelter-less are only a problem when they are among us, in spaces we want to be in, physically, socially, and economically. And so policing "disorder" can be understood as a form of land-use control, a way of "zoning" city streets and neighborhoods, to maintain their stability or, in some cases, to make those spaces more pliable for development.[123]

Neither the *Grants Pass* majority nor the dissent addresses this aspect of the relationship between vagrancy and urban land. But urban sociology has long understood the management of the poor through the lens of territory. In 1976, Harvey Molotch famously described the city as a "growth machine."[124] He argued that the city can best be understood as a competition among land-based elites for developmental resources, all toward the end of increasing land value. For "politically mobilized local elites, however split they might be on other issues," the "desire for growth provides the key operative motivation" and the "most important constraint upon available options for local initiative in social and economic reform."[125]

Viewed from this perspective, the return of vagrancy was predictable. That local businesses, homeowners, real estate and ancillary industries, and others with a stake in the local economy are interested in stable if not rising property values, and that city officials, naturally, will be responsive to their demands to "clean up the neighborhood" should be uncontroversial. The interests of city officials and the

---

[123] Richard Schragger, *The Limits of Localism*, 100 MICH. L. REV. 371, 405–15 (2001) [hereinafter Schragger, *Limits of Localism*]; *see also* KATHERINE BECKETT & STEVE HERBERT, BANISHED: THE NEW SOCIAL CONTROL IN URBAN AMERICA 3–15, 23–61, 85–139 (2010).

[124] Harvey Molotch, *The City as a Growth Machine: Toward a Political Economy of Place*, 82 AM. J. SOCIO. 309, 309 (1976).

[125] *Id.* at 310.

growth machine are aligned insofar as the city's tax base depends on maintaining a healthy business climate and an attractive and safe streetscape. Richer people pay more in taxes than poorer people. To city leaders and taxpayers, the homeless are a pure negative; they pay no taxes but cost the city in the provision of social services and put its very flourishing at risk.

Mike Davis, in *City of Quartz*, his now classic 1990 account of Los Angeles, provided a pointed description of how these interests generate a city obsessed with controlling marginal populations.[126] Davis welcomed us to "Fortress L.A.," "where the defense of luxury lifestyles is translated into a proliferation of new repressions in space and movement, undergirded by the ubiquitous 'armed response.'"[127] In the 1980s and 1990s, Los Angeles was a place of "bum-proof" bus benches, rounded at the edges to ensure against sleeping, and automatic sprinklers that would activate at random times during the night to soak those who might loiter. It was a place where restaurants locked up their trash behind steel gates and where the police promoted a policy of "containment" and engaged in periodic sweeps to rid the sidewalks of "cardboard condos."[128] (Again, note that the homelessness "crisis" did not just appear in the last decade.) Davis sketched a particularly dystopian vision of the city in which public space is privatized, abetted by an elaborate surveillance apparatus. The rich are protected by private security while those on the margins of society are shunted into increasingly dangerous spaces. On his account, the police were essentially adjuncts to the real-estate industry; the destitute were pushed out or contained to those narrow locations of the city that were not yet ripe for redevelopment.[129]

The territorial management of the urban poor has been a consistent, perhaps even the most enduring, theme in the sociology of the city.[130] In 1996, Robert Ellickson, a prominent Yale Law School professor, published *Controlling Chronic Misconduct in City Spaces: Of*

---

[126] *See generally* Mike Davis, City of Quartz: Excavating the Future in Los Angeles (1990).

[127] *Id.* at 223.

[128] *Id.* at 232–36.

[129] *Id.* at 244–60; *see also* Bernard E. Harcourt, *Policing L.A.'s Skid Row: Crime and Real Estate Redevelopment in Downtown Los Angeles [An Experiment in Real Time]*, 2005 U. Chi. Legal F. 325.

[130] For an intellectual history, see Mitchell Duneier, Ghetto: The Invention of a Place, the History of an Idea (2017). For an account of how the urban political economy

Panhandlers, Skid Rows, and Public-Space Zoning, which made explicit the link between regulating undesirables and regulating their location in city spaces.[131] Like Davis, Ellickson bemoaned the deterioration of the city's communal spaces. Unlike Davis, he attributed their declining vibrancy to their overuse by the aggressive panhandler, the overnight sleeper, and the chronic bench sitter. "By the early 1990s," Ellickson observed, "the increased disorderliness of the urban street scene had triggered a political backlash. Commentators began to report that the urban populace was suffering from 'compassion fatigue.'"[132]

His solution: Create red, yellow, and green zones across the city, defined as spaces in which certain activities are or are not tolerated by the police.[133] Green zones would be the most restrictive—no chronic street nuisances would be permitted—while in red zones, the destitute would be allowed to set up camp (within limits). Like the *Grants Pass* majority, Ellickson did not hesitate to characterize what homeless people must do on the streets—sleep, eat, sit—as regulable *conduct*, as nuisances. And he was quite comfortable to limit red zones to a very small slice of the city's communal spaces: five percent.[134] Ellickson's public-space zoning was a policy of containment. The anti-Amsterdam, he was explicit about his desire to bring back the old skid rows in order to sanitize the rest of the city. He was also aware that the homeless needed to exist *somewhere*. He was not prepared to exile them altogether.

Ellickson's urban space management scheme was heavily influenced by the "broken windows" theory of policing, which was at its height in the 1990s. Also called "order maintenance" or "quality of life" policing, it was meant to be responsive to the sense of growing disorder and criminality in the nation's cities.[135] It was especially popular in New York, where Rudolph Giuliani, the mayor from 1994–2001, pursued it with great vigor, promising to get rid of "homeless people, panhandlers, prostitutes, squeegee cleaners,

---

produces and sustains homelessness, see Don Mitchell, Mean Streets: Homelessness, Public Space, and the Limits of Capital (2020).

[131] Ellickson, *supra* note 21.

[132] *Id.* at 1167–68.

[133] *Id.* at 1220–22.

[134] *Id.* at 1221.

[135] Schragger, *Limits of Localism*, *supra* note 123, at 377.

squatters, graffiti artists, reckless bicyclists, and unruly youth."[136] The broken windows theory, promulgated in the first instance by James Q. Wilson and George Kelling in a 1982 *Atlantic* article, asserted that small forms of disorder and low-level criminality (like a broken window), if left unaddressed, would lead to more significant disorder and higher-level criminality.[137] On this theory, the police were urged to aggressively enforce prohibitions against panhandling, littering, vandalism, turnstile jumping, jaywalking, and street peddling. The belief was that such order maintenance would not only produce its own benefits but would prevent more serious crime as well.

It is notable that the Court's opinion in *Grants Pass* does not cite broken windows theory or explicitly rely on order maintenance policing, even as the majority clearly believes that there is a relationship between homeless encampments and criminality. In part, that may be because broken windows theory has been widely criticized, even in the popular literature.[138] The theory runs into trouble in three significant ways. First, the existence of low-level street disorder does not appear to have a causal relationship with serious crime.[139] Graffiti and turnstile jumping does not, it turns out, *cause* an increase in murders and rapes—though common underlying pathologies *might* be responsible for all kinds of crime. Second, the *perception* of disorder is at the heart of broken windows, but perceptions are unreliable. The actual signals of a materially disordered street (graffiti, litter, abandoned cars, broken windows) are discounted in certain neighborhoods but take on heightened significance in others.[140] In fact, one of the most important indicators of perceived disorder is *race*: People perceive

---

[136] Neil Smith, *Giuliani Time: The Revanchist 1990s*, 57 Soc. Text 1, 3 (1998).

[137] James Q. Wilson & George L. Kelling, *Broken Windows: The Police and Neighborhood Safety*, Atl. Monthly, Mar. 1982, at 29, 31.

[138] *See* Malcolm Gladwell, *The Tipping Point Revisited: Broken Windows*, Pushkin (Oct. 24, 2024), https://www.pushkin.fm/podcasts/revisionist-history/the-tipping-point-revisited-broken-windows; Emma Goldberg, *Malcolm Gladwell Holds His Ideas Loosely. He Thinks You Should, Too.*, N.Y. Times (Sept. 29, 2024), https://www.nytimes.com/2024/09/26/business/malcolm-gladwell-revenge-of-the-tipping-point.html. For an early critique, see Bernard E. Harcourt, Illusion of Order: The False Promise of Broken Windows Policing (2001).

[139] *See* Daniel T. O'Brien, Chelsea Farrell & Brandon C. Welsh, *Looking Through Broken Windows: The Impact of Neighborhood Disorder on Aggression and Fear of Crime Is an Artifact of Research Design*, 2 Ann. Rev. Criminology 53, 62–63 (2019); Robert J. Sampson, Great American City: Chicago and the Enduring Neighborhood Effect 126–29 (2012); *see also* Baher Azmy, Taking Back the Streets: Impact Litigation as Movement Law 43 (Nov. 12, 2024) (unpublished manuscript) (on file with authors).

[140] Sampson, *supra* note 139, at 130–31, 133–35, 137–40.

Black neighborhoods to be more disordered than they are and underperceive objective disorder in white neighborhoods.[141] Unsurprisingly, this means that, third, the aggressive enforcement of low-level criminality has a disproportionate effect on minority neighborhoods, with no corresponding reduction in serious crime—only additional harmful interactions between police and Black and brown citizens.[142]

The rise and fall of broken windows offers a lesson, though not one learned by the Court: Perceived crises of street disorder and the political demand to do something about crime often have the character of moral panics. The fear of imminent urban collapse of 1970s New York contributed to the policing approaches of the 1980s and 1990s. Today, San Francisco's homeless encampments are a sign to some commentators of the deep failures of urban liberalism and of the impending demise of the American city.[143] These predictions of urban disintegration are not creations of the twentieth or twenty-first centuries. They reflect an underlying anti-urbanism that has long resided deep within the American psyche, from Thomas Jefferson to Donald Trump.[144] The city is always on the verge of collapse, for in every age it is beset by hordes of immigrants, the poor, the vicious, the criminal, or the corrupt.[145] As Jane Jacobs observed in her classic *The Death and Life of Great American Cities*, there is a long tradition of treating the city's problems as so unsolvable as to require its dismantling, its thoroughgoing bulldozered renewal, or its dispersal and deconcentration.[146] The disease-free, crime-free, homeless-free suburbs beckon.

Of course, homelessness is not a made-up problem, nor is it readily solved. Some portion of the homeless suffer from mental illness and substance abuse. Deinstitutionalizing the mentally ill—mainly by closing the hospitals where the sick had been formerly warehoused—was

---

[141] *Id.* at 137–40, 145–46.

[142] Azmy, *supra* note 139 (manuscript at 43–46).

[143] Nathan Heller, *What Happened to San Francisco, Really?*, New Yorker (Oct. 16, 2023), https://www.newyorker.com/magazine/2023/10/23/what-happened-to-san-francisco-really; Danny Westneat, *West Coast Cities Start to Confront the Limits of the Liberal Dream*, Seattle Times (Sept. 30, 2023, 6:00 AM), https://www.seattletimes.com/seattle-news/west-coast-cities-start-to-confront-the-limits-of-the-liberal-dream.

[144] Steven Conn, Americans Against the City: Anti-Urbanism in the Twentieth Century 11 (2014); Richard Schragger, *The Attack on American Cities*, 96 Tex. L. Rev. 1163, 1212 (2017) [hereinafter Schragger, *Attack on American Cities*].

[145] Schragger, *Attack on American Cities*, *supra* note 144, at 1195–1215.

[146] Jane Jacobs, The Death and Life of Great American Cities 27–35 (1961).

carried out in the 1970s and 1980s, but without sufficient foresight. Funds for outpatient services and supportive housing were not forthcoming; the mentally ill were left to fend for themselves.[147] Providing adequate services to troubled people is challenging, especially in eras of social-welfare austerity.

Nevertheless, one should be a bit cynical about the episodic use of aggressive policing to address an ongoing social problem. Giuliani's reign brought us what became known as "Giuliani time,"[148] characterized by homeless sweeps, zero-tolerance policing, and dramatically rising incarceration rates.[149] New York City Mayor Michael Bloomberg followed up with an aggressive use of stop-and-frisk, a regime that, at its height, resulted in 686,000 stops of New York citizens *per year*.[150] Most of the stops, it appears, were pretextual. A federal district judge, ruling that the NYPD violated the Constitution, ultimately determined that the police overwhelmingly stopped Black and Latino residents[151] and the "hit rate" (i.e., a stop that helped detect a crime or revealed a weapon) was a miniscule six percent.[152] In Chicago, the city adopted an anti-gang loitering ordinance targeting those gang members "remaining in any one place for no apparent purpose."[153] That statute was defended on order-maintenance grounds. The city asserted that "norms of order are critical to keeping social influence pointed away from, rather than toward criminality; the spectacle of open gang activity, vandalism, aggressive panhandling, and other forms of disorder transmits signals that cause both lawbreakers and law-abiders to behave in ways conducive

---

[147] On the failures of deinstitutionalization, see Chris Koyanagi, *Learning from History: Deinstitutionalization of People with Mental Illness as Precursor to Long-Term Care Reform*, Kaiser Comm'n on Medicaid & the Uninsured (2007), https://www.kff.org/wp-content/uploads/2013/01/7684.pdf (discussing the history and failings of deinstitutionalization of people with mental illness in the United States). On the relationship between deinstitutionalization and homelessness, see Petr Winkler et al., *Deinstitutionalized Patients, Homelessness, and Imprisonment: A Systematic Review*, 208 Brit. J. Psychiatry 421 (2016) (contesting claim that deinstitutionalization caused homelessness).

[148] The term gained currency after the 1997 beating and sodomizing of Abner Louima, a Haitian immigrant, by white police officers, who allegedly chanted during the assault (referring to the previous mayor), "It's Giuliani time, not Dinkins time," though Louima is reported to have later retracted that element of the assault. *See* Smith, *supra* note 136, at 2.

[149] *Id.*

[150] Azmy, *supra* note 139 (manuscript at 2).

[151] *Id.* (manuscript at 50); Floyd v. City of New York, 959 F. Supp. 2d 540, 557 (S.D.N.Y. 2013).

[152] *Floyd*, 959 F. Supp. 2d at 558.

[153] Schragger, *Limits of Localism*, *supra* note 123, at 371.

to crime."[154] But in a 6-3 decision in 1999, *City of Chicago v. Morales*, the Supreme Court struck down the ordinance on void-for-vagueness grounds, following *Papachristou*.[155] Notably, the *Grants Pass* majority does not mention *Morales*.

There is no evidence that the Chicago police lost a potent tool of crime prevention with the loss of the city's gang-loitering ordinance. In fact, just the opposite: Murder rates in Chicago dropped precipitously in the mid-2000s,[156] along with crime rates throughout the country. Stop-and-frisk in New York also had little to do with stopping crime. Crime rates in New York City did not seem to budge when stops went from 97,000 in 2002 to 686,000 in 2011.[157] Nor did crime explode, despite what some prognosticators predicted, after the city was ordered to curtail its use of stop-and-frisk.[158] The truth is that crime has fallen almost everywhere over the last forty years or so,[159] in cities of all kinds—whatever a given city's policing policy. There is little consensus among experts as to why.[160]

To be clear, none of this is to say that having significant numbers of destitute people on the streets and large-scale homeless encampments in or on the fringes of our major cities are not serious social problems. Indeed, their existence is cause for alarm and an indictment of our flawed social safety net, the lack of housing opportunities, a failing mental health regime, and our inability to address a long-standing substance abuse crisis.

---

[154] *Id.* at 380 (quoting Brief for the Petitioner at 15, City of Chicago v. Morales, 527 U.S. 41 (1999) (No. 97-1121)).

[155] *Morales*, 527 U.S. at 51.

[156] Following the Supreme Court's 1999 ruling in *Morales*, the number of murders dropped from 631 in 2000 to 448 in 2005, with the number decreasing each year in between. The number of murders in the ten years prior to *Morales* (1990–1999) averaged about 829 per year, while in the ten years following *Morales* (2000–2009) the number of murders averaged about 532, an average decrease of almost 300 murders per year. *Annual Reports*, CHI. POLICE DEP'T, https://www.chicagopolice.org/statistics-data/statistical-reports/annual-reports.

[157] Azmy, *supra* note 139 (manuscript at 45) (citing *Floyd*, 959 F. Supp. 2d at 591–603).

[158] *Id.* (manuscript at 60).

[159] On the great crime decline and its causes, see Oliver Roeder, Lauren-Brooke Eisen & Julia Bowling, *What Caused the Crime Decline?*, BRENNAN CTR. FOR JUST. (2015), https://www.brennancenter.org/our-work/research-reports/what-caused-crime-decline.

[160] For a summary of the literature, see Vanessa Barker, *Explaining the Great American Crime Decline: A Review of Blumstein and Wallman, Goldberger and Rosenfeld, and Zimring*, 35 LAW & SOC. INQUIRY 489, 490–92 (2010) (observing that "researchers have had a difficult time explaining the [crime] decline . . . there is no consensus, no single most important cause").

But it is important to observe (though the Court does not) that our most recent homelessness "crisis" has emerged at a moment when U.S. cities are enjoying a multi-decades-long "urban resurgence."[161] Starting in the early 2000s, American cities experienced a "reversal of fortunes."[162] Downtown populations began to stabilize or increase after the decades-long declines that had accompanied the post-war flight to the suburbs. In many formerly declining cities, including Detroit (which in 2013 declared the largest municipal bankruptcy in U.S. history[163]), property values have skyrocketed.[164] This resurgence has been global; people and businesses all over the world seem to have a renewed interest in living or locating in central cities.

Few commentators predicted this return of the city. It seemed more plausible that with the rise of instantaneous communications, online commerce, and rapid travel, the need to be physically located close to work or consumer goods would be outdated. Co-locating in physical space seemed like an old technology, made obsolete by the information technology revolution. The opposite occurred, however; cities seem to be more attractive than ever, even accounting for the distance-work revolution that accelerated with the COVID-19 pandemic.[165] Indeed, despite a perception of urban ills, the demand for urban real estate throughout the country seems to be bottomless. What we are witnessing in high-demand cities like New York and San Francisco is a burgeoning homeless population competing for space in places with some of the most expensive real estate in the world.

Of course, the close proximity of the dramatically rich and dramatically poor is not a coincidence at all. Cities have always been places where the rich and poor live only a few blocks or (at most) a few miles from one another, even if their lives rarely intersect. When they are

---

[161] Richard Schragger, City Power: Urban Governance in a Global Age 191–217 (2016).

[162] Ingrid Gould Ellen & Katherine O'Regan, *Reversal of Fortunes? Lower-Income Urban Neighborhoods in the U.S. in the 1990s*, 45 Urb. Stud. 845, 866 (2009).

[163] Jared Brey, *From the Edge of Bankruptcy to a Decade of Surpluses*, Governing (Oct. 10, 2024), https://www.governing.com/finance/from-the-edge-of-bankruptcy-to-a-decade-of-surpluses.

[164] The assessed value for real property (all classes) has increased each year since 2015, with a double-digit percent increase in value each of the past three years (2022–2024). *See How Do We Value Properties in Detroit?*, City of Detroit (Jan. 2024), https://detroitmi.gov/sites/detroitmi.localhost/files/2024-01/Detroit%20Values%20presentation%20January%202024.pdf.

[165] Konrad Putzier & Kate King, *American Cities Are Starting to Thrive Again. Just Not Near Office Buildings.*, Wall St. J. (May 30, 2023, 12:01 AM ET), https://www.wsj.com/articles/american-cities-are-starting-to-thrive-again-just-not-near-office-buildings-d839798f.

working, cities provide opportunities—in the form of education, increased wages, and access to jobs—for young people, immigrants, and rural and small-town in-migrants. One goes to the big city to make one's fortune. The richer the city, though, the greater the pressure on those neighborhoods that previously hosted the "down-and-out." As city living becomes more desirable, the places the poor can go—the Bowery and other skid rows—rapidly shrink. The cycles of urban economic boom and bust tend to disfavor the poor. In busts, the poor lack work; in booms, they get priced out of their homes or pushed out of the neighborhood.

If we are to tolerate a permanent underclass in our country (which history suggests we are inclined to do), then there must be a place for them to be, to exist in physical space.[166] We still talk about the "homeless" as if it were a temporary condition. In developing countries, acceptance of the inevitability of the landless poor leads to calling them squatters and their encampments informal settlements.[167] Indeed, it could be that the U.S. is approaching a time when the distribution of property is so pervasively unjust that it requires exceptional measures. In the meantime, *Grants Pass*'s narrow question of whether one can sleep on a bench in a public park seems somewhat unresponsive to the cycles of urban disinvestment and investment that have buffeted the American city especially over the last 150 years and certainly since the post-war suburban boom.[168] Nor does that narrow question address the perceived fragility of the city street, the abiding sense among urban dwellers and their elected officials that a neighborhood's stability or a downtown's economy can easily be undone by panhandlers, tent-dwellers, and chronic bench sitters.

At bottom, what divides the majority and dissent in *Grants Pass* is the perceived power of the homeless. Justice Sotomayor sees the use of criminal law to regulate the most powerless in society as obvious overreaching. The homeless are not a threat; they do not claim dominion over territory—just a place to sleep, to exist. They are "unpopular," "outcasts," indeed, "the most vulnerable among us."[169]

---

[166] On the "underclass" generally, see William Julius Wilson, The Truly Disadvantaged: The Inner City, the Underclass, and Public Policy 45–46 (1987).

[167] *See* K.D. Willis, *Squatter Settlements*, *in* International Encyclopedia of Human Geography 403, 403 (Rob Kitchin & Nigel Thrift eds., 2009).

[168] For a discussion, see Douglas W. Rae, City: Urbanism and its End (2003).

[169] City of Grants Pass v. Johnson, 144 S. Ct. 2202, 2243–44 (2024) (Sotomayor, J., dissenting).

By contrast, and for all his rhetorical sympathy, Gorsuch understands the homeless as exercising significant dominion over public spaces, an exercise that has to be countermanded by the state through its deployment of all possible resources, including the criminal law, and explicitly eschewing possible constitutional constraints. For Gorsuch, the power that the homeless exercise over urban territory is a serious threat to the city's residents, who are pushed out of the city's public spaces or made to feel uncomfortable and threatened on the public ways. Thus it has always been with the poor and unsheltered. To "take back the streets"[170] from the homeless requires a territorial contest in which their constitutional protection is entirely out of place.

IV. The Making and Unmaking of Constitutional Law

These competing visions of the vagrants' power are key to understanding the majority's and dissent's opposing answers to the constitutional law question in *Grants Pass*: Does the Eighth Amendment provide a basis for restricting the reach of a state's substantive criminal law as applied to those who lack housing?[171] The Court's answer in the negative has immediate consequences for where the homeless can sleep and what the Eighth Amendment prohibits. But what might otherwise seem a fairly narrow case has more significant consequences as well.

For one thing, both what the case itself says and the history it erases speak volumes about the Court's approach to the constitutional rights of the shelter-less poor. The vagrancy law challenge, along with myriad other cases and developments in law and policy in the 1960s and beyond, shifted the terrain on which both constitutional and policy decisions regarding homelessness were made. In *Papachristou* and other cases, the Court had understood the problem of homelessness at least in part from the perspective of the homeless themselves. *Grants Pass* clearly leaves that perspective to the dissent. Moreover, with the vagrancy revolution, the Court had placed constitutional heft behind the claims of the homeless, limiting what government officials could do to them. *Grants Pass* augurs a reversion to an earlier approach to the constitutional status of the poor and homeless. In rejecting even a narrow right to sleep in public when no other options exist, it places the homeless outside of the community of constitutional rights bearers.

---

[170] Azmy, *supra* note 139 (manuscript at 1).

[171] *Grants Pass*, 144 S. Ct. at 2226.

Perhaps more importantly, *Grants Pass* threatens our own concept of freedom, for how we treat the unhoused presents a basic test of society's respect for freedom for all. This was Jeremy Waldron's point in *Homelessness and the Issue of Freedom*, authored almost thirty-five years ago (at yet another moment of homeless "crisis").[172] Waldron argued that our ability to do anything, including exercising our basic liberties, depends on enjoying a property right (either private or communal) of some kind, however modest. Being in a physical place without a property right to it means that one is "utterly and at all times at the mercy of others" since "in order to exist, a person has to be somewhere."[173] The homeless person, Waldron observed, is thus "comprehensively unfree" to the extent that they are not allowed to engage in activities by right that require a physical location.[174] Because they have no right to any private place, Waldron pointed out, "[i]f sleeping is prohibited in public places, then sleeping is comprehensively prohibited to the homeless. If urinating is prohibited in public places (and if there are no public lavatories) then the homeless are simply unfree to urinate. These are not altogether comfortable conclusions, and they are certainly not comfortable for those who have to live with them."[175] Sotomayor's dissent makes the same point.

To be fair, Waldron's (and Sotomayor's) argument for freedom does not answer the key question that preoccupies the *Grants Pass* majority: Is the judiciary the correct branch to identify and enforce such freedom? Nor does their argument answer the broader question: Are judicially enforced rights effective in achieving their goals? The *Grants Pass* majority's central claim is that judicial rights-making interferes with an effective humanitarian policy response—an argument that (as we have noted) many of the cities of the Ninth Circuit also made.

This claim is not easily proven and is obviously contested. Have the Court's interventions in the vast number of institutions that it regulates through rights—workplaces, schools, hospitals, public accommodations, universities, churches, the military, the police, local governments—advanced our humanitarian goals or thwarted them? Presumably one's answer will depend on the context, but perhaps more

---

[172] Jeremy Waldron, *Homelessness and the Issue of Freedom*, 39 UCLA L. Rev. 295 (1991).

[173] *Id.* at 299, 300.

[174] *Id.* at 302.

[175] *Id.* at 315.

on one's philosophical or ideological commitments—especially with regard to which rights are viewed as indispensable.

What we can probably say is that providing a (limited) constitutional right to sleep, urinate, eat, or sit in public when there are no alternatives is second best to providing the necessary resources so that everyone can do those things in private, at least most of the time. Rights are a poor replacement for resources, though courts have played a role in forcing governments to redistribute to meet their constitutional obligations.[176] The relative effectiveness of such interventions is again grist for the historian.

The flip side to judicial effectiveness is whether local governments are better positioned than judges to address these issues. Do we trust local governments to use the criminal law sparingly—"a light-touch," as Gorsuch writes—to facilitate the provision of temporary shelter, with the goal of more permanent shelter?[177] The Court asserts that we should.

To be sure, there are citizens of good will all over the country who approach the problem of homelessness with compassion and are willing to spend local resources to address it in their towns. Homeless advocacy organizations can and do assert some political pressure on city councils. "Growth machine" politics is dominant but not inevitable. There is also the potential for self-interest. It is costly to put the homeless in jail; it requires policing, judging, and incarcerating large numbers of people. To the extent that the evidence tends to show that a punitive approach undermines crime prevention and just increases homelessness—that the street-to-jail-to-street-back-to-jail pipeline does little to address the underlying social and economic pathologies that lead to homelessness[178]—such officials might deploy social-welfare resources

---

[176] Notably, *Martin v. City of Boise* induced local governments and homeless advocacy groups in Oregon to negotiate and support a state law, passed in 2021, meant to "bring clarity and guidance for local governments in the management of outdoor space." Those same groups urged increased state funding for homeless services. *See Yes on HB 3115: Homelessness and Public Space*, League of Or. Cities & Or. L. Ctr., https://olis.oregonlegislature.gov/liz/2021R1/Downloads/FloorLetter/3212. HB 3115, as codified, requires local government public space regulations to be "objectively reasonable as to time, place and manner with regards to persons experiencing homelessness." Or. Rev. Stat. § 195.530(2) (2021).

[177] City of Grants Pass v. Johnson, 144 S. Ct. 2202, 2213 (2024).

[178] A recent study found no correlation between criminalization policies and a long-term reduction in homelessness. *See* Hannah Lebovits & Andrew Sullivan, Do Criminalization Policies Impact Local Homelessness? Exploring the Limits and Concerns of Socially Constructed Deviancy (Feb. 4, 2024) (unpublished manuscript), https://ssrn.com/abstract=4716230; *see also* Thea Sebastian, Hanna Love & Tahir Duckett, *Criminalizing Homelessness Can Lead to More*

even without the constitutional mandate *Grants Pass* has declined to impose.

But city officials might instead "race to the bottom," making the lives of the shelter-less so miserable that they move down the road to the next town or to the most convenient big city, where the homeless can more easily hide in plain sight. The game of "hot potato" that characterized the Anglo-American response to provision for the poor and homeless for centuries[179] is likely to return. The majority's celebration of local autonomy is selective here; compare this case to others in which the Court has insisted that some rights (Second Amendment or religious free exercise, for example) are too important to permit local variation. Federalism is valuable—against a baseline of rights. But *whose* rights is a matter of judicial politics.

Decentralization in the face of a collective-action problem can actually limit a city's power. San Francisco and Los Angeles may want to rethink a decision that allows local governments to avoid responsibility for providing for their own homeless. Suburban jurisdictions, rural towns, and small cities do not have the social-welfare resources of the larger cities, often by choice and sometimes by capacity. Grants Pass is one of those places. A city of about 40,000 in a rural Oregon county that has experienced deep revenue losses from the collapse of the logging industry, its burgeoning homeless population includes many long-time residents. The county is overwhelmingly white and aging, dominated by a generally libertarian, anti-tax, and anti-government conservative majority. But despite having some of the highest rates of opioid overdoses in the state, the starving of welfare services for the poor, even as the need has exploded, seems purposeful. Nine times between 2004 and 2016, Josephine County residents rejected measures that would shore up local finances and provide basic municipal services, opting instead for deep cuts in public safety, libraries, and social services.[180]

The Court's decision in *Grants Pass* might be a "win" for those kinds of places. But as we have already observed, unless society is willing to exile hundreds of thousands of people to the wilderness, homeless people will always need somewhere in the wider metropolitan region to go. And

---

Crime, GOVERNING (Oct. 9, 2024), https://www.governing.com/urban/criminalizing-homelessness-can-lead-to-more-crime.

[179] GOLUBOFF, VAGRANT NATION, *supra* note 8, at 15.

[180] *See* MICHELLE WILDE ANDERSON, THE FIGHT TO SAVE THE TOWN: REIMAGINING DISCARDED AMERICA 3, 121 (2022).

that means they will be in our towns and cities, even if corralled into "red zones." Indeed, Grants Pass has not "solved" its homeless problem. Following the Supreme Court decision, the city set aside two city-owned parcels for use as campsites for the unhoused. But these sites are isolated and potentially dangerous, and they are temporary.[181] Moreover, every local government is now equally empowered to threaten its homeless populations with imprisonment, likely further pushing the homeless into the larger urban centers. We have levelled down, not up.

To be sure, the constitutional rights at issue in *Grants Pass* are not likely to alter those underlying conditions. At most, a right to sleep in public when there are no available shelter beds gives the homeless some limited freedom from police harassment. Maybe that would be enough. Or maybe the police would find other ways to manage urban space as they did following the collapse of the formal vagrancy regime. In any case, the limited right the Court overturned in *Grants Pass* was at least more than nothing. It served as a baseline and maybe could have been a start to a more robust entitlement.[182]

In his 1991 article, Waldron observed that callousness to the rights of others is ultimately callousness for our own rights. Indeed, these points are related: The more we accept a race to the bottom; a starving of resources; an exclusion of the homeless from the community of constitutional rights bearers, the more we put our own rights at risk.[183] Who is included in the community of rights bearers exactly, and which rights do we bear? The answers to these questions are long contested and dynamic, and they are not apparent in the narrow opinions of *Grants Pass*. But the vagrancy law challenge played an important and largely unknown role in answering them some fifty years ago.

This brings us to the most surprising and perhaps broadest implication of *Grants Pass* that the history of vagrancy law enables us to see: the implications of the case for constitutionally protected fundamental rights in general. Vagrancy laws caught so many in their dragnet, which is the reason social movements of the 1960s viewed the vagrancy

---

[181] Jane Vaughan, *After Supreme Court Decision, Grants Pass Struggles to Make Long-Term Plan for Homelessness*, OPB (Sept. 19, 2024, 2:01 PM), https://www.opb.org/article/2024/09/19/after-us-supreme-court-decision-grants-pass-struggles-to-make-long-term-plan-for-homelessness.

[182] As noted above, the Ninth's Circuit's *Martin v. City of Boise* decision led to Oregon's adoption of a compromise state law meant to balance the interests of local governments and homeless populations. *See supra* note 176.

[183] Waldron, *supra* note 172, at 296.

challenge as essential to their respective struggles for freedom and equal rights. Because the laws were used against so many different types of people, and contested by so many different social movements, the cases invalidating them embraced a wide range of individual rights. This meant that the constitutional fate of the vagrant was bound up with the constitutional fate of the other major progressive social movements of the 1960s and 1970s. In other words, the vagrancy law challenge was about "them," the marginal and out of place who were targeted most frequently and systematically. But it was also about "us," anyone potentially subject to encroachment by unchecked police discretion, which, it turns out, is everyone. That is why Douglas's *Papachristou* paean to the social movements of the 1960s embraced not only the specific goals those movements sought, but an all-encompassing aspiration for "the right of dissent, . . . the right to be nonconformists[,] and the right to defy submissiveness" that produce "the feeling of independence and self-confidence, the feeling of creativity." The vagrancy revolution ultimately embraced us all.[184]

That becomes even more apparent when one understands the larger fundamental rights context in which *Papachristou* was decided in the early 1970s.[185] Three weeks before the Court heard arguments in *Papachristou*, the Court heard *Eisenstadt v. Baird*,[186] which concerned a state law restricting access to contraception. The week after hearing *Papachristou*, the Court heard argument in *Roe v. Wade*, the case challenging a Texas law that criminalized abortion.[187] These cases might seem far afield, but all three raised important questions about the content of constitutional rights, and several Justices—especially Justices Douglas and Brennan—understood their connection. For Douglas, authoring *Papachristou*, and Brennan, who was writing *Eisenstadt*, the *Papachristou-Eisenstadt-Roe* connection went to central constitutional questions: What was the content of fundamental rights, and where in the Constitution were they located? To what extent were such rights

---

[184] Goluboff, Vagrant Nation, *supra* note 8, at 334–36.

[185] *Id.* at 314–28; *see also* Risa Goluboff, *Dispatch from the Supreme Court Archives: Vagrancy, Abortion, and What the Links Between Them Reveal About the History of Fundamental Rights*, 62 Stan. L. Rev. 1361 (2010).

[186] *Eisenstadt* was argued November 17–18, 1971, and *Papachristou* was argued December 8, 1971. Eisenstadt v. Baird, 405 U.S. 438, 438 (1972); Papachristou v. City of Jacksonville, 405 U.S. 156, 156 (1972).

[187] *Roe* was first argued on December 13, 1971, and then reargued on October 11, 1972. Roe v. Wade, 410 U.S. 113, 113 (1973).

to be exercised in private (as in *Eisenstadt* and *Roe*) and to what extent in public (as in *Papachristou*)? The vagrancy, contraception, and abortion cases were connected, strategically and substantively, as they implicated these central issues, and their respective resolutions would set the path for the development of the Court's rights jurisprudence going forward.[188]

As we have noted, the Justices in conference had voted to base *Papachristou* on the void-for-vagueness doctrine of the Due Process Clause, but Douglas saw in the case an opportunity to identify and articulate a set of public-facing individual rights.[189] Douglas believed that the vagrancy laws criminalized protected conduct—particularly rights to be idle, to wander, to be unemployed, to enjoy the outdoors, to reject the bourgeois life and embrace the counterculture.[190] Eager to enshrine these rights into constitutional law, Douglas relied in his early drafts of *Papachristou* on the Ninth Amendment and then the Due Process Clause of the Fourteenth Amendment to describe and protect substantive fundamental rights and establish a broad vision of what the criminal law was not allowed to touch.[191]

Douglas shared his draft opinion with Justice Brennan, and it prompted Brennan to articulate his own view of fundamental rights in the context of both *Papachristou* and *Roe*. In a remarkable and highly unusual eleven-page memo to Douglas, Brennan offered a holistic view of the rights he deemed worthy of constitutional protection.[192] He structured basic liberties under three headings: freedom from bodily restraint and freedom to care for one's health and person; freedom of choice in basic decisions of life; and "autonomous control over the development and expression of one's intellect and personality."[193] After more than a decade of cases, in the vagrancy challenge and beyond, that had experimented with various ways of protecting individual liberty, both Douglas and Brennan thought the time had come for the Court to articulate something more systematic and definite.

Justice Blackmun, who was hard at work writing *Roe*, was not as sure. Though in conference the Justices had seemed to settle on a

---

188 Goluboff, Vagrant Nation, *supra* note 8, at 318–22.

189 *Id.* at 315.

190 *Id.*

191 *Id.* at 319–20.

192 *Id.* at 319.

193 *Id.*

fundamental rights basis for the opinion, Blackmun was initially inclined to use void for vagueness in *Roe* due to worries about "the more complex" issues fundamental rights raised.[194]

Ultimately, and apparently for strategic reasons, *Papachristou* and *Roe* switched doctrinal places.[195] Though Brennan appreciated and agreed with Douglas's *Papachristou* reasoning, he worried that the liberals would lose their majority—in both *Roe* and maybe in *Papachristou* too—if Douglas circulated his paean to mobility and nonconformity before *Roe*'s majority was committed. Indeed, once Justice Stewart made clear that a doctrinal embrace of broad individual rights in *Papachristou* would lose Douglas his vote, Douglas made void for vagueness the doctrinal basis for *Papachristou*.[196] At the same time, Brennan and Douglas convinced Blackmun to ground *Roe* in fundamental rights. *Roe* decriminalized first-term and most second-term abortions, telling legislatures that they had to respect a right of reproductive privacy.

In the end, then, *Roe*, following on *Griswold* and *Eisenstadt*, enshrined a constitutional right of private bodily autonomy.[197] *Papachristou*, on the other hand, did not fully achieve Douglas's vision of enshrining substantive public rights. The Jacksonville vagrancy ordinance failed because it licensed arbitrary and discriminatory arrests and convictions. The Court did not prevent legislatures from regulating certain conduct; it told them to do so with more specificity and to avoid either discriminatory enforcement that would systematically target "them" or arbitrary enforcement that might accidentally target "us."

Douglas's broad conception of rights nevertheless lived on in at least two ways. First, though no longer the holding of the case, all of Douglas's fundamental rights remained in *dicta* in *Papachristou*.[198] His language also found its way into the companion case to *Roe*, in a Douglas concurrence in *Doe v. Bolton*. Despite the void-for-vagueness holding of *Papachristou*, Douglas treated the case as if it had actually enshrined his broad set of fundamental rights.[199] These invisible threads connected the two cases, one involving a woman's right to choose to terminate a

[194] *Id.*

[195] *Id.* at 322.

[196] *Id.* at 322, 329.

[197] Roe v. Wade, 410 U.S. 113, 153–54 (1973).

[198] Papachristou v. City of Jacksonville, 405 U.S. 156, 164–68 (1972).

[199] Goluboff, Vagrant Nation, *supra* note 8, at 322; Doe v. Bolton, 410 U.S. 179, 209 (1973) (Douglas, J., concurring).

pregnancy and one about a woman's right to be in a car at night with whomever she wanted.

In erasing the history of vagrancy from *Grants Pass*, the Court also erases the threads that bound *Papachristou* to *Roe* and beyond—and that bound the de-moralization of poverty with the de-moralization of sexuality and reproduction. The stakes of the historical vacuum of *Grants Pass* are thus even higher once one realizes the relationship between the public-facing rights implicated by the vagrancy law challenge and the private-facing fundamental rights the Burger Court established in *Roe* and beyond and that the Roberts Court has recently revisited.

The Roberts Court has been more than willing—eager even—to overturn foundational and settled precedent.[200] It does not formally do so in this case. But by reading *Grants Pass* as a narrow case about the reach of *Robinson*, the Court engages in an institutional forgetting of the broader fundamental rights landscape that produced *Papachristou*. *Grants Pass* is defined as a case about the homeless, not about the criminal law writ large or police discretion or fundamental rights. *Grants Pass* understood narrowly is about the regulation of sleeping and camping in public. Understood broadly, it is intertwined with *Dobbs v. Jackson Women's Health Organization*'s rejection of a right of procreative privacy,[201] as *Roe*'s recognition of such a right was intertwined with *Papachristou*.

Conclusion

The truth is that we are a "vagrant nation" in two senses. The first, historical, sense refers to the long, multi-century existence of poor and shelter-less persons, regulated through the criminal law and to the mostly lost story of vagrancy law's constitutional revolution, only partially summarized here.[202] The second, societal, sense refers to our tolerance of a state of affairs in which the shelter-less have no rights to be in any particular place even though they have no physical situs in which to be. Waldron wrote of a "deeply frightening fact about the modern United States."[203] As a society, "we are willing to tolerate an economic system

[200] *See, e.g.*, Dobbs v. Jackson Women's Health Org., 597 U.S. 215 (2022); Loper Bright Enters. v. Raimondo, 144 S. Ct. 2244 (2024).

[201] *Dobbs*, 597 U.S. at 231.

[202] *See generally* Goluboff, Vagrant Nation, *supra* note 8.

[203] Waldron, *supra* note 172, at 304.

in which large numbers of people are homeless," but we seem unwilling to "allow those who are in this predicament to act as free agents, looking after their own needs, in public places—the only space available to them."[204] *Grants Pass* embodies this "frightening fact" and, in this way, likely tracks the views of many (or even most) Americans, who view the homeless as a menace and a blight—as exercising power in contested spaces—whatever sympathies they may express for them.

Grants Pass erases this history, and in so doing it also erases the links between us and them. It is not a charitable opinion, and it probably fails the candor test. It is almost certainly true that courts cannot easily address the endemic social and economic problems that gave rise to vagrancy laws and now to no-camping ordinances. But to pretend that ordinances that threaten and often deliver criminal punishment—both fines and jail time—somehow "help" individual homeless people or are effective tools in getting people the shelter that they desire is not credible. Those laws might help mayors and city councilors and governors win elections, but they are not going to "solve" a problem that we as a society seem mostly unwilling to solve.

Is the best response to the problem of homelessness a judicially enforced constitutional right to do some (limited) set of things (i.e., sleep in public) under certain (relatively narrow) conditions (i.e., when there are not enough shelter beds)? Of course not. But rejection of that narrow kind of right seems unduly harsh, even for a Court that has shown little compassion for the vulnerable.

As a matter of constitutional doctrine, no Court has yet to constitutionalize Justice Douglas's public-facing fundamental rights, and we would not expect any to do so in our lifetimes. Nevertheless, Douglas's *Papachristou* opinion, as published, has its own democratic power. Its void-for-vagueness holding captures harms that are both systematically discriminatory and can arbitrarily happen to anyone. Like the history of the vagrancy revolution generally and the lessons of the ongoing conflict about which people can occupy which urban spaces, it reminds us not to fetishize the difference between "us" and "them."

---

[204] *Id.*

ADRIAN VERMEULE

THE OLD REGIME AND THE LOPER BRIGHT "REVOLUTION"

On June 28, 2024, the Supreme Court decided *Loper Bright Enterprises v. Raimondo* and *Relentless, Inc. v. Department of Commerce*,[1] companion cases presenting the same question: whether *Chevron, U.S.A., Inc. v. Natural Resources Defense Council, Inc.*[2] should be overruled. The Court said "yes," and did overrule *Chevron*.[3] A number of popular articles and legal commentators immediately called the decision "revolutionary"[4] or, in a variant, the culmination of a "conservative counterrevolution"[5] against the administrative state. Others

Adrian Vermeule is the Ralph S. Tyler, Jr. Professor of Constitutional Law at Harvard Law School.

Author's note: Thanks to Sam Delmer for excellent research assistance and to multiple colleagues and friends for extensive discussion of these issues.

[1] 144 S. Ct. 2244 (2024).

[2] 467 U.S. 837 (1984).

[3] *Loper Bright*, 144 S. Ct. at 2273.

[4] *See, e.g.*, Adeola Adeosun, *Neil Gorsuch Leading 'Revolution' in Supreme Court Ruling*, Newsweek (June 30, 2024, 6:19 PM EDT), https://www.newsweek.com/neil-gorsuch-leading-revolution-supreme-court-ruling-shan-wu-1919288; Squire Patton Boggs, *The 2024 Revolution in Administrative Law*: Chevron *and Beyond*, YouTube (July 19, 2024), https://www.youtube.com/watch?v=XiR8ytgeBYY. For a large collection of varying initial responses to the decision ranging from skeptical to dramatic, see generally Cary Coglianese & Daniel E. Walters, *The Great Unsettling: Administrative Governance After* Loper Bright, 77 Admin. L. Rev. 1 (2025).

[5] *See* David L. Franklin, *This Supreme Court Has Betrayed Antonin Scalia's Legacy*, Slate (June 28, 2024, 4:36 PM), https://slate.com/news-and-politics/2024/06/supreme-court-opinions-antonin

The Supreme Court Review, 2025.
 https://doi.org/10.1086/735545

insisted that the central "grand narrative" of administrative law has now become, for better or for worse, the narrative propounded by libertarian and originalist critics of the administrative state.[6]

My own immediate reaction, published the day the decision came down, was different and more skeptical: *Loper Bright*, it seemed to me, was in large part a relabeling of *Chevron* deference as delegated agency discretion, rather than a dramatic change in the law.[7] I will expand on that view here, update it in light of later developments, and put it in a larger frame, offering a more general thesis—if you like, a different "grand narrative"—about *Loper Bright*, and about the broader libertarian and originalist attempt to curtail the administrative state through expanded judicial review of agency action.

The thesis runs this way. A commonplace of revolutions, and counterrevolutions, is that however dramatic they may be in the short run, in the long run they often produce less change than their proponents hope and their opponents fear. Sometimes revolutions or counterrevolutions even serve to cement into place, or indeed augment, the very structures and norms that the revolutionaries found most objectionable. Such a thesis was suggested as to the most dramatic upheaval of them all: the French Revolution of 1789. In *The Ancien Régime and the French Revolution*,[8] written in 1856 after a long series of revolutions and counterrevolutions of varying description, Alexis de Tocqueville argued not only that the Revolution was as much an outgrowth of earlier laws, institutions, and norms as a departure

---

-scalia-betrayal.html (describing *Loper Bright* both as part of a "conservative counterrevolution" and as a "revolution" that betrays the legacy of Justice Antonin Scalia as a proponent of *Chevron*).

[6] *See* Cass R. Sunstein, *Administrative Law's Grand Narrative* (Harvard Pub. L. Working Paper No. 24-21, 2024), https://ssrn.com/abstract=4986085 [hereinafter Sunstein, *Administrative Law's Grand Narrative*]; *see also* Cass R. Sunstein, *The Consequences of* Loper Bright 13 (Harvard Pub. L. Working Paper No. 24-29, 2024), https://ssrn.com/abstract=4881501 ("*Loper Bright* is a leading exhibit in the rise (and rise) of libertarian administrative law. . . .").

[7] *See* Adrian Vermeule, Chevron *by Any Other Name: From* 'Chevron *Deference' to* 'Loper Bright *Delegation*,' New Dig. (June 28, 2024), https://thenewdigest.substack.com/p/chevron-by-any-other-name. For a similarly skeptical view, although one focused on *Skidmore* deference rather than delegation, see Jonathan H. Adler, *From Deference to Respect – The Real Import of* Loper Bright, Reason (July 3, 2024, 1:36 PM), https://reason.com/volokh/2024/07/03/from-deference-to-respect-the-real-import-of-loper-bright. And for some suggestive remarks of Justice Kavanaugh along similar lines, see *infra* note 51 and accompanying text. For a piece that propounds essentially the same thesis on *Loper Bright* delegation as Vermeule, *supra*, see Thomas W. Merrill, Case Comment, *The Demise of Deference—and the Rise of Delegation to Interpret?*, 138 Harv. L. Rev. 227 (2024).

[8] Alexis de Tocqueville, The Ancien Régime and the French Revolution (Arthur Goldhammer trans., Cambridge Univ. Press 2011) (1856).

from them, but also that those laws, institutions and norms largely survived the Revolution; indeed, they were in a sense confirmed and strengthened by it, albeit clothed in new outward forms. For Tocqueville, the Revolution had "a first phase during which the French seemed to want to abolish everything from their past, and a second in which they would recover part of what they had left behind. Many of the laws and political traditions of the *Ancien Régime* suddenly disappeared in 1789 only to reappear a few years later, much as certain rivers plunge underground only to reemerge somewhat farther on, bringing the same waters to new shores."[9]

In what follows, I will suggest the possibility of a similar thesis, of course on a much smaller scale, as to the *Loper Bright* "revolution" and indeed the administrative law "revolution" more generally. (This point is equally relevant for those who describe *Loper Bright* as a counterrevolution against the administrative state; counterrevolutions also chronically promise more than they deliver, as the supporters of the Bourbon Restoration discovered after 1815.) There is a difference to be noted right away: In the case of *Loper Bright*, in contrast to the French Revolution, we do not yet have the advantage of time and hence of hindsight. We are still in the first of Tocqueville's two phases, in which revolutionaries hope and believe that the old regime of absolutism can be entirely extirpated. For the Court's radical critics of the administrative state, such as Justices Gorsuch and Thomas, we are in the bright dawn of the Year Zero, which is also (as the French revolutionaries themselves hoped) a restoration of the classical republic.

But it is already possible to see how *Loper Bright* both grew out of pre-existing legal doctrines, principles, and trends, and also to see how the chastening of the *Loper Bright* revolution could occur, leaving in place much of the old *Chevron* regime under different labels. Indeed, I will argue, the beginning of that process is already visible within the four corners of the majority opinion itself. Writing for the Court, its leading Girondin or moderate revolutionary, the Chief Justice, already attempts to temper the *Loper Bright* revolution, writing a roadmap for a broad recharacterization of "*Chevron* deference" as "*Loper Bright* delegation."[10] In some potentially broad range of the cases that would previously have been covered by the *Chevron* doctrine,

[9] *Id.* at 3.

[10] As previously argued in Vermeule, *supra* note 7.

courts will now say that Congress has explicitly or implicitly delegated discretionary policymaking authority to the agencies. In this framework, much of the review of the outer bounds of agency discretion that previously took place under the *Chevron* label will take place under the label of arbitrary-and-capricious review, but it is at best unclear how much will change in any operative sense, especially given that *Chevron* and arbitrariness review have long been held to overlap in part.[11] Furthermore, even apart from delegation, the Chief Justice's opinion for the Court leaves in place a robust *Skidmore* doctrine of "respect" for persuasive agency interpretations;[12] it also backhandedly confirms the idea associated with *NLRB v. Hearst Publications, Inc.* that courts owe agencies a form of deference as to "mixed questions," or the application of legal standards to facts, which is a form of policymaking discretion.[13] It is difficult, at least in the abstract, to identify with certainty any clear category of cases that will come out differently under the new regime than under the old one.

The overall impression that *Loper Bright* makes is a curiously schizophrenic one—ironically enough, the same impression that David Currie once attributed to *Crowell v. Benson*.[14] *Loper Bright* ostentatiously gives to the Court's Hamburgerians[15] with one hand while partly taking back the gift with the other. *Loper Bright*, in other words, gives a highly salient (apparent) victory to the forces of libertarian administrative law,[16] while also and simultaneously qualifying that

[11] Judulang v. Holder, 565 U.S. 42, 52 n.7 (2011) ("The Government urges us instead to analyze this case under the second step of the test we announced in *Chevron*. . . . Were we to do so, our analysis would be the same, because under *Chevron* step two, we ask whether an agency interpretation is 'arbitrary or capricious in substance.'" (internal citation omitted) (quoting Mayo Found. for Med. Educ. & Rsch. v. United States, 562 U.S. 44, 53 (2011))).

[12] Loper Bright Enters. v. Raimondo, 144 S. Ct. 2244, 2263 (2024).

[13] *Id.* at 2259–60; *see* NLRB v. Hearst Publ'ns, Inc., 322 U.S. 111, 131 (1944).

[14] *See* David P. Currie, The Constitution in the Supreme Court: The Second Century, 1888–1986, at 215 (1990) (explaining that in the second half of the opinion, "Hughes neatly refuted his own argument").

[15] *See* Philip Hamburger, Is Administrative Law Unlawful? (2014); *see also* Gutierrez-Brizuela v. Lynch, 834 F.3d 1142, 1151 (10th Cir. 2016) (Gorsuch, J., concurring) (citing Hamburger, *supra*, at 287–91); Dep't of Transp. v. Ass'n of Am. R.Rs., 575 U.S. 43, 71 (2015) (Thomas, J., concurring in the judgment) (citing Hamburger, *supra*, at 33–34, 35–36, 38). For my own views on Hamburgerism, see Adrian Vermeule, "*No*," 93 Tex. L. Rev. 1547 (2015).

[16] Cass R. Sunstein & Adrian Vermeule, *Libertarian Administrative Law*, 82 U. Chi. L. Rev. 393 (2015).

victory to such a degree as to raise serious questions about not only how much the law will change, but whether it will significantly change at all. In part, this curious two-step appears to be an effort on the part of the Chief Justice to both satisfy and yet also preempt the more radical originalist Justices to his right, the *Jacobins de droite*, Justices Gorsuch and Thomas. The latter would go even farther and eliminate some of the exceptions and qualifications the Court's opinion leaves in place, or indeed would even revive the constitutional nondelegation doctrine as a tool for the more systematic destruction of the administrative state.[17]

Only time will tell whether the Chief Justice is doomed to suffer the same fate as the Girondins of the early 1790s, who discovered to their great cost that revolutions are easier to unleash than to restrain and moderate. Even a revival of the constitutional nondelegation doctrine, however, promises more than it could deliver, as I will explain. In the long run, by far the best prediction is that, just as the basic structures of the *ancien régime* survived the Revolution and were even further cemented into place, so too with the administrative state and judicial deference to administrative interpretations of law—whether that deference is explicit or implicit and whether under the label of deference, of delegated policymaking discretion, or of mere respect.

Part I provides a brief requiem for the *ancien régime*. Part II lays out the main holdings of *Loper Bright*, details the thesis that the decision may change much less than might initially appear, and examines some of the many doctrinal questions raised and left open by the decision. In particular, I examine the possibility of interaction effects with the Court's other recent decisions on administrative law, and I suggest that those effects will not do much to exacerbate the effect of *Loper Bright*, in part because they cut in countervailing directions. Part III examines the main proposal of the Court's *Jacobins de droite*, who would revive the nondelegation doctrine as a constitutional matter, and argues that such a revival is both unlikely to occur and likely to be surprisingly inconsequential even if it does occur. I conclude that the anti-administrative revolution, dramatic though it may appear to those of us who are living through it, is likely to be at most a

[17] *See, e.g.*, *Ass'n of Am. R.Rs.*, 575 U.S. at 77 (Thomas, J., concurring in the judgment); Gundy v. United States, 588 U.S. 128, 179 (2019) (Gorsuch, J., dissenting).

marginal revolution—a mild and perhaps temporary correction to the "market" for administrative authority. Just as the French State after the Revolution emerged, in a sense, even more like itself, just under different forms and labels, so too with the administrative state after *Loper Bright.*

I. A Requiem for the Old Regime

Before focusing on the detailed holdings of *Loper Bright,* I begin with a brief but necessary funeral mass for the old regime, which the majority opinion dispatched with little ceremony and buried in an unmarked grave.

Two points are salient. The first is that the Court unmistakably distorted the history of deference doctrine, simply omitting important strands of case law that would have considerably complicated or even compromised its historical narrative. This is not the first time such a thing has happened, of course, but the overstated and simplistic historical narrative of *Loper Bright* comes perilously close to misinformation-by-omission. Second, in Tocquevillian spirit, I will suggest that the *Loper Bright* "revolution" is actually best seen as building upon and bringing to a culmination prior strands in the case law, rather than effecting a radical break with the past.

A. The History

The Court's historical narrative was simple. Federal courts had always asserted ultimate authority to interpret statues, de novo or independently. True, in some case law, including some very early case law from the Marshall Court—presumably at least probative evidence of the original understanding—the Justices had said that longstanding statutory constructions by the executive departments are worthy of "respect." But the *Loper Bright* Court saw this as merely a form of what today would be called *Skidmore* deference, more accurately called *Skidmore* "weight."[18] So too, the cases that spoke of deference in the 1940s, and that formed the immediate background

[18] Peter L. Strauss, *"Deference" Is Too Confusing—Let's Call Them* "Chevron *Space" and* "Skidmore *Weight,"* 112 Colum. L. Rev. 1143, 1145–46 (2012) ("'*Skidmore* weight' addresses the possibility that an agency's view on a given statutory question may in itself warrant respect by judges who themselves have ultimate interpretive authority. . . . It is not only that agencies have the credibility of their circumstances, but also that they can contribute to an efficient, predictable, and nationally uniform understanding of the law that would be disrupted by the variable results to

in place when the Administrative Procedure Act (APA) was enacted in 1946, were merely cases in which courts deferred to the application of legal standards to facts, an exercise not of legal interpretation but of policymaking. The text of the APA, on the Court's view, then plainly confirmed the (putatively) traditional position that federal courts are to decide "all relevant questions of law" for themselves.[19] In 1984, *Chevron* broke with the traditional view, creating a category of cases in which law-interpreting power was transferred from the courts to agencies, in violation of the APA. Over time, the *Chevron* framework became ever more complex, indeed byzantine, and eventually became so unworkable as to teeter on the brink of collapse. In this narrative, the overruling of *Chevron* was not so much a forward-looking change in the Court's approach to deference as a restoration of the original authority of courts, traditional in our constitutional order and confirmed by the text of the APA. Like the Parisian revolutionaries of 1789, the more articulate of whom saw themselves as (or at least claimed to be) restorers of classical republican liberty, the Court's narrative claims that it is merely restoring a fundamental principle governing the relationship between courts and agencies, one that is reflected in the APA's text.

The barest acquaintance with the Court's case law, however, suggests that something has gone badly wrong here. I refer not to *Chevron*, nor even to the case law of the 1940s, but rather to case law decided well before the full flowering of the administrative state. Consider a few of the Court's earlier and emphatic statements, *none* of which appear in the majority opinion.

> [W]here Congress has committed to the head of a department certain duties requiring the exercise of judgment and discretion, his action thereon, *whether it involve questions of law or fact*, will not be reviewed by the courts unless he has exceeded his authority or this Court should be of opinion that his action was clearly wrong. . . . [W]here the decision of questions of fact is committed by Congress to the judgment and discretion of the head of a department, his decision thereon is conclusive; and that even upon mixed questions of law and fact, *or of law alone*, his action will carry with it a strong presumption of its correctness, and the courts will not ordinarily

be expected from a geographically and politically diverse judiciary encountering the hardest . . . issues. . . .").

[19] Loper Bright Enters. v. Raimondo, 144 S. Ct. 2244, 2261 (2024) ("The APA . . . specifies that courts, not agencies, will decide '*all* relevant questions of law' arising on review of agency action . . . even those involving ambiguous laws . . . and set aside any such action inconsistent with the law as they interpret it.").

> review it, although they may have the power, and will occasionally exercise the right of so doing.[20]

> Whether [the executive officer] decided right or wrong, is not the question. Having jurisdiction to decide at all, he had necessarily jurisdiction, and *it was his duty to decide as he thought the law was*, and the courts have no power whatever under those circumstances to review his determination *by mandamus or injunction*.[21]

> In all cases of ambiguity, the contemporaneous construction, not only of the courts but of the departments, and even of the officials whose duty it is to carry the law into effect, is universally *held to be controlling*.[22]

Note that these cases are not subject to the Court's basic maneuver of treating all previous references to deference-like principles as no more than references to *Skidmore* "respect" or "weight" *avant la lettre*.[23] Instead these cases refer quite expressly to a stronger version of deference, under which delegated statutory discretion carries with it a presumption that agency legal interpretations are "controlling," even as to "law alone," unless they clearly exceed the boundaries of the agency's statutory authority—a decent short summary of what later would be called the *Chevron* framework. Indeed, ironically enough, it is also a decent short summary of one of the main holdings of *Loper Bright* itself, which at least to some large degree recreates the *Chevron* framework while claiming to overrule it, as I will suggest shortly. The truth is that there have always been multiple strands jostling in the Court's case law,[24] and these multiple strands reappeared within the *Chevron* framework itself. The opinion in *Loper Bright* elides this messy history in order to portray *Chevron* as a kind of fall from grace, an inexplicable departure from an original and longstanding baseline approach of de novo judicial interpretation in search of the single right answer.

Overruling *Chevron* is thus not a simple exercise, and it has been made less simple by the Court's transparently selective account of the history of deference law. Are cases such as the ones I have quoted

[20] Bates & Guild Co. v. Payne, 194 U.S. 106, 108–10 (1904) (emphasis added).

[21] U.S. *ex rel.* Riverside Oil Co. v. Hitchcock, 190 U.S. 316, 324–25 (1903) (emphasis added).

[22] Schell v. Fauché, 138 U.S. 562, 572 (1891) (emphasis added).

[23] *Loper Bright*, 144 S. Ct. at 2258–59 ("But the Court did not extend similar deference to agency resolutions of questions of *law*.... [S]uch deferential review ... was cabined to fact-bound determinations....").

[24] As the Court noted expressly as early as *Bates & Guild Co.*, 194 U.S. at 108–10.

here still good law? One might think the answer is a straightforward "no," but it is not so obvious that they are not. After all, the Court does not expressly overrule or even mention them, and they might even now be described as cases of statutory delegation. Still, one may expect that either they will be folded into the *Skidmore* doctrine or else treated as implicitly overruled by the Court's holding that de novo judicial interpretation is commanded by the text of the APA—even though one does not usually treat subsequently enacted statutes as overruling large swathes of prior case law unless they do so expressly.[25] In any case, however, what is clear is that the Court's failure to even address such problems, in the service of a simplistic narrative, is a failure not only of candor but of legal craft.

B. CONTINUITY

Just as Tocqueville argued, shockingly, that the Revolution had as much built upon prior institutions and policies as departed from them, so too with *Loper Bright*. I will argue in Part II below that the deference and quasi-deference doctrines that *Loper Bright* retains as part of the current law cover much or most of the *Chevron* terrain, especially insofar as *Loper Bright* relabels *Chevron* "deference" as "delegation," express or implied. Here, it suffices merely to point out that *Loper Bright*'s emphasis on delegation is not some sudden about-face by the Court. Rather it is best seen as a continuation and expansion of themes from *Chevron* itself—and from a notorious epicycle on *Chevron*, the *United States v. Mead Corporation* decision in 2001.[26]

The original *Chevron* opinion had of course framed its approach partly (but only partly) in terms of delegation, saying:

> If Congress has explicitly left a gap for the agency to fill, there is an express delegation of authority to the agency to elucidate a specific provision of the statute by regulation. Such legislative regulations are given controlling weight unless they are arbitrary, capricious, or manifestly contrary to the statute. Sometimes the legislative delegation to an agency on a particular question is implicit rather than explicit. In such a case, a court may not

[25] *Cf.* 5 U.S.C. § 559 ("[The subchapter of the Administrative Procedure Act (APA)] . . . do[es] not limit or repeal additional requirements imposed by statute or otherwise recognized by law. . . . [A s]ubsequent statute may not be held to supersede or modify this subchapter, [or] chapter 7 . . . except to the extent that it does so expressly.").

[26] 533 U.S. 218 (2001).

> substitute its own construction of a statutory provision for a reasonable interpretation made by the administrator of an agency.[27]

As we will see, this sounds rather strikingly like the crucial analysis of delegation in *Loper Bright*—at least if we carry out the essentially semantic trick of saying that the delegation-space of agency authority to which the *Chevron* Court refers[28] is itself the "one right answer" demanded by *Loper Bright*; and especially if, as I will argue, implicit as well as explicit delegations are and must be recognized by *Loper Bright*'s logic. Comparing this passage from *Chevron* with *Loper Bright*, one might be forgiven for wondering what, exactly, all the shouting is about, putting aside the fact that the two opinions speak about essentially the same legal situation in somewhat different language.

But the delegation theme was somewhat lost or downplayed in the years after *Chevron*. The majority opinion in *Mead* once again put delegation front and center in *Chevron* analysis,[29] holding that a tariff classification ruling had no claim to *Chevron* deference because there was "no indication that Congress intended such a ruling to carry the force of law. . . ."[30] *Mead*'s basic rationale was that the *Chevron* inquiry should be refocused on delegation. Adumbrating the passage from *Chevron* quoted above, the *Mead* Court expanded upon the theme of implied delegation, saying:

> Congress . . . may not have expressly delegated authority or responsibility to implement a particular provision or fill a particular gap. Yet it can still be apparent from the agency's generally conferred authority and other statutory circumstances that Congress would expect the agency to be able to speak with the force of law when it addresses ambiguity in the statute or fills a space in the enacted law, even one about which "Congress did not actually have an intent" as to a particular result.[31]

Implied delegations, in other words, could be indirectly inferred as a legal presumption, regardless of any inquiry into the actual intentions of actually existing legislators—inferred from what the *Mead* Court

---

[27] Chevron, U.S.A., Inc. v. Nat. Res. Def. Council, Inc., 467 U.S. 837, 843–44 (1984).

[28] Strauss, *supra* note 18, at 1145 ("'*Chevron* space' denotes the area within which an administrative agency has been statutorily empowered to act in a manner that creates legal obligation or constraints. . . .").

[29] *Mead*, 533 U.S. at 227. Indeed, *Loper Bright* seems to praise *Mead* as at least a step in the right direction, describing it as a "refinement[] . . . to match *Chevron*'s presumption to reality." Loper Bright Enters. v. Raimondo, 144 S. Ct. 2244, 2268 (2024).

[30] *Mead*, 533 U.S. at 221.

[31] *Id.* at 229 (quoting *Chevron*, 467 U.S. at 845).

called "indicator[s] of delegation."[32] For the *Mead* Court, *Chevron* "was simply a case recognizing that even without express authority to fill a specific statutory gap, circumstances pointing to implicit congressional delegation present a particularly insistent call for deference."[33] Therefore, "*Chevron* left *Skidmore* intact and applicable where statutory circumstances indicate no intent to delegate general authority to make rules with force of law. . . ."[34]

This view reorganizes the law of judicial review of agency legal interpretations around delegation. *Chevron* is merely a case about legal presumptions for inferring implied delegations, which must be evaluated partly at retail, and *Skidmore* survives in situations where no delegation of lawmaking authority can be inferred at all. As we will see, this regime is not far at all from the regime *Loper Bright* erects—with the added flourish in the latter decision that, after the process of legal interpretation is done, the courts insist that the answer at which they have arrived is the sole right answer, even if the *content* of that answer is that Congress has conferred upon the agency a statutorily delegated policymaking space. It is at best unclear what that extra flourish adds to the analysis, beyond the statement of a judicial mood, as I will also discuss. For now, the key Tocquevillian point is that the continuities between the old regime and the new are at least as striking as their discontinuities.

II. The Law of, and After, *Loper Bright*

Now for the main holdings of *Loper Bright*, their scope, and what if anything they change from the previous law.

A. THE BASELINE HOLDING

The Court's most basic holding was simple: Section 706 of the APA, which says "courts shall decide all relevant questions of law," requires courts to always and everywhere ascertain the single "best meaning" of the statute, and thus to decide all legal questions de novo, independently.[35] In contrast to *Chevron*, courts must not afford

---

[32] *Id.*

[33] *Id.* at 237.

[34] *Id.*

[35] Loper Bright Enters. v. Raimondo, 144 S. Ct. 2244, 2261–63 (2024).

agency legal interpretations controlling weight even in cases of ambiguity, although as we will see courts may still afford "deference" under *Skidmore*, more accurately weight or respect, to persuasive agency arguments about what statutes mean. Hence, *Chevron* was unlawful *ab initio*, wrong the day it was decided, and the Court overrules it.[36] The basic holding was accompanied by a rather unprofitable debate about stare decisis that I will largely ignore, except insofar as *Loper Bright* raises the question of what happens to previous decisions from the Court and lower courts that upheld agency actions at "*Chevron* Step Two" under ambiguous statutory schemes.

The main significance of the majority's decision to ground its holding in the APA is that the Court did not decide that Article III precludes *Chevron* of its own force. In theory that leaves open the possibility that Congress could enact a version of *Chevron* by amending the APA, although that seems extraordinarily unlikely. The concurrences by Justice Gorsuch and by Justice Thomas would have gone farther and decided the Article III question,[37] but those Justices also joined the more limited majority opinion.

B. CRITICAL QUALIFICATIONS

What exactly is the scope of *Loper Bright*? What is the prevailing law after the decision? The basic holding is importantly qualified in at least three major and critical ways. Later, I will consider some further nuances and the effect of *Loper Bright* on surrounding doctrines.

The first major qualification is that so-called "*Skidmore* deference" remains very much alive. Recall that the Court's basic method of cabining cases from the Marshall Court onwards that spoke of some form of deference to settled, longstanding or contemporaneous statutory constructions by the executive departments was to characterize all such cases as showing mere judicial "respect" for agency interpretations. Whether *Skidmore* deference even counts as a form of "deference," and what effect it has, are of course much-controverted

---

[36] *Id.* at 2273.

[37] *Id.* at 2274 (Thomas, J., concurring) ("I write separately to underscore the more fundamental problem: *Chevron* deference also violates our Constitution's separation of powers. . . ."); *id.* at 2285 (Gorsuch, J., concurring) ("*Chevron* deference . . . precludes courts from exercising the judicial power vested in them by Article III to say what the law is.").

questions. At least it seems clear that the sort of deference courts owe when Congress has expressly or impliedly delegated a legal space of policymaking authority to an agency is different in principle than the sort of weight or respect owed to persuasive agency interpretations under *Skidmore*. The former is authority-based deference, the latter merely epistemic.[38]

Second, although the Court's discussion is rather convoluted on this point, it seems to acknowledge the validity of what is sometimes called *Hearst* deference[39] on mixed questions of law and fact, or deference to the application of legal standards to facts. The main description of such cases centers on delegated discretion: In *Hearst*, *Gray v. Powell*,[40] and like cases "the Court applied deferential review upon concluding that a particular statute empowered an agency to decide how a broad statutory term applied to specific facts found by the agency."[41] The Court's view seems to be that the application of law to fact is a form of "policymaking," rather than law-interpretation per se.[42] Thus review of agency applications of law to fact seems to be shunted into arbitrariness review.[43] It is unclear that doing so changes very much, at least in the abstract; shortly I will discuss the possible interactions between arbitrariness review and the *Loper Bright* framework. Whether such a reframing of application of law to facts as policymaking makes much sense at a conceptual level is a different issue to which I also return.

Third and most importantly, the Court recognizes the validity of delegations of statutory authority to agencies to fill in statutory content. The best reading, arrived at de novo by the court, may itself just be that such a delegation exists. As the majority puts it, in a

---

[38] *Id.* at 2265 (majority opinion) ("And although exercising independent judgment is consistent with the "respect" historically given to Executive Branch interpretations . . . *Chevron* insists on much more." (citations omitted) (quoting Edwards' Lessee v. Darby, 25 U.S. (12 Wheat) 206, 210 (1827); and Skidmore v. Swift & Co., 323 U.S. 134, 140 (1944))).

[39] NLRB v. Hearst Publ'ns, 322 U.S. 111 (1944).

[40] Gray v. Powell, 314 U.S. 402 (1941).

[41] *Loper Bright*, 144 S. Ct. at 2259.

[42] *Id.* at 2268 ("That is not to say that Congress cannot or does not confer discretionary authority on agencies. . . . But to stay out of discretionary policymaking left to the political branches, judges need only fulfill their obligations under the APA. . . .").

[43] *Id.* at 2261 ("Section 706 *does* mandate that judicial review of agency policymaking . . . be deferential.").

seemingly bland aside that will doubtless be critical to the legal status of agency legal interpretations in the future:

> In a case involving an agency, of course, the statute's meaning may well be that the agency is authorized to exercise a degree of discretion. Congress has often enacted such statutes. For example, some statutes expressly delegate to an agency the authority to give meaning to a particular term. Others empower an agency to prescribe rules to fill up the details of a statutory scheme, or to regulate subject to the limits imposed by a term or phrase that leaves agencies with flexibility, such as "appropriate" or "reasonable." When the best reading of a statute is that it delegates discretionary authority to an agency, the role of the reviewing court under the APA is, as always, to independently interpret the statute and effectuate the will of Congress subject to constitutional limits. The court fulfills that role by recognizing constitutional delegations, "fix[ing] the boundaries of [the] delegated authority," H. Monaghan, Marbury and the Administrative State, 83 Colum. L. Rev. 1, 27 (1983), and ensuring the agency has engaged in reasoned decisionmaking within those boundaries. By doing so, a court upholds the traditional conception of the judicial function that the APA adopts.[44]

Significantly, the Court here quotes and cites with approval the remarkably prescient article by Henry Monaghan, written in 1983 just before *Chevron* was decided, that argues that independent, de novo statutory interpretation by courts is entirely consistent with "deference." Monaghan's central point was that there was no logical inconsistency between saying two different things: (1) the constitutional power and duty of judges to say what the law is, and the APA's instruction to courts to decide all relevant questions of law, require judges to decide all legal questions independently; (2) agencies rather than courts may have the authority to fill in the details of statutory gaps or ambiguities.[45] The reason those two things are consistent is simple. When judges identify the "best reading" of the statute, that best reading might itself just be that an explicit or implicit congressional delegation of such authority to the agency has occurred. The consequence of all this is that some large but uncertain fraction of what used to be called "*Chevron* deference" can now be relabeled

---

[44] *Id.* at 2263 (citations and internal quotation marks omitted); *see also id.* at 2268 (noting that Congress can "confer discretionary authority on agencies").

[45] Henry P. Monaghan, Marbury *and the Administrative State*, 83 COLUM. L. REV. 1, 6 (1983) ("Where deference exists, the court must specify the boundaries of agency authority, *within which the agency is authorized to fashion authoritatively part, often a large part, of the meaning of the statute*." (emphasis added)).

"*Loper Bright* delegation." Cases that used to be labeled as "deference to reasonable agency interpretations of ambiguous statutes" will now be called "independent judicial interpretation that identifies a single best answer, an answer that consists of a delegation of discretionary authority to agencies within a given range."

The resulting regime represents a retail rather than wholesale version of *Chevron*. Whereas *Chevron* was said to rest on a general presumption that gaps and ambiguities represented a delegation to agencies, judges will now have to decide, statute by statute and problem by problem, whether a *Loper Bright* delegation is the best reading of the statute.[46] But it is also true that *Chevron* was always already a retail regime, in the sense that judges always had to decide, statute by statute and problem by problem, what decision Congress had made about the issue at hand. At most, the *Loper Bright* majority and dissent disagree over whether agency authorization to fill in gaps and ambiguities should be understood as a general guiding presumption, or instead as a case-by-case conclusion.[47] But as general presumptions have always had to be applied at retail in cases, it's hard to see that the wholesale-to-retail transition will make any major difference, legally or substantively. Even if *Loper Bright* delegation is best understood as a retail version of *Chevron*, a relabeled version of *Chevron* it remains.

1. *Implied Delegations?* Does Monaghan's logic, adopted by the Court, cover implied delegations as well as express delegations? I believe that it does. As such, *Loper Bright* should be read as a "hermeneutic of continuity" with the preceding law. Recall that both *Mead* and *Chevron* recognized the possibility of implied delegations. And the logic of doing so seems airtight even under the "single best reading" approach. After all, if judges conclude, all things considered, that

[46] *Cf. Loper Bright*, 144 S. Ct. at 2263–64 ("As an early proponent (and later critic) of *Chevron* recounted, courts during [the period of the APA] thus identified delegation of discretionary authority to agencies on a 'statute-by-statute basis.'" (quoting Antonin Scalia, *Judicial Deference to Administrative Interpretations of Law*, 1989 Duke L.J. 511, 516)).

[47] *Compare id.* at 2265–66 ("*Chevron* cannot be reconciled with the APA ... by presuming that statutory ambiguities are implicit delegations to agencies.... Courts instead understand that such statutes... have a single, best meaning." (citations omitted)), *with id.* at 2297 (Kagan, J., dissenting) ("[*Chevron*'s rule of deferring to reasonable agency constructions if the statute is ambiguous], the Court has long explained, rests on a presumption about legislative intent—about what Congress wants when a statute it has charged an agency with implementing contains an ambiguity or gap.").

Congress implicitly but unmistakably delegated a space of lawmaking discretion to the agency, that too just is the best reading.

The *Loper Bright* Court does not expressly say that the relevant delegations can themselves be implied rather than express. But the structure of its discussion suggests that even after *Loper Bright*, implied delegations have the same status as express ones.[48] The natural reading of the Court's discussion is that the Court mentions express delegations, such as the authority to define a statutory term, merely as one illustrative example of delegation. But the Court does not say that all delegations must be express, and it does not even purport to offer an exhaustive list of the varied types of statutory delegations.[49] Some of the Court's other examples are not easy to describe as examples of express delegation, or at least could just as well be effected by implied as well as express delegation. Consider the power to "fill up the details" of a statutory scheme, a power that in any given case might be discerned not from express delegation, but simply from Congress's leaving essential details incompletely specified. The whole thrust of the Court's approach in *Loper Bright* is that the court is to identify the best reading, all things considered, and that holds whether the relevant delegation is express or implied. To be sure, the Court rejected the *Chevron* idea that statutory gaps and ambiguities should be generally presumed to represent implied delegations at wholesale,[50] but that does not mean that an implied delegation cannot be found at retail in a particular case.

This reading is reinforced by a background principle of legal interpretation and a point of administrative law doctrine. The background interpretive principle posits that absent some special rule of clear statement, legal instruments may speak either expressly or by implication, so long as the ordinary meaning of the instrument, all things considered, is best read to so indicate. Ordinarily, absent some

[48] The next few paragraphs draw upon material initially published as Adrian Vermeule, *Implied Delegations After* Loper, YALE J. ON REGUL.: NOTICE & COMMENT (July 9, 2024), https://www.yalejreg.com/nc/implied-delegations-after-loper-by-adrian-vermeule.

[49] As the Court likes to remind us, we are not to read judicial opinions as though they are comprehensive statutes. *See, e.g.*, Nat'l Pork Producers Council v. Ross, 598 U.S. 356, 373 (2023); Brown v. Davenport, 596 U.S. 118, 141 (2022); Borden v. United States, 593 U.S. 420, 443 n.9 (2021) (plurality opinion). *See generally* Margaret H. Lemos, *Should Judicial Opinions Be Read Like Statutes?* (Duke L. Sch. Pub. L. & Legal Theory Working Paper No. 2024-51, 2024), https://ssrn.com/abstract=4911985 (collecting cases).

[50] *Loper Bright*, 144 S. Ct. at 2265 ("*Chevron* cannot be reconciled with the APA . . . by presuming that statutory ambiguities are implicit delegations to agencies.").

special canon of interpretation, what a legislature may do explicitly, it may do implicitly. The foundation of that principle is sheer common sense. After all, in every other sort of human communication, we often understand by implication something that has not been expressly said. Indeed, in any normal communicative context, it is impossible that everything should be expressly said.

The point of administrative law doctrine is that to read *Loper Bright* to require that all delegations be express would threaten to make the major questions doctrine redundant. That doctrine requires (roughly speaking) that delegations must be express when, but only when, they authorize the agency to decide a question of major economic or political significance. It does not, however, say that all delegations must be express, period. In other words, to read *Loper Bright* as erecting a heretofore unknown global clear statement rule against all delegated authority, one requiring that all delegations (not just major delegations) must be express, would go even farther than the Court has gone with the major questions doctrine. This seems an implausible reading, at least until the Justices inform us otherwise. After all, as I mention shortly, the discussion in *Loper Bright* itself seemed to indicate that the major questions doctrine remains part of the law, a point that would have been unnecessary if that doctrine had been subsumed in an even broader rule that all delegation, of whatever scope and importance, must be clearly stated. The best reading of the Court's discussion, then, is that even under *Loper Bright*, delegation of authority may be implied as well as express.

Overall, taken together with what seems to be the continuing validity of *Skidmore* and *Hearst*, I suspect that there is less to *Loper Bright* than meets the eye. Even after *Loper Bright* there is a rather large domain in which courts that would have deferred under *Chevron* can still defer, just with a different legal framework. Of course it is true that, we may confidently expect, at least some cases will come out differently than under the *Chevron* regime. But the *Chevron* regime was itself heavily qualified by the time of its demise, and agencies and courts had for some time been used to avoiding it or at least not putting too much reliance on it. And as we have seen, there is much more continuity across the triptych of *Chevron*, *Mead*, and *Loper Bright* than initially appears. Delegation is a central concept in all three, and all three acknowledge that—within whatever fairly loose boundaries the constitutional nondelegation doctrine allows—Congress may "delegate" or grant to agencies a legal space within which to create binding rules, whether through rulemaking or adjudication. The task of the judge, in all three decisions, is to determine the outer boundaries of the relevant delegations. If *Loper Bright* now describes that task as determining the one right answer to statutory meaning, that is more a *façon de parler* than an about-face.

And indeed the Court's frequent swing voter, Justice Kavanaugh, seemed to reach the same conclusion. In public remarks delivered after the decision, Justice Kavanaugh described *Loper Bright* as "a course correction consistent with the separation of powers to make sure that the executive branch is acting within the authorization granted to it by Congress" and urged:

> [D]on't over-read *Loper Bright*, oftentimes Congress will grant a broad authorization to an executive agency. So it's really important as a neutral umpire to respect the line that Congress has drawn, when it's granted broad authorization, not to unduly hinder the executive branch when performing its congressional authorized functions, but at the same time not allowing the executive branch, as it could with *Chevron* in its toolkit, to go beyond the congressional authorization.[51]

If *Loper Bright* just means that agencies may not go beyond the boundaries of "broad" congressional authorization, it reiterates, in different language, a legal constraint as old as the hills.[52] And even if the best reading of *Loper Bright* is more consequential, contrary to the account I have offered, Justice Kavanaugh's position as the Court's (frequent) swing voter makes his view, and my view, something of a self-fulfilling prophecy.

So far, cases in the lower courts cut in various directions, unsurprisingly. An illustrative pair of cases that have attracted early attention[53] are from the Seventh and Fifth Circuits, respectively. In the first, the court upheld, under *Loper Bright*, a rule of the Consumer Financial Protection Bureau that barred discrimination against not

---

[51] *A Conversation with Brett Kavanaugh Transcript*, Cath. Univ. of Am. (Sept. 26, 2024), https://cit.catholic.edu/a-conversation-with-brett-kavanaugh-transcript.

[52] *See, e.g.*, Little v. Barreme, 6 U.S. (2 Cranch) 170 (1804); Kendall v. U.S. *ex rel.* Stokes, 37 U.S. 524 (1838).

[53] *See* Christopher N. LaVigne, Kimberly Pallen, Jordan Garmen & Vahe Mesropyan, *Employment Update: Recent Decisions and Agency Actions*, N.Y. L.J. (Nov. 4, 2024, 8:00 AM), https://www.law.com/newyorklawjournal/2024/11/04/employment-update-recent-decisions-and-agency-actions.

only applicants for credit, but also prospective applicants.[54] The court of appeals pointed to the broad statutory delegation of rulemaking authority in the Equal Credit Opportunity Act, which vested the Bureau with the power to make rules "necessary or proper to effectuate the purposes of this title" and "to prevent circumvention or evasion thereof."[55] In the contrasting case, the court of appeals held that a Department of Labor rule clarifying the circumstances under which employers could reduce the wages of employees who receive tips was contrary to the Fair Labor Standards Act.[56] Note that it is by no means clear that these cases are in any sense inconsistent. The best reading of the statute, all things considered, may just be that in the first case there was a delegation and the agency stayed within its boundaries, whereas in the second case, the agency exceeded the boundaries of its authority. If this all sounds vaguely familiar, that is no accident; it is the same sort of discussion that happened under the pre-existing *Chevron* regime.

C. POLICYMAKING AND INTERPRETATION

A corollary of the view I have advanced is that *Loper Bright*'s efforts to relabel everything agencies do as "policymaking" rather than "interpretation"[57] is something of a red herring. The Justices in the majority seem to think, and indeed more or less said, that the sort of discretionary-choice-within-a-reasonable-range that the Monaghan relabeling leaves to agencies is best understood as "policymaking" rather than "interpretation." That understanding saves the appearances, as the theologians say, and allows the Justices to take themselves to be doing all the law, while the agencies only ever do policy. (In the loophole passage on delegation that I have quoted from the majority opinion, the majority included references to some famous cases of arbitrariness review, doubtless due to this conceptualization of discretionary-choice-within-a-reasonable-range as "policymaking.") But

---

[54] Consumer Fin. Prot. Bureau v. Townstone Fin., Inc., 107 F.4th 768, 776–77 (7th Cir. 2024).

[55] *Id.* at 776; *see also* Mayfield v. U.S. Dep't of Lab., 117 F.4th 611, 614 (5th Cir. 2024) (upholding the Department of Labor's Minimum Salary Rule under the "Department's explicitly delegated authority to define and delimit the terms of the [statute]").

[56] Rest. L. Ctr. v. U.S. Dep't of Lab., 120 F.4th 163, 174–75 (5th Cir. 2024).

[57] *See supra* notes 39–43 and accompanying text.

of course, as many pointed out under the *Chevron* regime,[58] the authorized agency choice of a specifying or concretizing interpretation within a reasonable range is itself always also policymaking within a "policy space." It is conceptually impossible for agencies to "choose policy" within a defined legal space granted by statute without first interpreting the statute to determine what the boundaries of the legal space are. Such choice by agencies is therefore both interpretation and policymaking, one hundred percent the one and one hundred percent the other, in a kind of hypostatic union of the administrative state. The Court's relabeling of agency interpretation as agency policymaking is but a corollary of the Court's more fundamental relabeling of *Chevron* deference as *Loper Bright* delegation. I have argued that the latter is more likely to confirm than to overturn the extant institutional relationship between courts and agencies, and so too with the former.

D. INTERACTION EFFECTS?

One entirely legitimate thought is that although *Loper Bright* may not represent an "avulsive change"[59] in administrative law taken in isolation, there may also be interaction effects with other decisions from this Term that change the surrounding legal and institutional context, and thus change the effect of the decision. Let me mention three candidates—two that possibly magnify the effect of *Loper Bright*, in the sense that they will provide scope for *Loper Bright* to be invoked to constrain agency discretion even more than the decision suggests on its own, and one that possibly dampens it.

1. *"Hard Look" Review.* The first possible interaction effect involves arbitrary and capricious review. In *Ohio v. EPA*,[60] decided the same week as *Loper Bright*, Justice Gorsuch wrote for the Court to overturn an Environmental Protection Agency (EPA) Federal Implementation Plan for ozone air quality standards, saying that the EPA had not adequately explained its plan in light of ongoing litigation that had in effect exempted a number of states from the plan—a problem that, the Court said, had been adequately raised during the comment

[58] *See, e.g.*, E. Donald Elliott, Chevron *Matters: How the* Chevron *Doctrine Redefined the Roles of Congress, Courts and Agencies in Environmental Law*, 16 VILL. ENV'T L.J. 1 (2005).

[59] United States v. Mead Corp., 533 U.S. 218, 239 (2001) (Scalia, J., dissenting).

[60] 603 U.S. 279 (2024).

period.[61] The decision has been criticized for taking an inconsistent stance towards, on the one hand, comments by regulated parties in agency proceedings, and on the other agency rationales issued in those same proceedings; the Court read the former for all they could possibly be worth while reading EPA's own rationale grudgingly.[62] If *Ohio v. EPA* portends a general revival of "hard look" review, pervasively skeptical of the reasoning behind agency action, then it will magnify the effect of *Loper Bright* in the sense that claims that used to be decided at *Chevron* Step Two will now be channeled into arbitrariness review, which will also be heavy-handed. Although scholars like Jeffrey Pojanowski have urged the Court to adopt a model of "neoclassical administrative law," under which the Court will review legal questions de novo but apply arbitrariness review deferentially across the board,[63] *Ohio v. EPA* suggests that there is no reason to think that the Court has adopted such a model in general.

Conversely, however, it would be wildly premature to discern any trend towards heightened "hard look" review in the Court's recent arbitrariness decisions. Overall, those decisions display no consistent pattern. Consider the strikingly deferential arbitrariness decision written by Justice Kavanaugh in *FCC v. Prometheus Radio Project*[64] in 2021. *Prometheus* involved the Federal Communications Commission (FCC)'s repeal of certain of its ownership rules on the ground that the rules were no longer necessary to promote competition, localism, or viewpoint diversity. The repeal was challenged on the ground that the record did not adequately support the FCC's conclusions; in particular, the claim ran, the FCC had not provided adequate reason to conclude that the repeal would not harm minority and female interests. A unanimous Court brusquely rejected the challenge, with the striking formulation, reminiscent of the *Chevron* regime, that arbitrary and capricious review requires only that agency

---

[61] *Id.* at 296.

[62] *See* Daniel Deacon, Ohio v. EPA *and the Future of APA Arbitrariness Review*, Yale J. on Regul.: Notice & Comment (June 27, 2024), https://www.yalejreg.com/nc/ohio-v-epa-and-the-future-of-apa-arbitrariness-review.

[63] *See* Jeffrey A. Pojanowski, *Neoclassical Administrative Law*, 133 Harv. L. Rev. 852, 857 (2020) ("The neoclassical approach rejects judicial deference on legal questions while respecting the policy choices that agencies legislate in the discretionary space Congress has given them."). For a response questioning whether such a framework is feasible after failing in the past, see Adrian Vermeule, *Neo-?*, 133 Harv. L. Rev. F. 103 (2020).

[64] 592 U.S. 414 (2021).

action fall within a "zone of reasonableness."[65] To be sure, there have been other more aggressive arbitrariness decisions in recent years as well,[66] but no larger trend or pattern emerges.

2. *Delayed Challenges to Agency Action.* A second and potentially far more consequential interaction effect arises from the Court's decision in *Corner Post, Inc. v. Board of Governors of the Federal Reserve System.*[67] Decided shortly after *Loper Bright*, *Corner Post* read the general fallback six-year time limit for APA claims against agency action[68]—for example, a facial challenge that a rule exceeds the agency's authority under its organic statute—to start running not at the time of the final agency action, but at the time of injury to the plaintiff.[69] The time limit, in the Court's view, should be read as a statute of limitations, not a statute of repose.[70]

Although *Corner Post* seems esoteric, it is potentially highly consequential. It means that if an agency rule was finalized decades ago, survived challenges at the time, and has structured and organized a whole sector of industry since then, a newly injured plaintiff can bring a facial challenge against it even today—inter alia, by forming a new corporation or other entity that is now injured by the rule. It is entirely legitimate to think that this will magnify the effect of *Loper Bright*.

In my view, *Corner Post* was perhaps the worst decision of the Term from the standpoint of legal craft. It suffers from a kind of blindness to the fact that statutes are more than strings of text with putatively ordinary meaning; rather they are instruments of government that have to fit into a larger structure of law and legal institutions. Myopically reading a particular text in a way that potentially destabilizes whole industries and the settled course of administrative lawmaking

[65] *Id.* at 423 ("A court [reviewing under the arbitrary-and-capricious standard] simply ensures that the agency has acted within a zone of reasonableness and, in particular, has reasonably considered the relevant issues and reasonably explained the decision.").

[66] *See, e.g.*, Dep't of Homeland Sec. v. Regents of the Univ. of Cal., 591 U.S. 1, 26–28 (2020) (holding that the Department of Homeland Security's rescission of Deferred Action for Child Arrivals (DACA) was arbitrary and capricious for not addressing all aspects of the program).

[67] 144 S. Ct. 2440 (2024).

[68] 28 U.S.C. § 2401(a).

[69] *Corner Post*, 144 S. Ct. at 2450–52.

[70] *Id.* at 2452 ("Section 2401(a) thus operates as a statute of limitations rather than a statute of repose.").

verges on an absurd result—and even the most dedicated textualists have said that reading statutes to avoid absurd results is a good idea.[71] What matters for present purposes, however, is whether *Corner Post* will result in a more robust *Loper Bright* than would otherwise occur. And while it would be foolish to deny that *Corner Post* matters, there are several reasons for mild skepticism that the interaction between the two decisions will be quite as disastrous as it seems.

First, *Corner Post* only addressed the APA's general default fallback statute of limitations. Many major regulatory statutes contain their own limitations periods, which (in important cases) give, for example, sixty days from the final agency action to file a petition for review in the permissible court of appeals.[72] So the domain within which *Corner Post* matters is not wholly clear and may not be enormous.

Second, the Court noted two further limits: the ability of parties to petition for agency reconsideration of an extant rule under APA Sections 553(e) and 555(e), and then seek judicial review if the agency denies the petition; and the distinction between facial challenges and as-applied challenges. As-applied challenges raised as a defense in an agency enforcement proceeding were always exempt from the six-year statute of limitations under the predominant law in the lower courts (which the Court seemingly endorsed).[73] So as to those challenges, nothing has changed—although the Court noted that unregulated plaintiffs, harmed by the combination of the agency action and the action of directly regulated intermediaries, would not be able to raise their challenges as defenses in enforcement proceedings. Furthermore, *Corner Post* left open precisely which facial challenges are eligible for the Court's injury-focused approach. We know that facial challenges to final regulations on the substantive ground that they violate the statute do qualify, and this is a genuine interaction effect

[71] *See, e.g.*, City of Columbus v. Ours Garage & Wrecker Serv., Inc., 536 U.S. 424, 449 n.4 (2002) ("A possibility so startling . . . is well enough precluded by the rule that a statute should not be interpret to produce absurd results."); Linda D. Jellum, *But That Is Absurd! Why Specific Absurdity Undermines Textualism*, 76 Brook. L. Rev. 917, 918 n.3 (2011) (collecting this and other quotations).

[72] *See, e.g.*, 28 C.F.R. § 68.57 (2023) ("In cases arising under section 247B of the INA, any person aggrieved by a final agency order . . . may, within sixty (60) days after entry of the order, seek review of the final agency order in the United States Court of Appeals. . . .").

[73] "Regulated parties 'may always assail a regulation as exceeding the agency's statutory authority in enforcement proceedings against them' or 'petition an agency to reconsider a longstanding rule and then appeal the denial of that petition.'" *Corner Post*, 144 S. Ct. at 2458 (quoting Herr v. U.S. Forest Serv., 803 F.3d 809, 821–22 (6th Cir. 2015)).

with *Loper Bright*. However, the Court noted the possibility that there may be a category of injuries that can only be suffered by entities that exist at the time of the relevant agency action, such as a procedural claim that a notice of proposed rulemaking was inadequate.[74]

Finally, the interaction between *Loper Bright* and *Corner Post* may not cut only in one direction. It will change the selection of cases for litigation, in ways that might cause the Court to firm up the qualifications to *Loper Bright* that I laid out previously, or even to identify further limitations to *Corner Post*. We might imagine a set of cases in which aggressive lower courts entertain aggressive challenges to decades-old regulations, causing the Court to blanch. Of course, that is just one possibility and we can also imagine others.

3. *Standing*. So far, I have mentioned two possible interaction effects with cases decided around the same time as *Loper Bright* that might amplify the latter decision, resulting in greater judicial constraint on administrative discretion. But we should not overlook that the Court issued several quite restrictive standing decisions during the same Term as *Loper Bright*, demanding more specificity for factual showings, for claims of future injury, and for causal and remedial connections between the defendant or defendants' action(s) and the plaintiff's injury. In some cases, standing will now be more of a problem for challenges to agency action than it was before. Consider *FDA v. Alliance for Hippocratic Medicine*,[75] which rejected challenges to the Food and Drug Administration's approval of mifepristone on standing grounds, reading the relevant requirements strictly.[76] If injury, causation, and redressability are now harder to show, the effect of *Corner Post* is dampened. The standing problems become especially important as to unregulated plaintiffs who assert some sort of indirect injury by virtue of the interaction between the agency action and the behavior of directly regulated intermediaries.[77] It is not hard to imagine, at least in the abstract, that the standing hurdle will substantially constrain the effect of *Corner Post* as to such parties, although here too the direction of the doctrine is simply uncertain.

---

[74] *Id.* at 2459 n.8 ("It also may be that some injuries can only be suffered by entities that existed at the time of the challenged action.").

[75] 602 U.S. 367 (2024).

[76] *Id.* at 386–95.

[77] Susan C. Morse, *Time Bars for Administrative Procedure Claims After* Corner Post, 114 CALIF. L. REV. (forthcoming 2026) (manuscript at 25–30), https://ssrn.com/abstract=4909489.

E. OPEN LEGAL QUESTIONS

Loper Bright raises any number of further legal questions that it will doubtless take the courts years to work through. I will mention only a few of the largest questions and briefly sketch some possible paths for future law.

1. *Major Questions?* It has been argued that *Loper Bright* eliminates the major questions doctrine.[78] The thinking is that the major questions doctrine is either now unnecessary or even positively contrary to the *Loper Bright* approach, given that the courts are now tasked with identifying a single right answer. After all, once the predicate conditions for the major questions doctrine are met, the doctrine instructs courts to determine whether Congress *clearly* conferred the relevant major authorization on the agency. But that inquiry seems to diverge from the right-answer question whether Congress did confer such authority on the agency, all things considered. If the answer to the latter question is "yes," then that ought to be the end of the story.

This argument seems unlikely to prevail, however, for both conceptual and pragmatic reasons. Conceptually, the mandate to identify a single right answer is not inconsistent with deploying either substantive canons or linguistic canons to help determine what the right answer is. There is an ongoing disagreement within the Court as to whether the major questions doctrine should be described as substantive, a subconstitutional mechanism for enforcing the nondelegation doctrine, or instead as linguistic, an ordinary inference from "text and context."[79] But on either account, *Loper Bright* cannot reasonably be read to eliminate all such canons from the judicial interpretive inquiry, a genuinely radical move. Pragmatically, the Court in *Loper Bright* itself adverted to the major questions doctrine (although, oddly, not by name) in terms that seem to implicitly reaffirm its continued existence, saying that "*Chevron* does not apply if the question at issue is one of 'deep economic and political significance'. . . .

---

[78] Richard J. Pierce, Jr., *Two Neglected Effects of* Loper Bright, Regul. Rev. (July 1, 2024), https://www.theregreview.org/2024/07/01/pierce-two-neglected-effects-of-loper-bright ("Taken together . . . *Ohio v. EPA* and *Loper Bright* . . . eliminate any plausible basis for the major questions doctrine.").

[79] For an account of the respective positions of Justices Gorsuch and Barrett on these issues, and for my deep skepticism about the latter's view, see Adrian Vermeule, *Text and "Context,"* Yale J. on Regul.: Notice & Comment (July 13, 2023), https://www.yalejreg.com/nc/text-and-context-by-adrian-vermeule.

We have instead expected Congress to delegate such authority 'expressly' if at all. . . ."[80] Especially in light of the dim prospects for a revival of the constitutional nondelegation doctrine—on which more below—it seems at best improbable that the Court will discard the doctrine that it has evolved as an interpretive substitute for that doctrine.[81]

2. Kisor/Auer *Deference?* Another crucial question is whether judicial deference to agency interpretations of their own rules survives *Loper Bright*. In *Kisor v. Wilkie*,[82] decided in 2019, a plurality of the Court retained the basic rule, most recently affirmed by Justice Scalia's opinion for the Court in *Auer v. Robbins*,[83] that courts should defer to reasonable agency interpretations of ambiguities of rules previously issued (or decided in adjudication) by the agencies themselves. Justice Kagan's plurality opinion in *Kisor*, however, heavily qualified the *Auer* doctrine by recognizing or adding both substantive and procedural limits.[84] Notably, the Chief Justice provided the fifth vote in *Kisor* on stare decisis grounds, distinguishing the question of *Auer* deference from the question of *Chevron* deference.[85]

The opinions in *Loper Bright* largely track the opinions in *Kisor*, just with the relevant Justices switched around and the opposite outcome. Justice Kagan's dissent in *Loper Bright* closely tracks her plurality opinion in *Kisor*, and the majority opinion in *Loper Bright* closely

---

[80] Loper Bright Enters. v. Raimondo, 144 S. Ct. 2244, 2269 (2024) (quoting King v. Burwell, 576 U.S. 473, 486 (2015)).

[81] In *Alliance for Fair Board Recruitment v. SEC*, 125 F.4th 159 (5th Cir. 2024) (en banc), the Fifth Circuit reviewed NASDAQ rules, approved by the Securities and Exchange Commission, that mandated disclosure about the racial, gender, and sexual diversity of company directors. The en banc panel held that the rules were inconsistent with the Securities Exchange Act of 1934, relying both on *Loper Bright* and the major questions doctrine; the panel said that the major questions doctrine "confirms our interpretation of the plain meaning" of the relevant statutory provisions. *Id.* at 168. This seems to track Justice Barrett's approach, under which "the MQD often usefully may be invoked as 'an additional point' that 'reinforces' the conclusion reached as a result of a 'best reading' analysis." *See* Randolph May, *What's Up First—MQD or BR?*, YALE J. ON REGUL.: NOTICE & COMMENT (Jan. 24, 2025), https://www.yalejreg.com/nc/whats-up-first-mqd-or-br-by-randolph-may (quoting Biden v. Nebraska, 600 U.S. 477, 520, 507, 521 (2023) (Barrett, J., concurring)).

[82] 588 U.S. 558 (2019).

[83] 519 U.S. 452 (1997).

[84] *Kisor*, 588 U.S. at 574–79 (clarifying that a court should not give *Auer* deference unless it is ambiguous after "exhausting all of the 'traditional tools' of construction," and that the rule must be a reasonable rule, held by the agency, implicating substantive expertise after "fair and considered judgment" (first quoting Chevron, U.S.A., Inc. v. Nat. Res. Def. Council, Inc., 467 U.S. 837, 843 n.9 (1984); and then quoting *Auer*, 519 U.S. at 462)).

[85] *Id.* at 590–91 (Roberts, C.J., concurring in part).

tracks the basic APA arguments offered by the dissents in *Kisor*. Furthermore, the complexity that characterized the *Chevron* framework in its developed (or decayed) form, which the *Loper Bright* majority condemned as excessive and confusing, could fairly be said to characterize the heavily qualified *Kisor* framework. All this implies that *Kisor* is vulnerable in the future on the same grounds that made *Chevron* vulnerable.

However, several cautions are necessary.[86] First, the Chief Justice's concurrence in the judgment in *Kisor* suggests that he sees relevant differences in the two contexts, at least as to the stare decisis question. It is unclear whether that view survives his achievement, if that is what it is, for assembling a majority to overrule *Chevron*, but if it does, then *Kisor* might survive with at least one other vote from the Court's center-right Justices. Second, if *Kisor/Auer* deference is overruled, some of the same major qualifications that appear in *Loper Bright* would appear in that decision as well. The Court would presumably say that where Congress is best read to have entrusted agencies with a zone of discretion, that discretion extends to the interpretation of their own prior rules, which is itself both interpretation and policymaking, inextricably fused in the way I have suggested above. And a version of *Skidmore* deference would survive in this context as well. Overall, one could well imagine a decision that does for *Kisor/Auer* deference what *Loper Bright* does for *Chevron* deference: reframe the relevant inquiry as a search for one right answer, but include within that right-answerism the concepts of delegation and of persuasive deference, thereby folding into it much of the same operative content as currently exists.

3. *Pre-Existing* Chevron *Cases and Statutory Stare Decisis?* The Court is explicit in *Loper Bright* that the holdings of prior cases that relied on the *Chevron* framework to find that specific agency actions are lawful—including the Clean Air Act holding of *Chevron* itself—are still subject to statutory stare decisis despite the change in interpretive

[86] I put aside the (correct) observation that the specific texts of the APA at issue in the two contexts are different, see Chad Squitieri, Auer *After* Loper Bright, Yale J. on Regul.: Notice & Comment (Oct. 15, 2024), https://www.yalejreg.com/nc/auer-after-loper-bright-by-chad-squitieri. *Compare* Loper Bright Enters. v. Raimondo, 144 S. Ct. 2244, 2260 (2024) (citing APA Section 706 for the rule that courts must "decide all relevant questions of law"), *with Kisor*, 588 U.S. at 581 (citing APA Section 706 for the rule that courts must "determine the meaning or applicability of the terms of agency action"). As Professor Squitieri notes, it is not at all obvious how this difference is legally relevant. *See* Squitieri, *supra*.

methodology.[87] This will protect a number of major rulemakings from the past forty years, and thus preserves the operative continuity between the *Loper Bright* regime and the *ancien régime*.

But of course this by no means answers all the critical legal questions. What if the prior case held that the agency action was permissible, but not mandatory, at *Chevron* Step Two? May the agency now switch to the opposite rule, and what sort of justification would it have to supply—would it now have to argue that the opposite rule is the single best statutory reading, uninfected by *Chevron*? In the latter scenario, however, it seems that the agency can still argue that the single best reading just is that the statute itself affords the agency a zone of discretion. One could spin out any number of scenarios, but what does seem clear is that it will take years to work out these details.

F. WHAT WAS THE POINT?

Let me now step back to address a natural question, and a large one. If the low-temperature view of *Loper Bright* that I have advanced is correct, what was all the fuss about? What if anything was the point of the "revolution" which so many have discerned in the decision? My main general answer, in counterintuitive Tocquevillian spirit, is that the anti-administrative revolution in a sense confirms and strengthens what went before. The basic reason is that what judges do is a product not only of legal doctrine, but of the broader legal and institutional environment in which doctrine takes shape; that environment can even change or color what doctrine means.

At least since *Crowell v. Benson*[88] in 1932, the Court has struggled with two large-scale conflicting imperatives, which I have elsewhere labeled the "deference dilemma."[89] The first imperative is that the administrative state not become "a government of a bureaucratic character alien to our system,"[90] as Chief Justice Hughes put it in *Crowell*, in order to justify both de novo judicial review of legal questions and of a subset of factual questions, involving so-called "constitutional facts" and "jurisdictional facts." Professor Louis Jaffe drew a crucial corollary in the middle of the twentieth century,

---

[87] *Loper Bright*, 144 S. Ct. at 2273.

[88] 285 U.S. 22 (1932).

[89] Adrian Vermeule, *The Deference Dilemma*, 31 Geo. Mason L. Rev. 619 (2024).

[90] *Crowell*, 285 U.S. at 57.

observing that "[t]he availability of judicial review is the necessary condition, psychologically if not logically, of a system of administrative power which purports to be legitimate, or legally valid."[91]

The second imperative, however, is captured by Justice Antonin Scalia's observation, in his famous 1989 article defending *Chevron*,[92] that the legal and institutional conditions in which judges now work have changed in ways that have affected the demand for, and the necessity of, deference itself. Scalia wrote that deference to agency legal interpretations "is a more rational presumption today than it would have been thirty years ago—which explains the change in the law. Broad delegation to the Executive is the hallmark of the modern administrative state; agency rulemaking powers are the rule rather than, as they once were, the exception. . . ."[93] In an environment in which agencies are given broad and sometimes ill-defined statutory authority to, for example, regulate "unreasonable risk[s] of injury to health or the environment,"[94] putatively de novo judicial interpretation can no longer be what it once was. Judges who really try to interpret such a statute for themselves would have to decide what exactly counts as an "unreasonable risk"—a task for which nothing in their legal training equips them, and from which even the most confident judge might flinch.

At first blush, it seems that *Loper Bright* opts emphatically for the first of these two imperatives and returns to the straightforward *Crowell* baseline of fully independent judicial determination of statutory questions. But that appearance is misleading because massive delegation of statutory authorities to agencies has changed the landscape of administrative law. The problem for the Court is that the statutory and regulatory environment, and indeed the whole development of the institutions of the American state, are so radically different now than in 1932 that the posture of the judiciary cannot but be different as well. De novo interpretation of broad, open-ended delegations of complex regulatory tasks is just not the same sort of interpretive task as the sort of statutory interpretation that common-law judges did. Interpreting the Toxic Substances Control Act is not

---

[91] Louis L. Jaffe, Judicial Control of Administrative Action 320 (1965).

[92] Antonin Scalia, *Judicial Deference to Administrative Interpretations of Law*, 1989 Duke L.J. 511.

[93] *Id.* at 516.

[94] Toxic Substances Control Act, 15 U.S.C. § 2605.

the same order of legal problem as interpreting "no vehicles in the park," although legal education lags in this regard.

In such an environment, we might expect to see sensible judges committed to de novo legal interpretation attempting to square the circle. They would do so by proclaiming loudly that legal interpretation is for the courts, while adding, somewhat less loudly, that of course the content of the single right answer at which the judges arrive may itself yield the conclusion that agencies get to say what the operative legal rules are. In the world of broad delegations, the combination of a conspicuous headline victory for legal conservative-libertarians with a relabeling that preserves much of the institutional substance of the *Chevron* regime seems an ideal path to steer between Scylla and Charybdis, to navigate the deference dilemma. And that is exactly what we do see in *Loper Bright.*

1. *Expressing a Mood.* On this view, at the level of the Court as an institutional working majority, one that expects to be in control of the law for some time to come, *Loper Bright* may best be taken to "express[] a mood," as Justice Frankfurter said of Congress in *Universal Camera.*[95] To be sure, the expression of a mood, whether by the Court or by Congress, is easy to mock as "merely" symbolic, but symbols are powerful things. The decision has a signaling effect that is not easy to capture in articulated legal doctrine, but that also radiates beyond the official doctrine. The diffuse effect of the Court's mood, the background music of *Loper Bright*, may be to embolden lower courts.

On the other hand, *Loper Bright* suggests that the Chief Justice and a subset of his colleagues are very much attuned to the deeper institutional and structural rationales that animated *Chevron* deference in the first place. The Chief Justice is nothing if not institutionally sensitive, and he is surely aware that a regime of genuinely de novo interpretation, without *Loper Bright*'s major qualifications and especially its large loophole for delegation, is potentially a recipe for disaster. The Court spent much of the past Term overturning decisions from overly aggressive lower appellate courts, most conspicuously the Fifth Circuit.[96] In that world, the combination of an apparent headline victory for legal conservative-libertarians with a relabeling

---

[95] Universal Camera Corp. v. NLRB, 340 U.S. 474, 487 (1951).

[96] *See, e.g.*, Moody v. NetChoice, LLC, 603 U.S. 707 (2024); Gonzalez v. Trevino, 602 U.S. 653 (2024); FDA v. All. for Hippocratic Med., 602 U.S. 367 (2024); Consumer Fin.

that preserves much of the institutional substance of the *Chevron* regime seems an ideal recipe for a Tocquevillian pseudo-revolution. Most courts, including most of the Supreme Court majority, do not want to be in the position of deciding for themselves what counts as, for example, an "unreasonable risk of toxicity." Only time will tell which of these forces will predominate, but it would be foolish to bet that the operative landscape of judicial review of agency action will look markedly different in 2044 than it did in 1984.

III. The *Jacobins de Droite*

In *Loper Bright*, as I mentioned, the Chief Justice plays the Court's leading Girondin—the moderate revolutionary who hopes to go so far, and no farther. To his right flank are the Justices we might call the *Jacobins de droite*, Justices Gorsuch and Thomas, who press for more rigorous and throughgoing revolutionary action. Although both joined the majority opinion, both also filed lengthy separate concurrences that laid out a more ambitious vision: a revival of the so-called "nondelegation doctrine" at the constitutional level.[97] From one standpoint, Justices Gorsuch and Thomas are asking exactly the right question, whatever the validity of the answers they give. As I have argued, the basic legal situation identified by Justice Scalia as the main engine of *Chevron* deference, now largely relabeled as "*Loper Bright* delegation," is that Congress has granted an indefinite range of broad and open-ended authorizations to the agencies. In that world, no adjustment of the doctrine concerning judicial review of agency statutory interpretations is likely to seriously curtail agency discretion, for the simple reason that judges know how little they know, and—under whatever doctrinal label—will flinch from the task

Prot. Bureau v. Cmty. Fin. Servs. Ass'n of Am., Ltd., 601 U.S. 416 (2024); Murthy v. Missouri, 603 U.S. 43 (2024); United States v. Rahimi, 602 U.S. 680 (2024).

[97] In a somewhat ambiguous jab at the majority's reformulation of deference as delegated policymaking discretion, Justice Thomas wrote that "*Chevron* deference 'cannot be salvaged' by recasting it as deference to an agency's 'formulation of policy.' . . . If that were true, *Chevron* would mean that 'agencies are unconstitutionally exercising legislative Powers vested in Congress.'" Loper Bright Enters. v. Raimondo, 144 S. Ct. 2244, 2275 (Thomas, J., concurring) (quoting Baldwin v. United States, 140 S. Ct. 690, 691 (2020) (Thomas, J., dissenting from the denial of certiorari)). This view rests on a theory of nondelegation that is different and far more extreme than the standard theory, as explained in Stephen G. Breyer, Richard B. Stewart, Cass R. Sunstein, Adrian Vermeule & Michael Herz, Administrative Law and Regulatory Policy: Problems, Text, and Cases 45–46 (9th ed. 2022).

of genuinely independent review. By attempting to revive the constitutional nondelegation doctrine, the *Jacobins de droite* are striking at (what they see as) the root of the problem.

In my longstanding view, amplified by more recent scholarship, the originalist credentials of the constitutional nondelegation doctrine are desperately thin.[98] Furthermore, and more generally, the expansive statutory authorities given to the executive branch that have accumulated over the course of American history are not plausibly described as a kind of "abdication" by Congress. Rather they are the product of a sustained course of action by Congress, as an institution extended over time, to build the administrative state. The fundamental logic of the nondelegation argument—that Congress must itself specify substantive policy because of the unique deliberative and democratic features of the lawmaking process laid out in Article I—is self-defeating; the same logic implies that Congress will, deliberating democratically, decide to grant statutory authority to the agencies when the public interest will be best served by doing so.[99]

For present purposes, however, I will bracket these familiar arguments to focus on two different and mutually related questions: How likely is a genuine revival of the constitutional nondelegation doctrine, and how much difference would it make if it were revived? My answers to these two questions are "highly unlikely" and "not much," respectively.

As for the prospects of a genuine revival, that possibility has been a staple of the conservative-libertarian legal movement time out of mind, at least since Justice Rehnquist's concurrence in the *Benzene Case*.[100] It is a staple of judicial concurrences, of Federalist Society panels, and of student notes. Legal conservative-libertarians breathlessly await the eschaton. But where constitutional nondelegation shows surprisingly little influence is in actual law. So far, at least, it

---

[98] *See* Eric A. Posner & Adrian Vermeule, *Interring the Nondelegation Doctrine*, 69 U. Chi. L. Rev. 1721, 1733–41 (2002) ("What is true of legislative precedent from early Congresses is also true of early judicial precedent; in the latter setting, as in the former, there is nothing to indicate that the nondelegation metaphor can boast a venerable pedigree."); Julian Davis Mortenson & Nicholas Bagley, *Delegation at the Founding*, 121 Colum. L. Rev. 277, 282 (2021) ("The nondelegation doctrine has nothing to do with the Constitution as it was originally understood.").

[99] Adrian Vermeule, Law's Abnegation 43–44 (2016).

[100] Indus. Union Dep't, AFL-CIO v. Am. Petroleum Inst., 448 U.S. 607, 671 (1980) (Rehnquist, J., concurring).

has been a case of "jam yesterday and jam tomorrow, but never jam today."[101]

The Court's most recent sustained encounter with the constitutional nondelegation doctrine, *Gundy v. United States*,[102] more or less fizzled out. Justice Kagan's plurality opinion[103] offered a constrained reading of the statute and then, with this reading in hand, straightforwardly rejected the nondelegation challenge under the longstanding "intelligible principle" test, partly on the ground that the statute as so construed was no broader or more discretionary than a myriad of other authorities that the Court had upheld over the decades and indeed centuries since the Founding.[104] Justice Alito wrote a somewhat tortuous concurrence in which he declined to vote to declare the statute unconstitutional under current law, but said that he might reconsider if a majority of the Court were willing to do so.[105]

Overall, it is hard to see *Gundy* as anything but a kind of flinch. The Court as a body showed little apparent appetite for any real revival of the constitutional nondelegation doctrine, and subsequent attempts to find a vehicle for revisiting the issue have attracted little support. In *Allstates Refractory Contractors, LLC v. Su*,[106] the Court recently denied a petition for certiorari from a Sixth Circuit decision that upheld against a nondelegation challenge a central provision of the Occupational Safety and Health Act: the Occupational Safety and Health Administration's power to enact and enforce any workplace safety standard that it deems "reasonably necessary or appropriate." That issue had sparked much excitable academic discussion,[107] and it typifies the sort of broad open-ended authority that will make *Loper Bright* delegation operationally similar to *Chevron*

---

[101] *See* Adrian Vermeule, *Never Jam Today*, YALE J. ON REGUL.: NOTICE & COMMENT (June 20, 2019), https://www.yalejreg.com/nc/never-jam-today-by-adrian-vermeule.

[102] 588 U.S. 128 (2019).

[103] As Justice Kavanaugh did not participate, the Kagan opinion was actually for four of the eight participating Justices.

[104] *Gundy*, 588 U.S. at 146 (plurality opinion).

[105] *Id.* at 148–49 (Alito, J., concurring) ("If a majority of this Court were willing to reconsider the approach we have taken for the past 84 years, I would support that effort. But because a majority is not willing to do that, it would be freakish to single out the provision at issue here for special treatment.").

[106] 144 S. Ct. 2490 (2024).

[107] *See, e.g.*, Cass R. Sunstein, *Is OSHA Unconstitutional?*, 94 VA. L. REV. 1407 (2008).

deference.[108] The only Justices to dissent from that denial were Justices Gorsuch and Thomas, who seem unable to spark much interest among their colleagues for their project of mounting a heroic *défense de la république*. In general, the major questions doctrine, which Gorsuch (but not Justice Barrett) sees as implementing the nondelegation doctrine as a subconstitutional matter, has become a kind of substitute for enforcement of nondelegation at the constitutional level.

But suppose that the dam finally breaks, as it might someday; there is currently a bit of ferment in the lower courts, mostly as to the so-called issue of "private delegations" pushed by ambitious decisions of the Fifth Circuit.[109] Suppose that Justice Gorsuch's *Gundy* dissent were written into the law. What if anything would change? Probably not much. That dissent proposed a nominal narrowing of the constitutional test. Rejecting the "intelligible principle" formulation, Gorsuch would have limited the valid categories of delegated statutory authority to (1) executive fact-finding and application of law to fact; (2) "fill[ing] up the details" of statutory schemes in which the basic policy choices have been made by Congress; and (3) assignment to the executive or judicial branches of "certain non-legislative responsibilities."[110] The problem with this approach is that it is unclear how much ice would really be cut by eliminating the "intelligible principle" test. Most or all of the broad and open-ended grants of statutory authority to which Justice Scalia adverted could be said, with a straight face at least, to fall into one or the other, or a combination, of Justice Gorsuch's categories of valid delegation. Were the Court to formally abandon the "intelligible principle" test, one might well see one or two dramatic headline invalidations of federal statutes, followed by a relapse towards the status quo ante. An analogy here is to the Court's Commerce Clause jurisprudence, in which the

---

[108] *See* Vermeule, *supra* note 7.

[109] The Court recently granted a certiorari petition from the United States in a case in which the Fifth Circuit invalidated a statutory authority of the Federal Communications Commission on "private nondelegation" grounds. *See* Consumers' Rsch. v. FCC, 109 F.4th 743 (5th Cir. 2024) (en banc), *cert. granted*, No. 24-354, 2024 WL 4864036 (U.S. Nov. 22, 2024). It is noteworthy, however, that we do not see the opposite and more telling case of the Court granting cert in a case in which the lower court *denied* a nondelegation claim. The latter, unlike the former, would suggest a real appetite for a change in the law.

[110] *Gundy*, 588 U.S. at 157–59 (Gorsuch, J., dissenting).

dramatic revival of judicial limits in *United States v. Lopez*[111] did not, in the end, turn out to be the harbinger of dramatic change.

Conclusion: A Marginal Revolution

In earlier work,[112] I compared the growth of the administrative state and the limited scope of judicial review—"deference" in the old language, "delegated discretion" in the new—to the stock market, which rises over time but not in a perfectly linear way. At any given moment, cutbacks, corrections or retrenchments occur and loom very large for the people living at those moments. Yet over a longer time scale, the market tends to return to its growth trendline. So too, while the administrative state can be shaped, constrained and curtailed at various margins by specific decisions, the secular trend is likely to persist. I still think this is a helpful frame.

Tocqueville's account of his times, however, supplies a more apt "grand narrative"[113] for our times. What it captures, and what the stock market analogy fails to capture, is the sheer ideological passion of many of the participants in the conservative-libertarian legal movement—the patent fact that many of *Chevron*'s critics in the bar and the academy, and some of the Justices who voted to overrule *Chevron*, are gripped by no less than a kind of revolutionary fervor for "anti-administrativism."[114] And the narrative parallel is only enhanced when we realize that among the Justices who voted to overrule *Chevron* are some, like the Chief Justice and perhaps to a lesser degree Justice Kavanaugh, who play the part of more moderate revolutionaries, and who seem to have tried to preempt the *Jacobins de droite* from taking things too far. It is very much an open question in the short run whether the moderates will succeed in arresting the course of the revolution, taking it so far and no farther. One recalls that the original Girondins ended up beneath the blade. But Tocqueville's whole point, his striking thesis, is that whether or not the moderate revolutionaries succeed or, as in his case, fail, nonetheless in the longer run the Revolution merely served to reinforce and

[111] 514 U.S. 549 (1995).

[112] Vermeule, *supra* note 99, at 12.

[113] *Cf.* Sunstein, *Administrative Law's Grand Narrative*, *supra* note 6.

[114] Gillian E. Metzger, *The Supreme Court, 2016 Term—Foreword: 1930s Redux: The Administrative State Under Siege*, 131 Harv. L. Rev. 1, 4 (2017).

consolidate the order against which it rebelled. The laws and customs of the *ancien régime* were reintroduced in new forms and under new labels. Whatever happens in the next year, or five years, I believe that a few decades on, one will look back and say: so too with *Chevron* and *Loper Bright*.

ADAM A. DAVIDSON

THE SOCIETY CASES

Introduction

Commentators have begun to smell something rotten in the state of One First Street. In a series of cases, the Supreme Court has apparently taken a notably decarceral turn. While the law professoriate and *New York Times* set might be expected to welcome this jurisprudential shift with glee, instead the Court has caused much consternation. As Josh Chafetz recently described the moves, the Court has "ruled that federal law must be interpreted so as not to cover behavior that looks, to any reasonable observer, sketchy as hell."[1] The *New York Times* editorial board stated that the defendant's actions in one of the cases "certainly looked corrupt" and called on the decision "to be narrowly construed."[2]And those cases involving the Trump presidency and January 6 assault on the Capitol have

Adam A. Davidson is an Assistant Professor of Law at the University of Chicago Law School.

Author's note: I thank Will Baude, Josh Chafetz, Raff Donelson, Sarah Fackrell, Kim Forde-Mazrui, Thomas Frampton, Rachel Harmon, William Hubbard, Darrell Miller, Farah Peterson, Chris Schmidt, Chris Williams, and participants in the Langston Midwest Writing Workshop, the UVA Criminal Law Colloquium, and the Chicago-Kent Faculty Workshop for helpful comments and conversations. I also thank the Paul H. Leffmann Fund for research support.

[1] Josh Chafetz, *Corruption and the Supreme Court*, 36 Yale J.L. & Human. (forthcoming 2025) (manuscript at 3), https://ssrn.com/abstract=4971946.

[2] Editorial Board, *A Narrow Ruling on Public Corruption*, N.Y. Times (June 28, 2016), https://www.nytimes.com/2016/06/29/opinion/a-narrow-ruling-on-public-corruption.html.

The Supreme Court Review, 2025.
 https://doi.org/10.1086/735607

ignited more (perhaps justified) fury than this Article could possibly hope to recount.[3]

That unexpected reaction is because these pro-defendant cases all appear to be of a certain type. They involve crimes allegedly committed by a whiter, wealthier group than the typical criminal defendant. These cases involve public corruption, potential insurrection, and at times even the former President of the United States. And overwhelmingly, the Court has reached pro-defendant outcomes that defy the typical story of tough-on-crime jurisprudence handed down by a Republican-stacked Supreme Court.

This relatively simple narrative of positive outcomes for favored groups fits neatly within the political story told about the current conservative Supreme Court.[4] But that simple narrative also obscures an important facially race- and class-neutral doctrinal move that allows the Court to achieve its goals (whether they are political or not). Further, it does not explain why liberal Justices who would seem opposed to this project of cementing race-class hierarchies do not uniformly oppose either the outcome or the reasoning in these cases.

Commentators are correct that these cases raise problems for those who would oppose racial and class-based hierarchies. But they have misdiagnosed that problem's operation by focusing on the racial, class-based, and political predilections of the individual Justices. In doing so, they have overlooked both the race and class-neutral problem that the Court is trying to solve in these cases and how the Court's solution to that problem structurally furthers inequality.

What commentators have missed is that these cases are part of an older, broader, but largely unrecognized set that addresses a recurring issue the Court faces. In these cases, the Court must address when the usual structure of the law fails. That usual structure allows for broad substantive liability that is checked primarily by the discretionary choices of individual governmental actors. But in these cases, that structure causes harms that do not arise in the mine-run case. Usually, but not always, this problem arises in criminal cases because this structural choice is at our criminal legal system's core.

---

[3] *See, e.g.*, David M. Driesen, *Donald Trump and the Collapse of Checks and Balances*, 77 SMU L. Rev. F. 199 (2024); Adam Liptak, *Echoes of* Roe v. Wade *in Decision Granting Immunity to Trump*, N.Y. Times (July 29, 2024), https://www.nytimes.com/2024/07/29/us/trump-immunity-roe-v-wade.html.

[4] *See, e.g.*, Elie Mystal, *Supreme Court Preview: This Term, It Can Always Get Worse*, Nation (Sept. 29, 2023), https://www.thenation.com/article/society/supreme-court-term-2023.

Because of the doctrinal move the Court uses to address this problem, I call these cases the Society Cases. In them, the Court takes what is formally a case against a person in their individual capacity and injects into it that person's societal role. This injection then allows the Court to treat this societally important person differently, and almost always with greater substantive or procedural protection, than a similarly situated person who did not have that role, based on the societal disruption the suit would cause. These cases extend beyond the public corruption issues on which commentators have focused to involve Presidents, other governmental and pseudo-governmental officials at all levels, and even political protestors. In some cases, where the person's role is especially prominent—like those involving Presidents—the Court uses the person's role to shape formal doctrine, essentially negating the idea that the individual and their role are truly separate. This extreme form of the move has deeply troubled both dissenting Justices and commentators, as the Court has used it to place some individuals nearly beyond the reach of both civil and criminal law. In other, less extreme, cases, the Court uses the person's role to shape its reasoning, explaining why assumptions about the checks and balances that usually guide its analysis no longer hold.

But because our society is one that is suffused with race and class hierarchy, the societal roles that the Court recognizes disproportionately belong to a wealthier, whiter set of people than the usual defendant. As a result, the Court creates a dual system of justice, where disproportionately wealthy, white, and societally important defendants receive substantive and procedural protections that the vast majority do not.

Despite this race- and class-based disproportionality, this Article argues that the Justices are right to analyze how someone's societal role changes the assumptions and considerations that go into deciding a case. The alternative—ignoring the different status of these atypical litigants—would lead to a more artificial analysis that could cause unintended harms.

Because of this, the Society Cases create a tension for the pro-equality jurist: He or she can do what seems correct in the case before them, but in doing so they will further entrench the race and class hierarchies they otherwise would fight against. But the bigoted, anti-equality jurist faces no such tension; the outcomes called for by both their bigotry and their neutral analysis are the same. What's more, the bigoted jurist is able to hide their bigotry behind neutral terms, while the pro-equality jurist is more likely to require race- and class-conscious analysis to advance their aims. The Society Cases thus serve as an example of the power and perniciousness of structural inequality in action.

While there are numerous issues that the Society Cases raise, this Article has the limited goal of uncovering the Court's use of this analytical move and beginning to explore the doctrinal and societal ramifications of it. It does not, however, try to definitively put any given case into or outside of the category of the Society Cases. As I will discuss, while there is a definite core of Society Cases, the boundaries of that category are contestable. For example, in some of these cases, the Court might use the analytical move I identify here, but other commentators might argue that move is surplusage because its force is swamped by the strength of the Court's other analyses. Others might argue that this move of combining the individual with their societal role is one of numerous possible proxies the Court (or the courts) use to identify broader societal impacts, and so all of those proxy cases should be included in the category. This Article does not seek to completely refute these possibilities and is instead content with the more modest goal of beginning the academic project of highlighting and exploring the existence and results of the Court's blending of individuals with their societal roles.

The remainder of this Article proceeds in three Parts. Part I seeks to identify the analytical move that marks one of the Society Cases. It focuses on three groups of litigants where the Court has blended the individual with their societal role: comparatively powerful political and economic figures, current and former Presidents, and political protestors (of a sort). It then turns to cases that suggest the category's possible borders.

Having described and defined the Society Cases in Part I, Part II defends them. While it does not seek to defend any of these cases on their merits, it does defend the existence of the category. Given the background doctrinal structure of broad liability cabined by individual discretion that the Court is acting against, the Court correctly recognizes that the Society Cases will have different effects and raise different concerns than cases involving the usual defendant. It seems uncontroversial to say that a civil suit involving the President is likely to cause greater disruption than one involving almost anyone else. And the charging of a government official, private executive, or political protestor raises heightened concerns about improper targeting that do not arise in the usual criminal case. By analyzing the individual alongside their societal role, the Court provides more transparent and holistic analyses of the cases before it. Part II further defends the Society Cases not for what they are, but for what they could be. It argues that while these cases have overwhelmingly been used to grant additional protection to litigants with societal roles that make them more powerful than the typical criminal or civil rights litigant, the same blend of individual and societal considerations could lead the courts to hold those powerful actors to a higher standard.

Part III returns to the race-class problem that began this Article to complicate this otherwise positive story about the Society Cases. It argues that the problem with the Society Cases is not the cases themselves, but the necessity of their existence. In these cases, the Court must deviate from the usual legal structure it has created because it did not make room for the important societal roles held by the "usual" defendants in the cases that populate the criminal legal system. It is in part because the Court previously discounted the societal roles of those people to virtual nothingness that the system of broad liability cabined by rarely checked individual discretion was allowed to take hold in our criminal system, and in turn that this system was able to wreak havoc on those Blacker, Browner, and poorer parts of society that the Court ignored. The Society Cases, this Part argues, represent a window into the alternate reality where the whole society received the level of respect the Court affords the "high" society defendants in the Society Cases.[5]

Finally, Part III argues that the Society Cases represent an example of structural inequality in action.[6] Because they sit atop race and class hierarchies, the differential treatment that the Society Cases calls for further entrenches these hierarchies. This exposes the depth and power of structural, as opposed to individual, racism and other inequality.

---

[5] *Cf.* Henry Mitchell, *Senator Sam Ervin: The Lion of Watergate at Home in the South Looking Back on His Career and the Constitution*, WASH. POST (Dec. 19, 1982), https://www.washingtonpost.com/archive/lifestyle/1982/12/19/senator-sam-ervin/8d105831-48e9-462f-97d7-9d64c56ef609 ("When Nixon and Mitchell started in on their 'no-knock' business, I fought hard against it, and it was clear that blacks would be the major victims of it. They weren't going to use it against high-society people.").

[6] At times, this Article will refer to structural racism instead of structural inequality more broadly. Though the problems discussed here affect numerous intersecting lines of identity and oppression including race, class, and gender, the majority of the work from which this Part draws focuses on race, and so the terminology used reflects this.

I. Identifying the Society Cases

Identifying the Society Cases involves unearthing a common root that binds together three related branches of cases. In the first, the Court faces criminal prosecutions that impact well-connected political and economic defendants. The second branch is functionally the most extreme version of the first, involving cases in which one of the litigants is the President, sued at least arguably outside of their governmental capacity. Finally, it is the third branch that uncovers the link between them all. Here, the Court faces a defendant who, despite being relatively powerless themself, takes actions that are motivated by engagement with the political sphere or are part of governmental processes.

By analyzing each of these branches together, it becomes clear that the Court adjusts its usual interpretative lens in order to protect the political and economic spheres of our society from the usual reach of the criminal law. In order to see this difference, it is important to set out how the criminal law usually operates.

A. Breadth and Discretion in the Criminal Law

Understanding the Society Cases first requires understanding the system created by the Court's typical criminal jurisprudence. Although not every Society Case is a criminal law case, they seem to make up the core of the category. That is because in the usual criminal case, the Court has enabled two interconnected features of our criminal legal system that it seeks to cabin in Society Cases: breadth and discretion.

The criminal law is broad, by which I mean a shocking number of behaviors are criminalized. The federal code alone contains thousands of different crimes.[7] It is so sweeping that it led one professor to remark, "There is no one in the United States over the age of 18 who cannot be indicted for some federal crime. . . . That is not an exaggeration."[8] Observing the criminal law's breadth is, at this point, uncontroversial. It was "old news" when William Stuntz observed it

---

[7] Despite a surprising number of efforts, no one has actually managed to count them all. *See* Gary Fields & John R. Emshwiller, *Many Failed Efforts to Count Nation's Federal Criminal Laws*, Wall St. J. (July 23, 2011), https://www.wsj.com/articles/SB10001424052702304319804576389601079728920.

[8] *Id.* (quoting Professor John Baker).

in 2001,[9] and as Stuntz notes, scholars had been decrying the breadth of the criminal code since at least the 1960s.[10] Despite some occasional actions against type,[11] the Court has largely allowed this breadth to flourish. Indeed, even in those cases where the Court has narrowed substantive criminal laws that could affect many people, it has taken half measures.[12] Of course, one overarching reason for this is a simple doctrinal reality: The vast majority of criminal law stems from states' broad police powers,[13] while the limitations the Court imposes come from the comparatively narrow set of rights imposed by the Constitution.

Despite nearly everyone having apparently violated some criminal law, the reason most of us don't live in constant fear of our local prosecutor is the other major feature of our criminal system: discretion. Even if we, as a society, wanted to enforce every criminal law on the books to the fullest extent possible, the amount of resources—in time, money, and people—it would take to do so makes the goal functionally impossible. "The end point of this progression is clear: criminal codes that cover everything and decide nothing, that serve only to delegate power to district attorneys' offices and police departments."[14]

Ultimately, this means that no one is completely safe from the criminal system's reach. A sufficiently motivated—by good or ill—police officer or prosecutor can use the criminal law's breadth to target nearly anyone.[15] Again, in the usual case, the Court has been

---

[9] William J. Stuntz, *The Pathological Politics of Criminal Law*, 100 Mich. L. Rev. 505, 507 (2001).

[10] *Id.* at 505 n.2.

[11] Justice Gorsuch, for instance, has sought to revive the rule of lenity across several recent cases. *See, e.g.*, Pulsifer v. United States, 601 U.S. 124, 184–85 (2024) (Gorsuch, J., dissenting); Snyder v. United States, 603 U.S. 1, 20 (2024) (Gorsuch, J., concurring); Wooden v. United States, 595 U.S. 360, 395 (2022) (Gorsuch, J., concurring).

[12] *See* Daniel S. Harawa, *Lemonade: A Racial Justice Reframing of the Roberts Court's Criminal Jurisprudence*, 110 Calif. L. Rev. 681, 727–29 (2022) (noting how the Court did tamp down on some attempts by states to have broad vagrancy and anti-gang laws, although it has allowed others to continue).

[13] *See, e.g.*, Wendy Sawyer & Peter Wagner, *Mass Incarceration: The Whole Pie 2024*, Prison Pol'y Initiative (Mar. 14, 2024), https://www.prisonpolicy.org/reports/pie2024.html (finding that approximately 1.5 million of the 1.9 million incarcerated people in the United States are held in state and local facilities).

[14] Stuntz, *supra* note 9, at 509.

[15] The grand jury could be a bulwark against this but has long failed to serve as a meaningful check in the typical case. *See, e.g.*, Andrew D. Leipold, *Why Grand Juries Do Not (and Cannot) Protect the Accused*, 80 Cornell L. Rev. 260, 264 (1995) (arguing that "as currently constructed, grand juries not only do not, but cannot, protect the accused from unfounded

fine with this state of affairs. Indeed, if anything, it has bolstered it by expanding doctrines like qualified and absolute immunity that protect police, prosecutors, and other state actors from liability.[16]

But the Society Cases represent an anomaly in the Court's usual criminal jurisprudence. Whereas the Court is often content to allow the breadth of legislative enactments to be checked by the discretionary choices of other criminal system actors, in the Society Cases the Court provides the check itself. It does so not only by limiting the discretion of police or prosecutors, but also by narrowing the reach of the substantive law.

That is not to say that every case in which the Court narrows the substantive law fits under the umbrella of the Society Cases. Instead, it is the reason for the Court's narrowing that drives the label. While the Society Cases utilize the usual tools of statutory and constitutional interpretation, in them the Court evinces an additional concern that if the criminal law is allowed to reach as far as the government would like, some other part of society—usually the political, but sometimes the economic sphere—will be overly and improperly affected.

B. Powerful People

In the first group of Society Cases, the Court finds itself judging the prosecution of people who wield significant political or economic power and are facing prosecution for allegedly wielding that power improperly. To be clear, the powerful people discussed in this Section are not necessarily the most powerful people in the country (although some may approach that distinction). They are powerful in comparison to the typical criminal defendant who is an economically poor racial minority. The Bureau of Justice Statistics reported that in 2022, only thirty-one percent of people in state and federal prison were white,[17] while white, non-Hispanic people were over fifty-eight percent of the people represented in the Census.[18] And one 2015

charges"); Kate Levine, *How We Prosecute the Police*, 104 Geo. L.J. 745, 755–57 (2016) (describing how prosecutors used grand juries to protect police who killed Black people from indictment).

[16] *See generally* Joanna Schwartz, Shielded: How the Police Became Untouchable (2023); Adam A. Davidson, *The Shadow of the Law of the Police*, 122 Mich. L. Rev. 1035 (2024).

[17] E. Ann Carson, *Prisons Report Series Preliminary Data Release, 2022*, Bureau Just. Stat. (Sept. 2023), https://bjs.ojp.gov/preliminary-data-release-prisons.

[18] *Quick Facts Population Estimates July 1, 2024*, U.S. Census Bureau, https://www.census.gov/quickfacts/fact/table/US/PST045224.

study, for example, found that more than sixty percent of the families of incarcerated people it surveyed had a household income below $25,000, while only twelve percent of respondents had a household income over $50,000.[19] Unsurprisingly, these families struggled to pay the over $13,000 of "conviction-related costs, including restitution and attorney fees" that they incurred on average, with two in three reporting that they struggled to meet basic needs because of these costs.[20] In a darkly ironic turn, the amount of money—$13,000—that the families of typical incarcerated people reported as debilitating is the same amount as the alleged gratuity taken in the case to which I now turn.

Portage, Indiana seems like an unlikely location to begin a discussion of the Society Cases, but even in small towns there can be big money. In 2013, Portage, Indiana awarded several contracts totaling over a million dollars to a local truck company for garbage trucks.[21] The next year, that company gave James Snyder, Portage's mayor, a check for $13,000 for "consulting services."[22] Federal prosecutors took a different view of that exchange and charged Snyder with accepting an illegal gratuity.[23] Snyder was convicted by a jury, and his conviction was affirmed by the Seventh Circuit.[24]

In *Snyder v. United States*, the Supreme Court reversed. Most of the reasons for that reversal were what one would expect in a case interpreting a criminal statute. For example, the text, history, and structure of the statute suggested that it was intended only to cover bribery instead of both bribery and gratuities.[25] Likewise, reading 18 U.S.C. § 666(a)(1)(B) to cover both gratuities and bribery would mean that Congress inexplicably created a statutory scheme for state and local officials that was both less precise and more punishing than for

---

[19] Saneta deVuono-powell, Chris Schweidler, Alicia Walters & Azadeh Zohrabi, *Who Pays? The True Cost of Incarceration on Families*, Ella Baker Ctr. 55 (2015), https://static.prisonpolicy.org/scans/who-pays%20Ella%20Baker%20report.pdf. By comparison, the median U.S. household income in 2015 was $55,775. Kirby G. Posey, *Household Income: 2015*, U.S. Census Bureau (Sept. 2016), https://www.census.gov/content/dam/Census/library/publications/2016/acs/acsbr15-02.pdf.

[20] deVuono-powell, Schweidler, Walters & Zohrabi, *supra* note 19, at 13.

[21] Snyder v. United States, 603 U.S. 1, 9 (2024).

[22] *Id.*

[23] *Id.* (citing 18 U.S.C. § 666(a)(1)(B)).

[24] *Id.* at 10.

[25] *Id.* at 10–13.

federal officials committing the same conduct.[26] And as Justice Gorsuch pointed out in his concurrence, lenity seemed to be an unspoken thumb on the scale.[27]

But unlike these usual bits of statutory interpretation, the Court also relied on a reason befitting one of the Society Cases: federalism. Because Snyder was not an ordinary individual defendant, but a political figure using political power, the Court found this additional analysis necessary.

The government's broad interpretation of the statute, the Court said, "would significantly infringe on bedrock federalism principles."[28] By subjecting state and local political actors to this far-reaching criminal liability, the Court worried that Congress may have gone too far in upsetting the balance those sub-national governments created for the acceptable relationship between their political actors and constituents.[29] Indeed, the Court tips its hand several places in the opinion to signal the strength of this concern. In the opening paragraphs, Justice Kavanaugh lays out the expansiveness of the government's interpretation by writing, "Section 666 does not supplement those state and local rules by subjecting 19 million state and local officials to up to 10 years in federal prison for accepting even commonplace gratuities."[30] Later, in describing the facts of the case, he is careful to note that Snyder was never prosecuted, or even disciplined, at the state or local level for accepting this money.[31]

The result was an admonition to the government that the Court stated it had made "time and again": "[T]he Court 'cannot construe a criminal statute on the assumption that the Government will use it responsibly.'"[32] That admonition is true and had come through in a variety of ways in different cases, as the Court's citations showed.

For example, the Court cited *Ciminelli v. United States* and *Kelly v. United States*, both of which involved the Court chiding the government

---

[26] *Id.* at 13–14, 15–17.

[27] *Id.* at 20–21 (Gorsuch, J., concurring).

[28] *Id.* at 14 (majority opinion).

[29] *See id.* (noting that the sub-national governments' "differing approaches reflect nuanced state and local policy judgments about when gifts expressing appreciation to public officials for their past acts cross the line from the innocuous to the problematic").

[30] *Id.* at 5.

[31] *Id.* at 9.

[32] *Id.* at 17 (quoting McDonnell v. United States, 579 U.S. 550, 576 (2016)).

for (with the lower courts' approval) using fraud statutes to create what amounted to federal criminal good governance standards.[33] And in *Percoco v. United States*, the Court expressly worried that the government's theory of prosecution would invade the normal political process by disrupting the long history of "*éminence grises*, individuals who lacked any formal government position but nevertheless exercised very strong influence over government decisions."[34] Its language in *McDonnell v. United States* was especially striking. The sort of federalism concerns the Court would return to in *Snyder* reared their head.[35] But more than this, the Court recounted how nearly one hundred former high-ranking government officials warned that the government's "breathtaking expansion of public-corruption law" used to prosecute former-Governor McDonnell "would likely chill federal officials' interactions with the people they serve and thus damage their ability effectively to perform their duties."[36]

The exact contours of the Court's analysis shift from case to case as it seeks to rein in the government's aggressiveness. But from *Percoco* to *Ciminelli* to *McDonnell* and beyond, it is telling that every case the Court martialed for this point in *Snyder* involved either a political defendant or a defendant with outsized economic or political might.[37]

These cases represent one branch of the Society Cases. In them, the Court—through explicit statements and implicit analysis—protects defendants with significant power in the political or economic sphere from the consequences of the sort of broadly interpreted criminal law it allows to run rampant in most of the criminal system. It does this through a variety of tools. Federalism plays a key role in some cases, but that is not the only tool the Court uses. In others the Court does not introduce an unexpected formal doctrine, but

---

[33] *See* Ciminelli v. United States, 598 U.S. 306, 316 (2023); Kelly v. United States, 590 U.S. 391, 403–04 (2020).

[34] Percoco v. United States, 598 U.S. 319, 330 (2023).

[35] *McDonnell*, 579 U.S. at 576–77.

[36] *Id.* at 575.

[37] *See, e.g., id.* at 555 (former Virginia governor and his wife); Skilling v. United States, 561 U.S. 358, 367 (2010) (former Enron executive); *Percoco*, 598 U.S. at 322 (former "top aide to the Governor of New York"); *Ciminelli*, 598 U.S. at 310 (owner of a construction company who conspired with a government advisor to win a $750 million project in Buffalo, New York); *Kelly*, 590 U.S. at 394 ("The case's cast of characters are public officials who worked at or with the Port Authority and had political ties to New Jersey's then-Governor Chris Christie.").

instead tilts its statutory interpretation to raise concerns about the consequences of troubling behavior by powerful actors that other legal actors seemed more than willing to punish.

For example, *Skilling v. United States*, which involved a former Enron executive, was one round in the fight between the Court, Congress, and federal prosecutors over the reach of honest services fraud.[38] Federal prosecutors used the mail and wire fraud statute to reach a broad swath of potential conduct under the umbrella of honest services fraud, and Congress obliged their attempts, going so far as to amend the statute in the late 1980s after the Court limited its reach.[39] In Skilling's case that allegedly fraudulent conduct included "undisclosed self-dealing by a public official or private employee—*i.e.*, the taking of official action by the employee that furthers his own undisclosed financial interests while purporting to act in the interests of those to whom he owes a fiduciary duty."[40] The lower courts were largely willing to go along with this breadth, but the Court interpreted the criminal prohibition on honest services fraud to encompass only bribery and kickback schemes.[41] As such, honest services fraud became a narrow crime for the powerful, but unsophisticated, defendant. Powerful, in that it can only be committed by those with sufficient power to be the target of such a bribe or kickback, and unsophisticated, because unlike Skilling, they must lack the sophistication to engage in schemes for personal profit that do not involve directly taking bribes or kickbacks.

Compare this treatment with the Court's analysis of Skilling's impartial jury claim. Although it vacated his conviction because of the government's overreach with the honest services fraud statute, the Court did not give Skilling's impartial jury claim such friendly treatment. This, in many ways, was no surprise. District courts are given wide leeway in conducting trials, and included in this is a "proper[] resistan[ce] to second-guessing the trial judge's estimation of a juror's impartiality, for that judge's appraisal is ordinarily influenced by a host of factors impossible to capture fully in the record."[42] Of course,

---

[38] *Skilling*, 561 U.S. at 400–01 (recounting this history).

[39] *See id.*

[40] *Id.* at 409 (quoting Brief for United States at 43–44, *Skilling*, 561 U.S. 358 (No. 08-1394)).

[41] *See id.* at 368.

[42] *Id.* at 386.

the Court may have been just as skeptical of lower courts' ability to wield this discretion as it was of the government's ability to cabin the scope of the criminal law.[43] But while an honest services fraud conviction is likely only to impact the politically or economically connected, as the Court's cases show, an impartial jury claim has much broader reach. While some highly publicized trials are, like Skilling's, the result of a high-profile defendant, many others are caused by the public fascination with more regular, albeit gruesome, crimes.[44]

Notably, however, Justice Sotomayor's dissent on this point highlighted the societal importance of Skilling and Enron to the impartial jury claim. She would have granted him relief because she found the district court's *voir dire* insufficient in the face of how "[t]he sudden collapse of Enron directly affected thousands of people in the Houston area and shocked the entire community" resulting in an "accompanying barrage of local media coverage was massive in volume and often caustic in tone."[45]

This is not to say that the Court's concern with the criminal law reaching into the political and economic spheres is the only issue driving these cases. It almost certainly is not. But whether because of explicit concerns or implicit biases, the Court does appear to treat concerns about the criminal law's breadth and prosecutorial discretion with more care in the Society Cases than in the ordinary course.

Of course, one might quibble with these examples or wish to substitute others for a variety of reasons. *Skilling*, in particular, sits closer to the Society Cases' border because the blend of the individual and their societal role is largely implicit, at least within the majority opinion. But it seems clear that, even if it is far from the only reason, the blend of the individual with their societal role is at least influencing the Court's analysis in these cases. Indeed, it is hardly ever the case that this analytical move is the only piece of analysis the Court does. In some cases, the move hardly seems necessary. The Court in *Snyder* offered "six reasons, taken together ... text, statutory history, statutory structure, statutory punishments, federalism, and fair

---

[43] *Cf.* Chafetz, *supra* note 1 (manuscript at 29) (noting that the Court privileges the status of courts over other governmental actors).

[44] *See Skilling*, 561 U.S. at 379–81 (discussing several murder cases which led to outsized media attention and findings of prejudiced juries).

[45] *Id.* at 427 (Sotomayor, J., concurring in part).

notice" to reach its conclusion.[46] At least arguably, the Court could have focused entirely on those reasons germane only to the individual prosecution to reach the same outcome. But it is because of this that the Society Cases are of interest. That the Court in *Snyder*, for example, chose not to focus entirely on the individual suggests that the issue the Society Cases raise—the lack of fit between a particular defendant's societal role and the background assumptions of the criminal law—is a problem that is deeply concerning to the Court.

Perhaps more broadly, one might push against this idea that these cases suggest that the Society Cases are a special class because they are not the only time that the Court narrows substantive criminal law. After all, in other cases the Court polices the lines of substantive criminal law with no reflection on the political or economic sphere.[47] But that distinction misunderstands the category. As Part II will discuss further, this Article does not identify Society Cases by outcome, but by the presence of the Court's decision to blend its concerns for the individual with the concerns raised by that individual's societal role. That blend leads to narrowed substantive law in these cases, but in others it could mean *broader* liability.

C. PRESIDENTS

Cases involving the President could fall within the earlier discussion of those Society Cases involving powerful people generally. Alternately, one might argue that Presidents are *sui generis*, and including those cases involving Presidents distorts the image of the broader category of Society Cases. This Section charts a middle ground, arguing that cases involving the President in their personal capacity highlight several aspects of the Society Cases that might otherwise be obscured.

Three key insights arise when we turn to these presidential cases. First is that the Society Cases are not inherently tied to the criminal law. Instead, it is the failure of regular processes to account for the full impact of the case that identifies one of the Society Cases. Usually, this failure of regular processes is a systemic failure, that is,

---

[46] Snyder v. United States, 603 U.S. 1, 10 (2024).

[47] *See, e.g.*, Rehaif v. United States, 588 U.S. 225 (2019) (narrowing a gun possession statute through traditional statutory interpretation tools).

the combination of potentially broad liability cabined by lightly checked discretion invading into some place it usually does not touch—here, the presidency—that this Article has discussed thus far. Most Society Cases involve the criminal law because that combination of liability and discretion is at the core of our criminal system's functioning, but the criminal law is not the only place that this institutional arrangement arises.

Second, they illuminate most clearly the analytical move that defines the Society Cases. Despite being cases ostensibly about Presidents as individuals, the Court intertwines the person and the office in a way that grants greater protection to the individual. Sometimes this protection is created by outright limitations on the individual's liability.[48] But in other cases, it takes the form of requiring additional scrutiny before the individual can be acted against.[49]

Third, these cases illustrate that being part of the Society Cases does not demand that the powerful person achieves a total victory. Instead, cases involving Presidents show how the Court may both treat a dispute with the special dispensation that marks it as one of the Society Cases and hold even the most powerful individuals to account.

One of the most striking aspects of cases involving the President is just how otherwise mundane the disputes at the center of some of these cases are. *Trump v. Mazars USA, LLP* is about an otherwise ordinary congressional subpoena for tax documents.[50] *Clinton v. Jones* is about trial scheduling.[51] And *Nixon v. Fitzgerald* is, ultimately, a retaliatory firing dispute with a *West Wing* flair.[52] Absent their presidential twists, all of these cases were the sort of bog standard disputes that the courts decide every day. Perhaps even more than the criminal cases that make up the bulk of those discussed in this Article, the mere fact that these cases reach the Court at all signals their specialness.

---

[48] *See, e.g.*, Trump v. United States, 603 U.S. 593 (2024); Nixon v. Fitzgerald, 457 U.S. 731 (1982).

[49] *See, e.g.*, Clinton v. Jones, 520 U.S. 681, 708–09 (1997).

[50] 591 U.S. 848, 853 (2020).

[51] *Jones*, 520 U.S. at 686–89.

[52] *See Fitzgerald*, 457 U.S. at 733–41. *Trump v. Vance*, 591 U.S. 786 (2020), also falls within this description, as it involved a state grand jury subpoena similar to the congressional subpoena at issue in *Mazars*. *See id.* at 791.

But of course, these cases are special. Involving the President makes them so. And indeed, the presidency is so special, occupying such "a unique position in the constitutional scheme,"[53] that the presence of a President on one side of the "v." makes even otherwise mundane civil matters take on national importance.

This is because the structural problems that underlie the Society Cases are not limited to the criminal law. They may be more potent in criminal cases, but the structure of broad substantive law narrowed by discretionary choices of individual actors is a recurring theme in our legal system. Take *Mazars* as an example. "The congressional power to obtain information is 'broad' and 'indispensable.'"[54] That breadth includes "inquiries into the administration of existing laws, studies of proposed laws, and 'surveys of defects in our social, economic or political system for the purpose of enabling the Congress to remedy them.'"[55] Given the breadth of possible legislation Congress might pass, the scope of this power seems nearly limitless.[56]

But as the saying goes, Congress is a they, not an it. Congressional committees and subcommittees, not the entire Congress, ultimately issue subpoenas.[57] While this provides some checks as compared to the world where every sitting congressperson could issue a subpoena, it still allows for ample discretion that has garnered complaints from both sides of the aisle. Representative Jim Jordan issued over ninety subpoenas in his role as the chair of the House Select Subcommittee on the Weaponization of the Federal Government.[58] Unspoken in

[53] *Fitzgerald*, 457 U.S. at 749.

[54] *Mazars*, 591 U.S. at 862 (quoting Watkins v. United States, 354 U.S. 178, 187 (1957)).

[55] *Id.* (quoting *Watkins*, 354 U.S. at 187).

[56] Congress cannot issue subpoenas for law enforcement or general exposure purposes, but given the breadth of possible legislation, even if Congress's real purpose was law enforcement or exposure, the universe of information that Congress would not be able to obtain seems small. *See, e.g., id.* at 867 ("Any personal paper possessed by a President could potentially 'relate to' a conceivable subject of legislation, for Congress has broad legislative powers that touch a vast number of subjects. The President's financial records could relate to economic reform, medical records to health reform, school transcripts to education reform, and so on. Indeed, at argument, the House was unable to identify *any* type of information that lacks some relation to potential legislation." (citation omitted)).

[57] *See* Jane A. Hudiburg, Cong. Rsch. Serv., R44247, A Survey of House and Senate Committee Rules on Subpoenas 1–2 (2021).

[58] Michael Sozan & Alice Lillydahl, *Despite Defying His Own Lawful Subpoena, Rep. Jim Jordan Has Issued at Least 91 Subpoenas to Others*, Ctr. for Am. Progress (Aug. 1, 2024), https://www.americanprogress.org/article/despite-defying-his-own-lawful-subpoena-rep-jim-jordan-has-issued-at-least-91-subpoenas-to-others.

the Subcommittee's title is that the alleged "weaponization" is against conservative viewpoints.[59] By contrast, the House committee investigating the January 6 assault on the Capitol issued more than 100 subpoenas,[60] including one to Representative Jordan.[61] In the usual case, the courts are deeply reticent to cabin the discretion Congress uses to effect its subpoena powers. One large law firm counseled that "[a]s a practical matter, this means that courts generally will not interfere with a congressional subpoena absent a truly opprobrious violation of an individual's constitutional rights."[62] But that changes when the subpoena involves the President.

In *Mazars* the Court added four limitations[63] to the usual practice of evaluating a congressional subpoena. In order to avoid conflict between Congress and the executive branch, it required courts to "carefully assess whether the asserted legislative purpose warrants the significant step of involving the President and his papers."[64] This meant that the subpoena should not stand if Congress sought "access to the President's personal papers when other sources could provide Congress the information it needs."[65] In addition to this necessity requirement, the Court required the subpoena to be narrow: "no broader than reasonably necessary to support Congress's legislative objective."[66] Third, courts had to look closely at Congress's basis for its legislative purpose, "[t]he more detailed and substantial the evidence . . . the better."[67] Finally, despite the Court's repeated holdings

---

[59] Lexis Schapitl & Claudia Grisales, *House Panel on 'Weaponization' of the Government's First Hearing Takes Aim at DOJ, FBI*, NPR (Feb. 9, 2023, 5:51 PM ET), https://www.npr.org/2023/02/09/1155459408/house-panel-on-weaponization-of-the-federal-government-will-hold-its-first-heari.

[60] Zach Schonfeld, *Here's a List of the People Who Have Been Subpoenaed by the Jan. 6 Committee*, Hill (June 7, 2022, 2:06 PM ET), https://thehill.com/homenews/house/3514712-heres-a-list-of-the-people-who-have-been-subpoenaed-by-the-jan-6-committee.

[61] Sozan & Lillydahl, *supra* note 58.

[62] Hon. David M. McIntosh, Hon. Mark Gitenstein & Sean P. McDonnell, *Understanding Your Rights in Response to a Congressional Subpoena*, Mayer Brown (2014), https://docs.pogo.org/resource/2018/7_white-paper-congressional-subpoena.pdf.

[63] More accurately, the Court laid out four examples of the type of considerations that were relevant to evaluating congressional subpoenas to the President but recognized that "[o]ther considerations may be pertinent as well; one case every two centuries does not afford enough experience for an exhaustive list." Trump v. Mazars USA, LLP, 591 U.S. 848, 871 (2020).

[64] *Id.* at 869.

[65] *Id.* at 870.

[66] *Id.*

[67] *Id.*

that the distraction and time of responding to litigation are not by themselves enough to prevent the President from having to respond,[68] the Court held that "burdens imposed by a congressional subpoena should be carefully scrutinized, for they stem from a rival political branch that has an ongoing relationship with the President and incentives to use subpoenas for institutional advantage."[69]

What this all highlights is that the issues that might trigger the extra scrutiny that signals one of the Society Cases span the civil-criminal divide. Instead, what matters is the interaction between the individual litigant's role in society and how effectively the Court believes the usual balance of substantive law and discretion accounts for that role. The unique nature of the presidency, and so of the President, tilts that calculation heavily towards intervention in even the most otherwise mundane civil matters, showing how systems that the Court believes work perfectly well for the ninety-nine percent of cases may still need adjusting for the one percent.[70]

Ultimately, even in these otherwise mundane matters, the Court's treatment of the issues before it serves to make acting against the societally important defendant more difficult. Sometimes this occurs because the Court narrows the applicable substantive liability, but in other cases the Court erects additional procedural or evidentiary hurdles that litigants and the lower courts must overcome to hold these important defendants accountable.

But these additional hurdles are not an inevitability. It is a repeated theme in the Society Cases, and cases involving the President are no exception, that the lower courts treat the case like any other, only for the Supreme Court to highlight the non-standard issues that were rejected below.

For example, in discussing *Mazars*, I noted that subpoenas involving the President are looked at more skeptically. But the more accurate description of that phenomenon is that they are looked at more skeptically by the Supreme Court. In the lead up to *Mazars*, the Second and D.C. Circuits found irrelevant or downplayed, respectively,

[68] This includes the Court's repeating this holding in a case decided the same day. *See* Trump v. Vance, 591 U.S. 786, 801–02 (2020).

[69] *Mazars*, 591 U.S. at 871.

[70] *See, e.g.*, Clinton v. Jones, 520 U.S. 681, 684 (1997) (trial scheduling).

the separation of powers issues that the Supreme Court believed were the heart of the case.[71]

Likewise, in the criminal cases involving both Presidents and other individuals, the lower courts regularly treated these cases much like any other, only for the Supreme Court to uplift the separation of powers, federalism, or other issues that denote the case as being part of the Society Cases. This occurred in the numerous honest services fraud and government misconduct convictions that were overturned by the Court discussed in the previous Section. But it also occurred in cases like *Trump v. United States*,[72] in which the Supreme Court found a presidential immunity that the D.C. Circuit rejected in full.[73] And as I will discuss in the next Section, the lower courts and Supreme Court differed significantly along similar lines in their interpretation of the Sarbanes-Oxley Act of 2002 in *Fischer v. United States*.[74]

This differential treatment between the various levels of the judiciary raises the second insight analyzing presidential cases teaches us about the Society Cases. While litigants, and often lower courts, separate the individual from the office, the Supreme Court unifies the two in ways that grant additional protection even when defendants have allegedly acted in their personal capacity.

This conflation takes different forms, but in its least controversial form it seems not only defensible, but correct. In this least controversial form, the Court merely says that it is a relevant consideration whether some aspect of litigation will impede the President from carrying out their duties.[75] At its core, this is just a variation on the sorts of choices about case management that judges make in every piece of litigation every day. Just like a judge might grant a continuance so a litigant does not have to miss work, they might grant one so the President, well, does not have to miss (constitutionally mandated) work. And indeed, in these sorts of cases, the Court has rejected

[71] *Mazars*, 591 U.S. at 866.

[72] Trump v. United States, 603 U.S. 593, 642 (2024) ("The President therefore may not be prosecuted for exercising his core constitutional powers, and he is entitled, at a minimum, to a presumptive immunity from prosecution for all his official acts.").

[73] United States v. Trump, 91 F.4th 1173, 1189 (D.C. Cir.), *vacated and remanded*, 603 U.S. 593 (2024) ("[W]e reject all three potential bases for immunity both as a categorical defense to federal criminal prosecutions of former Presidents and as applied to this case in particular.").

[74] 603 U.S. 480, 483.

[75] *See, e.g.*, Trump v. Vance, 591 U.S. 786, 810 (2020).

arguments that some sort of formal heightened-need standard is necessary to protect the President from distraction or otherwise vexatious litigation.[76] Instead, the Court has simply reiterated the importance of the President's role in our constitutional structure, highlighting how the President can delay or escape the demands of litigation by showing how those demands "would impede his constitutional duties."[77]

While this sort of analysis seems simple, the conflation between person and office becomes much more controversial and complicated when the allegation involves acts the President took while in office. *Trump v. United States* is, for good and ill, the most instructive case. There, the Court considered then-former-President Trump's potential criminal liability for allegedly conspiring to overturn the November 2020 presidential election.[78] Given that he was the President at the time of the alleged actions, the question from the Court's perspective was whether he could be held criminally liable for "official actions" he took as President.[79] The Court said that, at least presumptively and possibly absolutely, he could not.[80] This built on the Court's previous holding in *Fitzgerald* that the President also could not be held civilly liable for damages for his official acts.[81]

The rationale for both of these holdings makes sense from the perspective that the President—the person—and the presidency—the office—are, realistically, inseparable. In order to prevent the President (the person) from placing their own fears of individual criminal or civil liability above what they believe to be the best course of action for the country, the Court believed that a strong form of immunity was necessary.[82] If we want the President to take "bold and unhesitating action," this, again, makes sense.[83]

---

[76] *See, e.g., id.* at 807–09 (rejecting a heightened-need standard in the context of a state grand jury subpoena).

[77] *Id.* at 810.

[78] *Trump*, 603 U.S. at 602.

[79] *Id.* at 605.

[80] *Id.* at 615.

[81] *See id.* at 611.

[82] *See id.* at 613 ("The danger [in criminally prosecuting a President] is akin to, indeed greater than, what led us to recognize absolute Presidential immunity from civil damages liability—that the President would be chilled from taking the 'bold and unhesitating action' required of an independent Executive." (quoting Nixon v. Fitzgerald, 457 U.S. 731, 745 (1982))).

[83] *Fitzgerald*, 457 U.S. at 745.

But this idea, that there is a person so special that they could flagrantly and intentionally violate the law with no civil or criminal recourse, offends some of the deepest beliefs people hold about this country. That fact comes shining through in the dissents in both *Fitzgerald* and *Trump*. Justice Blackmun perhaps stated it most powerfully:

> For me, the Court leaves unanswered his unanswerable argument that no man, not even the President of the United States, is absolutely and fully above the law. Until today, I had thought this principle was the foundation of our national jurisprudence. It now appears that it is not.[84]

And Justice Sotomayor laid out the potentially terrifying consequences:

> When he uses his official powers in any way, under the majority's reasoning, he now will be insulated from criminal prosecution. Orders the Navy's Seal Team 6 to assassinate a political rival? Immune. Organizes a military coup to hold onto power? Immune. Takes a bribe in exchange for a pardon? Immune. Immune, immune, immune. Let the President violate the law, let him exploit the trappings of his office for personal gain, let him use his official power for evil ends. Because if he knew that he may one day face liability for breaking the law, he might not be as bold and fearless as we would like him to be. That is the majority's message today.[85]

While this is the most extreme example of this phenomenon, the presence of this analytical move defines the Society Cases. The Court, in a case nominally about the personal liability of an individual, raises the effects that a verdict against them would have on those holding the societal office of that individual. By combining the individual with the societal, the Court reasons that additional hurdles and limitations—sometimes substantive, sometimes procedural—are justified before a person like this (and this person) can be held liable, if they can be held liable at all. The end result is that if the Court believes you are sufficiently important, you are likely to receive greater protections than a similarly situated other.

What may be surprising, then, is how rarely the President wins these cases. Indeed, *Fitzgerald* is the only case discussed thus far in which the suit against the President was dismissed as a result of the

---

[84] *Id.* at 797–98 (Blackmun, J., dissenting) (citations omitted); *see also Trump*, 603 U.S. at 657 (Sotomayor, J., dissenting) ("Today's decision ... makes a mockery of the principle, foundational to our Constitution and system of Government, that no man is above the law.").

[85] *Trump*, 603 U.S. at 685 (Sotomayor, J., dissenting).

Court's intervention.[86] In every other case, the President was forced to continue to litigate, albeit often with additional protections resulting from the Court's holding. Presidents Trump, Clinton, and Nixon were all required to respond to the subpoenas or otherwise engage in the litigation against them.[87] And even when facing criminal liability, President Trump did not convince the Court to dismiss the indictment.[88] Instead, he received an immunity of debated robustness, which required him to continue facing substantial criminal liability.[89]

Therefore the final takeaway from these presidential cases is not that the Court is unable or unwilling to hold powerful people accountable. Someone could hold "the most powerful job in the world,"[90] but they cannot totally escape the law. Instead, the lesson from these cases is that powerful people are treated differently in that they are afforded greater protections, even if they lose in the end.

D. POLITICAL (CRIMINAL) ACTION

To this point, one might wonder why these cases should be described as affecting society instead of merely affecting powerful, or well-connected, individuals. *Fischer* shows how the Court's concerns extend beyond any one individual to the structures of our society.

---

[86] Though the dissenters disagreed, *Fitzgerald* under that case's majority's view might not even belong to the Society Cases. That is because, as interpreted by the majority, all of the alleged actions Nixon took were official acts he took as the President, not actions that could be tied to him as an individual. 457 U.S. at 749.

[87] Clinton v. Jones, 520 U.S. 681, 684 (1997) (reversing the grant of a stay of trial until the end of President Clinton's presidency); United States v. Nixon, 418 U.S. 683, 707 (1974) (rejecting the claim of absolute privilege in response to a federal criminal subpoena); Trump v. Vance, 591 U.S. 786, 810 (2020) (same for state criminal subpoena); Trump v. Mazars USA, LLP, 591 U.S. 848, 869–71 (2020) (remanding for further consideration of the subpoena in light of the standards the Court set out).

[88] As others have noted, President Trump received a practical win in this case, even if he did not receive the full legal win he might have hoped for. The Court's addition of a robust immunity inquiry necessarily extended the time the litigation would take until the next election, which ultimately allowed him to delay the prosecution until the end of his second term, if not end it altogether through either the pardon process or his influence over the Justice Department. *See* Adam Liptak, *In Immunity Case, Trump Can Lose in Ways That Amount to a Win*, N.Y. Times (Apr. 24, 2024), https://www.nytimes.com/2024/04/24/us/trump-immunity-case-supreme-court.html.

[89] *See, e.g.*, *Trump*, 603 U.S. at 651 (Barrett, J., concurring) ("Properly conceived, the President's constitutional protection from prosecution is narrow.").

[90] *See* David A. Super, Opinion, *The American Presidency Is the Most Powerful Job in the World. Too Powerful.*, L.A. Times (Sept. 11, 2023), https://www.latimes.com/opinion/story/2024-09-11/presidency-immunity-founders-gun-safety.

The facts underlying *Fischer* were extraordinary, but the legal question that reached the Court was downright common. The Court was asked to determine the reach of a residual clause in a criminal statute,[91] a task it has taken on many times before.[92] The Court had not always looked favorably on these sorts of broad residual causes. It struck down the residual clause in the Armed Career Criminal Act, for example, as unconstitutionally vague.[93] And indeed, the Court had narrowed this sort of residual language within the Sarbanes-Oxley Act, the same act at issue in *Fischer*, a decade before *Fischer* was decided.[94] From this perspective, it was not entirely surprising that the Court in *Fischer* did not adopt the broad definition of "obstructs, influences, or impedes any official proceeding" that the government sought.[95] Instead, it narrowly construed 18 U.S.C. § 1512(c)(2) to require "that the defendant impaired the availability or integrity for use in an official proceeding of records, documents, objects, or as we earlier explained, other things used in the proceeding, or attempted to do so."[96]

But as with the presidential cases, it is not the outcome but the reasoning that makes *Fischer* one of the Society Cases. *Fischer* contains much of the reasoning one would expect to see from a case interpreting a criminal statute. The Court addresses arguments about plain language, surplusage, statutory context, and legislative history. But in the midst of this otherwise usual bit of statutory interpretation, the Court notes that the Government's "interpretation would criminalize a broad swath of prosaic conduct, exposing activists and lobbyists alike to decades in prison."[97] This could include "a peaceful protestor" who might ultimately "face a 20-year sentence."[98]

---

[91] Fischer v. United States, 603 U.S. 480, 485 (2024).

[92] *See, e.g.*, Johnson v. United States, 576 U.S. 591, 594 (2015) (noting that between 2007 and 2015, the "Court ha[d] decided four cases attempting to discern [the] meaning" of the residual clause of the Armed Career Criminal Act's "violent felony" definition).

[93] *See id.*

[94] *See* Yates v. United States, 574 U.S. 528, 531–32 (2015) (holding that 18 U.S.C. § 1519's prohibition on "alter[ing]" a "tangible object" was limited to a tangible object that is "used to record or preserve information").

[95] *Fischer*, 603 U.S. at 483 (quoting 18 U.S.C. § 1512(c)(2)).

[96] *Id.* at 498.

[97] *Id.* at 496.

[98] *Id.*

The dissent had a simple response to this problem. The statute has a high maximum and no minimum sentence because Congress thought "the prohibited conduct may run the gamut from major to minor,"[99] and so "trusted District Courts to impose sentences commensurate with the defendant's particular conduct."[100]

But this limitation was not good enough for the majority. There were other statutes that could cover the same conduct "with far lower maximum sentences."[101] As a result, "[i]t would be improper to substitute for those fine-grained statutory distinctions the charging discretion of prosecutors and the sentencing discretion of district courts."[102]

Three aspects of this argument make it surprising, if not exceptional, and so shed light on why the core of the Court's concern is the case's societal effect. The first is the aspect of the criminal system at the heart of this Article. Duplicative statutes are terribly common in the criminal law.[103] They enable prosecutors to overcharge (or undercharge) as they see fit in order to shape a defendant's criminal exposure and have greater leverage in negotiating a plea.[104] The Court's concern that there may be some overlap in *Fischer* thus rings hollow.

Second, the Court's refusal to recognize as a check not only the discretion of prosecutors, but of judges, is unusual, to say the least.[105] The federal criminal law is saturated with the discretion of these two actors. As already discussed, prosecutors control of charging grants them overwhelming power in the disposition of a criminal case. But to the extent there is another actor approaching them, it is the sentencing judge. In the federal system, sentencing judges are constrained

---

[99] *Id.* at 519 (Barrett, J., dissenting) (quoting *Yates*, 574 U.S. at 569 (Kagan, J., dissenting)).

[100] *Id.*

[101] *Id.* at 494 n.2 (majority opinion).

[102] *Id.*

[103] *See* William Ortman, *The Prosecution Bar*, 101 Wash. U. L. Rev. 123, 133 (2023) ("Overcharging is possible because American criminal statutes contain menus of overlapping offenses from which prosecutors may pick."); Stuntz, *supra* note 9, at 507 ("And federal and state codes alike are filled with overlapping crimes, such that a single criminal incident typically violates a half dozen or more prohibitions.").

[104] Ortman, *supra* note 103, at 133 ("Overcharging is legal, so long as all charges are supported by probable cause, frequently used, and an enormously valuable tool for inducing defendants to plead guilty.").

[105] *See, e.g.*, Chafetz, *supra* note 1 (manuscript at 2) (noting the differential treatment with which the Court describes the judiciary as against the other branches of government).

only by statutory maximums and minimums, and their decisions are reviewed with significant deference.[106]

Finally, notice what is absent from this argument: the First Amendment. The Court purports to be concerned with the statute's effect on protesting and obvious political speech like lobbying, but the constitutional amendment that would protect those things is not mentioned, much less discussed. Of course, one obvious reason for this lack of discussion is that Fischer, perhaps smartly given that his alleged underlying conduct was breaking into the Capitol and getting into a fight with police, did not raise a First Amendment defense.[107]

What the Court's treatment of this issue suggests is that it was not concerned with duplicative statutes, or prosecutorial or judicial discretion, generally, nor was it concerned with the vagaries of First Amendment jurisprudence. Instead, the Court was concerned with the effect that empowering prosecutors and sentencing judges would have on a particular aspect of society that this case represents. And that concern extends beyond the formal protections of the First Amendment.

This concern is unsurprising. The attack on the Capitol on January 6 that Fischer took part in was unquestionably violent, illegal, and just as surely, deeply political. While one would hope that the Court did not want to protect the exact form of this political action, it could rationally be concerned that broadly interpreting this statute would allow the government to target other less violent but still unpopular political actors in the future. That is especially so given that, as was the case here, the people being prosecuted may well be the political opponents of the party in power.

Through this lens, we can see why the Society Cases are not limited to those involving Presidents and other politically or economically powerful individuals. The same need for narrower substantive law and reduced discretion can arise when a regular citizen takes sufficiently powerful, extreme, or unpopular actions in these spheres, too.

E. THE OUTER BOUNDS OF THE SOCIETY CASES

This Part has thus far discussed the Society Cases primarily through exemplars. That is because identifying the Society Cases as a clearly

---

[106] *See* United States v. Booker, 543 U.S. 220 (2005); Gall v. United States, 552 U.S. 38 (2007).

[107] *See Fischer*, 603 U.S. at 484.

delineated group can be difficult. Since the Court does not explicitly state that it is making the analytical move identified here, the outer bounds of this category can be fuzzy. Indeed, the phenomenon described in this Article is, when sufficiently loosely defined, capacious enough to capture essentially every case in which the courts recognize that their decision will have effects on society beyond the dispute before them. In other words, nearly every precedential case might, in this overly loose sense, be one of the Society Cases.

But there are some lines that can be drawn. First, the Society Cases involve the Court adding procedural or analytic hurdles that are in addition to its normal analysis. So the Court will engage in the expected statutory interpretation questions, for example, but it will also deal with a separation of powers problem or an atypical suspicion of government discretion as a tool to cabin the worst outcomes. Second, and perhaps most importantly, the analytical move at the heart of the Society Cases is about the interaction between the societal role and the law, not about the interaction between the individual and the law. This is why many famous, societally impactful cases are not necessarily Society Cases. Two groups of cases help to illuminate these lines: those involving qualified immunity and individual rights cases.

Qualified immunity cases rarely involve powerful actors like Presidents or governors and instead provide protection for the many usually nameless officials who keep our governments functioning. It is hard to imagine *every* suit against a government official being equivalent to a suit against a governor, an Enron executive, or the President. But analytically, these cases seem to fit.

Begin with the core concern at the heart of the Society Cases: an untenable match between the stakes of the case and the usual balance of substantive breadth cabined by discretion. As for breadth, in these cases the courthouse doors are open (or at least the Court perceives them as open).[108] Particularly since incorporation, the growth of both federal and state governments in the twentieth century, and the use of Section 1983 to impose damages liability, the opportunities for government officials to be held liable for violating the Constitution are manifold.[109]

---

[108] *See* Schwartz, *supra* note 16, at 10–11 (noting that "some feared that *Monroe v. Pape* had opened the federal courthouse doors too wide").

[109] *See* Monroe v. Pape, 365 U.S. 167, 170–88 (1961) (noting the incorporation of the prohibition on unreasonable searches and seizures to the states and holding that an individual

And here too there is a discretionary check. Usually, the flood of civil litigation is stemmed by the same sorts of resource constraints and discretionary choices that operate in the criminal or government investigation sphere. Only here, the resource constraint is the cost in time and money of civil litigation against any possible, often meager, recovery, and the discretionary actors are the civil rights lawyers who screen cases for both sizable recoveries and meritoriousness.[110]

The Court has expressly stated its concern that these cases, ostensibly based on the individual wrongful action of a person acting outside of their official capacity (and doctrinally based on a legal fiction to this effect),[111] would have a broader effect on the operation of government by causing overdeterrence.[112] To combat this societal effect, it created immunity doctrines that act as an additional guard on top of the usual substantive and procedural constraints on civil liability. From this perspective, qualified immunity cases may be a core example of the Society Cases.

Why then do I say that they sit at the category's outer bounds? Perhaps the main objection would be that it is difficult to imagine that every Section 1983 civil rights case falls within the same category as a case against the President. Courts, after all, do not seem to be going out of their way to inject novel arguments into every case against a prison guard brought by a pro se incarcerated person.

But one way to see the difference between the Society Cases' core and periphery on this front is to recognize the distinction between the Court and the courts. The many qualified immunity decisions issued by the courts every year are not (or at least not always) part of

---

officer could be held liable under Section 1983 for violating that prohibition while acting under color of law).

[110] *See* Joanna C. Schwartz, *Civil Rights Ecosystems*, 118 Mich. L. Rev. 1539, 1559 (2020) ("[P]laintiffs' attorneys, who usually take civil rights cases on contingency, have strong incentives to select the cases most likely to win and decline the cases least likely to be successful.").

[111] *See* Scheuer v. Rhodes, 416 U.S. 232, 237 (1974) ("Ex parte Young teaches that when a state officer acts under a state law in a manner violative of the Federal Constitution, he 'comes into conflict with the superior authority of that Constitution, and he is in that case stripped of his official or representative character and is subjected in his person to the consequences of his individual conduct.'" (quoting *Ex parte* Young, 209 U.S. 123, 159–60 (1908))).

[112] *See* Harlow v. Fitzgerald, 457 U.S. 800, 814 (1982) (arguing that "it cannot be disputed seriously that claims frequently run against the innocent as well as the guilty—at a cost not only to the defendant officials, but to society as a whole," with costs including "the danger that fear of being sued will 'dampen the ardor of all but the most resolute, or the most irresponsible [public officials], in the unflinching discharge of their duties'" (quoting Gregoire v. Biddle, 177 F.2d 579, 581 (2d Cir. 1949))).

the Society Cases. That is because they do not fit one of that category's core factors: the courts adding unexpected hurdles to the resolution of the case as a result of a societal role. Instead, these decisions are best described as the lower courts' attempt at applying the Supreme Court's established jurisprudence. In other words, the doctrinal innovations and other derivations from the Court's trends that mark the Society Cases are absent.

The *Supreme Court's* immunity decisions, however, and particularly those involving qualified immunity, seem to fit the bill to a tee. As I have already discussed, the Court created the modern qualified immunity doctrine in order to address what it feared would be the wider societal ramifications of the usual processes of civil litigation against actors associated with the various branches of government.[113] This governmental functioning is of course part of society that it regularly recognizes as one to be protected from litigation-based interference. More than this, the Court until very recently has reached out to act against its trends to decide these cases. While the number of cases decided by the Court dwindled, it nevertheless would regularly grasp into the lower courts to decide qualified immunity cases.[114] And these cases were not charting new legal frontiers. Acting against its own instructions about the sorts of cases that it takes and decides, the Court was regularly engaging in what seemed to be error correction.[115] The Court's primary goal seemed to be telling (or, in some cases, chiding) the lower courts when they failed to treat with sufficient rigor the requirement for a constitutional violation to have crossed the bounds of clearly established law.[116]

More than this, as in the President cases, when the Court has dealt with the combination of qualified immunity and a particularly societally important person, the importance of that role has reshaped the law. In *Ashcroft v. Iqbal*, which involved alleged discrimination against Arab Muslims in the wake of 9/11 by the Attorney General and FBI Director, the Court's concern for the imposition of litigation on

---

[113] *See id.*

[114] *See* Adam A. Davidson, *Procedural Losses and the Pyrrhic Victory of Abolishing Qualified Immunity*, 99 Wash. U. L. Rev. 1459, 1471–72 (2022).

[115] *Id.* at 1473–74.

[116] *See, e.g.*, Kisela v. Hughes, 584 U.S. 100, 104 (2018) ("This Court has 'repeatedly told courts—and the Ninth Circuit in particular—not to define clearly established law at a high level of generality.'" (quoting City of San Francisco v. Sheehan, 575 U.S. 600, 613 (2015))).

high-ranking officials was part of the reason it both narrowed *Bivens* liability and expanded the reach of its then-new plausibility pleading standard.[117]

This discussion of qualified immunity highlights an additional feature of the Society Cases. These cases are disproportionately likely to come from the Supreme Court. Indeed, one easy way to see this is simply to note the number of reversals, and the reason for them, across the cases discussed thus far. The lower courts will often treat these cases like any other, leading the Supreme Court to reverse, at least in part, because of the greater weight it puts onto those factors, like the separation of powers or skepticism of deference to the government, that bring the case into the category of Society Cases. But the Supreme Court is also institutionally positioned to create Society Cases. It alone acts with an eye towards the full precedential ramifications of every case it decides. While lower courts are forced to decide cases through mandatory jurisdiction, the Court chooses almost every case on its docket.[118] And of course, while the lower courts can be overturned by the Supreme Court or disagreed with by their sister circuits, the Court does and must remain cognizant that it has the final word nationally. This institutional position makes the Supreme Court unlike any other court and perhaps allows it to recognize when some cases are not like any other cases.

Finally, one last way to draw a line around the Society Cases is to look at famous cases that hinge on a determination of individual rights. Distinguishing these cases highlights that the analytical move that defines the Society Cases is about the interaction between the societal role and the law, not about the relationship between the individual and the law. This means that many famous, societally impactful cases are not necessarily Society Cases.

Take as an example *Lawrence v. Texas*, which declared unconstitutional laws criminalizing consensual same-sex sexual conduct.[119] It is difficult, if not impossible, to say that *Lawrence* was not driven in part by the growing societal acceptance of LGBTQ+ people in United States society. But what distinguishes a case like *Lawrence* from the Society Cases is that the legal analysis hinged not on the

---

[117] *See* Ashcroft v. Iqbal, 556 U.S. 662 (2009).

[118] Relatedly, future analysis might interrogate how the Court's control of its docket through the certiorari process influences the Society Cases.

[119] 539 U.S. 558, 578 (2003).

relationship between the societal role of LGBTQ+ people and the law, but on the relationship between the *person* and the individual rights granted to them by the Constitution. That is not to say that a case involving individual rights can never be a Society Case. Instead, it is simply to say that a societally impactful individual rights case does not *automatically* become a Society Case.

II. Defending the Society Cases

A. Defending the Society Cases as They Are

> *In our judicial system, 'the public has a right to every man's evidence.' Since the earliest days of the Republic, 'every man' has included the President of the United States.*[120]
>
> *No man is above the law, and no man is below it.*[121]

These statements highlight the deep roots of the belief that in the eyes of the law, all persons are equal. It is that deeply embedded belief that makes the Society Cases an uncomfortable fit for our jurisprudence. These cases suggest that, by dint of the position they have attained, some people deserve special dispensation from the usual operation of the law. From this perspective, none of the Society Cases should exist, or at least none of them should have reached the Supreme Court. Instead, they should have been decided in the many tomes of the Federal Reporter, or the unpublished decisions of the District Courts, where the vast bulk of the criminal prosecutions, subpoenas, and trial scheduling decisions end up.

But the awkward truth is that the people in the Society Cases are differently situated than most other litigants. And the Court's treatment of them is a rational recognition of this difference. Of course, that is not to say that the Court gets it right in every one of these cases. Each of the Society Cases might be rightly or wrongly decided along numerous grounds. The Court may make a misstep in its statutory or constitutional analysis, or it may put too much or too little weight

---

[120] Trump v. Vance, 591 U.S. 786, 791 (2020); *id.* at 791 n.1 ("This maxim traces at least as far back as Lord Chancellor Hardwicke, in a 1742 parliamentary debate.").

[121] Victor Mather, *A Brief History of the Phrase 'No One Is Above the Law,'* N.Y. Times (June 13, 2024), https://www.nytimes.com/2024/06/13/us/politics/trump-biden-no-one-is-above-the-law.html (quoting President Theodore Roosevelt, Third Annual Message (Dec. 7, 1903), https://www.presidency.ucsb.edu/documents/third-annual-message-16).

onto those sorts of additional factors that raise the case into the category of the Society Cases.

Although this Part will not defend any of the Society Cases on the merits, it will defend their existence as a category. I argue that the Court is correct to be more skeptical of exercises of government discretion and the suitability of standard adjudication processes in the Society Cases. Additionally, recognizing and discussing what sets these cases apart is laudable because it encourages both judicial transparency and doctrinal development. In the alternative world where these cases are nominally treated like any other, it is difficult to imagine jurists managing to completely ignore that they involve powerful people like the President or political actions like the January 6 assault on the Capitol. Instead, judges' knowledge of those realities would fight against attempts at judicial impartiality, perhaps skewing these cases in recognizable, but unstated, ways. More than this, recognizing what makes these cases different allows the Court to engage thoughtfully with difficult issues that arise when the law reaches into the varying parts of our society.[122]

Perhaps the simplest reason to be skeptical of the government's exercise of discretion in cases like this one is that the government itself is skeptical of its ability to neutrally exercise its discretion in at least some of these cases. The use of special prosecutors is the most obvious example of this. At the federal level, special prosecutors are able to be appointed not only in cases of a conflict of interest but also in "other extraordinary circumstances."[123]

But even outside of those exceptional cases that involve a special prosecutor, more banal professional ambitions also warrant increased scrutiny in these cases. Participating in litigation involving high-profile people or incidents is one way for an ambitious lawyer to build the sort of reputation that can propel them to higher office.[124] Of course, this

---

[122] One response to this point is that perhaps courts should stay out of these conflicts altogether. But that is, ultimately, impossible. Because these issues arise in litigation, whether criminal or civil, the courts would always have to be involved at some level. But even if the courts chose to apply something like the political question or abstention doctrines to these cases, that decision still involves the courts engaging with these issues in order to explain why their refusal to recognize or exercise jurisdiction was proper.

[123] 28 C.F.R. § 600.1(a) (2024).

[124] *See, e.g.*, Sara Sun Beale, *Rethinking the Identity and Role of United States Attorneys*, 6 Ohio St. J. Crim. L. 369, 421 (2009) ("A U.S. Attorney, however appointed, has the opportunity to be involved in high profile cases and to develop the kinds of contacts and name recognition that could pave the way to elective office or a judicial appointment.").

sort of targeting of high-profile individuals has benefits and drawbacks that have long been the source of debate.[125] The takeaway here is simply that by recognizing that these cases involve not just an individual, but an individual with an important societal position, the Court can better address the full scope of issues that these cases present.

Take *Fischer* as an example. As alleged, Fischer's actions on January 6 obviously broke numerous laws.[126] Some of Fischer's charges, like "the felony offense of Assaulting, Resisting, or Impeding Certain Officers, in violation of 18 U.S.C. § 111(a)(1),"[127] even seem supported by Fischer's own Facebook posts, which claimed that he was inside the Capitol and "pushed police back about 25 feet."[128] And Fischer could even still have been found guilty of the 18 U.S.C. § 1512(c)(2) charge that the Court narrowed.[129] As Justice Jackson pointed out in concurrence, certifying the Electoral College vote was an "official proceeding [that] plainly used certain records, documents, or objects—including, among others, those relating to the electoral votes themselves," and "Fischer's conduct, as alleged here, involved the impairment (or the attempted impairment) of the availability or integrity of things used during the January 6 proceeding" in ways that might violate the statute.[130]

Fischer, then, is hardly a sympathetic individual, and his actions seem near the core of even the narrowed charge he faced. But by focusing entirely on Fischer as an individual criminal defendant, we miss the importance of the government's attempt to set a broad precedent. While not all protests are disruptive,[131] many are, and for many

---

[125] *See generally* Daniel C. Richman & William J. Stuntz, *Al Capone's Revenge: An Essay on the Political Economy of Pretextual Prosecution*, 105 Colum. L. Rev. 583 (2005).

[126] *See* Fischer v. United States, 603 U.S. 480, 484 (2024).

[127] United States v. Fischer, 64 F.4th 329, 333 (D.C. Cir. 2023); *see also* Miller v. United States, 144 S. Ct. 2706 (2024) (vacating and remanding for further consideration in light of *Fischer*); Lang v. United States, 144 S. Ct. 2706 (2024) (same).

[128] *Fischer*, 603 U.S. at 484.

[129] Fischer was one of the 1,500 January 6 defendants pardoned by President Trump on the first day of his second term. Fatima Moien, *Pardoned North Cornwall Police Officer Charged in Jan. 6 Riots Says He Did Nothing Wrong*, CBS 21 News (Jan. 22, 2025, 1:05 PM), https://local21news.com/news/local/former-lebanon-officer-gets-pardoned-for-jan-6-says-no-crimes-committed-donal-trump-president-pardons-executive-orders-lebanon-county-pa.

[130] *Fischer*, 603 U.S. at 505–06 (Jackson, J., concurring).

[131] *See* Laura Rene McNeal, *From Hoodies to Kneeling During the National Anthem: The Colin Kaepernick Effect and Its Implications for K-12 Sports*, 78 La. L. Rev. 145, 146–47 (2017) (describing Colin Kaepernick's "act of kneeling during the national anthem in protest of police brutality against African-American males").

that is both their point and the source of their effectiveness.[132] Even protests that do not physically disrupt or obstruct anyone can gain power from the incidental disruption they cause.[133]

The system for legal challenges to this type of issue is designed in a way that could seriously deter protest even if protestors are ultimately not convicted. A facial challenge on First Amendment grounds seems doomed from the outset, given that there is a clear core of document destruction activity that is not expressive, and so would not raise First Amendment hackles.[134] But, as Fischer's attorney noted, even an as-applied challenge would cause significant harm to a defendant.[135] That is because in our criminal system, often the process is the punishment.[136] At best, an as-applied challenge would happen only after an arrest, charging, and potentially pre-trial detention in a motion to dismiss the indictment. But those motions to dismiss indictments face an incredibly high standard because the government need provide only minimal information in the indictment.[137] As courts routinely note, "summary judgment does not exist in federal criminal procedure."[138] Whether the government's prosecution offends the Constitution, then, is likely only to be fully determinable at the close of the government's evidence at trial, when the full facts it is relying on are known.[139] In the meantime, the accused person must have the Sword of Damocles hanging over their head, whether they are incarcerated pre-trial or not, in the form of a possible twenty-year federal prison sentence.

---

[132] *See* Note, *Equity on the Campus: The Limits of Injunctive Regulation of University Protest*, 80 YALE L.J. 987, 996 & nn.53–56 (1971) (describing protests on college campuses).

[133] *See id.* at 996 n.54 (describing how the "inevitable accoutrements of any mass demonstration" may cause disruption); Transcript of Oral Argument at 51–59, *Fischer*, 603 U.S. 480 (No. 23-5572) (discussing protests that have occurred during Supreme Court argument and protestors blocking bridges).

[134] For similar reasons, a challenge based on the First Amendment overbreadth doctrine seems unavailing. *See* New York v. Ferber, 458 U.S. 747, 768–70 (1982).

[135] Transcript of Oral Argument, *supra* note 133, at 109–11.

[136] *See* Davidson, *supra* note 16, at 1046 (noting that "every [police] stop carries the risk of pretrial incarceration and disruptions to work, childcare, and other responsibilities as a natural result of detention, as well as the numerous consequences of even a 'minor' criminal conviction" (footnote omitted)). *See generally* MALCOLM M. FEELEY, THE PROCESS IS THE PUNISHMENT: HANDLING CASES IN A LOWER CRIMINAL COURT (1992).

[137] United States v. Phillips, 690 F. Supp. 3d 268, 276–79 (S.D.N.Y. 2023).

[138] United States v. Aiyer, 33 F.4th 97, 117 (2d Cir. 2022) (quoting United States v. Wedd, 993 F.3d 104, 121 (2d Cir. 2021)).

[139] *See, e.g.*, *Phillips*, 690 F. Supp. 3d at 292–93 (denying a pre-trial due process challenge as premature).

Of course, this is a variation of the same problem faced by every federal criminal defendant. But as is true in all of the Society Cases, here we think that something about these defendants' role in society makes them require exceptional protection. That something in this instance is the expressive, and sometimes expressly political, content of their allegedly criminal actions. Where formal criminal procedure and First Amendment doctrines fail to capture these concerns, the looser but more holistic analysis of the Society Cases can succeed.

That is, again, not to say that combining Fischer's individual conduct with his societal role led to the right outcome, or even that the Court engaged in the right societal analysis. It is only to say that ignoring that Fischer inhabited a distinct societal role that was intertwined with the individual conduct he was indicted for would be a worse, less fulsome analysis. That is so even though arguments related to the societal role do not fit within the legal tools that we usually use for statutory construction.

And ultimately, it is the allowance for a more holistic analysis that enables both the transparency and doctrinal development benefits that the Society Cases bring. Treating the defendants in the Society Cases as if they were similarly positioned to every other criminal defendant would require judges to ignore (or pretend to ignore) the other highly salient aspects of the case to which they are surely apprised. This, for a variety of reasons, seems unlikely. What's more, even though judges might be able to formally ignore these societal considerations, it seems likely that doctrine would continue to be shaped by these considerations *sub silentio*.

To explain why that is, we need not look beyond the criminal system, as critics have long suggested similar problems arise in the contexts of the exclusionary rule and jury nullification. "Exclusion [as a remedy] suffers a serious psychological problem. Judges are reluctant to free obviously guilty criminals."[140] The result of this reluctance is that, in the individual case, some judges make confounding factual determinations in suppression hearings,[141] but more broadly,

---

[140] Donald Dripps, *The Case for the Contingent Exclusionary Rule*, 38 Am. Crim. L. Rev. 1, 2 (2001); *see also* William J. Stuntz, *Warrants and Fourth Amendment Remedies*, 77 Va. L. Rev. 881, 911–13 (1991) (discussing the problem of judicial bias, in the form of having an "inherently unsympathetic" claimant, in suppression hearings).

[141] *See* Dripps, *supra* note 140, at 21–22 (discussing a case in which the district court credited the testimony of a law enforcement officer who "had given discredited testimony in another case" over a polygraph test, an uninvolved airline employee, and the fact that the

substantive constitutional protections shrink in order to avoid excluding evidence.[142] Despite the lack of transparent and honest reasoning by the judiciary, these actions do not go unnoticed. "Courthouse regulars will sometimes speak as though Fourth Amendment fraud were part of established jurisprudence."[143] Rules like "the kilogram exception" (meaning don't expect evidence to be suppressed if it's more than a kilogram of certain drugs) and the power of "'dropsy' testimony" (police saying that a defendant happened to drop the evidence law enforcement found, putting it into plain view) become well known, even if unwritten, rules.[144]

In the suppression context, judges must give at least some reasoning, and because suppression hearings are relatively common, these sorts of unspoken trends and rules are identifiable. But Society Cases seem noticeably rarer, and the sorts of doctrinal issues that drive them are, unlike in the suppression context, often orthogonal to the core legal issues that would be discussed if they were a "normal" case.

The Society Cases, then, would seem to suffer from the same psychological problems as those that arise in the suppression context, but they would be less readily susceptible to identification by litigators and commentators. Judges would be influenced by a desire to take account of a litigant's societal role but unable to do so forthrightly; they would be forced to twist the facts and law in unseemly, but predictable, directions.

Jury nullification takes this problem a step further and allows us to see what might happen when transparency is at its nadir. Jury nullification, "when jurors vote to acquit a defendant despite believing that the defendant is guilty under the law and that the prosecution has proved its case beyond a reasonable doubt," is an inherently available tactic in our system because of the secrecy of jury deliberations.[145] Despite its inherent nature, there are essentially no legal guiderails to shape the practice, and judges overwhelmingly resist it.[146] Indeed,

---

defendants did not have a key to locked suitcases (containing dozens of kilograms of cocaine) that they allegedly consented to a search of).

[142] *See id.* at 2–5 (discussing the Fourth Amendment and equal protection).

[143] *Id.* at 21.

[144] *See id.* at 20–21.

[145] Caisa Elizabeth Royer, *The Disobedient Jury: Why Lawmakers Should Codify Jury Nullification*, 102 Cornell L. Rev. 1401, 1402 (2017).

[146] *Id.*

the Second Circuit has gone so far as to hold that "trial courts have the duty to forestall or prevent" jury nullification, including by disallowing attorneys from presenting arguments for it.[147] As a result, while observers might speculate,[148] it is only possible to truly identify jury nullification if a juror comes out and says that's what they've done in a post-trial interview.

Jury nullification's black box thus gives a preview of what the Society Cases might look like if the courts were forced to address them purely within the context of the legal structure that would apply to an individual regardless of their societal position. In both nullification and the Society Cases, legal actors are forced to grapple with not only an individual who may have broken the law, but with the effect that individual's actions, and especially our legal system's response to those actions, has on society more broadly. And in both, the specter of differential treatment arises most often when the defendant is an obvious stand-in for some broader issue within society. Those issues are varied, ranging from the role of the President and other powerful actors,[149] to the value of protest of all kinds,[150] and even to race relations (whether laudably or maliciously),[151] homelessness,[152] and the ability of people to resist the government with force.[153] The question in all of these examples, as in the Society Cases, is not whether the societal impacts of their outcomes will be relevant, but how. Jury nullification shows that without a forthright Society Case-like analysis,

[147] *In re* United States, 945 F.3d 616, 626–27 (2d Cir. 2019).

[148] *See, e.g.*, Paul Butler, *Racially Based Jury Nullification: Black Power in the Criminal Justice System*, 105 Yale L.J. 677, 678–79 (1995) (describing the trial of former Washington D.C. Mayor Marion Berry).

[149] *See supra* Section I.B–C.

[150] *See supra* Section I.D.

[151] *See* United States v. Thomas, 116 F.3d 606, 616 (2d Cir. 1997) (discussing both "acquittals in fugitive slave cases" and "the two hung juries in the 1964 trials of Byron De La Beckwith in Mississippi for the murder of NAACP field secretary Medgar Evers, or the 1955 acquittal of J.W. Millam and Roy Bryant for the murder of fourteen-year-old Emmett Till"). *See generally* Butler, *supra* note 148.

[152] *See* Jonathan Edwards, *A Volunteer Was Cited for Feeding Homeless People. A Jury Acquitted Him.*, Wash. Post (Aug. 9, 2023), https://www.washingtonpost.com/nation/2023/08/09/houston-food-not-bombs-acquitted.

[153] *See, e.g.*, Tay Wiles, *Why the Bundy Crew Keeps Winning in Court*, High Country News (Aug. 31, 2017), https://www.hcn.org/articles/cliven-bundy-why-the-bundy-crowd-keeps-winning-in-court (discussing acquittals in cases about "the 2014 armed standoff between the federal government and supporters of rancher Cliven Bundy").

there would still be commentary about how litigants' societal roles impacted the outcome of cases. But commentators would be forced to speculate even more about the Court's now-unwritten motivations.

Thus far, this Part has argued that given the inevitable role that broader societal issues will play in these cases, the Court has rightly abandoned the idea that it should focus entirely on the individual by applying the general legal structure to that individual. Instead, by blending the individual and their societal role in the Society Cases, the Court enables a more transparent and holistic analysis of the issues that these important cases raise.

This limited defense is based on the Society Cases as they are. The Court has overwhelmingly used the blending of the individual and their societal role as a tool to give additional protections to people who are, if not powerful individually, part of a group that has significant economic, social, or political power. That, however, is not an inherent feature of the category.

B. DEFENDING THE SOCIETY CASES FOR WHAT THEY COULD BE

This Article has told a story about the Society Cases that is likely troubling to those who would oppose this country's race and class hierarchies. Even if the Society Cases are, as the preceding Section argued, on some level rightly decided, the fact that the beneficiaries of the additional legal protections they entail are disproportionately white and wealthy suggests that we should perhaps be skeptical that their effects are pro-social. Part I of this Article is replete with examples of the downsides of the Court's choice to blend the individual and societal role. The Court has protected government officials who appear plainly corrupt, violent and discriminatory law enforcement, and even alleged violent insurrectionists of both the protestor and presidential varieties.

This reality is reflective of the society in which the Court acts. As Part III discusses in more depth, the race and class skew of the Society Cases exists because the Court operates in a society that maintains race and class hierarchies that disproportionately exclude non-white and non-wealthy individuals from the halls of power. That is why the analytical move that identifies the Society Cases can both have racialized and classed effects and be race- and class-neutral, regardless of whether the Court acts with discriminatory intent or a pure desire to get the individual case before it correct. The possibility for the Society

Cases to further structural inequality is very real.[154] For these reasons, a reader would not be out-of-bounds in believing that the analytical move of blending the individual and societal role in the Society Cases should be rejected.

But even if this negative view describes the Society Cases as they are, another defense is possible based on what the Society Cases *could be*. To see this possibility, we can look again to qualified immunity, particularly to that brief moment in 2020 in which the entire country believed that we might have a Reconstruction-level racial reckoning. That time, which may now feel like a distant past, involved some genuinely shocking moments by the judiciary. Courts around the country issued statements recognizing the ongoing reality of individual and structural racism and issuing support for taking action on racial justice.[155] The Illinois Supreme Court, for example, announced the recruitment of a Chief Diversity and Inclusion Officer, saying, "Racism exists, whether it be actualized as individual racism, institutional racism or structural racism, and it undermines our democracy, the fair and equitable administration of justice, and severely diminishes individual constitutional protections and safeguards of full citizenship with the attendant rights and benefits sacred to all."[156] One Florida state court judge even resigned so that he could be free to speak about racial (in)justice.[157]

Other judges, though, did this work from the bench. Unsurprisingly, cases raising qualified immunity provided an excellent vehicle for judicial intervention in that moment. Some of those interventions were powerful, but unsurprising. Judge Carlton Reeves' opinion granting qualified immunity in *Jamison v. McClendon* gained significant

---

[154] *See infra* Section III.B.

[155] *See State Court Statements on Racial Justice*, NAT'L CTR. FOR ST. CTS., https://www.ncsc.org/consulting-and-research/areas-of-expertise/racial-justice/state-activities/state-court-statements-on-racial-justice (collecting such statements); *see also* Michael Catalano, Todd Curry, Michael Romano & Matthew Walz, *"We Are a Part of the Problem They Protest": Judges, Representation and Racial Justice Statements*, POLS., GRPS. & IDENTITIES 1 (2024) (exploring why state courts did and did not make racial justice statements in 2020).

[156] Press Release, Illinois Supreme Court, Supreme Court Releases Statement on Racial Justice, Next Steps for Judicial Branch (June 22, 2020), https://www.illinoiscourts.gov/News/378/Supreme-Court-Releases-Statement-on-Racial-Justice-Next-Steps-for-Judicial-Branch/news-detail [https://perma.cc/5CXM-UYKV].

[157] Mike Kiniry & Julie Glenn, *Senior Judge Retires to Speak up About Racial Inequality*, WGCU (Sept. 16, 2020, 11:44 AM EDT), https://news.wgcu.org/show/gulf-coast-life/2020-09-16/senior-judge-retires-to-speak-up-about-racial-inequality.

attention for its lengthy, heartbreaking discussion of the history and effects of unjustified, racialized police action and the doctrines that protect it.[158] Likewise, in *Stewart v. City of Euclid, Ohio*, Judge Bernice Donald lamented the majority's grant of qualified immunity, concluding her concurrence by stating:

> I find myself writing separately about the dangers of unchecked police powers with unsettling and increasing frequency. Six years ago, I dissented from a decision affirming summary judgment for several officers who killed Leroy Hughes, an African American man suffering from mental illness, by shocking him with tasers twelve times in five minutes. . . . In that dissent, I recalled the names of Amadou Diallo, Sean Bell, Oscar Grant, Jonathan Ferrell, and others. And I exhorted this Court and its readers not to "ignore the seeds of systemic inequalities sown in our Nation's history and lain bare by diligent review."
>
> We have new names today: George Floyd, Elijah McClain, Rayshard Brooks, and too many others. The world knows why they died. The same seeds whose bitter fruit killed Leroy Hughes killed them too. And on March 13, 2017, in Euclid, Ohio, they killed Luke Stewart. . . .
>
> Luke Stewart should be alive today. He was unarmed, unsuspected of committing a serious felony, and behind the wheel of a stationary vehicle when Rhodes opened fire into his torso, chest, neck, and wrist. Qualified immunity should not shield Rhodes from the consequences of that unreasonable decision.[159]

Both Judge Reeves and Judge Donald have been consistent proponents of civil rights, racial justice, and police accountability.[160] But at least for that summer, they were joined by what some would view as unlikely allies. To start, note that Judge Donald's opinion in *Stewart* was only a dissent in part. That is because the majority ultimately reversed the district court in two important respects.

The district court had dismissed Stewart's case against Euclid and several of its police officers entirely, but the majority revived Stewart's *state law* claims. It was able to do this for two reasons: First, Ohio's officer immunity was distinct from federal qualified immunity, protecting officers unless their "acts or omissions were with

---

[158] Jamison v. McClendon, 476 F. Supp. 3d 386, 402–09 (S.D. Miss. 2020); Carrie Johnson, *Judge, Shielding Cop via 'Qualified Immunity,' Asks Whether It Belongs in 'Dustbin,'* NPR (Aug. 6, 2020, 5:01 AM ET), https://www.npr.org/2020/08/06/899489809/judge-shielding-cop-via-qualified-immunity-asks-whether-it-belongs-in-dustbin.

[159] Stewart v. City of Euclid, 970 F.3d 667, 683–84 (6th Cir. 2020) (Donald, J., concurring in part) (citations omitted).

[160] *See, e.g.*, Sheffey v. City of Covington, 564 F. App'x 783, 796–97 (6th Cir. 2014) (Donald, J., dissenting); Green v. Thomas, 734 F. Supp. 3d 532, 547, 566 (S.D. Miss. 2024).

malicious purpose, in bad faith, or in a wanton or reckless manner," as opposed to violating clearly established law.[161] Second, and more importantly, the majority could take this step because it did something it did not have to do: It evaluated whether there was a substantive constitutional violation for use of excessive force and answered that there was.[162]

Qualified immunity, remember, has two prongs. One questions whether the law was clearly established on a particular point at a particular time, but the other asks whether there was a constitutional violation at all. Courts, importantly, do not have to, and often do not, decide whether a constitutional violation occurred, instead focusing on whether any possible violation was clearly established. But in *Stewart*, despite finding that there was no clearly established law on point, the Sixth Circuit decided to hold that the police officer's actions (at least when construed favorably to Stewart) constituted excessive force in violation of the Fourth Amendment.[163] And it was this holding that allowed the majority to further say that the officer should not have state law immunity.[164]

Stewart, by itself, bears only some of the hallmarks of a Society Case. The concurrence, but not the majority, highlights the importance that the officer's societal position has in the case. And the majority's treatment of the case, while departing from the most common course the courts take in qualified immunity cases, is fully contemplated by the Supreme Court's qualified immunity doctrine, which always reserves the option for the courts to answer the underlying constitutional question. Further, perhaps answering that question was the right call here simply because of the interaction between the federal constitutional question and Ohio state law.

But *Stewart* begins to look more anomalous if it is treated as one star in a constellation. I have discussed some of the others—the many judicial and non-judicial statements and actions that made up the summer of 2020. But the brightest star next to *Stewart* is another case

[161] *Stewart*, 970 F.3d at 677 (quoting Ohio Rev. Code Ann. § 2744.03(A)(6)(b) (West 2016)).

[162] *Id.* at 674.

[163] *Id.* at 672–74.

[164] *Id.* at 676–77.

involving the City of Euclid decided around the same time, *Wright v. City of Euclid, Ohio*.[165]

Both cases involved excessive force, and both involved a similarly egregious set of background facts giving rise to a *Monell* claim against the city. While Stewart's *Monell* claim failed because of a lack of clearly established law, Wright's claim succeeded. Looking at the facts of these cases shows why. The City of Euclid's use of force training was as ineffective as it was offensive, and it was *comically* offensive. So comical, in fact, that it included a video of a Chris Rock bit titled *How Not to Get Your Ass Kicked by the Police!* that made fun of Rodney King and included lines like "[e]verybody knows, if the police have to come and get you, they're bringing an ass kicking with 'em," and "[i]f have you to give a friend a ride, get a white friend. A white friend can be the difference between a ticket and a bullet in the ass."[166] It also contained several memes of police officers using blatantly unconstitutional force.[167] The same officer who did this training also reviewed the allegations of excessive force that the department received.[168] Perhaps unsurprisingly, neither he nor the police chief had ever "heard of a use-of-force incident by another Euclid officer that he deemed inappropriate."[169]

Even with these sorts of horrendous facts, it is surprising to see a court allow a *Monell* claim to proceed. *Monell* liability is notoriously difficult to prove. Critiques of the doctrine have abounded for decades,[170] and overcoming *Monell* is an even more arduous process than overcoming qualified immunity. Joanna Schwartz recently found that "[i]t is far more difficult for plaintiffs to prove *Monell* claims against municipalities than it is for plaintiffs to defeat qualified immunity when raised by individual government defendants."[171]

A *Monell* claim's success, while anomalous, is not so outrageous as to make a case become one of the Society Cases by itself. Instead, it is at best a signal that the societal roles in the case may be at play.

---

[165] Wright v. City of Euclid, 962 F.3d 852 (6th Cir. 2020).

[166] *Id.* at 862–63 (quoting InsaneNutter, *Chris Rock - How Not to Get Your Ass Kicked by the Police!*, YouTube (Feb. 2, 2007), https://www.youtube.com/watch?v=uj0mtxXEGE8 [https://perma.cc/NU2W-MGLN]).

[167] *Id.*

[168] *Id.*

[169] *Id.* at 864.

[170] *See* Joanna C. Schwartz, *Municipal Immunity*, 109 Va. L. Rev. 1181, 1198–1200 (2023).

[171] *Id.* at 1187.

Here the strongest signal that a societal role was shaping the opinion came in *Wright*'s conclusion. There, the Sixth Circuit ended its opinion not with a statement about *Monell* liability, or about constitutional law at all. Instead, it cited to the Law Enforcement Code of Ethics to espouse what it believed to be the role of police in society.[172] Far from engaging in the sort of bad behavior that occurred in this case, it was the duty of the police "to serve the community; to safeguard lives and property; to protect the innocent against deception, the weak against oppression or intimidation and the peaceful against violence or disorder; and to respect the constitutional rights of all to liberty, equality, and justice."[173]

Ultimately, what made this moment a shining example for what the Society Cases could be is how bipartisan the shift was. Both judges in the majority of *Stewart* were Republican appointees, and the author of *Wright*, Judge John K. Bush, was not only a Republican appointee but the previous head of his local chapter of the Federalist Society.[174]

Indeed, even the Supreme Court joined in this particular moment. In one of the few recent cases holding that a lower court went too far in granting qualified immunity, in *Taylor v. Riojas*, the Court found that prison guards holding Taylor in an especially squalid cell for six days were not entitled to qualified immunity because, even if there was a lack of squarely binding precedent, "any reasonable officer should have realized that Taylor's conditions of confinement offended the Constitution."[175] *Taylor* was decided per curiam, with only Justice Thomas registering his unwritten dissent.

But again, the sign that the Court was engaging in something beyond its standard-fare legal analysis came not in the main opinion, but in Justice Alito's concurrence. Justice Alito concurred not to dispute the Court's constitutional analysis, but to register his dissatisfaction with the fact the Court took the case at all. That concurrence mirrored the issues commentators have long raised with the Court's qualified

---

[172] *Wright*, 962 F.3d at 882.

[173] *Id.* (quoting *Law Enforcement Code of Ethics*, Int'l Ass'n of Chiefs of Police, https://web.archive.org/web/20200613153817/https://www.theiacp.org/resources/law-enforcement-code-of-ethics).

[174] Andrew Wolfson, *President Trump Taps Louisville Conservative John K. Bush for Court*, Louisville Courier J. (May 9, 2017, 8:24 AM ET), https://www.courier-journal.com/story/news/politics/2017/05/08/donald-trump-taps-louisville-conservative-john-k-bush-court/101426196.

[175] Taylor v. Riojas, 592 U.S. 7, 9 (2020).

immunity reversals—that they seemingly violated the Court's own rules for accepting certiorari because they "turn[] entirely on an interpretation of the record in one particular case" and "the asserted error consists of ... the misapplication of a properly stated rule of law."[176] Of course, what was different here is that the Court reversed a grant of qualified immunity instead of a denial.

What the cases discussed in this Section show is that although the Society Cases have often been used to protect the powerful, that is not a quality inherent to the category. Instead, recognizing that an individual has a societal role that the courts should be cognizant of could lead them to shape doctrines that protect the powerless and hold the powerful to a higher standard.

III. Race, Class, and Recognizing Society

This Article may be the first, but hopefully will not be the last, word on the Society Cases. That group of cases is simply too diverse and too important for every insight that might be found within them to be exhausted in a single work. But this Article will conclude with two additional insights that analyzing those cases uncovers. First, the Society Cases show that the structure of broad substantive liability and largely unchecked discretion that undergirds our criminal system was not an inevitability. Instead, had the Court recognized the societal impact of "normal" criminal cases as readily as they do the impact in the Society Cases, both narrower substantive law and more rigorously reviewed discretionary choices may have taken hold.

Second, the Society Cases provide a notable example of the downward spiral of structural inequality in action. The special dispensation for the whiter, richer defendants that the Society Cases involve turns race- and class-neutral adjudication into a tool for increasing inequality, masks prejudice by making the prejudiced and race-neutral-justified outcomes the same, and turns many of the most effective moves towards greater equality into suspect race- and class-conscious decision-making.

A. Recognizing the Whole Society

Much of the analysis thus far suggests that the Court's development of the Society Cases is a laudable twist in the Court's jurisprudence,

---

[176] *Id.* at 11 (Alito, J., concurring).

against which commentators have mistakenly fixed their ire. The Society Cases, I have argued, represent an example of the Court properly exercising its role as institutional shepherd to identify cases with outsized societal impact that, if treated like a standard case involving the same legal issues, might cause underappreciated ramifications in the political sphere or empower individual prosecutors (or prosecutor-like actors) to overwhelm the regular functioning of our societal systems. Despite the popular adage that "no one is above the law," it is clear to the point of obviousness that in many ways the President, a governor, or a political protestor—even a violent one—are differently situated from the average person committing a crime. Broadly stated, the argument for the Society Cases is simply that the Court is right to recognize and grapple with that difference instead of letting it pass by unnoticed, or perhaps more realistically, noticed but uncommented on.

But I do not mean to say that there is no problem with the Society Cases. Of course, that the category should exist does not mean that any case within that category was necessarily rightly decided. Beyond this, however, is a deeper issue.

The problem with the Society Cases is that they need to exist at all. This class of cases exists only because the Court has minimized the harm that these same issues cause in the full suite of its criminal jurisprudence.[177] Instead, only when a defendant bearing societal markers that the Court is willing to recognize appears before it does the Court fully appreciate the intrusion that a motivated prosecutor and sweeping criminal statutes can have. For much of the Court, too often the disproportionately Black, Brown, and poor parts of society that it allows to be encircled by the full stretch of the criminal legal system's power seem not to count as "society" worthy of similar protection.

There appear to be two hypotheses one might have about why the sort of special dispensation and protection exists for litigants in the Society Cases, but ultimately they present a false choice. One hypothesis would say that this is an inherent necessity—that wherever

[177] I focus here on the criminal law, but as with the Society Cases generally, the problem extends to all areas where the combination of broad substantive liability is cabined primarily by deferentially reviewed, if not entirely unreviewed, discretion. As discussed throughout the Article, the criminal law seems to be the most salient, largest, and most powerful area where this problem arises, and so it warrants the bulk of the Article's analysis.

we drew the lines around substantive liability and discretion, there would always be a need to treat these litigants to a different, even if not expressly higher, bar. But the other hypothesis would say that the Society Cases exist because the Court discounted to the point of nullity the societal impact in the many similar cases that it hears. And in part because of this discounting, the Court encouraged the system of broad substantive liability cabined by individual discretion for most that it finds intolerable in the Society Cases.

Ultimately, these two hypotheses can converge. The Society Cases do not demand a substantive outcome. Instead, they are about the level and type of analysis that goes into reaching the case's conclusion. Defendants win some Society Cases and lose others, but on the way to that outcome the Court always considers how the individual's societal role will affect the impact of its decision. If the Court had recognized the importance of societal roles throughout criminal law, the Society Cases might not need to exist. Instead, those cases that I call the Society Cases would simply receive the same level of analytical rigor that every other case did.

At this point, a note about what I am *not* arguing seems appropriate. This is not, or at least it need not be, a story about conscious bias. Nor is this an inherently political story, as the appointing party of the Justices is far from a one-to-one match for their votes in these cases. I am not arguing that the Society Cases exist because the members of the Court (or of the courts) are consciously denigrating the value of litigants outside of that class of cases. Indeed, they may believe they are doing the opposite in cases where the broader impact of their jurisprudence is particularly salient.[178] Instead, I am arguing that in the broader set of criminal cases, the functional working of the system built on broad liability and individual discretion is uncritically assumed to encompass any impact an individual's societal role might have, and so the Court feels no need to question—much less to upset—the legal structures it has helped create.[179] When I say that the Court

---

[178] *See, e.g.*, Utah v. Strieff, 579 U.S. 232, 243 (2016) (addressing the possibility of "dragnet searches"); *id.* at 252–54 (Sotomayor, J., dissenting).

[179] *Cf.* Bernard E. Harcourt, *The Influence of Systems Analysis on Criminal Law and Procedure: A Critique of a Style of Judicial Decision-Making* 37 (Columbia L. Sch. Pub. L. Rsch. Paper No. 14-562, 2013), https://scholarship.law.columbia.edu/cgi/viewcontent.cgi?article=3061&context=faculty_scholarship (criticizing the use of systems analytic thinking in judicial decision-making in criminal law and procedure because it "takes for granted the construction of social

does not recognize its broader criminal jurisprudence as impacting society, this is what I mean.

The Society Cases represent a window into an alternate world and show that that world is possible. Fully describing that alternate reality is far beyond the scope of this Article, but we can look to a few examples for a preview. Those examples are *Pulsifer v. United States*[180] and *Utah v. Strieff*.[181]

1. Pulsifer v. United States. The core of *Pulsifer* was a classic criminal law statutory interpretation question. The Court had to decide whether a provision of the First Step Act required defendants subjected to certain mandatory minimum sentences to have all of three traits (A, B, and C), or if having one of those three traits (A, B, or C) allowed them to instead receive an individualized sentence.[182] The vagaries of the statutory analysis are beyond this Article. Instead, what is important here are the arguments the Court did not discuss at all.

As Justice Gorsuch noted in dissent, the government's interpretation of the statute would "guarantee[] thousands more people in the federal criminal justice system will be denied a chance—just a chance—at an individualized sentence."[183] It is telling that even in dissent, Gorsuch does not discuss these thousands of people, and how their incarceration or freedom is likely to have extensive impacts on the communities to which they belong. Instead, Gorsuch gives a lengthy history of federal sentencing, including the rise in mandatory minimum sentences, the explosion of the federal prison population, and the subsequent pullback in the First Step Act.[184]

Given our current jurisprudential structures, that was likely the right move. That sort of statutory history is a regular feature of our

---

problems and the boundaries of social systems, and thereby insulates the formulation of the problem from deeper critical investigation").

[180] 601 U.S. 124 (2024).

[181] *Strieff*, 579 U.S. 232.

[182] *Pulsifer*, 601 U.S. at 155–56 (Gorsuch, J., dissenting). The media and dissent framed this case as the Court deciding whether "and" means "and" or whether "and" means "or." The Court said, ironically given this framing, that "and" means "or." *See* Daniel King, *Does "and" Really Mean "and"? Not Always, the Supreme Court Rules.*, Mother Jones (Mar. 29, 2024), https://www.motherjones.com/criminal-justice/2024/03/supreme-court-pulsifer-criminal-justice-drug-definitions-law.

[183] *Pulsifer*, 601 U.S. at 156 (Gorsuch, J., dissenting); *id.* at 160–61 (noting that the government's reading would lead to forty-four percent of drug offenders being eligible for relief while Pulsifer's would lead to sixty-six percent being eligible).

[184] *Id.* at 156–60.

statutory interpretation, and it raised an argument about statutory purpose that the majority felt forced to counter.[185]

But in a world where the analytical moves of the Society Cases were the norm, Gorsuch's dissent, and perhaps the entire case, might look very different. In that world, the Court would have grappled with how each of these individuals also held a role in our society. They may not be CEOs or Presidents, but they are mothers and fathers, sons and daughters, brothers and sisters, caregivers and employees and mentors and holders of all other sorts of relationships that mean that any sentence imposed on them has effects that extend far beyond themselves. All of a sudden, what appeared to be a staid statutory interpretation question instead raises issues—even if not, as the Society Cases show, the formal doctrine—of due process, equal protection, and cruel and unusual punishment, as the Court is forced to confront the effects of its decision on not only the sentenced person, but on the many non-litigants who would be negatively impacted. Perhaps *Pulsifer*'s outcome would be the same either way, but the analysis leading to that outcome would be different and more robust.

Note, however, that *Pulsifer* aligns with the Society Cases in another important way. Even if *Pulsifer* was decided differently, the additional societal analysis would not necessarily result in a different substantive outcome for the accused person. They may receive the exact same sentence in both worlds. Instead, in the current system, it is simply easier to impose that sentence. A universalization of the Society Cases means only that the outcomes the courts reach come at the end of a more rigorous and fulsome analysis. It would mean that instead of trusting prosecutors to only pursue cases with mandatory minimum sentences when people were deserving of that sentence, there might be additional checks in the forms of an adversarial process in front of a sentencing judge and appellate review.

2. Strieff *and Society Lost at Sea*. But sometimes Justices do attempt the sort of analysis I suggest they should here. Perhaps the most famous recent example is Justice Sotomayor's dissent in *Utah v. Strieff*. What set that dissent apart was not its constitutional analysis, but the explicit discussion of how the problems of suspicionless stops and mass amounts of criminal warrants extended far beyond the facts of the case before the Court, as well as the recognition of the

[185] *See id.* at 151–52 (majority opinion) (arguing that the First Step Act's decarceratory purposes did not necessarily require Pulsifer's more decarceratory interpretation of the statute).

disproportionate racial impact of who would be affected by the Court's approval of the Utah police's behavior.[186] Sotomayor described how generations of Black and Brown children had been given "the talk" about how to survive encounters with police who seemed all too eager to harm them, and how these people of color "are the canaries in the coal mine . . . who recognize that unlawful police stops corrode all our civil liberties and threaten all our lives."[187]

This dissent was powerful and impactful.[188] But the parts of it that gained the most attention also felt most unmoored from the rest of the analysis. I argue this was because Justice Sotomayor was attempting to bring a societal analysis to an area where societal impacts had long been deemed jurisprudentially irrelevant. Indeed, this can be easily seen in Sotomayor's citations. After a string of citations describing Supreme Court precedent, suddenly Sotomayor draws entirely from non-judicial commentary. Some of these citations are to law review articles, but many, and many of the most important, are instead to books by law professors for broader audiences or to authors whose only affiliation with the law is that they were, sometimes violently, subjected to it.[189]

What links these latter citations is that they, unlike the judiciary, have attempted to struggle with questions of the law's societal effects on those pieces of society to which they belong, and which the Court has been all too willing to ignore. Because of the lack of a readily available legal framework, Sotomayor was out to sea. She was forced to look to those frameworks developed by people who were not operating within, or necessarily thinking about, the constraints of a judicial decision. Sotomayor's first steps at implementing these frameworks within the judiciary were laudable, and they seem to have inspired others.[190] But their lack of a legal hook and clear analytical framework makes their implementation amorphous.

---

[186] *Strieff*, 579 U.S. at 254 (Sotomayor, J., dissenting).

[187] *Id.*

[188] *See* Kathryn Stanchi, *The Rhetoric of Racism in the United States Supreme Court*, 62 B.C. L. Rev. 1251, 1253 n.6 (2021) ("Justice Sonia Sotomayor's dissent in *Utah v. Strieff* is often recognized as a powerful antiracist dissent and yet she never uses the word 'racism.'"); Catherine M. Grosso & Barbara O'Brien, *Grounding Criminal Procedure*, 20 J. Gender Race & Just. 53, 76 (2017) (noting national media coverage of this dissent).

[189] *See Strieff*, 579 U.S. at 253–54 (Sotomayor, J., dissenting).

[190] *See, e.g.*, Green v. Thomas, 734 F. Supp. 3d 532, 547 (S.D. Miss. 2024) (discussing "Qualified Immunity's Racial Consequences").

I would suggest that the Society Cases are one place that future attempts by Sotomayor and others to engage in this type of analysis could find a legal footing. The Society Cases represent a place where the Court regularly shifts its analysis from the impact on the individual litigant before it to the effects its decision is likely to have more broadly because of that individual's place in society. This move allows the Court to engage both facts and doctrines that a purely individual-focused analysis would foreclose. And perhaps most importantly for an area like criminal law and procedure that is thickly covered with precedent, the Society Cases show that engaging in the societal analysis is a way to distinguish even well-established law.

That ability to upset established law seems especially pertinent here because the societal effects the courts have ignored are so large. The *Washington Post* once found that "America has locked up so many black people it has warped our sense of reality."[191] That analysis showed an unemployment rate that "would jump from 11 percent to 19 percent" for Black men between the ages of twenty-five and fifty-four if incarcerated people were included in our unemployment calculations.[192] Other commentators have found similarly disturbing economic effects.[193] And these costs are broad. As Paul Butler once wrote, they are

> measured in terms of the costs to the black community of having so many African-Americans, particularly males, incarcerated or otherwise involved in the criminal justice system. These costs are social and economic, and include the perceived dearth of men "eligible" for marriage, the large percentage of black children who live in female-headed households, the lack of male "role models" for black children, especially boys, the absence of wealth in the black community, and [as I have already discussed,] the large unemployment rate among black men.[194]

---

[191] Jeff Guo, *America Has Locked Up So Many Black People It Has Warped Our Sense of Reality*, Wash. Post (Feb. 16, 2016), https://www.washingtonpost.com/news/wonk/wp/2016/02/26/america-has-locked-up-so-many-black-people-it-has-warped-our-sense-of-reality.

[192] *Id.*

[193] *See, e.g.*, Harry J. Holzer, *Why Are Employment Rates So Low Among Black Men?*, Brookings Inst. (Mar. 1, 2021), https://www.brookings.edu/articles/why-are-employment-rates-so-low-among-black-men (discussing studies about the effects of incarceration on the earnings and labor participation of Black men).

[194] Butler, *supra* note 148, at 695 (footnotes omitted).

B. THE STRUCTURAL INEQUALITY OF THE SOCIETY CASES

This Article concludes with perhaps its most troubling observation. The Society Cases represent an example of the ability of race- and class-neutral analysis to nevertheless reproduce, and indeed to further, inequality along those lines. More than this, these cases show how building an ostensibly neutral structure atop one beset by inequality forces people who might wish to engage in equality-enhancing actions to choose between furthering equality and some other laudatory goal,[195] while at the same time allowing those who harbor prejudice to achieve their bigoted goals by wrapping them in neutral analysis.

Thus far, this Article has focused on what the Society Cases might tell us about the Court's criminal system jurisprudence. This Section turns to the question of whether the Society Cases might show us anything about our society. It posits that in the Society Cases we see an example of the troubling systemic choices that allow for the perpetuation and flourishing of modern race and class inequality.

As this Article has argued, the Court's treatment of the Society Cases as a distinct class is, if not totally correct, at least rational. But treating these cases differently creates two classes of criminal law: In one, the case focuses entirely on the individual, and the law may broadly regulate behavior while prosecutorial discretion over whom gets punished by that law goes nearly unquestioned by the courts. In the other, the individual is tied to their societal role, and so criminal statutes are more narrowly construed while the courts view prosecutorial choices with skepticism. The people subjected to this latter, more defendant-friendly form of the criminal legal system have been, and are likely to continue being, richer and whiter than those who must face the might of the criminal law at its zenith.[196]

---

[195] *Cf.* Daria Roithmayr, Reproducing Racism 82–92 (2014) (describing how job referral networks reproduce racial inequality even in the absence of ongoing racial prejudice).

[196] *Compare Labor Force Statistics from the Current Population Survey*, Bureau Lab. Stats. (2023), https://www.bls.gov/cps/cpsaat11.htm (reporting that white people were overrepresented in comparison to their percentage of the population in management occupations, including as both chief executives and general and operations managers), *and* Anna Brown & Sara Atske, *Black Americans Have Made Gains in U.S. Political Leadership, but Gaps Remain*, Pew Rsch. Ctr. (Jan. 22, 2021), https://www.pewresearch.org/short-reads/2021/01/22/black-americans-have-made-gains-in-u-s-political-leadership-but-gaps-remain (reporting on the "the upward yet uneven trajectory of Black political leadership in America"), *with U.S. Criminal Justice Data*, Sentencing Project, https://www.sentencingproject.org/research/us-criminal-justice

Importantly, this is so even if the courts are acting with no racial intent. This is a worrisome reality. As the Society Cases currently operate, judges acting race neutrally and in good faith could (and at least arguably do) entrench racial stratification with no desire to do so. And importantly, recognizing this structure puts the well-meaning, non-bigoted judge into a predicament. If they act race neutrally, deciding one of the Society Cases on its own terms without recognition of the racial differences inherent in the two systems created by the different classes of criminal cases, they are likely to entrench racial stratification. But if they treat one of the current Society Cases like every other criminal case, they are more likely to reach an outcome that allows the criminal law—and most disturbingly, individual criminal system actors—to have an outsized impact on parts of society where we may think criminal law should have no role to play at all.

There is thus a tension for an equality-advancing judge between what they believe to be the right outcome in the case before them and what outcome would reduce the inequalities in our society. But this tension is one-sided.

There is no similar tension for the anti-equality, prejudiced jurist. And so perhaps the most troubling part of this regime is not the possibility that the courts may further inequality even though they operate with no racial intent. Instead, the most troubling possibility is that the courts, or perhaps more specifically individual judges, could operate within this dual criminal legal regime *with racial prejudice*, but the rational operation of the system allows them to mask that prejudice while achieving their racially prejudiced goals. In other words, because the Society Cases sit on top of our racially stratified society, earnestly pursuing the non-racial goals that lead to the existence of that class of cases can also serve as a tool of racial subordination that furthers our society's racial stratification, just as if the perpetuation of racial bigotry had been the stated goal.[197]

-data (reporting Black/white and Latino/white imprisonment disparities nationally of 4.8 to 1 and 1.3 to 1, respectively).

[197] Of course, as discussed in Section II.B, just because the Society Cases currently operate in this way does not mean that they *must* operate in this way. One hope of this Article is that by raising the salience of the analytical move that the courts are making, judges and Justices will begin to think more carefully about the trends in substantive outcomes caused by their current use of this societal role-centering analysis. Indeed, as discussed later in this Article, one might imagine the pro-equality jurist using a neutral blending of the individual and their societal role in more mine-run cases as a countermeasure against the two-tiered system currently created by the Society Cases.

The Society Cases are not the only part of our systems that operate in this way, and I am not the first to identify this structural slide towards perpetual inequality. Perhaps most closely related is Daria Roithmayr's work on what she has called the lock-in model of inequality, in which she analogizes to the antitrust space and the benefits accruing from monopolization and cartelization.[198] Roithmayr discusses numerous examples of otherwise laudatory behavior—things like using one's network to find a friend a job,[199] attempting to maximize the value of one's home,[200] or basing admissions on a purportedly neutral standardized test[201]—that, because they operate against a history of racial cartelization, nevertheless serve to perpetuate the racial inequality of the past. Others have analyzed the discrimination-as-cartel model from the perspective of the Thirteenth Amendment,[202] and its potential role in disparate impact analysis.[203]

One might also view this problem through the lens of institutional or structural racism. Institutional racism, a term that "gained popularity in the 1970s and 1980s as a means of highlighting the continued systematic production of inequality, despite declines in overt acts of individual racial hostility,"[204] has been debated and discussed since its first introduction, and has no singular definition.[205] Ian Haney López defined it as "directed or undirected racial status-enforcement influenced in an unrecognized manner by racial institutions"[206] while also recognizing that others had utilized the term to mean either "intentional racism in institutions—that is, purposeful discrimination in formally organized settings" or "widespread race-neutral practices that impose harmful effects on minority communities, irrespective of

---

[198] *See generally* ROITHMAYR, *supra* note 195. *See also* Richard R.W. Brooks, *The Banality of Racial Inequality*, 124 YALE L.J. 2626 (2015).

[199] *See* ROITHMAYR, *supra* note 195, at 82–92.

[200] *See id.* at 93–108.

[201] *See id.* at 77–81.

[202] Darrell A.H. Miller, *Racial Cartels and the Thirteenth Amendment Enforcement Power*, 100 KY. L.J. 23 (2012).

[203] Ian Ayres, *Market Power and Inequality: A Competitive Conduct Standard for Assessing When Disparate Impacts Are Unjustified*, 95 CALIF. L. REV. 669 (2007).

[204] Ian F. Haney López, *Institutional Racism: Judicial Conduct and a New Theory of Racial Discrimination*, 109 YALE L.J. 1717, 1726–27 (2000).

[205] *See id.* at 1727 n.30 (citing numerous critical race theorists' analyses of the topic).

[206] *Id.* at 1811. "Racial institutions" are in turn defined as "any understanding of race that has come to be so widely shared within a community that it operates as an unexamined cognitive resource for understanding one's self, others, and the-way-the-world-is." *Id.* at 1809.

the actions or attitudes of individual decision makers."[207] Relatedly, structural racism builds on the institutional analysis to "shift[] our attention from the single, intra-institutional setting to inter-institutional arrangements and interactions."[208]

One way to view the Society Cases is as another example of the institutional racism that López found embedded in the courts. In the Los Angeles Superior Court, the judges' institutional "script requiring the nomination of personal and professional acquaintances" combined with the path institutionalism of assumptions about what made someone "qualified" to lead to unintentional discrimination against Mexican Americans in grand juror nominations.[209] Here, the Supreme Court's script states that certain litigants are entitled to special analytical dispensation, and the resulting substantive and procedural protections that come from that, as a result of their societal role. By contrast, the bulk of the people who come before it are to be treated as individuals separated entirely from the roles they play. Even in the rare cases where this script is challenged, the Court's path institutionalism allows the Justices to forge ahead because "the unrecognized boundaries for decision making" relegate relevant arguments against this treatment to beyond the borders of its doctrinal analysis.[210]

An inter-institutional, structural analysis adds to this insight. The Society Cases, after all, are not only about the Supreme Court. Instead, their existence and arguable necessity arises because of the standard operation of numerous criminal legal institutions including police departments, prosecutor's offices, and the lower courts. Indeed, an exhaustive structural analysis addressing the "cumulative [causation] within and across domains" would have to grapple not only with these criminal legal institutions.[211] It would also have to address the legal and political structures that make the defendants in the Society Cases have such an outsized societal impact that they are "too big to

---

[207] *Id.* at 1727.

[208] john a. powell, *Structural Racism: Building Upon the Insights of John Calmore*, 86 N.C. L. Rev. 791, 796 (2008); *see also* John O. Calmore, *Race/ism Lost and Found: The Fair Housing Act at Thirty*, 52 U. Mia. L. Rev. 1067, 1075 (1998) ("But racism reinforces synergisms of disadvantage over both space and time in ways that present an interlocking system of unfair and discriminatory disadvantage that makes it difficult to separate racial discrimination and 'life's unfairness' from racism itself.").

[209] López, *supra* note 204, at 1785.

[210] *See, e.g.*, Utah v. Strieff, 579 U.S. 232, 253–54 (2016) (Sotomayor, J., dissenting).

[211] powell, *supra* note 208, at 796.

fail," that is, that treating them equally could upset the normal functioning of the country. At the same time, this structural analysis would contend with the economic, political, and legal forces that allowed the Court (and courts) to relegate the societal importance of the vast majority of defendants to the system of broad liability and unchecked discretion that it finds intolerable in the Society Cases with little blowback.[212]

What is to be done? A first, best solution would recognize that this is a racialized and classed problem and address it explicitly with that reality at the center of the analysis.[213] But race consciousness, especially, is out of favor with the current Court.[214] That does not mean Justices should totally abandon these first, best, and most direct arguments and analysis. Creating a "jurisprudence in exile" can aid the day when the political and jurisprudential winds blow in a different direction.[215] Perhaps even more importantly, as Justice Sotomayor's writing in *Strieff* and other "great dissents" have shown, constitutional change is not limited to the Supreme Court, and laying bare these often unspoken inner workings can motivate the many other actors—from legislatures to commentators to the people more broadly—who help to create our constitutional ecosystem.[216]

---

[212] For one example, see John O. Calmore, *Racialized Space and the Culture of Segregation: "Hewing A Stone of Hope from A Mountain of Despair,"* 143 U. Pa. L. Rev. 1233, 1236 (1995) ("An analysis of racialized space is complex for many reasons, as it involves at least the consideration of politics and public policy, racially signified and symbolized conflicts, and aspects of hegemony, such as the construction of our 'common sense' understandings of everyday life.").

[213] *Cf.* Schuette v. Coal. to Defend Affirmative Action, 572 U.S. 291, 381 (2014) (Sotomayor, J., dissenting) ("In my colleagues' view, examining the racial impact of legislation only perpetuates racial discrimination. This refusal to accept the stark reality that race matters is regrettable. The way to stop discrimination on the basis of race is to speak openly and candidly on the subject of race, and to apply the Constitution with eyes open to the unfortunate effects of centuries of racial discrimination.").

[214] *See, e.g.*, Students for Fair Admissions, Inc. v. President & Fellows of Harvard Coll., 600 U.S. 181 (2023).

[215] *See* Richard M. Re, *Personal Precedent at the Supreme Court*, 136 Harv. L. Rev. 824, 841 n.5 (2023).

[216] *See, e.g.*, I Dissent: Great Opposing Opinions in Landmark Supreme Court Cases, at xi (Mark Tushnet ed., 2008) ("Our constitutional tradition celebrates the great dissenters. . . . On one level, the reason is clear: out of step with the prevailing constitutional views of their times, they were vindicated by history."); Paul Butler, *"A Long Step Down the Totalitarian Path": Justice Douglas's Great Dissent in* Terry v. Ohio, 79 Miss. L.J. 9, 16–19 (2009) (discussing the impacts of Justice William O. Douglas's dissents in numerous areas); *see also* Farah Peterson, *Our Constitutionalism of Force*, 122 Colum. L. Rev. 1539, 1540–42 (2022) (discussing the rise of popular constitutionalism and adding to it the history of popular violence as a tool of lawmaking).

But there are also more readily available doctrinal solutions. Because the ignored parts of society this Article has discussed are often racialized but not explicitly race-based, the Court could at least partially address the problem that underlies the Society Cases without triggering heightened scrutiny. Proposals to more rigorously consider someone's family or provider status, for example, have already begun to percolate in the courts.[217] And as discussed in the previous Section, the Court could draw on the Society Cases for legal analysis that incorporates the societal impacts of the criminal legal system more broadly. Doing so might allow the Court to begin moving away from the structure of broad liability and unrestricted discretion that it has cultivated thus far by distinguishing, instead of overruling, past precedents.

Conclusion

This Article has identified a category of the Court's jurisprudence that it calls the Society Cases. The Society Cases are those in which someone is sued or charged in their individual capacity, but the Court nevertheless considers the societal role they hold—President, financial executive, governmental actor, or political protestor, perhaps—to afford them protections based on that role. Usually, but not always, the Society Cases involve criminal prosecutions. This is because the harm that the Court pushes back against in these cases by blending the individual and societal position is that caused by a legal regime characterized by broad substantive liability that is cabined by the rarely checked discretion of individual governmental actors. And this description fits our criminal system to a tee.

Despite continued pronouncements that every person is equal before the law, the Society Cases' differential treatment seems at the least defensible, and often correct. That is because allowing an individual prosecutor or private litigant to target the defendants in the Society Cases could give them outsized power over the economic and political parts of our society in which we do not think they

[217] *See, e.g.*, Adam Davidson, Comment Letter to the U.S. Sentencing Commission on Proposed Priorities *909 (July 15, 2024), https://www.ussc.gov/sites/default/files/pdf/amendment-process/public-comment/202407/89FR48029_public-comment_R.pdf#page=904 (joining "the Tzedek Association's call for changes to the Guidelines that explicitly guide judges' discretion when considering the effects that a sentence will have on others beyond the sentenced individual").

should be able to intervene. The Court's treatment of these cases is simply recognizing and attempting to address the reality that these individuals simply are not separable from the societal office they hold.

But that does not mean the Society Cases' existence is entirely praiseworthy. Instead, they are a necessary jurisprudential intervention only because the Court diminished the relevance of the societal roles that the vast majority of the defendants before them play. As a result, the broad liability and unchecked discretionary choices the Court finds intolerable in the Society Cases have helped the criminal system to wreak havoc on the Blacker, Browner, and poorer parts of society that are the bulk of the criminal legal system's targets.

This is an example of structural inequality in action. The Court pursues a line of analysis that, as this Article argues, is both race- and class-neutral and seems correct given the background it acts against. But that background is one that is steeped in race and class hierarchy, and because of this inequality, the Court's formally race- and class-neutral differential treatment helps to further those unjust inequalities it often claims to be fighting against.

All hope is not lost, however. The analytical move underlying the Society Cases does not inherently further inequality. While it has historically helped to create a stratified system of justice, if used differently, it can help to raise the societal roles that the Court has long ignored to the forefront or serve as a reason to hold the powerful to greater account.

DANIEL HEMEL

FORMALISM, FUNCTIONALISM, AND NONFUNCTIONALISM IN THE CONSTITUTIONAL LAW OF TAX

Introduction

Commentary on American public law frequently focuses on the clash between "formalism" and "functionalism." Formalists—according to Larry Alexander's definition—seek to apply the law without regard to the background reasons that the relevant law is meant to serve, even when the law's command "fails to serve those background reasons in a particular case."[1] By contrast, functionalists—as explained by Curtis Bradley—"explicitly take into account what they understand to be the purposes of a law when construing its scope" and seek to "ensure that there is a close fit between the purpose of the law and its application."[2] Although the definitions of formalism and functionalism are both disputed, and although the

Daniel Hemel is a Professor of Law at New York University School of Law.

Author's note: Thanks to Jake Brooks, David Gamage, Rick Pildes, Lawrence Solum, David Strauss, and workshop participants at William & Mary Law School for thoughtful comments on earlier drafts.

[1] Larry Alexander, *"With Me, It's All er Nuthin'": Formalism in Law and Morality*, 66 U. Chi. L. Rev. 530, 530 (1999).

[2] Curtis A. Bradley, *The Irrepressible Functionalism in U.S. Foreign Relations Law*, *in* Foreign Relations Law ix, ix–x (Curtis A. Bradley ed., 2019).

The Supreme Court Review, 2025.
 https://doi.org/10.1086/735428

classification of specific cases as "formalist" or "functionalist" is often contested, the formalism/functionalism dichotomy has proven to be a useful framework for understanding the Supreme Court's jurisprudence in areas such as the separation of powers,[3] foreign relations,[4] and the law of democracy.[5]

In cases concerning the Constitution's fiscal provisions, a third alternative has emerged that is neither formalist nor functionalist: what we might call "nonfunctionalism." Nonfunctionalism reflects the belief that certain clauses of the Constitution do not serve any ongoing purpose and should be construed so that they accomplish as little as possible, if anything at all. Sometimes, nonfunctionalism masquerades as hypertextualist formalism: For example, the Court has interpreted the Origination Clause—which requires that all revenue-raising bills originate in the House of Representatives[6]—as permitting the Senate to introduce its own tax measures by formally taking a House-passed bill and replacing all of the substantive language.[7] Yet whereas a formalist might seek to construe the text of the Origination Clause without allowing her view of the clause's purpose to color her judgment, Origination Clause nonfunctionalists resort to a hypertextual reading precisely because they deem the clause to be purposeless.[8]

---

[3] *See* Peter L. Strauss, *The Place of Agencies in Government: Separation of Powers and the Fourth Branch*, 84 COLUM. L. REV. 573 (1984); Peter L. Strauss, *Formal and Functional Approaches in Separation-of-Powers Questions—A Foolish Inconsistency?*, 72 CORNELL L. REV. 488 (1987).

[4] *See* Bradley, *supra* note 2.

[5] *See* Richard H. Pildes, *Formalism and Functionalism in the Constitutional Law of Politics*, 35 CONN. L. REV. 1525, 1528 (2003) (observing that "the law of democracy remains one of the last bastions of legal formalism in constitutional law" and arguing for a more functionalist approach).

[6] U.S. CONST. art. I, § 7, cl. 1.

[7] *See* Flint v. Stone Tracy Co., 220 U.S. 107, 142–43 (1911).

[8] For example, Joseph Thorndike justifies Origination Clause nonfunctionalism on the ground that the Seventeenth Amendment—which mandates the direct election of Senators—obviates the provision's initial rationale (to place the taxing power in the hands of House members who "were directly elected by the people"). *See* Joseph Thorndike, *The Origination Clause? Let It Go*, FORBES (Aug. 7, 2014, 11:45 AM EDT), https://www.forbes.com/sites/taxanalysts/2014/08/07/the-origination-clause-let-it-go. Long before the Seventeenth Amendment, Justice Joseph Story argued that unlike in Britain—where the origination requirement ensured that the taxing power lay in the hands of the elected House of Commons rather than the hereditary House of Lords—the requirement was of "little importance" in the U.S. context because "the senators are in a just sense equally representatives of the people." 1 JOSEPH STORY, COMMENTARIES ON THE CONSTITUTION OF THE UNITED STATES 620–21, §§ 876, 878 (Thomas M. Cooley ed., Boston, Little, Brown & Co. 4th ed. 1873) (1833). Story argued for a narrow construction of the Clause's scope—and a broad interpretation of the Senate's amendment

Nonfunctionalism characterizes the Court's approach not only to the Origination Clause but also to the Uniformity Clause, which provides that "all Duties, Imposts, and Excises shall be uniform throughout the United States."[9] In the 1983 case *United States v. Ptasynski*, the Court upheld an excise tax on crude oil that was plainly not "uniform throughout the United States" because it explicitly exempted oil from northern Alaska.[10] In contrast to the Court's Origination Clause case law, *Ptasynski* is the opposite of hypertextualist formalism: The Court in that case excused Congress's facial violation of the Uniformity Clause's plain text, deferring instead to lawmakers' judgment that Alaskan oil "merited favorable treatment" based on the "disproportionate costs and difficulties" of oil extraction in Arctic and sub-Arctic regions.[11] But as with the Origination Clause, the Court's Uniformity Clause jurisprudence effectively renders the provision a "dead letter."[12] As Ari Glogower puts it, "the Court has interpreted the Article I, Section 8 uniformity requirement in a manner that practically reads this provision out of the Constitution."[13]

While the Court has steered toward nonfunctionalism in its Origination Clause and Uniformity Clause jurisprudence, it has zigzagged over time in its approach to the Direct Tax Clauses, which require that all "direct" taxes be apportioned among the states based on population.[14] (The first of the two Direct Tax Clauses—Article I, Section Two, Clause Three—initially included the infamous three-fifths compromise, specifying that a slave should count for sixty percent of a free person in calculating the population of each state.) In the Supreme Court's first encounter with the Direct Tax Clauses, the 1796 case *Hylton v. United*

---

power—in order to ensure that the provision would not pose "a practical obstruction to the legislation of a free government." *Id.* at 620, § 877.

[9] U.S. CONST. art. I, § 8, cl. 1.

[10] 462 U.S. 74, 77, 85–86 (1983).

[11] *See id.* at 78–79, 85–86.

[12] *Compare* Adriaan Lanni & Adrian Vermeule, *Constitutional Design in the Ancient World*, 64 STAN. L. REV. 907, 922 (2012) (observing that the Origination Clause has become "largely a dead letter"), *with* Stephen J. Lubben, *PROMESA and the Bankruptcy Clause: A Reminder About Uniformity*, 12 BROOK. J. CORP. FIN. & COM. L. 53, 66 (2017) (observing that the Uniformity Clause "has essentially been rendered something of a dead letter").

[13] Ari Glogower, *The Constitutional Limits to the Taxing Power*, 93 FORDHAM L. REV. 781, 791 (2024).

[14] *See* U.S. CONST. art. I, § 2, cl. 3 ("Representatives and direct Taxes shall be apportioned among the several States . . . according to their respective Numbers"); *id.* art. I, § 9, cl. 4 ("No Capitation, or other direct, Tax shall be laid, unless in Proportion to the Census. . . .").

States, Justice Chase wrote that if any tax is too difficult to apportion on the basis of population, then the apportionment requirement does not apply—in other words, that the apportionment requirement can never limit the types of taxes that Congress can impose.[15] And for nearly the next century, the Court never struck down any revenue-raising measure on the ground that it was a direct tax requiring apportionment. But ninety-nine years after *Hylton*, a closely divided Court reversed course in *Pollock v. Farmers' Loan and Trust Co.* and adopted a sweeping definition of direct taxes, resulting in the invalidation of the second-ever federal income tax.[16]

Pollock precipitated a popular backlash, and the Court beat a "strategic retreat"[17] from its position of Direct Tax Clause maximalism in a series of early twentieth century cases that declined to extend *Pollock* beyond its facts.[18] Congress and the states responded, too, with the Sixteenth Amendment—ratified in 1913—which exempted all "taxes on incomes" from the apportionment requirement.[19] But the Court soon swung again, holding in the 1920 case *Eisner v. Macomber* that an unapportioned tax on a "stock dividend"—in effect, a stock split—violated the Direct Tax Clauses and fell outside the Sixteenth Amendment's scope because it applied to shareholders who had not "realized" gain in the form of money or payment in kind.[20]

Macomber is widely regarded as a triumph of formalistic interpretation.[21] But it was also something of a one-hit wonder. Over the next twenty years, the Court embraced an expansive definition of "income" and a correspondingly narrow view of the apportionment requirement's reach,[22] leading future Harvard Law professor Stanley Surrey

---

[15] 3 U.S. (3 Dall.) 171, 174 (1796) (opinion of Chase, J.).

[16] 157 U.S. 429 (1895).

[17] Bruce Ackerman, *Taxation and the Constitution*, 99 Colum. L. Rev. 1, 33 (1999).

[18] *See* Knowlton v. Moore, 178 U.S. 41, 83 (1900) (holding that a federal tax on bequests is not a direct tax); Spreckels Sugar Refin. Co. v. McLain, 192 U.S. 397, 413 (1904) (holding that a federal tax on the gross receipts of petroleum refineries, sugar refineries, and pipelines is not a direct tax); Flint v. Stone Tracy Co., 220 U.S. 107, 150 (1911) (holding that a federal tax on corporate income is not a direct tax).

[19] U.S. Const. amend. XVI.

[20] 252 U.S. 189, 212–13 (1920).

[21] *See, e.g.*, William B. Barker, *Statutory Interpretation, Comparative Law, and Economic Theory: Discovering the Ground of Income Taxation*, 40 San Diego L. Rev. 821, 840 (2003).

[22] *See, e.g.*, Helvering v. Bruun, 309 U.S. 461, 469 (1940); Helvering v. Horst, 311 U.S. 112, 115–19 (1940).

to conclude in 1941 that "the formalistic doctrine of realization proclaimed by [*Macomber*] is not a constitutional mandate."[23] In more than eight decades since Surrey wrote those words, the Court has never officially overruled *Macomber*, yet it also has not invalidated any federal tax for failure to satisfy the apportionment requirement.

Moore v. United States, which reached the Supreme Court in October Term 2023, offered the Justices an opportunity to resurrect—or to inter—*Macomber*'s holding that a tax on unrealized gains is a direct tax that lies outside the Sixteenth Amendment's income tax carveout. *Moore* involved a challenge to the "mandatory repatriation tax," part of the Tax Cuts and Jobs Act of 2017, which applied to American shareholders of foreign corporations that had accumulated earnings abroad. The case drew particular attention because a ruling for the Moores could have doomed not only the 2017 mandatory repatriation tax but also the Biden Administration's proposal for a "billionaire minimum income tax," which—had it not stalled in Congress—would have taxed ultra-high net worth individuals on a portion of their unrealized gains each year.[24]

By a seven-to-two margin, the Justices rejected the Moores' challenge.[25] But that lopsided vote count masked deep divisions among the Justices in the majority. Justice Kavanaugh, joined by four of his colleagues, sidestepped the question of whether a tax on unrealized gains can qualify as an income tax under the Sixteenth Amendment, concluding that the Moores would lose even if *Macomber* remains good law. By contrast, Justice Barrett—joined by Justice Alito—fully embraced *Macomber*'s realization requirement but concluded that the Moores' challenge nonetheless failed because of an ill-considered concession that the couple's lawyer made at oral argument.

Notably, neither Justice Kavanaugh nor Justice Barrett articulated a functional theory of the Direct Tax Clauses, and neither opinion sought to explain what purposes—if any—the Constitution's direct tax limitations continue to serve in the aftermath of the Sixteenth Amendment. Perhaps surprisingly, the only opinion in *Moore* that

---

[23] Stanley S. Surrey, *The Supreme Court and the Federal Income Tax: Some Implications of the Recent Decisions*, 35 Ill. L. Rev. Nw. U. 779, 791 (1941).

[24] *See, e.g.*, Joe Miller & Stephen Foley, *How the US Supreme Court Could Thwart a Prospective Wealth Tax*, Fin. Times (Dec. 3, 2023), https://www.ft.com/content/6b700a29-0ebd-493a-9888-01046bfb8592.

[25] 144 S. Ct. 1680 (2024).

engaged in familiar functionalist reasoning was the dissent by Justice Thomas, a jurist otherwise "known for his formalism."[26] Only Thomas, joined in his dissent by Justice Gorsuch, identified a clear purpose for the Direct Tax Clauses: to preserve the federalist system by protecting the states' property tax base from congressional encroachment.[27] And only Thomas explained how his application of the law would further that underlying purpose: by distinguishing income, which Congress can tax without apportionment, from wealth, which—under Thomas's vision—would be the exclusive taxing province of the states except "in emergencies."[28] Justice Jackson, for her part, appeared to endorse a nonfunctionalist reading of the Direct Tax Clauses, arguing in a solo concurrence that constraints on Congress's taxing power should come not from the Constitution but from the electoral process.[29]

The fractured decision in *Moore* invites reflection on the roles of formalism, functionalism, and nonfunctionalism in the constitutional law of tax. For formalists, *Moore* presses the question of whether text and precedent on their own can definitively resolve contemporary controversies over the scope of Congress's taxing power. For functionalists, Justice Thomas's dissent in *Moore* offers the most creative account in any Supreme Court opinion to date of the Direct Tax Clauses' underlying purposes, though as we shall see, Thomas's theory is not the only plausible functionalist account of the Direct Tax Clauses and may not ultimately be the most persuasive. Meanwhile, Justice Jackson's concurrence raises the question of when, if ever, nonfunctionalism is a legitimate approach to constitutional interpretation—a question with implications that extend well beyond the sphere of taxation.

Part I of this Article provides a brief overview of the dispute in *Moore* and summarizes the Justices' opinions in the case, underlining their formalist, functionalist, and nonfunctionalist elements. Part II, the heart of the analysis, evaluates the arguments for—and against—formalist, functionalist, and nonfunctionalist approaches to the constitutional law of tax. It explains why formalism yields indeterminate

[26] Tara Leigh Grove, *Which Textualism?*, 134 HARV. L. REV. 265, 307 n.167 (2020).

[27] *Moore*, 144 S. Ct. at 1714–15 (Thomas, J., dissenting).

[28] *Id.* at 1715.

[29] *Id.* at 1699 (Jackson, J., concurring).

answers to the most important modern-day questions regarding the scope of Congress's taxing power but also why indeterminacy may not be fatal to the formalist enterprise. It goes on to scrutinize Justice Thomas's base protection theory of the Direct Tax Clauses—the only functionalist account offered by any of the Justices in *Moore*—and demonstrates that the base protection theory could yield doctrinal conclusions starkly different from those that Thomas draws. In particular, it shows how taxes on unrealized gains—and even broad-based wealth taxes—could be justified on functionalist grounds if supporters were willing to spar with Thomas on functionalist terrain. Finally, it illustrates several ways that one might motivate a nonfunctionalist approach to the Direct Tax Clauses while also underscoring the shortcomings of Justice Jackson's own justification for nonfunctionalism. The upshot of the Article's analysis is not that any one of these approaches—formalism, functionalism, or nonfunctionalism—is clearly better than the others. Rather, each approach—viewed sympathetically—reflects a different strategy for using law to manage moral, social, and economic conflict, and examining these three approaches in the specific context of tax can yield general lessons that inform constitutional interpretation in a deeply polarized society.

I. More About *Moore*

In 2006, Charles and Kathleen Moore, a married couple living in Washington state, invested $40,000 in a company called KisanKraft, an Indian corporation co-founded by Charles's friend and former Microsoft colleague Ravi Agrawal to supply Indian farmers with basic tools and equipment. By 2017, KisanKraft had generated hundreds of thousands of dollars in profits but had not paid any dividends to shareholders.[30] That year, Congress—as part of an overhaul of the U.S. international tax regime—enacted a one-time tax on Americans who held significant stakes in foreign corporations that had accumulated earnings overseas.[31] As a result of the mandatory repatriation tax, the Moores paid an additional $14,729 to the Internal Revenue Service.[32]

---

[30] *See* Marie Sapirie, *Persons of the Year: The Moores: The Constitution, Realization, and Two Tax Everymen*, 181 Tax Notes Fed. 2091, 2091 (2023).

[31] I.R.C. § 965.

[32] *Moore*, 144 S. Ct. at 1686.

In 2019, the Moores sued the federal government for a refund, arguing that the mandatory repatriation tax—like the tax struck down in *Macomber*—is a tax on unrealized gains and thus not a tax on "incomes" authorized by the Sixteenth Amendment. The district court and the Ninth Circuit both rejected the Moores' argument, finding that subsequent Supreme Court and lower court cases have effectively eviscerated *Macomber*'s realization holding.[33] The Ninth Circuit denied rehearing en banc over a fiery dissent by Judge Bumatay, who accused the *Moore* panel of gutting the apportionment requirement when "only the people have the power to declare a constitutional provision a dead letter."[34]

The Moores took their case to the Supreme Court, which granted certiorari in June 2023 on the question of "[w]hether the Sixteenth Amendment authorizes Congress to tax unrealized sums without apportionment among the states."[35] But when the Court handed down its decision a year later, it left that question unanswered. "We do not decide," wrote Justice Kavanaugh, "whether realization is required for an income tax."[36] For that reason, the Court's ruling was widely regarded as "narrow."[37]

Narrow though the Court's holding was, the four opinions in *Moore* showcase the broad spectrum of jurisprudential approaches—including formalism, functionalism, and nonfunctionalism—that have characterized the Court's constitutional tax case law through the centuries. Justice Kavanaugh's majority opinion—which cobbled together a coalition of himself, Chief Justice Roberts, and Justices Sotomayor, Kagan, and Jackson—focuses on the fact that KisanKraft had realized income even though the Moores themselves had not. Kavanaugh notes that "[i]n general, Congress taxes the income of American business entities such as corporations and partnerships in one of two ways"[38]: It

[33] *See* Moore v. United States, No. C19-1539, 2020 WL 6799022, at *2–3 (W.D. Wash. Nov. 19, 2020); Moore v. United States, 36 F.4th 930, 935–38 (9th Cir. 2022).

[34] Moore v. United States, 53 F.4th 507, 515 (9th Cir. 2022) (Bumatay, J., dissenting from denial of rehearing en banc).

[35] Moore v. United States, 143 S. Ct. 2656 (2023); Petition for Writ of Certiorari at i, *Moore*, 144 S. Ct. 1680 (No. 22-800).

[36] *Moore*, 144 S. Ct. at 1696.

[37] *See, e.g.*, Andy Grewal, Moore *Decides Less*, TaxProf Blog (June 26, 2024), https://taxprof.typepad.com/taxprof_blog/2024/06/grewal-moore-decides-less.html; Leslie Samuels, *Some Preliminary Reflections on* Moore, 115 Tax Notes Int'l 679, 680 (2024).

[38] *Moore*, 144 S. Ct. at 1685.

taxes corporate income at the entity level and partnership income on a pass-through basis, attributing the partnership's income to the partnership's owners and taxing them on their allocated portions. Yet in the 1925 case *Burk-Waggoner Oil Association v. Hopkins*, the Court allowed Congress to tax a state-law partnership as if it were a corporation, imposing tax at the entity level rather than the owner level.[39] Kavanaugh reasons that the same principle works in reverse: Congress may choose to tax state-law corporations (and, by extension, foreign-law corporations) as though they are partnerships, imposing tax at the owner level rather than the entity level.[40]

Justice Kavanaugh goes on to observe that several significant tax provisions that long predate the mandatory repatriation tax—most notably, the subpart F rules for passive foreign income—also tax corporate shareholders on their pro rata portion of a corporation's earnings.[41] "And those tax provisions, if suddenly eliminated, would deprive the U.S. Government and the American people of trillions in lost tax revenue," Kavanaugh continues, adding that "[t]he Constitution does not require that fiscal calamity." Kavanaugh arguably catastrophizes the matter: The subpart F rules—important as they are—generate less than $10 billion per year, not "trillions."[42] Still, in emphasizing the fiscal impact—overstated or not—of a ruling for the Moores, Kavanaugh's opinion is openly consequentialist.

Yet consequentialism is not—or at least need not be—the same thing as functionalism. As Rick Pildes observes, consequentialists "compare the total social welfare in competing states of affairs and then . . . choose legal rules that will generate the end state with the highest total welfare."[43] By contrast, functionalism—at least as defined at the outset—does not license a judge to impose her own social

---

[39] *See id.* at 1689 (citing Burk-Waggoner Oil Ass'n v. Hopkins, 269 U.S. 110, 114 (1925)).

[40] *See id.* at 1690.

[41] *See id.* at 1692–93.

[42] *See id.* at 1696; *cf.* Daniel Bunn, Alan Cole, William McBride & Garrett Watson, *How the* Moore *Supreme Court Case Could Reshape Taxation of Unrealized Income*, Tax Found. (Aug. 30, 2023), https://taxfoundation.org/research/all/federal/moore-v-united-states-tax-unrealized-income (estimating that the repeal of subpart F would cost the federal government $5.8 billion in fiscal year 2025, rising to $9.4 billion by fiscal year 2033). As for the S corporation and partnership tax regimes, which likewise tax shareholders (or partners) on their portion of an enterprise's income, taxpayers generally choose these business forms over the standard C corporation because they believe that partnership or S corporation status will *reduce* their overall tax bill.

[43] Richard H. Pildes, *Forms of Formalism*, 66 U. Chi. L. Rev. 607, 609 (1999).

welfare calculus on the law. Rather, a functionalist judge interprets laws to advance what she understands to be the purposes embodied in those laws—which may, but need not, produce what she thinks are the best near-term consequences for the country or for humanity.

Justice Kavanaugh's opinion is thus consequentialist but not functionalist, at least when functionalism is understood in these terms. Kavanaugh never examines the purposes of the Direct Tax Clauses or the realization requirement. Nor does he explain the purposes underlying the rule in *Burk-Waggoner* that Congress can tax a state-law partnership's realized income at the entity level—and thus never explains why this same rule should be applied in reverse to authorize taxation of a corporation's realized income at the owner level. Kavanaugh's purpose-agnostic approach may have been pragmatic: He needed to knit together a five-Justice coalition that—as we shall see—included at least one member, Justice Jackson, who appears to view constitutional constraints on Congress's taxing power as purposeless. Yet as we will also see, Kavanaugh's purpose-agnosticism leaves him without the resources to respond to the separate opinion of Justice Barrett, who offers a different reading of the same precedent.

Whereas Justice Kavanaugh withholds judgment on *Macomber*'s continued vitality, Justice Barrett embraces *Macomber* without reservation. Since *Macomber*, she writes, the Supreme Court "has never abandoned the core requirement that that income must be realized to be taxable without apportionment."[44] Barrett acknowledges that under *Burk-Waggoner*, Congress can tax a state-law partnership as a corporation, at least under certain circumstances. But, she argues, the rule in *Burk-Waggoner* does not—contra Kavanaugh—work in reverse:

> *Burk-Waggoner* . . . held that for tax purposes, Congress could treat a partnership like a corporation when it acts like a corporation. We did not decide whether Congress may treat a *corporation like a partnership—e.g.*, attributing its income to shareholders—when, in truth and substance, it operates as a corporation.[45]

In one respect, Barrett's opinion echoes the tax-law principle of "substance over form": The Court allowed Congress to tax Burk-Waggoner Oil Association like a corporation, according to Barrett,

[44] *Moore*, 144 S. Ct. at 1701 (Barrett, J., concurring in the judgment) (some internal quotation marks omitted).

[45] *Id.* at 1706.

because even though the enterprise was formally a partnership under state law, it functioned like a corporation. Yet in another respect, Barrett's opinion is as rigidly formalistic as Kavanaugh's. Like the majority opinion, Barrett never explains what purposes are served by the apportionment requirement or the realization rule or the holding of *Burk-Waggoner*. The disagreement between Kavanaugh and Barrett regarding the proper reading of *Burk-Waggoner* thus has a "he says, she says" quality: Kavanaugh reads the case one way, Barrett reads the case another way, and neither gives us any reason why one reading is more authentic to the purposes underlying the Direct Tax Clauses or the Sixteenth Amendment.

The Kavanaugh and Barrett opinions are alike in another way, too: They both reach the same bottom-line result that the Moores lose. According to Barrett, the Moores lose because they "have conceded that subpart F is constitutional," even though "subpart F is not meaningfully different from the [mandatory repatriation tax] in how it attributes corporate income to shareholders."[46] Given this concession, Barrett concludes that the Moores have not met their burden of showing why they are entitled to a refund.[47]

Kavanaugh and Barrett's opinions are thus doubly different from the dissent by Justice Thomas, which—unlike the other opinions in the case—employs functionalist reasoning and reaches the opposite bottom-line result. To be sure, Justice Thomas does not ignore text or precedent. But in contrast to Kavanaugh and Barrett, Thomas articulates a specific purpose served by the Constitution's direct tax limitations: to shield the states' property tax base from congressional encroachment.

According to Thomas, the Direct Tax Clauses were—from the outset—"a critical aspect of the balance between state and federal power in the original design of the Constitution."[48] In Thomas's telling, the Constitution—because it barred states from printing money[49] and limited their ability to tax imports and exports[50]—left states to rely on direct taxes for revenue.[51] The apportionment

---

[46] *Id.* at 1709.

[47] *See id.*

[48] *Id.* at 1712 (Thomas, J., dissenting).

[49] U.S. Const. art. I, § 10, cl. 1.

[50] *Id.* art. I, § 10, cl. 2.

[51] *Moore*, 144 S. Ct. at 1714 (Thomas, J., dissenting).

requirement served to discourage Congress from intruding on the states' direct tax base. Although the Constitution did not ban federal direct taxation entirely, the cumbersome apportionment requirement ensured that "the Federal Government would impose direct taxes only sparingly, as needed to supplement the revenue from imposts in emergencies."[52]

Justice Thomas acknowledges that after ratification, it was "not entirely clear" how to distinguish between direct and indirect taxes, even though the distinction was—according to Thomas's account—"an important component of the founding compromise."[53] Thomas goes on to recount the decades of litigation starting with *Hylton* and leading up to the Court's conclusion—in the 1881 case *Springer v. United States*—that "*direct taxes*, within the meaning of the Constitution, are only capitation taxes . . . and taxes on real estate."[54] Yet as Thomas notes, *Springer*'s conclusion soon came under attack in the 1895 *Pollock* case, which he calls "the single most important piece of context for understanding the Sixteenth Amendment."[55]

Pollock concerned the constitutionality of the second federal income tax, enacted in 1894. (The first federal income tax, enacted during the Civil War, was repealed in 1872.) The Court in *Pollock* heard oral argument twice. After the first argument, the Court held that since a tax on real property is a direct tax, a tax on the income from real property is a direct tax, too—in other words, that income cannot be distinguished from source.[56] In *Pollock II*, the Court extended the holding of *Pollock I* from real property to personal property,[57]

---

[52] *Id.* at 1715. Thomas's base protection account of the Direct Tax Clauses tracks an argument advanced by West Virginia and sixteen other states in their amicus brief supporting the Moores. *See* Brief of Amici Curiae State of West Virginia et al. in Support of Petitioners at 10–11, *Moore*, 144 S. Ct. 1680 (No. 22-800); *see also* W. Elliot Brownlee, Federal Taxation in America: A History 35 (3rd ed. 2016) (noting that the Direct Tax Clauses reflected—among other influences—a concern "that the new national government might preempt the use of property taxation by state and local governments"); Erik M. Jensen, *The Taxing Power, the Sixteenth Amendment, and the Meaning of "Incomes,"* 33 Ariz. St. L.J. 1057, 1077 n.105 (2001) (noting that one purpose of the Direct Tax Clauses was "to ensure the states would have a tax base").

[53] *Moore*, 144 S. Ct. at 1715 (Thomas, J., dissenting).

[54] Springer v. United States, 102 U.S. 586, 602 (1880).

[55] *Moore*, 144 S. Ct. at 1717 (Thomas, J., dissenting).

[56] Pollock v. Farmers' Loan & Tr. Co. (*Pollock I*), 157 U.S. 429, 583 (1895).

[57] Pollock v. Farmers' Loan & Tr. Co. (*Pollock II*), 158 U.S. 601, 637 (1895).

notwithstanding *Springer*'s statement that taxes on personal property are indirect.

Justice Thomas recognizes, as he must, that the Sixteenth Amendment overturned *Pollock*—at least in part. But according to Thomas, the Sixteenth Amendment overturned only one holding of *Pollock*: that income cannot be distinguished from source. As he puts it, "[t]he only thing the Amendment changed about the Constitution was to abolish *Pollock*'s rule that an income tax is a direct tax if a tax on the source of the income would be a direct tax."[58] In his reading, the Sixteenth Amendment "left everything else in place"—including the rule that taxes on personal property are direct taxes.[59] And "[b]ecause the Sixteenth Amendment requires a way to distinguish between income and source, it includes a realization requirement"[60]—a requirement that, Thomas goes on to conclude, the mandatory repatriation tax does not satisfy.[61]

Thomas also engages in familiar formalist reasoning, citing dictionary definitions from around the time of the Sixteenth Amendment that ostensibly support his interpretation of "income" as entailing a realization requirement.[62] His is not a wholly functionalist analysis. Yet uniquely among the four opinions in the case, Justice Thomas identifies a function not only for the Direct Tax Clauses but also for the realization requirement: to preserve a distinction between income and property and thereby protect the states' property tax base from federal invasion.

In that last respect, Thomas's opinion contrasts most starkly with the solo concurrence of Justice Jackson. While joining the majority opinion in full, Jackson writes separately to emphasize that the judicial role in tax disputes "should be limited" and Congress's view should be "controlling."[63] Quoting Justice John Marshall Harlan's dissent in *Pollock II*, Jackson argues that the remedy for any congressional abuse of the taxing power "is to be found at the ballot-box,"

[58] *Moore*, 144 S. Ct. at 1720 (Thomas, J., dissenting).

[59] *Id.*

[60] *Id.* at 1721.

[61] *See id.* at 1723–25.

[62] *See id.* at 1722.

[63] *See id.* at 1697, 1699 (Jackson, J., dissenting).

not in the courtroom.[64] Although she does not go so far as to say explicitly that the Direct Tax Clauses should be rendered entirely nonfunctional, she never explains what function the Direct Tax Clauses would serve under her expansive vision of Congress's tax authority.

Given how often constitutional debates are framed in formalist-versus-functionalist terms, the nonfunctionalist (or nearly nonfunctionalist) approach suggested by Justice Jackson's solo concurrence might seem like a sharp break from tradition. Yet as noted at the outset, nonfunctionalism in the constitutional law of tax has a long lineage—a lineage tracing back to Justice Chase's 1796 opinion in *Hylton*. And although historical pedigree is not enough to make the case for nonfunctionalism, it is perhaps enough to persuade us not to dismiss Jackson's approach out of hand. The next Part takes seriously the case for nonfunctionalism—as well as for formalism and functionalism—seeking to fill in the justificatory blanks that all four *Moore* opinions leave.

II. Interpreting the Direct Tax Clauses and the Sixteenth Amendment

Formalism, functionalism, and nonfunctionalism each come in multiple flavors. The purest form of formalism—what Rick Pildes calls "apurposive rule-following"[65]—seeks to adjudicate legal disputes based on rules found in authoritative sources such as texts and precedents without any reference to the substantive goals underlying those rules.[66] Pure formalism does not resolve the question of which sources are authoritative—for example, whether stare decisis can trump the original public meaning of constitutional text. Yet pure formalists of the originalist and precedentialist variety agree that the rule, not the purpose underlying the rule, ought to control.

Pure functionalism elevates what pure formalism subordinates: the substantive goals underlying textual and precedential rules. A pure functionalist might conclude that a textual or precedential rule mandates Result A in a particular case yet still choose Result B because she believes that B better serves the purposes underlying the rule.

---

[64] *See id.* (quoting Pollock v. Farmers' Loan & Tr. Co. (*Pollock II*), 158 U.S. 601, 680 (1895) (Harlan, J., dissenting)).

[65] Pildes, *supra* note 43, at 612–15.

[66] *See* Alexander, *supra* note 1, at 531.

Ptasynski, the Uniformity Clause case mentioned above,[67] arguably illustrates the pure functionalist approach. In *Ptasynski*, the Court reasoned that even though Article I, Section Eight, Clause One formally requires geographic uniformity in taxation, the purpose underlying that provision is to prevent Congress from granting an "undue preference" to one state over another.[68] Although the crude oil excise tax in *Ptasynski* exempted oil from northern Alaska, the Court determined that the preference for Alaskan oil was not "undue"—and thus did not violate the Uniformity Clause's purpose—because the "fragile economy," "harsh environment," and "remote location" of Alaska's northerly regions all made it more expensive to drill for crude oil there.[69]

Ptasynski alternatively might be interpreted as an example of nonfunctionalism. Since lawmakers almost always will be able to cite some economic rationale for geographic differentiation, *Ptasynski* effectively renders the Uniformity Clause nugatory.[70] *Ptasynski* thus illustrates the blurriness of the line between functionalism and nonfunctionalism: A functionalist might interpret a rule to serve a very narrow purpose, while a nonfunctionalist might construe the same rule to serve no purpose at all.

Along with pure formalism, pure functionalism, and pure nonfunctionalism, we can imagine various hybrids. For example, a decisionmaker might use text or precedent to narrow her range of interpretive options and then select the option that—in her view—best serves the purpose underlying the relevant law. (We might call this "functionalism within formalism.") Or if the decisionmaker concludes that the law serves no useful purpose, she might choose—from among textually or precedentially permissible interpretations—the option that accomplishes the least ("nonfunctionalism within formalism"). To be sure, some formalists might argue that "functionalism within formalism" and "nonfunctionalism within formalism" are not formalism at all, since they violate formalism's core commitment to apurposive rule-following. The goal here is not to adjudicate boundary disputes

---

[67] *See supra* text accompanying note 10.

[68] United States v. Ptasynski, 462 U.S. 74, 86 (1983).

[69] *Id.* at 85.

[70] *See* Gale Ann Norton, *The Limitless Federal Taxing Power*, 8 HARV. J.L. & PUB. POL'Y 591, 604 (1985).

among formalism, functionalism, and nonfunctionalism but to explore and evaluate how these three approaches—in their paradigmatic instantiations—would seek to settle the most important open questions in the constitutional law of tax.

A. FORMALISM

Formalism is often thought to require that law be "relatively determinate"[71]—that interpretation of the relevant legal materials leads to "one and only one outcome either in all cases or in some significant and contested range of cases."[72] Determinacy is not, on its own, an incontrovertible justification for formalism: Some consequentialists—for example—might argue that judges and legal decisionmakers should choose the outcome that maximizes overall welfare even if text or precedent point determinately to a different result. Still, even if determinacy does not lead ineluctably to formalism, indeterminacy over a significant and contested range of cases would undermine one argument for formalism: that it fosters more efficient resolution of disputes than functionalism or consequentialism would.[73]

The two most significant and contested contemporary controversies over Congress's constitutional taxing power concern wealth taxes and mark-to-market income taxes. Several prominent politicians on the left—including Senators Elizabeth Warren and Bernie Sanders—have rallied around the idea of a two percent wealth tax on households with net worth over $50 million.[74] Former President Biden, for his part, proposed a "billionaire minimum income tax" that—despite the word "billionaire" in the title—would have applied to the unrealized gains of households with net worth over $100 million.[75] Neither of these proposals is likely to become law in a Trump-Vance Administration (though back in 1999, Donald Trump—then a prospective candidate for the Reform Party presidential nomination—did propose a one-time wealth tax of 14.25 percent on individuals with

[71] *See* Alexander, *supra* note 1, at 544.

[72] Brian Leiter, *Legal Formalism and Legal Realism: What Is the Issue?*, 16 Legal Theory 111, 111 (2010).

[73] *See* Alexander, *supra* note 1, at 544–45.

[74] *See* Ultra-Millionaire Tax Act of 2024, S. 4017, 118th Cong.

[75] *See* Libin Zhang, *Billionaires, Millionaires, and Other Defined Terms in 2023*, 182 Tax Notes Fed. 145 (2024).

$10 million or more in net worth to pay off the national debt[76]). Yet if and when Democrats regain control of Congress and the White House down the road, wealth and mark-to-market income tax proposals are both likely to reenter the national policy conversation.

Problematically for formalists, the relevant constitutional texts and applicable judicial precedents generate indeterminate conclusions regarding both proposals. Start with the text of the Direct Tax Clauses. Even as those provisions were being crafted, the definition of "direct tax" was recognized as nebulose. An oft-cited passage in James Madison's notes from the Constitutional Convention mentions Rufus King of Massachusetts asking his fellow delegates, "[W]hat was the precise meaning of *direct* taxation?" According to Madison, "No one answd."[77] William Paterson, a Convention delegate and later a Supreme Court Justice, acknowledged in the 1796 *Hylton* case that although he was confident that capitation taxes and land taxes were direct taxes, he was uncertain whether the category extended beyond that, adding that "perhaps" a general tax on personal property would be a direct tax, too.[78]

Even if one accepts a narrow definition of "direct taxes" as limited to uniform per capita taxes and real property taxes, the implications for modern-day tax controversies remain ambiguous. If a wealth tax like Senator Warren's includes real property within the base, does that make it a direct tax requiring apportionment? The Constitution's text does not tell us. The term "direct tax" could be read to include capitation taxes and taxes exclusively on real property, or it could be read to include capitation taxes and all taxes that include real property within the base. Formalism offers few resources with which to resolve that interpretive dispute.

A similar murk surrounds the meaning of the word "income"— or "incomes"—in the Sixteenth Amendment, which carves out an

---

[76] *See* Phil Hirschkorn, *Trump Proposes Massive One-Time Tax on the Rich*, CNN (Nov. 9, 1999), https://www.cnn.com/ALLPOLITICS/stories/1999/11/09/trump.rich/index.html.

[77] 2 The Records of the Federal Convention of 1787, at 350 (Max Farrand ed., 1911) [hereinafter Farrand's Records].

[78] Hylton v. United States, 3 U.S. (3 Dall.) 171, 177 (1796) (opinion of Paterson, J.). Even the meaning of "capitation" is unclear: Though modern-day dictionaries define "capitation" as a uniform per capita payment, the term was sometimes used in the eighteenth century— including by Adam Smith—to refer to taxes that varied based on an individual's wealth. *See* 2 Adam Smith, An Inquiry into the Nature and Causes of the Wealth of Nations 526 (London, W. Strahan & T. Cadell 1776); James R. Campbell, *Dispelling the Fog About Direct Taxation*, 1 Brit. J. Am. Legal Stud. 109, 124–29 (2012).

exemption from the apportionment requirement for "taxes on incomes, from whatever source derived." In a recent study, legal scholars Thomas Lee, Lawrence Solum, and James Phillips and linguist Jesse Egbert examine 978 uses of the word "income" or its plural in American English from 1900 to 1912 and conclude that "there were no examples of *income(s)* clearly referring to unrealized gain."[79] And if unrealized gains are not "income," then the Sixteenth Amendment would not authorize Congress to adopt a mark-to-market income tax, though there would still remain the question of whether a mark-to-market income tax is a direct tax in the first place.

Yet as Lee and coauthors emphasize, their linguistic analysis is based on a general corpus of fiction and nonfiction texts,[80] not an examination of tax-specific sources. And in the lead-up to the ratification of the Sixteenth Amendment, tax specialists sometimes did use the term "income" to encompass unrealized gains. For example, the Treasury Department promulgated regulations in 1911 that construed the term "income" for purposes of a corporate excise tax to include the "increase in the value of unsold property" if reflected on a corporation's books.[81] Thus, at least by the time that Delaware, New Mexico, and Wyoming ratified the Sixteenth Amendment in February 1913, thereby pushing the amendment over the constitutionally requisite three-quarters threshold, the idea that "income" could include unrealized gains was not entirely foreign to the American legal lexicon. Lee and coauthors argue that for originalists, the definition of income "as used in *common speech*"—not the meaning "implicit in the technicalities of pre-1913 tax statutes"—should control.[82] Jake Brooks and David Gamage respond that lay readers at the time of ratification

---

[79] *See* Thomas R. Lee, Lawrence B. Solum, James C. Phillips & Jesse Egbert, *Corpus Linguistics and the Original Public Meaning of the Sixteenth Amendment*, 73 Duke L.J. Online 159, 163 (2024). For a critique of Lee et al.'s analysis, see Brief of Amici Curiae Professors of Tax Law, Legal History, and Computational Science in Support of Respondent at 13–20, Moore v. United States, 144 S. Ct. 1680 (2024) (No. 22-800).

[80] *See* Lee et al., *supra* note 79, at 163 & n.13.

[81] *See* T.D. 1742 § 43, 14 Treas. Dec. Int. Rev. 123, 127 (1911). For further examples of Treasury decisions construing "income" under the 1909 Act to include unrealized gains, see John R. Brooks & David Gamage, *The Original Meaning of the Sixteenth Amendment*, 102 Wash. U. L. Rev. 1, 44–45 (2024). As Brooks and Gamage note, Wisconsin's 1911 income tax statute defined "income" to include the estimated rental value of owner-occupied real estate—an indication that at least one state legislature that ratified the Sixteenth Amendment understood "income" to include more than cash and in-kind proceeds realized through sales and exchanges. *See id.* at 49; 1911 Wis. Sess. Laws 484, 485.

[82] *See* Lee et al., *supra* note 79, at 188.

would have understood the Sixteenth Amendment to be using the term "income" in a technical legal sense.[83] Lurking in the background is a larger debate—implicating both textualism and originalism—as to whether statutory and constitutional provisions should be interpreted from the perspective of the "ordinary English speaker" or the "ordinary lawyer."[84]

To be sure, formalists need not be textualists or originalists. In theory, a formalist could acknowledge that the original meanings of "direct tax" and "incomes" are ambiguous but that judicial precedent settles the matter. Unfortunately for formalists, the precedent is not much clearer than the text.

As noted above, the Supreme Court stated in the 1881 case *Springer* that "direct taxes, within the meaning of the Constitution, are only capitation taxes . . . and taxes on real estate."[85] But *Pollock*, the later-in-time decision, held (1) that income cannot be distinguished from source, and (2) that direct taxes include taxes on personal property as well as real property.[86] Furthermore, *Macomber* interpreted the Sixteenth Amendment as abrogating only the first of *Pollock*'s two holdings and also as incorporating a realization requirement into the definition of "income."[87] Accordingly, one might conclude (1) that as a matter of precedent wealth taxes are direct taxes subject to the apportionment requirement whether or not they include real property in the base, and (2) that taxes on unrealized gains are direct taxes, too, because they fall outside the Sixteenth Amendment's carveout for "income" taxes.

This is, indeed, what Justice Barrett's formalist concurrence in *Moore* concludes. But even if Barrett correctly reads the relevant precedents, the Supreme Court's meta-precedent—its precedent about

---

83 Brooks & Gamage, *supra* note 81, at 11–12.

84 *Cf.* Amy Coney Barrett, *Congressional Insiders and Outsiders*, 84 U. Chi. L. Rev. 2193, 2209 (2017) (distinguishing the "ordinary English speaker" and "ordinary lawyer" perspectives in the statutory interpretation context). *Compare* Lawrence B. Solum, *The Public Meaning Thesis: An Originalist Theory of Constitutional Meaning*, 101 B.U. L. Rev. 1953, 1957 (2021) (advancing the thesis that "the original meaning of the constitutional text is best understood as its public meaning: roughly, the meaning that the text had for competent speakers of American English at the time each provision of the text was framed and ratified"), *with* John O. McGinnis & Michael B. Rappaport, *The Constitution and the Language of the Law*, 59 Wm. & Mary L. Rev. 1321, 1325–26 (2018) (arguing that "the Constitution is written in the distinctive idiom of the law," which often differs from "standard, everyday English").

85 102 U.S. 586, 602 (1880).

86 *See* Pollock v. Farmers' Loan & Tr. Co. (*Pollock II*), 158 U.S. 601, 618 (1895).

87 *See* Eisner v. Macomber, 252 U.S. 189, 205–06, 212 (1920).

precedent—permits the Court to overrule "egregiously wrong" decisions that have "caused significant negative jurisprudential or real-world consequences."[88] As Alex Zhang notes, "the majority view" among tax scholars is that the Court in *Macomber* "got it wrong,"[89] but whether *Macomber* was *egregiously* wrong is up for debate. Thus, even if the Court's precedents lead to determinate conclusions regarding the constitutionality of wealth and mark-to-market income taxes (e.g., because *Macomber* bars both), the Court's meta-precedent casts a cloud over its first-degree precedents.

Insofar as formalists ground their approach on values of predictability and certainty, the indeterminacy of the relevant texts and precedents (and meta-precedents) would seem to make formalism a poor fit in the direct tax domain.[90] But predictability and certainty are not the only bases upon which formalism might be justified, and they might not even be the strongest reasons for adopting a formalist approach. If all we cared about were predictability and certainty, then we could adopt a rule that any tax lawfully enacted by Congress is ipso facto constitutional, thus removing any doubt after the time of enactment about the tax's validity. (In other words, we could be constitutional nonfunctionalists.) Or we could provide for fast-track review of any constitutional challenge to a tax statute at the Supreme Court, which could authoritatively settle the matter.[91]

Yet formalism potentially serves other values beyond predictability and certainty. For example, Larry Alexander argues that formalism can successfully mediate moral conflict in societies whose members disagree deeply about what morality requires in concrete cases.[92] Although Alexander himself argues that rules "must be determinate" in order to fulfill this conflict-resolution function,[93] we

---

[88] *See* Ramos v. Louisiana, 590 U.S. 83, 115, 121–23 (2020) (Kavanaugh, J., concurring) (synthesizing stare decisis factors).

[89] Alex Zhang, *Rethinking* Eisner v. Macomber *and the Future of Structural Tax Reform*, 92 Geo. Wash. L. Rev. 179, 187 n.48 (2024).

[90] *Cf.* Philip P. Frickey, *Revisiting the Revival of Theory in Statutory Interpretation: A Lecture in Honor of Irving Younger*, 84 Minn. L. Rev. 199, 207–08 (1999) (observing—in the context of statutory interpretation—that "[i]f the new formalism has not resulted in greater predictability and certainty. . . , it has failed on its own terms").

[91] *See* Pildes, *supra* note 43, at 613 (noting that "[d]eterminate rules are not the only means of providing institutional settlement" and that the Supreme Court "can authoritatively settle moral conflicts if its institutional role is socially accepted as legitimate").

[92] *See* Alexander, *supra* note 1, at 532–34, 540–45.

[93] *See id.* at 546.

can reformulate Alexander's argument to deemphasize determinacy. According to this reformulation, even if reasonable people can disagree about whether the term "direct taxes" included personal property taxes circa 1787 or whether the word "income" encompassed unrealized gains circa 1913, what matters is that these are semantic disagreements and not moral ones. They do not, for example, require participants to articulate and defend controversial views about the requirements of distributive justice. Formalism thus turns the temperature of legal controversies down several notches.

Of course, semantic disagreements about the meaning of "direct taxes" circa 1787 or "income" circa 1913 carry moral stakes insofar as they implicate what sorts of policies Congress can pursue to address economic inequality. And participants in these semantic debates may arrive at positions that—consciously or subconsciously—reflect their first-order moral beliefs. Yet even if this "attitudinal model" of legal interpretation is accurate—even if moral beliefs and personal policy preferences are the strongest influence on how judges and other legal decisionmakers interpret texts and precedents[94]—the empirical accuracy of the attitudinal model is not a knock-down argument against formalism. First, formalists might argue that judges and other legal decisionmakers should strive to set aside their moral beliefs and personal policy preferences even if many real-world judges do not. Second, formalists might argue that even if moral beliefs and personal policy preferences inevitably influence interpretation, judges and legal decisionmakers still should justify their interpretations in formalist—rather than consequentialist or other moral—terms. The virtue of formalism, or so the argument goes, is that it sublimates normative disagreement and thereby allows participants in interpretive debates to avoid "moral combat."[95]

The case for formalism on conflict-avoidance grounds—the idea that formalist reasoning defuses moral disagreement and thereby helps to maintain social peace—is, admittedly, uneasy. For one thing, the best way to manage moral disagreement may be to acknowledge it rather than to repress it. For another, excluding moral reasoning from legal interpretation does not necessarily prevent moral combat; it

[94] *See* Jeffrey A. Segal & Alan J. Champlin, *The Attitudinal Model*, *in* Routledge Handbook of Judicial Behavior 17, 17 (Robert M. Howard & Kirk A. Randazzo eds., 2017).

[95] *See* Larry Alexander & Emily Sherwin, The Rule of Rules: Morality, Rules, and the Dilemmas of Law 14 (2001).

simply shifts the combat zone from the domain of law to the domain of ordinary politics. Tax inevitably implicates questions of distributive justice, and even if judges do not appeal to moral arguments in tax cases, presumably the politicians who make tax law in the first instance still will.

Formalists might respond to the last point by emphasizing the distinction between legislating and judging. It is one thing for a majority of duly elected Senators and House members to pass tax legislation that reflects their and their constituents' moral views. But it is another thing, or so the argument goes, for unelected and unaccountable judges to impose their own moral views on a deeply divided nation. The losers in the latter case have reason to be doubly offended: Not only have their moral views been disregarded, but their votes have been, too. And for that reason, nonformalist judging may be especially threatening to social peace.

Summing up: In the area of direct taxation, the indeterminacy of text and precedent leads to indeterminate conclusions for the case for formalism. Determinacy is not a sufficient justification for formalism, but it may not be a necessary condition either. To be sure, the case for formalism would be stronger if the relevant texts and precedents were clearer, since formalism would then bring the additional benefit of predictability. Yet even without that, one can sketch out a potentially plausible argument for a formalist approach to the Direct Tax Clauses and the Sixteenth Amendment—an argument that could cross-apply to any number of other areas where constitutional interpretation implicates deep moral divisions.

B. FUNCTIONALISM

Formalism and functionalism are, in one sense, polar opposites: Whereas formalists apply legal rules without regard to the underlying purposes of those rules, functionalists give purpose pride of place. Yet in another respect, formalism and functionalism can be understood as parallel and potentially complementary strategies for managing moral disagreement and social conflict. This notion of functionalism as—like formalism—a strategy for avoiding moral combat is arguably immanent in the work of legal theorist Ronald Dworkin, who by his own account began his legal career as a tax lawyer.[96]

---

[96] *See* Edward J. McCaffery, *Taxing Wealth Seriously*, 70 TAX L. REV. 305, 305 n.∗ (2017). Stephen Guest describes Dworkin's early career at the law firm Sullivan & Cromwell

Although Dworkin is sometimes described as a "formalist,"[97] Dworkin's theory of "law as integrity" is perhaps best characterized as "functionalism within formalism." Dworkin argues that judges and other legal decisionmakers should choose the interpretation of a statute that "provides the best case for what the plain words of the statute plainly require"[98]—an argument that, he says, extends to the Constitution as well.[99] A judge applying Dworkin's approach is functionalist—not consequentialist—because he "is not trying to reach what he believes is the best substantive result, but to find the best justification he can of a past legislative event."[100] Yet Dworkin's functionalism operates within formalism—not outside—insofar as it does not permit a judge to ignore text or precedent altogether.[101]

In illustrating this approach in his magisterial book *Law's Empire*, Dworkin offers the evocative metaphor of judges as successive authors of a "chain novel," with each picking up the plot where the last one left off. In Dworkin's metaphor, "[e]ach novelist aims to make a single novel of the material he has been given" so that "it can be construed as the work of a single author rather than, as in the fact, the product of many different hands."[102] And the novelist has not fulfilled her task, according to Dworkin, if she "leaves unexplained some major structural aspect of the text."[103]

But why *should* a judge (or other legal decisionmaker) interpret a law to advance what she perceives to be the law's underlying purpose rather than—say—her own conception of the good? In attempting to answer that question, Dworkin gestures to the goal of molding a

---

somewhat differently, writing that Dworkin "dealt mainly with international commercial transactions" but not mentioning any particular tax focus. STEPHEN GUEST, RONALD DWORKIN 12 (3d ed. 2013).

[97] Brian Leiter describes Dworkin as a "sophisticated formalist," but Leiter is using "formalism" here in contradistinction to "realism," not in contradistinction to "functionalism." According to Leiter, Dworkin "remains within the formalist camp because he sees the law as rationally determinate and . . . he denies that [judges'] decisions are not bound by authoritative legal standards." Brian Leiter, *Positivism, Formalism, Realism*, 99 COLUM. L. REV. 1138, 1146 (1999) (reviewing ANTHONY SEBOK, LEGAL POSITIVISM IN AMERICAN JURISPRUDENCE (1998)).

[98] RONALD DWORKIN, LAW'S EMPIRE 338 (1986).

[99] *Id.* at 379.

[100] *Id.* at 338.

[101] *See id.* at 401.

[102] *Id.* at 229–30.

[103] *Id.* at 230.

"true community" out of a "morally pluralistic society,"[104] but his normative argument for "law as integrity" remains—as others have observed—incomplete.[105] Perhaps that incompleteness is fitting if we think of *Law's Empire* as itself a chain novel in progress. And although Dworkin never finished the novel himself, fellow legal philosopher Jeremy Waldron—who was once Dworkin's colleague and is now mine—has picked up where Dworkin left off in explaining why "law as integrity" might be a worthy aspiration.

As Waldron notes, "you can imagine a community in which a major victory by one faction is pursued by the victors in a sort of year-zero fashion, so that it is as though their opponents never existed politically, never had any achievements; their statutes—along with their statues—are all torn down."[106] According to Waldron, law as integrity rejects that conquistadorial approach to political competition. As Waldron puts it:

> Integrity requires winners to moderate their self-righteousness, to accept a principled understanding of their victory, and to be willing to submit to a principled understanding of their opponents' victories too. . . . By treating the legacy of our victories and our opponents' victories as common ground for us all, we change the meaning of what it is to suffer a political defeat, and we mitigate the antagonism and resentment on one side or the other that political conflict involves.[107]

So understood, law as integrity—or in this Article's terminology, functionalism within formalism—suggests an optimistic perspective on the possibility of building consensus in a morally pluralistic society. It contrasts with the pessimism implicit in Alexander's argument for pure formalism, behind which looms "a brooding omnipresence of moral dissensus and irresolvable conflict."[108] Functionalism seeks to forge a "true community" by taking seriously the normative reasons motivating the constitutional and legislative work product of different political factions. Pure formalism, on the contrary, steers clear of explicitly normative reasoning on the view that

---

[104] *See id.* at 213–15.

[105] For one skeptical account of "law as integrity," see Andrei Marmor, *Integrity in* Law's Empire (Cornell L. Sch. Rsch. Paper No. 19-28, 2019), https://ssrn.com/abstract=3422173.

[106] Jeremy Waldron, *The Rise and Decline of Integrity* 14–15 (N.Y.U. Sch. L. Pub. L. Working Paper No. 19-49, 2020), https://ssrn.com/abstract=3463479.

[107] *Id.* at 15.

[108] *See* Pildes, *supra* note 43, at 616.

admitting moral arguments into legal interpretation will exacerbate the same antagonisms and resentments that functionalism aims to allay.

As applied to the constitutional law of tax, functionalism calls on judges to interpret the Direct Tax Clauses, the Sixteenth Amendment, and the Constitution's other tax provisions "in the best light possible."[109] It rejects interpretations that would render the Direct Tax Clauses nonfunctional, for in that case, the judge-as-chain-novelist has not fulfilled her assignment. But beyond that, judges who share a general commitment to functionalism will not necessarily agree on a particular plot line. Justice Thomas's dissent offers one functional account of the Direct Tax Clauses, according to which those provisions protect the states' property tax base from congressional encroachment and thereby require a realization rule to distinguish income from wealth. Although that is not the only possible functionalist account of the Direct Tax Clauses, the absence of any competing functionalist reading of the Direct Tax Clauses in *Moore* may leave the mistaken impression that Justice Thomas's theory is the only functionalist game in town.

To see how functionalism might lead to doctrinal conclusions that differ from Thomas's, consider first Thomas's claim that the purpose of the Direct Tax Clauses is to protect the states' property tax base from federal encroachment. Thomas's account struggles to explain why the Direct Tax Clauses nonetheless allow *apportioned* direct taxes. Although Thomas notes that "[t]he Federalists' defense of the new national taxing power stressed that the Federal Government would impose direct taxes only sparingly,"[110] he offers no reason why anyone else should have credited the Federalists' defense. He quotes Alexander Hamilton's argument that in light of the apportionment requirement, direct taxes "never can oppress a particular state, by an unequal imposition,"[111] but Hamilton's argument is notably different from Thomas's base protection rationale. For Thomas, the Direct Tax Clauses serve to limit federal taxation of property, leaving that tax base to the states. For Hamilton, the Direct Tax Clauses serve to

---

[109] *See* Dworkin, *supra* note 98, at 244.

[110] Moore v. United States, 144 S. Ct. 1680, 1715 (2024) (Thomas, J., dissenting).

[111] *See id.* (quoting 3 The Debates in the Several State Conventions on the Adoption of the Federal Constitution 365 (Jonathan Elliot ed., 1836)).

ensure that Congress—when it lays direct taxes—does not discriminate against disfavored states.

The difference between Hamilton's antidiscrimination rationale and Thomas's base protection rationale bears important implications for the constitutionality of an unapportioned federal wealth tax. If the Direct Tax Clauses serve an antidiscrimination function, then an unapportioned federal tax on all wealth might be less problematic than an unapportioned federal tax on real property, as the former would not favor industry-heavy states over their land-rich agricultural counterparts. Thus, Hamilton's antidiscrimination rationale provides a reason for reading the term "direct taxes" to include federal real property taxes but not to include federal wealth taxes that apply equally to both real and personal property.

Even if one accepts Thomas's base protection rationale as the function of the Direct Tax Clauses, that conclusion does not answer the question of whether the category of "direct" taxes includes only capitation and real property taxes (as *Springer* holds) or whether it extends further to personal property taxes (per *Pollock*). Although state and local property taxes were widespread in the early American republic, they mostly applied to real property.[112] That remains the case today: According to Census Bureau data, taxes on real property account for approximately ninety-eight percent of all property tax revenues collected by state and local governments.[113] Thus, insofar as the purpose of the Direct Tax Clauses was—and is—to protect the states' historic tax base from congressional encroachment, it is not obvious that this purpose would justify reading the term "direct taxes" to include personal property taxes, which were not circa 1787—and are still not—a significant source of state or local revenue.

---

[112] *See* Glenn W. Fisher, The Worst Tax? A History of the Property Tax in America 39 tbl.3.1 (1996) (noting that every state had a land tax in 1796, but only four out of sixteen taxed personal property beyond horses and cattle); Edward T. Howe & Donald J. Reeb, *The Historical Evolution of State and Local Tax Systems*, 78 Soc. Sci. Q. 109, 111 (1997) (noting that as of 1796, "real property components (*i.e.*, land and buildings) constituted most of the property tax base" in the states). The rise of state-level "general property taxes"—which applied broadly to real and personal property—was primarily an early- to mid-nineteenth-century phenomenon. *See* Mabel Newcomer, *The Decline of the General Property Tax*, 6 Nat'l Tax J. 38, 45 (1953).

[113] U.S. Gov't Accountability Off., GAO-09-521, Real Estate Tax Deduction: Taxpayers Face Challenges in Determining What Qualifies; Better Information Could Improve Compliance 2 n.4 (2009), https://www.gao.gov/products/gao-09-521 (citing Census Bureau data from 2006). Although more recent data does not appear to be available, there is little reason to believe that the percentage has changed dramatically since 2006.

Thomas's functionalist account also flounders when he states that the "only way" to draw a distinction between income and wealth is through a realization requirement.[114] Certainly, many economists would bristle at that claim. The "economic conception of income," or the "Schanz-Haig-Simons definition," posits that an individual's income is the sum of her consumption and the change in her net worth in a given period, whether or not the change in net worth is realized.[115] That definition—rooted in the late-nineteenth-century work of German scholar Georg von Schanz and subsequently elaborated by American economists Robert Haig and Henry Simons in the 1920s and 1930s—provides another way to distinguish income from wealth: Income is the flow of wealth between two moments in time, while wealth is the total stock of value at a given moment in time.

Concededly, the Schanz-Haig-Simons definition of income is vague as to the relevant time period; a court that sought to distinguish income from wealth via the Schanz-Haig-Simons concept would need to set some outer bound on the interval over which "income" could be measured.[116] But while that would require courts to engage in line-drawing (e.g., to say that a tax on the change in an individual's net worth over a year is an "income" tax but a tax on the change in an individual's net worth over a lifetime is a wealth tax), law often requires courts to engage in line-drawing. A realization rule similarly requires courts to engage in line-drawing insofar as courts must determine when something other than a sale constitutes a realization event. Indeed, a realization requirement may not even work to distinguish income from wealth, because a wealth tax—like an income tax—can be realization-based. As Robin Morgan notes, the government can impose a realization-based wealth tax by waiting until assets are sold and then taxing the entirety of an asset's value, not just the change in the asset's value over a given period.[117] Put another way, a

---

[114] *See Moore*, 144 S. Ct. at 1709, 1722 (Thomas, J., dissenting).

[115] *See* David White, *The Impact of Economic Theory on Capital Gains Tax Reform Proposals*, *in* Capital Gains Taxation: A Comparative Analysis of Key Issues 30, 38, 48 (Michael Littlewood & Craig Elliffe eds., 2017).

[116] Without some temporal bound, the Schanz-Haig-Simons concept of income would fail to distinguish income from wealth because "[a]ll our wealth reflects an increase in our economic power from the moment of birth." Daniel J. Hemel, *The Low and High Stakes of* Moore, 180 Tax Notes Fed. 563, 565 (2023).

[117] *See* Robin Morgan, *Are There Differences Between Wealth and Income Taxation? Yes, but Less Than We Think*, 76 Tax L. Rev. 325, 357 (2023).

realization requirement is neither necessary nor sufficient to distinguish income from wealth.

All of which is to say that Justice Thomas's functionalist account of the Constitution's direct tax provisions is tenuous at best. Interpreted in their best light, the Direct Tax Clauses arguably serve an antidiscrimination function rather than a state tax base protection function, and even if one views the Direct Tax Clauses in base protection terms, those provisions still could be read—consistent with their base protection purpose—to permit unapportioned federal wealth and mark-to-market income taxes. Yet by failing to articulate any functionalist alternative to Thomas's account, the other Justices in *Moore* effectively ceded the field to Thomas. Thomas's functionalist theory of the Direct Tax Clauses—flawed though it may be—will remain the reigning functionalist account of the Constitution's direct tax provisions as long as no one else shows up to the fight.

C. NONFUNCTIONALISM

Whereas functionalists seek to interpret constitutional provisions in their "best light," nonfunctionalists adopt an approach of "lights out," construing constitutional provisions so that they accomplish as little as possible, if anything at all. Importantly, this is not the same as saying that a provision is "nonjusticiable": A provision may be nonjusticiable—in the sense of being inappropriate for judicial resolution—but still normatively binding on nonjudicial actors such as the Executive and Congress.[118] Still other constitutional provisions may be—in Larry Sager's words—"legally valid to their full conceptual limits" but "underenforced by the federal judiciary," even if not altogether nonjusticiable.[119] Sager offers, as an example, the rational basis strand of Fourteenth Amendment equal protection doctrine: State and local officials are subject to a normatively binding obligation to treat all persons within their jurisdiction equally, even though federal courts rarely enforce that obligation outside certain limited contexts (e.g., race, religion, national origin, and gender).[120] Nonjusticiability and

---

[118] *See, e.g.*, Luther v. Borden, 48 U.S. (7 How.) 1, 42 (1849) (stating that "it rests with Congress to decide" how to interpret and enforce the Republican Guarantee Clause).

[119] Lawrence Gene Sager, *Fair Measure: The Legal Status of Underenforced Constitutional Norms*, 91 Harv. L. Rev. 1212, 1221 (1978).

[120] *See id.* at 1215–17.

underenforcement kick the interpretive can to the other branches or the states. Nonfunctionalism asserts that the can is empty.

Put another way, nonjusticiability and underenforcement speak to the *who* of constitutional interpretation: whether the courts or the political branches should be responsible for determining the meaning of constitutional provisions. By contrast, nonfunctionalism—like formalism and functionalism—addresses the *how* of constitutional interpretation: which methods should interpreters apply and which values should they seek to vindicate when they construe constitutional commands. (In its strongest form, nonfunctionalism would not even recognize constitutional provisions as normatively binding commands.) To illustrate the distinction, one could coherently maintain that a provision is nonjusticiable *and* that nonjudicial actors (e.g., federal and state legislators and executive branch officials) ought to interpret the provision formalistically or functionally. By the same token, one could remain committed to judicial supremacy—the idea that the judiciary is the authoritative interpreter of the Constitution—while also believing that certain constitutional provisions should be construed as nonfunctional. Moreover, nonfunctionalism—like functionalism—can operate within or outside formalism: in the former case, by favoring the least functional reading of text and/or precedent; in the latter case, by ignoring text and precedent altogether.

Nonfunctionalism also comes in narrower and broader varieties. A narrow nonfunctionalist approach to the Direct Tax Clauses would straiten the scope of direct taxation without taking aim at other constitutional provisions. Calvin Johnson offers one version of a narrow nonfunctionalist theory of the Direct Tax Clauses, arguing that "[t]he formula for apportionment was brought into the Constitution solely because the formula counted each slave as three-fifths of a person" and that with slavery a thing of the past, the Direct Tax Clauses are "devoid of any remaining constitutional purpose."[121] Bruce Ackerman takes the argument a step further and writes that the Direct Tax Clauses are not only obsolete, but "tainted."[122] According to Ackerman,

[121] Calvin H. Johnson, *Apportionment of Direct Taxes: The Foul-Up in the Core of the Constitution*, 7 Wm. & Mary Bill Rts. J. 1, 41–42 (1998); *accord* John R. Brooks & David Gamage, *Taxation and the Constitution, Reconsidered*, 76 Tax L. Rev. 75, 89 (2022) ("[T]he meaning of 'direct tax' is inextricably bound up with slavery and the Three-Fifths Clause in a way that makes the term effectively meaningless today.").

[122] Ackerman, *supra* note 17, at 4.

"American law should leave no stone unturned in its effort to root out any residue of its original compromise with slavery—and the 'direct tax' clause is a small, but potentially damaging, stone."[123]

The records of the Constitutional Convention provide a shaky foundation for the claim that the Direct Tax Clauses exist solely to shield slavery from taxation. The first delegate to propose that "direct" taxes be apportioned on the same basis as representatives—on July 12, 1787—was Gouverneur Morris,[124] the most outspoken opponent of slavery at the Convention[125] and a critic of the Three-Fifths Clause.[126] At the time, one group of delegates favored the allocation of representatives based on a periodic census, with each enslaved person counting for three-fifths of a free person.[127] Morris, by contrast, proposed that the Convention should establish the initial allocation of representatives and that Congress should be allowed to make any further changes itself.[128] Morris—who represented Pennsylvania at the Convention but whose family owned a sprawling estate in New York—argued that property "was the main object of Govt.," and thus "certainly it ought to be one measure of the influence due to those who were to be affected by the Governmt."[129] His goal was to protect the power of richer seaboard states vis-à-vis the poorer states soon to emerge along the frontier—*not* to entrench the power of the slaveholding South vis-à-vis the North.

Morris introduced the first direct tax resolution—"Provided always that direct Taxation ought to be proportioned according to representation"[130]—in response to the critique that legislators would use their authority over the allocation of representatives to aggrandize their own states' power. As historian Howard Ohline observes, "the assumption was that congressmen would not indiscriminately increase the representation of their states if the same action resulted

---

[123] *Id.* at 58.

[124] 1 Farrand's Records, *supra* note 77, at 591–92.

[125] *See* William Michael Treanor, *Gouverneur Morris and the Drafting of the Federalist Constitution*, 21 Geo. J.L. & Pub. Pol'y 1, 3 (2023).

[126] *See* Howard A. Ohline, *Republicanism and Slavery: Origins of the Three-Fifths Clause in the United States Constitution*, 28 Wm. & Mary Q. 563, 568 (1971).

[127] *See id.* at 579.

[128] *See id.* at 540.

[129] *Id.* at 533.

[130] *See* 1 Farrand's Records, *supra* note 77, at 589.

in an increase of their direct taxes."[131] The Convention coalesced quickly around the idea that direct taxes should be allocated on the same basis as representation—perhaps unsurprisingly given that only a few years had passed since American revolutionaries rallied around the slogan "taxation without representation is tyranny." Even the advocates for a census-based allocation of representatives—such as the South Carolinian Pierce Butler—"admitt[ed] the justice of Mr. Govr. Morris's motion,"[132] which passed unanimously.[133]

Thus, although it is true that the direct tax language entered the Constitution with the issue of slavery looming in the background, it is much harder to argue that the language is "inextricably bound up with ... the Three-Fifths Clause."[134] The idea of linking representation to the apportionment of direct taxes emerged as part of an *alternative* to having any population-based formula for allocating representatives, with or without the Three-Fifths Clause. Ultimately, Morris won the battle but lost the war: He persuaded his fellow delegates to tie direct taxation to representation, but the Convention nonetheless voted the next day to allocate representatives in the lower House according to a decennial Census, with the infamous three-fifths rule for counting the enslaved.[135]

A careful reading of the Convention records thus supports the conclusion that Morris's original purpose for introducing his direct tax resolution became obsolete, but it became obsolete long before the Thirteenth Amendment abolished slavery. Morris's purpose was to peel away support for a census-based allocation of representatives, but within a day, that gambit failed. Less than two weeks later, Morris proposed that the apportionment requirement for direct taxes be stricken from the Constitution, adding that he "had only meant it as a bridge to assist us over a certain gulph; having passed the gulph the bridge may be removed."[136] But to the extent that Morris's direct tax

---

[131] *See* Ohline, *supra* note 126, at 580.

[132] *See* 1 FARRAND'S RECORDS, *supra* note 77, at 592. Madison's notes add that "Mr. Mason admitted the justice of the principle," "General Pinkney liked the idea," and "Mr. Wilson approved the principle." *Id.*

[133] *See id.* at 589, 592–93.

[134] *Contra* Brooks & Gamage, *supra* note 121, at 89.

[135] *See* 1 FARRAND'S RECORDS, *supra* note 77, at 597.

[136] 2 FARRAND'S RECORDS, *supra* note 77, at 106. In his notes on the Convention, Madison added—in a footnote to Morris's "gulph" remark—that that the "object" of the direct tax proviso "was to lessen the eagerness on one side, & the opposition on the other, to the share

proposal was "linked to a deeply discredited ideology,"[137] it was not the ideology of slavery, which Morris resolutely opposed. It was an anti-populist ideology that sought to shield private property from redistributive claims—an ideology which lost out in the fight over the allocation of representatives but suffuses much of the rest of the Constitution, from the structure of the Senate and the indirect election of Presidents to the life-tenured judiciary and the steep obstacles to ratification of amendments.[138]

The obsolescence of Morris's original reason for introducing his direct tax resolution does not necessarily weaken either the case for formalism or the case for functionalism. On the formalist side, most modern-day originalists elevate the original public meaning of constitutional texts, not the original intentions of the delegates to the Constitutional Convention. Since the Convention debates were conducted in secret—and records of the proceedings were not published until decades later[139]—members of the public would not have understood that Morris introduced the direct tax language as part of a multidimensional chess game over the allocation of representatives. Functionalists, for their part, do not claim that they are seeking to recover the actual motives underlying a particular text or precedent. The fact that Morris renounced the direct tax proviso after he lost the battle over allocation of representatives would not, therefore, give functionalists significant pause. Recall that for functionalists—or at least, for functionalists in a Dworkinian mode—law as integrity obligates them to make "the best case" for what the "plain words of [the Constitution] plainly require."[140] The Direct Tax Clauses plainly

---

of representation claimed by the S[outhern] States on account of the Negroes." *See id.* at 106 n.∗. However, Madison's footnote is inconsistent with his own notes from the July 12 debate and the Convention Journal, both of which show that the delegates unanimously approved the linkage between direct taxes and representation before they decided whether to allocate representatives by population and before they settled on the three-fifths formula. *See* 1 *id.* at 589–93. On Madison's post hoc attempt to justify the three-fifths compromise—along with his efforts to downplay Morris's objection to slavery—see Mary Sarah Bilder, Madison's Hand: Revising the Constitutional Convention 163–64 (2015).

[137] *See* Brooks & Gamage, *supra* note 121, at 99.

[138] Michael J. Klarman, The Framers' Coup: The Making of the United States Constitution 607, 625–28 (2016).

[139] *See* Bilder, *supra* note 136, at 225 (noting the 1819 publication of the Convention's official records); *id.* at 1 (1840 publication of Madison's notes).

[140] *See* Dworkin, *supra* note 98, at 338.

remain a part of the Constitution, even if Morris wished that his handiwork had been resected.

At the same time, evidence from the Constitutional Convention does not defeat the case for direct tax nonfunctionalism, though it suggests that the case for nonfunctionalism must be based on something more than an "effort to root out any residue of [the] original compromise with slavery."[141] For example, a proponent of narrow nonfunctionalism might argue that the Direct Tax Clauses, as supplemented by the Sixteenth Amendment, do little to protect the states' property tax base from federal intrusion and thus that Thomas's base protection rationale for the Direct Tax Clauses is implausible. In support of this argument, a narrow nonfunctionalist might note that according to modern public finance theory, an income tax—by reducing the after-tax return from saving—encourages individuals to consume their wealth immediately and thereby shrinks the property tax base.[142] According to this view, restricting Congress's power to tax property does little to preserve the states' revenue-raising capacity because an income tax—even when limited to realized gains—still encroaches upon state revenue-raising.

Proponents of narrow nonfunctionalism might argue further that the Direct Tax Clauses are not only an ineffectual means of protecting the states' property tax base from federal encroachment but also an unnecessary means. Building on Herbert Wechsler's "political safeguards of federalism"[143] and Larry Kramer's later elaboration on Wechsler's theme,[144] a narrow nonfunctionalist might argue that the remarkably durable two-party system obviates the need for the Direct Tax Clauses because the interests of national-level officials are well aligned with their co-partisans at the state and local level. In other words, Congress is unlikely to enact a federal tax that undermines state revenue-raising capacity too severely because members of Congress do not want to kneecap their party allies. The Direct

[141] *Contra* Ackerman, *supra* note 17, at 58.

[142] For a clear and concise explanation of the relationship between income taxation and savings incentives, see Joseph Bankman & David A. Weisbach, *The Superiority of an Ideal Consumption Tax over an Ideal Income Tax*, 58 Stan. L. Rev. 1413, 1417–19 (2006).

[143] *See* Herbert Wechsler, *The Political Safeguards of Federalism: The Rôle of the States in the Composition and Selection of the National Government*, 54 Colum. L. Rev. 543 (1954).

[144] *See* Larry D. Kramer, *Putting the Politics Back into the Political Safeguards of Federalism*, 100 Colum. L. Rev. 215, 219 (2000).

Tax Clauses, or so the argument goes, function only to prevent Congress from doing what Congress would not do anyway.[145]

A broader form of nonfunctionalism might look beyond the Direct Tax Clauses and take aim at the very notion that a two-century-old Constitution should constrain the menu of policy options in a modern-day democracy. Broad nonfunctionalists might argue that our "proslavery Constitution" is rotten to the core—that the legacy of slavery permeates not only the explicit slavery-related provisions such as the Three-Fifths Clause,[146] the Slave Trade Clause,[147] and the Fugitive Slave Clause,[148] but also the Electoral College,[149] the Article V amendment process,[150] the Fifth Amendment Takings Clause,[151] and many others. According to this view, Ackerman's argument that we should "root out any residue of [the] original compromise with slavery" requires us to take a nonfunctionalist chainsaw to the entire document.

Apart from the issue of slavery, broad nonfunctionalists might contest the core idea of "constitutionalism": that certain issues of moral, social, and economic significance should be removed from the

---

[145] Ari Glogower points to another possible reason for narrow nonfunctionalism in the direct tax domain: A broad interpretation of the Direct Tax Clauses "shields the rich from taxation, while allowing potentially onerous tax burdens on lower-income taxpayers." *See* Glogower, *supra* note 13, at 817. Yet to the extent that the Direct Tax Clauses limit the taxation of the rich, that may be—even from the perspective of the working class—a feature rather than a bug. As Nobel Prize-winning economists Finn Kydland and Edward Prescott note, a working-class majority "might rationally choose to have a constitution which limits their power . . . to expropriate the wealth of the capitalist class" in order to induce capital owners to make long-term investments that ultimately raise overall wages. Finn E. Kydland & Edward C. Prescott, *Rules Rather Than Discretion: The Inconsistency of Optimal Plans*, 85 J. Pol. Econ. 473, 486 (1977). For further discussion of Kydland and Prescott's argument and its application to the Direct Tax Clauses, see Daniel J. Hemel, *Capital Taxation in the Middle of History*, 99 N.Y.U. L. Rev. 1554, 1560–61, 1579–87 (2024).

[146] U.S. Const. art. I, § 2, cl. 3.

[147] *See id.* art. I, § 9, cl. 1 (preventing Congress from banning the importation of slaves prior to 1808 and limiting the duty on imported slaves to ten dollars per person).

[148] *See id.* art. IV, § 2, cl. 3 (requiring states to return fugitive slaves).

[149] *See* Paul Finkelman & Gabriel J. Chin, *How We Know the US Constitution Was Proslavery*, 9 Const. Stud. 1, 16 (2024) (observing that the Constitution allocated electors based on congressional representation and thus reflected the Three-Fifths Clause, thereby "giving the slave states extra power in electing the president").

[150] *See id.* at 17 ("Art. V's requirement of a three-fourths majority of the states to ratify any amendment to the Constitution gave the slave states a perpetual veto over any constitutional changes.").

[151] *See id.* at 26 (noting that as a result of the Takings Clause, emancipation through ordinary legislative action "would have bankrupted the nation").

domain of majoritarian rule.[152] Broad nonfunctionalists might start from the same premise as formalism and functionalism—that the fundamental challenge for law in a pluralistic polity is to mediate moral disagreement while maintaining social cohesion, or at least social peace—but follow that premise to a starkly different conclusion. They might argue that moral disagreements are best resolved through the give-and-take of ordinary politics, which leaves opportunities for compromise, coalition formation, and change over time. Constitutionalism, by contrast, encourages individuals and groups to frame their claims in absolutist terms—in the language of inalienable rights and hard-and-fast proscriptions instead of flexible accommodations and mutually beneficial bargains.

These arguments for nonfunctionalism, narrow or broad, are certainly contestable. The key point here, though, is that the case for nonfunctionalism can be made on principled grounds. A judge or other legal decisionmaker may have good reasons for favoring the narrowest possible interpretation of a constitutional provision or even for rejecting constitutional constraints altogether. Put another way, nonfunctionalism is not necessarily lawless: Rather, a judge or other legal decisionmaker who reads the Direct Tax Clauses nonfunctionally is choosing to respect one source of law—the federal tax statutes enacted by a democratically accountable Congress—instead of an indeterminate and arguably archaic bicentenarian text.

But while there are potentially persuasive arguments for nonfunctionalism in and beyond the direct tax domain, those arguments do not appear in Justice Jackson's concurrence. Justice Jackson does not explain why the remedy for abuses of the taxing power "is to be found at the ballot-box"[153] when the courthouse doors remain open to other constitutional claims. Justice Jackson's concurrence thus leaves her vulnerable to the charge of "checkerboard" constitutionalism,[154] where some constitutional provisions are interpreted formally or functionally while others are construed to minimize their efficacy. Whatever benefits nonfunctionalism might bring in terms of increasing predictability or facilitating political compromise, these benefits are lost

---

[152] *See* Martin Loughlin, Against Constitutionalism 1–7, 192–202 (2022) (defining and criticizing "constitutionalism").

[153] Moore v. United States, 144 S. Ct. 1680, 1699 (2024) (Jackson, J., concurring).

[154] *Cf.* Dworkin, *supra* note 98, at 179 (using the term "'checkerboard' laws" to describe laws that systematically treat likes unalike).

when nonfunctionalism is scattershot: when individual judges or other legal decisionmakers decide—for undisclosed reasons—to breathe life into some constitutional provisions but not others.

It may be too much to ask of a single Justice that she propound a principled justification for direct tax nonfunctionalism in the first direct tax case she has ever faced.[155] More fairly, this Article's analysis of nonfunctionalism culminates with a challenge rather than a critique. The challenge for narrow nonfunctionalists is to explain why we should read the Direct Tax Clauses so that they accomplish nearly nothing even as we continue to read other constitutional provisions for all they are worth. The challenge for broad nonfunctionalists is to articulate a theory explaining why the entire Constitution should not be normatively binding on modern-day majorities—a more demanding task than merely explaining why unelected judges should defer to the constitutional interpretations of the legislature and the executive. In sum, nonfunctionalism is a potentially defensible approach to the interpretation of specific constitutional provisions and perhaps to the document as a whole, but to be defensible, it needs to be defended.

Conclusion

The formalism/functionalism dichotomy offers a useful—though partial—framework for understanding controversies over the interpretation of the Direct Tax Clauses and the Sixteenth Amendment. This Article endeavors to intervene in the formalism/functionalism

---

[155] Elie Mystal suggests that beyond the direct tax context, Justice Jackson may be a practitioner of nonfunctionalism within formalism, to use this Article's terminology. "Jackson's view," according to Mystal's interpretation, boils down to this: "If the Constitution is clear, then of course the courts should step in. But if it's not, it makes no sense to have unelected rulers place their interpretations over and above those of the representatives that people actually voted for." Elie Mystal, *Ketanji Brown Jackson Is Redefining What It Means to Be a Liberal Justice*, NATION (Aug. 5, 2024), https://www.thenation.com/article/society/ketanji-brown-jackson-legal-philosphy.

Mystal's distillation of Jackson's judicial philosophy, if accurate, still leaves the question of whether Jackson is a nonfunctionalist or a judicial passivist—whether she thinks that constitutional provisions (outside of "clear" rules) are not normatively binding on anyone or whether she thinks that those provisions, though still normatively binding, are not suitable for judicial enforcement. Moreover, if her objections to constitutionalism are broad (e.g., based on the view that the dead hand of the past should not constrain modern-day majorities), then it is not clear why she would make an exception for cases where the Constitution is itself clear. Again, it may not be reasonable to demand answers to these questions from a first-year Justice. The key point is that nonfunctionalism—whether narrow or broad, and whether inside or outside formalism—requires a defense, though in Jackson's case, that defense may well be forthcoming.

debate while elevating a third candidate: nonfunctionalism. With respect to formalism, the Article underscores the indeterminacy of text and precedent in the direct tax domain while also acknowledging that formalism might be justifiable on conflict-avoidance grounds even when formalist methods do not yield determinate outcomes in many cases. The Article also seeks to show why functionalism, as distinct from consequentialism, might be an attractive means of maintaining social cohesion and why functionalism in the direct tax context need not lead to the same conclusions that the only functionalist opinion in *Moore* derives. Finally, the Article identifies nonfunctionalism as a potentially principled alternative to formalism and functionalism—an alternative that has deep historical roots in the constitutional law of tax but that is defended only shallowly in the one nonfunctionalist opinion in *Moore*.

Zooming further out, all three approaches—formalism, functionalism, and nonfunctionalism—can be understood as different strategies for managing moral conflict. Formalism pursues that objective by modulating the language of legal argument—by inducing participants in constitutional controversies to frame their claims in semantic and/or doctrinal rather than moral terms. Functionalism takes a different tack, seeking to construct a unifying normative vision out of a sequence of constitutional provisions and precedents in an attempt to forge consensus among competing ideologies and interests. Nonfunctionalism, for its part, intentionally leaves the work of consensus-building to the domain of ordinary politics. Which approach most effectively achieves the goal of social cohesion is a contestable—and empirical—question. *Moore* does not resolve that question—indeed, *Moore* itself resolves very little. But *Moore* provides a lens into that debate, widening our field of vision to include the nonfunctionalist alternative to formalism and functionalism while bringing the merits and demerits of each approach into clearer focus.

ANTHONY J. CASEY AND
JOSHUA C. MACEY

PURDUE PHARMA AND THE NEW BANKRUPTCY EXCEPTIONALISM

On its surface, the Supreme Court's decision in *Harrington v. Purdue Pharma L.P.*[1] is about whether the text of the United States Bankruptcy Code gives courts the authority to approve nonconsensual third-party releases in Chapter 11.[2] Section 1123(b)(6) of the Code allows Chapter 11 plans of reorganization to "include any other appropriate provision not inconsistent with the applicable provisions of this title."[3] The question posed to the Court in *Purdue* was whether that language encompasses nonconsensual third-party releases. The

Anthony J. Casey is the Donald M. Ephraim Professor of Law and Economics at the University of Chicago Law School and the Faculty Director of the Center on Law and Finance. Joshua C. Macey is an Associate Professor of Law at Yale Law School.

Authors' note: The Richard Weil Faculty Research Fund and the Paul H. Leffmann Fund provided generous research support to Casey. We are grateful to William Baude for his excellent comments and to Kelly Bu, Emma Lotts, and Elaine Wang for their excellent research assistance.

[1] 603 U.S. 204 (2024).

[2] *Id.* at 209. Nonconsensual third-party releases are court orders that release nondebtor third parties from claims of liability when not all claimholders consent to the release. These releases are often provided as part of a settlement in exchange for contributions from the party benefitting from the releases. The orders often include channeling injunctions that prevent the claimholders from bringing their claims against the nondebtors and force them instead to bring their claims exclusively against a settlement fund.

[3] 11 U.S.C. § 1123(b)(6).

The Supreme Court Review, 2025.
 Published by The University of Chicago Press. https://doi.org/10.1086/735879

majority concluded it does not. Justice Kavanaugh, writing for a four-Justice dissent, disagreed.

Although both the majority and dissent anchored their arguments in the text of Section 1123, non-textual concerns featured prominently in both opinions. For his part, Justice Kavanaugh emphasized that bankruptcy law is designed to address the kind of collective-action problems that arise in mass tort cases like *Purdue*.[4] He further argued that third-party releases are an important tool in facilitating a collective resolution.[5] The majority, by contrast, expressed concern that bankruptcy courts operate as if they have a "roving commission to resolve all such problems that happen [their] way, blind to the role other mechanisms (legislation, class actions, multi-district litigation, consensual settlements, among others) play in addressing them."[6]

A version of this concern has long troubled courts and academics, who have argued that bankruptcy courts exercise too much discretion and too much power. These critiques typically refer to a concept of "bankruptcy exceptionalism." Often the concern is that a non-Article III tribunal (the bankruptcy court) wields Article III powers.[7] As we explain in Part I, we are skeptical that there is anything exceptional about these powers. All courts exercise discretion and fill gaps, and bankruptcy court discretion is firmly rooted in the text of the Bankruptcy Code and subject to de novo review in an Article III tribunal.[8] Still, since the Code was enacted, the concern that bankruptcy courts possess too much authority and too much discretion has been the basis of numerous constitutional decisions limiting the power of bankruptcy courts.

An important but misunderstood feature of the *Purdue* decision, however, is that the Supreme Court did not address any constitutional

[4] *Purdue Pharma L.P.*, 603 U.S. at 227–28 (Kavanaugh, J., dissenting).

[5] *Id.* at 234–36.

[6] *Id.* at 220 (majority opinion).

[7] N. Pipeline Constr. Co. v. Marathon Pipe Line Co., 458 U.S. 50 (1982); Stern v. Marshall, 564 U.S. 462 (2011).

[8] The discretion of the bankruptcy courts is quite routine and provided for by the text of the Bankruptcy Code. Sometimes the Code allocates discretion to the courts by using broad language (like "appropriate"). Other times it invokes the language of equity (like "fair and equitable"). There is nothing particularly exceptional about these grants of discretion. As Justice Scalia wrote more than twenty-five years ago, drafting a law requires a decision about whether to set ex ante rules or to leave matters to ex post judicial discretion. And a court announcing a judicial doctrine must decide how much discretion to leave to future courts. *See generally* Antonin Scalia, *The Rule of Law as a Law of Rules*, 56 U. Chi. L. Rev. 1175 (1989).

issues, at least not directly. With regard to Article III, the Second Circuit, in affirming the use of third-party releases, had decided that de novo review by an Article III court was required but noted it was providing that review.[9] Thus, the question before the Supreme Court was not whether a bankruptcy court could approve the releases, but whether an Article III court hearing bankruptcy cases could. And yet, the majority repeatedly framed its inquiry as being about the power of *bankruptcy* courts.[10]

As a result, the opinion is flush with exceptionalist rhetoric about expansive bankruptcy court power while the holding does not address the issue head on. Instead, the Court develops a new statutory canon of constraint that narrowly construes terms in the Bankruptcy Code—like "appropriate," "necessary," and "fair and equitable"—to cabin judicial authority in bankruptcy cases.[11] This, we argue, represents a new bankruptcy exceptionalism in which broad statutory provisions that should be interpreted by their plain meaning are narrowed to constrain the powers of bankruptcy courts.

This new bankruptcy exceptionalism will be disruptive to bankruptcy practice—far beyond what the *Purdue* Court contemplated. The Court explicitly left several issues like consensual releases and full-satisfaction plans unresolved. Those issues are now percolating through the lower courts, producing inconsistent approaches by different judges—even those within the same district.[12] And many other innovative bankruptcy tools which find support in the broad language

---

[9] *In re* Purdue Pharma L.P., 69 F.4th 45, 68 (2d Cir. 2023), *rev'd sub nom.* Harrington v. Purdue Pharma L.P., 603 U.S. 204 (2024).

[10] *Purdue Pharma L.P.*, 603 U.S. at 218 ("[W]e do not think paragraph (6) affords a bankruptcy court the authority the plan proponents suppose."); *id.* ("Doubtless, paragraph (6) operates to confer additional authorities on a bankruptcy court. But the catchall cannot be fairly read to endow a bankruptcy court with the 'radically different' power to discharge the debts of a nondebtor without the consent of affected nondebtor claimants." (citations omitted)); *id.* at 218–19 ("Each of those 'other' paragraphs authorizes a bankruptcy court to adjust claims without consent only to the extent such claims concern the debtor."); *id.* at 219 ("The dissent neglects why a bankruptcy court may resolve derivate claims under paragraph (3). . . ."); *id.* at 220 ("[N]o one (save perhaps the dissent) thinks it provides a bankruptcy court with a roving commission to resolve all such problems that happen its way. . . .").

[11] Indeed, the Supreme Court's recent bankruptcy jurisprudence repeatedly emphasizes its intention to interpret the Code to narrow the discretion of bankruptcy courts. *See infra* Section II.B. Meanwhile, the Third Circuit announced a new good-faith filing requirement that will curtail the scope of cases that can come before a bankruptcy judge. *See In re* LTL Mgmt., LLC, 64 F.4th 84 (3d Cir. 2023).

[12] *See infra* Part III.

of the Code are now in doubt. These include substantive consolidation, third-party injunctions, and for-cause dismissal. Indeed, one of the foundational pillars of Chapter 11's statutory structure is its requirement that a plan can be confirmed only if it "does not discriminate unfairly, and is fair and equitable" to dissenting impaired classes.[13] This language carries with it a long history of doctrine, judicial gloss, and discretionary invocation to prevent debtor misbehavior.[14] It does not, however, come with a statutory definition.

A canon of narrowing broad language and constraining bankruptcy judges thus draws into question the scope and meaning of these provisions and many of the common tools of the practice. If this new approach sticks, it could create barriers to collective resolution by incentivizing parties, lawyers, and bankruptcy judges to find workarounds that are immune to appellate scrutiny.

This Article explores these developments in three parts. Part I describes and critiques conventional scholarly claims about bankruptcy exceptionalism. Part II presents the Supreme Court's approach to bankruptcy over the last four decades. While the Court has historically questioned the constitutionality of bankruptcy courts in a direct fashion, we speculate that *Purdue* marks the culmination of the Court's shift toward a canon that reads broad provisions in the Code narrowly to protect Article III power while avoiding direct constitutional questions. Part III considers how this new bankruptcy exceptionalism will affect bankruptcy practice and incentivize costly workarounds.

I. The Scholarly Account of Bankruptcy Exceptionalism

Justice Gorsuch's majority opinion was expressing a familiar sentiment about the U.S. bankruptcy system. For years, scholars and courts have asserted, often critically, that federal bankruptcy powers are exceptional.[15] For example, Pamela Foohey and Jonathan Lipson

---

[13] 11 U.S.C. § 1129(b).

[14] It has even made its way into the insolvency laws of several other jurisdictions around the world.

[15] *See, e.g.*, Jonathan C. Lipson, *Debt and Democracy: Towards a Constitutional Theory of Bankruptcy*, 83 Notre Dame L. Rev. 605, 611 (2008) ("Bankruptcy appears to result in exceptions to conventional notions about the treatment of a variety of constitutional protections involving, among others, property, due process, and religious liberty."); Jonathan M. Seymour, *Against Bankruptcy Exceptionalism*, 89 U. Chi. L. Rev. 1925, 1956 (2022) ("[B]ankruptcy scholars are close to consensus that *some* kind of bankruptcy exceptionalism exists, whether typified by the

recently celebrated the *Purdue* decision for pushing back against bankruptcy exceptionalism, which in their view "reflects a willingness to bend the rule of law."[16] Likewise, Jonathan Seymour has praised recent Supreme Court decisions for rejecting "bankruptcy exceptionalism," arguing exceptionalism "exacerbates corrosive trends within the bankruptcy system that cannot readily be corrected by other courts, especially in the field of corporate reorganizations."[17]

What exactly do scholars and courts mean when they describe bankruptcy courts as exceptional? At first glance, some common descriptions seem unremarkable. Bankruptcy courts fill gaps, find exceptions to general rules, craft equitable remedies, and take account of unwritten norms. But so do judges in all courts in the United States.[18] So there would need to be something distinctive about bankruptcy courts and bankruptcy practice—something more fundamental—to set them apart.

To us the most plausible account of the bankruptcy exceptionalism critique would reflect a concern that bankruptcy courts are using the Code's broad grants of authority—for example Sections like 105(a)

---

claim that the bankruptcy court is a 'court of equity' with broad equitable powers, by a distinctly equitable flavor of statutory interpretation, or in some other form.").

[16] Jonathan C. Lipson & Pamela Foohey, *The End(s) of Bankruptcy Exceptionalism:* Purdue Pharma *and the Problem of Social Debt*, 46 Cardozo L. Rev. (forthcoming 2025), https://ssrn.com/abstract=5025124.

[17] Seymour, *supra* note 15, at 1930.

[18] Perhaps not Justice Gorsuch. But he is an outlier. During his confirmation hearings, one of his Tenth Circuit dissenting opinions refusing to find an equitable exception to a statute was widely criticized. The case—commonly referred to as the "frozen trucker case"—involved a truck driver who was fired for driving his employer's truck to safety to avoid life-threatening cold. The majority of the Tenth Circuit upheld findings by the Department of Labor (DOL) and an administrative law judge (ALJ) that the termination violated a law prohibiting discharge where an employee "refuses to operate a vehicle" because of unsafe conditions. TransAm Trucking, Inc. v. Admin. Rev. Bd., 833 F.3d 1206 (10th Cir. 2016). Then-Judge Gorsuch dissented, explaining that the driver *operated* the vehicle and the statute only protected *refusal to operate*. He explained that neither the DOL, nor the ALJ, nor the Tenth Circuit had the power to read an exception into the statute. Far from labeling the majority as "exceptionalist" for its broad interpretation, critics viewed Gorsuch's position as the exception. One scholar argued that Gorsuch's approach revealed that that he might be unfit for the Supreme Court. Jed Shugerman, *Neil Gorsuch and the 'Frozen Trucker,'* Slate (Mar. 21, 2017, 10:38 AM), https://slate.com/news-and-politics/2017/03/neil-gorsuchs-arrogant-frozen-trucker-opinion-shows-he-wants-to-be-like-scalia.html.

Justice Gorsuch's reasoning in the frozen trucker case is of a kind with his *Purdue* opinion. Both are formalist approaches exhibiting a distrust of judicial discretion exercised in the first instance by non-Article III judges. Similar themes can also be found in his concurrence in *Loper Bright Enterprises v. Raimondo*, 603 U.S. 369 (2024), which was decided the day after *Purdue* and overruled the *Chevron* doctrine. *Id.* at 416 (Gorsuch, J., concurring).

and 1123(b)(6)[19]—to resolve issues that would ordinarily be adjudicated elsewhere but, because of the exigencies of financial distress, can more efficiently be resolved in a single proceeding. To understand this as problematic assumes that Article III courts should play a special role in private litigation, and that the availability of appellate review does not protect that special role.[20] A critic of exceptionalism might also worry here that bankruptcy courts are resolving too many issues too quickly, and in a manner inconsistent with due process or Article III values.[21]

In the remainder of this Part, we explore these different accounts of bankruptcy exceptionalism. We start with the weak version focused on the exercise of equitable discretion and then move to more substantial claims grounded in constitutional concerns of due process, structure, and separation of powers.

A. THE WEAK VERSION OF EXCEPTIONALISM: DISCRETION

Some critics describe bankruptcy courts as exceptional for exercising discretion. Because this same discretion is exercised by other federal and state courts, in our view, these accounts reflect an anti-bankruptcy bias that has long permeated academic scholarship.

One account suggests there are both benign and malignant forms of bankruptcy exceptionalism. Of the benign, the authors say:

> [I]n truth we are all exceptionalists to some extent. No one seriously argues that bankruptcy courts lack equitable discretion to recognize exceptions to general rules. . . .[22]

This description is puzzling. Remove the word bankruptcy and the passage describes a common feature in law. Equitable discretion—the

[19] Section 105(a) gives bankruptcy courts authority to "issue any order, process, or judgment that is necessary or appropriate to carry out the provisions of this title." 11 U.S.C. § 105(a). Section 1123(b)(6), as discussed, gives bankruptcy courts authority to "include" in a reorganization plan "any other appropriate provision not inconsistent with the applicable provisions of this title." 11 U.S.C. § 1123(b)(6).

[20] Though beyond the scope of this Article, we think that the Article III requirement is satisfied by claimants' right to appeal bankruptcy court decisions to an Article III court. *See* Anthony J. Casey & Aziz Z. Huq, *The Article III Problem in Bankruptcy*, 82 U. Chi. L. Rev. 1155 (2015); *see also* Anthony J. Casey & Joshua C. Macey, *The Bankruptcy Tribunal*, 96 Am. Bankr. L.J. 749 (2022).

[21] *Cf.* Anthony J. Casey & Joshua C. Macey, *Bankruptcy by Another Name*, 133 Yale L.J.F. 1016 (2024).

[22] Lipson & Foohey, *supra* note 16 (manuscript at 7).

power to fashion exceptions to general rules—is part of the day-to-day functioning of courts, as is the power to grant traditional equitable remedies when appropriate.[23] Of course, the exercise of equitable discretion comes up more often in some cases than others.[24] A case seeking an injunction will look different from a case seeking contract damages. But common-law systems have been working out those differences since long before the Constitution's Bankruptcy Clause was drafted.

At times, critics of bankruptcy exceptionalism shift between using the term "equity" in the colloquial sense of discretion and the more formal sense of the doctrines and remedies available in a traditional court of chancery.[25] Talk of bankruptcy courts as "courts of equity"[26] would seem to invoke the latter use of the term, but the discussion is rarely that precise. In identifying the acts of equitable discretion in bankruptcy cases, the criticism is often more about everyday discretion pursuant to statutory grants of authority.

The *Purdue* case highlights the imprecision. The direct question to the Court was unquestionably about a statutory grant of discretion. The debtors' argument relied primarily on the power granted in Section 1123(b)(6) to defend the releases.[27] But nonconsensual third-party releases are structured as channeling injunctions to protect the estate, which are traditional equitable remedies. And so, one would expect some discussion of equity in the more formal sense. Indeed, as we pointed out in an amicus brief, examples of nondebtor releases imposed by the Lord Chancellor date at least as far back as 1619.[28]

---

[23] *See* Henry E. Smith, *Equity as Meta Law*, 130 YALE L.J. 1050, 1057–58 (2021) ("[E]quity in American law is a response to universal problems in legal systems and human institutions generally."); *see also* Samuel L. Bray, *The System of Equitable Remedies*, 63 UCLA L. REV 530 (2016).

[24] Smith, *supra* note 23, at 1143–44 (identifying equity as useful in cases that present problems of "polycentricity, conflicting rights, and opportunism"). *See generally* Samuel L. Bray, *Equity, Law and the Seventh Amendment*, 100 TEX. L. REV. 467 (2022) (identifying equity's role in case aggregation).

[25] *See* Samuel L. Bray, A Student's Guide to the Meanings of Equity (Apr. 21, 2021) (unpublished manuscript), https://ssrn.com/abstract=3821861.

[26] *See, e.g.*, Pepper v. Litton, 308 U.S. 295, 304 (1939).

[27] *See* Brief for Debtor Respondents at 19, Harrington v. Purdue Pharma L.P., 603 U.S. 204 (2024) (No. 23-124), 2023 WL 7042400.

[28] *See* Tiffin v. Hart (Eng. Ct. Ch. 1618–19), *in* REPORTS OF CASES DECIDED BY FRANCIS BACON, BARON VERULAM, VISCOUNT ST. ALBANS, LORD CHANCELLOR OF ENGLAND, IN THE HIGH COURT OF CHANCERY (1617–1621), at 161 (John Ritchie ed., 1932); Brief of Amici Curiae Law Professors in Support of Respondents at 9, *Purdue Pharma L.P.*, 603 U.S. 204 (No. 23-124).

Likewise, the Second Circuit had noted that releases should be viewed against the "backdrop of equity."[29] But the Court's opinion eschews any reference to equitable remedies and focuses instead on colloquial discretion.

In any event, bankruptcy courts are federal courts, and the federal judicial system has not recognized a distinction between courts of law and equity since 1938.[30] The federal courts today are not structured separately such that some administer law and others equity. Rather, federal courts simply issue equitable remedies (in the traditional sense) or exercise equitable discretion (colloquially) as circumstances require.[31] Within any case, a federal court might invoke the formal law-equity distinction when determining which remedies and procedures are available in a particular dispute.[32]

To foreshadow a bit, the Court's dismissive approach to formal equitable doctrines in bankruptcy cases is consistent with our view of a new bankruptcy exceptionalism. One would think equitable remedies are still available in all federal cases. The notion that this would not be true in a bankruptcy case is exceptional.

---

[29] *In re* Purdue Pharma L.P., 69 F.4th 45, 79 (2d Cir. 2023) (citing *United States v. Energy Resources Co., Inc.*, 495 U.S. 545 (1990), for the proposition that Section 1123(b)(6) should be read as conferring authority "deriving from bankruptcy courts' status as 'courts of equity'").

[30] Certain courts within the United States do still function as courts of equity. The Delaware Court of Chancery, which presides over the nation's most complex corporate and business governance cases, famously does. As a result, complex corporate issues that go before that court are decided by judges arguably exercising discretion and invoking broader remedies than their counterparts in the Delaware Superior Court, which operates as a court of law. One might argue that Delaware's structure is "exceptional"—it is one of only three states that still maintains separate equity courts—but the structure is one with a long historical pedigree.

Other states have started to create specialized business courts in attempts to compete with Delaware. They seek to replicate the specialization of the Delaware Court of Chancery, but without the specific qualities of a court of equity.

[31] One noteworthy aspect of this structure is that large corporate bankruptcy proceedings supplant Delaware's equitable proceedings when it comes to corporate governance claims even though they do not distinguish between law and equity. But this, too, is not "exceptional." It is a feature of any proceeding in a federal court that could otherwise have been brought in a state court of equity, such as those brought under diversity jurisdiction.

[32] Samuel Bray has argued that there is still a system of equity that exists within the unified federal courts. Bray, *supra* note 23. And the distinction still controls the Seventh Amendment right to a civil jury. Whether a litigant in federal court has a right to a jury turns in part on whether a case would have been brought in a court of law or equity in 1791. This vestige of the law-equity divide applies and is enforced in all federal cases, including bankruptcy cases. Notably, however, the Seventh Amendment does not apply to cases in state court. A party litigating in state court is not entitled to a jury under the Seventh Amendment even if the case arose from federal substantive law. *See* Minneapolis & St. Louis R. Co. v. Bombolis, 241 U.S. 211, 223 (1916).

Another criticism of bankruptcy courts as exceptional comes from Seymour, who has presented the most thorough and sophisticated account of bankruptcy exceptionalism. He observes:

> Everywhere in bankruptcy, judges alter rights, create remedies, and steer cases out of fidelity to unwritten norms that seek to advance what those within the bankruptcy culture understand to be the better and more efficient functioning of the bankruptcy system. Various scholars have attempted to describe and systemize these norms.[33]

Again, we ask: What is exceptional here? It is easy for those in a certain field to convince themselves that what they are doing is "special" or "unique." But unwritten norms appear throughout our legal system, and courts regularly challenge or push back on those norms.[34] Recounting specific unwritten norms is useful to understanding bankruptcy law,[35] just as it is useful in understanding other areas of law. Bankruptcy cases may require the exercise of judicial discretion *more often* than civil cases,[36] but bankruptcy courts use the same methods and procedures as other courts.[37] Thus, whatever differences exist are a matter of degree rather than kind. The claim that bankruptcy courts are exceptional because they craft remedies, alter rights, and observe or rely on unwritten norms strikes us as a peculiarly narrow and parochial view.

---

[33] Seymour, *supra* note 15, at 1938; *see also* Laura N. Coordes, *Narrowing Equity in Bankruptcy*, 94 Am. Bankr. L.J. 303, 325 (2020) (describing the practice of "equitable interpretation" in which bankruptcy courts select whatever interpretation of the Code promotes bankruptcy values).

[34] *See* William Baude, Jud Campbell & Stephen E. Sachs, *General Law and the Fourteenth Amendment*, 76 Stan. L. Rev 1185 (2024); William Baude, *Beyond Textualism*, 46 Harv. J.L. & Pub. Pol'y 1331 (2023).

[35] *See* Douglas G. Baird, The Unwritten Law of Corporate Reorganizations (2022); Vincent S.J. Buccola, *Unwritten Law and the Odd Ones Out*, 131 Yale L.J. 2559 (2022) (reviewing Baird, *supra*).

[36] One of us has argued that bankruptcy courts exist and are valuable because bankruptcy cases pose incomplete contracting problems at higher rates than other cases. Anthony J. Casey, *Chapter 11's Renegotiation Framework and the Purpose of Corporate Bankruptcy*, 120 Colum. L. Rev. 1709, 1744–45 (2020). Having specialist courts with experience in a particular issue is useful. A specialist court will be more adept at reaching the right outcome, but that doesn't mean they are applying a different law or procedure.

[37] We are unaware of any empirical study suggesting that bankruptcy judges exercise discretion in a different way or more often than other judges.

B. THE STRONG VERSION OF EXCEPTIONALISM: AUTHORITY, STRUCTURE, AND DUE PROCESS

The previous Section deals with some of the rhetoric used in discussing bankruptcy exceptionalism. Other accounts suggest the underlying concern is about the constitutionality of bankruptcy procedure. We turn now to those accounts.

1. *Substantive Authority*. Congress's authority to create bankruptcy law comes from the Constitution's Bankruptcy Clause.[38] The substantive limits of this power are broad but untested.[39] Often, then, the real question is about statutory interpretation: What has Congress authorized?

One criticism of bankruptcy courts as exceptional is that they exercise more authority than granted to them by Congress. That position, however, disregards the plain text of the Bankruptcy Code, which contains broad language delegating discretion and authority to courts. The discretionary powers bankruptcy courts possess are based not on an antiquarian notion that they are "courts of equity" or that they exercise "equitable powers," but rather on specific provisions of the Bankruptcy Code that delegate authority to bankruptcy courts and empower the courts to respond to novel or complex issues. For example, Section 1123(b)(6) gives a bankruptcy court authority to approve a plan that includes "any other appropriate provision not inconsistent with the applicable provisions of this title."[40] Section 1112(b) allows a court to dismiss a case "for cause."[41] Section 364(d) provides that a court "may authorize" the debtor to obtain credit if certain conditions are met, including a finding that the affected parties have received "adequate protection."[42] Section 510(c) provides that a court "may under principles of equitable subordination, subordinate an allowed claim to all or part of another allowed claim or all or part of

[38] U.S. Const. art. I, § 8, cl. 4.

[39] *See* Siegel v. Fitzgerald, 596 U.S. 464, 473 (2022) ("[T]he subject of bankruptcies is incapable of final definition, and includes nothing less than the subject of the relations between a debtor and his creditors." (cleaned up)). *But see* Ralph Brubaker, *Mass Torts, The Bankruptcy Power, and the Constitutional Limits on Mandatory No-Opt-Out Settlements*, 23 Fla. St. U. Bus. Rev. 1, 17 (2024) (arguing that there must be some limit related to limited funds).

[40] 11 U.S.C. § 1123(b)(6).

[41] *Id.* § 1112(b).

[42] *Id.* § 364(d).

an allowed interest to all or part of another allowed interest."[43] Section 1129(a) requires that a plan of reorganization have been "proposed in good faith."[44] And Section 1129(b) requires that a nonconsensual plan be "fair and equitable" and that it not "discriminate unfairly" to be approved.[45] These provisions all explicitly delegate policymaking authority and discretion to bankruptcy courts, establishing clear statutory grounds for flexible and responsive judicial decision-making.

And then there is Section 105(a), which gives bankruptcy courts authority to "issue any order, process, or judgment that is necessary or appropriate to carry out the provisions of this title."[46] This language allows for some gap-filling by bankruptcy judges.[47] While Section 105(a) gets a lot of attention and is criticized as a source of bankruptcy exceptionalism, it is quite the opposite. The language of 105(a) mirrors the language of the All Writs Act,[48] originally enacted in 1789, which grants similar powers to other federal courts. Thus, Section 105(a) merely gives bankruptcy courts the same powers that other courts possess elsewhere.[49]

2. *Procedural Authority and Constitutional Structure*. Procedurally things are a bit more complicated. Congress established an elaborate and complicated system for the adjudication of bankruptcy matters. And one exceptionalist criticism of that system is that bankruptcy courts issue judgments untethered from constitutional limitations on

---

[43] *Id.* § 510(c).

[44] *Id.* § 1129(a)(3).

[45] *Id.* § 1129(b).

[46] *Id.* § 105(a).

[47] 2 Collier on Bankruptcy ¶ 105.01 (Richard Levin & Henry J. Sommer eds., 16th ed. 2022) (noting the "power to fill in gaps" derived from Section 105(a)).

[48] 28 U.S.C. § 1651 ("The Supreme Court and all courts established by Act of Congress may issue all writs necessary or appropriate in aid of their respective jurisdictions and agreeable to the usages and principles of law.").

[49] The All Writs Act has, however, been interpreted more broadly by the Supreme Court than Section 105(a). It has formed the basis for the expansions of its shadow docket. Stephen I. Vladeck, *The Solicitor General and the Shadow Docket*, 133 Harv. L. Rev. 123, 124–28 (2019); William Baude, *Foreword: The Supreme Court's Shadow Docket*, 9 N.Y.U. J.L. & Liberty 1 (2015). This point has not been lost on litigants. During a February 2025 confirmation hearing, the debtor's attorneys in the bankruptcy of Red River Talc LLC argued that (notwithstanding the decision in *Purdue*) the power to issue nonconsensual third-party releases can be found in the All Writs Act. *See* Debtor's Memorandum of Law in Support of Confirmation of the Second Amended Prepackaged Chapter 11 Plan of Reorganization of Red River Talc LLC at 204–12, *In re* Red River Talc LLC, No. 24-90505 (Bankr. S.D. Tex. Feb. 20, 2025), Doc. No. 1075.

their power.[50] Bankruptcy judges are not "Article III" judges,[51] but they are adjudicating disputes over private rights that arguably fall under the exclusive judgment power of Article III and state courts.[52] This argument rests on a view that the Constitution protects property and liberty interests by making Article III judges, who have lifetime tenure and salary protections, available to adjudicate private disputes among individual litigants.

By this reasoning, constitutional protections are lost when non-Article III bankruptcy courts adjudicate controversies involving private rights. The argument implies bankruptcy courts should be courts of *extremely* limited jurisdiction. What is exceptional is not the power they exercise, but the fact that a non-Article III court is exercising that power. That is, when bankruptcy judges exercise equitable powers—even those based on the text of the Bankruptcy Code—a constitutional exceptionalist would argue they must be reined in to protect the structure created by Article III. Perhaps the bankruptcy system, by granting appellate authority to district courts, is immune to some versions of this critique, but a very strong commitment to Article III exceptionalism might perceive even that to be insufficient.

As a practical matter, we think that critique overstates things. Bankruptcy courts are subject to appellate review, which should alleviate structural concerns, at least if one accepts the appellate model of judicial review.[53] And, as a formal matter, the powers created by the Bankruptcy Code are ultimately vested in Article III district courts, which have jurisdiction over bankruptcy and related matters.[54] While the district courts do (as a matter of course) refer bankruptcy cases to bankruptcy judges in their districts,[55] they always retain the power of

---

[50] *See* Coordes, *supra* note 33; Diane Lourdes Dick, *Equitable Powers and Judicial Discretion: A Survey of U.S. Bankruptcy Judges*, 94 Am. Bankr. L.J. 265, 269–73, 279–81, 284–95 (2020).

[51] They are not appointed by the President with the advice and consent of the Senate and do not enjoy lifetime tenure and protected compensation. Stern v. Marshall, 564 U.S. 462, 486 (2011).

[52] *Cf.* William Baude, *The Judgment Power*, 96 Geo. L.J. 1807 (2008) (defining the judgment power).

[53] *See* Thomas W. Merrill, *Article III, Agency Adjudication, and the Origins of the Appellate Model of Administrative Law*, 111 Colum. L. Rev. 939 (2011).

[54] 28 U.S.C. § 1334.

[55] *Id.* § 157. Thus, while it is common to talk about the powers of bankruptcy courts, it is perhaps more technically accurate to speak of bankruptcy *cases* or refer to a "bankruptcy tribunal." *See* Casey & Macey, *supra* note 20.

appellate review[56] and can withdraw the reference to take a case back.[57] Thus, although bankruptcy courts are the courts of first instance for virtually all bankruptcy cases, they exercise that power as adjuncts to, and subject to the discretion of, an Article III district court judge.[58]

3. *Due Process*. A final constitutional challenge is that bankruptcy courts fail to protect due process rights. Because bankruptcy courts are resolving private rights disputes outside of the direct control of Article III there is a risk of depriving parties of their right to a jury, forcing parties to give up choice of law rights, or coercing premature settlements. According to those who hold this view, bankruptcy law's pursuit of judicial efficiency is in tension with due process values. While we are skeptical of such due process arguments—for reasons set forth elsewhere[59]—they do reflect a recurring concern about the constitutionality of certain bankruptcy practices.[60]

II. Exceptionalism in the Courts

Courts have occasionally echoed these concerns about bankruptcy exceptionalism, often cabining bankruptcy court power on formalist grounds. Until recently, this formalism reflected a structural commitment to the special place of Article III courts.

A. HISTORICALLY

Throughout the twentieth century, judicial review of bankruptcy exceptionalism tracked the constitutional concerns described in the previous Part. The Supreme Court sometimes limited bankruptcy authority and sometimes accommodated broad discretion, but when the Court worried that bankruptcy practice did not provide sufficient due process or Article III review, it considered the constitutionality of the practice head on and issued a constitutional ruling.

The most direct challenge to the constitutionality of bankruptcy courts came in the early 1980s, in *Northern Pipeline Construction Co. v.*

---

[56] In certain instances, the bankruptcy court's judgment is advisory and only becomes final after de novo review at the district court. *See Stern*, 564 U.S. at 475; 28 U.S.C. §§ 157–158.

[57] 28 U.S.C. § 157(d).

[58] It is not surprising then that critics speak in terms of constraining bankruptcy court power. We adopt that same convention from here on.

[59] Bankruptcy makes jury trials available, gives parties the right to appeal adverse judgments, and absent a single bankruptcy proceeding for resolving distressed firms, claimants or plaintiffs who bring suit late are likely to be left with nothing. *See generally* Casey & Macey, *supra* note 21.

[60] Sergio Campos & Samir D. Parikh, *Due Process Alignment in Mass Restructurings*, 91 Fordham L. Rev. 325 (2022).

Marathon Pipe Line Co., which involved the power to adjudicate contract disputes.[61] A divided court announced that bankruptcy courts did not have that power. It was relevant to the Justices deciding *Northern Pipeline* that bankruptcy courts were neither territorial courts nor military courts-martial and that the case in question was not a public rights dispute.[62] As a result, bankruptcy courts did not, according to Justice Brennan's plurality decision, fall within any of the historic exceptions to the requirements of Article III.[63]

The *Northern Pipeline* decision led to the passage of the Bankruptcy Amendments and Federal Judgeship Act of 1984 (BAFJA), which made bankruptcy judges "a unit of the district court."[64] BAFJA seemingly endorsed the appellate review model in which non-Article III courts can be allowed to adjudicate private disputes if certain "jurisdictional" facts are subject to de novo review in an Article III court.[65]

To the extent that criticisms of bankruptcy exceptionalism are aimed at bankruptcy courts (a) deciding private rights disputes and (b) lacking Article III status, it is worth noting that members of the Supreme Court personally contributed to making bankruptcy courts exceptional in this way. In the early 1980s, Congress considered two reforms to respond to the *Northern Pipeline* decision. One would have afforded bankruptcy judges Article III status.[66] The other proposed to give jurisdiction to district court judges who were given authority to refer cases to bankruptcy judges.[67] Chief Justice Warren Burger lobbied against the first proposal arguing it "would dilute the

[61] 458 U.S. 50 (1982).

[62] *Id.* at 70 (plurality opinion).

[63] *Id.* at 76.

[64] Bankruptcy Amendments and Federal Judgeship Act of 1984, Pub. L. No. 98-353, § 151, 98 Stat. 333, 336 ("In each judicial district, the bankruptcy judges in regular active service shall constitute a unit of the district court to be known as the bankruptcy court for that district. Each bankruptcy judge, as a judicial officer of the district court, may exercise the authority conferred under this chapter with respect to any action, suit, or proceeding and may preside alone and hold a regular or special session of the court, except as otherwise provided by law or by rule or order of the district court.").

[65] *See* Merrill, *supra* note 53, at 944 ("The appellate review model—which cast Article III courts in the familiar role of reviewing records made by other tribunals and resolving questions of law—came to be seen as solving this danger of 'contamination' of the judicial power by involvement in matters of administration."); *cf. id.* at 945 ("The critical point is that the tension perceived by modern commentators between the language of Article III and the use of non-Article III agencies to adjudicate disputes under federal law was largely invisible during the years when the appellate review model was adopted.").

[66] H.R. 1401, 98th Cong., 129 Cong. Rec. H512 (daily ed. Feb. 10, 1983).

[67] H.R. 3257, 98th Cong. (1983).

prestige and quality of the Federal judiciary."[68] Thus, if bankruptcy courts are exceptional when they exercise powers that properly belong to Article III courts, that is at least partially the fault of a Supreme Court Justice who was worried about degrading the status and prestige of non-bankruptcy Article III courts.

After *Northern Pipeline*, the next major case to address the constitutionality of bankruptcy courts was not about bankruptcy at all. It was instead about the constitutionality of adjudication by the Commodities Futures Trading Commission (CFTC). Even so, the case, *CFTC v. Schor*,[69] was widely understood to implicate the same Article III issue that had been raised four years earlier in *Northern Pipeline*. In *Schor*, the Supreme Court held that the CFTC had authority to adjudicate the kinds of private law disputes that *Northern Pipeline* had held unconstitutional.[70] Crucially, however, the Court pointed out that parties had consented to adjudication by the CFTC:

> Congress gave the CFTC the authority to adjudicate such matters, but the decision to invoke this forum is left entirely to the parties and the power of the federal judiciary to take jurisdiction of these matters is unaffected. In such circumstances, separation of powers concerns are diminished, for it seems self-evident that just as Congress may encourage parties to settle a dispute out of court or resort to arbitration without impermissible incursions on the separation of powers, Congress may make available a quasi-judicial mechanism through which willing parties may, at their option, elect to resolve their differences.[71]

Read together, *Northern Pipeline* and *Schor* create the impression that Article III courts must be available to hear certain private rights disputes, though the *Schor* Court carved out an exception when parties consent to a non-Article III adjudicatory forum.[72]

Over the next thirty years, the Supreme Court considered the constitutionality of bankruptcy court adjudication on a few more

---

[68] *See* Stuart Taylor Jr., *Business and the Law: Dispute on Bankruptcy*, N.Y. Times (June 24, 1984), https://www.nytimes.com/1984/07/24/business/business-and-the-law-bitter-dispute-on-bankruptcy.html; *see also Bankruptcy Amendments and Federal Judgeship Act of 1984*, Nat'l Conf. of Bankr. Judges (Dec. 15, 2023), https://ncbj.org/bankruptcy-amendments-and-federal-judgeship-act-of-1984.

[69] 478 U.S. 833 (1986).

[70] *Id.* at 857.

[71] *Id.* at 855.

[72] The Supreme Court formally extended this line of reasoning to bankruptcy in 2015. *See* Wellness Int'l Network v. Sharif, 575 U.S. 665, 679 (2015) ("[W]e conclude that allowing bankruptcy litigants to waive the right to Article III adjudication of *Stern* claims does not usurp the constitutional prerogatives of Article III courts.").

occasions. For example, in 1989, in *Granfinanciera, S.A. v. Nordberg*, the Court held that the Seventh Amendment guaranteed the right to a jury trial for fraudulent transfer claims even though Congress had designated such claims as "core" proceedings triable by a bankruptcy judge without a jury.[73] As in *Purdue*, the Court recognized that the constitutional right could "impede swift resolution of bankruptcy proceedings and increase the expense of Chapter 11 reorganizations."[74] But these practical considerations were "insufficient to overcome the Seventh Amendment's clear command."[75] Then, in 2011, in *Stern v. Marshall*, the Court ruled that bankruptcy courts could not issue final judgments involving state law counterclaims.[76] Once again, the statutory designation of such claims as "core" was irrelevant to the constitutional analysis.[77] The Court later tempered this ruling when it announced that the Constitution could tolerate bankruptcy court judgments over private rights when those judgments are subject to de novo review by an Article III court.[78]

But the formal doctrine that emerged between 1982 and 2011 paints only a partial picture of bankruptcy practice in that period. Despite occasionally striking down bankruptcy court judgments on constitutional grounds, for decades the Supreme Court and courts of appeals tolerated broad exercises of bankruptcy court authority—either by reading the language of the Code broadly or by not reviewing bankruptcy court decisions.[79] To that end, courts tolerated bankruptcy court innovations that allowed bankruptcy judges to blur corporate formalities,[80] order nonconsensual third-party releases,[81]

---

[73] Granfinanciera, S.A. v. Nordberg, 492 U.S. 33, 49 (1989).

[74] *Id.* at 63.

[75] *Id.*

[76] 564 U.S. 462, 482 (2011).

[77] *Id.* at 477–78.

[78] Exec. Benefits Ins. Agency v. Arkison, 573 U.S. 25, 28 (2014).

[79] *See, e.g.*, United States v. Energy Res. Co., 495 U.S. 545, 549 (1990) (reading Sections 105(a) and 1123(b)(6) as providing "broad authority to modify creditor-debtor relationships").

[80] *See, e.g.*, *In re* Bonham, 229 F.3d 750, 771 (9th Cir. 2000) (allowing for substantive consolidation); *see also In re* Owens Corning, 419 F.3d 195, 208 (3d Cir. 2007) ("Whatever the rationale, courts have permitted substantive consolidation as an equitable remedy in certain circumstances.").

[81] Before *Purdue*, six circuits allowed nonconsensual third-party releases, and they did so by reading the Code broadly (and, in our view, correctly). *See In re* Metromedia Fiber Network, Inc., 416 F.3d 136, 141 (2d Cir. 2005); *In re* Millennium Lab Holdings II, LLC, 945 F.3d 126, 139 (3d Cir. 2019); *In re* A.H. Robins Co., 880 F.2d 694, 701–02 (4th Cir. 1989); *In re*

dismiss cases for being filed in bad faith,[82] and approve settlements that might deviate from the strict requirements of absolute priority.[83] These innovations occurred quietly as district and circuit courts tolerated bankruptcy court discretion based on the broad language of the Code, and they did so while largely leaving due process and Article III concerns unaddressed.

B. *PURDUE* AND THE CONSTITUTIONALITY OF BANKRUPTCY COURTS

Recently, however, the Supreme Court has begun to avoid constitutional decisions in bankruptcy cases, opting instead to narrowly construe the text of the Code.[84] Our reading of *Purdue* suggests this is part of a trend of reading broad provisions of the Bankruptcy Code narrowly to avoid constitutional questions about court structure. Though the courts never explicitly say so, they have adopted something like a canon—seemingly rooted in notions of due process and structural separation of powers concerns—of narrowing the Code's text.[85]

The majority in *Purdue* provided a purely statutory explanation for its decision. It argued that nearby text in the Code—found in Sections 1123(b)(1)–(5)—authorizes only specific plan provisions dealing with claims held by the debtor. And so, Justice Gorsuch wrote for the majority, "other appropriate provisions" must be similarly limited to provisions directly relating to claims and property of the

Dow Corning Corp., 280 F.3d 648, 656–60 (6th Cir. 2002); *In re* Airadigm Commc'ns, Inc., 519 F.3d 640, 655–57 (7th Cir. 2008); *In re* Seaside Eng'g & Surveying, Inc., 780 F.3d 1070, 1075–79 (11th Cir. 2015). Three circuits prohibited them. *See In re* Pac. Lumber Co., 584 F.3d 229, 252 (5th Cir. 2009); *In re* Lowenschuss, 67 F.3d 1394, 1401–02 (9th Cir. 1995); *In re* W. Real Estate Fund, Inc., 922 F.2d 592, 600 (10th Cir. 1990) (per curiam), *modified sub nom.* Abel v. West, 932 F.2d 898 (10th Cir. 1991).

[82] *See, e.g.*, *In re* Integrated Telecom Express, Inc., 384 F.3d 108, 118 (3d Cir. 2004) (dismissing a case for not being filed in good faith).

[83] *See, e.g.*, *In re* Iridium Operating LLC, 478 F.3d 452, 464 (2d Cir. 2007) ("[T]he bankruptcy court, in its discretion, could endorse a settlement that does not comply in some minor respects with the priority rule if the parties to the settlement justify, and the reviewing court clearly articulates the reasons for approving, a settlement that deviates from the priority rule.").

[84] Jonathan Seymour has described this practice as "structural or holistic textualism." Seymour, *supra* note 15, at 1953.

[85] *See, e.g.*, Czyzewski v. Jevic Holding Corp., 580 U.S. 451 (2017); Law v. Siegel, 571 U.S. 415, 424 (2014) ("The Code's meticulous—not to say mind-numbingly detailed—enumeration of exemptions and exceptions to those exemptions confirms that courts are not authorized to create additional exceptions.").

debtor.[86] The dissent, by contrast, felt the text's plain meaning—particularly, the fact that Section 1123(b)(6) allows the inclusion of any "appropriate provision not inconsistent" with other provisions of the Code[87]—gives courts presiding over Chapter 11 proceedings discretion to approve plan provisions that are necessary to resolve complex issues that arise when firms are in financial distress.[88]

By our reading, however, non-textual concerns were the driving force behind the majority's decision. Like the cases described in the previous Section, the majority in *Purdue* expressed a concern about structural issues that could be posed by third-party releases. The structural concerns stand out when the Court expresses unease about a "roving commission," and when it frames the question before it as one about the authority of bankruptcy courts rather than addressing the actual question before it, which dealt with the power of an *Article III court presiding over a bankruptcy case*.

In fact, one of the most notable parts of *Purdue* is that the case satisfied the Article III requirements the Supreme Court had established a decade earlier. As a formal matter, the bankruptcy court order had been subject to and ultimately approved under de novo review in an Article III court (here, the Second Circuit).[89] The case thus came to the Court as one not about the power of a bankruptcy court but about the power of an Article III court hearing a bankruptcy case to approve third-party releases. No direct constitutional claims were even raised on appeal.[90]

Yet, the Supreme Court felt compelled to hold that the *bankruptcy court* had gone too far in resolving claims against third parties. At one

---

[86] Harrington v. Purdue Pharma L.P., 603 U.S. 204, 218–19 (2024) ("Each of those 'other' paragraphs authorizes a bankruptcy court to adjust claims without consent only to the extent such claims concern the debtor. From this, it follows naturally that an 'appropriate provision' adopted pursuant to the catchall that purports to extinguish claims without consent should be similarly constrained.").

[87] The most obvious provisions of the Code limiting what can be in a plan are found in Section 1129, which provides an extensive list of requirements that a plan must meet before it is approved. 11 U.S.C. § 1129.

[88] *Purdue Pharma L.P.*, 603 U.S. at 240 (Kavanaugh, J., dissenting) ("The Court has explained on numerous occasions that the 'ordinary meaning' of a statute authorizing appropriate relief 'confers broad discretion' on a court." (quoting Sch. Comm. v. Dep't of Ed., 471 U.S. 359, 369 (1985))).

[89] As the Second Circuit explained, "the practical import of the *Stern* issue is nonexistent given that only conclusions of law are at issue here, requiring our de novo review under any standard." *In re* Purdue Pharma L.P., 69 F.4th 45, 69 (2d Cir. 2023).

[90] Brief for the Petitioner at 41, *Purdue Pharma L.P.*, 603 U.S. 204 (No. 23-124), 2023 WL 6220089 (presenting only a constitutional avoidance argument).

point, the majority announced that "a bankruptcy court's powers are not limitless."[91] But no one had argued that they were.[92] Again, the case was about whether the Second Circuit was endowed with the power to approve third-party releases after a de novo review.[93]

Driving the point home, although the Court claimed it was engaging in ordinary statutory interpretation, the majority opinion contains a number of passages that would fit comfortably with constitutional arguments from earlier decades. For example, the majority emphasized that the third parties in *Purdue* [94] were "seek[ing] an injunction 'permanently and forever' foreclosing similar suits in the future. And they seek all this without the consent of those affected."[95] Later, the majority appears to invoke due process values by claiming that Purdue's theory of nonconsensual third-party releases "suggests those claims can be bargained away without the consent of those affected, as if the claims were somehow Purdue's own property."[96]

Perhaps most importantly, the majority opinion suggested that a broad theory of Section 1123(b)(6) would have been inconsistent with the history and tradition of the judicial power:

> No one has directed us to a statute or case suggesting American courts in the past enjoyed the power in bankruptcy to discharge claims brought by nondebtors against other nondebtors, all without the consent of those affected. Surely, if Congress had meant to reshape traditional practice so profoundly in the present bankruptcy code, extending to courts the capacious new power the plan proponents claim, one might have expected it to say so expressly 'somewhere in the [c]ode itself.'[97]

---

[91] *Purdue Pharma L.P.*, 603 U.S. at 220.

[92] The limitations on third-party releases in a plan or reorganization are found in 11 U.S.C. § 1129. The Second Circuit had gone to great lengths to set out the contours of those limitations. *See Purdue Pharma L.P.*, 69 F.4th at 75–77.

[93] By contrast, the Court announced that bankruptcy courts were not endowed with the power to extinguish nondebtor claims against nondebtors. *Purdue Pharma L.P.*, 603 U.S at 220–21.

[94] The releases in the case were granted in favor of the members of the Sackler family who had previously owned and managed the company. *Id.* at 211.

[95] *Id.* at 215.

[96] *Id.* at 220; *see also id.* at 222 ("Yet they seek a judicial order that would extinguish virtually all claims against them for fraud, willful injury, and even wrongful death, all without the consent of those who have brought and seek to bring such claims. In each of these ways, the Sacklers seek to pay less than the code ordinarily requires and receive more than it normally permits.").

[97] *Id.* at 224.

These quotes are all framed as reasons to adopt a narrow understanding of Section 1123(b)(6), but they resemble the structural arguments that had for decades persuaded the Supreme Court to constitutionally limit bankruptcy courts' judgment power. For example, in pointing out that nonconsensual third-party releases would give Purdue a property right in plaintiffs' claims, the majority hints—without saying so outright—that nonconsensual third-party releases would amount to an unconstitutional taking, or at least that they would raise property-rights concerns. Similarly, concerns about "roving" and "limitless" bankruptcy court powers resemble concerns that bankruptcy courts are exercising Article III powers. And the resort to history and tradition suggests that Congress needs to provide a clear—in our view, impossibly clear[98]—statement if it wants to "reshape traditional practice" by expanding bankruptcy court powers to include the right to order nonconsensual third-party releases. Those concerns all appear to have been on the minds of the Justices and likely influenced the Court's interpretation of the text of the Bankruptcy Code.

Because the Court did not explicitly base its ultimate decision on these concerns, we cannot prove the constitutional matters were the primary driver for the Court's decision. After all, the Court never says it is engaged in constitutional avoidance. But on our read, the opinion—with its asides about structure and history and tradition, its references to the authority of the bankruptcy court, and its forced rendering of

---

[98] Imagine a legislative drafter who did want to grant broad discretion to courts in approving plans of reorganization. This drafter wants plans to conform with all the requirements set forth explicitly in other provisions of the Code, especially Section 1129. But beyond that, the drafter wants to give the parties and the courts leeway. How would that drafter accomplish her objective?

Section 1123(b)(6) provides that a plan can approve any appropriate provisions not inconsistent with other provisions of the Code. That is the most direct way of achieving this hypothetical drafter's objective. By our reading, the other items listed in Sections 1123(b)(1)–(5) are specific things that the drafters worried might be viewed by courts as inconsistent with other provisions. So they specifically listed them as allowable.

Perhaps a more adept drafter would have put Section 1123(b)(6) first to convey the point. Beyond that option, there are not many other ways to say that parties can include any appropriate provisions in a plan as long as they are not prohibited elsewhere.

Justice Gorsuch avoids this problem by assuming that the question is not how a drafter would grant broad authority that includes releases but rather how a drafter would specifically authorize these exact types of releases. Those are meaningfully different drafting goals. The Court's approach requires Congress to add to the Section 1123(b) list as every case reveals a new option. That approach undermines the discretionary language, and, by the Court's logic, every addition further constrains discretion and narrows the set of other appropriate provisions.

the *ejusdem generis* interpretive principle[99]—reveals a driving concern that nonconsensual third-party releases would curtail plaintiffs' property rights and assign Article III powers to non-Article III courts.

Purdue is the clearest and most important example to date in which the Supreme Court interpreted the Bankruptcy Code narrowly to limit the powers of non-Article III judges and to mitigate perceived constitutional infirmities. But it is not the only instance in which the Court has voiced a concern about the scope of the Bankruptcy Code. For example, in *Mission Products Holdings, Inc. v. Tempnology, LLC*, a case about the right to reject intellectual property licenses in bankruptcy, the Supreme Court observed: "The Code of course aims to make reorganizations possible. But it does not permit anything and everything that might advance that goal."[100] In *Czyzewski v. Jevic Holding Corp.*, the Court rejected a procedural maneuver, known as a "structured dismissal," that was used to circumvent the Code's absolute priority requirement.[101] While the holding of the case was narrow, the Court's opinion noted: "The importance of the priority system leads us to expect more than simple statutory silence if, and when, Congress were to intend a major departure."[102] Some lower courts have read this statement to create a clear-statement requirement for interpreting Code provisions that might conflict with absolute priority.[103] Other lower courts have taken *Jevic* even further, inferring a general policy against bankruptcy court gap-filling.[104] Finally, *Jevic* itself built on an earlier case, *Law v. Siegel*, where the

[99] *Purdue Pharma L.P.*, 603 U.S. at 618–21.

[100] Mission Prod. Holdings, Inc. v. Tempnology, LLC, 587 U.S. 370, 386 (2019).

[101] 580 U.S. 451, 465 (2017).

[102] *Id.*

[103] *See, e.g.*, *In re* Hertz Corp., 120 F.4th 1181, 1200 (3d Cir. 2024) ("[T]he Supreme Court concluded [absolute priority] applied everywhere absent a clear statement authorizing a departure.").

[104] *See, e.g.*, *In re* Serta Simmons Bedding, LLC, 125 F.4th 555, 589 (5th Cir. 2025) (citing *Jevic* for the need for a "textual hook" to approve certain bankruptcy settlements); *In re* George Wash. Bridge Bus Station Dev. Venture LLC, 65 F.4th 43, 52 (2d Cir. 2023) (citing *Jevic* for the proposition that statutory silence should be read to constrain bankruptcy courts); *In re* Purdue Pharma L.P., 635 B.R. 26, 37 (Bankr. S.D.N.Y. 2021), *rev'd*, 69 F.4th 45 (2d Cir. 2023), *rev'd sub nom.* Harrington v. Purdue Pharma L.P., 603 U.S. 204 (2024) (citing *Jevic* for the principle that rare case exceptions "will no longer do"). Some bankruptcy judges have pushed back on this reading of *Jevic*. *See In re* Genesis Glob. Holdco, LLC, 660 B.R. 439, 488 (Bankr. S.D.N.Y. 2024) (approving a settlement over a *Jevic*-based objection); *In re* Nine W. Holdings, Inc., 588 B.R. 678, 690 (Bankr. S.D.N.Y. 2018) (overruling a *Jevic*-based exception and noting that the Court had left open the possibility of "Code-related objectives that [other] violating distributions serve" (quoting *Jevic*, 580 U.S. at 468)).

Court also made a point of noting that statutory silence "does not give courts discretion to grant or withhold exemptions based on whatever considerations they deem appropriate."[105]

None of these cases directly confronted a constitutional challenge to any particular bankruptcy practice. Nor did they state explicitly that they were limiting bankruptcy court authority to correct a constitutional infirmity in the U.S. bankruptcy system. Nonetheless, in each case, the Court went out of its way to express its concern that bankruptcy courts were exercising too much authority. And in each one, the Court suggested—as have the scholarly critics of bankruptcy exceptionalism—that such authority is inconsistent with rule of law principles.

In that respect, the bankruptcy cases before the Court are consistent with a new bankruptcy exceptionalism where the Court—concerned about proper judicial authority—reads broad grants of authority in the Bankruptcy Code more narrowly than it might elsewhere. For example, as noted above, the Court has taken a much different approach in dealing with broad grants of discretion that run directly and exclusively to Article III courts.[106]

* * *

So does *Purdue* create or curtail exceptionalism? The question is partly semantic, and the answer depends on how one defines bankruptcy exceptionalism. If bankruptcy exceptionalism means that it is exceptional for non-Article III courts to adjudicate disputes that ordinarily fall under the authority of Article III courts, then *Purdue* indirectly limits bankruptcy exceptionalism by announcing a limitation on all courts hearing bankruptcy cases. The non-exceptional approach would be for Article III or state courts to adjudicate private disputes among individuals. *Purdue* has ensured that a swath of those

---

[105] 571 U.S. 415, 423 (2014); *see also* City of Chicago v. Fulton, 592 U.S. 154, 166 (2021) (Sotomayor, J., concurring) ("[A]ny gap left by the Court's ruling today is best addressed by rule drafters and policymakers, not bankruptcy judges.").

[106] As discussed above, the All Writs Act has formed the basis for the Court's shadow docket, *see supra* note 49, and has been invoked routinely by lower courts to justify broad injunctions, including in mass tort cases, *see, e.g.*, Stott v. Cap. Fin. Servs., Inc., 277 F.R.D. 316 (N.D. Tex. 2011); Next Level Commc'ns LP v. DSC Commc'ns Corp., 179 F.3d 244 (5th Cir. 1999); *In re* Johns-Manville Corp., 27 F.3d 48 (2d Cir. 1994); *In re* Baldwin-United Corp., 770 F.2d 328 (2d Cir. 1985); *In re* Corrugated Container Antitrust Litig., 659 F.2d 1332 (5th Cir. 1981); United States v. N.Y. Tel. Co., 434 U.S. 159 (1977); Teas v. Twentieth Century-Fox Film Corp., 413 F.2d 1263 (5th Cir. 1969).

cases will never be resolved before a bankruptcy judge. One can debate whether this is a good outcome. We think it is not.

Besides the merits of which forum should adjudicate these cases, the majority's interpretive approach also introduces significant uncertainty for bankruptcy courts and practitioners. Instead of confronting the Article III question directly, the Court invented a new kind of bankruptcy exceptionalism by distorting the substantive provisions of the Bankruptcy Code to sidestep underlying procedural concerns about the structural design of the bankruptcy courts. While this constitutional avoidance may have facilitated agreement among a majority of the Court, it has already bred confusion and inconsistency in the lower courts. It is to that problem that we now turn.

III. *Purdue*'s Effect on Substantive Bankruptcy Law and Practice

Many bankruptcy practices exist because judges and lawyers responded creatively to changes in capital markets. Given how little guidance the text itself provides, and how much uncertainty there is about the new structural canon of bankruptcy interpretation, an enormous number of bankruptcy doctrines are vulnerable to Supreme Court reversal. We do not believe the Court will reverse every practice, but the lack of a limiting principle in *Purdue* could be just as harmful, since corporations and bankruptcy attorneys have little guidance about which bankruptcy principles remain acceptable and which do not. Ironically, then, the Court's attempt to constrain bankruptcy judges will incentivize unruly and strategic approaches by judges and practitioners. The following Sections provide specific examples of how *Purdue* threatens future bankruptcy cases in distinct ways.

A. Mass Tort Settlements in Bankruptcy

Most obviously, *Purdue* will change the landscape for settling mass torts in bankruptcy. The *Purdue* Court identified a list of issues upon which it did not pass judgment. These included *consensual* third-party releases, plans that provide for full satisfaction of claims against a third-party nondebtor, and substantially consummated plans.[107] The

[107] Harrington v. Purdue Pharma L.P., 603 U.S. 204, 226 (2024).

dissent was skeptical that these and other practices could survive the majority opinion, and they are now live issues in the lower courts.

1. Purdue *Itself—Preliminary Injunctions and Other Mass Tort Workarounds.* The Court's ruling in *Purdue* did not end settlement discussions in that case. After the opinion was issued, the bankruptcy judge extended the injunctions against nondebtor litigation to try to secure a global settlement. Across the board, bankruptcy courts have been quick to affirm their power to temporarily enjoin nondebtor litigation during the pendency of bankruptcy proceedings. But the test for granting those injunctions has changed. As one judge explained:

> Accordingly, to the extent a debtor sought to justify a preliminary injunction on the notion that it was likely to succeed on the merits by ultimately obtaining a third-party release, such an argument would now need to fail in light of *Purdue Pharma*.[108]

At the same time, the court explained that preliminary injunctions of third-party claims are still "appropriate where the assertion of those claims would interfere with the debtor's reorganization efforts."[109]

And that is how *Purdue* has proceeded. Litigation against the Sacklers is still enjoined while the parties continue to negotiate toward a near-global settlement. Reports and court filings suggest they are close to a deal. But the parties have had to add creative mechanisms to protect against the risk of holdouts. According to one report, while the Sacklers have increased their settlement offer by $500 million, they have also added a condition requiring the claimants "to set aside as much as $800 million in an account akin to a legal-defense fund for the billionaires to fight such cases [brought by the hold outs]."[110]

This structure is still subject to judicial approval and plan voting, but it provides a glimpse of the workarounds that might be attempted if mass tort cases are to be settled without nonconsensual releases in bankruptcy court.

---

[108] *In re* Parlement Techs., Inc., 661 B.R. 722, 726 (Bankr. D. Del. 2024); *see also In re* Coast to Coast Leasing, LLC, 661 B.R. 621, 623 (Bankr. N.D. Ill. 2024); *In re* Purdue Pharma L.P., No. 19-23649, 2024 WL 4894349 (S.D.N.Y. Nov. 26, 2024).

[109] *Parlement Techs, Inc.*, 661 B.R. at 728.

[110] Jan Hoffman, *Sacklers Up Their Offer to Settle Purdue Opioids Cases, with a New Condition*, N.Y. Times (Jan. 23, 2025), https://www.nytimes.com/2025/01/23/health/sacklers-purdue-settlement-opioids.html.

2. Boy Scouts of America—*Equitable Mootness and Full Satisfaction.* In its concluding paragraph in *Purdue*, the Court noted the following:

> Nor do we have occasion today to express a view on what qualifies as a consensual release or pass upon a plan that provides for the full satisfaction of claims against a third-party nondebtor. Additionally, because this case involves only a stayed reorganization plan, we do not address whether our reading of the bankruptcy code would justify unwinding reorganization plans that have already become effective and been substantially consummated.[111]

The Court's specific mention of full satisfaction and substantial consummation were likely included specifically with the bankruptcy of Boy Scouts of America in mind.[112]

The *Boy Scouts* case presents perhaps the most compelling case for nonconsensual third-party releases. The bankruptcy resulted from over eighty thousand claims of sexual abuse brought against the Boys Scouts of America and tens of thousands of its affiliates.[113] The plan of reorganization in that case created a multi-billion-dollar settlement trust for victims funded by contributions from thousands of entities including the Boy Scouts of America, local Boy Scouts councils, chartered organizations (which operated or sponsored local Boy Scouts programs and include small and large churches and charitable organizations),

---

[111] *Purdue Pharma L.P.*, 603 U.S. at 226.

[112] The Court had received amicus briefing on how its decision in *Purdue* might affect that case. *See* Brief of Ad Hoc Group of Local Councils of the Boy Scouts of America as *Amicus Curiae* Supporting Debtor Respondents, *Purdue Pharma L.P.*, 603 U.S. 204 (No. 23–124), 2023 WL 7184149; Brief for the Boy Scouts of America as *Amicus Curiae* in Support of Respondent, *Purdue Pharma L.P.*, 603 U.S. 204 (No. 23–124). The Court also received an application to stay the implementation of the plan of reorganization in the Boy Scouts of America bankruptcy pending the Court's decision in *Purdue*. *See* Application for a Stay of the Bankruptcy Plan Presently Being Implemented in the United States Bankruptcy Court for the District of Delaware (No. 22-1237), Lujan Claimants v. Boy Scouts of Am., No. 23A741 (U.S. Feb. 5, 2024). Justice Alito had granted a temporary stay for the Court to consider that motion. *See* Order, *Boy Scouts of Am.*, No. 23A741 (U.S. Feb. 16, 2024) (Alito, J., in chambers). The Court denied the application six days later. *See* Order in Pending Case, *Boy Scouts of Am.*, No. 23A741 (U.S. Feb. 22, 2024). The Boy Scouts case was also mentioned during oral argument and around a dozen times in Justice Kavanaugh's dissent. *See* Transcript of Oral Argument at 54, *Purdue Pharma L.P.*, 603 U.S. 204 (No. 23–124); *Purdue Pharma L.P.*, 603 U.S. at 229, 238, 256, 264, 273, 275 n.7, 278 (Kavanaugh, J., dissenting).

[113] *See In re* Boy Scouts of Am., 642 B.R. 504, 558, 664 (Bankr. D. Del. 2022), *supplemented*, No. 20-10343, 2022 WL 20541782 (Bankr. D. Del. Sept. 8, 2022), *aff'd*, 650 B.R. 87 (D. Del. 2023).

and insurers of those parties.[114] To facilitate this settlement the plan included broad releases for these participating parties. Notably, and in contrast to the *Purdue* case, the releases in the *Boy Scouts* case do not include any individual who directly committed (or was alleged to have committed) an act of abuse.[115]

The Boy Scouts' plan was confirmed by the bankruptcy court and now sits under consideration before the Third Circuit.[116] Opponents of the plan argue it should be rejected under the reasoning of *Purdue* because local councils, chartering organizations, and insurers are receiving nonconsensual nondebtor releases.[117]

But proponents of the plan make two arguments for why it should survive the *Purdue* decision. First, at the time of the *Purdue* decision, the Boy Scouts' plan was already confirmed and had been making payouts to victims for over a year. Thus, they argue, it was "substantially consummated," and the case is "equitably moot."[118] Because the *Purdue* Court specifically declined to opine on substantial consummation, one might expect the Third Circuit to affirm the case, drawing some comfort that the Supreme Court will not step in to reverse.

That said, there is considerable disagreement among judges about the notion that a bankruptcy case becomes immune to appellate review simply because there are limits to the available relief upon reversal. We do not expect equitable mootness to be a long-lived doctrine. Unlike third-party releases, it is actually a doctrine unmoored from statutory authority, which is likely to offend the Court's sense of textualism. On top of that, it is a judge-made doctrine that shields bankruptcy judges from Article III review.[119] If our analysis above is

[114] *See id.*; *see also* Third Modified Fifth Amended Chapter 11 Plan of Reorganization (with Technical Modifications) for Boy Scouts of America and Delaware BSA, LLC, *Boy Scouts of Am.*, No. 20-10343 (Bankr. D. Del. Aug. 29, 2022) [hereinafter Boy Scouts Plan].

[115] *See* Boy Scouts Plan, *supra* note 114.

[116] *See In re* Boy Scouts of Am., No. 23-01664 (3d Cir. Apr. 10, 2023).

[117] Lujan Claimants Supplemental Brief re: Effect of *Purdue* on Appeal, *Boy Scouts of Am.*, No. 23-01664 (3d Cir. Aug. 7, 2024).

[118] Supplemental Brief of Appellees Boy Scouts of America, the Ad Hoc Committee of Local Councils and the Coalition of Abused Scouts for Justice, *Boy Scouts of Am.*, No. 23-01664 (3d Cir. Aug. 7, 2024) [hereinafter Supplemental Brief of Appellees]; *see also* Supplemental Brief of Appellee Future Claimants' Representative Regarding the Effect of *Harrington v. Purdue Pharma L.P.*, *Boy Scouts of Am.*, No. 23-01664 (3d Cir. Aug. 7, 2024).

[119] To be clear, we do not think this example proves the account of bankruptcy exceptionalism. Rather it is just an instance of the phenomenon common to all of law where one judicial doctrine developed by lower courts is inconsistent with the approach preferred by the Supreme Court.

correct, that is exactly the kind of doctrine that keeps formalist Justices up at night. Indeed, one Third Circuit judge—who currently sits on the panel for the *Boy Scouts* case—has criticized the equitable mootness doctrine several times, labelling it "legally ungrounded and practically unadministrable."[120]

The proponents of the plan in the *Boys Scouts* case might have two additional arrows in their quiver. First, Section 363(m) of the Code specifically protects certain asset sales from appellate review after they have been consummated.[121] The *Boy Scouts* settlement plan included the sale of insurance policies back to insurers for almost $1.6 billion free and clear of any claims against the policies[122] as part of the release structure.[123] These sales were bound up with the entire plan and the releases of other nondebtor entities and co-insured parties. A court might read Section 363(m) as protecting a consummated sale *and all intertwined transactions* from appellate review. As one might expect, the parties' briefs very in their views about how intertwined the sales are with other transactions.[124]

Finally, there is the argument about full-satisfaction plans, which proponents of the *Boy Scouts* settlement plan have leaned on before

[120] *In re* One2One Commc'ns, LLC, 805 F.3d 428, 438 (3d Cir. 2015) (Krause, J., concurring).

[121] 11 U.S.C. § 363(m); *see* Supplemental Brief of Appellees, *supra* note 118, at 16–18; Appellees Settling Insurers Supplemental Brief, *Boy Scouts of Am.*, No. 23-01664 (3d Cir. Aug. 7, 2024).

[122] There is an exception in the plan for claims belonging to one chartering organization that had potential claims as an additional insured party, the Archbishop of Agana, a Corporation Sole. *See* Boys Scouts Plan, *supra* note 114. The Archbishop was itself an entity in Chapter 11 bankruptcy proceedings. The bankruptcy court in *Boy Scouts* had ruled that a sale free of the Archbishop's interests would violate the automatic stay in the Archbishop's bankruptcy. *See In re* Boy Scouts of Am., 642 B.R. 504, 574 (Bankr. D. Del. 2022). This wrinkle demonstrates the naïveté of claims that releases were not needed in *Purdue* because the Sacklers could just file for bankruptcy themselves. Such a proceeding would not foster resolution but instead would complicate matters and create what is often referred to as the "dueling debtor" problem. *See id.* at 578 (describing "dueling debtor" cases); *see also* Harrington v. Purdue Pharma L.P., 603 U.S. 204, 273 (2024) (Kavanaugh, J., dissenting) ("And in cases involving hundreds of affiliated entities who share liability and share insurance, such as the Boy Scouts and the Catholic Church, it would be almost impossible to coordinate assets and ensure equitable victim recovery across hundreds of distinct bankruptcies.").

[123] *See Boy Scouts of Am.*, 642 B.R. at 538, 568–79.

[124] *See* Brief for Certain Contributing and Participating Chartered Organizations as *Amici Curiae* in Support of Affirmance at 4, 14, *Boy Scouts of Am.*, No. 23-01664 (3d Cir. Aug. 7, 2024) (urging "the Court to treat the Plan as the package deal that it is" despite arguments by insurers that the court "should uphold the buyback *even if* other aspects of the confirmation order, including the releases, are reversed").

the Third Circuit.[125] The concept is simple. If a claimant is paid the full amount it is owed by the third-party nondebtor, then there is nothing left to argue about, and the release cannot harm anyone. The full-satisfaction doctrine is most intuitive in an insurer or joint tortfeasor context. A victim who suffered $1 million in damages may be entitled to recover $1 million from either the debtor or a third party or both. But the victim is not entitled to recover *more* than $1 million in damages just because there might be two possible defendants. If the victim attempted to bring suit after fully recovering, the prior recovery would be a defense, and the case would be dismissed. And so, some courts have said that a bankruptcy court can release the victims' claims against the nondebtor when the debtor's estate is providing full satisfaction of the claim (here, $1 million).

But implementation of the doctrine is fraught. Set aside future claimants, where the full-satisfaction doctrine is meaningless, and one still must figure out who decides what counts as full satisfaction. At the time of a mass tort settlement, most victims have not had their individual claims litigated. The court does not know the amount of a particular objecting victim's claim against the nondebtor (or against the debtor for that matter).

What does it mean then to say that the claim against the nondebtor is fully satisfied by the settlement trust? This question has two components. First, how much is owed to the victim, and second, when will the money be made available to the victims? In the *Boy Scouts* case, the judge made a detailed factual finding based on expert testimony to the effect that there would be enough money in the settlement trust to pay all claims in full. This is essentially a statistical finding that all potential liabilities will likely be covered, but it is far from a certainty.[126]

As a practical matter, we think this method of achieving settlement promotes the public interest. But it is hard to see how it survives the holding in *Purdue*. The bankruptcy judge in *Purdue*, subject to review by the Second Circuit, made a factual determination that the victims would be worse off without the proposed settlement containing releases. The Supreme Court seems to have said that is insufficient to justify binding the holdouts. Things may be different, the

---

[125] *See* Supplemental Brief of Appellees, *supra* note 118, at 5–12.

[126] *See* Brubaker, *supra* note 39, at 10 (noting that it is impossible to know at confirmation if a mass tort plan is providing full payment).

Court says, when the bankruptcy court makes a factual finding that the settlement fully compensates victims. But what if the victims disagree? Under what statutory authority can they be bound?[127]

As Justice Kavanaugh noted in his dissent:

> Again, the only provision that could possibly supply authority to include those full-satisfaction releases in a bankruptcy plan is the catchall in § 1123(b)(6). Any contract-law theory would not work for full-satisfaction releases, given that holdout creditors often refuse to consent to full-satisfaction releases. So if full-satisfaction releases are to be allowed, § 1123(b)(6) must be read to reach creditor claims against non-debtors, even without consent.[128]

But that is exactly what the *Purdue* majority rejected.

One version of the full-satisfaction doctrine that might survive post-*Purdue* scrutiny would be for courts to allow channeling injunctions that require victims to bring cases against the fund until and unless the fund runs out of money. Such injunctions could be considered in aid of a rule that a tort victim is only entitled to one satisfaction[129] but would not bind victims to a release that may result in less than full payment. This would be consistent with the court's authority to enter injunctions either under Section 105(a)'s grant of power necessary to enforce a plan or the All Writs Act's grant of authority in aid of a court's jurisdiction.

Such releases would become ineffective if, years down the road, the fund ran out of money. It is not clear whether debtors would get behind that version of releases. On the one hand, if the funds truly are providing full satisfaction, the possibility of the fund running out should be negligible. On the other hand, the entire point of the releases is to provide finality in aid of settlement. Precisely because the number and magnitude of future claims is unknown and plagued by variance, the tail risk is high.

---

[127] It is possible that the Court will view things differently than in *Purdue* if the litigants find the right statutory authority. One argument put forward in the Red River Talc bankruptcy is that the authority for full-satisfaction releases (and nonconsensual releases more broadly) may lie in the All Writs Act. *See supra* note 49. In this way, the lawyers have astutely separated the argument for releases from the Bankruptcy Code and from the powers of a bankruptcy judge. Whether that is enough to distance the issue from the new bankruptcy exceptionalism remains to be seen, but it may be the strongest remaining argument (in the eyes of the Court) for releases.

[128] Harrington v. Purdue Pharma L.P., 603 U.S. 204, 264 (2024) (Kavanaugh, J., dissenting).

[129] *See* Aro Mfg. Co. v. Convertible Top Replacement Co., 377 U.S. 476, 512 (1964).

In the end, we suspect that the *Boy Scouts* settlement plan will survive. The Third Circuit will likely affirm the confirmation of the plan pointing to some or all the grounds discussed, and the Supreme Court will sit this one out. This is good news for the victims waiting for their recoveries, but the full-satisfaction doctrine seems unlikely to be the hook to justify future mass tort settlements. This uncertainty is bad news for victims in similar bankruptcy cases that are pending or yet to be filed, such as those involving sexual abuse allegations in dozens of Catholic Church dioceses.[130]

B. CONSENSUAL RELEASES—OPT-IN OR OPT-OUT?

During oral argument in *Purdue*, Justice Thomas repeatedly questioned whether the validity of consensual releases and nonconsensual releases were inextricably linked.[131] Justice Kavanaugh's dissent suggested they are. Noting that there was no other provision in the Code allowing for releases, he concluded that "the only provision that could possibly supply authority to include those [consensual] releases in the bankruptcy plan is the catchall in § 1123(b)(6)."[132]

The Court explicitly declined to answer the question, noting only that such releases "may rest on different legal grounds."[133] The problem is difficult because a consensual nondebtor release included in a bankruptcy plan is more than a private settlement contract. With a consensual release, a debtor is putting the release provision into a bankruptcy plan that is disclosed to and voted on by its creditors, asking the court to approve that plan, and essentially asking for a preemptive federal court order enforcing the terms of the release. The debtor may even condition approval of the plan upon reaching a certain threshold of consent.[134] Because this is all tied up in the Chapter 11

---

[130] *See* Marie T. Reilly, *Catholic Dioceses in Bankruptcy*, 49 SETON HALL L. REV. 871 app. A (2019) (listing diocese bankruptcies).

[131] *See* Transcript of Oral Argument at 6, 7, 33, 62, *Purdue Pharma L.P.*, 603 U.S. 204 (No. 23–124).

[132] *Purdue Pharma L.P.*, 603 U.S. at 264 (Kavanaugh, J., dissenting).

[133] *Id.* at 226 (majority opinion).

[134] The track record of multidistrict litigation (MDL) settlements shows that absent an aggregated voting mechanism that binds holdouts, parties work to construct mechanisms to coerce near unanimity. One example of such a mechanism is a settlement provision requiring that plaintiffs' lawyers withdraw from representing clients who do not settle. *See* Casey & Macey, *supra* note 21, at 1040; Elizabeth Chamblee Burch & Margaret S. Williams, *Repeat Players in Multidistrict Litigation: The Social Network*, 102 CORNELL L. REV. 1445, 1460–63

plan-confirmation process, the authority for such releases would lie in a provision of bankruptcy law, as opposed to state contract law.

Lower courts have unsurprisingly fractured in their post-*Purdue* approach to consensual releases. While no court has yet held consensual releases to be entirely off-limits, several courts have limited the means by which consent can be registered. The issue comes up most frequently in deciding whether consent can be achieved through opt-in or opt-out provisions. The bankruptcy courts have varied in their approaches to this issue. For example, one bankruptcy judge in Delaware explained, "[a]fter *Purdue Pharma*, a third-party release is no longer an ordinary plan provision that can properly be entered by 'default' in the absence of an objection."[135] The judge likened opt-out consent provisions in a plan to leaving a letter on a car's windshield stating that a failure to respond within ten days constitutes consent to a contract. He concluded: "[A] creditor cannot be deemed to consent to a third-party release without some affirmative expression of the creditor's consent."[136] That affirmative expression might take the form of a vote for a plan or some other form of opting in. Another bankruptcy judge in Delaware approved opt-out consent.[137]

In New York, one bankruptcy judge looked to state contract law to require affirmative written consent from each claimholder.[138] One invoked Federal Rule of Civil Procedure 23 to allow opt-out consent.[139] Another allowed opt-out releases where notice was robust and the circumstances suggested that the failure to opt-out was a

(2017). Lynn Baker and Andrew Bradt view these practices more favorably and defend the MDL process as one that mitigates the costs of litigating individually. *See* Lynn A. Baker & Andrew D. Bradt, *MDL Myths*, 101 Tex. L. Rev. 1521, 1541 (2023); Lynn A. Baker, *Mass Torts and the Pursuit of Ethical Finality*, 85 Fordham L. Rev. 1943 (2017).

[135] *In re* Smallhold, Inc., 665 B.R. 704, 709 (Bankr. D. Del. 2024).

[136] *Id.* at 711.

[137] Findings of Fact, Conclusions of Law, and Order (I) Approving the Disclosure Statement for, and Confirming, the Amended Joint Prepackaged Plan of Reorganization of Wheel Pros, LLC and Its Debtor Affiliates Pursuant to Chapter 11 of the Bankruptcy Code, and Granting Related Relief, *In re* Wheel Pros, LLC, No. 24-11939 (Bankr. D. Del. Oct. 15, 2024); Findings of Fact, Conclusions of Law and Order Confirming the Second Amended Joint Chapter 11 Plan of Reorganization of FTX Trading LTD and Its Debtor Affiliates, *In re* FTX Trading Ltd., No. 22-11068 (Bankr. D. Del. Oct. 8, 2024).

[138] *In re* Tonawanda Coke Corp., 662 B.R. 220, 223 (Bankr. W.D.N.Y. 2024).

[139] *In re* Roman Cath. Diocese of Syracuse, No. 20-30663, 2024 WL 5456196, at *2 (Bankr. N.D.N.Y. Nov. 14, 2024).

meaningful signal of consent.[140] In the Southern District of Texas, one bankruptcy judge reasoned that because the *Purdue* court explicitly declined to address consensual releases, he was bound only by local pre-*Purdue* precedent on what constituted consent.[141]

Of course, if we are right that the Court is driven by broader structural concerns, then perhaps the Court will find in the text a path to approving consensual releases (even those with opt-out consent). After all, in prior cases like *Wellness International Network v. Sharif* and *Schor*, the Court has already indicated that its structural concerns are greatly reduced when the parties consent.[142] But here, again, the Court's methodological approach introduces a great deal of uncertainty. Because it did not directly identify structure as the basis for its holding, practitioners are left to anticipate how the new bankruptcy exceptionalism will operate in future cases. And the lower courts are supposed to apply the holding of the case—not our view of its motivation.

C. CHAPTER 15

One area of bankruptcy practice that has become increasingly important was not mentioned in the *Purdue* opinion: cross-border proceedings. When a debtor has assets in multiple jurisdictions, there are complicated procedures involved in coordinating insolvency proceedings. A debtor might initiate its main insolvency proceedings in Hong Kong or the United Kingdom and then seek to enforce the results of those proceedings with regard to assets or creditors in the United States. The legal mechanism for so doing is recognition and enforcement of the foreign proceedings under Chapter 15 of the Bankruptcy Code.

But what if the foreign proceedings include nonconsensual nondebtor releases? Those releases are common in other jurisdictions. They are granted broadly in the United Kingdom, under certain circumstances in Hong Kong, and at least with respect to affiliate entities

---

[140] *In re* Spirit Airlines, Inc., No. 24-11988, 2025 WL 737068, at *12 (Bankr. S.D.N.Y. Mar. 7, 2025).

[141] *In re* Robertshaw US Holding Corp., 662 B.R. 300, 322 (Bankr. S.D. Tex. 2024). Because the Fifth Circuit had prohibited nonconsensual releases even before *Purdue*, the Texas courts had grappled with the question of consent for years and the relevant precedent was robust. *Id.*

[142] *See supra* notes 71–72 and accompanying text.

in many European jurisdictions. U.S. bankruptcy courts have routinely recognized foreign proceedings including third-party releases even when those exact releases would not have been available under Chapter 11.[143]

Purdue should change none of that. The principles of comity and foreign recognition that undergird Chapter 15 counsel courts to recognize and enforce foreign proceedings as long as the creditors received a "full and fair opportunity to be heard in a manner consistent with U.S. due process standards."[144] Nonrecognition is reserved for cases where the foreign proceedings are "manifestly contrary to the public policy of the United States."[145]

It would be surprising for a court to hold that nonconsensual nondebtor releases were manifestly against the public policy of the United States. While the Court struck down the use of nonconsensual releases, it never suggested that they were fundamentally at odds with public policy. Even after *Purdue*, nonconsensual third-party releases are still available in cases involving asbestos (under Section 524(g) of the Bankruptcy Code), and the Court made a point of noting that "Congress may choose to add to the bankruptcy code special rules for opioid-related bankruptcies as it has for asbestos-related cases."[146] In the wake of *Purdue*, several courts have already recognized foreign proceedings with nonconsensual releases, holding they were not contrary to public policy.[147]

And yet, the Office of the United States Trustee has come out strongly on this issue, already challenging the Chapter 15 recognition of a Hong Kong proceeding on the ground that after *Purdue* all nonconsensual nondebtor releases are contrary to the public policy of the United States. The Trustee argued:

> [T]he relief requested is "manifestly contrary to public policy" because third-party releases may not be imposed without consent through a bankruptcy plan under United States law. *Harrington v. Purdue Pharma, L.P.*, 603 U.S. ___, 144 S. Ct. 2071 (2024). Accordingly, the Court cannot

[143] *See, e.g.*, *In re* Metcalfe & Mansfield Alt. Invs., 421 B.R. 685, 696 (Bankr. S.D.N.Y. 2010); *In re* Avanti Commc'ns Group PLC, 582 B.R. 603, 617 (Bankr. S.D.N.Y. 2018).

[144] *Avanti Commc'ns Group PLC*, 582 B.R. at 618.

[145] 11 U.S.C. § 1506. The foreign orders must also "sufficiently protect" the interests of creditors. *Id.* § 1522(a).

[146] Harrington v. Purdue Pharma L.P., 603 U.S. 204, 226 (2024).

[147] *See, e.g.*, *In re* Americanas S.A., No. 23-10092, 2024 WL 3506637 (Bankr. S.D.N.Y. July 22, 2024).

grant comity and enforce the nonconsensual third-party releases issued through a scheme in the Hong Kong Proceeding.[148]

The Trustee's choice to object in this particular case is surprising since the releases in question are fairly run-of-the mill, involving inter-company guaranties of a Chinese property developer (as opposed to tort claims arising out of operations in the United States). With those facts, the case is likely to result in a bankruptcy court opinion supporting the recognition of foreign proceedings with nondebtor releases.

The Trustee also appears to be indifferent to the necessity of such releases in other global jurisdictions where nondebtor releases are essential to coordinating insolvency proceedings that involve multi-entity debtors. Most large business are made up of several legal entities. Thus, the enterprise includes a parent entity and many subsidiaries. The parent and subsidiaries might be liable on the same debt.[149] It is difficult in those situations to resolve the liabilities of one

---

[148] Limited Objection of United States Trustee to the Verified Petition Under Chapter 15 for Recognition of a Foreign Main Proceeding and Related Relief at 2, *In re* Yuzhou Grp. Holdings Co., No. 24-11441 (Bankr. S.D.N.Y. Sept. 25, 2024) [hereinafter Yuzhou Trustee Objection].

The Office of the United States Trustee, along with the International Development Finance Corporation, raised similar concerns related to the Chapter 15 recognition of the Mexican Concurso Plan of Crédito Real. *See* United States Trustee's Reservation of Rights to Petitioner's Verified Petition for Recognition of Foreign Main Proceeding and Motion for Order Granting Full Force and Effect the Concurso Plan and Related Relief Pursuant to 11 U.S.C. §§ 105, 1507(a), 1509(b), 1515, 1520 and 1521, at 4, *In re* Crédito Real, S.A.B. de C.V., No. 25-10208 (Bankr. S.D.N.Y. Mar. 6, 2025) ("The U.S. Trustee is reviewing these and other provisions of the Recognition Order to ensure it is consistent with the relief that can be recognized under sections 1507, 1520, and 1521 and Supreme Court precedent in *Harrington v. Purdue Pharma L.P.*, 603 U.S. 204 (2024) and is currently engaged in discussions with the Chapter 15 Debtor regarding his concerns."); Objection of United States International Development Finance Corporation to Verified Petition for Recognition of Foreign Main Proceeding and Motion for Order Granting Full Force and Effect the Concurso Plan and Related Relief Pursuant to 11 U.S.C. §§ 105, 1507(a), 1509(b), 1515, 1520 and 1521, at 4, *Crédito Real, S.A.B. de C.V.*, No. 25-10208 (Bankr. S.D.N.Y. Mar. 4, 2025) ("The Concurso Plan cannot be recognized in its current form, because the Third-Party Release is not authorized by the Bankruptcy Code and is manifestly contrary to the public policy of the United States.").

These arguments were rejected by the Order Granting (I) Recognition of Foreign Main Proceeding, (II) Full Force and Effect to Concurso Plan and Certain Related Relief, *Crédito Real, S.A.B. de C.V.*, No. 25-10208 (Bankr. S.D.N.Y. Mar. 11, 2025); *see also* Angélica Serrano-Román, *Credito Real Restructuring Nets U.S. Recognition Despite Objection*, Bloomberg L. (Mar. 11, 2025, 5:48 PM EDT), https://news.bloomberglaw.com/litigation/credito-real-restructuring-nets-us-recognition-despite-objection ("'Purdue only goes so far here,' Horan said during the hearing. 'Purdue is expressly limited to a Chapter 11 case and Chapter 11 and Chapter 15 are very different animals.'").

[149] *See* Anthony J. Casey, *The New Corporate Web: Tailored Entity Partitions and Creditors' Selective Enforcement*, 124 Yale L.J. 2680 (2015).

entity without resolving the liabilities of the others. In the United States, this problem can be solved by bringing the bankruptcy cases for all of the affiliates into one proceeding. This "administrative consolidation" allows all the cases to be heard before the same judge. When it comes time to approve releases, all of the entities are debtors, and some courts even let the parties vote on one plan that covers the whole enterprise.[150] The upshot is that there are no "nondebtors."

That procedural mechanism is not always available in other jurisdictions, many of which would require separate proceedings—sometimes in front of different courts—for each entity.[151] This introduces coordination problems when it comes time to vote on the final resolution of the cases. Many of those jurisdictions address the problem with nondebtor releases. They allow one anchor debtor to initiate a proceeding and then propose a resolution that includes nonconsensual nondebtor releases for affiliates.[152]

The bankruptcy of multi-entity debtors with cross-liabilities requires at least one of these two mechanisms (releases or administrative consolidation) to function. Blocking third-party releases in Chapter 15 could make it impossible for insolvency proceedings from jurisdictions like the United Kingdom, Hong Kong, the Netherlands, and Germany to be effectively enforced in the United States.

Down the road, precedent allowing recognition is likely to form the foundation of a more radical maneuver when *United States*-based companies seeking nondebtor releases take their insolvency cases to another country. As we have explained in other work, there is little stopping a U.S. debtor from initiating insolvency proceedings abroad and then using Chapter 15 to enforce those proceedings in the United States. For this strategy to work, the debtor needs two things: 1) a welcoming jurisdiction—like the United Kingdom—that permits

---

[150] *See* Suzanne T. Brindise, *Choosing the 'Per-Debtor' Approach to Plan Confirmation in Multi-Debtor Chapter 11 Proceedings*, 108 Nw. U. L. Rev. 1355, 1369 (2014).

[151] *See* Nina Wouters & Alla Raykin, *Corporate Group Cross-Border Insolvencies Between the United States & European Union: Legal & Economic Developments*, 29 Emory Bankr. Devs. L.J. 387, 405 (2013) (noting that procedural consolidation is available in some but not other jurisdictions); *see also* INSOL Int'l, The Restructuring of Corporate Groups: A Global Analysis of Substantive, Procedural and Synthetic Group Procedures (2022).

[152] *See, e.g.*, Ilya Kokorin, *Third Party Releases in Insolvency of Multinational Enterprise Groups*, 18 Eur. Co. & Fin. L. Rev. 107, 139 (2021) ("Third-party releases facilitate centralised one-point-of-entry resolution of group distress.").

insolvency forum shopping and views nondebtor releases favorably;[153] and 2) post-*Purdue* Chapter 15 precedent recognizing and enforcing foreign plans with nondebtor releases. The Trustee's objection in *Yuzhou Group Holdings Co.* is likely to produce the latter.[154]

D. WHAT LIES AHEAD?

The list of practices drawn into question by *Purdue* is seemingly endless. For example, bankruptcy courts regularly grant exculpations to protect the debtor's agents and fiduciaries from lawsuits related to work performed during the bankruptcy. Like third-party releases, these provisions find no express authorization in the Code outside of Section 1123(b)(6). Similarly, some bankruptcy courts have taken to issuing "gatekeeping" injunctions.[155] These measures essentially require a litigant to come before the bankruptcy court asking permission to proceed with certain claims against nondebtors (usually insiders or fiduciaries). Again, there is no direct statutory provision other than Section 1123(b)(6) on point.

Doctrines like substantive consolidation, the true-sale doctrine, debt recharacterization,[156] and vote designation are all on similarly

---

[153] Already in the months since *Purdue*, one debtor has succeeded in doing something just short of what we describe. *See In re* Mega Newco Ltd., No. 24-12031, 2025 WL 601463 (Bankr. S.D.N.Y. Feb. 24, 2025). The debtor, based in Mexico, sought to restructure debt obligations created under U.S. law. *Id.* Rather than file in the United States or Mexico—whose laws made the restructuring complicated—it created a U.K. subsidiary, which voluntarily took on the debt liabilities. *Id.* at ∗1–2. That subsidiary then initiated U.K. proceedings which resulted in a Scheme of Arrangement that included nonconsensual nondebtor releases. *Id.* The subsidiary then sought and received Chapter 15 recognition in the Southern District of New York. *Id.* at *4.

In granting recognition, the bankruptcy court noted a potential for abuse but observed that there were no objections nor any "contention or evidence that the structure at issue here had been used in an unfair way and had thwarted third-party expectations." *Id.*

[154] *See* Yuzhou Trustee Objection, *supra* note 148. Without the objection, the proceedings would likely have been recognized with little or no comment from the court and without producing meaningful precedent.

[155] *See, e.g., In re* Highland Cap. Mgmt., L.P., 48 F.4th 419, 439 (5th Cir. 2022).

[156] As Diane Dick explains:

> Through the doctrine of recharacterization, bankruptcy courts treat certain debt investments in the debtor as equity investments; the decision is generally made on the basis of a nonexclusive multifactor balancing test that considers such factors as the adequacy of the debtor's capitalization, the relationship between the debtor and the supposed lender, and the corporation's ability to obtain financing from outside parties.

Diane Lourdes Dick, *Tactical Restructurings*, 93 FORDHAM L. REV. 1, 8, n.35 (2024).

shaky footing.[157] As are common sense rulings that prohibit the diversion of assets to the families of insiders.[158] Similarly, the procedural matter of administrative consolidation, which often allows creditors to treat large multi-entity enterprises as one for voting and other administrative purposes,[159] cannot be fully justified by the plain text of the Code nor of the Federal Rules of Bankruptcy Procedure.[160]

Even more fundamentally, bankruptcy courts have long assumed the power to dismiss cases that were not filed in good faith. But if one reads the Code the way the majority did in *Purdue*, even this power is in doubt. Section 1112(b) of the code allows dismissal for cause. But it then provides a list of sixteen instances that would constitute "cause," each one relating to behavior of the debtor *after filing*.[161] In contrast,

---

[157] *See* Seymour, *supra* note 15, at 1943 (including substantive consolidation and recharacterization in the list of exceptional bankruptcy tools).

[158] *See, e.g.*, *In re* Castleton Plaza, LP, 707 F.3d 821 (7th Cir. 2013) (going beyond the text of the statute to prohibit a plan that provided new equity to the spouse of the debtor's old equity holder).

[159] These practices are particularly important in resolving cross-liabilities within corporate groups, especially when nonconsensual nondebtor releases are on the table. *See supra* notes 150–153 and accompanying text.

[160] *See* Fed. R. Bankr. P. 1015(a).

[161] The listed items are:

> (A). substantial or continuing loss to or diminution of the estate and the absence of a reasonable likelihood of rehabilitation;
> (B). gross mismanagement of the estate;
> (C). failure to maintain appropriate insurance that poses a risk to the estate or to the public;
> (D). unauthorized use of cash collateral substantially harmful to 1 or more creditors;
> (E). failure to comply with an order of the court;
> (F). unexcused failure to satisfy timely any filing or reporting requirement established by this title or by any rule applicable to a case under this chapter;
> (G). failure to attend the meeting of creditors convened under section 341(a) or an examination ordered under rule 2004 of the Federal Rules of Bankruptcy Procedure without good cause shown by the debtor;
> (H). failure timely to provide information or attend meetings reasonably requested by the United States trustee (or the bankruptcy administrator, if any);
> (I). failure timely to pay taxes owed after the date of the order for relief or to file tax returns due after the date of the order for relief;
> (J). failure to file a disclosure statement, or to file or confirm a plan, within the time fixed by this title or by order of the court;
> (K). failure to pay any fees or charges required under chapter 123 of title 28;
> (L). revocation of an order of confirmation under section 1144;
> (M). inability to effectuate substantial consummation of a confirmed plan;
> (N). material default by the debtor with respect to a confirmed plan;
> (O). termination of a confirmed plan by reason of the occurrence of a condition specified in the plan; and
> (P). failure of the debtor to pay any domestic support obligation that first becomes payable after the date of the filing of the petition.

11 U.S.C. § 1112(b)(4).

good faith filing deals exclusively with things that occurred up until the moment of filing. The *Purdue* Court's invocation of the *ejusdem generis* canon suggests then that dismissal for cause can never include lack of good faith nor any other pre-filing causes. Are bankruptcy courts that require good faith at filing operating with a roving commission?

This all leaves the bankruptcy law in a state of great uncertainty. We do not think any legislative reforms are likely to change that. Nor, however, do we suggest bankruptcy courts and lawyers will abandon all innovative practices and just close shop.[162] Rather, we suspect the bankruptcy practice will start (has already started![163]) erecting workarounds to avoid the effect of the Court's new bankruptcy exceptionalism. Ironically, we expect that *Purdue* will be a catalyst in creating a real and pernicious gap between the "law on the books" and the "law on the ground." As Article III courts set up formalist barriers to the operation of the Code as written, the practice will be forced to adopt more evasive and contrived workarounds. Injunctions will be structured to dissuade or bind hold outs. The scope of injunctions,[164] exculpations, and gatekeeping clauses will be expanded (at least until the courts of appeal prohibit them altogether). Releases will migrate to settlements[165] and going concern sales[166] that are entered long

[162] Some expect other innovations to emerge. Ralph Brubaker has speculated that a district court hearing a bankruptcy case has the power to consolidate all debtor and nondebtor tort claims into one massive proceeding using 28 U.S.C § 157(b)(5). Ralph Brubaker, *Mandatory Aggregation of Mass Tort Litigation in Bankruptcy*, 131 Yale L.J.F. 960 (2022). We are skeptical about this reading of Section 157(b)(5) and even more so that such a reading would be upheld by the Supreme Court.

[163] *See infra* notes 165–166 and accompanying text.

[164] *See, e.g.*, *In re* Hal Luftig Co., No. 22-11617, 2025 WL 586757, at *18 (Bankr. S.D.N.Y. Feb. 24, 2025) (holding that *Purdue* did not prohibit confirmation orders enjoining litigation against nondebtors for the five-year life of a small-business plan under Subchapter V of Chapter 11).

[165] *See, e.g.*, *In re* Bird Global, Inc., No. 23-20514 (Bankr. S.D. Fla. Aug. 12, 2024), Doc. No. 1254 (approving nonconsensual releases in a settlement, noting, "*Purdue* did not address approval of settlement agreements under Federal Rule of Bankruptcy Procedure 9019 or sales of a debtor's property under 11 U.S.C. § 363 of the Bankruptcy Code, both of which are applicable in this case"), *aff'd sub nom.* Wright v. Bird Global, No. 24-23086 (S.D. Fla. Aug. 21, 2024) (holding that *Purdue* did not preclude releases where "the Debtors rely on the provisions of §§ 105, 363, 1123(b)(3)(A), 1123(b)(4), and Federal Rule of Bankruptcy Procedures 9019"); *In re* Roman Cath. Diocese of Rockville Centre, 665 B.R. 71 (Bankr. S.D.N.Y. 2024) (approving nonconsensual third-party releases as part of a settlement); *see also In re* Centro Grp., LLC, No. 21-11364, 2021 WL 5158001, at *3 (11th Cir. Nov. 5, 2021) (distinguishing settlement "bar orders" from releases included in a plan of confirmation).

[166] *In re* Hopeman Brothers, Inc., No. 24-32428, 2025 WL 297652, at *4 (Bankr. E.D. Va. Jan. 24, 2025) (approving nonconsensual releases after *Purdue* in a sale and settlement order

before the plan and structured to be irreversible. Plans might be structured to accelerate mootness. Debtors will push the envelope on what counts as full satisfaction. And so on, until it is just bankruptcy exceptionalism feeding on bankruptcy exceptionalism.

Conclusion

Purdue is an oddity. By our reading, the Court distorted the meaning of the statutory text to jealously protect Article III power. Rather than directly rebuke Congress for allowing non-Article III courts to share Article III power, the Court has adopted a canon allowing it to ignore the statutes produced by Congress. The canon could also be viewed as an analogue to the major questions doctrine that the Court has applied to administrative agencies. Again, the oddity is in applying this doctrine to cases that are brought before Article III courts. In a sense, the Court is altering the interpretation of statute rather than directly rebuking Congress for what it views as the original sin: delegating judicial authority to a non-Article III entity.[167] Ironically, in doing so it constrains the power of all courts—Article III included—to resolve complex bankruptcy cases. That is exceptional. And it is a recipe for unruliness.

and noting that "the Court has not found, and has not been pointed to, any decision extending *Purdue*'s decision to § 363 sales").

[167] Alternatively, the original sin could be viewed as not creating Article III bankruptcy courts, but that decision was itself the product of Article III judicial lobbying. *See supra* Section II.A.